Handy Road Atlas
A-Z GREAT BRITAIN

CONTENTS

Geographers' A-Z Map Company Ltd.

Fairfield Road, Borough Green, Sevenoaks, Kent TN15 8PP
Telephone : 01732 781000 (Enquiries & Trade Sales)
01732 783422 (Retail Sales)

Edition 22 2014   Copyright © Geographers' A-Z Map Company Ltd.
An AtoZ publication

D0259928

English	French	German
MOTORWAY	Autoroute	Autobahn
MOTORWAY UNDER CONSTRUCTION	Autoroute en construction	Autobahn im Bau
MOTORWAY PROPOSED	Autoroute prévue	Geplante Autobahn
MOTORWAY JUNCTIONS WITH NUMBERS Unlimited interchange **4** Limited interchange **5**	Echangeur numéroté Echangeur non limité **4** Echangeur limité **5**	Autobahnanschlußstelle mit Nummer Unbeschränkter Fahrtrichtungswechsel **4** Beschränkter Fahrtrichtungswechsel **5**
MOTORWAY SERVICE AREA **HESTON** with access from one carriageway only	Aire de services d'autoroute **HESTON** à sens unique	Rastplatz oder Raststätte **HESTON** Einbahn
MAJOR ROAD SERVICE AREAS with 24 hour Facilities Primary Route **LEEMING** Class A Road **OLDBURY**	Aire de services de route prioriataire Ouverte 24h sur 24 Route à grande circulation **LEEMING** Route de type A **OLDBURY**	Raststätte Durchgehend geöffnet Hauptverkehrsstraße **LEEMING** A-Straße **OLDBURY**
TRUCKSTOP (Selected)	Choix d'aire pour poids lourds	Auswahl von Fernfahrerrastplatz
PRIMARY ROUTE **A41**	Route à grande circulation **A41**	Hauptverkehrsstraße **A41**
PRIMARY ROUTE JUNCTION WITH NUMBER **5**	Echangeur numéroté **5**	Hauptverkehrsstraßenkreuzung mit Nummer **5**
PRIMARY ROUTE DESTINATION **DOVER**	Route prioritaire, direction **DOVER**	Hauptverkehrsstraße Richtung **DOVER**
DUAL CARRIAGEWAYS (A & B Roads)	Route à deux chaussées séparées (route A & B)	Zweispurige Schnellstraße (A- und B-Straßen)
CLASS A ROAD **A129**	Route de type A **A129**	A-Straße **A129**
CLASS B ROAD **B177**	Route de type B **B177**	B-Straße **B177**
NARROW MAJOR ROAD (Passing Places)	Route prioritaire étroite (possibilité de dépassement)	Schmale Hauptverkehrsstaße (mit Überholmöglichkeit)
MAJOR ROADS UNDER CONSTRUCTION	Route prioritaire en construction	Hauptverkehrsstaße im Bau
MAJOR ROADS PROPOSED	Route prioritaire prévue	Geplante Hauptverkehrsstaße
GRADIENT 1:5(20%) & STEEPER (Ascent in direction of arrow)	Pente égale ou supérieure à 20% (dans le sens de la montée)	20% Steigung und steiler (in Pfeilrichtung)
TOLL *TOLL*	Péage *TOLL*	Gebührenpflichtig *TOLL*
MILEAGE BETWEEN MARKERS *8*	Distance en milles entre les flèches *8*	Strecke zwischen Markierungen in Meilen *8*
RAILWAY AND STATION	Voie ferrée et gare	Eisenbahnlinie und Bahnhof
LEVEL CROSSING AND TUNNEL	Passage à niveau et tunnel	Bahnübergang und Tunnel
RIVER OR CANAL	Rivière ou canal	Fluß oder Kanal
COUNTY OR UNITARY AUTHORITY BOUNDARY	Limite des comté ou de division administrative	Grafschafts- oder Verwaltungsbezirksgrenze
NATIONAL BOUNDARY	Frontière nationale	Landesgrenze
BUILT-UP AREA	Agglomération	Geschlossene Ortschaft
VILLAGE OR HAMLET	Village ou hameau	Dorf oder Weiler
WOODED AREA	Zone boisée	Waldgebiet
SPOT HEIGHT IN FEET · 813	Altitude (en pieds) · 813	Höhe in Fuß · 813
HEIGHT ABOVE SEA LEVEL 400' - 1,000' 122m - 305m 1,000' - 1,400' 305m - 427m 1,400' - 2,000' 427m - 610m 2,000' + 610m +	Altitude par rapport au niveau de la mer 400' - 1,000' 122m - 305m 1,000' - 1,400' 305m - 427m 1,400' - 2,000' 427m - 610m 2,000' + 610m +	Höhe über Meeresspiegel 400' - 1,000' 122m - 305m 1,000' - 1,400' 305m - 427m 1,400' - 2,000' 427m - 610m 2,000' + 610m +
NATIONAL GRID REFERENCE (Kilometres) ¹⁰⁰	Coordonnées géographiques nationales (Kilometres) ¹⁰⁰	Nationale geographische Koordinaten (Kilometer) ¹⁰⁰
PAGE CONTINUATION ▲ **48**	Suite à la page indiquée ▲ **48**	Seitenfortsetzung ▲ **48**

0 1 2 3 4 5	10	15	20 Miles
0 1 2 3 4 5	10	15	20	25	30 Kilometres

Tourist Information | Information | Touristeninformationen

Tourist Information		Information		Touristeninformationen	
AIRPORT	✈	Aéroport	✈	Flughafen	✈
AIRFIELD	✈	Terrain d' aviation	✈	Flugplatz	✈
HELIPORT	🚁	Héliport	🚁	Hubschrauberlandeplatz	🚁
BATTLE SITE AND DATE	⚔ *1066*	Champ de bataille et date	⚔ *1066*	Schlachtfeld und Datum	⚔ *1066*
CASTLE (Open to Public)	🏰	Château (ouvert au public)	🏰	Schloss / Burg (für die Öffentlichkeit zugänglich)	🏰
CASTLE WITH GARDEN (Open to Public)	🏰	Château avec parc (ouvert au public)	🏰	Schloß mit Garten (für die Öffentlichkeit zugänglich)	🏰
CATHEDRAL, ABBEY, CHURCH, FRIARY, PRIORY	✝	Cathédrale, abbaye, église, monastère, prieuré	✝	Kathedrale, Abtei, Kirche, Mönchskloster, Kloster	✝
COUNTRY PARK	🌳	Parc régional	🌳	Landschaftspark	🌳
FERRY (Vehicular, sea)	⛴	Bac (véhicules, mer)	⛴	Fähre (Autos, meer)	⛴
(Vehicular, river)	⛴	(véhicules, rivière)	⛴	(Autos, fluß)	⛴
(Foot only)	🚶	(Piétons)	🚶	(nur für Personen)	🚶
GARDEN (Open to Public)	✿	Jardin (ouvert au public)	✿	Garten (für die Öffentlichkeit zugänglich)	✿
GOLF COURSE (9 Hole)	⛳	Terrain de golf (9 trous)	⛳	Golfplatz (9 Löcher)	⛳
(18 Hole)	⛳	(18 trous)	⛳	(18 Löcher)	⛳
HISTORIC BUILDING (Open to Public)	🏛	Monument historique (ouvert au public)	🏛	Historisches Gebäude (für die Öffentlichkeit zugänglich)	🏛
HISTORIC BUILDING WITH GARDEN (Open to Public)	🏛	Monument historique avec jardin (ouvert au public)	🏛	Historisches Gebäude mit Garten (für die Öffentlichkeit zugänglich)	🏛
HORSE RACECOURSE	🐎	Hippodrome	🐎	Pferderennbahn	🐎
LIGHTHOUSE	♟	Phare	♟	Leuchtturm	♟
MOTOR RACING CIRCUIT	🏎	Circuit automobile	🏎	Automobilrennbahn	🏎
MUSEUM, ART GALLERY	🖼	Musée	🖼	Museum, Galerie	🖼
NATIONAL PARK	▬▬	Parc national	▬▬	Nationalpark	▬▬
NATIONAL TRUST PROPERTY		National Trust Property		National Trust-Eigentum	
(Open)	*NT*	(ouvert)	*NT*	(geöffnet)	*NT*
(Restricted Opening)	*NT*	(heures d'ouverture)	*NT*	(beschränkte Öffnungszeit)	*NT*
(National Trust for Scotland)	*NTS NTS*	(National Trust for Scotland)	*NTS NTS*	(National Trust for Scotland)	*NTS NTS*
NATURE RESERVE OR BIRD SANCTUARY	🐦	Réserve naturelle botanique ou ornithologique	🐦	Natur- oder Vogelschutzgebiet	🐦
NATURE TRAIL OR FOREST WALK	🍀	Chemin forestier, piste verte	🍀	Naturpfad oder Waldweg	🍀
PLACE OF INTEREST	*Monument* •	Site, curiosité	*Monument* •	Sehenswürdigkeit	*Monument* •
PICNIC SITE	⛱	Lieu pour pique-nique	⛱	Picknickplatz	⛱
RAILWAY, STEAM OR NARROW GAUGE	🚂	Chemin de fer, à vapeur ou à voie étroite	🚂	Eisenbahn, Dampf- oder Schmalspurbahn	🚂
THEME PARK	🎡	Centre de loisir	🎡	Vergnügungspark	🎡
TOURIST INFORMATION CENTRE	🛈	Syndicat d'initiative	🛈	Information	🛈
VIEWPOINT (360 degrees)	☀	Vue panoramique (360 degrés)	☀	Aussichtspunkt (360 Grade)	☀
(180 degrees)	☀	(180 degrés)	☀	(180 Grade)	☀
VISITOR INFORMATION CENTRE	🆅	Centre d'information touristique	🆅	Besucherzentrum	🆅
WILDLIFE PARK	⚘	Réserve de faune	⚘	Wildpark	⚘
WINDMILL	🛞	Moulin à vent	🛞	Windmühle	🛞
ZOO OR SAFARI PARK	🐘	Parc ou réserve zoologique	🐘	Zoo oder Safari-Park	🐘

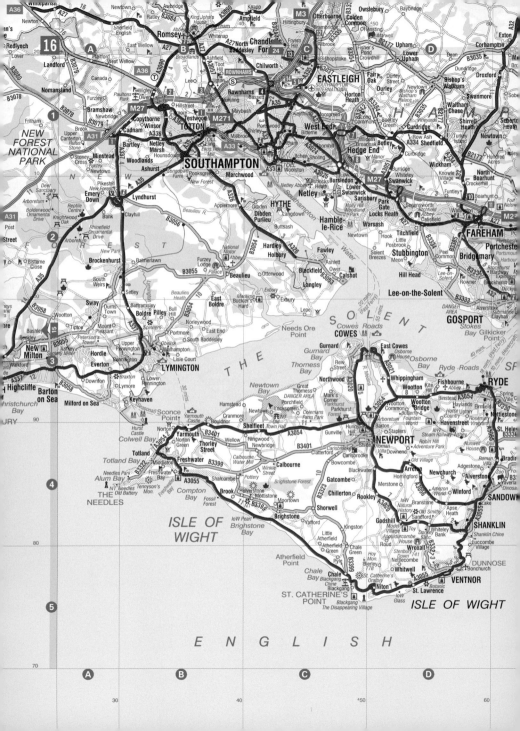

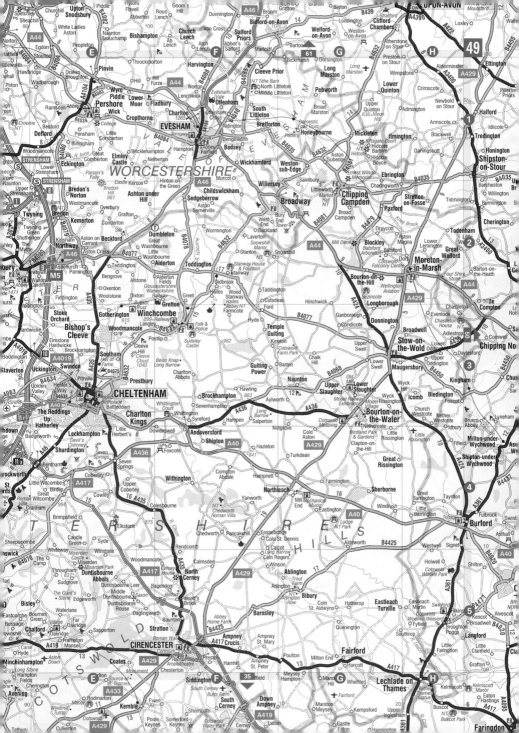

10 20 30 40

Ⓐ Ⓑ ▲ 68 Ⓒ Ⓓ

❶

90

❷

80

❸

C A R D I G A N   B A Y

(B A E   C E R E D I G I O N)

70

❹

60

Aberaeron

New Quay
(Ceinewydd)
Ⓜ Marine Wildlife Centre
Ffos-y-ffin
A482

Llwyncelyn

Maen-y-
groes
Gilfachreda

Cross Inn
New Quay
Honey Farm
Llanarth
B4342
Oakford
(Derwen Gam)
B4342

Cwmtudu

Nanternis
Caerwedros
Pen-cae
Geneva

Ynys-Lochtyn

Llwyndafydd
Synod Inn
(Post-Mawr)
Mydroilyn

❺

Blaen Celyn

Llangranog
Pontgarreg
A487
Plwmp

*Cardigan
Island*

Penbryn
Morfa
B4334
Pentregat
A486
B4338
Talgarreg
B4459
Ⓒ

• Cardigan Island
Coastal Farm Park
Gwbert
Rainforest
Centre
Felinwynt
Parcllyn
Aberporth
Samau
Brynhoffnant

Tresaith

250
Cemaes Head

Allt-y-goed
Ⓐ
B4548
Cippyn
Pwllvgranant
10
Y Ferwig
A487
44
Blaenannerch Ⓑ
*West Wales
Aberporth*
B4333
Tan-y-groes
15
Internal Fire
Ⓒ
B4334
Capel
Cynon
Bwlch-y-fadfa
Ⓓ

Tremain
Blaenporth
B4333

Glynarthen
*Curlew Weavers
Woollen Mill*
Rhydlewis
Ffostrasol
40

Castle
B4546
Penparc
Pantgwyn
Noyadd
Trefawr
Beulah
**Bettws
Ifan**
Brithdir
Felin
Wnda
Hawen
11
Pont-sian
12

Cardigan
(Aberteifi)
St. Dogmaels
Troedyraur
Penrhiw-pal

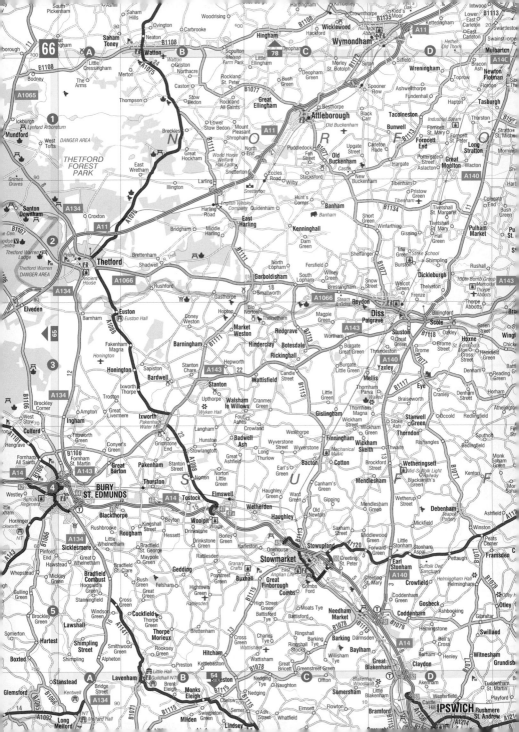

CAERNARFON BAY
(BAE CAERNARFON)

A B 80 C D

A4 7

A4E7

Pontllyfni

Aberdesach

Clynnog-fawr

St. Beuno
St. Beuno's Well

Slate Works

Capel Uchaf

Bwlchderwin

Bwlch Mawr
1671

1

Trefor

Trwyn y
Gorlech

Yr Eifl

Nant
Gwrtheyrn

1712
Gyrn Ddu

Cenin

Llanaelhaearn
Tre'r Ceiri
Hillfort

Carreg Ddu

Porth
Dinllaen

Pistyll

Llithfaen

B4417

Pencaenewydd
St. Cybi's Well

Llangybi

40

Morfa
Nefyn

Nefyn

Lleyn Historical
& Maritime

Fron

Pentre-
uchaf

Rhos-
fawr

Llanarmon

B4354

Groesffordd

Edern

B4412

Garn
Boduan

B4354

Y Ffor

Llanystumdwy
Dwyfor Ranch

Porth
Ysglaig

Rhos-y-llan

Glanrhyd

Boduan

Denio

Penarth Fawr
Medieval House

Abererch

Chwilog

A499

Tudweiliog

Rhos-ddu

Dinas
Garn Fadryn
Fort

Ffalnewydd

Llannor

Pen-ychain

2

Porth
Colmon

Penllech

Llangwnnadl

Pen-y-graig

Janiestyn

Garn
Fadryn

Bryn-mawr

Sarn
Meyllteyrn

Rhyd-y-
clafdy

Pwllheli

Marian-y-de

Marian-y-mor

Carreg yr
Imbill

Penrhos

Y Gamlas

A499

30

Penrhyn
Mawr

Porth Oer

Rhydlios

Rhoshirwaun

Bryncroes

Bottwnnog

B4413

Amytho

Llanbedrog

Trwyn
Llanbedrog

B4415

B4417

Braich Anelog

Anelog

Penycaerau

Rhiw

Plas yn
Rhiw

Llawr Dref

Llangian

A499

St. Tudwal's Road

Aberdaron

Llanfaelrhys

Llanengan

Abersoch

Braich y Pwll

Uwchmynydd

Aberdaron
Bay

Ynys Gwylan-fawr

Bwlchtocyn

Sarn Bach

Machroes

3

Pen y Cil

BARDSEY SOUND
(SWNT ENLLI)

Cilan
Uchaf

Trwyn yr
Wylfa

St. Tudwal's
Islands

Abbey

Bardsey Island
(Ynys Enlli)

Trwyn
Cilan

20

CARDIGAN BAY

(BAE CEREDIGION)

4

10

5

The Skerries
(Ynysoedd y Moelrhoniaid)

Middle Mouse
(Ynys Badrig)

West Mouse
(Maen y Bugael)

Carmel Head
(Trwyn y Gader)

East Mouse
(Ynys Amlwch)

Porth
Wen

Bull Bay
(Porthllechog)

Bull Bay
(Porth
Llechog)

Amlwch
Port

Amlwch

Cemaes
Bay

Cemlyn
Bay

Penrhyn
Wylfa

Llanbadrig

Burwen

B5111

Tregele

Cemaes

A5025

Penysarn

Llanfairynghornwy

Llanfechell

Bodewryd

Thomas
Chapel

Mynydd
Mechell

Rhosgoch

Carreglefn

Parys
Mountain

Gadfa

Llyn
Llygeirian

Llandyfrydog

Church Bay
(Porth Swtan)

Llanddyfnan

Llanfflewyn

Rhosybol

Penygraigwen

City Dulas

HOLYHEAD BAY
(BAE CAERGYBI)

Llanfaethlu

Swtan Rhydwyn

Llanrhyddlad

Llanynghenedl

Gwredog

Llyn Alaw

Raof

Holyhead to:
Dublin 3hrs. 15mins.
Dublin 1hr. 50mins.
(Fast Ferry)
Dun Laoghaire 1hr. 50mins.
(Fast Ferry, Seasonal)

Llanbabo

Llanddeusant

Mein Hirion

Tregwehelyd
Standing Stone

Llyn Alaw

Llanerchymedd

Maenaddwyn

Bachau

Llanfwrog

Breakwater

A5025

Carmel

B5112

Station

12

Capel
Coch

Gogarth
Bay

Porth-y-felin

Caer y Twr
Hillfort

Salt Island

Fort

HOLYHEAD
(Caergybi)

ANGLESEY

B5111

B5109

13

Ellin's
Tower

Hut
Circles

Stryd

A5

Penrhos

Llanfachraeth

Pen-lyn

Tryfil

Capel
Coca

Penrhos Feilw
Standing Stones

Kingsland

Llyn Llywenan

Llanywenddwy

(YNYS

MÔN

Porth
Dafarch

Ty Mawr
Standing
Stone

Burial
Chamber

Newlands
Park

Bodedern

Llanfaelog
Y Fali

Presaddfed
Burial Chambers

Trefor

Llangwyllog

B5111

Trearddur

B4545

Four Mile
Bridge

Caergeiliog

Bryngwran

A5

Bodffordd

Cefni
Reservoir

Llanfaes

Mona

Llangefni

YNYS

Llyn Dinam

Llyn-Trafiwll

A55

A5

Rhoscolyn

Llanfairyn-
neubwll

Llyn
Penrhyn

Capel
Gwyn

Llangristiolus

A51

GYBI

St. Gwenfaen's
Well

Cymyran
Bay

Valley

Ty Newydd
Burial
Chamber

Dothan

ANGLESEY

Gwalchmai

Heneglwys

Rhostrehwfa

A5

Rhosneigr

Llanfaelog

Bryn Du

Pencarnisiog

Cerrigceinwen

Dôl Dryfol
Tomb

Capel Mawr

Pentre Berw

Soar

B4422

A5025

Barclodiad Y Gawres
Grave

Bethel

Trefdraeth

Llangwylan
-isaf

Llangadwaladr

Malltraeth

B4419

Anglesey

Aberffraw

St. Cwyfan's
'The Church in the Sea'

A4080

Hermon

Malltraeth Sands

Llangaffo

Bodowyr
Dolmen

Castell
Bryn Gwyn

Aberffraw
Bay

Bodorgan

Dwyran

Foel
Farm Park

16

B4419

Newborough
(Niwbwrch)

Newborough
Forest

Anglesey
Model Village

Malltraeth
Bay

Llanddwyn Island
(Ynys Llanddwyn)

Llanddwyn
Bay

Abermenai
Point

Foryd
Bay

Llantaglan

Saron

CAERNARFON BAY

Caernarfon

Airworld

Llanwnda

Dinas
Dinlle

Llandwrog

(BAE CAERNARFON)

A499

Inigo Jones
Slate Works

A487

Pontllyfni

Aberdesach

Clynnog-fawr

Tai'n Lon

Capel
Uchaf

St. Beuno

St. Beuno's
Well

Bwlch Mawr
1671

Bwlchderwin

Trefor

Yr Eifl

1712
Gyrn Ddu

Trwyn y
Gorlech

N O R T H

S E A

heddlethorpe
St. Helen

Seal Sanctuary &
Wildlife Centre

Mablethorpe
Lifeboat Station
Ye Olde
Curiosity

Trusthorpe

Thorpe

Sutton on Sea

oy
rsh

Sandilands

A1111

Hannah

A52

Markby

Thurlby

Huttoft   Anderby
              Creek

R E

B1440   13   Anderby
Drainage

sthorpe

Mumby   Authorpe
             Row

Cumberworth

Bontthorpe   Helsey

loughby   **Hogsthorpe**   **Chapel**
                            St. Leonards

Sloothby

Hasthorpe   Stackholme
             End   Hardys
                          Animal
             Addlethorpe   Farm
on   **Ingoldmells**
arsh   Orby   Ingoldmells
              Orby   Point
              Marsh   Skegness   Butlin's
                       (Ingoldmells)
                       Water
                       Leisure Park   **Seathorne**
              Winthorpe

Burgh   Natureland
le Marsh   A158   Church   Seal Sanctuary
              Farm   Bottons
the   Pleasure Beach
sh   Mooti Village

Thorpe   **SKEGNESS**
St. Peter   Croft

              5   Seacroft
                   Croft Marsh
Magdalen
Wainfleet   Gibraltar Point
All Saints   Gibraltar
Mary
Toft   V

A52

DANGER AREA

Deeps

Boston

Scolt Head
Island

Brancaster Bay   Holkham Ba

Holme

90

80

70

60

1

2

3

4

5

POINT OF AYRE

Rue Point

The Ayres

The Ayres

The Lhen

Cranstal

Bride

A16

The Ayres

A10

Dhowin

A17

Shellag Point

Jurby West

Jurby East

B13

Andreas

A19

B3

Crosses

A9

Regaby

B7

Ramsey Bay

Jurby Head

Jurby

Ballasalla

B5

Sandygate

A13

St. Jude's

A17

A14

Civil War Fort

B14

Lhergy Frissel

Ramsey

The Cronk

Ballaugh

Sulby

Dhoor Grove

A13

Churchtown

A3

Glen Auldyn

Port e Vullen

A15

Maughold Head

Orrisdale

Orrisdale Head

A10

Curraghs

A3 T.T. Course

B8

Ravensdale

Gate

Elfin Glen

A2

Lezayre

Maughold

Crosses

Ballajora

Port Mooar

Glen Wyllin

Bishopscourt Glen

Kirk Michael

Slieau Dhoo
1601

Snaefell

T.T. Course

1854 North Barrule

Clagh Ouyr

Corrany

Cornaa

Glen Mona

Manx Electric Railway

Port Cornaa

Ballaleigh

Ballaugh Glen Mooar

Barregarrow

B10

Gob y Deigan

Sulby Resr.

Gate

Snaefell Mountain Railway

Dhoon

Bulgham Bay

Knocksharry

Cronk-y-Voddy

Lambfell Moar

Rhenass Waterfall

Colden
1599

Injebreck Resr.

Great-Laxey Mine Railway

Laxey Glen

Laxey Wheel

Dhoon Glen

Old Laxey

Laxey Head

St. Patrick's Isle

Peel

Ballagyr

A20

Glen Helen

Ballig

Slieau Ruy
1570

Laxey

Ballaheannagh

B11

B12

Ballacannell

Laxey Bay

Contrary Head

Patrick

A30

St. John's

A1

Hill

Greeba Castle

Baldwin

B21

Baldrine

Clay Head

I S L E   O F   M A N

Dalby Point

Glen Maye

Maye

Lower Foxdale

Fairy

T.T. Course

Crosby

Glen Vine

Strang

(Hillberry)

B22

Onchan

Groudle Glen Railway

Port Groudle

Niarbyl

Dalby

A27

Foxdale

B35

Garth

B26

Union Mills

B32

A1

Willaston

Groudle Glen

Onchan Head

Niarbyl Bay

A36

B36

A24

Braaid

Cooil

Spring Valley

Kewaigue

DOUGLAS

Manx

Douglas Bay

1586 Hill-South Barrule

Close Clark

30

A25

B37

Quine's Hill

A5

A25

Douglas Head

Stroin Vuigh

B39

Ballamodha

Newtown

Horse's Hill

A6

Port Soderick

Little Ness

Kerristal

Fleshwick Bay

Lingague

Ronague

Grenaby

B29

B30

A25

Isle of Man Steam railway

B40

A25

Santon Head

Ballabeg

A5

Bradda Head

Bradda

Surby

Colby

A5

A7

Ballasalla

ISLE OF MAN

Bradda Glen

Port Erin

Railway

Cregneash

St. Mary

Castletown

Derby Fort

Derbyhaven

St. Michael's Island

The Howe

Chambered Cairn

The Sound

Kitterland

National Folk

Four Roads

The A5

Port St. Mary

Ship Burial

Nautical

Old House of Keys

Dreswick Point

SPANISH HEAD

Calf of Man

PAGE NOT CONTINUED

Douglas to:
Belfast 2hrs. 45mins.
(Fast Ferry, Seasonal)
Birkenhead 4hrs. 15mins.
(Seasonal)
Heysham 3hrs. 30mins.
Dublin 2hrs. 45mins.
(Fast Ferry, Seasonal)
Liverpool 2hrs. 30mins.
(Fast Ferry, Seasonal)

90   400   10   20   90

1

80

N O R T H   S E A

2

70

Fast Castle
Head
Fast
Castle
Telegraph
Hill
Lumsdaine
Cross Law ·744
Coldingham Moor
ST. ABB'S HEAD
St. Abb's
Head
St. Abbs
Lifeboat
Station
Coldingham
Bay
Priory
Lifeboat Station

11

point

Houndwood
Coldingham
B6438
A1107
Eyemouth
Gunsgreenhill

3

859
Horseley
Hill
Water
Reston
18
Ayton
Burnmouth
Ross

60

Auchencrow

Chirnside
B6437
B6355
12
Lamberton
Marshall
Meadows

Edrom
Chirnside-
bridge
15
Whiteadder
Water
Tithe
Barn Clappers
Foulden
Conundrum
Farm
Haddon
Hill
1333
A6105
A1
Bell
Tower

Allanton
B6437

4

Hutton
B6460
Paxton
B6461
Castle
BERWICK-
UPON-TWEED
Tweedmouth
Lifeboat Station
Spittal

Whitsome

B6460
Fishwick
Paxton
House
B6461
Chain Bridge
Honey Farm
East
Ord
2
Pot o'
Doodle Do
Redshin
Cove

650

Horndean
Horncliffe
B6354
Scremerston

Ladykirk
Norham
Murton
Thornton
Murton

Swinton
B6470
Norham
Station
Upsettlington
B6470
Shoreswood
Shoresdean
West
Allerdean
Cheswick

Simprim
Twizel
Bridge
12
Grindon
Felkington
Berrington Law
Berrington
B6525
Haggerston
Goswick

5

Castle
Heaton
Stone Circle
Duddo
Bowsden
Beal
Fenham

LINDISFARNE
HOLY ISLAND
Keel
Head

Lennel
Melkington
NORTHUMBERLAND
Barmoor
West Kyloe
A1
Fenwick
Lindisfarne
Centre
Holy
Island
Priory
NT Lindisfarne
Castle Point
Burrows
Hole

stream
Cornhill-
on-Tweed
Etal
Heatherslaw
Light Railway
Waterford
Hall
Lowick
East
Kyloe
121
Kyloe
Hills
Buckton

West
Learmouth
A697
East
Learmouth
Flodden Field
Monument
Crookham
Branxton
Ford
B6353
B6354
B6525
West
Kyloe
Elwick
Ross
Budle
Bay
Chapel NT
Bamburgh
FARNE
ISLANDS
Staple
Sound
Inner

Pressen
Flodden
Field
Flodden
B6525
Holburn
St. Cuthbert's
Cave
Detchant
342

40

20

650

50

60

70

80

90

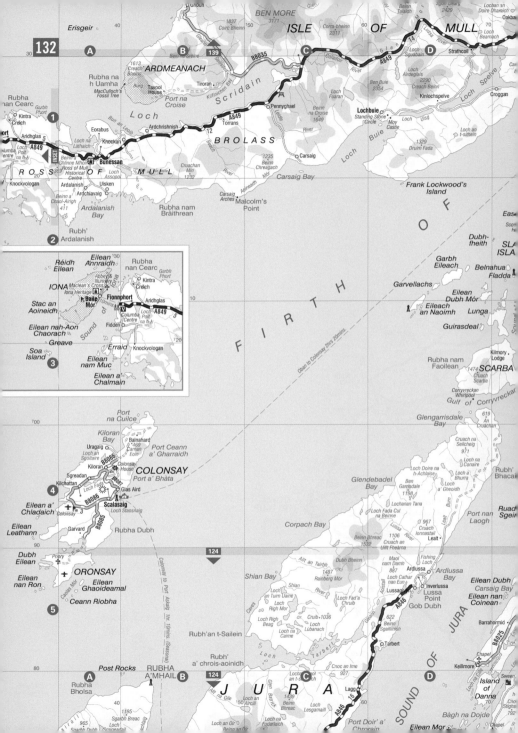

A   B   C   D

100   10   20   30

80

1

70

2

60

3

750

4

5

40

30

100   10   20   30

COLL

TIREE

Oban to Lochboisdale 5hrs. 20mins. (Seasonal)

Oban to Castlebay 5hrs.

Cairns of Co.

Eag na Maoile

Eilean Mór

Rubha Mór

Bousd

Cornaigmore

Sorisdale

Rubh'a' Bhinnein

Loch Fada

B8072

Rubha Hogh

Grishipoll

Cliad Bay

Bagh Feisdlum

Clabhach

Loch Clad

B8071

Arinagour

Hogh Bay

340 Ben Nogh

Loch nan Cinneachan

Loch Fatharna

Totronald

Loch Anlaimh

Stables

Coll

Uig

Acha

B8070

Eilean Ornsay

Feall Bay

5

Oban to Tiree 3hrs. 20mins. (Seasonal)

Calgary Point

Port na h-Eathar

Tiree to Barra 2hrs. 45mins. (Seasonal)

Gunna

Crossapol Bay

Soa

Freisland Bay

Port a' Mhurain

Coll to Tiree 55mins.

Treshn

Miodar

Carnan

Vaul Bay

Vaul

Salum

Caolas

Rubhà Dubh

H E B R I D

Hough Skerries

Balephetrish Bay

Loch Riaghain

Ruaig

Cairn na Burgh Beg

Cornaigmore

Sraid Ruadh

Balevullin

Balephetrish

B8068

Gott

Kirkapol

Gott Bay

Fladda

Kilmoluaig

Cornaigbeg

Kenovay

TIREE (Port Adhair Thiriodh)

Hough

Kilkenneth

Moss

Scarinish

An Iodhlann

Baugh

Loch an Eilein

Lunga

Sandaig

Middleton

Barrapol

Heylipol

Heanish

Rubha Tràigh an Duin

Port Mor

Island Life

Crossapol

B8065

2

B8066

TIREE

Treshnish Isles

Bac Mor or Dutchman's Cap

Port Bharrapool

Loch a' Phuill

Hynish Bay

Bac Beag

Balephuil

B8067

Balephuil Bay

Mannal

Balemartine

West Hynish

Hynish

Port Sniog

Skerryvore Lighthouse

I N N E R

Réidh Eilean

Eilean Annraidh

Rub nan Ce

30

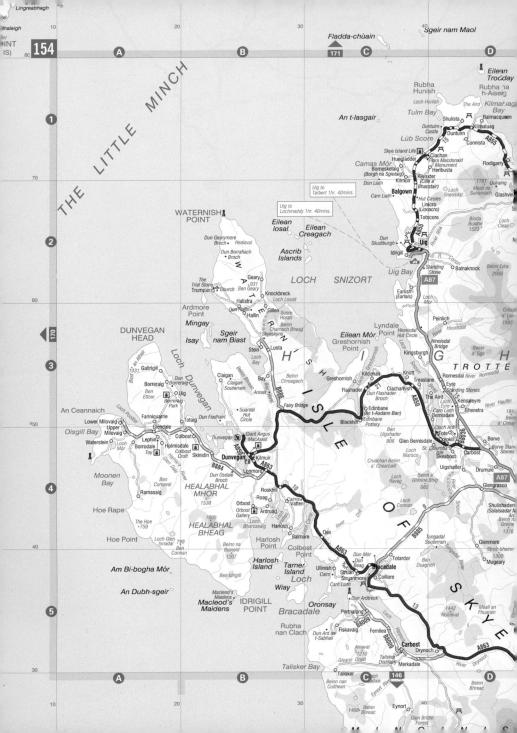

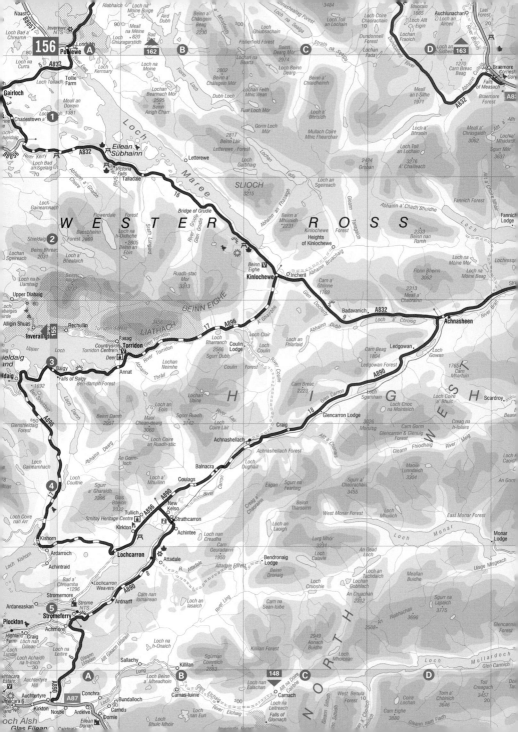

Spey Bay

300   10   20   30   70

1

Caves
Covesea   Fisheries &
Community   **Branderburgh**
Stotfield
Well   B9040   Seatown
Hopeman   Lossiemouth   **Lossiemouth**
Burghead   B9040   Lossie
Duffus   Forest   Tugnet
Cummingstown   B9012   St. Peter's   Ice House   WDCS
Roseisle   Kirk   DANGER   Wildlife Centre
Roseisle   Duffus   AREA   Spey Bay   **2**
Burghead Bay   College   Loch   Urquhart   Spey   Auchenhalrig   Porttannachy
Roseisle   of Roseisle   Spynie   Stone Circle   Viaduct   Nether
Forest   Moray   Spynie   **Kingston**   Dallachy   Broad
Findhorn   Motor   Palace   Lochhill   **Garmouth**   Bogmoor   Lower
Findhorn   Quarrywood   Urquhart   Auchenreath
Heritage   Cathedral   Upper Dallachy
Centre   Kinloss   Newton   12   **Bishopmill**   **Elgin**   **Urquhart**   Newlands
Coltfield   **New**   Ashgrove   **Lhanbryde**   **Mosstodloch**   Baxters
Culbin Forest   Alves   Dallas Dhu   Glen Moray   **Elgin**   Sheriffston   **Fochabers**
Findhorn   Distillery   Linkwood   Moss   Crofts   Spey   Speymouth
Bay   **Kinloss**   Lantern   Glassgreen   of Barmuckity   Cowfords   of Dipple   Ordiequish   Forest
Kintessack   Kinloss Abbey   A96   Miltonduff   Castle   Cooper   Loch   **3**
Falconer Stone   Distillery   Scotsburn   Tower   na Bo   Inchberry   Wood of Ordiequish
Broom   Nelson Tower   Muir of   Clackmarras   Cranloch   A96
of Moy   Lochaber   Miltonduff   Thornshill   Longmorn   Orton   1019
FORRES   Rafford   Forresterseat   Upper   Whitewreath   Auchroisk   Malcolmburn   Hill of
Whiterow   Califer   Heldon Hill   Barnhill   Bogside   Coleburn   Teindland   Distillery   Mulderie
Balnageith   Moor   Pluscarden Abbey   Teindland   B9015   Mulben
Conicaval   of Granary   Black Burn   Coleburn   Forest   A95
Logie   Damhead   Pluscarden   Kellas   Glenlattererach   Rosarie Forest   1111
Logie   Branchill   Hill of the   Reservoir   Pikey Hill   Glen of Rothes   Hill of Towie
Carnach   Romach   Wangie   1164   B9015
Dunphail   Loch   Dallas   Cairn Uish   Burn   **Rothes**   Ben Aigan
Newtyle Forest   **Dallas**   1197   1546
Glenernie   Meikle Hill   Glen Grant   Maggieknockater
932   Distillery
Knock of   1218   Lennoch Burn   Rothes   A95
Braemoray   Mill Buie   Carn na   Cairn Cattoch
1495   Cailliche   Elchies Forest 1210   Craigellachie   Speyside   Keith & Dufftown Railway   **4**
Dava   1324   Braehead   Bridge   Way   (Whisky Line)
Loch   Cardhu   **Archiestown**   B9102   **Craigellachie**   Tullich   111
Noir   Distillery   Robertstown   Macallan   Speyside   Lock
Loch   Cardow   Distillery   Cooperage   Park   **Balvenie**
Upper   Lossie   Carn Kitty   Upper Knockando   Dalmunach   Speyview   **Charlestown**   Glenfiddich
Derraid   1712   Knockando   Carron   **of Aberlour**   **Dufftown**   Distillery
Distillery   Glenallachie   Balvenie   Milltown of
Glaschoil   Larig Hill   Distillery   Distillery   Auchindoun
Cottartown   1783   Scootmore   Birchview   Milltown   Kirktown   **5**
Breag Liath   Forest   B9138   of Edinville   of Mortlach   'Giant's
1473   **Dava**   Marypark   A95   Chair'   Auchindoun
Ballieward   Glenfarclas   Meikle   1599
Dellefure   Dalwey   Inveravon Stones   Distillery   Conval   Laggan   The Scalp
Dulan Water   1867
Beinn   1800   B9102   B9137   Bellelegash   Drummin   BEN RINNES   Glenfiddich
Mhor 1545   Carn na   Craggarmore   Ballindalloch   Castle   2759   Bridgend
Loine   Distillery   Castle   Drummin   Glen   Ardwell
587   Advie   Tormore   Bridge   Castle   B9008   Fiddich
Ruigh   Upper   Distillery   of Avon   1605   B9009   Glenfiddich   Black Water   1872
arrach   Grantown   Auchnagallin   Carnacay   Lodge   Round Hill
Craggan   **Grantown-on-Spey**   300   **E**   **F**   **151**   Drumin   Shenval   **G**   **H**   30
Beinn   B9102   Castle   Glenlivet   Auchbreck   Corryhabbie Hill   Glenlitic   Cab
Mhor   Cromdale   Drumin   Glenlivet Distillery   2561   Forest
Speybridge   Knock   Haughs of Cromdale   Packhorse   Castleton   Cairn   Carn an t-Suidhe   Inverha
HILLS OF CROMDALE   Earth House   Bridge   Muldonich   2401
B9136   **Tomnavoulin**   1795   Blackwater   Forest
Carn Daimh

A940   A96   B9010   B9011   B9089   B9040   A941   B9135   A941   B9103   B9015A   B9104   A98   A96   B9103   A95   B9103   B9102   A95   B9138   B9008   B9009   B9137   B9102   A939   A940   A95   B9136   B9102

Seisiadar
A

A   B   C   C

1

2

171

3

900

Ullapool to
Stornoway 2hrs. 40mins.

Camas Eilean
Ghlais
Reiff

Eilean
Mullagrach
Isle Rist

Glas-leac
Mór

Tanera Beg

Summe

Glas-leac
Beag

Eilean Dubh

Priest Island   Bottle
Island

4

Greenstone
Point

Loch na
Doire
Duinne   Opinan   Rubha
Beag

Loch nan
Clachan
Geala   Mellon
Udrigle   Statt
Poir

Loch a'
Choire   Gruinard
Island

Slaggan Bay   Loch an
t-Slagain   Achgarve   Gruinard
Bay   Mungasd

Eilean Furadh
Mór   513   Beinn Dearg Mhòr   Laide   Gruinard
House

Rubha
nan
Sasan   Mellon
Charles   A832   First Coast

Rubha
Reidh   Camas
Mór   Loch an
Draing   Cove   Ormiscaig   Sand   Second
Coast

B8057   Aultbea   Loch
na Bà

An Cuaidh
972   Loch Airigh
an Eilein   Mellangaun

Loch
Squod   Isle of Ewe   Drumchork   Beinn Dearg
Bad Chailleach
897

Melvaig   Loch a'
Bhaid-
luachraich

Aultgrishan   Midtown   Loch
Fada

5   Seana Chamas   Cnoc Breac
962   Brae   Loch Ewe   Loch
Mhic' Ille
Riabhaich   Loch na
Moine Buige

B8021   Naast   Aird
Dubh

Peterburn   Loch Bad a'
Chreamh   Meall
na Mèine
.820   Bad
Bog

Port Erradale   Loch
nan
Llagh   Inverewe
NTS   Londubh   Loch
Ghuragarstidh

North
Erradale   Poolewe

A   155   B   Big Sand   River   Loch na
Curra   C   Blar Eiv   Loch
Kernsary   D

Longa
Island   Caolas Beag   Lonemore   Mial   B802   Strath   A832   Loch Tollaidh   Tollie
Farm   Loch na
Moine

Smithstown   Heritage   80   Gairloch   Meall an
Doirein   Lochan
Beannach Mòr
2595

Loch Gairloch   Beinn
Eilean   Aigh Charr

60   70   80   90

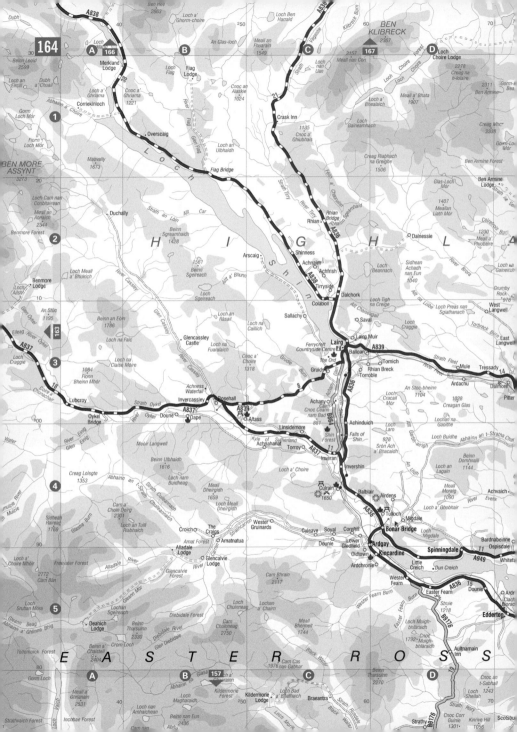

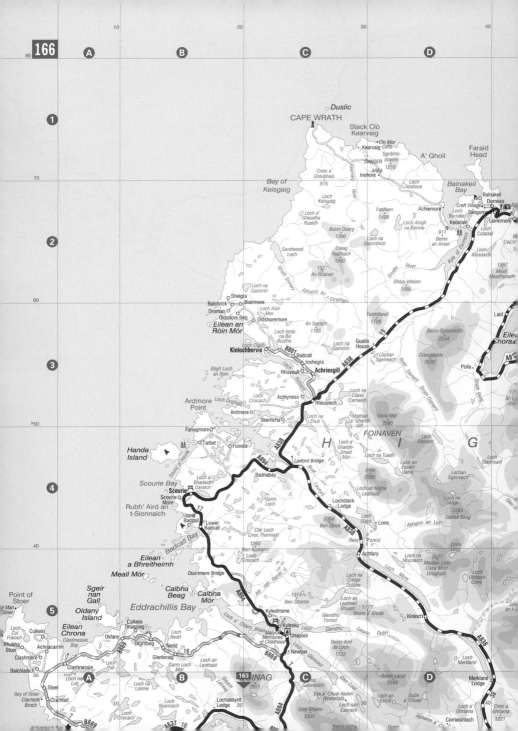

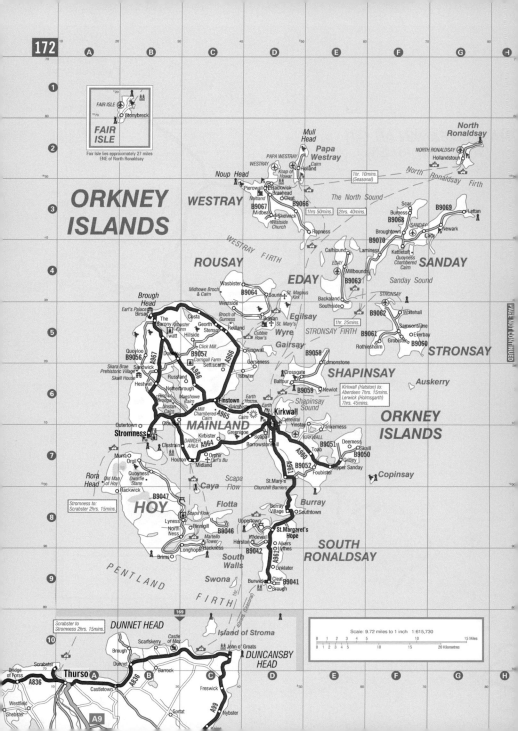

ORKNEY ISLANDS

FAIR ISLE

FAIR ISLE

Stonybreck

Fair Isle lies approximately 27 miles
ENE of North Ronaldsay

WESTRAY

Noup Head
Pierowall
Rackwick
Brackhead
Cleat
B9067
Midbea
Skelwick
Westside
Church
Rapness

Mull
Head

PAPA WESTRAY

**Papa
Westray**
Knap of
Howar
Holland
Cairn

1hr. 10mins.
(Seasonal)

The North Sound

**North
Ronaldsay**

NORTH RONALDSAY
Hollandstoun

North Ronaldsay Firth

Scar
Burness
B9068
Broughtown
Laminess
Lady

B9069
Lettan
Newark

1hrs 50mins.
2hrs. 40mins.

SANDAY

Calfsound
Kettletoft
Quoyness
Chambered
Cairn

ROUSAY

Wasbister
Midhowe Broch
& Cairn
Westside
Broch of
Gurness
Sourin
St. Magnus
Kirk
Egilsay
Evie
St. Mary's
Wyre
Cubbie
Row's
Gairsay

EDAY

B9064

EDAY
Millbounds
B9063
Backaland
Southside

Sanday Sound

STRONSAY

B9062
Whitehall
Samsonslane

STRONSAY

B9061
Grobister
Rothieshcolm

Everbay
B9060

1hr. 25mins.

STRONSAY FIRTH

**Brough
Head**
Earl's Palace
Birsay
The
Barony
Kirbister
Farm
Quoyloo
B9056
Skara Brae
Prehistoric Village
Skaill House
Sandwick
Hestwall
Costa
Geonh
Stenso
Redland
Hillside
Twatt
Dounby
Click Mill
Corrigall Farm
Settiscarth
Russland
Netherbrough
Maeshowe
Cairn
Ring of
Brodgar
Unstan
Cairn

Isbister
Tankerness
Gorseness
Tingwall

Crossgate
Balfour
Edmonstone

SHAPINSAY

B9059
Newlot

Auskerry

Kirkwall (Hatston) to:
Aberdeen 7hrs. 15mins.
Lerwick (Holmsgarth)
7hrs. 45mins.

**ORKNEY
ISLANDS**

MAINLAND

Finstown
Grimbister
Mill
Chambered
Cairn
Clousta
Kirbister
A964
DANGER
AREA
Orphir
Earl's Bu
Midland
Houton
Clestrain
Murra
Orgil
Quoyness
Dwarfie
Stane
Rackwick

Stromness
Outertown

Earth
House
Cairn

Kirkwall
Cathedral
Yinstay

Greengloe
Scapa
Borrowstonehill
St. Mary's
Churchill Barriers

Shapinsay
Sound

KIRKWALL
B9051
B9050
Toab
Skaill
Gritley
Foubister
Upper Sanday

Deerness

Copinsay

HOY

Rora
Head
Old Man
of Hoy

Scapa
Flow

Caya

Flotta

Lyness
North
Ness
Ounildil
Martello
Tower
Hackness
Longhope
Brims

South
Walls

Swona

Burray
Village
Uppertown
Herston
Widewall
B9042

Burray
Southtown

**St. Margaret's
Hope**

Aikers
Lythes
Linkdater

B9046
B9047

Stromness to:
Scrabster 2hrs. 15mins.

Burwick
Cleat
Brough
B9041

**SOUTH
RONALDSAY**

PENTLAND

FIRTH

Island of Stroma

DUNNET HEAD

Scrabster to
Stromness 2hrs. 15mins.

169

Scarfskerry
Brough
Castle
of Mey
John o' Groats
**DUNCANSBY
HEAD**

Scale: 9.72 miles to 1 inch   1:615,730
0   1   2   3   4   5   10   15 Miles
0 1 2 3 4 5   10   15   20 Kilometres

Scrabster
Bridge
of Forss
A836
Thurso
Castletown
A836
Barrock
Dunnet
Freswick
Sortat
Nybster
A99

Westfield
Shebster
A9

PAGE 170 CONTINUED

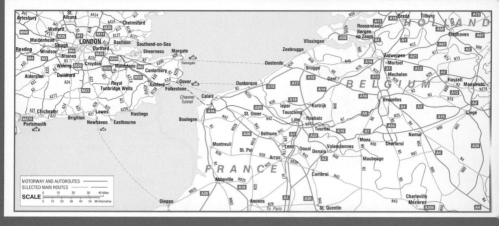

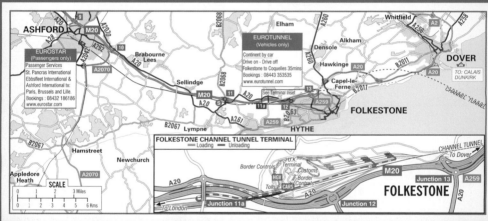

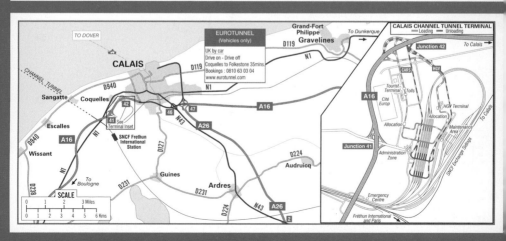

Mileage Chart

The distances for the mileage chart have been compiled by using a combination of Primary Routes and Motorways between any two towns shown.

To find the distance between any two towns shown, follow the horizontal line of one town and the vertical line of the other; at the intersection read off the mileage.

ie : Horizontal - LONDON
                 Intersection 216 miles
    Vertical - LIVERPOOL

Key to Route Planning Map Pages

PRIMARY ROUTES, shown in green throughout this Atlas, are a national network of recommended through routes which complement the motorway system. Selected places of major traffic importance are known as Primary Route Destinations and, on road signs, have a green background.

ABERDEEN
449 ABERYSTWYTH
181 324 AYR
400 114 272 BIRMINGHAM
330 159 196 124 BRADFORD
562 258 441 169 263 BRIGHTON
503 122 375 88 215 129 BRISTOL
447 198 366 102 156 117 167 CAMBRIDGE
505 106 377 106 233 168 42 201 CARDIFF
217 232 89 183 107 345 286 256 288 CARLISLE
437 134 297 18 124 157 102 84 129 200 COVENTRY
397 137 269 41 88 188 134 99 159 180 43 DERBY
340 192 239 95 40 232 184 117 210 150 94 57 DONCASTER
558 315 477 195 284 81 194 118 233 393 180 208 244 DOVER
125 340 75 284 198 466 377 326 379 91 303 266 212 444 EDINBURGH
553 199 425 161 282 170 75 232 107 336 166 213 257 244 439 EXETER
148 430 136 391 305 568 478 456 486 198 415 387 345 591 131 549 FORT WILLIAM
148 322 36 291 203 468 378 355 384 96 313 282 245 491 46 449 100 GLASGOW
445 109 317 53 171 152 35 132 53 228 59 93 149 189 331 107 435 324 GLOUCESTER
520 258 411 170 224 130 203 64 234 323 152 167 185 129 397 262 524 419 171 HARWICH
443 96 315 151 158 330 204 252 209 226 167 156 169 358 316 279 423 323 189 331 HOLYHEAD
107 492 198 449 353 620 536 490 558 260 458 421 369 601 157 607 63 162 496 554 481 INVERNESS
505 268 420 156 210 125 206 54 240 311 138 155 171 127 381 264 510 409 177 21 307 538 IPSWICH
269 182 139 151 62 324 235 215 232 50 170 136 99 344 141 307 248 146 200 279 180 310 268 KENDAL
357 235 255 139 68 243 228 134 239 165 123 94 37 254 230 290 367 255 195 204 218 387 189 127 KINGSTON UPON HULL
316 171 198 119 9 256 209 144 226 111 117 74 32 275 190 279 309 208 167 217 162 345 197 72 60 LEEDS
407 155 294 43 99 163 118 70 140 214 24 30 73 183 282 189 412 312 83 146 182 431 125 166 98 97 LEICESTER
376 208 249 87 80 207 170 88 192 178 76 53 41 206 247 241 376 274 135 152 204 402 124 140 46 72 52 LINCOLN
327 120 199 99 67 267 180 179 169 110 113 90 89 294 201 240 308 213 142 265 95 370 236 75 126 73 110 118 LIVERPOOL
321 128 204 87 37 252 167 159 188 117 99 53 51 273 208 239 315 215 132 230 120 363 211 72 96 42 95 87 34 MANCHESTER
273 233 181 174 69 316 265 196 287 92 175 130 84 316 147 337 279 192 230 266 226 306 253 77 88 64 154 127 134 106 MIDDLESBROUGH
230 266 146 209 98 345 300 232 312 58 209 165 115 350 104 369 237 153 263 297 257 263 287 88 130 96 188 153 167 136 40 NEWCASTLE UPON TYNE
476 270 348 163 185 174 234 62 256 280 142 142 169 351 284 478 378 193 72 289 505 44 249 145 178 112 103 222 177 221 252 NORWICH
381 155 267 54 78 191 140 84 165 188 52 15 48 210 256 218 386 286 108 165 177 410 140 141 92 72 27 37 107 68 128 159 118 NOTTINGHAM
485 151 335 68 167 106 73 92 106 267 57 101 138 142 358 151 465 365 57 101 183 142 358 157 101 126 223 175 162 76 113 68 157 218 253 159 104 OXFORD
680 301 552 269 394 279 184 343 218 463 278 316 369 355 551 109 663 561 217 374 388 715 375 419 412 391 310 359 353 344 449 481 393 323 261 PENZANCE
87 366 85 336 245 509 412 370 422 134 346 309 254 485 43 487 103 59 362 439 360 113 424 184 273 233 326 290 244 254 191 148 394 299 404 598 PERTH
589 232 461 203 325 206 111 274 159 372 209 254 300 286 485 43 592 490 150 305 322 648 305 348 299 281 379 412 327 255 333 231 429 284 299 172 96 PLYMOUTH
575 231 440 147 274 50 95 132 138 357 132 184 231 137 448 127 555 455 114 161 303 603 158 308 268 245 166 209 254 237 315 360 200 191 83 235 486 170 PORTSMOUTH
526 180 399 103 213 79 77 90 112 309 90 138 184 115 402 141 506 406 75 129 264 554 126 263 209 207 113 168 193 197 264 295 152 129 25 251 445 184 60 READING
529 178 383 121 245 82 53 140 101 312 113 159 207 158 400 91 510 408 73 177 262 569 177 265 251 230 137 213 208 287 318 200 162 65 201 443 132 43 57 SALISBURY
355 173 235 79 40 225 163 121 193 154 75 35 21 268 230 245 352 250 139 185 164 387 176 102 66 33 68 46 74 40 102 133 144 37 137 361 273 293 228 160 203 SHEFFIELD
388 73 260 47 100 216 116 140 107 171 64 67 114 249 262 175 369 267 77 114 208 292 175 137 112 79 123 59 67 166 203 196 86 105 286 309 218 195 147 150 85 SHREWSBURY
547 213 401 128 235 64 75 129 122 330 114 167 201 150 433 106 528 426 98 157 287 590 162 276 249 230 139 235 215 288 320 190 162 60 47 476 149 20 47 23 206 175 SOUTHAMPTON
520 258 431 152 220 85 177 64 211 342 129 168 185 89 395 226 548 438 152 57 303 549 57 283 200 213 139 156 255 225 262 299 99 160 105 337 439 269 117 98 132 197 173 126 SOUTHEND-ON-SEA
374 108 243 47 75 217 127 137 140 150 64 36 74 236 241 202 348 248 95 201 122 410 179 121 117 78 55 87 56 36 142 173 171 55 118 311 287 241 201 147 168 50 35 183 199 STOKE-ON-TRENT
496 76 368 124 220 209 80 236 41 279 150 184 244 264 370 154 477 375 91 279 172 578 279 249 262 229 174 226 168 187 293 323 286 178 144 266 446 196 175 147 136 202 124 159 245 159 SWANSEA
213 584 304 557 461 728 644 589 640 352 552 529 475 706 262 715 169 268 604 657 589 108 654 402 492 453 544 510 463 471 410 367 613 519 621 823 220 758 709 662 664 506 523 682 659 502 631 THURSO
437 96 309 29 135 162 62 119 73 220 46 82 118 197 306 136 418 311 28 168 105 361 182 185 140 107 88 36 142 173 151 118 311 267 151 237 217 57 244 350 177 166 95 101 103 49 124 150 65 WORCESTER
312 193 201 129 94 269 227 151 237 116 129 84 33 269 187 289 314 214 181 232 185 344 200 81 38 24 108 76 96 65 48 83 176 84 174 400 331 257 217 244 54 132 244 214 114 268 450 164 YORK
501 206 390 118 203 53 118 58 150 305 97 128 165 76 373 171 503 403 101 79 264 527 76 264 188 196 102 143 216 200 246 278 114 130 55 282 416 214 74 39 84 161 160 78 43 160 187 636 110 203 LONDON

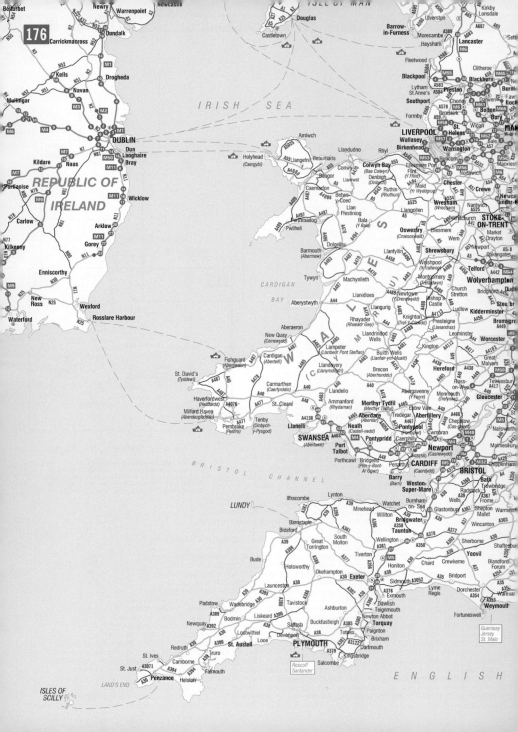

REFERENCE

MOTORWAY WITH NUMBER	M4 (S) Service Area
MOTORWAY (Under Construction/Proposed)	
MOTORWAY JUNCTIONS	
PRIMARY ROUTE	A5
A ROAD	A272
NATIONAL BOUNDARY	
TOWNS SHOWN IN THE MILEAGE CHART	**NORWICH**

SCALE

0   10   20   30   40 Miles
0   10   20   30   40   50   60 Kilometres

NORTH SEA

CHANNEL

FRANCE

ISLE OF WIGHT

GUERNSEY

St. Peter Port

JERSEY

St. Helier

Jersey and Guernsey lie 85 miles south of Weymouth

N

OUTER HEBRIDES

ISLE OF LEWIS
(EILEAN LEODHAIS)

Stornoway
(Steòrnabhagh)

Tarbert
(Tairbeart)

HARRIS
(NA HEARADH)

Leverburgh
(An t-Ob)

Lochmaddy
(Loch nam Madadh)

NORTH UIST
(UIBHIST A TUATH)

BENBECULA
(BEINN NA FAOGHLA)

Dunvegan

Portree

RAASAY

SOUTH UIST
(UIBHIST A DEAS)

Lochboisdale
(Loch Baghasdail)

ISLE OF SKYE

Kyle of
Lochalsh

BARRA
(BARRAIGH)

Castlebay
(Bàgh a' Chaisteil)

CANNA

RÙM

EIGG

MUCK

Mallaig

Arisaig

INNER HEBRIDES

COLL

TIREE

ISLE OF MULL

IONA

Tobermory

Kilchoan

Acharacle

Lochaline

COLONSAY

JURA

ISLAY

Port Ellen

GIGHA

Brodick

ISLE OF ARRAN

ISLE OF BUTE

Rothesay

Kennacraig

Largs

Tayinloan

Lochgilphead

Inveraray

Oban

Crianlarich

Callander

Doune

Dunblane

Loch Lomond

Helensburgh

Dumbarton

Greenock

Clydebank

GLASGOW

Paisley

Hamilton

East Kilbride

Motherwell

Airdrie

Falkirk

Stirling

Alloa

Dunfermline

EDINBURGH

Kinross

Perth

Dundee

Kirkcaldy

Glenrothes

Methil

Cupar

Auchterarder

Crieff

Aberfeldy

Dunkeld

Blairgowrie

Pitlochry

Kirriemuir

Forfar

Brechin

Braemar

Ballater

Kingussie

Newtonmore

Aviemore

Grantown-on-Spey

Fort Augustus

Invermoriston

Invergarry

Spean Bridge

Fort William

Glencoe

SCOTLAND

Loch Ness

Inverness

Nairn

Forres

Elgin

Keith

Dufftown

Huntly

Fochabers

Lossiemouth

Moray Firth

Cromarty

Invergordon

Alness

Dingwall

Fortrose

Strathcarron

Achnasheen

Kinlochewe

Torridon

Shieldaig

Gairloch

Poolewe

Ullapool

Lochinver

Scourie

Lairg

Bonar Bridge

Tain

Dornoch

Golspie

Brora

Helmsdale

Lochcarron

Tongue

Thurso

Scrabster

Wick

Braemar

Firth of Forth

Musselburgh

Dalkeith

Livingston

Bathgate

Bonnybridge

Kilsyth

Kirkintilloch

Wemyss Bay

Dunoon

Gourock

Cumbernauld

Coatbridge

Bellshill

Lanark

Lauder

Peebles

Galashiels

Selkirk

Hawick

Biggar

Moffat

Langholm

Lockerbie

Annan

Carlisle

Dumfries

Castle Douglas

Dalbeattie

Kirkcudbright

Gatehouse of Fleet

Newton Stewart

Wigtown

Whithorn

Cairnryan

Stranraer

New Galloway

Sanquhar

Cumnock

Mauchline

Kilmarnock

Troon

Prestwick

Ayr

Maybole

Girvan

Irvine

Ardrossan

Stevenston

Campbeltown

Solway Firth

Maryport

Workington

Whitehaven

Egremont

Ravenglass

Cockermouth

Keswick

Ambleside

Coniston

ISLE OF MAN

Peel

Ramsey

Douglas

NORTHERN IRELAND

Portrush

Portstewart

Ballycastle

Coleraine

Ballymoney

Londonderry

Letterkenny

Strabane

Omagh

Enniskillen

Monaghan

Armagh

Dungannon

Lough Neagh

Antrim

Ballymena

Crumlin

Larne

BELFAST

Downpatrick

Newcastle

Newtownards

Strangford Lough

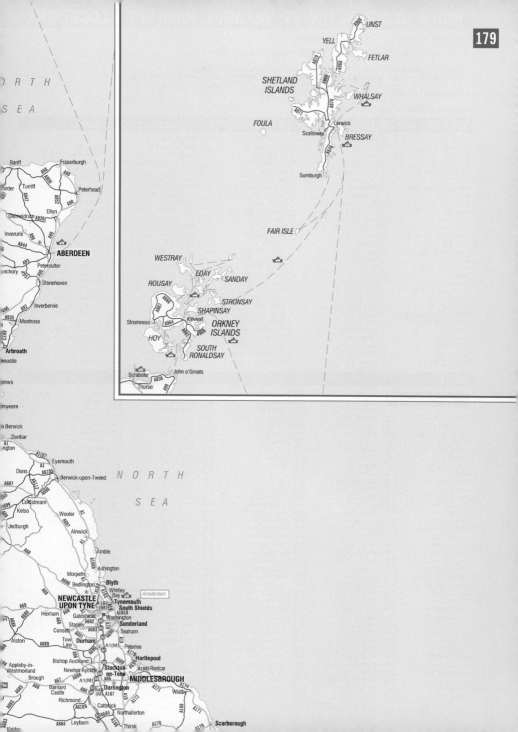

INDEX TO CITIES, TOWNS, VILLAGES, HAMLETS & LOCATIONS

(1) A strict alphabetical order is used e.g. An Dùnan follows Andreas but precedes Andwell.

(2) The map reference given refers to the actual map square in which the town spot or built-up area is located and not to the place name.

(3) Where two or more places of the same name occur in the same County or Unitary Authority, the nearest large town is also given; e.g. Achiemore. *High* . . . .2D **166** (nr. Durness) indicates that Achiemore is located in square 2D on page **166** and is situated near Durness in the Unitary Authority of Highland.

(4) Only one reference is given although due to page overlaps the place may appear on more than one page.

(5) Major towns and destinations are shown in bold, i.e. **Aberdeen.** *Aber* 3G **153**

COUNTIES and UNITARY AUTHORITIES with the abbreviations used in this index

Aberdeen : *Aber*
Aberdeenshire : *Abers*
Angus : *Ang*
Argyll & Bute : *Arg*
Bath & N E Somerset : *Bath*
Bedford : *Bed*
Blackburn with Darwen : *Bkbn*
Blackpool : *Bkpl*
Blaenau Gwent : *Blae*
Bournemouth : *Bour*
Bracknell Forest : *Brac*
Bridgend : *B'end*
Brighton & Hove : *Brig*
Bristol : *Bris*
Buckinghamshire : *Buck*
Caerphilly : *Cphy*
Cambridgeshire : *Cambs*
Cardiff : *Card*
Carmarthenshire : *Carm*
Central Bedfordshire : *C Beds*
Ceredigion : *Cdgn*
Cheshire East : *Ches E*
Cheshire West & Chester : *Ches W*
Clackmannanshire : *Clac*
Conwy : *Cnwy*
Cornwall : *Corn*
Cumbria : *Cumb*
Darlington : *Darl*
Denbighshire : *Den*
Derby : *Derb*
Derbyshire : *Derbs*
Devon : *Devn*
Dorset : *Dors*
Dumfries & Galloway : *Dum*
Dundee : *D'dee*
Durham : *Dur*
East Ayrshire : *E Ayr*
East Dunbartonshire : *E Dun*
East Lothian : *E Lot*
East Renfrewshire : *E Ren*
East Riding of Yorkshire : *E Yor*
East Sussex : *E Sus*
Edinburgh : *Edin*
Essex : *Essx*
Falkirk : *Falk*
Fife : *Fife*
Flintshire : *Flin*
Glasgow : *Glas*
Gloucestershire : *Glos*
Greater London : *G Lon*
Greater Manchester : *G Man*
Gwynedd : *Gwyn*
Halton : *Hal*
Hampshire : *Hants*
Hartlepool : *Hart*
Herefordshire : *Here*
Hertfordshire : *Herts*
Highland : *High*
Inverclyde : *Inv*
Isle of Anglesey : *IOA*
Isle of Man : *IOM*
Isle of Wight : *IOW*
Isles of Scilly : *IOS*
Kent : *Kent*
Kingston upon Hull : *Hull*
Lancashire : *Lanc*
Leicester : *Leic*
Leicestershire : *Leics*
Lincolnshire : *Linc*
Luton : *Lutn*
Medway : *Medw*
Merseyside : *Mers*
Merthyr Tydfil : *Mer T*
Middlesbrough : *Midd*
Midlothian : *Midl*
Milton Keynes : *Mil*
Monmouthshire : *Mon*
Moray : *Mor*
Neath Port Talbot : *Neat*
Newport : *Newp*
Norfolk : *Norf*
Northamptonshire : *Nptn*
North Ayrshire : *N Ayr*
North East Lincolnshire : *NE Lin*
North Lanarkshire : *N Lan*
North Lincolnshire : *N Lin*
North Somerset : *N Som*
Northumberland : *Nmbd*
North Yorkshire : *N Yor*
Nottingham : *Nott*
Nottinghamshire : *Notts*
Orkney : *Orkn*
Oxfordshire : *Oxon*
Pembrokeshire : *Pemb*
Perth & Kinross : *Per*
Peterborough : *Pet*
Plymouth : *Plym*
Poole : *Pool*
Portsmouth : *Port*
Powys : *Powy*
Reading : *Read*
Redcar & Cleveland : *Red C*
Renfrewshire : *Ren*
Rhondda Cynon Taff : *Rhon*
Rutland : *Rut*
Scottish Borders : *Bord*
Shetland : *Shet*
Shropshire : *Shrp*
Slough : *Slo*
Somerset : *Som*
Southampton : *Sotn*
South Ayrshire : *S Ayr*
Southend-on-Sea : *S'end*
South Gloucestershire : *S Glo*
South Lanarkshire : *S Lan*
South Yorkshire : *S Yor*
Staffordshire : *Staf*
Stirling : *Stir*
Stockton-on-Tees : *Stoc T*
Stoke-on-Trent : *Stoke*
Suffolk : *Suff*
Surrey : *Surr*
Swansea : *Swan*
Swindon : *Swin*
Telford & Wrekin : *Telf*
Thurrock : *Thur*
Torbay : *Torb*
Torfaen : *Torf*
Tyne & Wear : *Tyne*
Vale of Glamorgan, The : *V Glam*
Warrington : *Warr*
Warwickshire : *Warw*
West Berkshire : *W Ber*
West Dunbartonshire : *W Dun*
Western Isles : *W Isl*
West Lothian : *W Lot*
West Midlands : *W Mid*
West Sussex : *W Sus*
West Yorkshire : *W Yor*
Wiltshire : *Wilts*
Windsor & Maidenhead : *Wind*
Wokingham : *Wok*
Worcestershire : *Worc*
Wrexham : *Wrex*
York : *York*

INDEX

A

Abbas Combe. *Som* . . . 4C **22**
Abberley. *Worc* . . . 4B **60**
Abberley Common. *Worc* . . . 4B **60**
Abberton. *Essx* . . . 4D **54**
Abberton. *Worc* . . . 5D **61**
Abberwick. *Nmbd* . . . 3F **121**
Abbess Roding. *Essx* . . . 4F **53**
Abbey. *Devn* . . . 1E **13**
Abbey-cwm-hir. *Powy* . . . 3C **58**
Abbeydale. *S Yor* . . . 2H **85**
Abbeydale Park. *S Yor* . . . 2H **85**
Abbey Dore. *Here* . . . 2G **47**
Abbey Gate. *Devn* . . . 3F **13**
Abbey Hulton. *Stoke* . . . 1D **72**
Abbey St Bathans. *Bord* . . . 3D **130**
Abbeystead. *Lanc* . . . 4E **97**
Abbeytown. *Cumb* . . . 4C **112**
Abbey Village. *Lanc* . . . 2E **91**
Abbey Wood. *G Lon* . . . 3F **39**
Abbots Ann. *Hants* . . . 2B **24**
Abbots Bickington. *Devn* . . . 1D **11**
Abbots Bromley. *Staf* . . . 3E **73**
Abbotsbury. *Dors* . . . 4A **14**
Abbotsham. *Devn* . . . 4E **19**
Abbotskerswell. *Devn* . . . 2E **9**
Abbots Langley. *Herts* . . . 5A **52**
Abbots Leigh. *N Som* . . . 4A **34**
Abbotsley. *Cambs* . . . 5B **64**
Abbots Morton. *Worc* . . . 5E **61**
Abbots Ripton. *Cambs* . . . 3B **64**
Abbot's Salford. *Warw* . . . 5E **61**
Abbotstone. *Hants* . . . 3D **24**
Abbots Worthy. *Hants* . . . 3C **24**
Abcott. *Shrp* . . . 3F **59**
Abdon. *Shrp* . . . 2H **59**
Abenhall. *Glos* . . . 4B **48**
Aber. *Cdgn* . . . 1E **45**
Aberaeron. *Cdgn* . . . 4D **56**
Aberafan. *Neat* . . . 3G **31**
Aberaman. *Rhon* . . . 5D **46**
Aberangell. *Powy* . . . 4H **69**
Aberarad. *Carm* . . . 1H **43**
Aberarder. *High* . . . 1A **150**
Aberargie. *Per* . . . 2D **136**
Aberarth. *Cdgn* . . . 4D **57**
Aberavon. *Neat* . . . 3G **31**
Aber-banc. *Cdgn* . . . 1D **44**
Aberbargoed. *Cphy* . . . 2E **33**
Aberbechan. *Powy* . . . 1D **58**
Aberbeeg. *Blae* . . . 5F **47**
Aberbowlan. *Carm* . . . 2G **45**
Aberbran. *Powy* . . . 3C **46**
Abercanaid. *Mer T* . . . 5D **46**
Abercarn. *Cphy* . . . 2F **33**
Abercastle. *Pemb* . . . 1C **42**
Abercegir. *Powy* . . . 5H **69**
Aberchalder. *High* . . . 3F **149**
Aberchirder. *Abers* . . . 3D **160**
Abercorn. *W Lot* . . . 2D **129**
Abercraf. *Powy* . . . 4B **46**
Abercregan. *Neat* . . . 2B **32**
Abercrombie. *Fife* . . . 3H **137**
Abercwmboi. *Rhon* . . . 2D **32**
Abercych. *Pemb* . . . 1C **44**
Abercynon. *Rhon* . . . 2D **32**
Aber-Cywarch. *Gwyn* . . . 4A **70**
Aberdalgie. *Per* . . . 1C **136**
Aberdar. *Rhon* . . . 5C **46**
Aberdare. *Rhon* . . . 5C **46**
Aberdaron. *Gwyn* . . . 3A **68**
Aberdaugleddau. *Pemb* . . . 4D **42**
Aberdeen. *Aber* . . . 3G **153**
Aberdeen (Dyce) Airport. *Aber* . . . 2F **153**
Aberdesach. *Gwyn* . . . 5D **80**
Aberdour. *Fife* . . . 1E **129**
Aberdovey. *Gwyn* . . . 1F **57**
Aberdulais. *Neat* . . . 5A **46**
Aberdyfi. *Gwyn* . . . 1F **57**
Aberedw. *Powy* . . . 1D **46**
Abereiddy. *Pemb* . . . 1B **42**
Abererch. *Gwyn* . . . 2C **68**
Aberfan. *Mer T* . . . 5D **46**
Aberfeldy. *Per* . . . 4F **143**
Aberffraw. *IOA* . . . 4C **80**
Aberffrwd. *Cdgn* . . . 3F **57**
Aberford. *W Yor* . . . 1E **93**
Aberfoyle. *Stir* . . . 3E **135**
Abergarw. *B'end* . . . 3C **32**
Abergarwed. *Neat* . . . 5B **46**
Abergavenny. *Mon* . . . 4G **47**
Abergele. *Cnwy* . . . 3B **82**
Aber-Giar. *Carm* . . . 1F **45**
Abergorlech. *Carm* . . . 2F **45**
Abergwaun. *Pemb* . . . 1D **42**
Abergwesyn. *Powy* . . . 5A **58**
Abergwili. *Carm* . . . 3E **45**
Abergwynfi. *Neat* . . . 2B **32**
Abergwyngregyn. *Gwyn* . . . 3F **81**
Abergynolwyn. *Gwyn* . . . 5F **69**
Aberhafesp. *Powy* . . . 1C **58**
Aberhonddu. *Powy* . . . 3D **46**
Aberhosan. *Powy* . . . 1H **57**
Aberkenfig. *B'end* . . . 3B **32**
Aberlady. *E Lot* . . . 2A **130**
Aberlemno. *Ang* . . . 3E **145**
Aberllefenni. *Gwyn* . . . 5G **69**
Abermaw. *Gwyn* . . . 4F **69**
Abermeurig. *Cdgn* . . . 5E **57**
Aber-miwl. *Powy* . . . 1D **58**
Abermule. *Powy* . . . 1D **58**
Abernant. *Carm* . . . 2H **43**
Abernant. *Rhon* . . . 5D **46**
Abernethy. *Per* . . . 2D **136**
Abernyte. *Per* . . . 5B **144**
Aber-oer. *Wrex* . . . 1E **71**
Aberpennar. *Rhon* . . . 2D **32**
Aberporth. *Cdgn* . . . 5B **56**
Aberriw. *Powy* . . . 5D **70**
Abersoch. *Gwyn* . . . 3C **68**
Abersychan. *Torf* . . . 5F **47**
Abertawe. *Swan* . . . 3F **31**
Aberteifi. *Cdgn* . . . 1B **44**
Aberthin. *V Glam* . . . 4D **32**
Abertillery. *Blae* . . . 5F **47**
Abertridwr. *Cphy* . . . 3E **32**
Abertridwr. *Powy* . . . 4C **70**
Abertyleri. *Blae* . . . 5F **47**
Abertysswg. *Cphy* . . . 5E **47**
Aberuthven. *Per* . . . 2B **136**
Aber Village. *Powy* . . . 3E **46**
Aberyscir. *Powy* . . . 3D **46**
Aberystwyth. *Cdgn* . . . 2E **57**
Abhainn Suidhe. *W Isl* . . . 7C **171**
Abingdon-on-Thames. *Oxon* . . . 2C **36**
Abinger Common. *Surr* . . . 1C **26**
Abinger Hammer. *Surr* . . . 1B **26**
Abington. *S Lan* . . . 2B **118**
Abington Pigotts. *Cambs* . . . 1D **52**
Ab Kettleby. *Leics* . . . 3E **74**
Ab Lench. *Worc* . . . 5E **61**
Ablington. *Glos* . . . 5G **49**
Ablington. *Wilts* . . . 2G **23**
Abney. *Derbs* . . . 3F **85**
Aboyne. *Abers* . . . 4C **152**
Abram. *G Man* . . . 4E **90**
Abriachan. *High* . . . 5H **157**
Abridge. *Essx* . . . 1F **39**
Abronhill. *N Lan* . . . 2A **128**
Abson. *S Glo* . . . 4C **34**
Abthorpe. *Nptn* . . . 1E **51**
Aby. *Linc* . . . 3D **88**
Acaster Malbis. *York* . . . 5H **99**
Acaster Selby. *N Yor* . . . 5H **99**
Accott. *Devn* . . . 3G **19**
Accrington. *Lanc* . . . 2F **91**
Acha. *Arg* . . . 3C **138**
Achachork. *High* . . . 4D **155**
Achadh a' Chuirn. *High* . . . 1E **147**
Achahoish. *Arg* . . . 2F **125**
Achaleven. *Arg* . . . 5D **140**
Achallader. *Arg* . . . 4H **141**
Acha Mor. *W Isl* . . . 5F **171**
Achanalt. *High* . . . 2E **157**
Achandunie. *High* . . . 1A **158**
Ach'an Todhair. *High* . . . 1E **141**
Achany. *High* . . . 3C **164**
Achaphubuil. *High* . . . 1E **141**
Acharacle. *High* . . . 2A **140**
Acharn. *Ang* . . . 1B **144**
Acharn. *Per* . . . 4E **143**
Acharole. *High* . . . 3E **169**
Achateny. *High* . . . 2G **139**
Achavanich. *High* . . . 4D **169**
Achdalieu. *High* . . . 1E **141**
Achduart. *High* . . . 3E **163**
Achentoul. *High* . . . 5A **168**
Achfary. *High* . . . 5C **166**
Achfrish. *High* . . . 2C **164**
Achgarve. *High* . . . 4C **162**
Achiemore. *High* . . . 2D **166** (nr. Durness)
Achiemore. *High* . . . 3A **168** (nr. Thurso)
A'Chill. *High* . . . 3A **146**
Achiltibuie. *High* . . . 3E **163**
Achina. *High* . . . 2H **167**
Achinahuagh. *High* . . . 2F **167**
Achindarroch. *High* . . . 3E **141**
Achinduich. *High* . . . 3C **164**
Achinduin. *Arg* . . . 5C **140**
Achininver. *High* . . . 2F **167**
Achintee. *High* . . . 4B **156**

Ashgill—Bagby

Ashgill. *S Lan* 5A **128**
Ash Green. *Warw* 2H **61**
Ashgrove. *Mor* 2G **159**
Ashill. *Devn* 1D **12**
Ashill. *Norf* 5A **78**
Ashill. *Som* 1G **13**
Ashingdon. *Essx* 1C **40**
Ashington. *Nmbd* 1F **115**
Ashington. *W Sus* 4C **26**
Ashkirk. *Bord* 2G **119**
Ashlett. *Hants* 2C **16**
Ashleworth. *Glos* 3D **48**
Ashley. *Cambs* 4F **65**
Ashley. *Ches E* 2B **84**
Ashley. *Dors* 2G **15**
Ashley. *Glos* 2E **35**
Ashley. *Hants* 3A **16**
(nr. New Milton)
Ashley. *Hants* 3B **24**
(nr. Winchester)
Ashley. *Kent* 1H **29**
Ashley. *Nptn* 1E **63**
Ashley. *Staf* 2B **72**
Ashley. *Wilts* 5D **34**
Ashley Green. *Buck* 5H **51**
Ashley Heath. *Dors* 2G **15**
Ashley Heath. *Staf* 2B **72**
Ashley Moor. *Here* 4G **59**
Ash Magna. *Shrp* 2H **71**
Ashmanhaugh. *Norf* 3F **79**
Ashmansworth. *Hants* 1C **24**
Ashmansworthy. *Devn* 1D **10**
Ashmead Green. *Glos* 2C **34**
Ashmill. *Devn* 3D **11**
(nr. Holsworthy)
Ash Mill. *Devn* 4A **20**
(nr. South Molton)
Ashmore. *Dors* 1E **15**
Ashmore Green. *W Ber* 5D **36**
Ashover. *Derbs* 4A **86**
Ashow. *Warw* 3H **61**
Ash Parva. *Shrp* 2H **71**
Ashperton. *Here* 1B **48**
Ashprington. *Devn* 3E **9**
Ash Priors. *Som* 4E **21**
Ashreigney. *Devn* 1G **11**
Ash Street. *Suff* 1D **54**
Ashtead. *Surr* 5C **38**
Ash Thomas. *Devn* 1D **12**
Ashton. *Corn* 4D **4**
Ashton. *Here* 4H **59**
Ashton. *Inv* 2D **126**
Ashton. *Nptn* 2H **63**
(nr. Oundle)
Ashton. *Nptn* 1F **51**
(nr. Roade)
Ashton. *Pet* 5A **76**
Ashton Common. *Wilts* 1E **23**
Ashton Hayes. *Ches W* 4H **83**
Ashton-in-Makerfield. *G Man* 4D **90**
Ashton Keynes. *Wilts* 2F **35**
Ashton under Hill. *Worc* 2E **49**
Ashton-under-Lyne. *G Man* 1D **84**
Ashton upon Mersey. *G Man* 1B **84**
Ashurst. *Hants* 1B **16**
Ashurst. *Kent* 2G **27**
Ashurst. *Lanc* 4C **90**
Ashurst. *W Sus* 4C **26**
Ashurst Wood. *W Sus* 2F **27**
Ash Vale. *Surr* 1G **25**
Ashwater. *Devn* 3D **11**
Ashwell. *Herts* 2C **52**
Ashwell. *Rut* 4F **75**
Ashwellthorpe. *Norf* 1D **66**
Ashwick. *Som* 2B **22**
Ashwicken. *Norf* 4G **77**
Ashwood. *Staf* 2C **60**
Askam in Furness. *Cumb* 2B **96**
Askern. *S Yor* 3F **93**
Askerswell. *Dors* 3A **14**
Askett. *Buck* 5G **51**
Askham. *Cumb* 2G **103**
Askham. *Notts* 3E **87**
Askham Bryan. *York* 5H **99**
Askham Richard. *York* 5H **99**
Askrigg. *N Yor* 5C **104**
Askwith. *N Yor* 5D **98**
Aslackby. *Linc* 2H **75**
Aslacton. *Norf* 1D **66**
Aslockton. *Notts* 1E **75**
Aspatria. *Cumb* 5C **112**
Aspenden. *Herts* 3D **52**
Asperton. *Linc* 2B **76**
Aspley Guise. *C Beds* 2H **51**
Aspley Heath. *C Beds* 2H **51**
Aspull. *G Man* 4E **90**
Asselby. *E Yor* 2H **93**
Assington. *Suff* 2C **54**
Assington Green. *Suff* 5G **65**
Astbury. *Ches E* 4C **84**
Astcote. *Nptn* 5D **62**
Asterby. *Linc* 3B **88**
Asterley. *Shrp* 5F **71**
Asterton. *Shrp* 1F **59**
Asthall. *Oxon* 4A **50**
Asthall Leigh. *Oxon* 4B **50**
Astle. *High* 4E **165**
Astley. *G Man* 4F **91**
Astley. *Shrp* 4H **71**
Astley. *Warw* 2H **61**
Astley. *Worc* 4B **60**
Astley Abbotts. *Shrp* 1B **60**
Astley Bridge. *G Man* 3F **91**
Astley Cross. *Worc* 4C **60**
Aston. *Ches E* 1A **72**
Aston. *Ches W* 3H **83**
Aston. *Derbs* 2F **85**
(nr. Hope)
Aston. *Derbs* 2F **73**
(nr. Sudbury)
Aston. *Flin* 4F **83**
Aston. *Here* 4G **59**
Aston. *Herts* 3C **52**
Aston. *Oxon* 5B **50**
Aston. *Shrp* 1C **60**
(nr. Bridgnorth)
Aston. *Shrp* 3H **71**
(nr. Wem)
Aston. *S Yor* 2B **86**
Aston. *Staf* 1B **72**
Aston. *Telf* 5A **72**
Aston. *W Mid* 1E **61**
Aston. *Wok* 3F **37**
Aston Abbotts. *Buck* 3G **51**
Aston Botterell. *Shrp* 2A **60**
Aston-by-Stone. *Staf* 2D **72**
Aston Cantlow. *Warw* 5F **61**
Aston Clinton. *Buck* 4G **51**
Aston Crews. *Here* 3B **48**
Aston Cross. *Glos* 2E **49**
Aston End. *Herts* 3C **52**
Aston Eyre. *Shrp* 1A **60**
Aston Fields. *Worc* 4D **60**
Aston Flamville. *Leics* 1B **62**
Aston Ingham. *Here* 3B **48**
Aston juxta Mondrum. *Ches E* 5A **84**
Astonlane. *Shrp* 1A **60**
Aston le Walls. *Nptn* 5B **62**
Aston Magna. *Glos* 2G **49**
Aston Munslow. *Shrp* 2H **59**
Aston on Carrant. *Glos* 2E **49**
Aston on Clun. *Shrp* 2F **59**
Aston-on-Trent. *Derbs* 3B **74**
Aston Pigott. *Shrp* 5F **71**
Aston Rogers. *Shrp* 5F **71**
Aston Rowant. *Oxon* 2F **37**
Aston Sandford. *Buck* 5F **51**
Aston Somerville. *Worc* 2F **49**
Aston Subedge. *Glos* 1G **49**
Aston Tirrold. *Oxon* 3D **36**
Aston Upthorpe. *Oxon* 3D **36**
Astrop. *Nptn* 2D **50**
Astwick. *C Beds* 2C **52**
Astwood. *Mil* 1H **51**
Astwood Bank. *Worc* 4E **61**
Aswarby. *Linc* 2H **75**
Aswardby. *Linc* 3C **88**
Atcham. *Shrp* 5H **71**
Atch Lench. *Worc* 5E **61**
Athelhampton. *Dors* 3C **14**
Athelington. *Suff* 3E **66**
Athelney. *Som* 4G **21**
Athelstaneford. *E Lot* 2B **130**
Atherfield Green. *IOW* 5C **16**
Atherington. *Devn* 4F **19**
Atherington. *W Sus* 5B **26**
Athersley. *S Yor* 4D **92**
Atherstone. *Warw* 1H **61**
Atherstone on Stour. *Warw* 5G **61**
Atherton. *G Man* 4E **91**
Ath-Tharracail. *High* 2A **140**
Atlow. *Derbs* 1G **73**
Attadale. *High* 5B **156**
Attenborough. *Notts* 2C **74**
Atterby. *Linc* 1G **87**
Atterley. *Shrp* 1A **60**
Atterton. *Leics* 1A **62**
Attleborough. *Norf* 1C **66**
Attleborough. *Warw* 1A **62**
Attlebridge. *Norf* 4D **78**
Atwick. *E Yor* 4F **101**
Atworth. *Wilts* 5D **34**
Auberrow. *Here* 1H **47**
Aubourn. *Linc* 4G **87**
Aucharnie. *Abers* 4D **160**
Auchattie. *Abers* 4D **152**
Auchavan. *Ang* 2A **144**
Auchbreck. *Mor* 1G **151**
Auchenback. *E Ren* 4G **127**
Auchenblae. *Abers* 1G **145**
Auchenbrack. *Dum* 5G **117**
Auchenbreck. *Arg* 1B **126**
Auchencairn. *Dum* 4E **111**
(nr. Dalbeattie)
Auchencairn. *Dum* 1A **112**
(nr. Dumfries)
Auchencarroch. *W Dun* 1F **127**
Auchencrow. *Bord* 3E **131**
Auchendennan. *W Dun* 1E **127**
Auchendinny. *Midl* 3F **129**
Auchengray. *S Lan* 4C **128**
Auchenhalrig. *Mor* 2A **160**
Auchenheath. *S Lan* 5B **128**
Auchenlochan. *Arg* 2A **126**
Auchenmade. *N Ayr* 5E **127**
Auchenmalg. *Dum* 4H **109**
Auchentiber. *N Ayr* 5E **127**
Auchenvennel. *Arg* 1D **126**
Auchindrain. *Arg* 3H **133**
Auchininna. *Abers* 4D **160**
Auchinleck. *Dum* 2B **110**
Auchinleck. *E Ayr* 2E **117**
Auchinloch. *N Lan* 2H **127**
Auchinstarry. *N Lan* 2A **128**
Auchleven. *Abers* 1D **152**
Auchlochan. *S Lan* 1H **117**
Auchlunachan. *High* 5F **163**
Auchmillan. *E Ayr* 2E **117**
Auchmithie. *Ang* 4F **145**
Auchmuirbridge. *Per* 3E **136**
Auchmull. *Ang* 1E **145**
Auchnacree. *Ang* 4G **161**
Auchnafree. *Per* 5F **143**
Auchnagallin. *High* 5E **159**
Auchnagatt. *Abers* 4G **161**
Aucholzie. *Abers* 4H **151**
Auchreddie. *Abers* 4F **161**
Auchterarder. *Per* 2B **136**
Auchteraw. *High* 3F **149**
Auchterderran. *Fife* 4E **136**
Auchterhouse. *Ang* 5C **144**
Auchtermuchty. *Fife* 2E **137**
Auchterneed. *High* 3G **157**
Auchtertool. *Fife* 4E **136**
Auchtertyre. *High* 1G **147**
Auchtubh. *Stir* 1E **135**
Auckengill. *High* 2F **169**
Auckley. *S Yor* 4G **93**
Audenshaw. *G Man* 1D **84**
Audlem. *Ches E* 1A **72**
Audley. *Staf* 5B **84**
Audley End. *Essx* 2F **53**
Audmore. *Staf* 3C **72**
Auds. *Abers* 2D **160**
Aughertree. *Cumb* 1D **102**
Aughton. *E Yor* 1H **93**
Aughton. *Lanc* 3E **97**
(nr. Lancaster)
Aughton. *Lanc* 4B **90**
(nr. Ormskirk)
Aughton. *S Yor* 2B **86**
Aughton. *Wilts* 1H **23**
Aughton Park. *Lanc* 4C **90**
Auldearn. *High* 3D **158**
Aulden. *Here* 5G **59**
Auldgirth. *Dum* 1G **111**
Auldhouse. *S Lan* 4H **127**
Ault a' chruinn. *High* 1B **148**
Aultbea. *High* 5C **162**
Aultdearg. *High* 2E **157**
Aultgrishan. *High* 5B **162**
Aultguish Inn. *High* 1F **157**
Ault Hucknall. *Derbs* 4B **86**
Aultibea. *High* 1H **165**
Aultiphurst. *High* 2A **168**
Aultivullin. *High* 2A **168**
Aultmore. *Mor* 3B **160**
Aultnamain Inn. *High* 5D **164**
Aunby. *Linc* 4H **75**
Aunsby. *Linc* 2H **75**
Aust. *S Glo* 3A **34**
Austerfield. *S Yor* 1D **86**
Austin Fen. *Linc* 1C **88**
Austrey. *Warw* 5G **73**
Austwick. *N Yor* 3G **97**
Authorpe. *Linc* 2D **88**
Authorpe Row. *Linc* 3E **89**
Avebury. *Wilts* 5G **35**
Avebury Trusloe. *Wilts* 5F **35**
Aveley. *Thur* 2G **39**
Avening. *Glos* 2D **35**
Averham. *Notts* 5E **87**
Aveton Gifford. *Devn* 4C **8**
Avielochan. *High* 2D **150**
Aviemore. *High* 2C **150**
Avington. *Hants* 3D **24**
Avoch. *High* 3B **158**
Avon. *Hants* 3G **15**
Avonbridge. *Falk* 2C **128**
Avon Dassett. *Warw* 5B **62**
Avonmouth. *Bris* 4A **34**
Avonwick. *Devn* 3D **8**
Awbridge. *Hants* 4B **24**
Awliscombe. *Devn* 2E **13**
Awre. *Glos* 5C **48**
Awsworth. *Notts* 1B **74**
Axbridge. *Som* 1H **21**
Axford. *Hants* 2E **24**
Axford. *Wilts* 5H **35**
Axminster. *Devn* 3F **13**
Axmouth. *Devn* 3F **13**
Aycliffe Village. *Dur* 2F **105**
Aydon. *Nmbd* 3D **114**
Aykley Heads. *Dur* 5F **115**
Aylburton. *Glos* 5B **48**
Aylburton Common. *Glos* 5B **48**
Ayle. *Nmbd* 5A **114**
Aylesbeare. *Devn* 3D **12**
Aylesbury. *Buck* 4G **51**
Aylesby. *NE Lin* 4F **95**
Aylescott. *Devn* 1G **11**
Aylesford. *Kent* 5B **40**
Aylesham. *Kent* 5G **41**
Aylestone. *Leic* 5C **74**
Aylmerton. *Norf* 2D **78**
Aylsham. *Norf* 3D **78**
Aylton. *Here* 2B **48**
Aylworth. *Glos* 3G **49**
Aymestrey. *Here* 4G **59**
Aynho. *Nptn* 2D **50**
Ayot Green. *Herts* 4C **52**
Ayot St Lawrence. *Herts* 4B **52**
Ayot St Peter. *Herts* 4C **52**
Ayr. *S Ayr* 2C **116**
Ayreville. *Torb* 2E **9**
Aysgarth. *N Yor* 1C **98**
Ayshford. *Devn* 1D **12**
Ayside. *Cumb* 1C **96**
Ayston. *Rut* 5F **75**
Ayton. *Bord* 3F **131**
Aywick. *Shet* 3G **173**
Azerley. *N Yor* 2E **99**

B

Babbacombe. *Torb* 2F **9**
Babbinswood. *Shrp* 3F **71**
Babb's Green. *Herts* 4D **53**
Babcary. *Som* 4A **22**
Babel. *Carm* 2B **46**
Babell. *Flin* 3D **82**
Babingley. *Norf* 3F **77**
Bablock Hythe. *Oxon* 5C **50**
Babraham. *Cambs* 5E **65**
Babworth. *Notts* 2D **86**
Bac. *W Isl* 3G **171**
Bachau. *IOA* 2D **80**
Bacheldre. *Powy* 1E **59**
Bachymbyd Fawr. *Den* 4C **82**
Backaland. *Orkn* 4E **172**
Backbarrow. *Cumb* 1C **96**
Backe. *Carm* 3G **43**
Backfolds. *Abers* 3H **161**
Backford. *Ches W* 3G **83**
Backhill. *Abers* 5E **161**
Backhill of Clackriach. *Abers* 4G **161**
Backies. *High* 3F **165**
Backmuir of New Gilston. *Fife* 3G **137**
Back of Keppoch. *High* 5E **147**
Back Street. *Suff* 5G **65**
Backwell. *N Som* 5H **33**
Backworth. *Tyne* 2G **115**
Bacon End. *Essx* 4G **53**
Baconsthorpe. *Norf* 2D **78**
Bacton. *Here* 2G **47**
Bacton. *Norf* 2F **79**
Bacton. *Suff* 4C **66**
Bacton Green. *Norf* 2F **79**
Bacup. *Lanc* 2G **91**
Badachonacher. *High* 1A **158**
Badachro. *High* 1G **155**
Badanloch Lodge. *High* 5H **167**
Badavanich. *High* 3D **156**
Badbury. *Swin* 3G **35**
Badby. *Nptn* 5C **62**
Badcall. *High* 3C **166**
Badcaul. *High* 4E **163**
Baddeley Green. *Stoke* 5D **84**
Baddesley Clinton. *W Mid* 3G **61**
Baddesley Ensor. *Warw* 1G **61**
Baddidarach. *High* 1E **163**
Baddoch. *Abers* 5F **151**
Badenscallie. *High* 3E **163**
Badenscoth. *Abers* 5E **160**
Badentarbat. *High* 2E **163**
Badgall. *Corn* 4C **10**
Badgers Mount. *Kent* 4F **39**
Badgeworth. *Glos* 4E **49**
Badgworth. *Som* 1G **21**
Badicaul. *High* 1F **147**
Badingham. *Suff* 4F **67**
Badlesmere. *Kent* 5E **40**
Badlipster. *High* 4E **169**
Badluarach. *High* 4D **163**
Badminton. *S Glo* 3D **34**
Badnaban. *High* 1E **163**
Badnabay. *High* 4C **166**
Badnagie. *High* 5D **168**
Badnellan. *High* 3F **165**
Badninish. *High* 4E **165**
Badrallach. *High* 4E **163**
Badsey. *Worc* 1F **49**
Badshot Lea. *Surr* 2G **25**
Badsworth. *W Yor* 3E **93**
Badwell Ash. *Suff* 4B **66**
Bae Cinmel. *Cnwy* 2B **82**
Bae Colwyn. *Cnwy* 3A **82**
Bae Penrhyn. *Cnwy* 2H **81**
Bagby. *N Yor* 1G **99**

Bag Enderby—Barroway Drove

Bag Enderby. *Linc* 3C 88
Bagendon. *Glos* 5F 49
Bagginswood. *Shrp* 2A 60
Bàgh a Chàise. *W Isl* 1E 170
Bàgh a' Chaisteil. *W Isl* 9B 170
Bagham. *Kent* 5E 41
Baghasdal. *W Isl* 7C 170
Bagh Mor. *W Isl* 3D 170
Bagh Shiarabhagh. *W Isl* 8C 170
Bagillt. *Flin* 3E 83
Baginton. *Warw* 3H 61
Baglan. *Neat* 2A 32
Bagley. *Shrp* 3G 71
Bagley. *Som* 2H 21
Bagnall. *Staf* 5D 84
Bagnor. *W Ber* 5C 36
Bagshot. *Surr* 4A 38
Bagshot. *Wilts* 5B 36
Bagstone. *S Glo* 3B 34
Bagthorpe. *Norf* 2G 77
Bagthorpe. *Notts* 5B 86
Bagworth. *Leics* 5B 74
Bagwy Llydiart. *Here* 3H 47
Baildon. *W Yor* 1B 92
Baildon Green. *W Yor* 1B 92
Baile Ailein. *W Isl* 5E 171
Baile an Truiseil. *W Isl* 2F 171
Baile Boidheach. *Arg* 2F 125
Baile Glas. *W Isl* 3D 170
Bailemeonach. *Arg* 4A 140
Baile Mhanaich. *W Isl* 3C 170
Baile Mhartainn. *W Isl* 1C 170
Baile Mor. *Arg* 2A 132
Baile Mor. *W Isl* 2C 170
Baile nan Cailleach. *W Isl* 3C 170
Baile Raghaill. *W Isl* 2C 170
Bailey Green. *Hants* 4E 25
Baileyhead. *Cumb* 1G 113
Bailiesward. *Abers* 5B 160
Bail' Iochdrach. *W Isl* 3D 170
Baillieston. *Glas* 3H 127
Bailrigg. *Lanc* 4D 97
Bail' Uachdraich. *W Isl* 2D 170
Bail Ur Tholastaidh. *W Isl* 3H 171
Bainbridge. *N Yor* 5C 104
Bainsford. *Falk* 1B 128
Bainshole. *Abers* 5D 160
Bainton. *E Yor* 4D 100
Bainton. *Oxon* 3D 50
Bainton. *Pet* 5H 75
Baintown. *Fife* 3F 137
Baker Street. *Thur* 2H 39
Bakewell. *Derbs* 4G 85
Bala. *Gwyn* 2B 70
Balachuirn. *High* 4E 155
Balbeg. *High* 5G 157
(nr. Cannich)
Balbeg. *High* 1G 149
(nr. Loch Ness)
Balbeggie. *Per* 1D 136
Balblair. *High* 4C 164
(nr. Bonar Bridge)
Balblair. *High* 2B 158
(nr. Invergordon)
Balblair. *High* 4H 157
(nr. Inverness)
Balby. *S Yor* 4F 93
Balcathie. *Ang* 5F 145
Balchladich. *High* 1E 163
Balchraggan. *High* 4H 157
Balchrick. *High* 3B 166
Balcombe. *W Sus* 2E 27
Balcombe Lane. *W Sus* 2E 27
Balcurvie. *Fife* 3F 137
Baldersby. *N Yor* 2F 99
Baldersby St James. *N Yor* 2F 99
Balderstone. *Lanc* 1E 91
Balderton. *Ches W* 4F 83
Balderton. *Notts* 5F 87
Baldinnie. *Fife* 2G 137
Baldock. *Herts* 2C 52
Baldrine. *IOM* 3D 108
Baldslow. *E Sus* 4C 28
Baldwin. *IOM* 3C 108
Baldwinholme. *Cumb* 4E 113
Baldwin's Gate. *Staf* 2B 72
Bale. *Norf* 2C 78
Balearn. *Abers* 3H 161
Balemartine. *Arg* 4A 138
Balephretrish. *Arg* 4B 138
Balephuil. *Arg* 4A 138
Balerno. *Edin* 3E 129
Balevullin. *Arg* 4A 138
Balfield. *Ang* 2E 145
Balfour. *Orkn* 6D 172
Balfron. *Stir* 1G 127
Balgaveny. *Abers* 4D 160
Balgonar. *Fife* 4C 136
Balgowan. *High* 4A 150
Balgown. *High* 2C 154
Balgrochan. *E Dun* 2H 127
Balgy. *High* 3H 155
Balhalgardy. *Abers* 1E 153
Baliasta. *Shet* 1H 173
Baligill. *High* 2A 168
Balintore. *Ang* 3B 144
Balintore. *High* 1C 158
Balintraid. *High* 1B 158
Balk. *N Yor* 1G 99
Balkeerie. *Ang* 4C 144
Balkholme. *E Yor* 2A 94
Ball. *Shrp* 3F 71
Ballabeg. *IOM* 4B 108
Ballacannell. *IOM* 3D 108
Ballacarnane Beg. *IOM* 3C 108
Ballachulish. *High* 3E 141
Ballagyr. *IOM* 3B 108
Ballajora. *IOM* 2D 108
Ballaleigh. *IOM* 3C 108
Ballamodha. *IOM* 4B 108
Ballantrae. *S Ayr* 1F 109
Ballards Gore. *Essx* 1D 40
Ballasalla. *IOM* 4B 108
(nr. Castletown)
Ballasalla. *IOM* 2C 108
(nr. Kirk Michael)
Ballater. *Abers* 4A 152
Ballaugh. *IOM* 2C 108
Ballencrieff. *E Lot* 2A 130
Ballencrieff Toll. *W Lot* 2C 128
Ballentoul. *Per* 2F 143
Ball Hill. *Hants* 5C 36
Ballidon. *Derbs* 5G 85
Balliemore. *Arg* 1B 126
(nr. Dunoon)
Balliemore. *Arg* 1F 133
(nr. Oban)
Ballieward. *High* 5E 159
Ballig. *IOM* 3B 108
Ballimore. *Stir* 2E 135
Ballingdon. *Suff* 1B 54
Ballinger Common. *Buck* 5H 51
Ballingham. *Here* 2A 48
Ballingry. *Fife* 4D 136
Ballinluig. *Per* 3G 143
Ballintuim. *Per* 3A 144
Balliveolan. *Arg* 4C 140
Balloan. *High* 3C 164
Balloch. *High* 4B 158
Balloch. *N Lan* 2A 128
Balloch. *Per* 2H 135
Balloch. *W Dun* 1E 127
Ballochan. *Abers* 4C 152
Ballochgoy. *Arg* 3B 126
Ballochmyle. *E Ayr* 2E 117
Ballochroy. *Arg* 4F 125
Balls Cross. *W Sus* 3A 26
Ball's Green. *E Sus* 2F 27
Ballygown. *Arg* 4F 139
Ballygrant. *Arg* 3B 124
Ballymichael. *N Ayr* 2D 122
Balmacara. *High* 1G 147
Balmaclellan. *Dum* 2D 110
Balmacqueen. *High* 1D 154
Balmaha. *Stir* 4D 134
Balmalcolm. *Fife* 3F 137
Balmalloch. *N Lan* 2A 128
Balmeanach. *High* 5E 155
Balmedie. *Abers* 2G 153
Balmerino. *Fife* 1F 137
Balmerlawn. *Hants* 2B 16
Balmore. *E Dun* 2H 127
Balmore. *High* 4B 154
Balmuir. *Ang* 5D 144
Balmullo. *Fife* 1G 137
Balmurrie. *Dum* 3H 109
Balnaboth. *Ang* 2C 144
Balnabruaich. *High* 1B 158
Balnabruich. *High* 5D 168
Balnacoil. *High* 2F 165
Balnacra. *High* 4B 156
Balnacroft. *Abers* 4G 151
Balnageith. *Mor* 3E 159
Balnaglaic. *High* 5G 157
Balnagrantach. *High* 5G 157
Balnaguard. *Per* 3G 143
Balnahard. *Arg* 4B 132
Balnain. *High* 5G 157
Balnakeil. *High* 2D 166
Balnaknock. *High* 2D 154
Balnamoon. *Abers* 3G 161
Balnamoon. *Ang* 2E 145
Balnapaling. *High* 2B 158
Balornock. *Glas* 3H 127
Balquhidder. *Stir* 1E 135
Balsall. *W Mid* 3G 61
Balsall Common. *W Mid* 3G 61
Balscote. *Oxon* 1B 50
Balsham. *Cambs* 5E 65
Balstonia. *Thur* 2A 40
Baltasound. *Shet* 1H 173
Balterley. *Staf* 5B 84
Baltersan. *Dum* 3B 110
Balthangie. *Abers* 3F 161
Baltonsborough. *Som* 3A 22
Balvaird. *High* 3H 157
Balvaird. *Per* 2D 136
Balvenie. *Mor* 4H 159
Balvicar. *Arg* 2E 133
Balvraid. *High* 2G 147
Balvraid Lodge. *High* 5C 158
Bamber Bridge. *Lanc* 2D 90
Bamber's Green. *Essx* 3F 53
Bamburgh. *Nmbd* 1F 121
Bamford. *Derbs* 2G 85
Bamfurlong. *G Man* 4D 90
Bampton. *Cumb* 3G 103
Bampton. *Devn* 4C 20
Bampton. *Oxon* 5B 50
Bampton Grange. *Cumb* 3G 103
Banavie. *High* 1F 141
Banbury. *Oxon* 1C 50
Bancffosfelen. *Carm* 4E 45
Banchory. *Abers* 4D 152
Banchory-Devenick. *Abers* 3G 153
Bancycapel. *Carm* 4E 45
Bancyfelin. *Carm* 3H 43
Banc-y-ffordd. *Carm* 2E 45
Banff. *Abers* 2D 160
Bangor. *Gwyn* 3E 81
Bangor-is-y-coed. *Wrex* 1F 71
Bangors. *Corn* 3C 10
Bangor's Green. *Lanc* 4B 90
Banham. *Norf* 2C 66
Bank. *Hants* 2A 16
Bankend. *Dum* 3B 112
Bankfoot. *Per* 5H 143
Bankglen. *E Ayr* 3E 117
Bankhead. *Aber* 2F 153
Bankhead. *Abers* 3D 152
Bankhead. *S Lan* 5B 128
Bankland. *Som* 4G 21
Bank Newton. *N Yor* 4B 98
Banknock. *Falk* 2A 128
Banks. *Cumb* 3G 113
Banks. *Lanc* 2B 90
Bankshill. *Dum* 1C 112
Bank Street. *Worc* 4A 60
Bank, The. *Ches E* 5C 84
Bank, The. *Shrp* 1A 60
Bank Top. *Lanc* 4D 90
Banners Gate. *W Mid* 1E 61
Banningham. *Norf* 3E 78
Banniskirk. *High* 3D 168
Bannister Green. *Essx* 3G 53
Bannockburn. *Stir* 4H 135
Banstead. *Surr* 5D 38
Bantham. *Devn* 4C 8
Banton. *N Lan* 2A 128
Banwell. *N Som* 1G 21
Banyard's Green. *Suff* 3F 67
Bapchild. *Kent* 4D 40
Bapton. *Wilts* 3E 23
Barabhas. *W Isl* 3F 171
Barabhas Iarach. *W Isl* 2F 171
Baramore. *High* 1A 140
Barassie. *S Ayr* 1C 116
Baravullin. *Arg* 4D 140
Barbaraville. *High* 1B 158
Barber Booth. *Derbs* 2F 85
Barber Green. *Cumb* 1C 96
Barbhas Uarach. *W Isl* 2F 171
Barbieston. *S Ayr* 3D 116
Barbon. *Cumb* 1F 97
Barbourne. *Worc* 5C 60
Barbridge. *Ches E* 5A 84
Barbrook. *Devn* 2H 19
Barby. *Nptn* 3C 62
Barby Nortoft. *Nptn* 3C 62
Barcaldine. *Arg* 4D 140
Barcheston. *Warw* 1A 50
Barclose. *Cumb* 3F 113
Barcombe. *E Sus* 4F 27
Barcombe Cross. *E Sus* 4F 27
Barden. *N Yor* 5E 105
Barden Scale. *N Yor* 4C 98
Bardfield End Green. *Essx* 2G 53
Bardfield Saling. *Essx* 3G 53
Bardnabeinne. *High* 4E 164
Bardney. *Linc* 4A 88
Bardon. *Leics* 4B 74
Bardon Mill. *Nmbd* 3A 114
Bardowie. *E Dun* 2G 127
Bardrainney. *Inv* 2E 127
Bardsea. *Cumb* 2C 96
Bardsey. *W Yor* 5F 99
Bardsley. *G Man* 4H 91
Bardwell. *Suff* 3B 66
Bare. *Lanc* 3D 96
Barelees. *Nmbd* 1C 120
Barewood. *Here* 5F 59
Barford. *Hants* 3G 25
Barford. *Norf* 5D 78
Barford. *Warw* 4G 61
Barford St John. *Oxon* 2C 50
Barford St Martin. *Wilts* 3F 23
Barford St Michael. *Oxon* 2C 50
Barfrestone. *Kent* 5G 41
Bargeddie. *N Lan* 3A 128
Bargod. *Cphy* 2E 33
Bargoed. *Cphy* 2E 33
Bargrennan. *Dum* 2A 110
Barham. *Cambs* 3A 64
Barham. *Kent* 5G 41
Barham. *Suff* 5D 66
Barharrow. *Dum* 4D 110
Bar Hill. *Cambs* 4C 64
Barholm. *Linc* 4H 75
Barkby. *Leics* 4D 74
Barkestone-le-Vale. *Leics* 2E 75
Barkham. *Wok* 5F 37
Barking. *G Lon* 2F 39
Barking. *Suff* 5C 66
Barkingside. *G Lon* 2F 39
Barking Tye. *Suff* 5C 66
Barkisland. *W Yor* 3A 92
Barkston. *Linc* 1G 75
Barkston Ash. *N Yor* 1E 93
Barkway. *Herts* 2D 53
Barlanark. *Glas* 3H 127
Barlaston. *Staf* 2C 72
Barlavington. *W Sus* 4A 26
Barlborough. *Derbs* 3B 86
Barlby. *N Yor* 1G 93
Barlestone. *Leics* 5B 74
Barley. *Herts* 2D 53
Barley. *Lanc* 5H 97
Barley Mow. *Tyne* 4F 115
Barleythorpe. *Rut* 5F 75
Barling. *Essx* 2D 40
Barlings. *Linc* 3H 87
Barlow. *Derbs* 3H 85
Barlow. *N Yor* 2G 93
Barlow. *Tyne* 3E 115
Barmby Moor. *E Yor* 5B 100
Barmby on the Marsh. *E Yor* 2G 93
Barmer. *Norf* 2H 77
Barming. *Kent* 5B 40
Barming Heath. *Kent* 5B 40
Barmoor. *Nmbd* 1E 121
Barmouth. *Gwyn* 4F 69
Barmpton. *Darl* 3A 106
Barmston. *E Yor* 4F 101
Barmulloch. *Glas* 3H 127
Barnack. *Pet* 5H 75
Barnacle. *Warw* 2A 62
Barnard Castle. *Dur* 3D 104
Barnard Gate. *Oxon* 4C 50
Barnardiston. *Suff* 1H 53
Barnbarroch. *Dum* 4F 111
Barnburgh. *S Yor* 4E 93
Barnby. *Suff* 2G 67
Barnby Dun. *S Yor* 4G 93
Barnby in the Willows. *Notts* 5F 87
Barnby Moor. *Notts* 2D 86
Barnes. *G Lon* 3D 38
Barnes Street. *Kent* 1H 27
Barnet. *G Lon* 1D 38
Barnetby le Wold. *N Lin* 4D 94
Barney. *Norf* 2B 78
Barnham. *Suff* 3A 66
Barnham. *W Sus* 5A 26
Barnham Broom. *Norf* 5C 78
Barnhead. *Ang* 3F 145
Barnhill. *D'dee* 5D 145
Barnhill. *Mor* 3F 159
Barnhill. *Per* 1D 136
Barnhills. *Dum* 2E 109
Barningham. *Dur* 3D 105
Barningham. *Suff* 3B 66
Barnoldby le Beck. *NE Lin* 4F 95
Barnoldswick. *Lanc* 5A 98
Barns Green. *W Sus* 3C 26
Barnsley. *Glos* 5F 49
Barnsley. *Shrp* 1B 60
Barnsley. *S Yor* 4D 92
Barnstaple. *Devn* 3F 19
Barnston. *Essx* 4G 53
Barnston. *Mers* 2E 83
Barnstone. *Notts* 2E 75
Barnt Green. *Worc* 3E 61
Barnton. *Ches W* 3A 84
Barnwell. *Cambs* 5D 64
Barnwell. *Nptn* 2H 63
Barnwood. *Glos* 4D 48
Barons Cross. *Here* 5G 59
Barony, The. *Orkn* 5B 172
Barr. *Dum* 4G 117
Barr. *S Ayr* 5B 116
Barra Airport. *W Isl* 8C 170
Barrachan. *Dum* 5A 110
Barrahormid. *Arg* 1F 125
Barrapol. *Arg* 4A 138
Barrasford. *Nmbd* 2C 114
Barravullin. *Arg* 3F 133
Barregarrow. *IOM* 3C 108
Barrhead. *E Ren* 4G 127
Barrhill. *S Ayr* 1H 109
Barri. *V Glam* 5E 32
Barrington. *Cambs* 1D 53
Barrington. *Som* 1G 13
Barripper. *Corn* 3D 4
Barrmill. *N Ayr* 4E 127
Barrock. *High* 1E 169
Barrow. *Lanc* 1F 91
Barrow. *Rut* 4F 75
Barrow. *Shrp* 5A 72
Barrow. *Som* 3C 22
Barrow. *Suff* 4G 65
Barroway Drove. *Norf* 5E 77

Bissoe. Corn 4B 6
Bisterne. Hants 2G 15
Bisterne Close. Hants 2H 15
Bitchfield. Linc 3G 75
Bittadon. Devn 2F 19
Bittaford. Devn 3C 8
Bittering. Norf 4B 78
Bitterley. Shrp 3H 59
Bitterne. Sotn 1C 16
Bitteswell. Leics 2C 62
Bitton. S Glo 5B 34
Bix. Oxon 3F 37
Bixter. Shet 6E 173
Blaby. Leics 1C 62
Blackawton. Devn 3E 9
Black Bank. Cambs 2E 65
Black Barn. Linc 3D 76
Blackborough. Devn 2D 12
Blackborough. Norf 4F 77
Blackborough End. Norf 4F 77
Black Bourton. Oxon 5A 50
Blackboys. E Sus 3G 27
Blackbrook. Derbs 1H 73
Blackbrook. Mers 1H 83
Blackbrook. Staf 2B 72
Blackbrook. Surr 1C 26
Blackburn. Abers 2F 153
Blackburn. Bkbn 2E 91
Blackburn. W Lot 3C 128
Black Callerton. Tyne 3E 115
Black Carr. Norf 1C 66
Black Clauchrie. S Ayr 1H 109
Black Corries. High 3G 141
Black Crofts. Arg 5D 140
Black Cross. Corn 2D 6
Blackden Heath. Ches E 3B 84
Blackditch. Oxon 5C 50
Blackdog. Abers 2G 153
Black Dog. Devn 2B 12
Blackdown. Dors 2G 13
Blackdyke. Cumb 4C 112
Blacker Hill. S Yor 4D 92
Blackfen. G Lon 3F 39
Blackfield. Hants 2C 16
Blackford. Cumb 3E 113
Blackford. Per 3A 136
Blackford. Shrp 2H 59
Blackford. Som 2H 21
(nr. Burnham-on-Sea)
Blackford. Som 4B 22
(nr. Wincanton)
Blackfordby. Leics 4H 73
Blackgang. IOW 5C 16
Blackhall. Edin 2F 129
Blackhall. Ren 3F 127
Blackhall Colliery. Dur 1B 106
Blackhall Mill. Tyne 4E 115
Blackhall Rocks. Dur 1B 106
Blackham. E Sus 2F 27
Blackheath. Essx 3D 54
Blackheath. G Lon 3E 39
Blackheath. Suff 3G 67
Blackheath. Surr 1B 26
Blackheath. W Mid 2D 61
Black Heddon. Nmbd 2D 115
Blackhill. Abers 4H 161
Blackhill. High 3C 154
Black Hill. Warw 5G 61
Blackhills. Abers 2G 161
Blackhills. High 3D 158
Blackjack. Linc 2B 76
Blackland. Wilts 5F 35
Black Lane. G Man 4F 91
Blackleach. Lanc 1C 90
Blackley. G Man 4G 91
Blackley. W Yor 3B 92
Blacklunans. Per 2A 144
Blackmill. B'end 3C 32
Blackmoor. G Man 4E 91
Blackmoor. Hants 3F 25
Blackmoor Gate. Devn 2G 19
Blackmore. Essx 5G 53
Blackmore End. Essx 2H 53
Blackmore End. Herts 4B 52

Black Mount. Arg 4G 141
Blackness. Falk 2D 128
Blacknest. Hants 2F 25
Blackney. Dors 3H 13
Blacknoll. Dors 4D 14
Black Notley. Essx 3A 54
Blacko. Lanc 5A 98
Black Pill. Swan 3F 31
Blackpool. Bkpl 1B 90
Blackpool. Devn 4E 9
Blackpool Airport. Lanc 1B 90
Blackpool Corner. Devn 3G 13
Blackpool Gate. Cumb 2G 113
Blackridge. W Lot 3C 128
Blackrock. Arg 3B 124
Blackrock. Mon 4F 47
Blackrod. G Man 3E 90
Blackshaw. Dum 3B 112
Blackshaw Head. W Yor 2H 91
Blackshaw Moor. Staf 5E 85
Blacksmith's Green. Suff 4D 66
Blacksnape. Bkbn 2F 91
Blackstone. W Sus 4D 26
Black Street. Suff 2H 67
Black Tar. Pemb 4D 43
Blackthorn. Oxon 4E 50
Blackthorpe. Suff 4B 66
Blacktoft. E Yor 2B 94
Blacktop. Aber 3F 153
Black Torrington. Devn 2E 11
Blacktown. Newp 3F 33
Blackwall Tunnel. G Lon 2E 39
Blackwater. Corn 4B 6
Blackwater. Hants 1G 25
Blackwater. IOW 4D 16
Blackwater. Som 1F 13
Blackwaterfoot. N Ayr 3C 122
Blackwell. Darl 3F 105
Blackwell. Derbs 5B 86
(nr. Alfreton)
Blackwell. Derbs 3F 85
(nr. Buxton)
Blackwell. Som 4D 20
Blackwell. Warw 1H 49
Blackwell. Worc 3D 61
Blackwood. Cphy 2E 33
Blackwood. Dum 1G 111
Blackwood. S Lan 5A 128
Blackwood Hill. Staf 5D 84
Blacon. Ches W 4F 83
Bladnoch. Dum 4B 110
Bladon. Oxon 4C 50
Blaenannerch. Cdgn 1C 44
Blaenau Dolwyddelan. Cnwy 5F 81
Blaenau Ffestiniog. Gwyn 1G 69
Blaenavon. Torf 5F 47
Blaenawey. Mon 4F 47
Blaen Celyn. Cdgn 5C 56
Blaen Clydach. Rhon 2C 32
Blaendulais. Neat 5B 46
Blaenffos. Pemb 1F 43
Blaengarw. B'end 2C 32
Blaen-geuffordd. Cdgn 2F 57
Blaengwrach. Neat 5B 46
Blaengwynfi. Neat 2B 32
Blaenllechau. Rhon 2D 32
Blaenpennal. Cdgn 4F 57
Blaenplwyf. Cdgn 3E 57
Blaenporth. Cdgn 1C 44
Blaenrhondda. Rhon 2C 32
Blaen-y-coed. Carm 2H 43
Blaenycwm. Cdgn 2G 57
Blagdon. N Som 1A 22
Blagdon. Torb 2E 9
Blagdon Hill. Som 1F 13
Blagill. Cumb 5A 114
Blaguegate. Lanc 4C 90
Blaich. High 1E 141
Blain. High 2A 140
Blaina. Blae 5F 47
Blair Atholl. Per 2F 143
Blair Drummond. Stir 4G 135
Blairgowrie. Per 4A 144

Blairhall. Fife 1D 128
Blairingone. Per 4B 136
Blairlogie. Stir 4H 135
Blairmore. Abers 5B 160
Blairmore. Arg 1C 126
Blairmore. High 3B 166
Blairquhanan. W Dun 1F 127
Blaisdon. Glos 4C 48
Blakebrook. Worc 3C 60
Blakedown. Worc 3C 60
Blake End. Essx 3H 53
Blakemere. Here 1G 47
Blakeney. Glos 5B 48
Blakeney. Norf 1C 78
Blakenhall. Ches E 1B 72
Blakenhall. W Mid 1C 60
Blakeshall. Worc 2C 60
Blakesley. Nptn 5D 62
Blanchland. Nmbd 4C 114
Blandford Camp. Dors 2E 15
Blandford Forum. Dors 2D 15
Blandford St Mary. Dors 2D 15
Bland Hill. N Yor 4E 98
Blandy. High 2G 167
Blanefield. Stir 2G 127
Blankney. Linc 4H 87
Blantyre. S Lan 4H 127
Blarmachfoldach. High 2E 141
Blarnalearoch. High 4F 163
Blashford. Hants 2G 15
Blaston. Leics 1F 63
Blatchbridge. Som 2C 22
Blathaisbhal. W Isl 1D 170
Blatherwycke. Nptn 1G 63
Blawith. Cumb 1B 96
Blaxhall. Suff 5F 67
Blaxton. S Yor 4G 93
Blaydon. Tyne 3E 115
Bleadney. Som 2H 21
Bleadon. N Som 1G 21
Blean. Kent 4F 41
Bleasby. Linc 2A 88
Bleasby. Notts 1E 74
Bleasby Moor. Linc 2A 88
Blebocraigs. Fife 2G 137
Bleddfa. Powy 4E 58
Bledington. Glos 3H 49
Bledlow. Buck 5F 51
Bledlow Ridge. Buck 2F 37
Blencarn. Cumb 1H 103
Blencogo. Cumb 5C 112
Blendworth. Hants 1F 17
Blenheim. Oxon 5D 50
Blennerhasset. Cumb 5C 112
Bletchingdon. Oxon 4D 50
Bletchingley. Surr 5E 39
Bletchley. Mil 2G 51
Bletchley. Shrp 2A 72
Bletherston. Pemb 2E 43
Bletsoe. Bed 5H 63
Blewbury. Oxon 3D 36
Blickling. Norf 3D 78
Blidworth. Notts 5C 86
Blindburn. Nmbd 3C 120
Blindcrake. Cumb 1C 102
Blindley Heath. Surr 1E 27
Blindmoor. Som 1F 13
Blisland. Corn 5A 10
Blissford. Hants 1G 15
Bliss Gate. Worc 3B 60
Blisworth. Nptn 5E 63
Blithbury. Staf 3E 73
Blitterlees. Cumb 4C 112
Blockley. Glos 2G 49
Blofield. Norf 5F 79
Blofield Heath. Norf 4F 79
Blo' Norton. Norf 3C 66
Bloomfield. Bord 2H 119
Blore. Staf 1F 73
Blount's Green. Staf 2E 73
Bloxham. Oxon 2C 50
Bloxholm. Linc 5H 87
Bloxwich. W Mid 5E 73

Bloxworth. Dors 3D 15
Blubberhouses. N Yor 4D 98
Blue Anchor. Som 2D 20
Blue Anchor. Swan 3E 31
Blue Bell Hill. Kent 4B 40
Blue Row. Essx 4D 54
Bluetown. Kent 5D 40
Blundeston. Suff 1H 67
Blunham. C Beds 5A 64
Blunsdon St Andrew.
  Swin 3G 35
Bluntington. Worc 3C 60
Bluntisham. Cambs 3C 64
Blunts. Corn 2H 7
Blurton. Stoke 1C 72
Blyborough. Linc 1G 87
Blyford. Suff 3G 67
Blymhill. Staf 4C 72
Blymhill Lawns. Staf 4C 72
Blyth. Nmbd 1G 115
Blyth. Notts 2D 86
Blyth. Bord 5E 129
Blyth Bank. Bord 5E 129
Blyth Bridge. Bord 5E 129
Blythburgh. Suff 3G 67
Blythe Bridge. Staf 1D 72
Blythe Marsh. Staf 1D 72
Blythe, The. Staf 3E 73
Blyton. Linc 1F 87
Boarhills. Fife 2H 137
Boarhunt. Hants 2E 16
Boarshead. E Sus 2G 27
Boar's Head. G Man 4D 90
Boars Hill. Oxon 5C 50
Boarstall. Buck 4E 51
Boasley Cross. Devn 3F 11
Boath. High 1H 157
Boat of Garten. High 2D 150
Bobbing. Kent 4C 40
Bobbington. Staf 1C 60
Bobbingworth. Essx 5F 53
Bocaddon. Corn 3F 7
Bocking. Essx 3A 54
Bocking Churchstreet. Essx 3A 54
Boddam. Abers 4H 161
Boddam. Shet 10E 173
Boddington. Glos 3D 49
Bodedern. IOA 2C 80
Bodelwyddan. Den 3C 82
Bodenham. Here 5H 59
Bodenham. Wilts 4G 23
Bodewryd. IOA 1C 80
Bodfari. Den 3C 82
Bodffordd. IOA 3D 80
Bodham. Norf 1D 78
Bodiam. E Sus 3B 28
Bodicote. Oxon 2C 50
Bodieve. Corn 1D 6
Bodinnick. Corn 3F 7
Bodle Street Green. E Sus 4A 28
Bodmin. Corn 2E 7
Bodnant. Cnwy 3H 81
Bodney. Norf 1H 65
Bodorgan. IOA 4C 80
Bodrane. Corn 2G 7
Bodsham. Kent 1F 29
Boduan. Gwyn 2C 68
Bodymoor Heath. Warw 1F 61
Bogallan. High 3A 158
Bogbrae Croft. Abers 5H 161
Bogend. S Ayr 1C 116
Boghall. Midl 3F 129
Boghall. W Lot 3C 128
Boghead. S Lan 5A 128
Bogindollo. Ang 3D 144
Bogmoor. Mor 2A 160
Bogniebrae. Abers 4C 160
Bognor Regis. W Sus 3H 17
Bograxie. Abers 2E 152
Bogside. N Lan 4B 128
Bog, The. Shrp 1F 59
Bogton. Abers 3D 160
Bogue. Dum 1D 110
Bohenie. High 5E 149

Bohortha. Corn 5C 6
Bokiddick. Corn 2E 7
Bolam. Dur 2E 105
Bolam. Nmbd 1D 115
Bolberry. Devn 5C 8
Bold Heath. Mers 2H 83
Boldon. Tyne 3G 115
Boldon Colliery. Tyne 3G 115
Boldre. Hants 3B 16
Boldron. Dur 3D 104
Bole. Notts 2E 87
Bolehall. Staf 5G 73
Bolehill. Derbs 5G 85
Bolenowe. Corn 5A 6
Boleside. Bord 1G 119
Bolham. Devn 1C 12
Bolham Water. Devn 1E 13
Bolingey. Corn 3B 6
Bollington. Ches E 3D 84
Bolney. W Sus 3D 26
Bolnhurst. Bed 5H 63
Bolshan. Ang 3F 145
Bolsover. Derbs 3B 86
Bolsterstone. S Yor 1G 85
Bolstone. Here 2A 48
Boltachan. Per 3F 143
Boltby. N Yor 1G 99
Bolton. Cumb 2H 103
Bolton. E Lot 2B 130
Bolton. E Yor 4B 100
Bolton. G Man 4F 91
Bolton. Nmbd 3F 121
Bolton Abbey. N Yor 4C 98
Bolton-by-Bowland. Lanc 5G 97
Boltonfellend. Cumb 3F 113
Boltongate. Cumb 5D 112
Bolton Green. Lanc 3D 90
Bolton-le-Sands. Lanc 3D 97
Bolton Low Houses.
  Cumb 5D 112
Bolton New Houses. Cumb 5D 112
Bolton-on-Swale. N Yor 5F 105
Bolton Percy. N Yor 5H 99
Bolton Town End. Lanc 3D 97
Bolton upon Dearne. S Yor 4E 93
Bolton Wood Lane. Cumb 5D 112
Bolventor. Corn 5B 10
Bomarsund. Nmbd 1F 115
Bomere Heath. Shrp 4G 71
Bonar Bridge. High 4D 164
Bonawe. Arg 5E 141
Bonby. N Lin 3D 94
Boncath. Pemb 1G 43
Bonchester Bridge. Bord 3H 119
Bonchurch. IOW 5D 16
Bond End. Staf 4F 73
Bondleigh. Devn 2G 11
Bonds. Lanc 5D 97
Bonehill. Devn 5H 11
Bonehill. Staf 5F 73
Bo'ness. Falk 1C 128
Boney Hay. Staf 4E 73
Bonham. Wilts 3C 22
Bonhill. W Dun 2E 127
Boningale. Shrp 5C 72
Bonjedward. Bord 2A 120
Bonkle. N Lan 4B 128
Bonnington. Ang 5E 145
Bonnington. Edin 3E 129
Bonnington. Kent 2E 29
Bonnybank. Fife 3F 137
Bonnybridge. Falk 1B 128
Bonnykelly. Abers 3F 161
Bonnyrigg. Midl 3G 129
Bonnyton. Ang 5C 144
Bonnytown. Fife 2H 137
Bonsall. Derbs 5G 85
Bont. Mon 4G 47
Bontddu. Gwyn 4F 69
Bont Dolgadfan. Powy 5A 70
Bontgoch. Cdgn 2F 57
Bonthorpe. Linc 3D 89
Bont-newydd. Cnwy 3C 82

Bontnewydd. *Gwyn* 4D 81	Bosherston. *Pemb* 5D 42	Bousd. *Arg* 2D 138	Boyton. *Corn* 3D 10
(nr. Caernarfon)	Bosley. *Ches E* 4D 84	Boustead Hill. *Cumb* 4D 112	Boyton. *Suff* 1G 55
Bont Newydd. *Gwyn* 1G 69	Bossall. *N Yor* 3B 100	Bouth. *Cumb* 1C 96	Boyton. *Wilts* 3E 23
(nr. Llan Ffestiniog)	Bossiney. *Corn* 4A 10	Bouthwaite. *N Yor* 2D 98	Boyton Cross. *Essx* 5G 53
Bontuchel. *Den* 5C 82	Bossingham. *Kent* 1F 29	Boveney. *Buck* 3A 38	Boyton End. *Essx* 2G 53
Bonvilston. *V Glam* 4D 32	Bossington. *Som* 2B 20	Boveridge. *Dors* 1F 15	Boyton End. *Suff* 1H 53
Bon-y-maen. *Swan* 3F 31	Bostadh. *W Isl* 4D 171	Boverton. *V Glam* 5C 32	Bozeat. *Nptn* 5G 63
Booker. *Buck* 2G 37	Bostock Green. *Ches W* 4A 84	Bovey Tracey. *Devn* 5B 12	Braaid. *IOM* 4C 108
Booley. *Shrp* 3H 71	**Boston.** *Linc* 1C 76	Bovingdon. *Herts* 5A 52	Braal Castle. *High* 2D 168
Boorley Green. *Hants* 1D 16	Boston Spa. *W Yor* 5G 99	Bovingdon Green. *Buck* 3G 37	Brabling Green. *Suff* 4E 67
Boosbeck. *Red C* 3D 106	Boswarthen. *Corn* 3B 4	Bovinger. *Essx* 5F 53	Brabourne. *Kent* 1F 29
Boot. *Cumb* 4C 102	Boswinger. *Corn* 4D 6	Bovington Camp. *Dors* 4D 14	Brabourne Lees. *Kent* 1E 29
Booth. *W Yor* 2A 92	Botallack. *Corn* 3A 4	Bow. *Devn* 2H 11	Brabster. *High* 2F 169
Boothby Graffoe. *Linc* 5G 87	Botany Bay. *G Lon* 1D 39	Bowbank. *Dur* 2C 104	Bracadale. *High* 5C 154
Boothby Pagnell. *Linc* 2G 75	Botcheston. *Leics* 5B 74	Bow Brickhill. *Mil* 2H 51	Bracara. *High* 4F 147
Booth Green. *Ches E* 2D 84	Botesdale. *Suff* 3C 66	Bowbridge. *Glos* 5D 48	Braceborough. *Linc* 4H 75
Booth of Toft. *Shet* 4F 173	Bothal. *Nmbd* 1F 115	Bowburn. *Dur* 1A 106	Bracebridge. *Linc* 4G 87
Boothstown. *G Man* 4F 91	Bothampstead. *W Ber* 4D 36	Bowcombe. *IOW* 4C 16	Bracebridge Heath. *Linc* 4G 87
Boothville. *Nptn* 4E 63	Bothamsall. *Notts* 3D 86	Bowd. *Devn* 4E 12	Braceby. *Linc* 2H 75
Booth Wood. *W Yor* 3A 92	Bothel. *Cumb* 1C 102	Bowden. *Devn* 4E 9	Bracewell. *Lanc* 5A 98
Bootle. *Cumb* 1A 96	Bothenhampton. *Dors* 3H 13	Bowden. *Bord* 1H 119	Brackenber. *Cumb* 3A 104
Bootle. *Mers* 1F 83	Bothwell. *S Lan* 4H 127	Bowden Hill. *Wilts* 5E 35	Brackenfield. *Derbs* 5A 86
Booton. *Norf* 3D 78	Botley. *Buck* 5H 51	Bowdens. *Som* 4H 21	Brackenlands. *Cumb* 5D 112
Booze. *N Yor* 4D 104	Botley. *Hants* 1D 16	Bowderdale. *Cumb* 4H 103	Brackenthwaite. *Cumb* 5D 112
Boquhan. *Stir* 1G 127	Botley. *Oxon* 5C 50	Bowdon. *G Man* 2B 84	Brackenthwaite. *N Yor* 4E 99
Boraston. *Shrp* 3A 60	Botloe's Green. *Glos* 3C 48	Bower. *Nmbd* 1A 114	Brackla. *B'end* 4C 32
Borden. *Kent* 4C 40	Botolph Claydon. *Buck* 3F 51	Bowerchalke. *Wilts* 4F 23	Brackla. *High* 3C 158
Borden. *W Sus* 4G 25	Botolphs. *W Sus* 5C 26	Bowerhill. *Wilts* 5E 35	Bracklesham. *W Sus* 3G 17
Bordlands. *Bord* 5E 129	Bottacks. *High* 2G 157	Bower Hinton. *Som* 1H 13	Brackletter. *High* 5D 148
Bordley. *N Yor* 3B 98	Bottesford. *Leics* 2F 75	Bowermadden. *High* 2E 169	Brackley. *Nptn* 2D 50
Bordon. *Hants* 3G 25	Bottesford. *N Lin* 4B 94	Bowers. *Staf* 2C 72	Brackley Hatch. *Nptn* 1E 51
Boreham. *Essx* 5A 54	Bottisham. *Cambs* 4E 65	Bowers Gifford. *Essx* 2C 40	Brackloch. *High* 1F 163
Boreham. *Wilts* 2D 23	Bottlesford. *Wilts* 1G 23	Bowershall. *Fife* 4C 136	**Bracknell.** *Brac* 5G 37
Boreham Street. *E Sus* 4A 28	Bottomcraig. *Fife* 1F 137	Bowertower. *High* 2E 169	Braco. *Per* 3H 135
Borehamwood. *Herts* 1C 38	Bottom o' th' Moor. *G Man* 3E 91	Bowes. *Dur* 3C 104	Bracobrae. *Mor* 3C 160
Boreland. *Dum* 5D 118	Botton. *N Yor* 4D 107	Bowgreave. *Lanc* 5D 97	Bracon. *N Lin* 4A 94
Boreston. *Devn* 3D 8	Botton Head. *Lanc* 3F 97	Bowhousebog. *N Lan* 4B 128	Bracon Ash. *Norf* 1D 66
Borestone Brae. *Stir* 4H 135	Bottreaux Mill. *Devn* 4B 20	Bowithick. *Corn* 4B 10	Bradbourne. *Derbs* 5G 85
Boreton. *Shrp* 5H 71	Botus Fleming. *Corn* 2A 8	Bowland Bridge. *Cumb* 1D 96	Bradbury. *Dur* 2A 106
Borgh. *W Isl* 8B 170	Botwnnog. *Gwyn* 2B 68	Bowlees. *Dur* 2C 104	Bradda. *IOM* 4A 108
(on Barra)	Bough Beech. *Kent* 1F 27	Bowley. *Here* 5H 59	Bradden. *Nptn* 1E 51
Borgh. *W Isl* 3C 170	Boughrood. *Powy* 2E 47	Bowlhead Green. *Surr* 2A 26	Bradenham. *Buck* 2G 37
(on Benbecula)	Boughspring. *Glos* 2A 34	Bowling. *W Dun* 2F 127	Bradenham. *Norf* 5B 78
Borgh. *W Isl* 1E 170	Boughton. *Norf* 5F 77	Bowling. *W Yor* 1B 92	Bradenstoke. *Wilts* 4F 35
(on Berneray)	Boughton. *Nptn* 4E 63	Bowling Bank. *Wrex* 1F 71	Bradfield. *Essx* 2E 55
Borgh. *W Isl* 2G 171	Boughton. *Notts* 4D 86	Bowling Green. *Worc* 5C 60	Bradfield. *Norf* 2E 79
(on Isle of Lewis)	Boughton Aluph. *Kent* 1E 29	Bowlish. *Som* 2B 22	Bradfield. *W Ber* 4E 36
Borghastan. *W Isl* 3D 171	Boughton Green. *Kent* 5B 40	Bowmanstead. *Cumb* 5E 102	Bradfield Combust. *Suff* 5A 66
Borgh na Sgiotaig. *High* 1C 154	Boughton Lees. *Kent* 1E 28	Bowmore. *Arg* 4B 124	Bradfield Green. *Ches E* 5A 84
Borgie. *High* 3G 167	Boughton Malherbe. *Kent* 1C 28	Bowness-on-Solway. *Cumb* . . .3D 112	Bradfield Heath. *Essx* 3E 55
Borgue. *Dum* 5D 110	Boughton Monchelsea. *Kent* . . .5B 40	Bowness-on-Windermere.	Bradfield St Clare. *Suff* 5B 66
Borgue. *High* 1H 165	Boughton under Blean. *Kent* 5E 41	*Cumb* 5F 103	Bradfield St George. *Suff* 4B 66
Borley. *Essx* 1B 54	Boulby. *Red C* 3E 107	Bow of Fife. *Fife* 2F 137	Bradford. *Derbs* 4G 85
Borley Green. *Essx* 1B 54	Bouldnor. *IOW* 4B 16	Bowrietauld. *Ang* 4E 145	Bradford. *Devn* 2E 11
Borley Green. *Suff* 4B 66	Bouldon. *Shrp* 2H 59	Bowscale. *Cumb* 1E 103	Bradford. *Nmbd* 1F 121
Borlum. *High* 1H 149	Boulmer. *Nmbd* 3G 121	Bowsden. *Nmbd* 5F 131	**Bradford.** *W Yor* 1B 92
Bornais. *W Isl* 6C 170	Boulston. *Pemb* 3D 42	Bowside Lodge. *High* 2A 168	Bradford Abbas. *Dors* 1A 14
Bornesketaig. *High* 1C 154	Boultham. *Linc* 4G 87	Bowston. *Cumb* 5F 103	Bradford Barton. *Devn* 1B 12
Boroughbridge. *N Yor* 3F 99	Boulton. *Derb* 2A 74	Bow Street. *Cdgn* 2F 57	Bradford Leigh. *Wilts* 5D 34
Borough Green. *Kent* 5H 39	Boundary. *Staf* 1D 73	Bowthorpe. *Norf* 5D 78	Bradford-on-Avon. *Wilts* 5D 34
Borras Head. *Wrex* 5F 83	Bounds. *Here* 2B 48	Box. *Glos* 5D 48	Bradford-on-Tone. *Som* 4E 21
Borreraig. *High* 3A 154	Bourn. *Cambs* 5C 64	Box. *Wilts* 5D 34	Bradford Peverell. *Dors* 3B 14
Borrobol Lodge. *High* 1F 165	Bournbrook. *W Mid* 2E 61	Boxbush. *Glos* 3B 48	Bradiford. *Devn* 3F 19
Borrodale. *High* 4A 154	Bourne. *Linc* 3H 75	Box End. *Bed* 1A 52	Brading. *IOW* 4E 16
Borrowash. *Derb* 2B 74	Bourne End. *Bed* 4H 63	Boxford. *Suff* 1C 54	Bradley. *Ches W* 3H 83
Borrowby. *N Yor* 1G 99	Bourne End. *Buck* 3G 37	Boxford. *W Ber* 4C 36	Bradley. *Derbs* 1G 73
(nr. Northallerton)	Bourne End. *C Beds* 1H 51	Boxgrove. *W Sus* 5A 26	Bradley. *Glos* 2C 34
Borrowby. *N Yor* 3E 107	Bourne End. *Herts* 5A 52	Box Hill. *Wilts* 5D 34	Bradley. *Hants* 2E 25
(nr. Whitby)	**Bournemouth.** *Bour* 3F 15	Boxley. *Kent* 5B 40	Bradley. *NE Lin* 4F 95
Borrowston. *High* 4F 169	Bournemouth Airport. *Dors* 3G 15	Boxmoor. *Herts* 5A 52	Bradley. *N Yor* 1C 98
Borrowstonehill. *Orkn* 7D 172	Bournes Green. *Glos* 5E 49	Box's Shop. *Corn* 2C 10	Bradley. *Staf* 4C 72
Borrowstoun. *Falk* 1C 128	Bournes Green. *S'end* 2D 40	Boxted. *Essx* 2C 54	Bradley. *W Mid* 1D 60
Borstal. *Medw* 4B 40	Bourne, The. *Surr* 2G 25	Boxted. *Suff* 5H 65	Bradley. *W Yor* 2B 92
Borth. *Cdgn* 2F 57	Bournheath. *Worc* 3D 60	Boxted Cross. *Essx* 2D 54	Bradley. *Wrex* 5F 83
Borthwick. *Midl* 4G 129	Bournmoor. *Dur* 4G 115	Boxworth. *Cambs* 4C 64	Bradley Cross. *Som* 1H 21
Borth-y-Gest. *Gwyn* 2E 69	Bournville. *W Mid* 2E 61	Boxworth End. *Cambs* 4C 64	Bradley Green. *Ches W* 1H 71
Borve. *High* 4D 154	Bourton. *Dors* 3C 22	Boyden End. *Suff* 5G 65	Bradley Green. *Som* 3F 21
Borwick. *Lanc* 2E 97	Bourton. *N Som* 5G 33	Boyden Gate. *Kent* 4G 41	Bradley Green. *Warw* 5G 73
Bosbury. *Here* 1B 48	Bourton. *Oxon* 3H 35	Boylestone. *Derbs* 2F 73	Bradley Green. *Worc* 4D 61
Boscastle. *Corn* 3A 10	Bourton. *Shrp* 1H 59	Boylestonfield. *Derbs* 2F 73	Bradley in the Moors. *Staf* 1E 73
Boscombe. *Bour* 3G 15	Bourton. *Wilts* 5F 35	Boyndie. *Abers* 2D 160	Bradley Mount. *Ches E* 3D 84
Boscombe. *Wilts* 3H 23	Bourton on Dunsmore. *Warw* . . .3B 62	Boynton. *E Yor* 3F 101	Bradley Stoke. *S Glo* 3B 34
Boscoppa. *Corn* 3E 7	Bourton-on-the-Hill. *Glos* 2G 49	Boys Hill. *Dors* 1B 14	Bradlow. *Here* 2C 48
Bosham. *W Sus* 2G 17	Bourton-on-the-Water. *Glos* 3G 49	Boythorpe. *Derbs* 4A 86	Bradmore. *Notts* 2C 74

Bradmore. *W Mid* 1C 60	
Bradninch. *Devn* 2D 12	
Bradnop. *Staf* 5E 85	
Bradpole. *Dors* 3H 13	
Bradshaw. *G Man* 3F 91	
Bradstone. *Devn* 4D 11	
Bradwall Green. *Ches E* 4B 84	
Bradway. *S Yor* 2H 85	
Bradwell. *Derbs* 2F 85	
Bradwell. *Essx* 3B 54	
Bradwell. *Mil* 2G 51	
Bradwell. *Norf* 5H 79	
Bradwell-on-Sea. *Essx* 5D 54	
Bradwell Waterside. *Essx* 5C 54	
Bradworthy. *Devn* 1D 10	
Brae. *High* 5C 162	
Brae. *Shet* 5E 173	
Braeantra. *High* 1H 157	
Braefield. *High* 5G 157	
Braefindon. *High* 3A 158	
Braegrum. *Per* 1C 136	
Braehead. *Ang* 3F 145	
Braehead. *Dum* 4B 110	
Braehead. *Mor* 4G 159	
Braehead. *Orkn* 3D 172	
Braehead. *S Lan* 1H 117	
(nr. Coalburn)	
Braehead. *S Lan* 4C 128	
(nr. Forth)	
Braehoulland. *Shet* 4D 173	
Braemar. *Abers* 4F 151	
Braemore. *High* 5C 168	
(nr. Dunbeath)	
Braemore. *High* 1D 156	
(nr. Ullapool)	
Brae of Achnahaird. *High* 2E 163	
Brae Roy Lodge. *High* 4F 149	
Braeside. *Abers* 5G 161	
Braeside. *Inv* 2D 126	
Braes of Coul. *Ang* 3B 144	
Braetongue. *High* 3F 167	
Braeval. *Stir* 3E 135	
Braevallich. *Arg* 3G 133	
Brafferton. *Darl* 2F 105	
Brafferton. *N Yor* 2G 99	
Brafield-on-the-Green. *Nptn* . . .5F 63	
Bragar. *W Isl* 3E 171	
Bragbury Green. *Herts* 3C 52	
Bragleenbeg. *Arg* 1G 133	
Braichmelyn. *Gwyn* 4F 81	
Braides. *Lanc* 4D 96	
Braidwood. *S Lan* 5B 128	
Braigo. *Arg* 3A 124	
Brailsford. *Derbs* 1G 73	
Braintree. *Essx* 3A 54	
Braiseworth. *Suff* 3D 66	
Braishfield. *Hants* 4B 24	
Braithwaite. *Cumb* 2D 102	
Braithwaite. *S Yor* 3G 93	
Braithwaite. *W Yor* 5C 98	
Braithwell. *S Yor* 1C 86	
Brakefield Green. *Norf* 5C 78	
Bramber. *W Sus* 4C 26	
Brambledown. *Kent* 3D 40	
Brambridge. *Hants* 4C 24	
Bramcote. *Notts* 2C 74	
Bramcote. *Warw* 2B 62	
Bramdean. *Hants* 4E 24	
Bramerton. *Norf* 5E 79	
Bramfield. *Herts* 4C 52	
Bramfield. *Suff* 3F 67	
Bramford. *Suff* 1E 54	
Bramhall. *G Man* 2C 84	
Bramham. *W Yor* 5G 99	
Bramhope. *W Yor* 5E 99	
Bramley. *Hants* 1E 25	
Bramley. *S Yor* 1B 86	
Bramley. *Surr* 1B 26	
Bramley. *W Yor* 1C 92	
Bramley Green. *Hants* 1E 25	
Bramley Head. *N Yor* 4D 98	
Bramley Vale. *Derbs* 4B 86	
Bramling. *Kent* 5G 41	
Brampford Speke. *Devn* 3C 12	

Brampton—Broad Street

Brampton. *Cambs* 3B 64
Brampton. *Cumb* 2H 103
(nr. Appleby-in-Westmorland)
Brampton. *Cumb* 3G 113
(nr. Carlisle)
Brampton. *Linc* 3F 87
Brampton. *Norf* 3E 78
Brampton. *S Yor* 4E 93
Brampton. *Suff* 2G 67
Brampton Abbotts. *Here* 3B 48
Brampton Ash. *Nptn* 2E 63
Brampton Bryan. *Here* 3F 59
Brampton en le Morthen. *S Yor* 2B 86
Bramshall. *Staf* 2E 73
Bramshaw. *Hants* 1A 16
Bramshill. *Hants* 5F 37
Bramshott. *Hants* 3G 25
Branault. *High* 2G 139
Brancaster. *Norf* 1G 77
Brancaster Staithe. *Norf* 1G 77
Brancepeth. *Dur* 1F 105
Branch End. *Nmbd* 3D 114
Branchill. *Mor* 3E 159
Brand End. *Linc* 1C 76
Branderburgh. *Mor* 1G 159
Brandesburton. *E Yor* 5F 101
Brandeston. *Suff* 4E 67
Brand Green. *Glos* 3C 48
Brandhill. *Shrp* 3G 59
Brandis Corner. *Devn* 2E 11
Brandish Street. *Som* 2C 20
Brandiston. *Norf* 3D 78
Brandon. *Dur* 1F 105
Brandon. *Linc* 1G 75
Brandon. *Nmbd* 3E 121
Brandon. *Suff* 2G 65
Brandon. *Warw* 3B 62
Brandon Bank. *Cambs* 2F 65
Brandon Creek. *Norf* 1F 65
Brandon Parva. *Norf* 5C 78
Brandsby. *N Yor* 2H 99
Brandy Wharf. *Linc* 1H 87
Brane. *Corn* 4B 4
Bran End. *Essx* 3G 53
Branksome. *Pool* 3F 15
Bransbury. *Hants* 2C 24
Bransby. *Linc* 3G 87
Branscombe. *Devn* 4E 13
Bransford. *Worc* 5B 60
Bransgore. *Hants* 3G 15
Bransholme. *Hull* 1D 94
Bransley. *Shrp* 3A 60
Branston. *Leics* 3F 75
Branston. *Linc* 4H 87
Branston. *Staf* 3G 73
Branston Booths. *Linc* 4H 87
Branstone. *IOW* 4D 16
Bransty. *Cumb* 3A 102
Brant Broughton. *Linc* 5G 87
Brantham. *Suff* 2E 54
Branthwaite. *Cumb* 1D 102
(nr. Caldbeck)
Branthwaite. *Cumb* 2B 102
(nr. Workington)
Brantingham. *E Yor* 2C 94
Branton. *Nmbd* 3E 121
Branton. *S Yor* 4G 93
Branton Green. *N Yor* 3G 99
Branxholme. *Bord* 3G 119
Branxton. *Nmbd* 1C 120
Brassington. *Derbs* 5G 85
Brasted. *Kent* 5F 39
Brasted Chart. *Kent* 5F 39
Bratch, The. *Staf* 1C 60
Brathens. *Abers* 4D 152
Bratoft. *Linc* 4D 88
Brattleby. *Linc* 2G 87
Bratton. *Som* 2C 20
Bratton. *Telf* 4A 72
Bratton. *Wilts* 1E 23
Bratton Clovelly. *Devn* 3E 11
Bratton Fleming. *Devn* 3G 19
Bratton Seymour. *Som* 4B 22
Braughing. *Herts* 3D 53
Braulen Lodge. *High* 5E 157
Braunston. *Nptn* 4C 62
Braunstone Town. *Leic* 5C 74
Braunston-in-Rutland. *Rut* 5F 75
Braunton. *Devn* 3E 19
Brawby. *N Yor* 2B 100
Brawl. *High* 2A 168
Brawlbin. *High* 3C 168
Bray. *Wind* 3A 38
Braybrooke. *Nptn* 2E 63
Brayford. *Devn* 3G 19
Bray Shop. *Corn* 5D 10
Braystones. *Cumb* 4B 102
Brayton. *N Yor* 1G 93
Bray Wick. *Wind* 4G 37
Brazacott. *Corn* 3C 10
Brea. *Corn* 4A 6
Breach. *W Sus* 2F 17
Breachwood Green. *Herts* 3B 52
Breacleit. *W Isl* 4D 171
Breaden Heath. *Shrp* 2G 71
Breadsall. *Derbs* 1A 74
Breadstone. *Glos* 5C 48
Breage. *Corn* 4D 4
Breakachy. *High* 4G 157
Breakish. *High* 1E 147
Bream. *Glos* 5B 48
Breamore. *Hants* 1G 15
Bream's Meend. *Glos* 5B 48
Brean. *Som* 1F 21
Breanais. *W Isl* 5B 171
Brearton. *N Yor* 3F 99
Breascleit. *W Isl* 4E 171
Breaston. *Derbs* 2B 74
Brecais Àrd. *High* 1E 147
Brecais Iosal. *High* 1E 147
Brechfa. *Carm* 2F 45
Brechin. *Ang* 3F 145
Breckles. *Norf* 1B 66
Brecon. *Powy* 3D 46
Brecon Beacons. *Powy* 3C 46
Bredbury. *G Man* 1D 84
Brede. *E Sus* 4C 28
Bredenbury. *Here* 5A 60
Breden's Norton. *Worc* 2E 49
Bredfield. *Suff* 5E 67
Bredgar. *Kent* 4C 40
Bredhurst. *Kent* 4B 40
Bredicot. *Worc* 5D 60
Bredon. *Worc* 2E 49
Bredwardine. *Here* 1G 47
Breedon on the Hill. *Leics* 3B 74
Breibhig. *W Isl* 9B 170
(on Barra)
Breibhig. *W Isl* 4G 171
(on Isle of Lewis)
Breich. *W Lot* 3C 128
Breightmet. *G Man* 3F 91
Breighton. *E Yor* 1H 93
Breinton. *Here* 2H 47
Breinton Common. *Here* 2H 47
Breiwick. *Shet* 7F 173
Brelston Green. *Here* 3A 48
Bremhill. *Wilts* 4E 35
Brenachie. *High* 1B 158
Brenchley. *Kent* 1A 28
Brendon. *Devn* 2A 20
Brent Cross. *G Lon* 2D 38
Brent Eleigh. *Suff* 1C 54
Brentford. *G Lon* 3C 38
Brentingby. *Leics* 4E 75
Brent Knoll. *Som* 1G 21
Brent Pelham. *Herts* 2E 53
Brentwood. *Essx* 1H 39
Brenzett. *Kent* 3E 28
Brereton. *Staf* 4E 73
Brereton Cross. *Staf* 4E 73
Brereton Green. *Ches E* 4B 84
Brereton Heath. *Ches E* 4C 84
Bressingham. *Norf* 2C 66
Bretby. *Derbs* 3G 73
Bretford. *Warw* 3B 62
Bretforton. *Worc* 1F 49
Bretherdale Head. *Cumb* 4G 103
Bretherton. *Lanc* 2C 90
Brettenham. *Norf* 2B 66
Brettenham. *Suff* 5B 66
Bretton. *Flin* 4F 83
Bretton. *Pet* 5A 76
Brewer Street. *Surr* 5E 39
Brewlands Bridge. *Ang* 2A 144
Brewood. *Staf* 5C 72
Briantspuddle. *Dors* 3D 14
Bricket Wood. *Herts* 5B 52
Bricklehampton. *Worc* 1E 49
Bride. *IOM* 1D 108
Bridekirk. *Cumb* 1C 102
Bridell. *Pemb* 1B 44
Bridestowe. *Devn* 4F 11
Brideswell. *Abers* 5C 160
Bridford. *Devn* 4B 12
Bridge. *Corn* 4A 6
Bridge. *Kent* 5F 41
Bridge. *Som* 2G 13
Bridge End. *Bed* 5H 63
Bridge End. *Cumb* 5D 102
(nr. Broughton in Furness)
Bridge End. *Cumb* 5E 113
(nr. Dalston)
Bridge End. *Linc* 2A 76
Bridge End. *Shet* 8E 173
Bridgefoot. *Ang* 5C 144
Bridgefoot. *Cumb* 2B 102
Bridge Green. *Essx* 2E 53
Bridgehampton. *Som* 4A 22
Bridge Hewick. *N Yor* 2F 99
Bridgehill. *Dur* 4D 115
Bridgemary. *Hants* 2D 16
Bridgemere. *Ches E* 1B 72
Bridgemont. *Derbs* 2E 85
Bridgend. *Abers* 5C 160
(nr. Huntly)
Bridgend. *Abers* 5H 161
(nr. Peterhead)
Bridgend. *Ang* 2E 145
(nr. Brechin)
Bridgend. *Ang* 4C 144
(nr. Kirriemuir)
Bridgend. *Arg* 4F 133
(nr. Lochgilphead)
Bridgend. *Arg* 3B 124
(on Islay)
Bridgend. *B'end* 3C 32
Bridgend. *Cumb* 3F 103
Bridgend. *Devn* 4B 8
Bridgend. *Fife* 2F 137
Bridgend. *High* 3F 157
Bridgend. *Mor* 5A 160
Bridgend. *Per* 1D 136
Bridgend. *W Lot* 2D 128
Bridgend of Lintrathen.
Ang 3B 144
Bridgeness. *Falk* 1D 128
Bridge of Alford. *Abers* 2C 152
Bridge of Allan. *Stir* 4G 135
Bridge of Avon. *Mor* 5F 159
Bridge of Awe. *Arg* 1H 133
Bridge of Balgie. *Per* 4C 142
Bridge of Brown. *High* 1F 151
Bridge of Cally. *Per* 3A 144
Bridge of Canny. *Abers* 4D 152
Bridge of Dee. *Dum* 3E 111
Bridge of Don. *Aber* 2G 153
Bridge of Dun. *Ang* 3F 145
Bridge of Dye. *Abers* 5D 152
Bridge of Earn. *Per* 2D 136
Bridge of Ericht. *Per* 3C 142
Bridge of Feugh. *Abers* 4E 152
Bridge of Forss. *High* 2C 168
Bridge of Gairn. *Abers* 4A 152
Bridge of Gaur. *Per* 3C 142
Bridge of Muchalls.
Abers 4F 153
Bridge of Oich. *High* 3F 149
Bridge of Orchy. *Arg* 5H 141
Bridge of Walls. *Shet* 6D 173
Bridge of Weir. *Ren* 3E 127
Bridge Reeve. *Devn* 1G 11
Bridgerule. *Devn* 2C 10
Bridge Sollers. *Here* 1H 47
Bridge Street. *Suff* 1B 54
Bridgetown. *Devn* 2E 9
Bridgetown. *Som* 3C 20
Bridge Town. *Warw* 5G 61
Bridge Trafford.
Ches W 3G 83
Bridgeyate. *S Glo* 4B 34
Bridgham. *Norf* 2B 66
Bridgnorth. *Shrp* 1B 60
Bridgtown. *Staf* 5D 73
Bridgwater. *Som* 3G 21
Bridlington. *E Yor* 3F 101
Bridport. *Dors* 3H 13
Bridstow. *Here* 3A 48
Brierfield. *Lanc* 1G 91
Brierley. *Glos* 4B 48
Brierley. *Here* 5G 59
Brierley. *S Yor* 3E 93
Brierley Hill. *W Mid* 2D 60
Brierton. *Hart* 1B 106
Briestfield. *W Yor* 3C 92
Brigg. *N Lin* 4D 94
Briggate. *Norf* 3F 79
Briggswath. *N Yor* 4F 107
Brigham. *Cumb* 1B 102
Brigham. *E Yor* 4E 101
Brighouse. *W Yor* 2B 92
Brighstone. *IOW* 4C 16
Brightgate. *Derbs* 5G 85
Brighthampton. *Oxon* 5B 50
Brightholmlee. *S Yor* 1G 85
Brightley. *Devn* 3G 11
Brightling. *E Sus* 3A 28
Brightlingsea. *Essx* 4D 54
Brighton. *Brig* 5E 27
Brighton. *Corn* 3D 6
Brighton Hill. *Hants* 2E 24
Brightons. *Falk* 2C 128
Brightwalton. *W Ber* 4C 36
Brightwalton Green. *W Ber* 4C 36
Brightwell. *Suff* 1F 55
Brightwell Baldwin. *Oxon* 2E 37
Brightwell-cum-Sotwell. *Oxon* 2D 36
Brigmerston. *Wilts* 2G 23
Brignall. *Dur* 3D 104
Brig o'Turk. *Stir* 3E 135
Brigsley. *NE Lin* 4F 95
Brigsteer. *Cumb* 1D 97
Brigstock. *Nptn* 2G 63
Brill. *Buck* 4E 51
Brill. *Corn* 4E 5
Brilley. *Here* 1F 47
Brimaston. *Pemb* 2D 42
Brimfield. *Here* 4H 59
Brimington. *Derbs* 3B 86
Brimley. *Devn* 5B 12
Brimpsfield. *Glos* 4E 49
Brimpton. *W Ber* 5D 36
Brims. *Orkn* 9B 172
Brimscombe. *Glos* 5D 48
Brimstage. *Mers* 2F 83
Brincliffe. *S Yor* 2H 85
Brind. *E Yor* 1H 93
Brindle. *Lanc* 2E 90
Brindley. *Ches E* 5H 83
Brindley Ford. *Stoke* 5C 84
Brineton. *Staf* 4C 72
Bringhurst. *Leics* 1F 63
Brington. *Cambs* 3H 63
Brinian. *Orkn* 5D 172
Briningham. *Norf* 2C 78
Brinkhill. *Linc* 3C 88
Brinkley. *Cambs* 5F 65
Brinklow. *Warw* 3B 62
Brinkworth. *Wilts* 3F 35
Brinscall. *Lanc* 2E 91
Brinscombe. *Som* 1H 21
Brinsley. *Notts* 1B 74
Brinsty Common. *Here* 5A 60
Brinsworth. *S Yor* 2B 86
Brinton. *Norf* 2C 78
Brisco. *Cumb* 4F 113
Brisley. *Norf* 3B 78
Brislington. *Bris* 4B 34
Brissenden Green. *Kent* 2D 28
Bristol. *Bris* 4A 34
Bristol International Airport.
N Som 5A 34
Briston. *Norf* 2C 78
Britannia. *Lanc* 2G 91
Britford. *Wilts* 4G 23
Brithdir. *Cphy* 5E 47
Brithdir. *Cdgn* 1D 44
Brithdir. *Gwyn* 4G 69
Briton Ferry. *Neat* 3G 31
Britwell Salome. *Oxon* 2E 37
Brixham. *Torb* 3F 9
Brixton. *Devn* 3B 8
Brixton. *G Lon* 3E 39
Brixton Deverill. *Wilts* 3D 22
Brixworth. *Nptn* 3E 63
Brize Norton. *Oxon* 5B 50
Broad Alley. *Worc* 4C 60
Broad Blunsdon. *Swin* 2G 35
Broadbottom. *G Man* 1D 85
Broadbridge. *W Sus* 2G 17
Broadbridge Heath. *W Sus* 2C 26
Broad Campden. *Glos* 2G 49
Broad Chalke. *Wilts* 4F 23
Broadclyst. *Devn* 3C 12
Broadfield. *Inv* 2E 127
Broadfield. *Pemb* 4F 43
Broadfield. *W Sus* 2D 26
Broadford. *High* 1E 147
Broadford Bridge. *W Sus* 3B 26
Broadgate. *Cumb* 1A 96
Broad Green. *Cambs* 5F 65
Broad Green. *C Beds* 1H 51
Broad Green. *Worc* 3D 61
(nr. Bromsgrove)
Broad Green. *Worc* 5B 60
(nr. Worcester)
Broadhaven. *High* 3F 169
Broad Haven. *Pemb* 3C 42
Broadheath. *G Man* 2B 84
Broad Heath. *Staf* 3C 72
Broadheath. *Worc* 4A 60
Broadhembury. *Devn* 2E 12
Broadhempston. *Devn* 2E 9
Broad Hill. *Cambs* 3E 65
Broad Hinton. *Wilts* 4G 35
Broadholm. *Derbs* 1A 74
Broadholme. *Linc* 3F 87
Broadlay. *Carm* 5D 44
Broad Laying. *Hants* 5C 36
Broadley. *Lanc* 3G 91
Broadley. *Mor* 2A 160
Broadley Common. *Essx* 5E 53
Broad Marston. *Worc* 1G 49
Broadmayne. *Dors* 4C 14
Broadmere. *Hants* 2E 24
Broadmoor. *Pemb* 4E 43
Broad Oak. *Carm* 3F 45
Broad Oak. *Cumb* 5C 102
Broad Oak. *Devn* 3D 12
Broadoak. *Dors* 3H 13
(nr. Bridport)
Broad Oak. *Dors* 1C 14
(nr. Sturminster Newton)
Broad Oak. *E Sus* 4C 28
(nr. Hastings)
Broad Oak. *E Sus* 3H 27
(nr. Heathfield)
Broadoak. *Glos* 4B 48
Broadoak. *Hants* 1C 16
Broad Oak. *Here* 3H 47
Broad Oak. *Kent* 4F 41
Broadrashes. *Mor* 3B 160
Broads. *Norf* 5G 79
Broadsea. *Abers* 2G 161
Broad's Green. *Essx* 4G 53
Broadshard. *Som* 1H 13
Broadstairs. *Kent* 4H 41
Broadstone. *Pool* 3F 15
Broadstone. *Shrp* 2H 59
Broad Street. *E Sus* 4C 28

Broad Street—Budlake

Broad Street. *Kent* 1F **29** (nr. Ashford)
Broad Street. *Kent* 5C **40** (nr. Maidstone)
Broad Street Green. *Essx* 5B **54**
Broad, The. *Here* 4G **59**
Broad Town. *Wilts* 4F **35**
Broadwas. *Worc* 5B **60**
Broadwath. *Cumb* 4F **113**
Broadway. *Carm* 5D **45** (nr. Kidwelly)
Broadway. *Carm* 3G **43** (nr. Laugharne)
Broadway. *Pemb* 3C **42**
Broadway. *Som* 1G **13**
Broadway. *Suff* 3F **67**
Broadway. *Worc* 2G **49**
Broadwell. *Glos* 4A **48** (nr. Cinderford)
Broadwell. *Glos* 3H **49** (nr. Stow-on-the-Wold)
Broadwell. *Oxon* 5A **50**
Broadwell. *Warw* 4B **62**
Broadwell House. *Nmbd* 4C **114**
Broadwey. *Dors* 4B **14**
Broadwindsor. *Dors* 2H **13**
Broadwoodkelly. *Devn* 2G **11**
Broadwoodwidger. *Devn* 4E **11**
Broallan. *High* 4G **157**
Brobury. *Here* 1G **47**
Brochel. *High* 4E **155**
Brockamin. *Worc* 5B **60**
Brockbridge. *Hants* 1E **16**
Brockdish. *Norf* 3E **66**
Brockencote. *Worc* 3C **60**
Brockenhurst. *Hants* 2A **16**
Brocketsbrae. *S Lan* 1H **117**
Brockford Street. *Suff* 4D **66**
Brockhall. *Nptn* 4D **62**
Brockham. *Surr* 1C **26**
Brockhampton. *Glos* 3E **49** (nr. Bishop's Cleeve)
Brockhampton. *Glos* 3F **49** (nr. Sevenhampton)
Brockhampton. *Here* 2A **48**
Brockhill. *Bord* 2F **119**
Brockholes. *W Yor* 3B **92**
Brockhouse. *S Yor* 2C **86**
Brockhurst. *Hants* 2D **16**
Brocklesby. *Linc* 3E **95**
Brockley. *N Som* 5H **33**
Brockley Corner. *Suff* 3H **65**
Brockley Green. *Suff* 1H **53** (nr. Bury St Edmunds)
Brockley Green. *Suff* 5H **65** (nr. Haverhill)
Brockleymoor. *Cumb* 1F **103**
Brockmoor. *W Mid* 2C **60**
Brockton. *Shrp* 2F **59** (nr. Bishop's Castle)
Brockton. *Shrp* 5B **72** (nr. Madeley)
Brockton. *Shrp* 1H **59** (nr. Much Wenlock)
Brockton. *Shrp* 5F **71** (nr. Pontesbury)
Brockton. *Staf* 2C **72**
Brockton. *Telf* 4B **72**
Brockweir. *Glos* 5A **48**
Brockworth. *Glos* 4D **49**
Brocton. *Staf* 4D **72**
Brodick. *N Ayr* 2E **123**
Brodie. *Mor* 3D **159**
Brodiesord. *Abers* 3C **160**
Brodsworth. *S Yor* 4F **93**
Brogaig. *High* 2D **154**
Brogborough. *C Beds* 2H **51**
Brokenborough. *Wilts* 3E **35**
Broken Cross. *Ches E* 3C **84**
Bromborough. *Mers* 2F **83**
Bromdon. *Shrp* 2A **60**
Brome. *Suff* 3D **66**
Brome Street. *Suff* 3D **66**
Bromeswell. *Suff* 5F **67**
Bromfield. *Cumb* 5C **112**
Bromfield. *Shrp* 3G **59**
Bromford. *W Mid* 1F **61**
Bromham. *Bed* 5H **63**
Bromham. *Wilts* 5E **35**
Bromley. *G Lon* 4F **39**
Bromley. *Herts* 3E **53**
Bromley. *Shrp* 1B **60**
Bromley Cross. *G Man* 3F **91**
Bromley Green. *Kent* 2D **28**
Bromley Wood. *Staf* 3F **73**
Brompton. *Medw* 4B **40**
Brompton. *N Yor* 5A **106** (nr. Northallerton)
Brompton. *N Yor* 1D **100** (nr. Scarborough)
Brompton. *Shrp* 5H **71**
Brompton-on-Swale. *N Yor* 5F **105**
Brompton Ralph. *Som* 3D **20**
Brompton Regis. *Som* 3C **20**
Bromsash. *Here* 3B **48**
Bromsberrow. *Glos* 2C **48**
Bromsberrow Heath. *Glos* 2C **48**
Bromsgrove. *Worc* 3D **60**
Bromstead Heath. *Staf* 4B **72**
Bromyard. *Here* 5A **60**
Bromyard Downs. *Here* 5A **60**
Bronaber. *Gwyn* 2G **69**
Broncroft. *Shrp* 2H **59**
Brongest. *Cdgn* 1D **44**
Brongwyn. *Cdgn* 1C **44**
Bronington. *Wrex* 2G **71**
Bronllys. *Powy* 2E **47**
Bronnant. *Cdgn* 4F **57**
Bronwydd Arms. *Carm* 3E **45**
Bronydd. *Powy* 1F **47**
Bronygarth. *Shrp* 2E **71**
Brook. *Carm* 4G **43**
Brook. *Hants* 1A **16** (nr. Cadnam)
Brook. *Hants* 4B **24** (nr. Romsey)
Brook. *IOW* 4B **16**
Brook. *Kent* 1E **29**
Brook. *Surr* 1B **26** (nr. Guildford)
Brook. *Surr* 2A **26** (nr. Haslemere)
Brooke. *Norf* 1E **67**
Brooke. *Rut* 5F **75**
Brookenby. *Linc* 1B **88**
Brookend. *Glos* 5B **48**
Brook End. *Worc* 1D **48**
Brookfield. *Lanc* 1D **90**
Brookfield. *Ren* 3F **127**
Brookhouse. *Lanc* 3E **97**
Brookhouse Green. *Ches E* 4C **84**
Brookhouses. *Staf* 1D **73**
Brookhurst. *Mers* 2F **83**
Brookland. *Kent* 3D **28**
Brooklands. *G Man* 1B **84**
Brooklands. *Shrp* 1H **71**
Brookmans Park. *Herts* 5C **52**
Brooks. *Powy* 1D **58**
Brooksby. *Leics* 4D **74**
Brooks Green. *W Sus* 3C **26**
Brook Street. *Essx* 1G **39**
Brook Street. *Kent* 2D **28**
Brook Street. *W Sus* 3E **27**
Brookthorpe. *Glos* 4D **48**
Brookville. *Norf* 1G **65**
Brookwood. *Surr* 5A **38**
Broom. *C Beds* 1B **52**
Broom. *Fife* 3F **137**
Broom. *Warw* 5E **61**
Broome. *Norf* 1F **67**
Broome. *Shrp* 1H **59** (nr. Cardington)
Broome. *Shrp* 2G **59** (nr. Craven Arms)
Broome. *Worc* 3D **60**
Broomedge. *Warr* 2B **84**
Broomend. *Abers* 2E **153**
Broome Park. *Nmbd* 3F **121**
Broomer's Corner. *W Sus* 3C **26**
Broomfield. *Abers* 5G **161**
Broomfield. *Essx* 4H **53**
Broomfield. *Kent* 4F **41** (nr. Herne Bay)
Broomfield. *Kent* 5C **40** (nr. Maidstone)
Broomfield. *Som* 3F **21**
Broomfleet. *E Yor* 2B **94**
Broom Green. *Norf* 3B **78**
Broomhall. *Ches E* 1A **72**
Broomhall. *Wind* 4A **38**
Broomhaugh. *Nmbd* 3D **114**
Broom Hill. *Dors* 2F **15**
Broomhill. *High* 1D **151** (nr. Grantown-on-Spey)
Broomhill. *High* 1B **158** (nr. Invergordon)
Broomhill. *Norf* 5F **77**
Broomhill. *S Yor* 4E **93**
Broom Hill. *Worc* 3D **60**
Broomhillbank. *Dum* 5D **118**
Broomholm. *Norf* 2F **79**
Broomlands. *Dum* 4C **118**
Broomley. *Nmbd* 3D **114**
Broom of Moy. *Mor* 3E **159**
Broompark. *Dur* 5F **115**
Broom's Green. *Glos* 2C **48**
Brora. *High* 3G **165**
Broseley. *Shrp* 5A **72**
Brotherhouse Bar. *Linc* 4B **76**
Brotheridge Green. *Worc* 1D **48**
Brotherlee. *Dur* 1C **104**
Brothertoft. *Linc* 1B **76**
Brotherton. *N Yor* 2E **93**
Brotton. *Red C* 2D **107**
Broubster. *High* 2C **168**
Brough. *Cumb* 3A **104**
Brough. *Derbs* 2F **85**
Brough. *E Yor* 2C **94**
Brough. *High* 1E **169**
Brough. *Notts* 5F **87**
Brough. *Orkn* 9D **172**
Brough. *Shet* 4F **173** (nr. Booth of Toft)
Brough. *Shet* 5G **173** (on Whalsay)
Broughall. *Shrp* 1H **71**
Brougham. *Cumb* 2G **103**
Brough Sowerby. *Cumb* 3A **104**
Broughton. *Cambs* 3B **64**
Broughton. *Flin* 4F **83**
Broughton. *Hants* 3B **24**
Broughton. *Lanc* 1D **90**
Broughton. *Mil* 2G **51**
Broughton. *Nptn* 3F **63**
Broughton. *N Lin* 4C **94**
Broughton. *N Yor* 2B **100** (nr. Malton)
Broughton. *N Yor* 4B **98** (nr. Skipton)
Broughton. *Oxon* 2C **50**
Broughton. *Bord* 1D **118**
Broughton. *Staf* 2B **72**
Broughton. *V Glam* 4C **32**
Broughton Astley. *Leics* 1C **62**
Broughton Beck. *Cumb* 1B **96**
Broughton Cross. *Cumb* 1B **102**
Broughton Gifford. *Wilts* 5D **35**
Broughton Green. *Worc* 4D **60**
Broughton Hackett. *Worc* 5D **60**
Broughton in Furness. *Cumb* 1B **96**
Broughton Mills. *Cumb* 5D **102**
Broughton Moor. *Cumb* 1B **102**
Broughton Park. *G Man* 4G **91**
Broughton Poggs. *Oxon* 5H **49**
Broughtown. *Orkn* 3F **172**
Broughty Ferry. *D'dee* 5D **144**
Brownbread Street. *E Sus* 4A **28**
Brown Candover. *Hants* 3D **24**
Brown Edge. *Lanc* 3B **90**
Brown Edge. *Staf* 5D **84**
Brownhill. *Bkbn* 1E **91**
Brownhill. *Shrp* 3G **71**
Brownhills. *Shrp* 2A **72**
Brownhills. *W Mid* 5E **73**
Brown Knowl. *Ches W* 5G **83**
Brownlow. *Ches E* 4C **84**
Brownlow Heath. *Ches E* 4C **84**
Brown's Green. *W Mid* 1E **61**
Brownshill. *Glos* 5D **49**
Brownston. *Devn* 3C **8**
Brownstone. *Devn* 2A **12**
Browston Green. *Norf* 5G **79**
Broxa. *N Yor* 5G **107**
Broxbourne. *Herts* 5D **52**
Broxburn. *E Lot* 2C **130**
Broxburn. *W Lot* 2D **129**
Broxholme. *Linc* 3G **87**
Broxted. *Essx* 3F **53**
Broxton. *Ches W* 5G **83**
Broxwood. *Here* 5F **59**
Broyle Side. *E Sus* 4F **27**
Brù. *W Isl* 3F **171**
Bruach Mairi. *W Isl* 4F **171**
Bruairnis. *W Isl* 8C **170**
Bruan. *High* 5F **169**
Bruar Lodge. *Per* 1F **143**
Brucehill. *W Dun* 2E **127**
Brucklay. *Abers* 3G **161**
Bruera. *Ches W* 4G **83**
Bruern Abbey. *Oxon* 3A **50**
Bruichladdich. *Arg* 3A **124**
Bruisyard. *Suff* 4F **67**
Bruisyard Street. *Suff* 4F **67**
Brumby. *N Lin* 4B **94**
Brund. *Staf* 4F **85**
Brundall. *Norf* 5F **79**
Brundish. *Norf* 1F **67**
Brundish. *Suff* 4E **67**
Brundish Street. *Suff* 3E **67**
Brunery. *High* 1B **140**
Brunswick Village. *Tyne* 2F **115**
Brunthwaite. *W Yor* 5C **98**
Bruntingthorpe. *Leics* 1D **62**
Brunton. *Fife* 1F **137**
Brunton. *Nmbd* 2G **121**
Brunton. *Wilts* 1H **23**
Brushford. *Devn* 2G **11**
Brushford. *Som* 4C **20**
Brusta. *W Isl* 1E **170**
Bruton. *Som* 3B **22**
Bryanston. *Dors* 2D **15**
Bryant's Bottom. *Buck* 2G **37**
Brydekirk. *Dum* 2C **112**
Brymbo. *Cnwy* 3H **81**
Brymbo. *Wrex* 5E **83**
Brympton D'Evercy. *Som* 1A **14**
Bryn. *Carm* 5F **45**
Bryn. *G Man* 4D **90**
Bryn. *Neat* 2B **32**
Bryn. *Shrp* 2E **59**
Brynamman. *Carm* 4H **45**
Brynberian. *Pemb* 1F **43**
Brynbryddan. *Neat* 2A **32**
Bryncae. *Rhon* 3C **32**
Bryncethin. *B'end* 3C **32**
Bryncir. *Gwyn* 1D **69**
Bryn-coch. *Neat* 3G **31**
Bryncroes. *Gwyn* 2B **68**
Bryncrug. *Gwyn* 5F **69**
Bryn Du. *IOA* 3C **80**
Bryn Eden. *Gwyn* 3G **69**
Bryneglwys. *Den* 1D **70**
Bryn Eglwys. *Gwyn* 4F **81**
Brynford. *Flin* 3D **82**
Bryn Gates. *G Man* 4D **90**
Bryn Golau. *Rhon* 3D **32**
Bryngwran. *IOA* 3C **80**
Bryngwyn. *Mon* 5G **47**
Bryngwyn. *Powy* 1E **47**
Bryn-henllan. *Pemb* 1E **43**
Brynhoffnant. *Cdgn* 5C **56**
Bryn-llwyn. *Flin* 2C **82**
Brynllywarch. *Powy* 2D **58**
Brynmawr. *Blae* 4E **47**
Bryn-mawr. *Gwyn* 2B **68**
Brynmenyn. *B'end* 3C **32**
Brynmill. *Swan* 3F **31**
Brynna. *Rhon* 3C **32**
Brynrefail. *Gwyn* 4E **81**
Brynrefail. *IOA* 2D **81**
Brynsadler. *Rhon* 3D **32**
Bryn-Saith Marchog. *Den* 5C **82**
Brynsiencyn. *IOA* 4D **81**
Brynteg. *IOA* 2D **81**
Brynteg. *Wrex* 5F **83**
Brynygwenyn. *Mon* 4G **47**
Bryn-y-maen. *Cnwy* 3H **81**
Buaile nam Bodach. *W Isl* 8C **170**
Bualintur. *High* 1C **146**
Bubbenhall. *Warw* 3A **62**
Bubwith. *E Yor* 1H **93**
Buccleuch. *Bord* 3F **119**
Buchanan Smithy. *Stir* 1F **127**
Buchanhaven. *Abers* 4H **161**
Buchanty. *Per* 1B **136**
Buchany. *Stir* 3G **135**
Buchley. *E Dun* 2G **127**
Buchlyvie. *Stir* 4E **135**
Buckabank. *Cumb* 5E **113**
Buckden. *Cambs* 4A **64**
Buckden. *N Yor* 2B **98**
Buckenham. *Norf* 5F **79**
Buckerell. *Devn* 2E **13**
Buckfast. *Devn* 2D **8**
Buckfastleigh. *Devn* 2D **8**
Buckhaven. *Fife* 4F **137**
Buckholm. *Bord* 1G **119**
Buckholt. *Here* 4A **48**
Buckhorn Weston. *Dors* 4C **22**
Buckhurst Hill. *Essx* 1F **39**
Buckie. *Mor* 2B **160**
Buckingham. *Buck* 2E **51**
Buckland. *Buck* 4G **51**
Buckland. *Glos* 2F **49**
Buckland. *Here* 5H **59**
Buckland. *Herts* 2D **52**
Buckland. *Kent* 1H **29**
Buckland. *Oxon* 2B **36**
Buckland. *Surr* 5D **38**
Buckland Brewer. *Devn* 4E **19**
Buckland Common. *Buck* 5H **51**
Buckland Dinham. *Som* 1C **22**
Buckland Filleigh. *Devn* 2E **11**
Buckland in the Moor. *Devn* 5H **11**
Buckland Monachorum. *Devn* 2A **8**
Buckland Newton. *Dors* 2B **14**
Buckland Ripers. *Dors* 4B **14**
Buckland St Mary. *Som* 1F **13**
Buckland-tout-Saints. *Devn* 4D **8**
Bucklebury. *W Ber* 4D **36**
Bucklegate. *Linc* 2C **76**
Buckleigh. *Devn* 4E **19**
Buckler's Hard. *Hants* 3C **16**
Bucklesham. *Suff* 1F **55**
Buckley. *Flin* 4E **83**
Buckley Green. *Warw* 4F **61**
Buckley Hill. *Mers* 1F **83**
Bucklow Hill. *Ches E* 2B **84**
Buckminster. *Leics* 3F **75**
Bucknall. *Linc* 4A **88**
Bucknall. *Stoke* 1D **72**
Bucknell. *Oxon* 3D **50**
Bucknell. *Shrp* 3F **59**
Buckpool. *Mor* 2B **160**
Bucksburn. *Aber* 3F **153**
Buck's Cross. *Devn* 4D **18**
Bucks Green. *W Sus* 2B **26**
Buckshaw Village. *Lanc* 2D **90**
Bucks Hill. *Herts* 5A **52**
Bucks Horn Oak. *Hants* 2G **25**
Buck's Mills. *Devn* 4D **18**
Buckton. *E Yor* 2F **101**
Buckton. *Here* 3F **59**
Buckton. *Nmbd* 1E **121**
Buckton Vale. *G Man* 4H **91**
Buckworth. *Cambs* 3A **64**
Budby. *Notts* 4D **86**
Bude. *Corn* 2C **10**
Budge's Shop. *Corn* 3H **7**
Budlake. *Devn* 2C **12**

Budle—Cadeby

Budle. Nmbd 1F 121
Budleigh Salterton. Devn 4D 12
Budock Water. Corn 5B 6
Buerton. Ches E 1A 72
Buffler's Holt. Buck 2E 51
Bugbrooke. Nptn 5D 62
Buglawton. Ches E 4C 84
Bugle. Corn 3E 6
Bugthorpe. E Yor 4B 100
Buildwas. Shrp 5A 72
Builth Road. Powy 5C 58
Builth Wells. Powy 5C 58
Bulbourne. Herts 4H 51
Bulby. Linc 3H 75
Bulcote. Notts 1D 74
Buldoo. High 2B 168
Bulford. Wilts 2G 23
Bulford Camp. Wilts 2G 23
Bulkeley. Ches E 5H 83
Bulkington. Warw 2A 62
Bulkington. Wilts 1E 23
Bulkworthy. Devn 1D 11
Bullamoor. N Yor 5A 106
Bull Bay. IOA 1D 80
Bullbridge. Derbs 5A 86
Bullgill. Cumb 1B 102
Bull Hill. Hants 3B 16
Bullinghope. Here 2A 48
Bull's Green. Herts 4C 52
Bullwood. Arg 2C 126
Bulmer. Essx 1B 54
Bulmer. N Yor 3A 100
Bulmer Tye. Essx 2B 54
Bulphan. Thur 2H 39
Bulverhythe. E Sus 5B 28
Bulwark. Abers 4G 161
Bulwell. Nott 1C 74
Bulwick. Nptn 1G 63
Bumble's Green. Essx 5E 53
Bun Abhainn Eadarra. W Isl 7D 171
Bunacaimb. High 5E 147
Bun a' Mhuillinn. W Isl 7D 170
Bunarkaig. High 5D 148
Bunbury. Ches E 5H 83
Bunchrew. High 4A 158
Bundalloch. High 1A 148
Bunessan. Arg 1A 132
Bungay. Suff 2F 67
Bunkegivie. High 2H 149
Bunker's Hill. Cambs 5D 76
Bunkers Hill. Linc 5B 88
Bunker's Hill. Norf 5H 79
Bunloit. High 1H 149
Bunnahabhain. Arg 2C 124
Bunny. Notts 3C 74
Bunoich. High 3F 149
Bunree. High 2E 141
Bunroy. High 5E 149
Buntait. High 5F 157
Buntingford. Herts 3D 52
Buntings Green. Essx 2B 54
Bunwell. Norf 1D 66
Burbage. Derbs 3E 85
Burbage. Leics 1B 62
Burbage. Wilts 5H 35
Burcher. Here 4F 59
Burchett's Green. Wind 3G 37
Burcombe. Wilts 3F 23
Burcot. Oxon 2D 36
Burcot. Worc 3D 61
Burcote. Shrp 1B 60
Burcott. Buck 3G 51
Burcott. Som 2A 22
Burdale. N Yor 3C 100
Burdrop. Oxon 2B 50
Bures. Suff 2C 54
Burford. Oxon 4A 50
Burford. Shrp 4H 59
Burf, The. Worc 4C 60
Burg. Arg 4E 139
Burgate Great Green. Suff 3C 66
Burgate Little Green. Suff 3C 66
Burgess Hill. W Sus 4E 27
Burgh. Suff 5E 67
Burgh by Sands. Cumb 4E 113
Burgh Castle. Norf 5G 79
Burghclere. Hants 5C 36
Burghead. Mor 2F 159
Burghfield. W Ber 5E 37
Burghfield Common. W Ber 5E 37
Burghfield Hill. W Ber 5E 37
Burgh Heath. Surr 5D 38
Burghill. Here 1H 47
Burgh le Marsh. Linc 4E 89
Burgh Muir. Abers 2E 153
Burgh next Aylsham. Norf 3E 78
Burgh on Bain. Linc 2B 88
Burgh St Margaret. Norf 4G 79
Burgh St Peter. Norf 1G 67
Burghwallis. S Yor 3F 93
Burgie. Mor 3E 159
Burham. Kent 4B 40
Buriton. Hants 4F 25
Burland. Ches E 5A 84
Burland. Shet 8E 173
Burlawn. Corn 2D 6
Burleigh. Brac 3A 38
Burleigh. Glos 5D 48
Burlescombe. Devn 1D 12
Burleston. Dors 3C 14
Burlestone. Devn 4E 9
Burley. Hants 2H 15
Burley. Rut 4F 75
Burley. W Yor 1C 92
Burley Gate. Here 1A 48
Burley in Wharfedale. W Yor 5D 98
Burley Street. Hants 2H 15
Burley Woodhead. W Yor 5D 98
Burlingjobb. Powy 5E 59
Burlington. Shrp 4B 72
Burlton. Shrp 3G 71
Burmantofts. W Yor 1D 92
Burmarsh. Kent 2F 29
Burmington. Warw 2A 50
Burn. N Yor 2F 93
Burnage. G Man 1C 84
Burnaston. Derbs 2G 73
Burnbanks. Cumb 3G 103
Burnby. E Yor 5C 100
Burncross. S Yor 1H 85
Burneside. Cumb 5G 103
Burness. Orkn 3F 172
Burneston. N Yor 1F 99
Burnett. Bath 5B 34
Burnfoot. E Ayr 4D 116
Burnfoot. Per 3B 136
Burnfoot. Bord 3H 119
(nr. Hawick)
Burnfoot. Bord 3G 119
(nr. Roberton)
Burngreave. S Yor 2A 86
Burnham. Buck 2A 38
Burnham. N Lin 3D 94
Burnham Deepdale. Norf 1H 77
Burnham Green. Herts 4C 52
Burnham Market. Norf 1H 77
Burnham Norton. Norf 1H 77
Burnham-on-Crouch. Essx 1D 40
Burnham-on-Sea. Som 2G 21
Burnham Overy Staithe. Norf 1H 77
Burnham Overy Town. Norf 1H 77
Burnham Thorpe. Norf 1A 78
Burnhaven. Abers 4H 161
Burnhead. Dum 5A 118
Burnhervie. Abers 2E 153
Burnhill Green. Staf 5B 72
Burnhope. Dur 5E 115
Burnhouse. N Ayr 4E 127
Burniston. N Yor 5H 107
Burnlee. W Yor 4B 92
Burnley. Lanc 1G 91
Burnleydam. Ches E 1A 72
Burnmouth. Bord 3F 131
Burn Naze. Lanc 5C 96
Burn of Cambus. Stir 3G 135
Burnopfield. Dur 4E 115
Burnsall. N Yor 3C 98
Burnside. Ang 3E 145
Burnside. E Ayr 3E 117
Burnside. Per 3D 136
Burnside. Shet 4D 173
Burnside. S Lan 4H 127
Burnside. W Lot 2D 129
(nr. Broxburn)
Burnside. W Lot 2D 128
(nr. Winchburgh)
Burntcommon. Surr 5B 38
Burntheath. Derbs 2G 73
Burnt Heath. Essx 3D 54
Burnt Hill. W Ber 4D 36
Burnt Houses. Dur 2E 105
Burntisland. Fife 1F 129
Burnt Oak. G Lon 1D 38
Burnton. E Ayr 4D 117
Burntstalk. Norf 2G 77
Burntwood. Staf 5E 73
Burntwood Green. Staf 5E 73
Burnt Yates. N Yor 3E 99
Burnwynd. Edin 3E 129
Burpham. Surr 5B 38
Burpham. W Sus 5B 26
Burradon. Nmbd 4D 121
Burradon. Tyne 2F 115
Burrafirth. Shet 1H 173
Burras. Corn 5A 6
Burraton. Corn 3A 8
Burravoe. Shet 3E 173
(nr. North Roe)
Burravoe. Shet 4G 173
(on Yell)
Burray Village. Orkn 8D 172
Burrells. Cumb 3H 103
Burrelton. Per 5A 144
Burridge. Devn 2G 13
Burridge. Hants 1D 16
Burrigill. High 5E 169
Burrill. N Yor 1E 99
Burringham. N Lin 4B 94
Burrington. Devn 1G 11
Burrington. Here 3G 59
Burrington. N Som 1H 21
Burrough End. Cambs 5F 65
Burrough Green. Cambs 5F 65
Burrough on the Hill. Leics 4E 75
Burrow. Devn 4D 12
Burrow. Som 2C 20
Burrowbridge. Som 4G 21
Burrowhill. Surr 4A 38
Burry. Swan 3D 30
Burry Green. Swan 3D 30
Burry Port. Carm 5E 45
Burscough. Lanc 3C 90
Burscough Bridge. Lanc 3C 90
Bursea. E Yor 1B 94
Burshill. E Yor 5E 101
Bursledon. Hants 2C 16
Burslem. Stoke 1C 72
Burstall. Suff 1D 54
Burstock. Dors 2H 13
Burston. Devn 2H 11
Burston. Norf 2D 66
Burston. Staf 2D 72
Burstow. Surr 1E 27
Burstwick. E Yor 2F 95
Burtersett. N Yor 1A 98
Burtholme. Cumb 3G 113
Burthorpe. Suff 4G 65
Burthwaite. Cumb 5F 113
Burtle. Som 2H 21
Burtoft. Linc 2B 76
Burton. Ches W 4H 83
(nr. Kelsall)
Burton. Ches W 3F 83
(nr. Neston)
Burton. Dors 3G 15
(nr. Christchurch)
Burton. Dors 3B 14
(nr. Dorchester)
Burton. Nmbd 1F 121
Burton. Pemb 4D 43
Burton. Som 2E 21
Burton. Wilts 4D 34
(nr. Chippenham)
Burton. Wilts 3D 22
(nr. Warminster)
Burton. Wrex 5F 83
Burton Agnes. E Yor 3F 101
Burton Bradstock. Dors 4H 13
Burton-by-Lincoln. Linc 3G 87
Burton Coggles. Linc 3G 75
Burton Constable. E Yor 1E 95
Burton Corner. Linc 1C 76
Burton End. Cambs 1G 53
Burton End. Essx 3F 53
Burton Fleming. E Yor 2E 101
Burton Green. W Mid 3G 61
Burton Green. Wrex 5F 83
Burton Hastings. Warw 2B 62
Burton-in-Kendal. Cumb 2E 97
Burton in Lonsdale. N Yor 2F 97
Burton Joyce. Notts 1D 74
Burton Latimer. Nptn 3G 63
Burton Lazars. Leics 4E 75
Burton Leonard. N Yor 3F 99
Burton on the Wolds. Leics 3C 74
Burton Overy. Leics 1D 62
Burton Pedwardine. Linc 1A 76
Burton Pidsea. E Yor 1F 95
Burton Salmon. N Yor 2E 93
Burton's Green. Essx 3B 54
Burton Stather. N Lin 3B 94
Burton upon Stather. N Lin 3B 94
Burton upon Trent. Staf 3G 73
Burton Wolds. Leics 3D 74
Burtonwood. Warr 1H 83
Burwardsley. Ches W 5H 83
Burwarton. Shrp 2A 60
Burwash. E Sus 3A 28
Burwash Common. E Sus 3H 27
Burwash Weald. E Sus 3A 28
Burwell. Cambs 4E 65
Burwell. Linc 3C 88
Burwen. IOA 1D 80
Burwick. Orkn 9D 172
Bury. Cambs 2B 64
Bury. G Man 3G 91
Bury. Som 4C 20
Bury. W Sus 4B 26
Burybank. Staf 2C 72
Bury End. Worc 2F 49
Bury Green. Herts 3E 53
Bury St Edmunds. Suff 4A 66
Burythorpe. N Yor 3B 100
Busbridge. Surr 1A 26
Busby. E Ren 4G 127
Busby. Per 1C 136
Buscot. Oxon 2H 35
Bush. Corn 2C 10
Bush Bank. Here 5G 59
Bushbury. W Mid 5D 72
Bushby. Leics 5D 74
Bushey. Dors 4E 15
Bushey. Herts 1C 38
Bushey Heath. Herts 1C 38
Bush Green. Norf 1C 66
(nr. Attleborough)
Bush Green. Norf 2E 66
(nr. Harleston)
Bush Green. Suff 5B 66
Bushley. Worc 2D 48
Bushley Green. Worc 2D 48
Bushmead. Bed 4A 64
Bushmoor. Shrp 2G 59
Bushton. Wilts 4F 35
Bushy Common. Norf 4B 78
Busk. Cumb 5H 113
Buslingthorpe. Linc 2H 87
Bussage. Glos 5D 49
Bussex. Som 3G 21
Busta. Shet 5E 173
Bustard Green. Essx 3G 53
Butcher's Cross. E Sus 3G 27
Butcombe. N Som 5A 34
Bute Town. Cphy 5E 46
Butleigh. Som 3A 22
Butleigh Wootton. Som 3A 22
Butlers Marston. Warw 5H 61
Butley. Suff 5F 67
Butley High Corner. Suff 1G 55
Butlocks Heath. Hants 2C 16
Butterburn. Cumb 2H 113
Buttercrambe. N Yor 4B 100
Butterknowle. Dur 2E 105
Butterleigh. Devn 2C 12
Buttermere. Cumb 3C 102
Buttermere. Wilts 5B 36
Buttershaw. W Yor 2B 92
Butterstone. Per 4H 143
Butterton. Staf 5E 85
(nr. Leek)
Butterton. Staf 1C 72
(nr. Stoke-on-Trent)
Butterwick. Dur 2A 106
Butterwick. Linc 1C 76
Butterwick. N Yor 2B 100
(nr. Malton)
Butterwick. N Yor 2D 101
(nr. Weaverthorpe)
Butteryhaugh. Nmbd 5A 120
Butt Green. Ches E 5A 84
Buttington. Powy 5E 71
Buttonbridge. Shrp 3B 60
Buttonoak. Shrp 3B 60
Buttsash. Hants 2C 16
Butt's Green. Essx 5A 54
Butt Yeats. Lanc 3E 97
Buxhall. Suff 5C 66
Buxted. E Sus 3F 27
Buxton. Derbs 3E 85
Buxton. Norf 3E 79
Buxworth. Derbs 2E 85
Bwcle. Flin 4E 83
Bwlch. Powy 3E 47
Bwlchderwin. Gwyn 1D 68
Bwlchgwyn. Wrex 5E 83
Bwlch-Llan. Cdgn 5E 57
Bwlchnewydd. Carm 3D 44
Bwlchtocyn. Gwyn 3C 68
Bwlch-y-cibau. Powy 4D 70
Bwlchyddar. Powy 3D 70
Bwlch-y-fadfa. Cdgn 1E 45
Bwlch-y-ffridd. Powy 1C 58
Bwlch y Garreg. Powy 1C 58
Bwlch-y-groes. Pemb 1G 43
Bwlch-y-sarnau. Powy 3C 58
Bybrook. Kent 1E 28
Byermoor. Tyne 4E 115
Byers Garth. Dur 5G 115
Byers Green. Dur 1F 105
Byfield. Nptn 5C 62
Byfleet. Surr 4B 38
Byford. Here 1G 47
Bygrave. Herts 2C 52
Byker. Tyne 3F 115
Byland Abbey. N Yor 2H 99
Bylchau. Cnwy 4B 82
Byley. Ches W 4B 84
Bynea. Carm 3E 31
Byram. N Yor 2E 93
Byrness. Nmbd 4B 120
Bystock. Devn 4D 12
Bythorn. Cambs 3H 63
Byton. Here 4F 59
Bywell. Nmbd 3D 114
Byworth. W Sus 3A 26

C

Cabourne. Linc 4E 95
Cabrach. Arg 3C 124
Cabrach. Mor 1A 152
Cabus. Lanc 5D 97
Cadbury. Devn 2C 12
Cadder. E Dun 2H 127
Caddington. C Beds 4A 52
Caddonfoot. Bord 1G 119
Cadeby. Leics 5B 74

Cadeby. *S Yor* ...4F 93
Cadeleigh. *Devn* ...2C 12
Cade Street. *E Sus* ...3H 27
Cadgwith. *Corn* ...5E 5
Cadham. *Fife* ...3E 137
Cadishead. *G Man* ...1B 84
Cadle. *Swan* ...3F 31
Cadley. *Lanc* ...1D 90
Cadley. *Wilts* ...1H 23
(nr. Ludgershall)
Cadley. *Wilts* ...5H 35
(nr. Marlborough)
Cadmore End. *Buck* ...2F 37
Cadnam. *Hants* ...1A 16
Cadney. *N Lin* ...4D 94
Cadole. *Flin* ...4E 82
Cadoxton-Juxta-Neath. *Neat* ...2A 32
Cadwell. *Herts* ...2B 52
Cadwst. *Den* ...2C 70
Caeathro. *Gwyn* ...4E 81
Caehopkin. *Powy* ...4B 46
Caenby. *Linc* ...2H 87
Caerau. *B'end* ...2B 32
Caerau. *Card* ...4E 33
Cae'r-bont. *Powy* ...4B 46
Cae'r-bryn. *Carm* ...4F 45
Caerdeon. *Gwyn* ...4F 69
Caerdydd. *Card* ...4E 33
Caerfarchell. *Pemb* ...2B 42
Caerffili. *Cphy* ...3E 33
Caerfyrddin. *Carm* ...4E 45
Caergeiliog. *IOA* ...3C 80
Caergwrle. *Flin* ...5F 83
Caergybi. *IOA* ...2B 80
Caerlaverock. *Per* ...2A 136
Caerleon. *Newp* ...2G 33
Caerlleon. *Carm* ...2G 43
Caerllion. *Newp* ...2G 33
Caernarfon. *Gwyn* ...4D 81
Caerphilly. *Cphy* ...3E 33
Caersws. *Powy* ...1C 58
Caerwedros. *Cdgn* ...5C 56
Caerwent. *Mon* ...2H 33
Caerwys. *Flin* ...3D 82
Caim. *IOA* ...2F 81
Caio. *Carm* ...2G 45
Cairinis. *W Isl* ...2D 170
Cairisiadar. *W Isl* ...4C 171
Cairminis. *W Isl* ...9C 171
Carnbaan. *Arg* ...4F 133
Cairnbulg. *Abers* ...2H 161
Cairndow. *Arg* ...2A 134
Cairness. *Abers* ...2H 161
Caimeyhill. *Fife* ...1D 128
Cairngarroch. *Dum* ...5F 109
Cairngorms. *High* ...3D 151
Cairnhill. *Abers* ...5D 160
Cairrie. *Abers* ...4B 160
Cairnorrie. *Abers* ...4F 161
Cairnryan. *Dum* ...3F 109
Caister-on-Sea. *Norf* ...4H 79
Caistor. *Linc* ...4E 95
Caistor St Edmund. *Norf* ...5E 79
Caistron. *Nmbd* ...4D 121
Cakebole. *Worc* ...3C 60
Calais Street. *Suff* ...1C 54
Calanais. *W Isl* ...4E 171
Calbost. *W Isl* ...6G 171
Calbourne. *IOW* ...4C 16
Calceby. *Linc* ...3C 88
Calcot. *Glos* ...4F 49
Calcot Row. *W Ber* ...4E 37
Calcott. *Kent* ...4F 41
Calcott. *Shrp* ...4G 71
Caldback. *Shet* ...1H 173
Caldbeck. *Cumb* ...1E 102
Caldbergh. *N Yor* ...1C 98
Caldecote. *Cambs* ...5C 64
(nr. Cambridge)
Caldecote. *Cambs* ...2A 64
(nr. Peterborough)
Caldecote. *Herts* ...2C 52
Caldecote. *Warw* ...1A 62

Caldecott. *Nptn* ...4G 63
Caldecott. *Oxon* ...2C 36
Caldecott. *Rut* ...1F 63
Calderbank. *N Lan* ...3A 128
Calder Bridge. *Cumb* ...4B 102
Calderbrook. *G Man* ...3H 91
Caldercruix. *N Lan* ...3B 128
Calder Grove. *W Yor* ...3D 92
Calder Mains. *High* ...3C 168
Caldermill. *S Lan* ...5H 127
Calder Vale. *Lanc* ...5E 97
Calderwood. *S Lan* ...4H 127
Caldescote. *Nptn* ...5D 62
Caldicot. *Mon* ...3H 33
Caldwell. *Derbs* ...4G 73
Caldwell. *N Yor* ...3E 105
Caldy. *Mers* ...2E 83
Calebrack. *Cumb* ...1E 103
Caledfwlch. *Carm* ...3G 45
Calf Heath. *Staf* ...5D 72
Calford Green. *Suff* ...1G 53
Calfsound. *Orkn* ...4E 172
Calgary. *Arg* ...3E 139
Califer. *Mor* ...3E 159
California. *Cambs* ...2E 65
California. *Falk* ...2C 128
California. *Norf* ...4H 79
California. *Suff* ...1E 55
Calke. *Derbs* ...3A 74
Calkalkille. *High* ...3F 155
Callaly. *Nmbd* ...4E 121
Callander. *Stir* ...3F 135
Callaughton. *Shrp* ...1A 60
Callendoun. *Arg* ...1E 127
Callestick. *Corn* ...3B 6
Calligarry. *High* ...3E 147
Callington. *Corn* ...2H 7
Callingwood. *Staf* ...3F 73
Callow. *Here* ...2H 47
Callow End. *Worc* ...5D 48
Callow Hill. *Wilts* ...3F 35
Callow Hill. *Worc* ...3B 60
(nr. Bewdley)
Callow Hill. *Worc* ...4E 61
(nr. Redditch)
Calmore. *Hants* ...1B 16
Calmsden. *Glos* ...5F 49
Calne. *Wilts* ...4E 35
Calow. *Derbs* ...3B 86
Calshot. *Hants* ...2C 16
Calstock. *Corn* ...2A 8
Calstone Wellington. *Wilts* ...5F 35
Calthorpe. *Norf* ...2D 78
Calthorpe Street. *Norf* ...3G 79
Calthwaite. *Cumb* ...5F 113
Calton. *N Yor* ...4B 98
Calton. *Staf* ...5F 85
Calveley. *Ches E* ...5H 83
Calver. *Derbs* ...3G 85
Calverhall. *Shrp* ...2A 72
Calverleigh. *Devn* ...1C 12
Calverley. *W Yor* ...1C 92
Calvert. *Buck* ...3E 51
Calverton. *Mil* ...2F 51
Calverton. *Notts* ...1D 74
Calvine. *Per* ...2F 143
Calvo. *Cumb* ...4C 112
Cam. *Glos* ...2C 34
Camaghael. *High* ...1F 141
Camas-luinie. *High* ...1B 148
Camasnacroise. *High* ...3C 140
Camastianavaig. *High* ...5E 155
Camasunary. *High* ...2D 146
Camault Muir. *High* ...4H 157
Camb. *Shet* ...2G 173
Camber. *E Sus* ...4D 28
Camberley. *Surr* ...5G 37
Camberwell. *G Lon* ...3E 39
Camblesforth. *N Yor* ...2G 93
Cambo. *Nmbd* ...1D 114
Cambois. *Nmbd* ...1G 115
Camborne. *Corn* ...3D 4
Cambourne. *Cambs* ...5C 64

Cambridge. *Cambs* ...5D 64
Cambridge. *Glos* ...5C 48
Cambrose. *Corn* ...4A 6
Cambus. *Clac* ...4A 136
Cambusbarron. *Stir* ...4G 135
Cambuskenneth. *Stir* ...4H 135
Cambuslang. *S Lan* ...3H 127
Cambusnethan. *N Lan* ...4B 128
Cambus o'May. *Abers* ...4B 152
Camden Town. *G Lon* ...2D 39
Cameley. *Bath* ...1B 22
Camelford. *Corn* ...4B 10
Camelon. *Falk* ...1B 128
Camelsdale. *Surr* ...2A 26
Camer's Green. *Worc* ...2C 48
Camerton. *Bath* ...1B 22
Camerton. *Cumb* ...1B 102
Camerton. *E Yor* ...2F 95
Camghouran. *Per* ...3C 142
Cammachmore. *Abers* ...4G 153
Cammeringham. *Linc* ...2G 87
Camore. *High* ...4E 165
Campbelton. *N Ayr* ...4C 126
Campbeltown. *Arg* ...3B 122
Campbeltown Airport. *Arg* ...3A 122
Cample. *Dum* ...5B 118
Campmuir. *Per* ...5B 144
Campsall. *S Yor* ...3F 93
Campsea Ashe. *Suff* ...5F 67
Camps End. *Cambs* ...1G 53
Camp, The. *Glos* ...5E 49
Campton. *C Beds* ...2B 52
Camptoun. *E Lot* ...2B 130
Camptown. *Bord* ...3A 120
Camrose. *Pemb* ...2D 42
Camserney. *Per* ...4F 143
Camster. *High* ...4E 169
Camus Croise. *High* ...2E 147
Camuscross. *High* ...2E 147
Camusdarach. *High* ...4E 147
Camusnagaul. *High* ...1E 141
(nr. Fort William)
Camusnagaul. *High* ...5E 163
(nr. Little Loch Broom)
Camusteel. *High* ...4G 155
Camusterrach. *High* ...4G 155
Camusvrachan. *Per* ...4D 142
Canada. *High* ...1A 16
Canadia. *E Sus* ...4B 28
Canaston Bridge. *Pemb* ...3E 43
Candlesby. *Linc* ...4D 88
Candle Street. *Suff* ...3C 66
Candy Mill. *S Lan* ...5D 128
Cane End. *Oxon* ...4E 37
Canewdon. *Essx* ...1C 40
Canford Cliffs. *Pool* ...4F 15
Canford Heath. *Pool* ...3F 15
Canford Magna. *Pool* ...3F 15
Cangate. *Norf* ...3F 79
Canham's Green. *Suff* ...4C 66
Canholes. *Derbs* ...3E 85
Canisbay. *High* ...1F 169
Canley. *W Mid* ...3H 61
Cann. *Dors* ...4D 22
Cann Common. *Dors* ...4D 23
Cannich. *High* ...5F 157
Cannington. *Som* ...3F 21
Cannock. *Staf* ...4D 73
Cannock Wood. *Staf* ...4E 73
Canonbie. *Dum* ...2E 113
Canon Bridge. *Here* ...1H 47
Canon Frome. *Here* ...1B 48
Canon Pyon. *Here* ...1H 47
Canons Ashby. *Nptn* ...5C 62
Canonstown. *Corn* ...3C 4
Canterbury. *Kent* ...5F 41
Cantley. *Norf* ...5F 79
Cantley. *S Yor* ...4G 93
Cantlop. *Shrp* ...5H 71
Canton. *Card* ...4E 33
Cantraybruich. *High* ...4B 158
Cantray. *High* ...4B 158
Cantraywood. *High* ...4B 158
Cantsdam. *Fife* ...4D 136

Cantsfield. *Lanc* ...2F 97
Canvey Island. *Essx* ...2B 40
Canwick. *Linc* ...4G 87
Canworthy Water. *Corn* ...3C 10
Caol. *High* ...1F 141
Caolas. *W Isl* ...9B 170
Caolas Liubharsaigh. *W Isl* ...4D 170
Caolas Stocinis. *W Isl* ...8D 171
Caoles. *Arg* ...4B 138
Caol Ila. *Arg* ...3C 124
Caol Loch Ailse. *High* ...1F 147
Caol Reatha. *High* ...1F 147
Capel. *Kent* ...1H 27
Capel. *Surr* ...1C 26
Capel Bangor. *Cdgn* ...2F 57
Capel Betws Lleucu. *Cdgn* ...5F 57
Capel Coch. *IOA* ...2D 80
Capel Curig. *Cnwy* ...5G 81
Capel Cynon. *Cdgn* ...1D 45
Capel Dewi. *Carm* ...3H 45
Capel Dewi. *Cdgn* ...2F 57
(nr. Aberystwyth)
Capel Dewi. *Cdgn* ...1E 45
(nr. Llandysul)
Capel Garmon. *Cnwy* ...5H 81
Capel Green. *Suff* ...1G 55
Capel Gwyn. *IOA* ...3C 80
Capel Gwynfe. *Carm* ...3H 45
Capel Hendre. *Carm* ...4F 45
Capel Isaac. *Carm* ...3F 45
Capel Iwan. *Carm* ...1G 43
Capel-le-Ferne. *Kent* ...2G 29
Capel Llanilterne. *Card* ...4D 32
Capel Mawr. *IOA* ...3D 80
Capel Newydd. *Pemb* ...1G 43
Capel St Andrew. *Suff* ...1G 55
Capel St Mary. *Suff* ...2D 54
Capel Seion. *Carm* ...4F 45
Capel Seion. *Cdgn* ...3F 57
Capel Uchaf. *Gwyn* ...1D 68
Capel-y-ffin. *Powy* ...2F 47
Capenhurst. *Ches W* ...3F 83
Capernwray. *Lanc* ...2E 97
Capheaton. *Nmbd* ...1D 114
Cappercleuch. *Bord* ...2E 119
Capplegill. *Dum* ...4D 118
Capton. *Devn* ...3E 9
Capton. *Som* ...3D 20
Caputh. *Per* ...5H 143
Caradon Town. *Corn* ...5C 10
Carbis Bay. *Corn* ...3C 4
Carbost. *High* ...5C 154
(nr. Loch Harport)
Carbost. *High* ...4D 154
(nr. Portree)
Carbrook. *S Yor* ...2A 86
Carbrooke. *Norf* ...5B 78
Carburton. *Notts* ...3D 86
Carcluie. *S Ayr* ...3C 116
Car Colston. *Notts* ...1E 74
Carcroft. *S Yor* ...3F 93
Cardenden. *Fife* ...4E 136
Cardeston. *Shrp* ...4F 71
Cardewlees. *Cumb* ...4E 113
Cardiff. *Card* ...4E 33
Cardiff International Airport.
  V Glam ...5D 32
Cardigan. *Cdgn* ...1B 44
Cardinal's Green. *Cambs* ...1G 53
Cardington. *Bed* ...1A 52
Cardington. *Shrp* ...1H 59
Cardinham. *Corn* ...2F 7
Cardno. *Abers* ...2G 161
Cardow. *Mor* ...4F 159
Cardross. *Arg* ...2E 127
Cardurnock. *Cumb* ...4C 112
Careby. *Linc* ...4H 75
Careston. *Arg* ...2E 145
Carew. *Pemb* ...4E 43
Carew Cheriton. *Pemb* ...4E 43
Carew Newton. *Pemb* ...4E 43
Carey. *Here* ...2A 48
Carfin. *N Lan* ...4A 128
Carfrae. *Bord* ...4B 130

Cargate Green. *Norf* ...4F 79
Cargenbridge. *Dum* ...2G 11
Cargill. *Per* ...5A 14
Cargo. *Cumb* ...4E 11
Cargreen. *Corn* ...2A 8
Carham. *Nmbd* ...1B 12
Carhampton. *Som* ...2D 20
Carharrack. *Corn* ...4B 6
Carie. *Per* ...3D 142
(nr. Loch Rannah)
Carie. *Per* ...5D 142
(nr. Loch Tay)
Carisbrooke. *IOW* ...4C 16
Cark. *Cumb* ...2C 96
Carkeel. *Corn* ...2A 8
Carlabhagh. *W Isl* ...3E 171
Carland Cross. *Corn* ...3C 6
Carlbury. *Darl* ...3F 105
Carlby. *Linc* ...4H 75
Carlecotes. *S Yor* ...4B 92
Carleen. *Corn* ...4D 4
Carlesmoor. *N Yor* ...2D 98
Carleton. *Cumb* ...4F 113
(nr. Carlisle)
Carleton. *Cumb* ...4B 102
(nr. Egremont)
Carleton. *Cumb* ...2G 103
(nr. Penrith)
Carleton. *Lanc* ...1B 90
Carleton. *N Yor* ...5B 98
Carleton. *W Yor* ...2E 93
Carleton Forehoe. *Norf* ...5C 78
Carleton Rode. *Norf* ...1D 66
Carleton St Peter. *Norf* ...5F 79
Carlidnack. *Corn* ...4E 5
Carlingcott. *Bath* ...1B 22
Carlin How. *Red C* ...3E 107
Carlisle. *Cumb* ...4F 113
Carloonan. *Arg* ...2H 133
Carlops. *Bord* ...4E 129
Carlton. *Bed* ...5G 63
Carlton. *Cambs* ...5F 65
Carlton. *Leics* ...5A 74
Carlton. *N Yor* ...1A 100
(nr. Helmsley)
Carlton. *N Yor* ...1C 98
(nr. Middleham)
Carlton. *N Yor* ...2G 93
(nr. Selby)
Carlton. *Notts* ...1D 74
Carlton. *S Yor* ...3D 92
Carlton. *Stoc T* ...2A 106
Carlton. *Suff* ...4F 67
Carlton. *W Yor* ...2D 92
Carlton Colville. *Suff* ...1H 67
Carlton Curlieu. *Leics* ...1D 62
Carlton Husthwaite. *N Yor* ...2G 99
Carlton in Cleveland. *N Yor* ...4C 106
Carlton in Lindrick. *Notts* ...2C 86
Carlton-le-Moorland. *Linc* ...5G 87
Carlton Miniott. *N Yor* ...1F 99
Carlton-on-Trent. *Notts* ...4E 87
Carlton Scroop. *Linc* ...1G 75
Carluke. *S Lan* ...4B 128
Carlyon Bay. *Corn* ...3E 7
Carmarthen. *Carm* ...4E 45
Carmel. *Carm* ...4F 45
Carmel. *Flin* ...3D 82
Carmel. *Gwyn* ...5D 81
Carmel. *IOA* ...2C 80
Carmichael. *S Lan* ...1B 118
Carmunnock. *Glas* ...4H 127
Carmyle. *S Lan* ...3H 127
Carmyllie. *Ang* ...4E 145
Carnaby. *E Yor* ...3F 101
Carnach. *High* ...1C 148
(nr. Lochcarron)
Carnach. *High* ...4E 163
(nr. Ullapool)
Carnach. *Mor* ...4E 159
Carnach. *W Isl* ...8E 171
Carnachy. *High* ...3H 167
Carnain. *Arg* ...3B 124
Carnais. *W Isl* ...4C 171

Charingworth—Church End

Charingworth. *Glos* 2G 49
Charlbury. *Oxon* 4B 50
Charlcombe. *Bath* 5C 34
Charlcutt. *Wilts* 4E 35
Charlecote. *Warw* 5G 61
Charles. *Devn* 3G 19
Charlesfield. *Dum* 3C 112
Charleshill. *Surr* 2G 25
Charleston. *Ang* 4C 144
Charleston. *Ren* 3F 127
Charlestown. *Aber* 3G 153
Charlestown. *Abers* 2H 161
Charlestown. *Corn* 3E 7
Charlestown. *Dors* 5B 14
Charlestown. *Fife* 1D 128
Charlestown. *G Man* 4G 91
Charlestown. *High* 1H 155 (nr. Gairloch)
Charlestown. *High* 4A 158 (nr. Inverness)
Charlestown. *W Yor* 2H 91
Charlestown of Aberlour. *Mor* 4G 159
Charles Tye. *Suff* 5C 66
Charlesworth. *Derbs* 1E 85
Charlton. *G Lon* 3F 39
Charlton. *Hants* 2B 24
Charlton. *Herts* 3B 52
Charlton. *Nptn* 2D 50
Charlton. *Nmbd* 1B 114
Charlton. *Oxon* 3C 36
Charlton. *Som* 1B 22 (nr. Radstock)
Charlton. *Som* 2B 22 (nr. Shepton Mallet)
Charlton. *Som* 4F 21 (nr. Taunton)
Charlton. *Telf* 4H 71
Charlton. *W Sus* 1G 17
Charlton. *Wilts* 3E 35 (nr. Malmesbury)
Charlton. *Wilts* 1G 23 (nr. Pewsey)
Charlton. *Wilts* 4G 23 (nr. Salisbury)
Charlton. *Wilts* 4E 23 (nr. Shaftesbury)
Charlton. *Worc* 1F 49 (nr. Evesham)
Charlton. *Worc* 3C 60 (nr. Stourport-on-Severn)
Charlton Abbots. *Glos* 3F 49
Charlton Adam. *Som* 4A 22
Charlton Down. *Dors* 3B 14
Charlton Horethorne. *Som* 4B 22
Charlton Kings. *Glos* 3E 49
Charlton Mackrell. *Som* 4A 22
Charlton Marshall. *Dors* 2E 15
Charlton Musgrove. *Som* 4C 22
Charlton-on-Otmoor. *Oxon* 4D 50
Charlton on the Hill. *Dors* 2D 15
Charlwood. *Hants* 3E 25
Charlwood. *Surr* 1D 26
Charlynch. *Som* 3F 21
Charminster. *Dors* 3B 14
Charmouth. *Dors* 3G 13
Charndon. *Buck* 3E 51
Charney Bassett. *Oxon* 2B 36
Charnock Green. *Lanc* 3D 90
Charnock Richard. *Lanc* 3D 90
Charsfield. *Suff* 5E 67
Chart Corner. *Kent* 5B 40
Charter Alley. *Hants* 1D 24
Charterhouse. *Som* 1H 21
Charterville Allotments. *Oxon* 4B 50
Chartham. *Kent* 5F 41
Chartham Hatch. *Kent* 5F 41
Chartridge. *Buck* 5H 51
Chart Sutton. *Kent* 5B 40
Chart, The. *Kent* 5F 39
Charvil. *Wok* 4F 37
Charwelton. *Nptn* 5C 62
Chase Terrace. *Staf* 5E 73
Chasetown. *Staf* 5E 73
Chastleton. *Oxon* 3H 49
Chasty. *Devn* 2D 10
Chatburn. *Lanc* 5G 97
Chatcull. *Staf* 2B 72
Chatham. *Medw* 4B 40
Chatham Green. *Essx* 4H 53
Chathill. *Nmbd* 2F 121
Chatley. *Worc* 4C 60
Chattenden. *Medw* 3B 40
Chatteris. *Cambs* 2C 64
Chattisham. *Suff* 1D 54
Chatton. *Nmbd* 2E 121
Chatwall. *Shrp* 1H 59
Chaulden. *Herts* 5A 52
Chaul End. *C Beds* 3A 52
Chawleigh. *Devn* 1H 11
Chawley. *Oxon* 5C 50
Chawston. *Bed* 5A 64
Chawton. *Hants* 3F 25
Chaxhill. *Glos* 4C 48
Cheadle. *G Man* 2C 84
Cheadle. *Staf* 1E 73
Cheadle Hulme. *G Man* 2C 84
Cheam. *Surr* 4D 38
Cheapside. *Wind* 4A 38
Chearsley. *Buck* 4F 51
Chebsey. *Staf* 3C 72
Checkendon. *Oxon* 3E 37
Checkley. *Ches E* 1B 72
Checkley. *Here* 2A 48
Checkley. *Staf* 2E 73
Chedburgh. *Suff* 5G 65
Cheddar. *Som* 1H 21
Cheddington. *Buck* 4H 51
Cheddleton. *Staf* 5D 84
Cheddon Fitzpaine. *Som* 4F 21
Chedglow. *Wilts* 2E 35
Chedgrave. *Norf* 1F 67
Chedington. *Dors* 2H 13
Chediston. *Suff* 3F 67
Chediston Green. *Suff* 3F 67
Chedworth. *Glos* 4F 49
Chedzoy. *Som* 3G 21
Cheeseman's Green. *Kent* 2E 29
Cheetham Hill. *G Man* 4G 91
Cheglinch. *Devn* 2F 19
Cheldon. *Devn* 1H 11
Chelford. *Ches E* 3C 84
Chellaston. *Derb* 2A 74
Chellington. *Bed* 5G 63
Chelmarsh. *Shrp* 2B 60
Chelmick. *Shrp* 1G 59
Chelmondiston. *Suff* 2F 55
Chelmorton. *Derbs* 4F 85
Chelmsford. *Essx* 5H 53
Chelsea. *G Lon* 3D 39
Chelsfield. *G Lon* 4F 39
Chelsham. *Surr* 5E 39
Chelston. *Som* 4E 21
Chelsworth. *Suff* 1C 54
Cheltenham. *Glos* 3E 49
Chelveston. *Nptn* 4G 63
Chelvey. *N Som* 5H 33
Chelwood. *Bath* 5B 34
Chelwood Common. *E Sus* 3F 27
Chelwood Gate. *E Sus* 3F 27
Chelworth. *Wilts* 2E 35
Chelworth Lower Green. *Wilts* 2F 35
Chelworth Upper Green. *Wilts* 2F 35
Chelynch. *Som* 2B 22
Cheney Longville. *Shrp* 2G 59
Chenies. *Buck* 1B 38
Chepstow. *Mon* 2A 34
Chequerfield. *W Yor* 2E 93
Chequers Corner. *Norf* 5D 77
Cherhill. *Wilts* 4F 35
Cherington. *Glos* 2E 35
Cherington. *Warw* 2A 50
Cheriton. *Devn* 2H 19
Cheriton. *Hants* 4D 24
Cheriton. *Kent* 2G 29
Cheriton. *Pemb* 5D 43
Cheriton. *Swan* 3D 30
Cheriton Bishop. *Devn* 3A 12
Cheriton Cross. *Devn* 3A 12
Cheriton Fitzpaine. *Devn* 2B 12
Cherrington. *Telf* 3A 72
Cherrybank. *Per* 1D 136
Cherry Burton. *E Yor* 5D 101
Cherry Green. *Herts* 3D 52
Cherry Hinton. *Cambs* 5D 65
Cherry Willingham. *Linc* 3H 87
Chertsey. *Surr* 4B 38
Cheselbourne. *Dors* 3C 14
Chesham. *Buck* 5H 51
Chesham. *G Man* 3G 91
Chesham Bois. *Buck* 1A 38
Cheshunt. *Herts* 5D 52
Cheslyn Hay. *Staf* 5D 73
Chessetts Wood. *Warw* 3F 61
Chessington. *G Lon* 4C 38
Chester. *Ches W* 4G 83
Chesterblade. *Som* 2B 22
Chesterfield. *Derbs* 3A 86
Chesterfield. *Staf* 5F 73
Chesterhope. *Nmbd* 1C 114
Chester-le-Street. *Dur* 4F 115
Chester Moor. *Dur* 5F 115
Chesters. *Bord* 3A 120
Chesterton. *Cambs* 4D 64 (nr. Cambridge)
Chesterton. *Cambs* 1A 64 (nr. Peterborough)
Chesterton. *Glos* 5F 49
Chesterton. *Oxon* 3D 50
Chesterton. *Shrp* 1B 60
Chesterton. *Staf* 1C 72
Chesterton Green. *Warw* 5H 61
Chesterwood. *Nmbd* 3B 114
Chestfield. *Kent* 4F 41
Cheston. *Devn* 3C 8
Cheswardine. *Shrp* 2B 72
Cheswell. *Telf* 4B 72
Cheswick. *Nmbd* 5G 131
Cheswick Green. *W Mid* 3F 61
Chetnole. *Dors* 2B 14
Chettiscombe. *Devn* 1C 12
Chettisham. *Cambs* 2E 65
Chettle. *Dors* 1E 15
Chetton. *Shrp* 1A 60
Chetwode. *Buck* 3E 51
Chetwynd Aston. *Telf* 4B 72
Cheveley. *Cambs* 4F 65
Chevening. *Kent* 5F 39
Chevington. *Suff* 5G 65
Chevithorne. *Devn* 1C 12
Chew Magna. *Bath* 5A 34
Chew Moor. *G Man* 4E 91
Chew Stoke. *Bath* 5A 34
Chewton Keynsham. *Bath* 5B 34
Chewton Mendip. *Som* 1A 22
Chichacott. *Devn* 3G 11
Chicheley. *Mil* 1H 51
Chichester. *W Sus* 2G 17
Chickerell. *Dors* 4B 14
Chickering. *Suff* 3E 66
Chicklade. *Wilts* 3E 23
Chicksands. *C Beds* 2B 52
Chickward. *Here* 5E 59
Chidden. *Hants* 1E 17
Chiddingfold. *Surr* 2A 26
Chiddingly. *E Sus* 4G 27
Chiddingstone. *Kent* 1G 27
Chiddingstone Causeway. *Kent* 1G 27
Chiddingstone Hoath. *Kent* 1F 27
Chideock. *Dors* 3H 13
Chidgley. *Som* 3D 20
Chidham. *W Sus* 2F 17
Chieveley. *W Ber* 4C 36
Chignall St James. *Essx* 5G 53
Chignall Smealy. *Essx* 4G 53
Chigwell. *Essx* 1F 39
Chigwell Row. *Essx* 1F 39
Chilbolton. *Hants* 2B 24
Chilcomb. *Hants* 4D 24
Chilcombe. *Dors* 3A 14
Chilcompton. *Som* 1B 22
Chilcote. *Leics* 4G 73
Childer Thornton. *Ches W* 3F 83
Child Okeford. *Dors* 1D 14
Childrey. *Oxon* 3B 36
Child's Ercall. *Shrp* 3A 72
Childswickham. *Worc* 2F 49
Childwall. *Mers* 2G 83
Childwick Green. *Herts* 4B 52
Chilfrome. *Dors* 3A 14
Chilgrove. *W Sus* 1G 17
Chilham. *Kent* 5E 41
Chilhampton. *Wilts* 3F 23
Chilla. *Devn* 2E 11
Chilland. *Hants* 3D 24
Chillaton. *Devn* 4E 11
Chillenden. *Kent* 5G 41
Chillerton. *IOW* 4C 16
Chillesford. *Suff* 5F 67
Chillingham. *Nmbd* 2E 121
Chillington. *Devn* 4D 9
Chillington. *Som* 1G 13
Chilmark. *Wilts* 3E 23
Chilmington Green. *Kent* 1D 28
Chilson. *Oxon* 4B 50
Chilsworthy. *Corn* 5E 11
Chilsworthy. *Devn* 2D 10
Chiltern Green. *C Beds* 4B 52
Chilthorne Domer. *Som* 1A 14
Chilton. *Buck* 4E 51
Chilton. *Devn* 2B 12
Chilton. *Dur* 2F 105
Chilton. *Oxon* 3C 36
Chilton Candover. *Hants* 2D 24
Chilton Cantelo. *Som* 4A 22
Chilton Foliat. *Wilts* 4B 36
Chilton Lane. *Dur* 1A 106
Chilton Polden. *Som* 3G 21
Chilton Street. *Suff* 1A 54
Chilton Trinity. *Som* 3F 21
Chilwell. *Notts* 2C 74
Chilworth. *Hants* 1C 16
Chilworth. *Surr* 1B 26
Chimney. *Oxon* 5B 50
Chimney Street. *Suff* 1H 53
Chineham. *Hants* 1E 25
Chingford. *G Lon* 1E 39
Chinley. *Derbs* 2E 85
Chinnor. *Oxon* 5F 51
Chipley. *Som* 4E 20
Chipnall. *Shrp* 2B 72
Chippenham. *Cambs* 4F 65
Chippenham. *Wilts* 4E 35
Chipperfield. *Herts* 5A 52
Chipping. *Herts* 2D 52
Chipping. *Lanc* 5F 97
Chipping Campden. *Glos* 2G 49
Chipping Hill. *Essx* 4B 54
Chipping Norton. *Oxon* 3B 50
Chipping Ongar. *Essx* 5F 53
Chipping Sodbury. *S Glo* 3C 34
Chipping Warden. *Nptn* 1C 50
Chipstable. *Som* 4D 20
Chipstead. *Kent* 5G 39
Chipstead. *Surr* 5D 38
Chirbury. *Shrp* 1E 59
Chirk. *Wrex* 2E 71
Chirmorie. *S Ayr* 2H 109
Chirnside. *Bord* 4E 131
Chirnsidebridge. *Bord* 4E 131
Chirton. *Wilts* 1F 23
Chisbridge Cross. *Buck* 3G 37
Chisbury. *Wilts* 5A 36
Chiselborough. *Som* 1H 13
Chiseldon. *Swin* 4G 35
Chiselhampton. *Oxon* 2D 36
Chiserley. *W Yor* 2A 92
Chislehurst. *G Lon* 4F 39
Chislet. *Kent* 4G 41
Chiswell. *Dors* 5B 14
Chiswell Green. *Herts* 5B 52
Chiswick. *G Lon* 3D 38
Chisworth. *Derbs* 1D 85
Chitcombe. *E Sus* 3C 28
Chithurst. *W Sus* 4G 25
Chittering. *Cambs* 4D 65
Chitterley. *Devn* 2C 12
Chitterne. *Wilts* 2E 23
Chittlehamholt. *Devn* 4G 19
Chittlehampton. *Devn* 4G 19
Chittoe. *Wilts* 5E 35
Chivelstone. *Devn* 5D 9
Chivenor. *Devn* 3F 19
Chobham. *Surr* 4A 38
Cholderton. *Wilts* 2H 23
Cholesbury. *Buck* 5H 51
Chollerford. *Nmbd* 2C 114
Chollerton. *Nmbd* 2C 114
Cholsey. *Oxon* 3D 36
Cholstrey. *Here* 5G 59
Chop Gate. *N Yor* 5C 106
Choppington. *Nmbd* 1F 115
Chopwell. *Tyne* 4E 115
Chorley. *Ches E* 5H 83
Chorley. *Lanc* 3D 90
Chorley. *Shrp* 2A 60
Chorley. *Staf* 4E 73
Chorleywood. *Herts* 1B 38
Chorlton. *Ches E* 5B 84
Chorlton-cum-Hardy. *G Man* 1C 84
Chorlton Lane. *Ches W* 1G 71
Choulton. *Shrp* 2F 59
Chrishall. *Essx* 2E 53
Christchurch. *Cambs* 1D 65
Christchurch. *Dors* 3G 15
Christchurch. *Glos* 4A 48
Christian Malford. *Wilts* 4E 35
Christleton. *Ches W* 4G 83
Christmas Common. *Oxon* 2F 37
Christon. *N Som* 1G 21
Christon Bank. *Nmbd* 2G 121
Christow. *Devn* 4B 12
Chryston. *N Lan* 2H 127
Chuck Hatch. *E Sus* 2F 27
Chudleigh. *Devn* 5B 12
Chudleigh Knighton. *Devn* 5B 12
Chulmleigh. *Devn* 1G 11
Chunal. *Derbs* 1E 85
Church. *Lanc* 2F 91
Churcham. *Glos* 4C 48
Church Aston. *Telf* 4B 72
Church Brampton. *Nptn* 4E 62
Church Brough. *Cumb* 3A 104
Church Broughton. *Derbs* 2G 73
Church Corner. *Suff* 2G 67
Church Crookham. *Hants* 1G 25
Churchdown. *Glos* 4D 48
Church Eaton. *Staf* 4C 72
Church End. *Cambs* 5D 65 (nr. Cambridge)
Church End. *Cambs* 2B 64 (nr. Sawtry)
Church End. *Cambs* 3C 64 (nr. Willingham)
Church End. *Cambs* 5C 76 (nr. Wisbech)
Church End. *C Beds* 3H 51 (nr. Dunstable)
Church End. *C Beds* 2B 52 (nr. Stotfold)
Church End. *E Yor* 4E 101
Church End. *Essx* 3H 53 (nr. Braintree)
Churchend. *Essx* 3G 53 (nr. Great Dunmow)
Church End. *Essx* 1F 53 (nr. Saffron Walden)
Churchend. *Essx* 1E 40 (nr. Southend-on-Sea)
Church End. *Glos* 5C 48
Church End. *Hants* 1E 25
Church End. *Linc* 2B 76 (nr. Donington)
Church End. *Linc* 1D 88 (nr. North Somercotes)
Church End. *Norf* 4E 77
Church End. *Warw* 1G 61 (nr. Coleshill)
Church End. *Warw* 1G 61 (nr. Nuneaton)
Church End. *Wilts* 4F 35

Church Enstone—Clyst Honiton

Church Enstone. *Oxon* 3B 50
Church Fenton. *N Yor* 1F 93
Church Green. *Devn* 3E 13
Church Gresley. *Derbs* 4G 73
Church Hanborough. *Oxon* 4C 50
Church Hill. *Ches W* 4A 84
Church Hill. *Worc* 4E 61
Church Hougham. *Kent* 1G 29
Church Houses. *N Yor* 5D 106
Churchill. *Devn* 2G 13 (nr. Axminster)
Churchill. *Devn* 2F 19 (nr. Barnstaple)
Churchill. *N Som* 1H 21
Churchill. *Oxon* 3A 50
Churchill. *Worc* 3C 60 (nr. Kidderminster)
Churchill. *Worc* 5D 60 (nr. Worcester)
Churchinford. *Som* 1F 13
Church Knowle. *Dors* 4E 15
Church Laneham. *Notts* 3F 87
Church Langley. *Essx* 5E 53
Church Langton. *Leics* 1E 62
Church Lawford. *Warw* 3B 62
Church Lawton. *Ches E* 5C 84
Church Leigh. *Staf* 2E 73
Church Lench. *Worc* 5E 61
Church Mayfield. *Staf* 1F 73
Church Minshull. *Ches E* 4A 84
Church Norton. *W Sus* 3G 17
Churchover. *Warw* 2C 62
Church Preen. *Shrp* 1H 59
Church Pulverbatch. *Shrp* 5G 71
Churchstanton. *Som* 1E 13
Church Stoke. *Powy* 1E 59
Churchstow. *Devn* 4D 8
Church Stowe. *Nptn* 5D 62
Church Street. *Kent* 3B 40
Church Stretton. *Shrp* 1G 59
Churchthorpe. *Linc* 1C 88
Churchtown. *Cumb* 5E 113
Churchtown. *Derbs* 4G 85
Churchtown. *Devn* 2G 19
Churchtown. *IOM* 2D 108
Churchtown. *Lanc* 5D 97
Church Town. *Leics* 4A 74
Churchtown. *Mers* 3B 90
Church Town. *N Lin* 4A 94
Churchtown. *Shrp* 2E 59
Church Village. *Rhon* 3D 32
Church Warsop. *Notts* 4C 86
Church Westcote. *Glos* 3H 49
Church Wilne. *Derbs* 2B 74
Churnsike Lodge. *Nmbd* 2H 113
Churston Ferrers. *Torb* 3F 9
Churt. *Surr* 3G 25
Churton. *Ches W* 5G 83
Churwell. *W Yor* 2C 92
Chute Standen. *Wilts* 1B 24
Chwilog. *Gwyn* 2D 68
Chwitffordd. *Flin* 3D 82
Chyandour. *Corn* 3B 4
Cilan Uchaf. *Gwyn* 3B 68
Cilcain. *Flin* 4D 82
Cilcennin. *Cdgn* 4E 57
Cilfrew. *Neat* 5A 46
Cilfynydd. *Rhon* 2D 32
Cilgerran. *Pemb* 1B 44
Cilgeti. *Pemb* 4F 43
Cilgwyn. *Carm* 3H 45
Cilgwyn. *Pemb* 1E 43
Ciliau Aeron. *Cdgn* 5D 57
Cill Amhlaidh. *W Isl* 4C 170
Cill Donnain. *High* 1G 165
Cill Donnain. *W Isl* 6C 170
Cille a' Bhacstair. *High* 2C 154
Cille Bhrighde. *W Isl* 7C 170
Cille Pheadair. *W Isl* 6C 170
Cilmaengwyn. *Neat* 5H 45
Cilmeri. *Powy* 5C 58
Cilmery. *Powy* 5C 58
Cilrhedyn. *Pemb* 1G 43
Cilsan. *Carm* 3F 45
Ciltalgarth. *Gwyn* 1A 70
Ciltwrch. *Powy* 1E 47
Cilybebyll. *Neat* 5H 45
Cilycwm. *Carm* 2A 46
Cimla. *Neat* 2A 32
Cinderford. *Glos* 4B 48
Cinderhill. *Derbs* 1A 74
Cippenham. *Slo* 2A 38
Cippyn. *Pemb* 1B 44
Cirbhig. *W Isl* 3E 171
Circebost. *W Isl* 4D 171
Cirencester. *Glos* 5F 49
City. *Powy* 1E 58
City. *V Glam* 4C 32
City Centre. *Stoke* 1C 72
City Dulas. *IOA* 2D 80
City (London) Airport. *G Lon* 2F 39
City of London. *G Lon* 2E 39
City, The. *Buck* 2F 37
Clabhach. *Arg* 3C 138
Clachaig. *Arg* 1C 126
Clachaig. *High* 3F 141 (nr. Kinlochleven)
Clachaig. *High* 2E 151 (nr. Nethy Bridge)
Clachamish. *High* 3C 154
Clachan. *Arg* 4F 125 (on Kintyre)
Clachan. *Arg* 4C 140 (on Lismore)
Clachan. *High* 2H 167 (nr. Bettyhill)
Clachan. *High* 2D 155 (nr. Staffin)
Clachan. *High* 1C 154 (nr. Uig)
Clachan. *High* 5E 155 (on Raasay)
Clachan Farm. *Arg* 2A 134
Clachan na Luib. *W Isl* 2D 170
Clachan of Campsie. *E Dun* 2H 127
Clachan of Glendaruel. *Arg* 1A 126
Clachan-Seil. *Arg* 2E 133
Clachan Shannda. *W Isl* 1D 170
Clachan Strachur. *Arg* 3H 133
Clachbreck. *Arg* 2F 125
Clachnaharry. *High* 4A 158
Clachtoll. *High* 1E 163
Clackmannan. *Clac* 4B 136
Clackmannanshire Bridge. *Clac* 1C 128
Clackmarras. *Mor* 3G 159
Clacton-on-Sea. *Essx* 4E 55
Cladach a Chaolais. *W Isl* 2C 170
Cladach Chairinis. *W Isl* 3D 170
Cladach Chirceboist. *W Isl* 2C 170
Cladich. *Arg* 1H 133
Cladswell. *Worc* 5E 61
Claggan. *High* 1F 141 (nr. Fort William)
Claggan. *High* 4A 140 (nr. Lochaline)
Claigan. *High* 3B 154
Clandown. *Bath* 1B 22
Clanfield. *Hants* 1E 17
Clanfield. *Oxon* 5A 50
Clanville. *Hants* 2B 24
Clanville. *Som* 3B 22
Claonaig. *Arg* 4G 125
Clapgate. *Dors* 2F 15
Clapgate. *Herts* 3E 53
Clapham. *Bed* 5H 63
Clapham. *Devn* 4B 12
Clapham. *G Lon* 3D 39
Clapham. *N Yor* 3G 97
Clapham. *W Sus* 5B 26
Clap Hill. *Kent* 2E 29
Clappers. *Bord* 4F 131
Clappersgate. *Cumb* 4E 103
Clapton. *Som* 2H 13 (nr. Crewkerne)
Clapton. *Som* 1B 22 (nr. Radstock)
Clapton-in-Gordano. *N Som* 4H 33
Clapton-on-the-Hill. *Glos* 4G 49
Clapworthy. *Devn* 4G 19
Clara Vale. *Tyne* 3E 115
Clarbeston. *Pemb* 2E 43
Clarbeston Road. *Pemb* 2E 43
Clarborough. *Notts* 2E 87
Clare. *Suff* 1A 54
Clarebrand. *Dum* 3E 111
Clarencefield. *Dum* 3B 112
Clarilaw. *Bord* 3H 119
Clark's Green. *Surr* 2C 26
Clark's Hill. *Linc* 3C 76
Clarkston. *E Ren* 4G 127
Clasheddy. *High* 2G 167
Clashindarroch. *Abers* 5B 160
Clashmore. *High* 5E 165 (nr. Dornoch)
Clashmore. *High* 1E 163 (nr. Stoer)
Clashnessie. *High* 5A 166
Clashnoir. *Mor* 1G 151
Clathick. *Per* 1H 135
Clathy. *Per* 2B 136
Clatt. *Abers* 1C 152
Clatter. *Powy* 1B 58
Clatterford. *IOW* 4C 16
Clatworthy. *Som* 3D 20
Claughton. *Lanc* 3E 97 (nr. Caton)
Claughton. *Lanc* 5E 97 (nr. Garstang)
Claughton. *Mers* 2F 83
Claverdon. *Warw* 4F 61
Claverham. *N Som* 5H 33
Clavering. *Essx* 2E 53
Claverley. *Shrp* 1B 60
Claverton. *Bath* 5C 34
Clawdd-coch. *V Glam* 4D 32
Clawdd-newydd. *Den* 5C 82
Clawson Hill. *Leics* 3E 75
Clawton. *Devn* 3D 10
Claxby. *Linc* 3D 88 (nr. Alford)
Claxby. *Linc* 1A 88 (nr. Market Rasen)
Claxton. *Norf* 5F 79
Claxton. *N Yor* 4A 100
Claybrooke Magna. *Leics* 2B 62
Claybrooke Parva. *Leics* 2B 62
Clay Common. *Suff* 2G 67
Clay Coton. *Nptn* 3C 62
Clay Cross. *Derbs* 4A 86
Claydon. *Oxon* 5B 62
Claydon. *Suff* 5D 66
Clay End. *Herts* 3D 52
Claygate. *Dum* 2E 113
Claygate. *Kent* 1B 28
Claygate. *Surr* 4C 38
Claygate Cross. *Kent* 5H 39
Clayhall. *Hants* 3E 16
Clayhanger. *Devn* 4D 20
Clayhanger. *W Mid* 5E 73
Clayhidon. *Devn* 1E 13
Clay Hill. *Bris* 4B 34
Clayhill. *E Sus* 3C 28
Clayhill. *Hants* 2B 16
Clayhithe. *Cambs* 4E 65
Clayholes. *Ang* 5E 145
Clay Lake. *Linc* 3B 76
Clayock. *High* 3D 168
Claypits. *Glos* 5C 48
Claypole. *Linc* 1F 75
Claythorpe. *Linc* 3D 88
Clayton. *G Man* 1C 84
Clayton. *S Yor* 4E 93
Clayton. *Staf* 1C 72
Clayton. *W Sus* 4E 27
Clayton. *W Yor* 1B 92
Clayton Green. *Lanc* 2D 90
Clayton-le-Moors. *Lanc* 1F 91
Clayton-le-Woods. *Lanc* 2D 90
Clayton West. *W Yor* 3C 92
Clayworth. *Notts* 2E 87
Cleadale. *High* 5C 146
Cleadon. *Tyne* 3G 115
Clearbrook. *Devn* 2B 8
Clearwell. *Glos* 5A 48
Cleasby. *N Yor* 3F 105
Cleat. *Orkn* 3D 172 (nr. Braehead)
Cleat. *Orkn* 9D 172 (nr. St Margaret's Hope)
Cleatlam. *Dur* 3E 105
Cleator. *Cumb* 3B 102
Cleator Moor. *Cumb* 3B 102
Cleckheaton. *W Yor* 2B 92
Cleedownton. *Shrp* 2H 59
Cleehill. *Shrp* 3H 59
Cleekhimin. *N Lan* 4A 128
Clee St Margaret. *Shrp* 2H 59
Cleestanton. *Shrp* 3H 59
Cleethorpes. *NE Lin* 4G 95
Cleeton St Mary. *Shrp* 3A 60
Cleeve. *N Som* 5H 33
Cleeve. *Oxon* 3E 36
Cleeve Hill. *Glos* 3E 49
Cleeve Prior. *Worc* 1F 49
Clehonger. *Here* 2H 47
Cleigh. *Arg* 1F 133
Cleish. *Per* 4C 136
Cleland. *N Lan* 4B 128
Clench Common. *Wilts* 5G 35
Clenchwarton. *Norf* 3E 77
Clennell. *Nmbd* 4D 120
Clent. *Worc* 3D 60
Cleobury Mortimer. *Shrp* 3A 60
Cleobury North. *Shrp* 2A 60
Clephanton. *High* 3C 158
Clerkhill. *High* 2H 167
Clestrain. *Orkn* 7C 172
Clevancy. *Wilts* 4F 35
Clevedon. *N Som* 4H 33
Cleveley. *Oxon* 3B 50
Cleveleys. *Lanc* 5C 96
Clevelode. *Worc* 1D 48
Cleverton. *Wilts* 3E 35
Clewer. *Som* 1H 21
Cley next the Sea. *Norf* 1C 78
Cliaid. *W Isl* 8B 170
Cliasmol. *W Isl* 7C 171
Clibberswick. *Shet* 1H 173
Cliburn. *Cumb* 2G 103
Cliddesden. *Hants* 2E 25
Clieves Hills. *Lanc* 4B 90
Cliff. *Warw* 1G 61
Cliffburn. *Ang* 4F 145
Cliffe. *Medw* 3B 40
Cliffe. *N Yor* 3F 105 (nr. Darlington)
Cliffe. *N Yor* 1G 93 (nr. Selby)
Cliff End. *E Sus* 4C 28
Cliffe Woods. *Medw* 3B 40
Clifford. *Here* 1F 47
Clifford. *W Yor* 5G 99
Clifford Chambers. *Warw* 5F 61
Clifford's Mesne. *Glos* 3B 48
Cliffsend. *Kent* 4H 41
Clifton. *Bris* 4A 34
Clifton. *C Beds* 2B 52
Clifton. *Cumb* 2G 103
Clifton. *Derbs* 1F 73
Clifton. *Devn* 2G 19
Clifton. *G Man* 4F 91
Clifton. *Lanc* 1C 90
Clifton. *Nmbd* 1F 115
Clifton. *N Yor* 5D 98
Clifton. *Nott* 2C 74
Clifton. *Oxon* 2C 50
Clifton. *S Yor* 1C 86
Clifton. *Stir* 5H 141
Clifton. *W Yor* 2B 92
Clifton. *Worc* 1D 48
Clifton. *York* 4H 99
Clifton Campville. *Staf* 4G 73
Clifton Hampden. *Oxon* 2D 36
Clifton Hill. *Worc* 4B 60
Clifton Reynes. *Mil* 5G 63
Clifton upon Dunsmore. *Warw* 3C 62
Clifton upon Teme. *Worc* 4B 60
Cliftonville. *Kent* 3H 41
Cliftonville. *Norf* 2F 79
Climping. *W Sus* 5A 26
Climpy. *S Lan* 4C 128
Clint. *N Yor* 4E 99
Clint Green. *Norf* 4C 78
Clintmains. *Bord* 1A 120
Cliobh. *W Isl* 4C 171
Clipiau. *Gwyn* 4H 69
Clippesby. *Norf* 4G 79
Clippings Green. *Norf* 4C 78
Clipsham. *Rut* 4G 75
Clipston. *Nptn* 2E 62
Clipston. *Notts* 2D 74
Clipstone. *Notts* 4C 86
Clitheroe. *Lanc* 5G 97
Cliuthar. *W Isl* 8D 171
Clive. *Shrp* 3H 71
Clivocast. *Shet* 1H 173
Clixby. *Linc* 4D 94
Clocaenog. *Den* 5C 82
Clochan. *Mor* 2B 160
Clochforbie. *Abers* 3F 161
Clock Face. *Mers* 1H 83
Cloddiau. *Powy* 5E 70
Cloddymoss. *Mor* 2D 159
Clodock. *Here* 3G 47
Cloford. *Som* 2C 22
Clola. *Abers* 4H 161
Clophill. *C Beds* 2A 52
Clopton. *Nptn* 2H 63
Clopton Corner. *Suff* 5E 66
Clopton Green. *Suff* 5G 65
Closeburn. *Dum* 5A 118
Close Clark. *IOM* 4B 108
Closworth. *Som* 1A 14
Clothall. *Herts* 2C 52
Clotton. *Ches W* 4H 83
Clough. *G Man* 3H 91
Clough. *W Yor* 3A 92
Clough Foot. *W Yor* 2H 91
Cloughton. *N Yor* 5H 107
Cloughton Newlands. *N Yor* 5H 107
Clouston. *Orkn* 6B 172
Clova. *Abers* 1B 152
Clova. *Ang* 1C 144
Clovelly. *Devn* 4D 18
Clovenfords. *Bord* 1G 119
Clovenstone. *Abers* 2E 153
Clovullin. *High* 2E 141
Clowne. *Derbs* 3B 86
Clows Top. *Worc* 3B 60
Cloy. *Wrex* 1F 71
Cluanie Inn. *High* 2C 148
Cluanie Lodge. *High* 2C 148
Cluddley. *Telf* 5A 72
Clun. *Shrp* 2F 59
Clunas. *High* 4C 158
Clunbury. *Shrp* 2F 59
Clunderwen. *Pemb* 3F 43
Clune. *High* 1B 150
Clunes. *High* 5E 148
Clungunford. *Shrp* 3F 59
Clunie. *Per* 4A 144
Clunton. *Shrp* 2F 59
Cluny. *Fife* 4E 137
Clutton. *Bath* 1B 22
Clutton. *Ches W* 5G 83
Clwt-y-bont. *Gwyn* 4E 81
Clwydfagwyr. *Mer T* 5D 46
Clydach. *Mon* 4F 47
Clydach. *Swan* 5G 45
Clydach Vale. *Rhon* 2C 32
Clydebank. *W Dun* 2G 127
Clydey. *Pemb* 1G 43
Clyffe Pypard. *Wilts* 4F 35
Clynder. *Arg* 1D 126
Clyne. *Neat* 5B 46
Clynelish. *High* 3F 165
Clynnog-fawr. *Gwyn* 1D 68
Clyro. *Powy* 1F 47
Clyst Honiton. *Devn* 3C 12

Clyst Hydon—Coombe

Clyst Hydon. *Devn* .2D 12
Clyst St George. *Devn* .4C 12
Clyst St Lawrence. *Devn* .2D 12
Clyst St Mary. *Devn* .3C 12
Clyth. *High* .5E 169
Cnip. *W Isl* .4C 171
Cnwcau. *Pemb* .1C 44
Cnwch Coch. *Cdgn* .3F 57
Coad's Green. *Corn* .5C 10
Coal Aston. *Derbs* .3A 86
Coalbrookdale. *Telf* .5A 72
Coalbrookvale. *Blae* .5F 47
Coalburn. *S Lan* .1H 117
Coalburns. *Tyne* .3E 115
Coalcleugh. *Nmbd* .5B 114
Coaley. *Glos* .5C 48
Coalford. *Abers* .4F 153
Coalhall. *E Ayr* .3D 116
Coalhill. *Essx* .1B 40
Coalpit Heath. *S Glo* .3B 34
Coal Pool. *W Mid* .5E 73
Coalport. *Telf* .5B 72
Coalsnaughton. *Clac* .4B 136
Coaltown of Balgonie. *Fife* .4F 137
Coaltown of Wemyss. *Fife* .4F 137
Coalville. *Leics* .4B 74
Coalville. *Mil* .5F 63
Coalway. *Glos* .4A 48
Coanwood. *Nmbd* .4H 113
Coat. *Som* .4H 21
Coatbridge. *N Lan* .3A 128
Coatdyke. *N Lan* .3A 128
Coate. *Swin* .3G 35
Coate. *Wilts* .5F 35
Coates. *Cambs* .1C 64
Coates. *Glos* .5E 49
Coates. *Linc* .2G 87
Coates. *W Sus* .4A 26
Coatham. *Red C* .2C 106
Coatham Mundeville. *Darl* .2F 105
Cobbaton. *Devn* .4G 19
Coberley. *Glos* .4E 49
Cobhall Common. *Here* .2H 47
Cobham. *Kent* .4A 40
Cobham. *Surr* .4C 38
Cobnash. *Here* .4G 59
Coburg. *Devn* .5B 12
Cockayne. *N Yor* .5D 106
Cockayne Hatley. *C Beds* .1C 52
Cock Bank. *Wrex* .1F 71
Cock Bridge. *Abers* .3G 151
Cockburnspath. *Bord* .2D 130
Cock Clarks. *Essx* .5B 54
Cockenzie and Port Seton. *E Lot* .2H 129
Cockerham. *Lanc* .4D 96
Cockermouth. *Cumb* .1C 102
Cockernhoe. *Herts* .3B 52
Cockfield. *Dur* .2E 105
Cockfield. *Suff* .5B 66
Cockfosters. *G Lon* .1D 39
Cock Gate. *Here* .4G 59
Cock Green. *Essx* .4G 53
Cocking. *W Sus* .1G 17
Cocking Causeway. *W Sus* .1G 17
Cockington. *Torb* .2F 9
Cocklake. *Som* .2H 21
Cocklaw. *Abers* .4H 161
Cocklaw. *Nmbd* .2C 114
Cockley Beck. *Cumb* .4D 102
Cockley Cley. *Norf* .5G 77
Cockmuir. *Abers* .3G 161
Cockpole Green. *Wind* .3G 37
Cockshutford. *Shrp* .2H 59
Cockshutt. *Shrp* .3G 71
Cockthorpe. *Norf* .1B 78
Cockwood. *Devn* .4C 12
Cockyard. *Derbs* .3E 85
Cockyard. *Here* .2H 47
Codda. *Corn* .5B 10
Coddenham. *Suff* .5D 66
Coddenham Green. *Suff* .5D 66
Coddington. *Ches W* .5G 83
Coddington. *Here* .1C 48
Coddington. *Notts* .5F 87
Codford St Mary. *Wilts* .3E 23
Codford St Peter. *Wilts* .3E 23
Codicote. *Herts* .4C 52
Codmore Hill. *W Sus* .3B 26
Codnor. *Derbs* .1B 74
Codrington. *S Glo* .4C 34
Codsall. *Staf* .5C 72
Codsall Wood. *Staf* .5C 72
Coed Duon. *Cphy* .2E 33
Coedely. *Rhon* .3D 32
Coedglasson. *Powy* .4C 58
Coedkernew. *Newp* .3F 33
Coed Morgan. *Mon* .4G 47
Coedpoeth. *Wrex* .5E 83
Coedway. *Powy* .4F 71
Coed-y-bryn. *Cdgn* .1D 44
Coed-y-paen. *Mon* .2G 33
Coed-yr-ynys. *Powy* .3E 47
Coed Ystumgwern. *Gwyn* .3E 69
Coelbren. *Powy* .4B 46
Coffinswell. *Devn* .2E 9
Cofton Hackett. *Worc* .3E 61
Cogan. *V Glam* .4E 33
Cogenhoe. *Nptn* .4F 63
Cogges. *Oxon* .5B 50
Coggeshall. *Essx* .3B 54
Coggeshall Hamlet. *Essx* .3B 54
Coggins Mill. *E Sus* .3G 27
Coignafearn Lodge. *High* .2A 150
Coig Peighinnean. *W Isl* .1H 171
Coig Peighinnean Bhuirgh. *W Isl* .2G 171
Coilleag. *W Isl* .7C 170
Coilliemore. *High* .1A 158
Coillore. *High* .5C 154
Coire an Fhuarain. *W Isl* .4E 171
Coity. *B'end* .3C 32
Cokhay Green. *Derbs* .3G 73
Col. *W Isl* .4G 171
Colaboll. *High* .2C 164
Colan. *Corn* .2C 6
Colaton Raleigh. *Devn* .4D 12
Colbost. *High* .4B 154
Colburn. *N Yor* .5E 105
Colby. *Cumb* .2H 103
Colby. *IOM* .4B 108
Colby. *Norf* .2E 78
Colchester. *Essx* .3D 54
Cold Ash. *W Ber* .5D 36
Cold Ashby. *Nptn* .3D 62
Cold Ashton. *S Glo* .4C 34
Cold Aston. *Glos* .4G 49
Coldbackie. *High* .3G 167
Cold Blow. *Pemb* .3F 43
Cold Brayfield. *Mil* .5G 63
Cold Cotes. *N Yor* .2G 97
Coldean. *Brig* .5E 27
Coldeast. *Devn* .5B 12
Colden. *W Yor* .2H 91
Colden Common. *Hants* .4C 24
Coldfair Green. *Suff* .4G 67
Coldham. *Cambs* .5D 76
Coldham. *Staf* .5C 72
Cold Hanworth. *Linc* .2H 87
Coldharbour. *Corn* .4B 6
Cold Harbour. *Dors* .3E 15
Coldharbour. *Glos* .5A 48
Coldharbour. *Kent* .5G 39
Coldharbour. *Surr* .1C 26
Cold Hatton. *Telf* .3A 72
Cold Hatton Heath. *Telf* .3A 72
Cold Hesledon. *Dur* .5H 115
Cold Hiendley. *W Yor* .3D 92
Cold Higham. *Nptn* .5D 62
Coldingham. *Bord* .3F 131
Cold Kirby. *N Yor* .1H 99
Coldmeece. *Staf* .2C 72
Cold Northcott. *Corn* .4C 10
Cold Norton. *Essx* .5B 54
Cold Overton. *Leics* .4F 75
Coldrain. *Per* .3C 136
Coldred. *Kent* .1G 29
Coldridge. *Devn* .2G 11
Cold Row. *Lanc* .5C 96
Coldstream. *Bord* .5E 131
Coldwaltham. *W Sus* .4B 26
Coldwell. *Here* .2H 47
Coldwells. *Abers* .5H 161
Coldwells Croft. *Abers* .1C 152
Cole. *Som* .3B 22
Colebatch. *Shrp* .2F 59
Colebrook. *Devn* .2D 12
Colebrooke. *Devn* .2A 12
Coleburn. *Mor* .3G 159
Coleby. *Linc* .4G 87
Coleby. *N Lin* .3B 94
Cole End. *Warw* .2G 61
Coleford. *Devn* .2A 12
Coleford. *Glos* .4A 48
Coleford. *Som* .2B 22
Colegate End. *Norf* .2D 66
Cole Green. *Herts* .4C 52
Cole Henley. *Hants* .1C 24
Colehill. *Dors* .2F 15
Coleman Green. *Herts* .4B 52
Coleman's Hatch. *E Sus* .2F 27
Colemere. *Shrp* .2G 71
Colemore. *Hants* .3F 25
Colemore Green. *Shrp* .1B 60
Coleorton. *Leics* .4B 74
Colerne. *Wilts* .4D 34
Colesbourne. *Glos* .4E 49
Colesden. *Bed* .5A 64
Coles Green. *Worc* .5B 60
Coleshill. *Buck* .1A 38
Coleshill. *Oxon* .2H 35
Coleshill. *Warw* .2G 61
Colestocks. *Devn* .2D 12
Colethrop. *Glos* .4D 48
Coley. *Bath* .1A 22
Colgate. *W Sus* .2D 26
Colinsburgh. *Fife* .3G 137
Colinton. *Edin* .3F 129
Colintraive. *Arg* .2B 126
Colkirk. *Norf* .3B 78
Collace. *Per* .5B 144
Collaton. *Devn* .5D 8
Collaton St Mary. *Torb* .2E 9
College of Roseisle. *Mor* .2F 159
Collessie. *Fife* .2E 137
Collier Row. *G Lon* .1F 39
Colliers End. *Herts* .3D 52
Collier Street. *Kent* .1B 28
Colliery Row. *Tyne* .5G 115
Collieston. *Abers* .1H 153
Collin. *Dum* .2B 112
Collingbourne Ducis. *Wilts* .1H 23
Collingbourne Kingston. *Wilts* .1H 23
Collingham. *Notts* .4F 87
Collingham. *W Yor* .5F 99
Collingtree. *Nptn* .5E 63
Collins Green. *Warr* .1H 83
Collins Green. *Worc* .5B 60
Colliston. *Ang* .4F 145
Colliton. *Devn* .2D 12
Collydean. *Fife* .3E 137
Collyweston. *Nptn* .5G 75
Colmonell. *S Ayr* .1G 109
Colmworth. *Bed* .5A 64
Colnbrook. *Slo* .3B 38
Colne. *Cambs* .3C 64
Colne. *Lanc* .5A 98
Colne Engaine. *Essx* .2B 54
Colney. *Norf* .5D 78
Colney Heath. *Herts* .5C 52
Colney Street. *Herts* .5B 52
Coln Rogers. *Glos* .5F 49
Coln St Aldwyns. *Glos* .5G 49
Coln St Dennis. *Glos* .4F 49
Colpitts Grange. *Nmbd* .4C 114
Colpy. *Abers* .5D 160
Colscott. *Devn* .1D 10
Colsterdale. *N Yor* .1D 98
Colsterworth. *Linc* .3G 75
Colston Bassett. *Notts* .2D 74
Colstoun House. *E Lot* .2B 130
Coltfield. *Mor* .2F 159
Colthouse. *Cumb* .5E 103
Coltishall. *Norf* .4E 79
Coltness. *N Lan* .4A 128
Colton. *Cumb* .1C 96
Colton. *Norf* .5D 78
Colton. *N Yor* .5H 99
Colton. *Staf* .3E 73
Colton. *W Yor* .1D 92
Colt's Hill. *Kent* .1H 27
Col Uarach. *W Isl* .4G 171
Colvend. *Dum* .4F 111
Colwall. *Here* .1C 48
Colwall Green. *Here* .1C 48
Colwell. *Nmbd* .2C 114
Colwich. *Staf* .3E 73
Colwick. *Notts* .1D 74
Colwinston. *V Glam* .4C 32
Colworth. *W Sus* .5A 26
Colwyn Bay. *Cnwy* .3A 82
Colyford. *Devn* .3F 13
Colyton. *Devn* .3F 13
Combe. *Devn* .2D 8
Combe. *Here* .4F 59
Combe. *Oxon* .4C 50
Combe. *W Ber* .5B 36
Combe Almer. *Dors* .3E 15
Combebow. *Devn* .4E 11
Combe Down. *Bath* .5C 34
Combe Fishacre. *Devn* .2E 9
Combe Florey. *Som* .3E 21
Combe Hay. *Bath* .1C 22
Combeinteignhead. *Devn* .5C 12
Combe Martin. *Devn* .2F 19
Combe Moor. *Here* .4F 59
Combe Raleigh. *Devn* .2E 13
Comberbach. *Ches W* .3A 84
Comberford. *Staf* .5F 73
Comberton. *Cambs* .5C 64
Comberton. *Here* .4G 59
Combe St Nicholas. *Som* .1G 13
Combpyne. *Devn* .3F 13
Combridge. *Staf* .2E 73
Combrook. *Warw* .5H 61
Combs. *Derbs* .3E 85
Combs. *Suff* .5C 66
Combs Ford. *Suff* .5C 66
Combwich. *Som* .2F 21
Comers. *Abers* .3D 152
Comhampton. *Worc* .4C 60
Comins Coch. *Cdgn* .2F 57
Comley. *Shrp* .1G 59
Commercial End. *Cambs* .4E 65
Commins. *Powy* .3D 70
Commins Coch. *Powy* .5H 69
Commondale. *N Yor* .3D 106
Common End. *Cumb* .2B 102
Common Hill. *Here* .2A 48
Common Moor. *Corn* .2G 7
Commonside. *Ches W* .3H 83
Common Side. *Derbs* .3H 85 (nr. Chesterfield)
Commonside. *Derbs* .1G 73 (nr. Derby)
Common, The. *Wilts* .3H 23 (nr. Salisbury)
Common, The. *Wilts* .3F 35 (nr. Swindon)
Compstall. *G Man* .1D 84
Compton. *Devn* .2E 9
Compton. *Hants* .4C 24
Compton. *Staf* .2C 60
Compton. *Surr* .1A 26
Compton. *W Ber* .3D 36
Compton. *W Sus* .1F 17
Compton. *Wilts* .1G 23
Compton Abbas. *Dors* .1D 14
Compton Abdale. *Glos* .4F 49
Compton Bassett. *Wilts* .4F 35
Compton Beauchamp. *Oxon* .3A 36
Compton Bishop. *Som* .1G 21
Compton Chamberlayne. *Wilts* .4F 23
Compton Dando. *Bath* .5B 34
Compton Dundon. *Som* .3H 21
Compton Greenfield. *S Glo* .3A 34
Compton Martin. *Bath* .1A 22
Compton Pauncefoot. *Som* .4B 22
Compton Valence. *Dors* .3A 14
Comrie. *Fife* .1D 128
Comrie. *Per* .1G 135
Conaglen. *High* .2E 14[illegible]
Conchra. *Arg* .1B 125
Conchra. *High* .1A 14[illegible]
Conder Green. *Lanc* .4D 96
Conderton. *Worc* .2E 49
Condicote. *Glos* .3G 49
Condorrat. *N Lan* .2A 128
Condover. *Shrp* .5G 71
Coneyhurst Common. *W Sus* .3C 26
Coneysthorpe. *N Yor* .2B 100
Coneythorpe. *N Yor* .4F 99
Coney Weston. *Suff* .3B 66
Conford. *Hants* .3G 25
Congdon's Shop. *Corn* .5C 10
Congerstone. *Leics* .5A 74
Congham. *Norf* .3G 77
Congleton. *Ches E* .4C 84
Congl-y-wal. *Gwyn* .1G 69
Congresbury. *N Som* .5H 33
Congreve. *Staf* .4D 72
Conham. *S Glo* .4B 34
Conicavel. *Mor* .3D 159
Coningsby. *Linc* .5B 88
Conington. *Cambs* .4C 64 (nr. Fenstanton)
Conington. *Cambs* .2A 64 (nr. Sawtry)
Conisbrough. *S Yor* .1C 86
Conisby. *Arg* .3A 124
Conisholme. *Linc* .1D 88
Coniston. *Cumb* .5E 102
Coniston. *E Yor* .1E 95
Coniston Cold. *N Yor* .4B 98
Conistone. *N Yor* .3B 98
Connah's Quay. *Flin* .4E 83
Connel. *Arg* .5D 140
Connel Park. *E Ayr* .3F 117
Connista. *High* .1D 154
Connor Downs. *Corn* .3C 4
Conock. *Wilts* .1F 23
Conon Bridge. *High* .3H 157
Cononley. *N Yor* .5B 98
Cononsyth. *Ang* .4E 145
Conordan. *High* .5E 155
Consall. *Staf* .1D 73
Consett. *Dur* .4E 115
Constable Burton. *N Yor* .5E 105
Constantine. *Corn* .4E 5
Constantine Bay. *Corn* .1C 6
Contin. *High* .3G 157
Contullich. *High* .1A 158
Conwy. *Cnwy* .3G 81
Conyer. *Kent* .4D 40
Conyer's Green. *Suff* .4A 66
Cooden. *E Sus* .5B 28
Cooil. *IOM* .4C 108
Cookbury. *Devn* .2E 11
Cookbury Wick. *Devn* .2D 11
Cookham. *Wind* .3G 37
Cookham Dean. *Wind* .3G 37
Cookham Rise. *Wind* .3G 37
Cookhill. *Worc* .5E 61
Cookley. *Suff* .3F 67
Cookley. *Worc* .2C 60
Cookley Green. *Oxon* .2E 37
Cookney. *Abers* .4F 153
Cooksbridge. *E Sus* .4F 27
Cooksey Green. *Worc* .4D 60
Cookshill. *Staf* .1D 72
Cooksmill Green. *Essx* .5G 53
Coolham. *W Sus* .3C 26
Cooling. *Medw* .3B 40
Cooling Street. *Medw* .3B 40
Coombe. *Corn* .1C 10 (nr. Bude)
Coombe. *Corn* .3D 6 (nr. St Austell)
Coombe. *Corn* .4C 6 (nr. Truro)

Craigton. *Abers* 3E 152
Craigton. *Ang* 5E 145
(nr. Carnoustie)
Craigton. *Ang* 3C 144
(nr. Kirriemuir)
Craigton. *High* 4A 158
Craigtown. *High* 3A 168
Craig-y-Duke. *Neat* 5H 45
Craigyloch. *Ang* 3B 144
Craig-y-nos. *Powy* 4B 46
Craik. *Bord* 4F 119
Crail. *Fife* 3H 137
Crailing. *Bord* 2A 120
Crailinghall. *Bord* 2A 120
Crakehill. *N Yor* 2G 99
Crakemarsh. *Staf* 2E 73
Crambe. *N Yor* 3B 100
Crambeck. *N Yor* 3B 100
Cramlington. *Nmbd* 2F 115
Cramond. *Edin* 2E 129
Cramond Bridge. *Edin* 2E 129
Cranage. *Ches E* 4B 84
Cranberry. *Staf* 2C 72
Cranborne. *Dors* 1F 15
Cranbourne. *Brac* 3A 38
Cranbrook. *Devn* 3D 12
Cranbrook. *Kent* 2B 28
Cranbrook Common. *Kent* 2B 28
Crane Moor. *S Yor* 4D 92
Crane's Corner. *Norf* 4B 78
Cranfield. *C Beds* 1H 51
Cranford. *G Lon* 3B 38
Cranford St Andrew. *Nptn* 3G 63
Cranford St John. *Nptn* 3G 63
Cranham. *Glos* 4D 49
Cranham. *G Lon* 2G 39
Crank. *Mers* 1H 83
Cranleigh. *Surr* 2B 26
Cranley. *Suff* 3D 66
Cranloch. *Mor* 3G 159
Cranmer Green. *Suff* 3C 66
Cranmore. *IOW* 3B 16
Cranmore. *Linc* 5A 76
Crannich. *Arg* 4G 139
Crannoch. *Mor* 3B 160
Cranoe. *Leics* 1E 63
Cransford. *Suff* 4F 67
Cranshaws. *Bord* 3C 130
Cranstal. *IOM* 1D 108
Crantock. *Corn* 2B 6
Cranwell. *Linc* 5H 87
Cranwich. *Norf* 1G 65
Cranworth. *Norf* 5B 78
Craobh Haven. *Arg* 3E 133
Craobhnaclag. *High* 4G 157
Crapstone. *Devn* 2B 8
Crarae. *Arg* 4G 133
Crask. *High* 2H 167
Crask Inn. *High* 1C 164
Crask of Aigas. *High* 4G 157
Craster. *Nmbd* 3G 121
Cratfield. *Suff* 3F 67
Crathes. *Abers* 4E 153
Crathie. *Abers* 4G 151
Crathie. *High* 4H 149
Crathorne. *N Yor* 4B 106
Craven Arms. *Shrp* 2G 59
Crawcrook. *Tyne* 3E 115
Crawford. *Lanc* 4D 90
Crawford. *S Lan* 2B 118
Crawforddyke. *S Lan* 4B 128
Crawfordjohn. *S Lan* 2A 118
Crawick. *Dum* 3G 117
Crawley. *Devn* 2F 13
Crawley. *Hants* 3C 24
Crawley. *Oxon* 4B 50
Crawley. *W Sus* 2D 26
Crawley Down. *W Sus* 2E 27
Crawley Side. *Dur* 5C 114
Crawshawbooth. *Lanc* 2G 91
Crawton. *Abers* 5F 153
Cray. *N Yor* 2B 98
Cray. *Per* 2A 144
Crayford. *G Lon* 3G 39
Crayke. *N Yor* 2H 99
Craymere Beck. *Norf* 2C 78
Crays Hill. *Essx* 1B 40
Cray's Pond. *Oxon* 3E 37
Crazies Hill. *Wok* 3F 37
Creacombe. *Devn* 1B 12
Creagan. *Arg* 4D 141
Creag Aoil. *High* 1F 141
Creag Ghoraidh. *W Isl* 4D 170
Creaguaineach Lodge. *High* 2H 141
Creamore Bank. *Shrp* 2H 71
Creaton. *Nptn* 3E 62
Creca. *Dum* 2D 112
Credenhill. *Here* 1H 47
Crediton. *Devn* 2B 12
Creebridge. *Dum* 3B 110
Creech. *Dors* 4E 15
Creech Heathfield. *Som* 4F 21
Creech St Michael. *Som* 4F 21
Creed. *Corn* 4D 6
Creekmoor. *Pool* 3E 15
Creekmouth. *G Lon* 2F 39
Creeting St Mary. *Suff* 5C 66
Creeting St Peter. *Suff* 5C 66
Creeton. *Linc* 3H 75
Creetown. *Dum* 4B 110
Creggans. *Arg* 3H 133
Cregneash. *IOM* 5A 108
Cregrina. *Powy* 5D 58
Creich. *Arg* 2B 132
Creich. *Fife* 1F 137
Creighton. *Staf* 2E 73
Creigiau. *Card* 3D 32
Cremyll. *Corn* 3A 8
Crendell. *Dors* 1F 15
Crepkill. *High* 4D 154
Cressage. *Shrp* 5H 71
Cressbrook. *Derbs* 3F 85
Cresselly. *Pemb* 4E 43
Cressing. *Essx* 3A 54
Cresswell. *Nmbd* 5G 121
Cresswell. *Staf* 2D 73
Cresswell Quay. *Pemb* 4E 43
Creswell. *Derbs* 3C 86
Creswell Green. *Staf* 4E 73
Cretingham. *Suff* 4E 67
Crewe. *Ches E* 5B 84
Crewe-by-Farndon. *Ches W* 5G 83
Crewgreen. *Powy* 4F 71
Crewkerne. *Som* 2H 13
Crews Hill. *G Lon* 5D 52
Crewton. *Derb* 2A 74
Crianlarich. *Stir* 1C 134
Cribbs Causeway. *S Glo* 3A 34
Cribyn. *Cdgn* 5E 57
Criccieth. *Gwyn* 2D 69
Crich. *Derbs* 5A 86
Crichton. *Midl* 3G 129
Crick. *Mon* 2H 33
Crick. *Nptn* 3C 62
Crickadarn. *Powy* 1D 46
Cricket Hill. *Hants* 5G 37
Cricket Malherbie. *Som* 1G 13
Cricket St Thomas. *Som* 2G 13
Crickham. *Som* 2H 21
Crickheath. *Shrp* 3E 71
Crickhowell. *Powy* 4F 47
Cricklade. *Wilts* 2F 35
Cricklewood. *G Lon* 2D 38
Cridling Stubbs. *N Yor* 2F 93
Crieff. *Per* 1A 136
Criftins. *Shrp* 2F 71
Criggion. *Powy* 4E 71
Crigglestone. *W Yor* 3D 92
Crimchard. *Som* 2G 13
Crimdon Park. *Dur* 1B 106
Crimond. *Abers* 3H 161
Crimonmogate. *Abers* 3H 161
Crimplesham. *Norf* 5F 77
Crimscote. *Warw* 1H 49
Crinan. *Arg* 4E 133
Cringleford. *Norf* 5D 78
Crinow. *Pemb* 3F 43
Cripplesease. *Corn* 3C 4
Cripplestyle. *Dors* 1F 15
Cripp's Corner. *E Sus* 3B 28
Croanford. *Corn* 5A 10
Crockenhill. *Kent* 4G 39
Crocker End. *Oxon* 3F 37
Crockerhill. *Hants* 2D 16
Crockernwell. *Devn* 3A 12
Crocker's Ash. *Here* 4A 48
Crockerton. *Wilts* 2D 22
Crocketford. *Dum* 2F 111
Crockey Hill. *York* 5A 100
Crockham Hill. *Kent* 5F 39
Crockhurst Street. *Kent* 1H 27
Crockleford Heath.
Essx 3D 54
Croeserw. *Neat* 2B 32
Croes-Goch. *Pemb* 1C 42
Croes Hywel. *Mon* 4G 47
Croes-lan. *Cdgn* 1D 45
Croesor. *Gwyn* 1F 69
Croesoswallt. *Shrp* 3E 71
Croesyceiliog. *Carm* 4E 45
Croesyceiliog. *Torf* 2F 33
Croes-y-mwyalch. *Torf* 2G 33
Croesywaun. *Gwyn* 5E 81
Croford. *Som* 4E 20
Croft. *Leics* 1C 62
Croft. *Linc* 4E 89
Croft. *Warr* 1A 84
Croftamie. *Stir* 1F 127
Croftfoot. *Glas* 3G 127
Croftmill. *Per* 5F 143
Crofton. *Cumb* 4E 112
Crofton. *W Yor* 3D 93
Crofton. *Wilts* 5A 36
Croft-on-Tees. *N Yor* 4F 105
Crofts. *Dum* 2E 111
Crofts of Benachielt. *High* 5D 169
Crofts of Dipple. *Mor* 3H 159
Crofty. *Swan* 3E 31
Croggan. *Arg* 1E 132
Croglin. *Cumb* 5G 113
Croich. *High* 4B 164
Croick. *High* 3A 168
Croig. *Arg* 3E 139
Cromarty. *High* 2B 158
Crombie. *Fife* 1D 128
Cromdale. *High* 1E 151
Cromer. *Herts* 3C 52
Cromer. *Norf* 1E 79
Cromford. *Derbs* 5G 85
Cromhall. *S Glo* 2B 34
Cromor. *W Isl* 5G 171
Cromra. *High* 5H 149
Cromwell. *Notts* 4E 87
Cronberry. *E Ayr* 2F 117
Crondall. *Hants* 2F 25
Cronk, The. *IOM* 2C 108
Cronk-y-Voddy. *IOM* 3C 108
Cronton. *Mers* 2G 83
Crook. *Cumb* 5F 103
Crook. *Dur* 1E 105
Crookdake. *Cumb* 5C 112
Crooke. *G Man* 4D 90
Crookedholm. *E Ayr* 1D 116
Crooked Soley. *Wilts* 4B 36
Crookes. *S Yor* 2H 85
Crookgate Bank. *Dur* 4E 115
Crookhall. *Dur* 4E 115
Crookham. *Nmbd* 1D 120
Crookham. *W Ber* 5D 36
Crookham Village. *Hants* 1F 25
Crooklands. *Cumb* 1E 97
Crook of Devon. *Per* 3C 136
Crookston. *Ren* 3G 127
Cropredy. *Oxon* 1C 50
Cropston. *Leics* 4C 74
Cropthorne. *Worc* 1E 49
Cropton. *N Yor* 1B 100
Cropwell Bishop. *Notts* 2D 74
Cropwell Butler. *Notts* 2D 74
Cros. *W Isl* 1H 171
Crosbie. *N Ayr* 5D 126
Crosbost. *W Isl* 5F 171
Crosby. *Cumb* 1B 102
Crosby. *IOM* 4C 108
Crosby. *Mers* 1F 83
Crosby. *N Lin* 3B 94
Crosby Court. *N Yor* 5A 106
Crosby Garrett. *Cumb* 4A 104
Crosby Ravensworth. *Cumb* 3H 103
Crosby Villa. *Cumb* 1B 102
Croscombe. *Som* 2A 22
Crosland Moor. *W Yor* 3B 92
Cross. *Som* 1H 21
Crossaig. *Arg* 4G 125
Crossapol. *Arg* 4A 138
Cross Ash. *Mon* 4H 47
Cross-at-Hand. *Kent* 1B 28
Crossbush. *W Sus* 5B 26
Crosscanonby. *Cumb* 1B 102
Crossdale Street. *Norf* 2E 79
Cross End. *Essx* 2B 54
Crossens. *Mers* 3B 90
Crossford. *Fife* 1D 128
Crossford. *S Lan* 5B 128
Cross Foxes. *Gwyn* 4G 69
Crossgate. *Orkn* 6D 172
Crossgate. *Staf* 2D 72
Crossgatehall. *E Lot* 3G 129
Crossgates. *Fife* 1E 129
Crossgates. *N Yor* 1E 101
Crossgates. *Powy* 4C 58
Cross Gates. *W Yor* 1D 92
Crossgill. *Lanc* 3E 97
Cross Green. *Devn* 4D 11
Cross Green. *Staf* 5D 72
Cross Green. *Suff* 5A 66
(nr. Cockfield)
Cross Green. *Suff* 5B 66
(nr. Hitcham)
Cross Hands. *Carm* 4F 45
(nr. Ammanford)
Crosshands. *Carm* 2F 43
(nr. Whitland)
Crosshands. *E Ayr* 1D 117
Cross Hill. *Derbs* 1B 74
Crosshill. *E Ayr* 2D 117
Crosshill. *Fife* 4D 136
Cross Hill. *Glos* 2A 34
Crosshill. *S Ayr* 4C 116
Crosshills. *High* 1A 158
Cross Hills. *N Yor* 5C 98
Cross Holme. *N Yor* 5C 106
Crosshouse. *E Ayr* 1C 116
Cross Houses. *Shrp* 5H 71
Crossings. *Cumb* 2G 113
Cross in Hand. *E Sus* 3G 27
Cross Inn. *Cdgn* 4E 57
(nr. Aberaeron)
Cross Inn. *Cdgn* 5C 56
(nr. New Quay)
Cross Inn. *Rhon* 3D 32
Crosskeys. *Cphy* 2F 33
Crosskirk. *High* 2C 168
Crosslands. *Cumb* 1C 96
Cross Lane Head. *Shrp* 1B 60
Cross Lanes. *Corn* 4D 5
Cross Lanes. *Dur* 3D 104
Cross Lanes. *N Yor* 3H 99
Crosslanes. *Shrp* 4F 71
Cross Lanes. *Wrex* 1F 71
Crosslee. *Ren* 3F 127
Crossmichael. *Dum* 3E 111
Crossmoor. *Lanc* 1C 90
Cross Oak. *Powy* 3E 46
Cross of Jackston. *Abers* 5E 161
Cross o' th' Hands. *Derbs* 1G 73
Crossroads. *Abers* 3G 153
(nr. Aberdeen)
Crossroads. *Abers* 4E 153
(nr. Banchory)
Crossroads. *E Ayr* 1D 116
Cross Side. *Devn* 4B 20
Cross Street. *Suff* 3D 66
Crosston. *Ang* 3E 145
Cross Town. *Ches E* 3B 84
Crossway. *Mon* 4H 47
Crossway. *Powy* 5C [illegible]8
Crossway Green. *Mon* 2A [illegible]4
Crossway Green. *Worc* 4C [illegible]
Crossways. *Dors* 4C 1[illegible]
Crosswell. *Pemb* 1F 4[illegible]
Crosswood. *Cdgn* 3F 5[illegible]
Crosthwaite. *Cumb* 5F 103
Croston. *Lanc* 3C 90
Crostwick. *Norf* 4E 79
Crostwight. *Norf* 3F 79
Crothair. *W Isl* 4D 171
Crouch. *Kent* 5H 39
Croucheston. *Wilts* 4F 23
Crouch Hill. *Dors* 1C 14
Croughton. *Nptn* 2D 50
Crovie. *Abers* 2F 161
Crow. *Hants* 2G 15
Crowan. *Corn* 3D 4
Crowborough. *E Sus* 2G 27
Crowcombe. *Som* 3E 21
Crowcroft. *Worc* 5B 60
Crowdecote. *Derbs* 4F 85
Crowden. *Derbs* 1E 85
Crowden. *Devn* 3E 11
Crowdhill. *Hants* 1C 16
Crowdon. *N Yor* 5G 107
Crow Edge. *S Yor* 4B 92
Crow End. *Cambs* 5C 64
Crowfield. *Nptn* 1E 50
Crowfield. *Suff* 5D 66
Crow Green. *Essx* 1G 39
Crow Hill. *Here* 3B 48
Crowhurst. *E Sus* 4B 28
Crowhurst. *Surr* 1E 27
Crowhurst Lane End. *Surr* 1E 27
Crowland. *Linc* 4B 76
Crowland. *Suff* 3C 66
Crowlas. *Corn* 3C 4
Crowle. *N Lin* 3A 94
Crowle. *Worc* 5D 60
Crowle Green. *Worc* 5D 60
Crowmarsh Gifford. *Oxon* 3E 36
Crown Corner. *Suff* 3E 67
Crownthorpe. *Norf* 5C 78
Crowntown. *Corn* 3D 4
Crows-an-wra. *Corn* 4A 4
Crowshill. *Norf* 5B 78
Crowthorne. *Brac* 5G 37
Crowton. *Ches W* 3H 83
Croxall. *Staf* 4F 73
Croxby. *Linc* 1A 88
Croxdale. *Dur* 1F 105
Croxden. *Staf* 2E 73
Croxley Green. *Herts* 1B 38
Croxton. *Cambs* 4B 64
Croxton. *Norf* 2B 78
(nr. Fakenham)
Croxton. *Norf* 2A 66
(nr. Thetford)
Croxton. *N Lin* 3D 94
Croxton. *Staf* 2B 72
Croxtonbank. *Staf* 2B 72
Croxton Green. *Ches E* 5H 83
Croxton Kerrial. *Leics* 3F 75
Croy. *High* 4B 158
Croy. *N Lan* 2A 128
Croyde. *Devn* 3E 19
Croydon. *Cambs* 1D 52
Croydon. *G Lon* 4E 39
Crubenbeg. *High* 4A 150
Crubenmore Lodge. *High* 4A 150
Cruckmeore. *Shrp* 5G 71
Cruckton. *Shrp* 4G 71
Cruden Bay. *Abers* 5H 161
Crudgington. *Telf* 4A 72
Crudie. *Abers* 3E 161
Crudwell. *Wilts* 2E 35
Cruft. *Devn* 3F 11
Crug. *Powy* 3D 58
Crughywel. *Powy* 4F 47
Crugmeer. *Corn* 1D 6
Crugybar. *Carm* 2G 45
Crug-y-byddar. *Powy* 2D 58
Crulabhig. *W Isl* 4D 171

Davyhulme—Dounie

Davyhulme. *G Man* 1B **84**
Daw Cross. *N Yor* 4E **99**
Dawdon. *Dur* 5H **115**
Dawesgreen. *Surr* 1D **26**
Dawley. *Telf* 5A **72**
Dawlish. *Devn* 5C **12**
Dawlish Warren. *Devn* 5C **12**
Dawn. *Cnwy* 3A **82**
Daws Heath. *Essx* 2C **40**
Dawshill. *Worc* 5C **60**
Daw's House. *Corn* 4D **10**
Dawsmere. *Linc* 2D **76**
Dayhills. *Staf* 2D **72**
Dayhouse Bank. *Worc* 3D **60**
Daylesford. *Glos* 3H **49**
Daywall. *Shrp* 2E **71**
Ddol. *Flin* 3D **82**
Ddol Cownwy. *Powy* 4C **70**
Deadman's Cross. *C Beds* 1B **52**
Deadwater. *Nmbd* 5A **120**
Deaf Hill. *Dur* 1A **106**
Deal. *Kent* 5H **41**
Dean. *Cumb* 2B **102**
Dean. *Devn* 2G **19** (nr. Combe Martin)
Dean. *Devn* 2H **19** (nr. Lynton)
Dean. *Dors* 1E **15**
Dean. *Hants* 1D **16** (nr. Bishop's Waltham)
Dean. *Hants* 3C **24** (nr. Winchester)
Dean. *Oxon* 3B **50**
Dean. *Som* 2B **22**
Dean Bank. *Dur* 1F **105**
Deanburnhaugh. *Bord* 3F **119**
Dean Cross. *Devn* 2F **19**
Deane. *Hants* 1D **24**
Deanich Lodge. *High* 5A **164**
Deanland. *Dors* 1E **15**
Deanlane End. *W Sus* 1F **17**
Dean Park. *Shrp* 4H **59**
Dean Prior. *Devn* 2D **8**
Dean Row. *Ches E* 2C **84**
Deans. *W Lot* 3D **128**
Deanscales. *Cumb* 2B **102**
Deanshanger. *Nptn* 2F **51**
Deanston. *Stir* 3G **135**
Dearham. *Cumb* 1B **102**
Dearne *S Yor* 4E **93**
Dearne Valley. *S Yor* 4D **93**
Debach. *Suff* 5E **67**
Debden. *Essx* 2F **53**
Debden Green. *Essx* 1F **39** (nr. Loughton)
Debden Green. *Essx* 2F **53** (nr. Saffron Walden)
Debenham. *Suff* 4D **66**
Dechmont. *W Lot* 2D **128**
Deddington. *Oxon* 2C **50**
Dedham. *Essx* 2D **54**
Dedham Heath. *Essx* 2D **54**
Deebank. *Abers* 4D **152**
Deene. *Nptn* 1G **63**
Deenethorpe. *Nptn* 1G **63**
Deepcar. *S Yor* 1G **85**
Deepcut. *Surr* 5A **38**
Deepdale. *Cumb* 1G **97**
Deepdale. *N Lin* 3D **94**
Deepdale. *N Yor* 2A **98**
Deeping Gate. *Pet* 5A **76**
Deeping St James. *Linc* 5A **76**
Deeping St Nicholas. *Linc* 4B **76**
Deerhill. *Mor* 3B **160**
Deerhurst. *Glos* 3D **48**
Deerhurst Walton. *Glos* 3D **49**
Deerness. *Orkn* 7E **172**
Defford. *Worc* 1E **49**
Defynnog. *Powy* 3C **46**
Deganwy. *Cnwy* 3G **81**
Deighton. *N Yor* 4A **106**
Deighton. *W Yor* 3B **92**
Deighton. *York* 5A **100**
Deiniolen. *Gwyn* 4E **81**
Delabole. *Corn* 4A **10**
Delamere. *Ches W* 4H **83**
Delfour. *High* 3C **150**
Dellieture. *High* 5E **159**
Dell, The. *Suff* 1G **67**
Delly End. *Oxon* 4B **50**
Delny. *High* 1B **158**
Delph. *G Man* 4H **91**
Delves. *Dur* 5E **115**
Delves, The. *W Mid* 1E **61**
Delvin End. *Essx* 2A **54**
Dembleby. *Linc* 2H **75**
Demelza. *Corn* 2D **6**
Denaby Main. *S Yor* 1B **86**
Denbeath. *Fife* 4F **137**
Denbigh. *Den* 4C **82**
Denbury. *Devn* 2E **9**
Denby. *Derbs* 1A **74**
Denby Common. *Derbs* 1B **74**
Denby Dale. *W Yor* 4C **92**
Denchworth. *Oxon* 2B **36**
Dendron. *Cumb* 2B **96**
Deneside. *Dur* 5H **115**
Denford. *Nptn* 3G **63**
Dengie. *Essx* 5C **54**
Denham. *Buck* 2B **38**
Denham. *Suff* 4G **65** (nr. Bury St Edmunds)
Denham. *Suff* 3D **66** (nr. Eye)
Denham Green. *Buck* 2B **38**
Denham Street. *Suff* 3D **66**
Denhead. *Abers* 5G **161** (nr. Ellon)
Denhead. *Abers* 3G **161** (nr. Strichen)
Denhead. *Fife* 2G **137**
Denholm. *Bord* 3H **119**
Denholme. *W Yor* 1A **92**
Denholme Clough. *W Yor* 1A **92**
Denholme Gate. *W Yor* 1A **92**
Denio. *Gwyn* 2C **68**
Denmead. *Hants* 1E **17**
Dennington. *Suff* 4E **67**
Denny. *Falk* 1B **128**
Denny End. *Cambs* 4D **65**
Dennyloanhead. *Falk* 1B **128**
Den of Lindores. *Fife* 2E **137**
Denshaw. *G Man* 3H **91**
Denside. *Abers* 4F **153**
Densole. *Kent* 1G **29**
Denston. *Suff* 5G **65**
Denstone. *Staf* 1F **73**
Denstroude. *Kent* 4F **41**
Dent. *Cumb* 1G **97**
Den, The. *N Ayr* 4E **127**
Denton. *Cambs* 2A **64**
Denton. *Darl* 3F **105**
Denton. *E Sus* 5F **27**
Denton. *G Man* 1D **84**
Denton. *Kent* 1G **29**
Denton. *Linc* 2F **75**
Denton. *Norf* 2E **67**
Denton. *Nptn* 5F **63**
Denton. *N Yor* 5D **98**
Denton. *Oxon* 5D **50**
Denver. *Norf* 5F **77**
Denwick. *Nmbd* 3G **121**
Deopham. *Norf* 5C **78**
Deopham Green. *Norf* 1C **66**
Depden. *Suff* 5G **65**
Depden Green. *Suff* 5G **65**
Deptford. *G Lon* 3E **39**
Deptford. *Wilts* 3F **23**
Derby. *Derb* 2A **74**
Derbyhaven. *IOM* 5B **108**
Derculich. *Per* 3F **143**
Dereham. *Norf* 4B **78**
Deri. *Cphy* 5E **47**
Derril. *Devn* 2D **10**
Derringstone. *Kent* 1G **29**
Derrington. *Shrp* 1A **60**
Derrington. *Staf* 3C **72**
Derriton. *Devn* 2D **10**
Derryguaig. *Arg* 5F **139**
Derry Hill. *Wilts* 4E **35**
Derrythorpe. *N Lin* 4B **94**
Dersingham. *Norf* 2F **77**
Dervaig. *Arg* 3F **139**
Derwen. *Den* 5C **82**
Derwen Gam. *Cdgn* 5D **56**
Derwenlas. *Powy* 1G **57**
Desborough. *Nptn* 2F **63**
Desford. *Leics* 5B **74**
Detchant. *Nmbd* 1E **121**
Dethick. *Derbs* 5H **85**
Detling. *Kent* 5B **40**
Deuchar. *Ang* 2D **144**
Deuddwr. *Powy* 4E **71**
Devauden. *Mon* 2H **33**
Devil's Bridge. *Cdgn* 3G **57**
Devitts Green. *Warw* 1G **61**
Devizes. *Wilts* 5F **35**
Devonport. *Plym* 3A **8**
Devonside. *Clac* 4B **136**
Devoran. *Corn* 5B **6**
Dewartown. *Midl* 3G **129**
Dewlish. *Dors* 3C **14**
Dewsbury. *W Yor* 2C **92**
Dewshall Court. *Here* 2H **47**
Dexbeer. *Devn* 2C **10**
Dhoon. *IOM* 3D **108**
Dhoor. *IOM* 2D **108**
Dhowin. *IOM* 1D **108**
Dial Green. *W Sus* 3A **26**
Dial Post. *W Sus* 4C **26**
Dibberford. *Dors* 2H **13**
Dibden. *Hants* 2C **16**
Dibden Purlieu. *Hants* 2C **16**
Dickleburgh. *Norf* 2D **66**
Didbrook. *Glos* 2F **49**
Didcot. *Oxon* 2D **36**
Diddington. *Cambs* 4A **64**
Diddlebury. *Shrp* 2H **59**
Didley. *Here* 2H **47**
Didling. *W Sus* 1G **17**
Didmarton. *Glos* 3D **34**
Didsbury. *G Man* 1C **84**
Didworthy. *Devn* 2C **8**
Digby. *Linc* 5H **87**
Digg. *High* 2D **154**
Diggle. *G Man* 4A **92**
Digmoor. *Lanc* 4C **90**
Digswell. *Herts* 4C **52**
Dihewyd. *Cdgn* 5D **57**
Dilham. *Norf* 3F **79**
Dilhorne. *Staf* 1D **72**
Dillarburn. *S Lan* 5B **128**
Dillington. *Cambs* 4A **64**
Dilston. *Nmbd* 3C **114**
Dilton Marsh. *Wilts* 2D **22**
Dilwyn. *Here* 5G **59**
Dimmer. *Som* 3B **22**
Dimple. *G Man* 3F **91**
Dinas. *Carm* 1G **43**
Dinas. *Gwyn* 5D **81** (nr. Caernarfon)
Dinas. *Gwyn* 2B **68** (nr. Tudweiliog)
Dinas Cross. *Pemb* 1E **43**
Dinas Dinlle. *Gwyn* 5D **80**
Dinas Mawddwy. *Gwyn* 4A **70**
Dinas Powys. *V Glam* 4E **33**
Dinbych. *Den* 4C **82**
Dinbych-y-Pysgod. *Pemb* 4F **43**
Dinckley. *Lanc* 1E **91**
Dinder. *Som* 2A **22**
Dinedor. *Here* 2A **48**
Dinedor Cross. *Here* 2A **48**
Dingestow. *Mon* 4H **47**
Dingle. *Mers* 2F **83**
Dingleden. *Kent* 2C **28**
Dingleton. *Bord* 1H **119**
Dingley. *Nptn* 2E **63**
Dingwall. *High* 3H **157**
Dinmael. *Cnwy* 1C **70**
Dinnet. *Abers* 4B **152**
Dinnington. *Som* 1H **13**
Dinnington. *S Yor* 2C **86**
Dinnington. *Tyne* 2F **115**
Dinorwig. *Gwyn* 4E **81**
Dinton. *Buck* 4F **51**
Dinton. *Wilts* 3F **23**
Dinworthy. *Devn* 1D **10**
Dipley. *Hants* 1F **25**
Dippen. *Arg* 2B **122**
Dippenhall. *Surr* 2G **25**
Dippertown. *Devn* 4E **11**
Dippin. *N Ayr* 3E **123**
Dipple. *S Ayr* 4B **116**
Diptford. *Devn* 3D **8**
Dipton. *Dur* 4E **115**
Dirleton. *E Lot* 1B **130**
Dirt Pot. *Nmbd* 5B **114**
Discoed. *Powy* 4E **59**
Diseworth. *Leics* 3B **74**
Dishforth. *N Yor* 2F **99**
Disley. *Ches E* 2D **85**
Diss. *Norf* 3D **66**
Disserth. *Powy* 5C **58**
Distington. *Cumb* 2B **102**
Ditchampton. *Wilts* 3F **23**
Ditcheat. *Som* 3B **22**
Ditchingham. *Norf* 1F **67**
Ditchling. *E Sus* 4E **27**
Ditteridge. *Wilts* 5D **34**
Dittisham. *Devn* 3E **9**
Ditton. *Hal* 2G **83**
Ditton. *Kent* 5B **40**
Ditton Green. *Cambs* 5F **65**
Ditton Priors. *Shrp* 2A **60**
Divach. *High* 1G **149**
Dixonfield. *High* 2D **168**
Dixton. *Glos* 2E **49**
Dixton. *Mon* 4A **48**
Dizzard. *Corn* 3B **10**
Dobcross. *G Man* 4H **91**
Dobs Hill. *Flin* 4F **83**
Dobson's Bridge. *Shrp* 2G **71**
Dobwalls. *Corn* 2G **7**
Doccombe. *Devn* 4A **12**
Dochgarroch. *High* 4A **158**
Docking. *Norf* 2G **77**
Docklow. *Here* 5H **59**
Dockray. *Cumb* 2E **103**
Doc Penfro. *Pemb* 4D **42**
Dodbrooke. *Devn* 4D **8**
Doddenham. *Worc* 5B **60**
Doddinghurst. *Essx* 1G **39**
Doddington. *Cambs* 1C **64**
Doddington. *Kent* 5D **40**
Doddington. *Linc* 4G **87**
Doddington. *Nmbd* 1D **121**
Doddington. *Shrp* 3A **60**
Doddiscombsleigh. *Devn* 4B **12**
Doddshill. *Norf* 2G **77**
Dodford. *Nptn* 4D **62**
Dodford. *Worc* 3D **60**
Dodington. *Som* 2E **21**
Dodington. *S Glo* 4C **34**
Dodleston. *Ches W* 4F **83**
Dods Leigh. *Staf* 2E **73**
Dodworth. *S Yor* 4D **92**
Doe Lea. *Derbs* 4B **86**
Dogdyke. *Linc* 5B **88**
Dogmersfield. *Hants* 1F **25**
Dogsthorpe. *Pet* 5B **76**
Dog Village. *Devn* 3C **12**
Dolanog. *Powy* 4C **70**
Dolau. *Powy* 4D **58**
Dolau. *Rhon* 3D **32**
Dolbenmaen. *Gwyn* 1E **69**
Doley. *Staf* 3B **72**
Dol-fach. *Powy* 5B **70** (nr. Llanbrynmair)
Dolfach. *Powy* 3B **58** (nr. Llanidloes)
Dolfor. *Powy* 2D **58**
Dolgarrog. *Cnwy* 4G **81**
Dolgellau. *Gwyn* 4G **69**
Dolgoch. *Gwyn* 5F **69**
Dol-gran. *Carm* 2E **45**
Dolhelfa. *Powy* 3B **58**
Doll. *High* 3F **165**
Dollar. *Clac* 4B **136**
Dolley Green. *Powy* 4E **59**
Dollwen. *Cdgn* 2F **57**
Dolphin. *Flin* 3D **82**
Dolphingstone. *E Lot* 2G **129**
Dolphinholme. *Lanc* 4E **97**
Dolphinton. *S Lan* 5E **129**
Dolton. *Devn* 1F **11**
Dolwen. *Cnwy* 3A **82**
Dolwyddelan. *Cnwy* 5G **81**
Dol-y-Bont. *Cdgn* 2F **57**
Dolyhir. *Powy* 5E **59**
Domgay. *Powy* 4E **71**
Doncaster. *S Yor* 4F **93**
Donhead St Andrew. *Wilts* 4E **23**
Donhead St Mary. *Wilts* 4E **23**
Doniford. *Som* 2D **20**
Donington. *Linc* 2B **76**
Donington. *Shrp* 5C **72**
Donington Eaudike. *Linc* 2B **76**
Donington le Heath. *Leics* 4B **74**
Donington on Bain. *Linc* 2B **88**
Donington South Ing. *Linc* 2B **76**
Donisthorpe. *Leics* 4H **73**
Donkey Street. *Kent* 2F **29**
Donkey Town. *Surr* 4A **38**
Donna Nook. *Linc* 1D **88**
Donnington. *Glos* 3G **49**
Donnington. *Here* 2C **48**
Donnington. *Shrp* 5H **71**
Donnington. *Telf* 4B **72**
Donnington. *W Ber* 5C **36**
Donnington. *W Sus* 2G **17**
Donyatt. *Som* 1G **13**
Doomsday Green. *W Sus* 2C **26**
Doonfoot. *S Ayr* 3C **116**
Doonholm. *S Ayr* 3C **116**
Dorback Lodge. *High* 2E **151**
Dorchester. *Dors* 3B **14**
Dorchester on Thames. *Oxon* 2D **36**
Dordon. *Warw* 5G **73**
Dore. *S Yor* 2H **85**
Dores. *High* 5H **157**
Dorking. *Surr* 1C **26**
Dorking Tye. *Suff* 2C **54**
Dormansland. *Surr* 1F **27**
Dormans Park. *Surr* 1E **27**
Dormanstown. *Red C* 2C **106**
Dormington. *Here* 1A **48**
Dormston. *Worc* 5D **61**
Dorn. *Glos* 2H **49**
Dorney. *Buck* 3A **38**
Dornie. *High* 1A **148**
Dornoch. *High* 5E **165**
Dornock. *Dum* 3D **112**
Dorrery. *High* 3C **168**
Dorridge. *W Mid* 3F **61**
Dorrington. *Linc* 5H **87**
Dorrington. *Shrp* 5G **71**
Dorsington. *Warw* 1G **49**
Dorstone. *Here* 1G **47**
Dorton. *Buck* 4E **51**
Dotham. *IOA* 3C **80**
Dottery. *Dors* 3H **13**
Doublebois. *Corn* 2F **7**
Dougarie. *N Ayr* 2C **122**
Doughton. *Glos* 2D **35**
Douglas. *IOM* 4C **108**
Douglas. *S Lan* 1H **117**
Douglastown. *Ang* 4D **144**
Douglas Water. *S Lan* 1A **118**
Doulting. *Som* 2B **22**
Dounby. *Orkn* 5B **172**
Doune. *High* 3C **150** (nr. Kingussie)
Doune. *High* 3B **164** (nr. Lairg)
Doune. *Stir* 3G **135**
Dounie. *High* 4C **164** (nr. Bonar Bridge)
Dounie. *High* 5D **164** (nr. Tain)

Dounreay. *High* 2B 168
Doura. *N Ayr* 5E 127
Dousland. *Devn* 2B 8
Dovaston. *Shrp* 3F 71
Dove Holes. *Derbs* 3E 85
Dovenby. *Cumb* 1B 102
Dover. *Kent* 1H 29
Dovercourt. *Essx* 2F 55
Doverdale. *Worc* 4C 60
Doveridge. *Derbs* 2F 73
Doversgreen. *Surr* 1D 26
Dowally. *Per* 4H 143
Dowbridge. *Lanc* 1C 90
Dowdeswell. *Glos* 4F 49
Dowlais. *Mer T* 5D 46
Dowland. *Devn* 1F 11
Dowlands. *Devn* 3F 13
Dowles. *Worc* 3B 60
Dowlesgreen. *Wok* 5G 37
Dowlish Wake. *Som* 1G 13
Downall Green. *Mers* 4D 90
Down Ampney. *Glos* 2F 35
Downderry. *Corn* 3H 7
(nr. Looe)
Downderry. *Corn* 3D 6
(nr. St Austell)
Downe. *G Lon* 4F 39
Downend. *IOW* 4D 16
Downend. *S Glo* 4B 34
Downend. *W Ber* 4C 36
Down Field. *Cambs* 3F 65
Downfield. *D'dee* 5C 144
Downgate. *Corn* 5D 10
(nr. Kelly Bray)
Downgate. *Corn* 5C 10
(nr. Upton Cross)
Downham. *Essx* 1B 40
Downham. *Lanc* 5G 97
Downham. *Nmbd* 1C 120
Downham Market. *Norf* 5F 77
Down Hatherley. *Glos* 3D 48
Downhead. *Som* 2B 22
(nr. Frome)
Downhead. *Som* 4A 22
(nr. Yeovil)
Downholland Cross. *Lanc* 4B 90
Downholme. *N Yor* 5E 105
Downies. *Abers* 4G 153
Downley. *Buck* 2G 37
Down St Mary. *Devn* 2H 11
Downside. *Som* 1B 22
(nr. Chilcompton)
Downside. *Som* 2B 22
(nr. Shepton Mallet)
Downside. *Surr* 5C 38
Down, The. *Shrp* 1A 60
Down Thomas. *Devn* 3B 8
Downton. *Hants* 3A 16
Downton. *Wilts* 4G 23
Downton on the Rock. *Here* 3G 59
Dowsby. *Linc* 3A 76
Dowsdale. *Linc* 4B 76
Dowthwaitehead. *Cumb* 2E 103
Doxey. *Staf* 3D 72
Doxford. *Nmbd* 2F 121
Doynton. *S Glo* 4C 34
Drabblegate. *Norf* 3E 78
Draethen. *Cphy* 3F 33
Draffan. *S Lan* 5A 128
Dragonby. *N Lin* 3C 94
Dragons Green. *W Sus* 3C 26
Drakelow. *Worc* 2C 60
Drakemyre. *N Ayr* 4D 126
Drakes Broughton. *Worc* 1E 49
Drakes Cross. *Worc* 3E 61
Drakewalls. *Corn* 5E 11
Draughton. *Nptn* 3E 63
Draughton. *N Yor* 4C 98
Drax. *N Yor* 2G 93
Draycot. *Oxon* 5E 51
Draycote. *Warw* 4B 62
Draycot Foliat. *Swin* 4G 35
Draycott. *Derbs* 2B 74
Draycott. *Glos* 2G 49

Draycott. *Shrp* 1C 60
Draycott. *Som* 1H 21
(nr. Cheddar)
Draycott. *Som* 4A 22
(nr. Yeovil)
Draycott. *Worc* 1D 48
Draycott in the Clay. *Staf* 3F 73
Draycott in the Moors. *Staf* 1D 73
Drayford. *Devn* 1A 12
Drayton. *Leics* 1F 63
Drayton. *Linc* 2B 76
Drayton. *Norf* 4D 78
Drayton. *Nptn* 4C 62
Drayton. *Oxon* 2C 36
(nr. Abingdon)
Drayton. *Oxon* 1C 50
(nr. Banbury)
Drayton. *Port* 2E 17
Drayton. *Som* 4H 21
Drayton. *Warw* 5F 61
Drayton. *Worc* 3D 60
Drayton Bassett. *Staf* 5F 73
Drayton Beauchamp. *Buck* 4H 51
Drayton Parslow. *Buck* 3G 51
Drayton St Leonard. *Oxon* 2D 36
Drebley. *N Yor* 4C 98
Dreenhill. *Pemb* 3D 42
Drefach. *Carm* 4F 45
(nr. Meidrim)
Drefach. *Carm* 2D 44
(nr. Newcastle Emlyn)
Drefach. *Carm* 2G 43
(nr. Tumble)
Drefach. *Cdgn* 1E 45
Dreghorn. *N Ayr* 1C 116
Drellingore. *Kent* 1G 29
Drem. *E Lot* 2B 130
Dreumasdal. *W Isl* 5C 170
Drewsteignton. *Devn* 3H 11
Driby. *Linc* 3C 88
Driffield. *E Yor* 4E 101
Driffield. *Glos* 2F 35
Drift. *Corn* 4B 4
Drigg. *Cumb* 5B 102
Drighlington. *W Yor* 2C 92
Drimnin. *High* 3G 139
Drimpton. *Dors* 2H 13
Dringhoe. *E Yor* 4F 101
Drinisiadar. *W Isl* 8D 171
Drinkstone. *Suff* 4B 66
Drinkstone Green. *Suff* 4B 66
Drointon. *Staf* 3E 73
Droitwich Spa. *Worc* 4C 60
Droman. *High* 3B 166
Dron. *Per* 2D 136
Dronfield. *Derbs* 3A 86
Dronfield Woodhouse. *Derbs* 3H 85
Drongan. *E Ayr* 3D 116
Dronley. *Ang* 5C 144
Droop. *Dors* 2C 14
Drope. *V Glam* 4E 32
Droxford. *Hants* 1E 16
Droylsden. *G Man* 1C 84
Druggers End. *Worc* 2C 48
Druid. *Den* 1C 70
Druidston. *Pemb* 3C 42
Druim. *High* 3D 158
Druimarbin. *High* 1E 141
Druim Fhearna. *High* 2E 147
Druimindarroch. *High* 5E 147
Drum. *Per* 3C 136
Drumbeg. *High* 5B 166
Drumblade. *Abers* 4C 160
Drumbuie. *Dum* 1C 110
Drumbuie. *High* 5G 155
Drumburgh. *Cumb* 4D 112
Drumchapel. *Glas* 2G 127
Drumchardine. *High* 4H 157
Drumchork. *High* 5C 162
Drumclog. *S Lan* 1F 117
Drumeldrie. *Fife* 3G 137
Drumelzier. *Bord* 1D 118

Drumfearn. *High* 2E 147
Drumgask. *High* 4A 150
Drumgelloch. *N Lan* 3A 128
Drumguish. *High* 4B 150
Drumin. *Mor* 5F 159
Drumindorsair. *High* 4G 157
Drumlamford House. *S Ayr* 2H 109
Drumlasie. *Abers* 3D 152
Drumlemble. *Arg* 4A 122
Drumlithie. *Abers* 5E 153
Drummoddie. *Dum* 5A 110
Drummond. *High* 2A 158
Drummore. *Dum* 5E 109
Drummuir. *Mor* 4A 160
Drumnadrochit. *High* 5H 157
Drumnagorrach. *Mor* 3C 160
Drumoak. *Abers* 4E 153
Drumrunie. *High* 3F 163
Drumry. *W Dun* 2G 127
Drums. *Abers* 1G 153
Drumsleet. *Dum* 2G 111
Drumsmittal. *High* 4A 158
Drums of Park. *Abers* 3C 160
Drumsturdy. *Ang* 5D 145
Drumtochty Castle. *Abers* 5D 152
Drumuie. *High* 4D 154
Drumuillie. *High* 1D 150
Drumvaich. *Stir* 3F 135
Drumwhindle. *Abers* 5G 161
Drunkendub. *Ang* 4F 145
Drury. *Flin* 4E 83
Drury Square. *Norf* 4B 78
Drybeck. *Cumb* 3H 103
Drybridge. *Mor* 2B 160
Drybridge. *N Ayr* 1C 116
Drybrook. *Glos* 4B 48
Drybrook. *Here* 4A 48
Dryburgh. *Bord* 1H 119
Dry Doddington. *Linc* 1F 75
Dry Drayton. *Cambs* 4C 64
Drym. *Corn* 3D 4
Drymen. *Stir* 1F 127
Drymuir. *Abers* 4G 161
Drynachan Lodge. *High* 5C 158
Drynie Park. *High* 3H 157
Drynoch. *High* 5D 154
Dry Sandford. *Oxon* 5C 50
Dryslwyn. *Carm* 3F 45
Dry Street. *Essx* 2A 40
Dryton. *Shrp* 5H 71
Dubford. *Abers* 2E 161
Dubiton. *Abers* 3D 160
Dubton. *Ang* 3E 145
Duchally. *High* 2A 164
Duck End. *Essx* 3G 53
Duckington. *Ches W* 5G 83
Ducklington. *Oxon* 5B 50
Duckmanton. *Derbs* 3B 86
Duck Street. *Hants* 2B 24
Dudbridge. *Glos* 5D 48
Duddenhoe End. *Essx* 2E 53
Duddingston. *Edin* 2F 129
Duddington. *Nptn* 5G 75
Duddleswell. *E Sus* 3F 27
Duddo. *Nmbd* 5F 131
Duddon. *Ches W* 4H 83
Duddon Bridge. *Cumb* 1A 96
Dudleston. *Shrp* 2F 71
Dudleston Heath. *Shrp* 2F 71
Dudley. *Tyne* 2F 115
Dudley. *W Mid* 2D 60
Dudston. *Shrp* 1E 59
Dudwells. *Pemb* 2D 42
Duffield. *Derbs* 1H 73
Dufftown. *Mor* 5F 159
Duffus. *Mor* 2F 159
Dufton. *Cumb* 2H 103
Duggleby. *N Yor* 3C 100
Duirinish. *High* 5G 155
Duisdalemore. *High* 2E 147
Duisdeil Mòr. *High* 2E 147
Duisky. *High* 1E 141

Dukesfield. *Nmbd* 4C 114
Dukestown. *Blae* 5E 47
Dukinfield. *G Man* 1D 84
Dulas. *IOA* 2D 81
Dulcote. *Som* 2A 22
Dulford. *Devn* 2D 12
Dull. *Per* 4F 143
Dullatur. *N Lan* 2A 128
Dullingham. *Cambs* 5F 65
Dullingham Ley. *Cambs* 5F 65
Dulnain Bridge. *High* 1D 151
Duloe. *Bed* 4A 64
Duloe. *Corn* 3G 7
Dulverton. *Som* 4C 20
Dulwich. *G Lon* 3E 39
Dumbarton. *W Dun* 2F 127
Dumbleton. *Glos* 2F 49
Dumcrieff. *Dum* 5C 118
Dumfin. *Arg* 1E 127
Dumfries. *Dum* 2A 112
Dumgoyne. *Stir* 1G 127
Dummer. *Hants* 2D 24
Dumpford. *W Sus* 4G 25
Dun. *Ang* 2F 145
Dunagoil. *Arg* 4B 126
Dunalastair. *Per* 3E 142
Dunan. *High* 1D 147
Dunball. *Som* 2G 21
Dunbar. *E Lot* 2C 130
Dunbeath. *High* 5D 168
Dunbeg. *Arg* 5C 140
Dunblane. *Stir* 3G 135
Dunbog. *Fife* 2E 137
Dunbridge. *Hants* 4B 24
Duncanston. *Abers* 1C 152
Duncanston. *High* 3H 157
Dunchideock. *Devn* 4B 12
Dunchurch. *Warw* 3B 62
Duncote. *Nptn* 5D 62
Duncow. *Dum* 1A 112
Duncrievie. *Per* 3D 136
Duncton. *W Sus* 4A 26
Dundee. *D'dee* 5D 144
Dundee Airport. *D'dee* 1F 137
Dundon. *Som* 3H 21
Dundonald. *S Ayr* 1C 116
Dundonnell. *High* 5E 163
Dundraw. *Cumb* 5D 112
Dundreggan. *High* 2F 149
Dundrennan. *Dum* 5E 111
Dundridge. *Hants* 1D 16
Dundry. *N Som* 5A 34
Dunecht. *Abers* 3E 153
Dunfermline. *Fife* 1D 129
Dunford Bridge. *S Yor* 4B 92
Dungate. *Kent* 5D 40
Dunge. *Wilts* 1D 23
Dungeness. *Kent* 4E 29
Dungworth. *S Yor* 2G 85
Dunham-on-the-Hill. *Ches W* 3G 83
Dunham-on-Trent. *Notts* 3F 87
Dunhampton. *Worc* 4C 60
Dunham Town. *G Man* 2B 84
Dunham Woodhouses. *G Man* 2B 84
Dunholme. *Linc* 3H 87
Dunino. *Fife* 2H 137
Dunipace. *Falk* 1B 128
Dunira. *Per* 1G 135
Dunkeld. *Per* 4H 143
Dunkerton. *Bath* 1C 22
Dunkeswell. *Devn* 2E 13
Dunkeswick. *N Yor* 5F 99
Dunkirk. *Kent* 5E 41
Dunkirk. *S Glo* 3C 34
Dunkirk. *Staf* 5C 84
Dunkirk. *Wilts* 5E 35
Dunk's Green. *Kent* 5H 39
Dunlappie. *Ang* 2E 145
Dunley. *Hants* 1C 24
Dunley. *Worc* 4B 60
Dunlop. *E Ayr* 5F 127
Dunmaglass Lodge. *High* 1H 149
Dunmore. *Arg* 3F 125

Dunmore. *Falk* 1B 128
Dunmore. *High* 4H 157
Dunnet. *High* 1E 169
Dunnichen. *Ang* 4E 145
Dunning. *Per* 2C 136
Dunnington. *E Yor* 4F 101
Dunnington. *Warw* 5E 61
Dunnington. *York* 4A 100
Dunningwell. *Cumb* 1A 96
Dunnockshaw. *Lanc* 2G 91
Dunoon. *Arg* 2C 126
Dunphail. *Mor* 4E 159
Dunragit. *Dum* 4G 109
Dunrostan. *Arg* 1F 125
Duns. *Bord* 4D 130
Dunsby. *Linc* 3A 76
Dunscar. *G Man* 3F 91
Dunscore. *Dum* 1F 111
Dunscroft. *S Yor* 4G 93
Dunsdale. *Red C* 3D 106
Dunsden Green. *Oxon* 4F 37
Dunsfold. *Surr* 2B 26
Dunsford. *Devn* 4B 12
Dunshalt. *Fife* 2E 137
Dunshillock. *Abers* 4G 161
Dunsley. *N Yor* 3F 107
Dunsley. *Staf* 2C 60
Dunsmore. *Buck* 5G 51
Dunsop Bridge. *Lanc* 4F 97
Dunstable. *C Beds* 3A 52
Dunstall. *Staf* 3E 73
Dunstall. *Staf* 3F 73
Dunstall Green. *Suff* 4G 65
Dunstall Hill. *W Mid* 1D 60
Dunstan. *Nmbd* 3G 121
Dunster. *Som* 2C 20
Duns Tew. *Oxon* 3C 50
Dunston. *Linc* 4H 87
Dunston. *Norf* 5E 79
Dunston. *Staf* 4D 72
Dunston. *Tyne* 3F 115
Dunstone. *Devn* 3B 8
Dunston Heath. *Staf* 4D 72
Dunsville. *S Yor* 4G 93
Dunswell. *E Yor* 1D 94
Dunsyre. *S Lan* 5D 128
Dunterton. *Devn* 5D 11
Duntisbourne Abbots. *Glos* 5E 49
Duntisbourne Leer. *Glos* 5E 49
Duntisbourne Rouse. *Glos* 5E 49
Duntish. *Dors* 2B 14
Duntocher. *W Dun* 2F 127
Dunton. *Buck* 3G 51
Dunton. *C Beds* 1C 52
Dunton. *Norf* 2A 78
Dunton Bassett. *Leics* 1C 62
Dunton Green. *Kent* 5G 39
Dunton Patch. *Norf* 2A 78
Duntulm. *High* 1D 154
Dunure. *S Ayr* 3B 116
Dunvant. *Swan* 3E 31
Dunvegan. *High* 4B 154
Dunwich. *Suff* 3G 67
Dunwood. *Staf* 5D 84
Durdar. *Cumb* 4F 113
Durgates. *E Sus* 2H 27
Durham. *Dur* 5F 115
Durham Tees Valley Airport.
Darl 3A 106
Durisdeer. *Dum* 4A 118
Durisdeermill. *Dum* 4A 118
Durkar. *W Yor* 3D 92
Durleigh. *Som* 3F 21
Durley. *Hants* 1D 16
Durley. *Wilts* 5H 35
Durley Street. *Hants* 1D 16
Durlow Common. *Here* 2B 48
Durnamuck. *High* 4E 163
Durness. *High* 2E 166
Durno. *Abers* 1E 152
Durns Town. *Hants* 3A 16
Duror. *High* 3D 141
Durran. *Arg* 3G 133
Durran. *High* 2D 169

Durrant Green—Easton Maudit

Durrant Green. *Kent* 2C 28
Durrants. *Hants* 1F 17
Durrington. *W Sus* 5C 26
Durrington. *Wilts* 2G 23
Dursley. *Glos* 2C 34
Dursley Cross. *Glos* 4B 48
Durston. *Som* 4F 21
Durweston. *Dors* 2D 14
Duston. *Nptn* 4E 62
Duthil. *High* 1D 150
Dutlas. *Powy* 3E 58
Duton Hill. *Essx* 3G 53
Dutson. *Corn* 4D 10
Dutton. *Ches W* 3H 83
Duxford. *Cambs* 1E 53
Duxford. *Oxon* 2B 36
Dwygyfylchi. *Cnwy* 3G 81
Dwyran. *IOA* 4D 80
Dyce. *Aber* 2F 153
Dyffryn. *B'end* 2B 32
Dyffryn. *Carm* 2H 43
Dyffryn. *Pemb* 1D 42
Dyffryn. *V Glam* 4D 32
Dyffryn Ardudwy. *Gwyn* 3E 69
Dyffryn Castell. *Cdgn* 2G 57
Dyffryn Ceidrych. *Carm* 3H 45
Dyffryn Cellwen. *Neat* 5B 46
Dyke. *Linc* 3A 76
Dyke. *Mor* 3D 159
Dykehead. *Ang* 2C 144
Dykehead. *N Lan* 3B 128
Dykehead. *Stir* 4E 135
Dykend. *Ang* 3B 144
Dykesfield. *Cumb* 4E 112
Dylife. *Powy* 1A 58
Dymchurch. *Kent* 3F 29
Dymock. *Glos* 2C 48
Dyrham. *S Glo* 4C 34
Dysart. *Fife* 4F 137
Dyserth. *Den* 3C 82

E

Eachwick. *Nmbd* 2E 115
Eadar Dha Fhadhail. *W Isl* 4C 171
Eagland Hill. *Lanc* 5D 96
Eagle. *Linc* 4F 87
Eagle Barnsdale. *Linc* 4F 87
Eagle Moor. *Linc* 4F 87
Eaglescliffe. *Stoc T* 3B 106
Eaglesfield. *Cumb* 2B 102
Eaglesfield. *Dum* 2D 112
Eaglesham. *E Ren* 4G 127
Eaglethorpe. *Nptn* 1H 63
Eagley. *G Man* 3F 91
Eairy. *IOM* 4B 108
Eakley Lanes. *Mil* 5F 63
Eakring. *Notts* 4D 86
Ealand. *N Lin* 3A 94
Ealing. *G Lon* 2C 38
Eallabus. *Arg* 3B 124
Eals. *Nmbd* 4H 113
Eamont Bridge. *Cumb* 2G 103
Earby. *Lanc* 5B 98
Earcroft. *Bkbn* 2E 91
Eardington. *Shrp* 1B 60
Eardisland. *Here* 5G 59
Eardisley. *Here* 1G 47
Eardiston. *Shrp* 3F 71
Eardiston. *Worc* 4A 60
Earith. *Cambs* 3C 64
Earlais. *High* 2C 154
Earle. *Nmbd* 2D 121
Earlesfield. *Linc* 2G 75
Earlestown. *Mers* 1H 83
Earley. *Wok* 4F 37
Earlham. *Norf* 5D 78
Earlish. *High* 2C 154
Earls Barton. *Nptn* 4F 63
Earls Colne. *Essx* 3B 54
Earls Common. *Worc* 5D 60
Earl's Croome. *Worc* 1D 48
Earlsdon. *W Mid* 3H 61
Earlsferry. *Fife* 3G 137
Earlsford. *Abers* 5F 161
Earl's Green. *Suff* 4C 66
Earlsheaton. *W Yor* 2C 92
Earl Shilton. *Leics* 1B 62
Earl Soham. *Suff* 4E 67
Earl Sterndale. *Derbs* 4E 85
Earlston. *E Ayr* 1D 116
Earlston. *Bord* 1H 119
Earl Stonham. *Suff* 5D 66
Earlstoun. *Dum* 1D 110
Earlswood. *Mon* 2H 33
Earlswood. *Warw* 3F 61
Earlyvale. *Bord* 4F 129
Earnley. *W Sus* 3G 17
Earsairidh. *W Isl* 9C 170
Earsdon. *Tyne* 2G 115
Earsham. *Norf* 2F 67
Earsham Street. *Suff* 3E 67
Earswick. *York* 4A 100
Eartham. *W Sus* 5A 26
Earthcott Green. *S Glo* 3B 34
Easby. *N Yor* 4C 106
(nr. Great Ayton)
Easby. *N Yor* 4E 105
(nr. Richmond)
Easdale. *Arg* 2E 133
Easebourne. *W Sus* 4G 25
Easenhall. *Warw* 3B 62
Eashing. *Surr* 1A 26
Easington. *Buck* 4E 51
Easington. *Dur* 5H 115
Easington. *E Yor* 3G 95
Easington. *Nmbd* 1F 121
Easington. *Oxon* 2C 50
(nr. Banbury)
Easington. *Oxon* 2E 37
(nr. Watlington)
Easington. *Red C* 3E 107
Easington Colliery. *Dur* 5H 115
Easington Lane. *Tyne* 5G 115
Easingwold. *N Yor* 3H 99
Easole Street. *Kent* 5G 41
Eassie. *Ang* 4C 144
Eassie and Nevay. *Ang* 4C 144
East Aberthaw. *V Glam* 5D 32
Eastacombe. *Devn* 4F 19
Eastacott. *Devn* 4G 19
East Allington. *Devn* 4D 8
East Anstey. *Devn* 4B 20
East Anton. *Hants* 2B 24
East Appleton. *N Yor* 5F 105
East Ardsley. *W Yor* 2D 92
East Ashley. *Devn* 1G 11
East Ashling. *W Sus* 2G 17
East Aston. *Hants* 2C 24
East Ayton. *N Yor* 1D 101
East Barkwith. *Linc* 2A 88
East Barnby. *N Yor* 3F 107
East Barnet. *G Lon* 1D 39
East Barns. *E Lot* 2D 130
East Barsham. *Norf* 2B 78
East Beach. *W Sus* 3G 17
East Beckham. *Norf* 1D 78
East Bedfont. *G Lon* 3B 38
East Bennan. *N Ayr* 3D 123
East Bergholt. *Suff* 2D 54
East Bierley. *W Yor* 2B 92
East Blatchington. *E Sus* 5F 27
East Bliney. *Norf* 4B 78
East Bloxworth. *Dors* 3D 15
East Boldre. *Hants* 2B 16
East Bolton. *Nmbd* 3F 121
Eastbourne. *Darl* 3F 105
Eastbourne. *E Sus* 5H 27
East Brent. *Som* 1G 21
East Bridge. *Suff* 4G 67
East Bridgford. *Notts* 1D 74
East Briscoe. *Dur* 3C 104
East Buckland. *Devn* 3G 19
(nr. Barnstaple)
East Buckland. *Devn* 4C 8
(nr. Thurlestone)
East Budleigh. *Devn* 4D 12
Eastburn. *W Yor* 5C 98
East Burnham. *Buck* 2A 38
East Burrafirth. *Shet* 6E 173
East Burton. *Dors* 4D 14
Eastbury. *Herts* 1B 38
Eastbury. *W Ber* 4B 36
East Butsfield. *Dur* 5E 115
East Butterleigh. *Devn* 2C 12
East Butterwick. *N Lin* 4B 94
Eastby. *N Yor* 4C 98
East Calder. *W Lot* 3D 129
East Carleton. *Norf* 5D 78
East Carlton. *Nptn* 2F 63
East Carlton. *W Yor* 5E 98
East Chaldon. *Dors* 4C 14
East Challow. *Oxon* 3B 36
East Charleton. *Devn* 4D 8
East Chelborough. *Dors* 2A 14
East Chiltington. *E Sus* 4E 27
East Chinnock. *Som* 1H 13
East Chisenbury. *Wilts* 1G 23
Eastchurch. *Kent* 3D 40
East Clandon. *Surr* 5B 38
East Claydon. *Buck* 3F 51
East Clevedon. *N Som* 4H 33
East Clyne. *High* 3F 165
East Clyth. *High* 5E 169
East Coker. *Som* 1A 14
Eastcombe. *Glos* 5D 49
East Combe. *Som* 3E 21
East Common. *N Yor* 1G 93
East Compton. *Som* 2B 22
East Cornworthy. *Devn* 3E 9
Eastcote. *G Lon* 2C 38
Eastcote. *Nptn* 5D 62
Eastcote. *W Mid* 3F 61
Eastcott. *Corn* 1C 10
Eastcott. *Wilts* 1F 23
East Cottingwith. *E Yor* 5B 100
Eastcourt. *Wilts* 5H 35
(nr. Pewsey)
Eastcourt. *Wilts* 2E 35
(nr. Tetbury)
East Cowes. *IOW* 3D 16
East Cowick. *E Yor* 2G 93
East Cowton. *N Yor* 4A 106
East Cramlington. *Nmbd* 2F 115
East Cranmore. *Som* 2B 22
East Creech. *Dors* 4E 15
East Croachy. *High* 1A 150
East Dean. *E Sus* 5G 27
East Dean. *Glos* 3B 48
East Dean. *Hants* 4A 24
East Dean. *W Sus* 4A 26
East Down. *Devn* 2G 19
East Drayton. *Notts* 3E 87
East Dundry. *N Som* 5A 34
East Ella. *Hull* 2D 94
East End. *Cambs* 3C 64
East End. *Dors* 3E 15
East End. *E Yor* 4F 101
(nr. Ulrome)
East End. *E Yor* 2F 95
(nr. Withernsea)
East End. *Hants* 3B 16
(nr. Lymington)
East End. *Hants* 5C 36
(nr. Newbury)
East End. *Herts* 3E 53
East End. *Kent* 3D 40
(nr. Minster)
East End. *Kent* 2C 28
(nr. Tenterden)
East End. *N Som* 4H 33
East End. *Oxon* 4B 50
East End. *Som* 1A 22
East End. *Suff* 2E 54
Easter Ardross. *High* 1A 158
Easter Balgedie. *Per* 3D 136
Easter Balmoral. *Abers* 4G 151
Easter Brae. *High* 2A 158
Easter Buckieburn. *Stir* 1A 128
Easter Bush. *Midl* 3F 129
Easter Compton. *S Glo* 3A 34
Easter Fearn. *High* 5D 164
Easter Galcantray. *High* 4C 158
Eastergate. *W Sus* 5A 26
Easterhouse. *Glas* 3H 127
Easter Howgate. *Midl* 3F 129
Easter Kinkell. *High* 3H 157
Easter Lednathie. *Ang* 2C 144
Easter Ogil. *Ang* 2D 144
Easter Ord. *Abers* 3F 153
Easter Quarff. *Shet* 8F 173
Easter Rhynd. *Per* 2D 136
Easter Skeld. *Shet* 7E 173
Easter Suddie. *High* 3A 158
Easterton. *Wilts* 1F 23
Eastertown. *Som* 1G 21
Easter Tulloch. *Abers* 1G 145
East Everleigh. *Wilts* 1H 23
East Farleigh. *Kent* 5B 40
East Farndon. *Nptn* 2E 62
East Ferry. *Linc* 1F 87
Eastfield. *N Lan* 3B 128
(nr. Caldercruix)
Eastfield. *N Lan* 3B 128
(nr. Harthill)
Eastfield. *N Yor* 1E 101
Eastfield. *S Lan* 3H 127
Eastfield Hall. *Nmbd* 4G 121
East Fortune. *E Lot* 2B 130
East Garforth. *W Yor* 1E 93
East Garston. *W Ber* 4B 36
Eastgate. *Dur* 1C 104
Eastgate. *Norf* 3D 78
East Ginge. *Oxon* 3C 36
East Gores. *Essx* 3B 54
East Goscote. *Leics* 4D 74
East Grafton. *Wilts* 5A 36
East Green. *Suff* 5F 65
East Grimstead. *Wilts* 4H 23
East Grinstead. *W Sus* 2E 27
East Guldeford. *E Sus* 3D 28
East Haddon. *Nptn* 4D 62
East Hagbourne. *Oxon* 3D 36
East Halton. *N Lin* 2E 95
East Ham. *G Lon* 2F 39
Eastham. *Mers* 2F 83
Eastham. *Worc* 4A 60
Eastham Ferry. *Mers* 2F 83
Easthampstead. *Brac* 5G 37
Easthampton. *Here* 4G 59
East Hanney. *Oxon* 2C 36
East Hanningfield. *Essx* 5A 54
East Hardwick. *W Yor* 3E 93
East Harling. *Norf* 2B 66
East Harlsey. *N Yor* 5B 106
East Harnham. *Wilts* 4G 23
East Harptree. *Bath* 1A 22
East Hartford. *Nmbd* 2F 115
East Harting. *W Sus* 1G 17
East Hatch. *Wilts* 4E 23
East Hatley. *Cambs* 5B 64
Easthaugh. *Norf* 4C 78
East Hauxwell. *N Yor* 5E 105
East Haven. *Ang* 5E 145
Eastheath. *Wok* 5G 37
East Heckington. *Linc* 1A 76
East Hedleyhope. *Dur* 5E 115
East Helmsdale. *High* 2H 165
East Hendred. *Oxon* 3C 36
East Heslerton. *N Yor* 2D 100
East Hoathly. *E Sus* 4G 27
East Holme. *Dors* 4D 15
Easthope. *Shrp* 1H 59
Easthorpe. *Essx* 3C 54
Easthorpe. *Leics* 2F 75
East Horrington. *Som* 2A 22
East Horsley. *Surr* 5B 38
East Horton. *Nmbd* 1E 121
Easthouses. *Midl* 3G 129
East Howe. *Bour* 3F 15
East Huntspill. *Som* 2G 21
East Hyde. *C Beds* 4B 52
East Ilsley. *W Ber* 3C 36
Eastington. *Devn* 2H 11
Eastington. *Glos* 4G 49
(nr. Northleach)
Eastington. *Glos* 5C 48
(nr. Stonehouse)
East Keal. *Linc* 4C 88
East Kennett. *Wilts* 5G 35
East Keswick. *W Yor* 5F 99
East Kilbride. *S Lan* 4H 127
East Kirkby. *Linc* 4C 88
East Knapton. *N Yor* 2C 100
East Knighton. *Dors* 4D 14
East Knowstone. *Devn* 4B 20
East Knoyle. *Wilts* 3D 23
East Kyloe. *Nmbd* 1E 121
East Lambrook. *Som* 1H 13
East Langdon. *Kent* 1H 29
East Langton. *Leics* 1E 63
East Langwell. *High* 3E 164
East Lavant. *W Sus* 2G 17
East Lavington. *W Sus* 4A 26
East Layton. *N Yor* 4E 105
Eastleach Martin. *Glos* 5H 49
Eastleach Turville. *Glos* 5G 49
East Leake. *Notts* 3C 74
East Learmouth. *Nmbd* 1C 120
Eastleigh. *Devn* 4E 19
(nr. Bideford)
East Leigh. *Devn* 2H 11
(nr. Crediton)
East Leigh. *Devn* 3C 8
(nr. Modbury)
Eastleigh. *Hants* 1C 16
East Lexham. *Norf* 4A 78
East Lilburn. *Nmbd* 2E 121
Eastling. *Kent* 5D 40
East Linton. *E Lot* 2B 130
East Liss. *Hants* 4F 25
East Lockinge. *Oxon* 3C 36
East Looe. *Corn* 3G 7
East Lound. *N Lin* 1E 87
East Lulworth. *Dors* 4D 14
East Lutton. *N Yor* 3D 100
East Lydford. *Som* 3A 22
East Lyng. *Som* 4G 21
East Mains. *Abers* 4D 152
East Malling. *Kent* 5B 40
East Marden. *W Sus* 1G 17
East Markham. *Notts* 3E 87
East Marton. *N Yor* 4B 98
East Meon. *Hants* 4E 25
East Mersea. *Essx* 4D 54
East Mey. *High* 1F 169
East Midlands Airport. *Leics* 3B 74
East Molesey. *Surr* 4C 38
Eastmoor. *Norf* 5G 77
East Morden. *Dors* 3E 15
East Morton. *W Yor* 5D 98
East Ness. *N Yor* 2A 100
East Newton. *E Yor* 1F 95
East Newton. *N Yor* 2A 100
Eastney. *Port* 3E 17
Eastnor. *Here* 2C 48
East Norton. *Leics* 5E 75
East Nynehead. *Som* 4E 21
East Oakley. *Hants* 1D 24
Eastoft. *N Lin* 3B 94
East Ogwell. *Devn* 5B 12
Easton. *Cambs* 3A 64
Easton. *Cumb* 4D 112
(nr. Burgh by Sands)
Easton. *Cumb* 2F 113
(nr. Longtown)
Easton. *Devn* 4H 11
Easton. *Dors* 5B 14
Easton. *Hants* 3D 24
Easton. *Linc* 3G 75
Easton. *Norf* 4D 78
Easton. *Som* 2A 22
Easton. *Suff* 5E 67
Easton. *Wilts* 4D 35
Easton Grey. *Wilts* 3D 35
Easton-in-Gordano. *N Som* 4A 34
Easton Maudit. *Nptn* 5F 63

Embleton. Dur	2B 106
Embleton. Nmbd	2G 121
Embo. High	4F 165
Emborough. Som	1B 22
Embo Street. High	4F 165
Embsay. N Yor	4C 98
Emery Down. Hants	2A 16
Emley. W Yor	3C 92
Emmbrook. Wok	5F 37
Emmer Green. Read	4F 37
Emmington. Oxon	5F 51
Emneth. Norf	5D 77
Emneth Hungate. Norf	5E 77
Empingham. Rut	5G 75
Empshott. Hants	3F 25
Emsworth. Hants	2F 17
Enborne. W Ber	5C 36
Enborne Row. W Ber	5C 36
Enchmarsh. Shrp	1H 59
Enderby. Leics	1C 62
Endmoor. Cumb	1E 97
Endon. Staf	5D 84
Endon Bank. Staf	5D 84
Enfield. G Lon	1E 39
Enfield Wash. G Lon	1E 39
Enford. Wilts	1G 23
Engine Common. S Glo	3B 34
Englefield. W Ber	4E 36
Englefield Green. Surr	3A 38
Engleseabrook. Ches E	5B 84
English Bicknor. Glos	4A 48
Englishcombe. Bath	5C 34
English Frankton. Shrp	3G 71
Enham Alamein. Hants	2B 24
Enmore. Som	3F 21
Ennerdale Bridge. Cumb	3B 102
Enniscaven. Corn	3D 6
Enoch. Dum	4A 118
Enochdhu. Per	2H 143
Ensay. Arg	4E 139
Ensbury. Bour	3F 15
Ensdon. Shrp	4G 71
Ensis. Devn	4F 19
Enson. Staf	3D 72
Enstone. Oxon	3B 50
Enterkinfoot. Dum	4A 118
Enville. Staf	2C 60
Eolaigearraidh. W Isl	8C 170
Eorabus. Arg	1A 132
Eoropaidh. W Isl	1H 171
Epney. Glos	4C 48
Epperstone. Notts	1D 74
Epping. Essx	5E 53
Epping Green. Essx	5E 53
Epping Green. Herts	5C 52
Epping Upland. Essx	5E 53
Eppleby. N Yor	3E 105
Epplewarth. E Yor	1D 94
Epsom. Surr	4D 38
Epwell. Oxon	1B 50
Epworth. N Lin	4A 94
Epworth Turbary. N Lin	4A 94
Erbistock. Wrex	1F 71
Erbusaig. High	1F 147
Erchless Castle. High	4G 157
Erdington. W Mid	1F 61
Eredine. Arg	3G 133
Eriboll. High	3E 167
Ericstane. Dum	3C 118
Eridge Green. E Sus	2G 27
Erines. Arg	2G 125
Eriswell. Suff	3G 65
Erith. G Lon	3G 39
Erlestoke. Wilts	1E 23
Ermine. Linc	3G 87
Ermington. Devn	3C 8
Ernesettle. Plym	3A 8
Erpingham. Norf	2D 78
Erriottwood. Kent	5D 40
Errogie. High	1H 149
Errol. Per	1E 137
Errol Station. Per	1E 137
Erskine. Ren	2F 127
Erskine Bridge. Ren	2F 127

Ervie. Dum	3F 109
Erwarton. Suff	2F 55
Erwood. Powy	1D 46
Eryholme. N Yor	4A 106
Eryrys. Den	5E 82
Escalls. Corn	4A 4
Escomb. Dur	1E 105
Escrick. N Yor	5A 100
Esgair. Carm	3D 45
(nr. Carmarthen)	
Esgair. Carm	3G 43
(nr. St Clears)	
Esgairgeiliog. Powy	5G 69
Esh. Dur	5E 115
Esher. Surr	4C 38
Esholt. W Yor	5D 98
Eshott. Nmbd	5G 121
Eshton. N Yor	4B 98
Esh Winning. Dur	5E 115
Eskadale. High	5G 157
Eskbank. Midl	3G 129
Eskdale Green. Cumb	4C 102
Eskdalemuir. Dum	5E 119
Eskham. Linc	1C 88
Esknish. Arg	3B 124
Esk Valley. N Yor	4F 107
Eslington Hall. Nmbd	3E 121
Espley Hall. Nmbd	5F 121
Esprick. Lanc	1C 90
Essendine. Rut	4H 75
Essendon. Herts	5C 52
Essich. High	5A 158
Essington. Staf	5D 72
Eston. Red C	3C 106
Estover. Plym	3B 8
Eswick. Shet	6F 173
Etal. Nmbd	1D 120
Etchilhampton. Wilts	5F 35
Etchingham. E Sus	3B 28
Etchinghill. Kent	2F 29
Etchinghill. Staf	4E 73
Etherley Dene. Dur	2E 105
Ethie Haven. Ang	4F 145
Etling Green. Norf	4C 78
Etloe. Glos	5B 48
Eton. Wind	3A 38
Eton Wick. Wind	3A 38
Etteridge. High	4A 150
Ettersgill. Dur	2B 104
Ettiley Heath. Ches E	4B 84
Ettington. Warw	1A 50
Etton. E Yor	5D 101
Etton. Pet	5A 76
Ettrick. Bord	3E 119
Ettrickbridge. Bord	2F 119
Etwall. Derbs	2G 73
Eudon Burnell. Shrp	2B 60
Eudon George. Shrp	2A 60
Euston. Suff	3A 66
Euxton. Lanc	3D 90
Evanstown. B'end	3C 32
Evanton. High	2A 158
Evedon. Linc	1H 75
Evelix. High	4E 165
Evendine. Here	1C 48
Evenjobb. Powy	4E 59
Evenley. Nptn	2D 50
Evenlode. Glos	3H 49
Even Swindon. Swin	3G 35
Evenwood. Dur	2E 105
Evenwood Gate. Dur	2E 105
Everbay. Orkn	5F 172
Evercreech. Som	3B 22
Everdon. Nptn	5C 62
Everingham. E Yor	5C 100
Everleigh. Wilts	1H 23
Everley. N Yor	1D 100
Eversholt. C Beds	2H 51
Evershot. Dors	2A 14
Eversley. Hants	5F 37
Eversley Centre. Hants	5F 37
Eversley Cross. Hants	5F 37
Everthorpe. E Yor	1C 94
Everton. C Beds	5B 64

Everton. Hants	3A 16
Everton. Mers	1F 83
Everton. Notts	1D 86
Evertown. Dum	2E 113
Evesbatch. Here	1B 48
Evesham. Worc	1F 49
Evington. Leic	5D 74
Ewden Village. S Yor	1G 85
Ewdness. Shrp	1B 60
Ewell. Surr	4D 38
Ewell Minnis. Kent	1G 29
Ewelme. Oxon	2E 37
Ewen. Glos	2F 35
Ewenny. V Glam	4C 32
Ewerby. Linc	1A 76
Ewes. Dum	5F 119
Ewesley. Nmbd	5E 121
Ewhurst. Surr	1B 26
Ewhurst Green. E Sus	3B 28
Ewhurst Green. Surr	2B 26
Ewlo. Flin	4F 83
Ewloe. Flin	4F 83
Ewood Bridge. Lanc	2F 91
Eworthy. Devn	3E 11
Ewshot. Hants	1G 25
Ewyas Harold. Here	3G 47
Exbourne. Devn	2G 11
Exbury. Hants	2C 16
Exceat. E Sus	5G 27
Exebridge. Som	4C 20
Exelby. N Yor	1E 99
Exeter. Devn	3C 12
Exeter International Airport.	
Devn	3D 12
Exford. Som	3B 20
Exfords Green. Shrp	5G 71
Exhall. Warw	5F 61
Exlade Street. Oxon	3E 37
Exminster. Devn	4C 12
Exmoor. Som	3B 20
Exmouth. Devn	4D 12
Exning. Suff	4F 65
Exton. Devn	4C 12
Exton. Hants	4E 24
Exton. Rut	4G 75
Exton. Som	3C 20
Exwick. Devn	3C 12
Eyam. Derbs	3G 85
Eydon. Nptn	5C 62
Eye. Here	4G 59
Eye. Pet	5B 76
Eye. Suff	3D 66
Eye Green. Pet	5B 76
Eyemouth. Bord	3F 131
Eyeworth. C Beds	1C 52
Eyhorne Street. Kent	5C 40
Eyke. Suff	5F 67
Eynesbury. Cambs	5A 64
Eynort. High	1B 146
Eynsford. Kent	4G 39
Eynsham. Oxon	5C 50
Eype. High	3D 154
(on Isle of Skye)	
Eyre. High	5E 155
(on Raasay)	
Eythorne. Kent	1G 29
Eyton. Here	4G 59
Eyton. Shrp	5F 71
(nr. Bishop's Castle)	
Eyton. Shrp	4F 71
(nr. Shrewsbury)	
Eyton. Wrex	1F 71
Eyton on Severn. Shrp	5H 71
Eyton upon the Weald Moors.	
Telf	4A 72

F

Faccombe. Hants	1B 24
Faceby. N Yor	4B 106
Faddiley. Ches E	5H 83
Fadmoor. N Yor	1A 100
Fagwyr. Swan	5G 45

Faichem. High	3E 149
Faifley. W Dun	2G 127
Fail. S Ayr	2D 116
Failand. N Som	4A 34
Failford. S Ayr	2D 116
Failsworth. G Man	4H 91
Fairbourne. Gwyn	4F 69
Fairbourne Heath. Kent	5C 40
Fairburn. N Yor	2E 93
Fairfield. Derbs	3E 85
Fairfield. Kent	3D 28
Fairfield. Worc	3D 60
(nr. Bromsgrove)	
Fairfield. Worc	1F 49
(nr. Evesham)	
Fairford. Glos	5G 49
Fair Green. Norf	4F 77
Fair Hill. Cumb	1G 103
Fairhill. S Lan	4A 128
Fair Isle Airport. Shet	1B 172
Fairlands. Surr	5A 38
Fairlie. N Ayr	4D 126
Fairlight. E Sus	4C 28
Fairlight Cove. E Sus	4C 28
Fairmile. Devn	3D 12
Fairmile. Surr	4C 38
Fairmilehead. Edin	3F 129
Fair Oak. Devn	1D 12
Fair Oak. Hants	1C 16
(nr. Eastleigh)	
Fair Oak. Hants	5D 36
(nr. Kingsclere)	
Fairoak. Staf	2B 72
Fair Oak Green. Hants	5E 37
Fairseat. Kent	4H 39
Fairstead. Essx	4A 54
Fairstead. Norf	4F 77
Fairwarp. E Sus	3F 27
Fairwater. Card	4E 33
Fairy Cross. Devn	4E 19
Fakenham. Norf	3B 78
Fakenham Magna. Suff	3B 66
Fala. Midl	3H 129
Fala Dam. Midl	3H 129
Falcon. Here	2B 48
Faldingworth. Linc	2H 87
Falfield. S Glo	2B 34
Falkenham. Suff	2F 55
Falkirk. Falk	2B 128
Falkland. Fife	3E 137
Fallin. Stir	4H 135
Fallowfield. G Man	1C 84
Falmer. E Sus	5E 27
Falmouth. Corn	5C 6
Falsgrave. N Yor	1E 101
Falstone. Nmbd	1A 114
Fanagmore. High	4B 166
Fancott. C Beds	3A 52
Fanellan. High	4G 157
Fangdale Beck. N Yor	5C 106
Fangfoss. E Yor	4B 100
Fankerton. Falk	1A 128
Fanmore. Arg	4F 139
Fanner's Green. Essx	4G 53
Fannich Lodge. High	2E 156
Fans. Bord	5C 130
Farcet. Cambs	1B 64
Far Cotton. Nptn	5E 63
Fareham. Hants	2D 16
Farewell. Staf	4E 73
Far Forest. Worc	3B 60
Farforth. Linc	3C 88
Far Green. Glos	5C 48
Far Hoarcross. Staf	3F 73
Faringdon. Oxon	2A 36
Farington. Lanc	2D 90
Farlam. Cumb	4G 113
Farleigh. N Som	5H 33
Farleigh. Surr	4E 39
Farleigh Hungerford. Som	1D 22
Farleigh Wallop. Hants	2E 24
Farleigh Wick. Wilts	5D 34
Farlesthorpe. Linc	3D 88
Farleton. Cumb	1E 97

Farleton. Lanc	3E 97
Farley. High	4G 157
Farley. N Som	4H 33
Farley. Shrp	5F 71
(nr. Shrewsbury)	
Farley. Shrp	5A 72
(nr. Telford)	
Farley. Staf	1E 73
Farley. Wilts	4H 23
Farley Green. Suff	5G 65
Farley Green. Surr	1B 26
Farley Hill. Wok	5F 37
Farley's End. Glos	4C 48
Farlington. N Yor	3A 100
Farlington. Port	2E 17
Farlow. Shrp	2A 60
Farmborough. Bath	5B 34
Farmcote. Glos	3F 49
Farmcote. Shrp	1B 60
Farmington. Glos	4G 49
Far Moor. G Man	4D 90
Farmoor. Oxon	5C 50
Farmtown. Mor	3C 160
Farnah Green. Derbs	1H 73
Farnborough. G Lon	4F 39
Farnborough. Hants	1G 25
Farnborough. Warw	1C 50
Farnborough. W Ber	3C 36
Farncombe. Surr	1A 26
Farndish. Bed	4G 63
Farndon. Ches W	5G 83
Farndon. Notts	5E 87
Farnell. Ang	3F 145
Farnham. Dors	1E 15
Farnham. Essx	3E 53
Farnham. N Yor	3F 99
Farnham. Suff	4F 67
Farnham. Surr	2G 25
Farnham Common. Buck	2A 38
Farnham Green. Essx	3E 53
Farnham Royal. Buck	2A 38
Farnhill. N Yor	5C 98
Farningham. Kent	4G 39
Farnley. N Yor	5E 98
Farnley Tyas. W Yor	3B 92
Farnsfield. Notts	5D 86
Farnworth. G Man	4F 91
Farnworth. Hal	2H 83
Far Oakridge. Glos	5E 49
Farr. High	2H 167
(nr. Bettyhill)	
Farr. High	3C 150
(nr. Inverness)	
Farr. High	3C 150
(nr. Kingussie)	
Farraline. High	1H 149
Farrington. Devn	3D 12
Farrington. Dors	1D 14
Farrington Gurney. Bath	1B 22
Far Sawrey. Cumb	5E 103
Farsley. W Yor	1C 92
Farthinghoe. Nptn	2D 50
Farthingstone. Nptn	5D 62
Farthorpe. Linc	3B 88
Fartown. W Yor	3B 92
Farway. Devn	3E 13
Fasag. High	3A 156
Fascadale. High	1G 139
Fasnacloich. Arg	4E 141
Fassfern. High	1E 141
Fatfield. Tyne	4G 115
Faugh. Cumb	4G 113
Fauld. Staf	3F 73
Fauldhouse. W Lot	3C 128
Faulkbourne. Essx	4A 54
Faulkland. Som	1C 22
Fauls. Shrp	2H 71
Faversham. Kent	4E 40
Fawdington. N Yor	2G 99
Fawfieldhead. Staf	4E 85
Fawkham Green. Kent	4G 39
Fawler. Oxon	4B 50
Fawley. Buck	3F 37

Ford—Gairloch

Ford. *Buck* 5F 51
Ford. *Derbs* 2B 86
Ford. *Devn* 4E 19
(nr. Bideford)
Ford. *Devn* 3C 8
(nr. Holbeton)
Ford. *Devn* 4D 9
(nr. Salcombe)
Ford. *Glos* 3F 49
Ford. *Nmbd* 1D 120
Ford. *Plym* 3A 8
Ford. *Shrp* 4G 71
Ford. *Som* 1A 22
(nr. Wells)
Ford. *Som* 4D 20
(nr. Wiveliscombe)
Ford. *Staf* 5E 85
Ford. *W Sus* 5B 26
Ford. *Wilts* 4D 34
(nr. Chippenham)
Ford. *Wilts* 3G 23
(nr. Salisbury)
Forda. *Devn* 3E 19
Ford Barton. *Devn* 1C 12
Fordcombe. *Kent* 1G 27
Fordell. *Fife* 1E 129
Forden. *Powy* 5E 71
Ford End. *Essx* 4G 53
Forder Green. *Devn* 2D 9
Ford Green. *Lanc* 5D 97
Fordham. *Cambs* 3F 65
Fordham. *Essx* 3C 54
Fordham. *Norf* 1F 65
Fordham Heath. *Essx* 3C 54
Ford Heath. *Shrp* 4G 71
Fordhouses. *W Mid* 5D 72
Fordie. *Per* 1G 135
Fordingbridge. *Hants* 1G 15
Fordington. *Linc* 3D 88
Fordon. *E Yor* 2E 101
Fordoun. *Abers* 1G 145
Ford Street. *Essx* 3C 54
Ford Street. *Som* 1E 13
Fordton. *Devn* 3B 12
Fordwells. *Oxon* 4B 50
Fordwich. *Kent* 5F 41
Fordyce. *Abers* 2C 160
Forebridge. *Staf* 3D 72
Foremark. *Derbs* 3H 73
Forest. *N Yor* 4F 105
Forestburn Gate. *Nmbd* 5E 121
Foresterseat. *Mor* 3F 159
Forest Green. *Glos* 2D 34
Forest Green. *Surr* 1C 26
Forest Hall. *Cumb* 4G 103
Forest Head. *Cumb* 4G 113
Forest Hill. *Oxon* 5D 50
Forest-in-Teesdale. *Dur* 2B 104
Forest Lodge. *Per* 1G 143
Forest Mill. *Clac* 4B 136
Forest Row. *E Sus* 2F 27
Forestside. *W Sus* 1F 17
Forest Town. *Notts* 4C 86
Forfar. *Ang* 3D 144
Forgandenny. *Per* 2C 136
Forge. *Powy* 1G 57
Forge Side. *Torf* 5F 47
Forge, The. *Here* 5F 59
Forgewood. *N Lan* 4A 128
Forgie. *Mor* 3A 160
Forgue. *Abers* 4D 160
Formby. *Mers* 4A 90
Forncett End. *Norf* 1D 66
Forncett St Mary. *Norf* 1D 66
Forncett St Peter. *Norf* 1D 66
Forneth. *Per* 4H 143
Fornham All Saints. *Suff* 4H 65
Fornham St Martin. *Suff* 4A 66
Forres. *Mor* 3E 159
Forrestfield. *N Lan* 3B 128
Forrest Lodge. *Dum* 1C 110
Forsbrook. *Staf* 1D 72
Forse. *High* 5E 169
Forsinard. *High* 4A 168
Forss. *High* 2C 168
Forstal, The. *Kent* 2E 29
Forston. *Dors* 3B 14
Fort Augustus. *High* 3F 149
Forteviot. *Per* 2C 136
Fort George. *High* 3B 158
Forth. *S Lan* 4C 128
Forthampton. *Glos* 2D 48
Forthay. *Glos* 2C 34
Forth Road Bridge. *Fife* 2E 129
Fortingall. *Per* 4E 143
Fort Matilda. *Inv* 2D 126
Forton. *Hants* 2C 24
Forton. *Lanc* 4D 97
Forton. *Shrp* 4G 71
Forton. *Som* 2G 13
Forton. *Staf* 3B 72
Forton Heath. *Shrp* 4G 71
Fortrie. *Abers* 4D 160
Fortrose. *High* 3B 158
Fortuneswell. *Dors* 5B 14
Fort William. *High* 1F 141
Forty Green. *Buck* 1A 38
Forty Hill. *G Lon* 1E 39
Forward Green. *Suff* 5C 66
Fosbury. *Wilts* 1B 24
Foscot. *Oxon* 3H 49
Fosdyke. *Linc* 2C 76
Foss. *Per* 3E 143
Fossebridge. *Glos* 4F 49
Foster Street. *Essx* 5E 53
Foston. *Derbs* 2F 73
Foston. *Leics* 1D 62
Foston. *Linc* 1F 75
Foston. *N Yor* 3A 100
Foston on the Wolds. *E Yor* 4F 101
Fotherby. *Linc* 1C 88
Fothergill. *Cumb* 1B 102
Fotheringhay. *Nptn* 1H 63
Foubister. *Orkn* 7E 172
Foula Airport. *Shet* 8A 173
Foul Anchor. *Cambs* 4D 76
Foulbridge. *Cumb* 5F 113
Foulden. *Norf* 1G 65
Foulden. *Bord* 4F 131
Foul Mile. *E Sus* 4H 27
Foulridge. *Lanc* 5A 98
Foulsham. *Norf* 3C 78
Fountainhall. *Bord* 5H 129
Four Alls, The. *Shrp* 2A 72
Four Ashes. *Staf* 5D 72
(nr. Cannock)
Four Ashes. *Staf* 2C 60
(nr. Kinver)
Four Ashes. *Suff* 3C 66
Four Crosses. *Powy* 5C 70
(nr. Llanerfyl)
Four Crosses. *Powy* 4E 71
(nr. Llanymynech)
Four Crosses. *Staf* 5D 72
Four Elms. *Kent* 1F 27
Four Forks. *Som* 3F 21
Four Gotes. *Cambs* 4D 76
Four Lane End. *S Yor* 4C 92
Four Lane Ends. *Lanc* 4E 97
Four Lanes. *Corn* 5A 6
Fourlanes End. *Ches E* 5B 84
Four Marks. *Hants* 3E 25
Four Mile Bridge. *IOA* 3B 80
Four Oaks. *E Sus* 3C 28
Four Oaks. *Glos* 3B 48
Four Oaks. *W Mid* 2G 61
Four Roads. *Carm* 5E 45
Four Roads. *IOM* 5B 108
Fourstones. *Nmbd* 3B 114
Four Throws. *Kent* 3B 28
Fovant. *Wilts* 4F 23
Foveran. *Abers* 1G 153
Fowey. *Corn* 3F 7
Fowlershill. *Abers* 2G 153
Fowley Common. *Warr* 1A 84
Fowlis. *Ang* 5C 144
Fowlis Wester. *Per* 1B 136
Fowlmere. *Cambs* 1E 53
Fownhope. *Here* 2A 48
Foxcombe Hill. *Oxon* 5C 50
Fox Corner. *Surr* 5A 38
Foxcote. *Glos* 4F 49
Foxcote. *Som* 1C 22
Foxdale. *IOM* 4B 108
Foxearth. *Essx* 1B 54
Foxfield. *Cumb* 1B 96
Foxham. *Wilts* 4E 35
Fox Hatch. *Essx* 1G 39
Foxhole. *Corn* 3D 6
Foxholes. *N Yor* 2E 101
Foxhunt Green. *E Sus* 4G 27
Fox Lane. *Hants* 1G 25
Foxley. *Norf* 3C 78
Foxley. *Nptn* 5D 62
Foxley. *Wilts* 3D 35
Foxlydiate. *Worc* 4E 61
Fox Street. *Essx* 3D 54
Foxt. *Staf* 1E 73
Foxton. *Cambs* 1E 53
Foxton. *Dur* 2A 106
Foxton. *Leics* 2D 62
Foxton. *N Yor* 5B 106
Foxup. *N Yor* 2A 98
Foxwist Green. *Ches W* 4A 84
Foxwood. *Shrp* 3A 60
Foy. *Here* 3A 48
Foyers. *High* 1G 149
Foynesfield. *High* 3C 158
Fraddam. *Corn* 3C 4
Fraddon. *Corn* 3D 6
Fradley. *Staf* 4F 73
Fradley South. *Staf* 4F 73
Fradswell. *Staf* 2D 73
Fraisthorpe. *E Yor* 3F 101
Framfield. *E Sus* 3F 27
Framingham Earl. *Norf* 5E 79
Framingham Pigot. *Norf* 5E 79
Framlingham. *Suff* 4E 67
Frampton. *Dors* 3B 14
Frampton. *Linc* 2C 76
Frampton Cotterell. *S Glo* 3B 34
Frampton Mansell. *Glos* 5E 49
Frampton on Severn. *Glos* 5C 48
Frampton West End. *Linc* 1B 76
Framsden. *Suff* 5D 66
Framwellgate Moor. *Dur* 5F 115
Franche. *Worc* 3C 60
Frandley. *Ches W* 3A 84
Frankby. *Mers* 2E 83
Frankfort. *Norf* 3F 79
Frankley. *Worc* 2D 61
Frank's Bridge. *Powy* 5D 58
Frankton. *Warw* 3B 62
Frankwell. *Shrp* 4G 71
Frant. *E Sus* 2G 27
Fraserburgh. *Abers* 2G 161
Frating Green. *Essx* 3D 54
Fratton. *Port* 2E 17
Freathy. *Corn* 3A 8
Freckenham. *Suff* 3F 65
Freckleton. *Lanc* 2C 90
Freeby. *Leics* 3F 75
Freefolk Priors. *Hants* 2C 24
Freehay. *Staf* 1E 73
Freeland. *Oxon* 4C 50
Freethorpe. *Norf* 5G 79
Freiston. *Linc* 1C 76
Freiston Shore. *Linc* 1C 76
Fremington. *Devn* 3F 19
Fremington. *N Yor* 5D 104
Frenchay. *Bris* 4B 34
Frenchbeer. *Devn* 4G 11
French Street. *Kent* 5F 39
Frenich. *Stir* 3D 134
Frensham. *Surr* 2G 25
Frenze. *Norf* 2D 66
Fresgoe. *High* 2B 168
Freshfield. *Mers* 4A 90
Freshford. *Bath* 5C 34
Freshwater. *IOW* 4B 16
Freshwater Bay. *IOW* 4B 16
Freshwater East. *Pemb* 5E 43
Fressingfield. *Suff* 3E 67
Freston. *Suff* 2E 55
Freswick. *High* 2F 169
Fretherne. *Glos* 5C 48
Frettenham. *Norf* 4E 79
Freuchie. *Fife* 3E 137
Freystrop. *Pemb* 3D 42
Friar's Gate. *E Sus* 2F 27
Friar Waddon. *Dors* 4B 14
Friday Bridge. *Cambs* 5D 76
Friday Street. *E Sus* 5H 27
Friday Street. *Surr* 1C 26
Fridaythorpe. *E Yor* 4C 100
Friden. *Derbs* 4F 85
Friern Barnet. *G Lon* 1D 39
Friesthorpe. *Linc* 2H 87
Frieston. *Linc* 1G 75
Frieth. *Buck* 2F 37
Friezeland. *Notts* 5B 86
Frilford. *Oxon* 2C 36
Frilsham. *W Ber* 4D 36
Frimley. *Surr* 1G 25
Frimley Green. *Surr* 1G 25
Frindsbury. *Medw* 4B 40
Fring. *Norf* 2G 77
Fringford. *Oxon* 3E 50
Frinsted. *Kent* 5C 40
Frinton-on-Sea. *Essx* 4F 55
Friockheim. *Ang* 4E 145
Friog. *Gwyn* 4F 69
Frisby. *Leics* 5E 74
Frisby on the Wreake. *Leics* 4D 74
Friskney. *Linc* 5D 88
Friskney Eaudyke. *Linc* 5D 88
Friston. *E Sus* 5G 27
Friston. *Suff* 4G 67
Fritchley. *Derbs* 5A 86
Fritham. *Hants* 1H 15
Frith Bank. *Linc* 1C 76
Frith Common. *Worc* 4A 60
Frithelstock. *Devn* 1E 11
Frithelstock Stone. *Devn* 1E 11
Frithsden. *Herts* 5A 52
Frithville. *Linc* 5C 88
Frittenden. *Kent* 1C 28
Frittiscombe. *Devn* 4E 9
Fritton. *Norf* 5G 79
(nr. Great Yarmouth)
Fritton. *Norf* 1E 67
(nr. Long Stratton)
Fritwell. *Oxon* 3D 50
Frizinghall. *W Yor* 1B 92
Frizington. *Cumb* 3B 102
Frobost. *W Isl* 6C 170
Frocester. *Glos* 5C 48
Frochas. *Powy* 5D 70
Frodesley. *Shrp* 5H 71
Frodingham. *N Lin* 3C 94
Frodsham. *Ches W* 3H 83
Froggat. *Derbs* 3G 85
Froghall. *Staf* 1E 73
Frogham. *Hants* 1G 15
Frogham. *Kent* 5G 41
Frogmore. *Devn* 4D 8
Frogmore. *Hants* 5G 37
Frogmore. *Herts* 5B 52
Frognall. *Linc* 4A 76
Frogshall. *Norf* 2E 79
Frogwell. *Corn* 2H 7
Frolesworth. *Leics* 1C 62
Frome. *Som* 2C 22
Fromefield. *Som* 2C 22
Frome St Quintin. *Dors* 2A 14
Fromes Hill. *Here* 1B 48
Fron. *Carm* 2A 46
Fron. *Gwyn* 2C 68
Fron. *Powy* 4C 58
(nr. Llandrindod Wells)
Fron. *Powy* 1D 58
(nr. Newtown)
Fron. *Powy* 5E 71
(nr. Welshpool)
Froncysyllte. *Wrex* 1E 71
Frongoch. *Gwyn* 2B 70
Fron Isaf. *Wrex* 1E 71
Fronoleu. *Gwyn* 2G [illegible]
Frosterley. *Dur* 1D 10[illegible]
Froxfield. *C Beds* 2H 5
Froxfield. *Wilts* 5A 3[illegible]
Froxfield Green. *Hants* 4F 25
Fryern Hill. *Hants* 4C 24
Fryerning. *Essx* 5G 53
Fryton. *N Yor* 2A 100
Fugglestone St Peter. *Wilts* 3G 23
Fulbeck. *Linc* 5G 87
Fulbourn. *Cambs* 5E 65
Fulbrook. *Oxon* 4A 50
Fulflood. *Hants* 3C 24
Fulford. *Som* 4F 21
Fulford. *Staf* 2D 72
Fulford. *York* 5A 100
Fulham. *G Lon* 3D 38
Fulking. *W Sus* 4D 26
Fuller's Moor. *Ches W* 5G 83
Fuller Street. *Essx* 4H 53
Fullerton. *Hants* 3B 24
Fulletby. *Linc* 3B 88
Full Sutton. *E Yor* 4B 100
Fullwood. *E Ayr* 4F 127
Fulmer. *Buck* 2A 38
Fulmodestone. *Norf* 2B 78
Fulnetby. *Linc* 3H 87
Fulney. *Linc* 3B 76
Fulstow. *Linc* 1C 88
Fulthorpe. *Stoc T* 2B 106
Fulwell. *Tyne* 4G 115
Fulwood. *Lanc* 1D 90
Fulwood. *Notts* 5B 86
Fulwood. *Som* 1F 13
Fulwood. *S Yor* 2G 85
Fundenhall. *Norf* 1D 66
Funtington. *W Sus* 2G 17
Funtley. *Hants* 2D 16
Funzie. *Shet* 2H 173
Furley. *Devn* 2F 13
Furnace. *Arg* 3H 133
Furnace. *Carm* 5F 45
Furnace. *Cdgn* 1F 57
Furner's Green. *E Sus* 3F 27
Furness Vale. *Derbs* 2E 85
Furneux Pelham. *Herts* 3E 53
Furzebrook. *Dors* 4E 15
Furzehill. *Devn* 2H 19
Furzehill. *Dors* 2F 15
Furzeley Corner. *Hants* 1E 17
Furzey Lodge. *Hants* 2B 16
Furzley. *Hants* 1A 16
Fyfield. *Essx* 5F 53
Fyfield. *Glos* 5H 49
Fyfield. *Hants* 2A 24
Fyfield. *Oxon* 2C 36
Fyfield. *Wilts* 5G 35
Fylde, The. *Lanc* 1B 90
Fylingthorpe. *N Yor* 4G 107
Fyning. *W Sus* 4G 25
Fyvie. *Abers* 5E 161

G

Gabhsann bho Dheas. *W Isl* 2G 171
Gabhsann bho Thuath. *W Isl* 2G 171
Gabroc Hill. *E Ayr* 4F 127
Gadbrook. *Surr* 1D 26
Gaddesby. *Leics* 4D 74
Gadfa. *IOA* 2D 80
Gadgirth. *S Ayr* 2D 116
Gaer. *Powy* 3E 47
Gaerwen. *IOA* 3D 81
Gagingwell. *Oxon* 3C 50
Gaick Lodge. *High* 5B 150
Gailey. *Staf* 4D 72
Gainford. *Dur* 3E 105
Gainsborough. *Linc* 1F 87
Gainsborough. *Suff* 1E 55
Gainsford End. *Essx* 2H 53
Gairletter. *Arg* 1C 126
Gairloch. *Abers* 3E 153

Glenboig—Great Bardfield

Glenboig. *N Lan* 3A 128
Glenborrodale. *High* 2A 140
Glenbranter. *Arg* 4A 134
Glenbreck. *Bord* 2C 118
Glenbrein Lodge. *High* 2G 149
Glenbrittle. *High* 1C 146
Glenbuchat Lodge. *Abers* 2H 151
Glenbuck. *E Ayr* 2G 117
Glenburn. *Ren* 3F 127
Glencalvie Lodge. *High* 5B 164
Glencaple. *Dum* 3A 112
Glencarron Lodge. *High* 3C 156
Glencarse. *Per* 1D 136
Glencassley Castle. *High* 3B 164
Glencat. *Abers* 4C 152
Glencoe. *High* 3F 141
Glen Cottage. *High* 5E 147
Glencraig. *Fife* 4D 136
Glendale. *High* 4A 154
Glendevon. *Per* 3B 136
Glendoebeg. *High* 3G 149
Glendoick. *Per* 1E 136
Glendoune. *S Ayr* 5A 116
Glenduckie. *Fife* 2E 137
Gleneagles. *Per* 3B 136
Glenegedale. *Arg* 4B 124
Glenegedale Lots. *Arg* 4B 124
Glenelg. *High* 2G 147
Glenernie. *Mor* 4E 159
Glenesslin. *Dum* 1F 111
Glenfarg. *Per* 2D 136
Glenfarquhar Lodge. *Abers* 5E 152
Glenferness Mains. *High* 4D 158
Glenfeshie Lodge. *High* 4C 150
Glenfiddich Lodge. *Mor* 5H 159
Glenfield. *Leics* 5C 74
Glenfinnan. *High* 5B 148
Glenfintaig Lodge. *High* 5E 149
Glenfoot. *Per* 2D 136
Glenfyne Lodge. *Arg* 2B 134
Glengap. *Dum* 4D 110
Glengarnock. *N Ayr* 4E 126
Glengolly. *High* 2D 168
Glengorm Castle. *Arg* 3F 139
Glengrasco. *High* 4D 154
Glenhead Farm. *Ang* 2B 144
Glenholm. *Bord* 1D 118
Glen House. *Bord* 1E 119
Glenhurich. *High* 2C 140
Glenkerry. *Bord* 3E 119
Glenkiln. *Dum* 2F 111
Glenkindle. *Abers* 2B 152
Glenkinglass Lodge. *Arg* 5F 141
Glenkirk. *Bord* 2C 118
Glenlean. *Arg* 1B 126
Glenlee. *Dum* 1D 110
Glenleraig. *High* 5B 166
Glenlichorn. *Per* 2G 135
Glenlivet. *Mor* 1F 151
Glenlochar. *Dum* 3E 111
Glenlochsie Lodge. *Per* 1H 143
Glenluce. *Dum* 4G 109
Glenmarskie. *High* 3F 157
Glenmassan. *Arg* 1C 126
Glenmavis. *N Lan* 3A 128
Glen Maye. *IOM* 4B 108
Glenmazeran Lodge. *High* 1B 150
Glenmidge. *Dum* 1F 111
Glen Mona. *IOM* 3D 108
Glenmore. *High* 2G 139
(nr. Glenborrodale)
Glenmore. *High* 3D 151
(nr. Kingussie)
Glenmore. *High* 4D 154
(on Isle of Skye)
Glenmoy. *Ang* 2D 144
Glennoe. *Arg* 5E 141
Glen of Coachford. *Abers* 4B 160
Glenogil. *Ang* 2D 144
Glen Parva. *Leics* 1C 62
Glenprosen Village. *Ang* 2C 144
Glenree. *N Ayr* 3D 122
Glenridding. *Cumb* 3E 103
Glenrosa. *N Ayr* 2E 123
Glenrothes. *Fife* 3E 137
Glensanda. *High* 4C 140
Glensaugh. *Abers* 1F 145
Glenshero Lodge. *High* 4H 149
Glensluain. *Arg* 4H 133
Glenstockadale. *Dum* 3F 109
Glenstriven. *Arg* 2B 126
Glen Tanar House. *Abers* 4B 152
Glentham. *Linc* 1H 87
Glenton. *Abers* 1D 152
Glentress. *Bord* 1E 119
Glentromie Lodge. *High* 4B 150
Glentrool Lodge. *Dum* 1B 110
Glentrool Village. *Dum* 2A 110
Glentruim House. *High* 4A 150
Glentworth. *Linc* 2G 87
Glenuig. *High* 1A 140
Glen Village. *Falk* 2B 128
Glen Vine. *IOM* 4C 108
Glenwhilly. *Dum* 2G 109
Glenzierfoot. *Dum* 2E 113
Glespin. *S Lan* 2H 117
Gletness. *Shet* 6F 173
Glewstone. *Here* 3A 48
Glib Cheois. *W Isl* 5F 171
Glinton. *Pet* 5A 76
Glooston. *Leics* 1E 63
Glossop. *Derbs* 1E 85
Gloster Hill. *Nmbd* 4G 121
Gloucester. *Glos* 4D 48
Gloucestershire Airport. *Glos* 3D 49
Gloup. *Shet* 1G 173
Glusburn. *N Yor* 5C 98
Glutt Lodge. *High* 5B 168
Glutton Bridge. *Staf* 4E 85
Gluvian. *Corn* 2D 6
Glympton. *Oxon* 3C 50
Glyn. *Cnwy* 3A 82
Glynarthen. *Cdgn* 1D 44
Glynbrochan. *Powy* 2B 58
Glyn Ceiriog. *Wrex* 2E 70
Glyncoch. *Rhon* 2D 32
Glyncorrwg. *Neat* 2B 32
Glynde. *E Sus* 5F 27
Glyndebourne. *E Sus* 4F 27
Glyndyfrdwy. *Den* 1D 70
Glyn Ebwy. *Blae* 5E 47
Glynllan. *B'end* 3C 32
Glyn-neath. *Neat* 5B 46
Glynogwr. *B'end* 3C 32
Glyntaff. *Rhon* 3D 32
Glyntawe. *Powy* 4B 46
Glynteg. *Carm* 2D 44
Gnosall. *Staf* 3C 72
Gnosall Heath. *Staf* 3C 72
Goadby. *Leics* 1E 63
Goadby Marwood. *Leics* 3E 75
Goatacre. *Wilts* 4F 35
Goathill. *Dors* 1B 14
Goathland. *N Yor* 4F 107
Goathurst. *Som* 3F 21
Goathurst Common. *Kent* 5F 39
Goat Lees. *Kent* 1E 28
Gobernuisgach Lodge. *High* 4E 167
Gobernuisgeach. *High* 5B 168
Gobhaig. *W Isl* 7C 171
Gobowen. *Shrp* 2F 71
Godalming. *Surr* 1A 26
Goddard's Corner. *Suff* 4E 67
Goddard's Green. *Kent* 2C 28
(nr. Benenden)
Goddard's Green. *Kent* 2B 28
(nr. Cranbrook)
Goddards Green. *W Sus* 3D 27
Godford Cross. *Devn* 2E 13
Godleybrook. *Staf* 1D 73
Godmanchester. *Cambs* 3B 64
Godmanstone. *Dors* 3B 14
Godmersham. *Kent* 5E 41
Godolphin Cross. *Corn* 3D 4
Godre'r-graig. *Neat* 5A 46
Godshill. *Hants* 1G 15
Godshill. *IOW* 4D 16
Godstone. *Staf* 2E 73
Godstone. *Surr* 5E 39
Goetre. *Mon* 5G 47
Goff's Oak. *Herts* 5D 52
Gogar. *Edin* 2E 129
Goginan. *Cdgn* 2F 57
Golan. *Gwyn* 1E 69
Golant. *Corn* 3F 7
Golberdon. *Corn* 5D 10
Golborne. *G Man* 1A 84
Golcar. *W Yor* 3A 92
Goldcliff. *Newp* 3G 33
Golden Cross. *E Sus* 4G 27
Golden Green. *Kent* 1H 27
Golden Grove. *Carm* 4F 45
Golden Grove. *N Yor* 4F 107
Golden Hill. *Pemb* 2D 43
Goldenhill. *Stoke* 5C 84
Golden Pot. *Hants* 2F 25
Golden Valley. *Glos* 3E 49
Golders Green. *G Lon* 2D 38
Goldhanger. *Essx* 5C 54
Gold Hill. *Norf* 1E 65
Golding. *Shrp* 5H 71
Goldington. *Bed* 5H 63
Goldsborough. *N Yor* 4F 99
(nr. Harrogate)
Goldsborough. *N Yor* 3F 107
(nr. Whitby)
Goldsithney. *Corn* 3C 4
Goldstone. *Kent* 4G 41
Goldstone. *Shrp* 3B 72
Goldthorpe. *S Yor* 4E 93
Goldworthy. *Devn* 4D 19
Golfa. *Powy* 3D 70
Gollanfield. *High* 3C 158
Gollinglith Foot. *N Yor* 1D 98
Golsoncott. *Som* 3D 20
Golspie. *High* 4F 165
Gomeldon. *Wilts* 3G 23
Gomersal. *W Yor* 2C 92
Gometra House. *Arg* 4E 139
Gomshall. *Surr* 1B 26
Gonalston. *Notts* 1D 74
Gonerby Hill Foot. *Linc* 2G 75
Good Easter. *Essx* 4G 53
Gooderstone. *Norf* 5G 77
Goodleigh. *Devn* 3G 19
Goodmanham. *E Yor* 5C 100
Goodmayes. *G Lon* 2F 39
Goodnestone. *Kent* 5G 41
(nr. Aylesham)
Goodnestone. *Kent* 4E 41
(nr. Faversham)
Goodrich. *Here* 4A 48
Goodrington. *Torb* 3E 9
Goodshaw. *Lanc* 2G 91
Goodshaw Fold. *Lanc* 2G 91
Goodstone. *Devn* 5A 12
Goodwick. *Pemb* 1D 42
Goodworth Clatford. *Hants* 2B 24
Goole. *E Yor* 2H 93
Goom's Hill. *Worc* 5E 61
Goonabarn. *Corn* 3D 6
Goonbell. *Corn* 4B 6
Goonhavern. *Corn* 3B 6
Goonvrea. *Corn* 4B 6
Goose Green. *Cumb* 1E 97
Goose Green. *S Glo* 3C 34
Gooseham. *Corn* 1C 10
Goosewell. *Plym* 3B 8
Goosey. *Oxon* 2B 36
Goosnargh. *Lanc* 1D 90
Goostrey. *Ches E* 3B 84
Gorcott Hill. *Warw* 4E 61
Gordon. *Bord* 5C 130
Gordonbush. *High* 3F 165
Gordonstown. *Abers* 3C 160
(nr. Cornhill)
Gordonstown. *Abers* 5E 160
(nr. Fyvie)
Gorebridge. *Midl* 3G 129
Gorefield. *Cambs* 4D 76
Gores. *Wilts* 1G 23
Gorgie. *Edin* 2F 129
Goring. *Oxon* 3E 36
Goring-by-Sea. *W Sus* 5C 26
Goring Heath. *Oxon* 4E 37
Gorleston-on-Sea. *Norf* 5H 79
Gornalwood. *W Mid* 1D 60
Gorran Churchtown. *Corn* 4D 6
Gorran Haven. *Corn* 4E 6
Gorran High Lanes. *Corn* 4D 6
Gors. *Cdgn* 3F 57
Gorsedd. *Flin* 3D 82
Gorseinon. *Swan* 3E 31
Gorseness. *Orkn* 6D 172
Gorseybank. *Derbs* 5G 85
Gorsgoch. *Cdgn* 5D 57
Gorslas. *Carm* 4F 45
Gorsley. *Glos* 3B 48
Gorsley Common. *Here* 3B 48
Gorstan. *High* 2F 157
Gorstella. *Ches W* 4F 83
Gorsty Common. *Here* 2H 47
Gorsty Hill. *Staf* 3E 73
Gortantaoid. *Arg* 2B 124
Gorteneorn. *High* 2A 140
Gortenfern. *High* 2A 140
Gorton. *G Man* 1C 84
Gosbeck. *Suff* 5D 66
Gosberton. *Linc* 2B 76
Gosberton Cheal. *Linc* 3B 76
Gosberton Clough. *Linc* 3A 76
Goseley Dale. *Derbs* 3H 73
Gosfield. *Essx* 3A 54
Gosford. *Oxon* 4D 50
Gosforth. *Cumb* 4B 102
Gosforth. *Tyne* 3F 115
Gosmore. *Herts* 3B 52
Gospel End Village. *Staf* 1C 60
Gosport. *Hants* 2E 16
Gossabrough. *Shet* 3G 173
Gossington. *Glos* 5C 48
Gossops Green. *W Sus* 2D 26
Goswick. *Nmbd* 5G 131
Gotham. *Notts* 2C 74
Gotherington. *Glos* 3E 49
Gott. *Arg* 4B 138
Goudhurst. *Kent* 2B 28
Goulceby. *Linc* 3B 88
Gourdon. *Abers* 1H 145
Gourock. *Inv* 2D 126
Govan. *Glas* 3G 127
Govanhill. *Glas* 3G 127
Goverton. *Notts* 1E 74
Goveton. *Devn* 4D 8
Govilon. *Mon* 4F 47
Gowanhill. *Abers* 2H 161
Gowdall. *E Yor* 2G 93
Gowerton. *Swan* 3E 31
Gowkhall. *Fife* 1D 128
Gowthorpe. *E Yor* 4B 100
Goxhill. *E Yor* 5F 101
Goxhill. *N Lin* 2E 94
Goxhill Haven. *N Lin* 2E 94
Goytre. *Neat* 3A 32
Grabhair. *W Isl* 6F 171
Graby. *Linc* 3H 75
Graffham. *W Sus* 4A 26
Grafham. *Cambs* 4A 64
Grafham. *Surr* 1B 26
Grafton. *Here* 2H 47
Grafton. *N Yor* 3G 99
Grafton. *Oxon* 5A 50
Grafton. *Shrp* 4G 71
Grafton. *Worc* 2E 49
(nr. Evesham)
Grafton. *Worc* 4H 59
(nr. Leominster)
Grafton Flyford. *Worc* 5D 60
Grafton Regis. *Nptn* 1F 51
Grafton Underwood. *Nptn* 2G 63
Grafty Green. *Kent* 1C 28
Graianrhyd. *Den* 5E 82
Graig. *Carm* 5E 45
Graig. *Cnwy* 3H 81
Graig. *Den* 3C 82
Graig-fechan. *Den* 5D 82
Graig Penllyn. *V Glam* 4C 32
Grain. *Medw* 3C 4
Grainsby. *Linc* 1B 8
Grainthorpe. *Linc* 1C 8
Grainthorpe Fen. *Linc* 1C 88
Graiselound. *N Lin* 1E 87
Gramasdail. *W Isl* 3D 170
Grampound. *Corn* 4D 6
Grampound Road. *Corn* 3D 6
Granborough. *Buck* 3F 51
Granby. *Notts* 2E 75
Grandborough. *Warw* 4B 62
Grandpont. *Oxon* 5D 50
Grandtully. *Per* 3G 143
Grange. *Cumb* 3D 102
Grange. *E Ayr* 1D 116
Grange. *Here* 3G 59
Grange. *Mers* 2E 83
Grange. *Per* 1E 137
Grange Crossroads. *Mor* 3B 160
Grange Hill. *G Lon* 1F 39
Grangemill. *Derbs* 5G 85
Grange Moor. *W Yor* 3C 92
Grangemouth. *Falk* 1C 128
Grange of Lindores. *Fife* 2E 137
Grange-over-Sands. *Cumb* 2D 96
Grangepans. *Falk* 1D 128
Grange, The. *N Yor* 5C 106
Grangetown. *Card* 4E 33
Grangetown. *Red C* 2C 106
Grange Villa. *Dur* 4F 115
Granish. *High* 2C 150
Gransmoor. *E Yor* 4F 101
Granston. *Pemb* 1C 42
Grantchester. *Cambs* 5D 64
Grantham. *Linc* 2G 75
Grantley. *N Yor* 3E 99
Grantlodge. *Abers* 2E 152
Granton. *Edin* 2F 129
Grantown-on-Spey. *High* 1E 151
Grantshouse. *Bord* 3E 130
Grappenhall. *Warr* 2A 84
Grasby. *Linc* 4D 94
Grasmere. *Cumb* 4E 103
Grasscroft. *G Man* 4H 91
Grassendale. *Mers* 2F 83
Grassgarth. *Cumb* 5E 113
Grassholme. *Dur* 2C 104
Grassington. *N Yor* 3C 98
Grassmoor. *Derbs* 4B 86
Grassthorpe. *Notts* 4E 87
Grateley. *Hants* 2A 24
Gratton. *Devn* 1D 11
Gratton. *Staf* 5D 84
Gratwich. *Staf* 2E 73
Graveley. *Cambs* 4B 64
Graveley. *Herts* 3C 52
Gravelhill. *Shrp* 4G 71
Gravel Hole. *G Man* 4H 91
Gravelly Hill. *W Mid* 1F 61
Graven. *Shet* 4F 173
Graveney. *Kent* 4E 41
Gravesend. *Kent* 3H 39
Grayingham. *Linc* 1G 87
Grayrigg. *Cumb* 5G 103
Grays. *Thur* 3H 39
Grayshott. *Hants* 3G 25
Grayson Green. *Cumb* 2A 102
Grayswood. *Surr* 2A 26
Graythorp. *Hart* 2C 106
Grazeley. *Wok* 5E 37
Grealin. *High* 2E 155
Greasbrough. *S Yor* 1B 86
Greasby. *Mers* 2E 83
Great Abington. *Cambs* 1F 53
Great Addington. *Nptn* 3G 63
Great Alne. *Warw* 5F 61
Great Altcar. *Lanc* 4B 90
Great Amwell. *Herts* 4D 52
Great Asby. *Cumb* 3H 103
Great Ashfield. *Suff* 4B 66
Great Ayton. *N Yor* 3C 106
Great Baddow. *Essx* 5H 53
Great Bardfield. *Essx* 2G 53

Great Barford—Grove

Great Barford. *Bed* 5A 64
Great Barr. *W Mid* 1E 61
Great Barrington. *Glos* 4H 49
Great Barrow. *Ches W* 4G 83
Great Barton. *Suff* 4A 66
Great Barugh. *N Yor* 2B 100
Great Bavington. *Nmbd* 1C 114
Great Bealings. *Suff* 1F 55
Great Bedwyn. *Wilts* 5A 36
Great Bentley. *Essx* 3E 54
Great Billing. *Nptn* 4F 63
Great Bircham. *Norf* 2G 77
Great Blakenham. *Suff* 5D 66
Great Blencow. *Cumb* 1F 103
Great Bolas. *Telf* 3A 72
Great Bookham. *Surr* 5C 38
Great Bosullow. *Corn* 3B 4
Great Bourton. *Oxon* 1C 50
Great Bowden. *Leics* 2E 63
Great Bradley. *Suff* 5F 65
Great Braxted. *Essx* 4B 54
Great Bricett. *Suff* 5C 66
Great Brickhill. *Buck* 2H 51
Great Bridgeford. *Staf* 3C 72
Great Brington. *Nptn* 4D 62
Great Bromley. *Essx* 3D 54
Great Broughton. *Cumb* 1B 102
Great Broughton. *N Yor* 4C 106
Great Budworth. *Ches W* 3A 84
Great Burdon. *Darl* 3A 106
Great Burstead. *Essx* 1A 40
Great Busby. *N Yor* 4C 106
Great Canfield. *Essx* 4F 53
Great Carlton. *Linc* 2D 88
Great Casterton. *Rut* 5H 75
Great Chalfield. *Wilts* 5D 34
Great Chart. *Kent* 1D 28
Great Chatwell. *Staf* 4B 72
Great Chesterford. *Essx* 1F 53
Great Cheverell. *Wilts* 1E 23
Great Chilton. *Dur* 1F 105
Great Chishill. *Cambs* 2E 53
Great Clacton. *Essx* 4E 55
Great Cliff. *W Yor* 3D 92
Great Clifton. *Cumb* 2B 102
Great Coates. *NE Lin* 3F 95
Great Comberton. *Worc* 1E 49
Great Corby. *Cumb* 4F 113
Great Cornard. *Suff* 1B 54
Great Cowden. *E Yor* 5G 101
Great Coxwell. *Oxon* 2A 36
Great Crakehall. *N Yor* 1E 99
Great Cransley. *Nptn* 3F 63
Great Cressingham. *Norf* 5H 77
Great Crosby. *Mers* 1F 83
Great Cubley. *Derbs* 2F 73
Great Dalby. *Leics* 4E 75
Great Doddington. *Nptn* 4F 63
Great Doward. *Here* 4A 48
Great Dunham. *Norf* 4A 78
Great Dunmow. *Essx* 3G 53
Great Durnford. *Wilts* 3G 23
Great Easton. *Essx* 3G 53
Great Easton. *Leics* 1F 63
Great Eccleston. *Lanc* 5D 96
Great Edstone. *N Yor* 1B 100
Great Ellingham. *Norf* 1C 66
Great Elm. *Som* 2C 22
Great Eppleton. *Tyne* 5G 115
Great Eversden. *Cambs* 5C 64
Great Fencote. *N Yor* 5F 105
Great Finborough. *Suff* 5C 66
Greatford. *Linc* 4H 75
Great Fransham. *Norf* 4A 78
Great Gaddesden. *Herts* 4A 52
Great Gate. *Staf* 1E 73
Great Gidding. *Cambs* 2A 64
Great Givendale. *E Yor* 4C 100
Great Glemham. *Suff* 4F 67
Great Glen. *Leics* 1D 62
Great Gonerby. *Linc* 2G 75
Great Gransden. *Cambs* 5B 64
Great Green. *Norf* 2E 67
Great Green. *Suff* 5B 66
(nr. Lavenham)
Great Green. *Suff* 3D 66
(nr. Palgrave)
Great Habton. *N Yor* 2B 100
Great Hale. *Linc* 1A 76
Great Hallingbury. *Essx* 4F 53
Greatham. *Hants* 3F 25
Greatham. *Hart* 2B 106
Greatham. *W Sus* 4B 26
Great Hampden. *Buck* 5G 51
Great Harrowden. *Nptn* 3F 63
Great Harwood. *Lanc* 1F 91
Great Haseley. *Oxon* 5E 51
Great Hatfield. *E Yor* 5F 101
Great Haywood. *Staf* 3D 73
Great Heath. *W Mid* 2H 61
Great Heck. *N Yor* 2F 93
Great Henny. *Essx* 2B 54
Great Hinton. *Wilts* 1E 23
Great Hockham. *Norf* 1B 66
Great Holland. *Essx* 4F 55
Great Horkesley. *Essx* 2C 54
Great Hormead. *Herts* 2E 53
Great Horton. *W Yor* 1B 92
Great Horwood. *Buck* 2F 51
Great Houghton. *Nptn* 5E 63
Great Houghton. *S Yor* 4E 93
Great Hucklow. *Derbs* 3F 85
Great Kelk. *E Yor* 4F 101
Great Kendale. *E Yor* 3E 101
Great Kimble. *Buck* 5G 51
Great Kingshill. *Buck* 2G 37
Great Langdale. *Cumb* 4D 102
Great Langton. *N Yor* 5F 105
Great Leighs. *Essx* 4H 53
Great Limber. *Linc* 4E 95
Great Linford. *Mil* 1G 51
Great Livermere. *Suff* 3A 66
Great Longstone. *Derbs* 3G 85
Great Lumley. *Dur* 5F 115
Great Lyth. *Shrp* 5G 71
Great Malvern. *Worc* 1C 48
Great Maplestead. *Essx* 2B 54
Great Marton. *Bkpl* 1B 90
Great Massingham. *Norf* 3G 77
Great Melton. *Norf* 5D 78
Great Milton. *Oxon* 5E 51
Great Missenden. *Buck* 5G 51
Great Mitton. *Lanc* 1F 91
Great Mongeham. *Kent* 5H 41
Great Moulton. *Norf* 1D 66
Great Munden. *Herts* 3D 52
Great Musgrave. *Cumb* 3A 104
Great Ness. *Shrp* 4F 71
Great Notley. *Essx* 3H 53
Great Oak. *Mon* 5G 47
Great Oakley. *Essx* 3E 55
Great Oakley. *Nptn* 2F 63
Great Offley. *Herts* 3B 52
Great Ormside. *Cumb* 3A 104
Great Orton. *Cumb* 4E 113
Great Ouseburn. *N Yor* 3G 99
Great Oxendon. *Nptn* 2E 63
Great Oxney Green. *Essx* 5G 53
Great Parndon. *Essx* 5E 53
Great Paxton. *Cambs* 4B 64
Great Plumpton. *Lanc* 1B 90
Great Plumstead. *Norf* 4F 79
Great Ponton. *Linc* 2G 75
Great Potheridge. *Devn* 1F 11
Great Preston. *W Yor* 2E 93
Great Raveley. *Cambs* 2B 64
Great Rissington. *Glos* 4G 49
Great Rollright. *Oxon* 2B 50
Great Ryburgh. *Norf* 3B 78
Great Ryle. *Nmbd* 3E 121
Great Ryton. *Shrp* 5G 71
Great Saling. *Essx* 3G 53
Great Salkeld. *Cumb* 1G 103
Great Sampford. *Essx* 2G 53
Great Sankey. *Warr* 2H 83
Great Saredon. *Staf* 5D 72
Great Saxham. *Suff* 4G 65
Great Shefford. *W Ber* 4B 36
Great Shelford. *Cambs* 5D 64
Great Shoddesden. *Hants* 2A 24
Great Smeaton. *N Yor* 4A 106
Great Snoring. *Norf* 2B 78
Great Somerford. *Wilts* 3E 35
Great Stainton. *Darl* 2A 106
Great Stambridge. *Essx* 1C 40
Great Staughton. *Cambs* 4A 64
Great Steeping. *Linc* 4D 88
Great Stonar. *Kent* 5H 41
Greatstone-on-Sea. *Kent* 3E 29
Great Strickland. *Cumb* 2G 103
Great Stukeley. *Cambs* 3B 64
Great Sturton. *Linc* 3B 88
Great Sutton. *Ches W* 3F 83
Great Sutton. *Shrp* 2H 59
Great Swinburne. *Nmbd* 2C 114
Great Tew. *Oxon* 3B 50
Great Tey. *Essx* 3B 54
Great Thirkleby. *N Yor* 2G 99
Great Thorness. *IOW* 3C 16
Great Thurlow. *Suff* 5F 65
Great Torr. *Devn* 4C 8
Great Torrington. *Devn* 1E 11
Great Tosson. *Nmbd* 4E 121
Great Totham North. *Essx* 4B 54
Great Totham South. *Essx* 4B 54
Great Tows. *Linc* 1B 88
Great Urswick. *Cumb* 2B 96
Great Wakering. *Essx* 2D 40
Great Waldingfield. *Suff* 1C 54
Great Walsingham. *Norf* 2B 78
Great Waltham. *Essx* 4G 53
Great Warley. *Essx* 1G 39
Great Washbourne. *Glos* 2E 49
Great Wenham. *Suff* 2D 54
Great Whelnetham. *Suff* 5A 66
Great Whittington. *Nmbd* 2D 114
Great Wigborough. *Essx* 4C 54
Great Wilbraham. *Cambs* 5E 65
Great Wilne. *Derbs* 2B 74
Great Wishford. *Wilts* 3F 23
Great Witchingham. *Norf* 3D 78
Great Witcombe. *Glos* 4E 49
Great Witley. *Worc* 4B 60
Great Wolford. *Warw* 2H 49
Greatworth. *Nptn* 1D 50
Great Wratting. *Suff* 1G 53
Great Wymondley. *Herts* 3C 52
Great Wyrley. *Staf* 5D 73
Great Wytheford. *Shrp* 4H 71
Great Yarmouth. *Norf* 5H 79
Great Yeldham. *Essx* 2A 54
Grebby. *Linc* 4D 88
Greeba Castle. *IOM* 3C 108
Greenbank. *Shet* 1G 173
Greenbottom. *Corn* 4B 6
Greenburn. *W Lot* 3C 128
Greencroft. *Dur* 4E 115
Greencroft Park. *Dur* 5E 115
Greendown. *Som* 1A 22
Greendykes. *Nmbd* 2E 121
Green End. *Bed* 1A 52
(nr. Bedford)
Green End. *Bed* 4A 64
(nr. St Neots)
Green End. *Herts* 2D 52
(nr. Buntingford)
Green End. *Herts* 3D 52
(nr. Stevenage)
Green End. *N Yor* 4F 107
Green End. *Warw* 2G 61
Greenfield. *Arg* 4B 134
Greenfield. *C Beds* 2A 52
Greenfield. *Flin* 3D 82
Greenfield. *G Man* 4H 91
Greenfield. *Oxon* 2F 37
Greenfoot. *N Lan* 3A 128
Greenford. *G Lon* 2C 38
Greengairs. *N Lan* 2A 128
Greengate. *Norf* 4C 78
Greengill. *Cumb* 1C 102
Greenhalgh. *Lanc* 1C 90
Greenham. *Dors* 2H 13
Greenham. *Som* 4D 20
Greenham. *W Ber* 5C 36
Green Hammerton. *N Yor* 4G 99
Greenhaugh. *Nmbd* 1A 114
Greenhead. *Nmbd* 3H 113
Green Heath. *Staf* 4D 73
Greenhill. *Dum* 2C 112
Greenhill. *Falk* 2B 128
Greenhill. *Kent* 4F 41
Greenhill. *S Yor* 2H 85
Greenhill. *Worc* 3C 60
Greenhills. *N Ayr* 4E 127
Greenhithe. *Kent* 3G 39
Greenholm. *E Ayr* 1E 117
Greenhow Hill. *N Yor* 3D 98
Greenigoe. *Orkn* 7D 172
Greenland. *High* 2E 169
Greenland Mains. *High* 2E 169
Greenlands. *Worc* 4E 61
Green Lane. *Shrp* 3A 72
Green Lane. *Warw* 4E 61
Greenlaw. *Bord* 5D 130
Greenlea. *Dum* 2B 112
Greenloaning. *Per* 3H 135
Greenmount. *G Man* 3F 91
Greenock. *Inv* 2D 126
Greenock Mains. *E Ayr* 2F 117
Greenodd. *Cumb* 1C 96
Green Ore. *Som* 1A 22
Greenrow. *Cumb* 4C 112
Greens. *Abers* 4F 161
Greensgate. *Norf* 4D 78
Greenside. *Tyne* 3E 115
Greensidehill. *Nmbd* 3D 121
Greens Norton. *Nptn* 1E 51
Greenstead Green. *Essx* 3B 54
Greensted Green. *Essx* 5F 53
Green Street. *Herts* 1C 38
Green Street. *Suff* 3D 66
Green Street Green. *G Lon* 4F 39
Green Street Green. *Kent* 3G 39
Greenstreet Green. *Suff* 1D 54
Green, The. *Cumb* 1A 96
Green, The. *Wilts* 3D 22
Green Tye. *Herts* 4E 53
Greenway. *Pemb* 2E 43
Greenway. *V Glam* 4D 32
Greenwell. *Cumb* 4G 113
Greenwich. *G Lon* 3E 39
Greet. *Glos* 2F 49
Greete. *Shrp* 3H 59
Greetham. *Linc* 3C 88
Greetham. *Rut* 4G 75
Greetland. *W Yor* 2A 92
Gregson Lane. *Lanc* 2D 90
Grein. *W Isl* 8B 170
Greinetobht. *W Isl* 1D 170
Greinton. *Som* 3H 21
Grenaby. *IOM* 4B 108
Grendon. *Nptn* 4F 63
Grendon. *Warw* 1G 61
Grendon Common. *Warw* 1G 61
Grendon Green. *Here* 5H 59
Grendon Underwood. *Buck* 3E 51
Grenofen. *Devn* 5E 11
Grenoside. *S Yor* 1H 85
Greosabhagh. *W Isl* 8D 171
Gresford. *Wrex* 5F 83
Gresham. *Norf* 2D 78
Greshornish. *High* 3C 154
Gressenhall. *Norf* 4B 78
Gressingham. *Lanc* 2E 97
Greta Bridge. *Dur* 3D 105
Gretna. *Dum* 3E 112
Gretna Green. *Dum* 3E 112
Gretton. *Glos* 2F 49
Gretton. *Nptn* 1G 63
Gretton. *Shrp* 1H 59
Grewelthorpe. *N Yor* 2E 99
Greygarth. *N Yor* 2D 98
Grey Green. *N Lin* 4A 94
Greylake. *Som* 3G 21
Greysouthen. *Cumb* 2B 102
Greystoke. *Cumb* 1F 103
Greystoke Gill. *Cumb* 2F 103
Greystone. *Ang* 4E 145
Greystones. *S Yor* 2H 85
Greywell. *Hants* 1F 25
Griais. *W Isl* 3G 171
Grianan. *W Isl* 4G 171
Gribthorpe. *E Yor* 1A 94
Gribun. *Arg* 5F 139
Griff. *Warw* 2A 62
Griffithstown. *Torf* 2F 33
Griffydam. *Leics* 4B 74
Griggs Green. *Hants* 3G 25
Grimbister. *Orkn* 6C 172
Grimeford Village. *Lanc* 3E 90
Grimethorpe. *S Yor* 4E 93
Griminis. *W Isl* 3C 170
(on Benbecula)
Griminis. *W Isl* 1C 170
(on North Uist)
Grimister. *Shet* 2F 173
Grimley. *Worc* 4C 60
Grimoldby. *Linc* 2C 88
Grimpo. *Shrp* 3F 71
Grimsargh. *Lanc* 1D 90
Grimsbury. *Oxon* 1C 50
Grimsby. *NE Lin* 3F 95
Grimscote. *Nptn* 5D 62
Grimscott. *Corn* 2C 10
Grimshaw. *Bkbn* 2F 91
Grimshaw Green. *Lanc* 3C 90
Grimsthorpe. *Linc* 3H 75
Grimston. *E Yor* 1F 95
Grimston. *Leics* 3D 74
Grimston. *Norf* 3G 77
Grimston. *York* 4A 100
Grimstone. *Dors* 3B 14
Grimstone End. *Suff* 4B 66
Grinacombe Moor. *Devn* 3E 11
Grindale. *E Yor* 2F 101
Grindhill. *Devn* 3E 11
Grindiscol. *Shet* 8F 173
Grindle. *Shrp* 5B 72
Grindleford. *Derbs* 3G 85
Grindleton. *Lanc* 5G 97
Grindley. *Staf* 3E 73
Grindley Brook. *Shrp* 1H 71
Grindlow. *Derbs* 3F 85
Grindon. *Nmbd* 5F 131
Grindon. *Staf* 5E 85
Gringley on the Hill. *Notts* 1E 87
Grinsdale. *Cumb* 4E 113
Grinshill. *Shrp* 3H 71
Grinton. *N Yor* 5D 104
Griomsidar. *W Isl* 5G 171
Grishipoll. *Arg* 3C 138
Grisling Common. *E Sus* 3F 27
Gristhorpe. *N Yor* 1E 101
Griston. *Norf* 1B 66
Gritley. *Orkn* 7E 172
Grittenham. *Wilts* 3F 35
Grittleton. *Wilts* 4D 34
Grizebeck. *Cumb* 1B 96
Grizedale. *Cumb* 5E 103
Grobister. *Orkn* 5F 172
Groby. *Leics* 5C 74
Groes. *Cnwy* 4C 82
Groes. *Neat* 3A 32
Groes-faen. *Rhon* 3D 32
Groesffordd. *Gwyn* 2B 68
Groesffordd. *Powy* 3D 46
Groeslon. *Gwyn* 5D 81
Groes-lwyd. *Powy* 4E 70
Groes-wen. *Cphy* 3E 33
Grogport. *Arg* 5G 125
Groigearraidh. *W Isl* 4C 170
Gromford. *Suff* 5F 67
Gronant. *Flin* 2C 82
Groombridge. *E Sus* 2G 27
Grosmont. *Mon* 3H 47
Grosmont. *N Yor* 4F 107
Groton. *Suff* 1C 54
Grove. *Dors* 5C 14
Grove. *Kent* 4G 41

Grove—Hannington

Grove. *Notts* 3E 87
Grove. *Oxon* 2B 36
Grovehill. *E Yor* 1D 94
Grove Park. *G Lon* 3F 39
Grovesend. *Swan* 5F 45
Grove, The. *Dum* 2A 112
Grove, The. *Worc* 1D 48
Grub Street. *Staf* 3B 72
Grudie. *High* 2F 157
Gruids. *High* 3C 164
Gruinard House. *High* 4D 162
Gruinart. *Arg* 3A 124
Grulinbeg. *Arg* 3A 124
Gruline. *Arg* 4G 139
Grummore. *High* 5G 167
Grundisburgh. *Suff* 5E 66
Gruting. *Shet* 7D 173
Grutness. *Shet* 10F 173
Gualachulain. *High* 4F 141
Gualin House. *High* 3D 166
Guardbridge. *Fife* 2G 137
Guarlford. *Worc* 1D 48
Guay. *Per* 4H 143
Gubblecote. *Herts* 4H 51
Guestling Green. *E Sus* 4C 28
Guestling Thorn. *E Sus* 4C 28
Guestwick. *Norf* 3C 78
Guestwick Green. *Norf* 3C 78
Guide. *Bkbn* 2F 91
Guide Post. *Nmbd* 1F 115
Guilden Down. *Shrp* 2F 59
Guilden Morden. *Cambs* 1C 52
Guilden Sutton. *Ches W* 4G 83
Guildford. *Surr* 1A 26
Guildtown. *Per* 5A 144
Guilsborough. *Nptn* 3D 62
Guilsfield. *Powy* 4E 70
Guineaford. *Devn* 3F 19
Guisborough. *Red C* 3D 106
Guiseley. *W Yor* 5D 98
Guist. *Norf* 3B 78
Guiting Power. *Glos* 3F 49
Gulberwick. *Shet* 8F 173
Gullane. *E Lot* 1A 130
Gulling Green. *Suff* 5H 65
Gulval. *Corn* 3B 4
Gumfreston. *Pemb* 4F 43
Gumley. *Leics* 1D 62
Gunby. *E Yor* 1H 93
Gunby. *Linc* 3G 75
Gundleton. *Hants* 3E 24
Gun Green. *Kent* 2B 28
Gun Hill. *E Sus* 4G 27
Gunn. *Devn* 3G 19
Gunnerside. *N Yor* 5C 104
Gunnerton. *Nmbd* 2C 114
Gunness. *N Lin* 3B 94
Gunnislake. *Corn* 5E 11
Gunsgreenhill. *Bord* 3F 131
Gunstone. *Staf* 5C 72
Gunthorpe. *Norf* 2C 78
Gunthorpe. *N Lin* 1F 87
Gunthorpe. *Notts* 1D 74
Gunthorpe. *Pet* 5A 76
Gunville. *IOW* 4C 16
Gupworthy. *Som* 3C 20
Gurnard. *IOW* 3C 16
Gurney Slade. *Som* 2B 22
Gurnos. *Powy* 5A 46
Gussage All Saints. *Dors* 1F 15
Gussage St Andrew. *Dors* 1E 15
Gussage St Michael. *Dors* 1E 15
Guston. *Kent* 1H 29
Gutcher. *Shet* 2G 173
Guthram Gowt. *Linc* 3A 76
Guthrie. *Ang* 3E 145
Guyhirn. *Cambs* 5D 76
Guyhirn Gull. *Cambs* 5C 76
Guy's Head. *Linc* 3D 77
Guy's Marsh. *Dors* 4D 22
Guyzance. *Nmbd* 4G 121
Gwaelod-y-garth. *Card* 3E 32
Gwaenynog Bach. *Den* 4C 82
Gwaenysgor. *Flin* 2C 82
Gwalchmai. *IOA* 3C 80
Gwastad. *Pemb* 2E 43
Gwaun-Cae-Gurwen. *Neat* 4H 45
Gwaun-y-bara. *Cphy* 3E 33
Gwbert. *Cdgn* 1B 44
Gweek. *Corn* 4E 5
Gwehelog. *Mon* 5G 47
Gwenddwr. *Powy* 1D 46
Gwennap. *Corn* 4B 6
Gwenter. *Corn* 5E 5
Gwernaffield. *Flin* 4E 82
Gwernesney. *Mon* 5H 47
Gwernogle. *Carm* 2F 45
Gwern-y-go. *Powy* 1E 58
Gwernymynydd. *Flin* 4E 82
Gwersyllt. *Wrex* 5F 83
Gwespyr. *Flin* 2D 82
Gwinear. *Corn* 3C 4
Gwithian. *Corn* 2C 4
Gwredog. *IOA* 2D 80
Gwyddelwern. *Den* 1C 70
Gwyddgrug. *Carm* 2E 45
Gwynfryn. *Wrex* 5E 83
Gwystre. *Powy* 4C 58
Gwytherin. *Cnwy* 4A 82
Gyfelia. *Wrex* 1F 71
Gyffin. *Cnwy* 3G 81

H

Habberley. *Shrp* 5F 71
Habblesthorpe. *Notts* 2E 87
Habergham. *Lanc* 1G 91
Habin. *W Sus* 4G 25
Habrough. *NE Lin* 3E 95
Haceby. *Linc* 2H 75
Hacheston. *Suff* 5F 67
Hackenthorpe. *S Yor* 2B 86
Hackford. *Norf* 5C 78
Hackforth. *N Yor* 5F 105
Hackleton. *Nptn* 5F 63
Hackman's Gate. *Worc* 3C 60
Hackness. *N Yor* 5G 107
Hackness. *Orkn* 8C 172
Hackney. *G Lon* 2E 39
Hackthorn. *Linc* 2G 87
Hackthorpe. *Cumb* 2G 103
Haclait. *W Isl* 4D 170
Haconby. *Linc* 3A 76
Hadden. *Bord* 1B 120
Haddenham. *Buck* 5F 51
Haddenham. *Cambs* 3D 64
Haddenham End. *Cambs* 3D 64
Haddington. *E Lot* 2B 130
Haddington. *Linc* 4G 87
Haddiscoe. *Norf* 1G 67
Haddo. *Abers* 5F 161
Haddon. *Cambs* 1A 64
Hademore. *Staf* 5F 73
Hadfield. *Derbs* 1E 85
Hadham Cross. *Herts* 4E 53
Hadham Ford. *Herts* 3E 53
Hadleigh. *Essx* 2C 40
Hadleigh. *Suff* 1D 54
Hadleigh Heath. *Suff* 1C 54
Hadley. *Telf* 4A 72
Hadley. *Worc* 4C 60
Hadley End. *Staf* 3F 73
Hadley Wood. *G Lon* 1D 38
Hadlow. *Kent* 1H 27
Hadlow Down. *E Sus* 3G 27
Hadnall. *Shrp* 3H 71
Hadstock. *Essx* 1F 53
Hadston. *Nmbd* 5G 121
Hady. *Derbs* 3A 86
Hadzor. *Worc* 4D 60
Haffenden Quarter. *Kent* 1C 28
Haggate. *Lanc* 1G 91
Haggbeck. *Cumb* 2F 113
Haggerston. *Nmbd* 5G 131
Haggrister. *Shet* 4E 173
Hagley. *Here* 1A 48
Hagley. *Worc* 2D 60
Hagnaby. *Linc* 4C 88
Hagworthingham. *Linc* 4C 88
Haigh. *G Man* 4E 90
Haigh Moor. *W Yor* 2C 92
Haighton Green. *Lanc* 1D 90
Haile. *Cumb* 4B 102
Hailes. *Glos* 2F 49
Hailey. *Herts* 4D 52
Hailey. *Oxon* 4B 50
Hailsham. *E Sus* 5G 27
Hail Weston. *Cambs* 4A 64
Hainault. *G Lon* 1F 39
Hainford. *Norf* 4E 78
Hainton. *Linc* 2A 88
Hainworth. *W Yor* 1A 92
Haisthorpe. *E Yor* 3F 101
Hakin. *Pemb* 4C 42
Halam. *Notts* 5D 86
Halbeath. *Fife* 1E 129
Halberton. *Devn* 1D 12
Halcro. *High* 2E 169
Hale. *Cumb* 2E 97
Hale. *G Man* 2B 84
Hale. *Hal* 2G 83
Hale. *Hants* 1G 15
Hale. *Surr* 2G 25
Hale Bank. *Hal* 2G 83
Halebarns. *G Man* 2B 84
Hales. *Norf* 1F 67
Hales. *Staf* 2B 72
Halesgate. *Linc* 3C 76
Hales Green. *Derbs* 1F 73
Halesowen. *W Mid* 2D 60
Hale Street. *Kent* 1A 28
Halesworth. *Suff* 3F 67
Halewood. *Mers* 2G 83
Halford. *Shrp* 2G 59
Halford. *Warw* 1A 50
Halfpenny. *Cumb* 1E 97
Halfpenny Furze. *Carm* 3G 43
Halfpenny Green. *Shrp* 1C 60
Halfway. *Carm* 2G 45
Halfway. *Powy* 2B 46
Halfway. *S Yor* 2B 86
Halfway. *W Ber* 5C 36
Halfway House. *Shrp* 4F 71
Halfway Houses. *Kent* 3D 40
Halgabron. *Corn* 4A 10
Halifax. *W Yor* 2A 92
Halistra. *High* 3B 154
Halket. *E Ayr* 4F 127
Halkirk. *High* 3D 168
Halkyn. *Flin* 3E 82
Hall. *E Ren* 4F 127
Hallam Fields. *Derbs* 1B 74
Halland. *E Sus* 4G 27
Hallands, The. *N Lin* 2D 94
Hallaton. *Leics* 1E 63
Hallatrow. *Bath* 1B 22
Hallbank. *Cumb* 5H 103
Hallbankgate. *Cumb* 4G 113
Hall Dunnerdale. *Cumb* 5D 102
Hallen. *S Glo* 3A 34
Hall End. *Bed* 1A 52
Hallgarth. *Dur* 5G 115
Hall Green. *Ches E* 5C 84
Hall Green. *Norf* 2D 66
Hall Green. *W Mid* 2F 61
Hall Green. *W Yor* 3D 92
Hall Green. *Wrex* 1G 71
Halliburton. *Bord* 5C 130
Hallin. *High* 3B 154
Halling. *Medw* 4B 40
Hallington. *Linc* 2C 88
Hallington. *Nmbd* 2C 114
Halloughton. *Notts* 5D 86
Hallow. *Worc* 5C 60
Hallow Heath. *Worc* 5C 60
Hallowsgate. *Ches W* 4H 83
Hallsands. *Devn* 5E 9
Hall's Green. *Herts* 3C 52
Hallspill. *Devn* 4E 19
Hallthwaites. *Cumb* 1A 96
Hall Waberthwaite. *Cumb* 5C 102
Hallwood Green. *Glos* 2B 48
Hallworthy. *Corn* 4B 10
Hallyne. *Bord* 5E 129
Halmer End. *Staf* 1C 72
Halmond's Frome. *Here* 1B 48
Halmore. *Glos* 5B 48
Halnaker. *W Sus* 5A 26
Halsall. *Lanc* 3B 90
Halse. *Nptn* 1D 50
Halse. *Som* 4E 21
Halsetown. *Corn* 3C 4
Halsham. *E Yor* 2F 95
Halsinger. *Devn* 3F 19
Halstead. *Essx* 2B 54
Halstead. *Kent* 4F 39
Halstead. *Leics* 5E 75
Halstock. *Dors* 2A 14
Halsway. *Som* 3E 21
Haltcliff Bridge. *Cumb* 1E 103
Haltham. *Linc* 4B 88
Haltoft End. *Linc* 1C 76
Halton. *Buck* 5G 51
Halton. *Hal* 2H 83
Halton. *Lanc* 3E 97
Halton. *Nmbd* 3C 114
Halton. *W Yor* 1D 92
Halton. *Wrex* 2F 71
Halton East. *N Yor* 4C 98
Halton Fenside. *Linc* 4D 88
Halton Gill. *N Yor* 2A 98
Halton Holegate. *Linc* 4D 88
Halton Lea Gate. *Nmbd* 4H 113
Halton Moor. *W Yor* 1D 92
Halton Shields. *Nmbd* 3D 114
Halton West. *N Yor* 4H 97
Haltwhistle. *Nmbd* 3A 114
Halvergate. *Norf* 5G 79
Halwell. *Devn* 3D 9
Halwill. *Devn* 3E 11
Halwill Junction. *Devn* 3E 11
Ham. *Devn* 2F 13
Ham. *Glos* 2B 34
Ham. *G Lon* 3C 38
Ham. *High* 1E 169
Ham. *Kent* 5H 41
Ham. *Plym* 3A 8
Ham. *Shet* 8A 173
Ham. *Som* 1F 13
(nr. Ilminster)
Ham. *Som* 4F 21
(nr. Taunton)
Ham. *Som* 4E 21
(nr. Wellington)
Ham. *Wilts* 5B 36
Hambleden. *Buck* 3F 37
Hambledon. *Hants* 1E 17
Hambledon. *Surr* 2A 26
Hamble-le-Rice. *Hants* 2C 16
Hambleton. *Lanc* 5C 96
Hambleton. *N Yor* 1F 93
Hambridge. *Som* 4G 21
Hambrook. *S Glo* 4B 34
Hambrook. *W Sus* 2F 17
Ham Common. *Dors* 4D 22
Hameringham. *Linc* 4C 88
Hamerton. *Cambs* 3A 64
Ham Green. *Here* 1C 48
Ham Green. *Kent* 4C 40
Ham Green. *N Som* 4A 34
Ham Green. *Worc* 4E 61
Ham Hill. *Kent* 4A 40
Hamilton. *Leics* 5D 74
Hamilton. *S Lan* 4A 128
Hammer. *W Sus* 3G 25
Hammersmith. *G Lon* 3D 38
Hammerwich. *Staf* 5E 73
Hammerwood. *E Sus* 2F 27
Hammill. *Kent* 5G 41
Hammond Street. *Herts* 5D 52
Hammoon. *Dors* 1D 14
Hamnavoe. *Shet* 8E 173
(nr. Burland)
Hamnavoe. *Shet* 3F 173
(on Yell)
Hamp. *Som* 3G 21
Hampden Park. *E Sus* 5H 27
Hampen. *Glos* 3F 49
Hamperden End. *Essx* 2F 53
Hamperley. *Shrp* 2G 59
Hampnett. *Glos* 4F 49
Hampole. *S Yor* 3F 93
Hampreston. *Dors* 3F 15
Hampstead. *G Lon* 2D 38
Hampstead Norreys. *W Ber* 4D 36
Hampsthwaite. *N Yor* 4E 99
Hampton. *Devn* 3F 13
Hampton. *G Lon* 3C 38
Hampton. *Kent* 4F 41
Hampton. *Shrp* 2B 60
Hampton. *Swin* 2G 35
Hampton. *Worc* 1F 49
Hampton Bishop. *Here* 2A 48
Hampton Fields. *Glos* 2D 35
Hampton Hargate. *Pet* 1A 64
Hampton Heath. *Ches W* 1H 71
Hampton in Arden. *W Mid* 2G 61
Hampton Loade. *Shrp* 2B 60
Hampton Lovett. *Worc* 4C 60
Hampton Lucy. *Warw* 5G 61
Hampton Magna. *Warw* 4G 61
Hampton on the Hill. *Warw* 4G 61
Hampton Poyle. *Oxon* 4D 50
Hampton Wick. *G Lon* 4C 38
Hamptworth. *Wilts* 1H 15
Hamrow. *Norf* 3B 78
Hamsey. *E Sus* 4F 27
Hamsey Green. *Surr* 5E 39
Hamstall Ridware. *Staf* 4F 73
Hamstead. *IOW* 3C 16
Hamstead. *W Mid* 1E 61
Hamstead Marshall. *W Ber* 5C 36
Hamsterley. *Dur* 4E 115
(nr. Consett)
Hamsterley. *Dur* 1E 105
(nr. Wolsingham)
Hamsterley Mill. *Dur* 4E 115
Hamstreet. *Kent* 2E 28
Ham Street. *Som* 3A 22
Hamworthy. *Pool* 3E 15
Hanbury. *Staf* 3F 73
Hanbury. *Worc* 4D 60
Hanbury Woodend. *Staf* 3F 73
Hanby. *Linc* 2H 75
Hanchurch. *Staf* 1C 72
Hand and Pen. *Devn* 3D 12
Handbridge. *Ches W* 4G 83
Handcross. *W Sus* 3D 26
Handforth. *Ches E* 2C 84
Handley. *Ches W* 5G 83
Handley. *Derbs* 4A 86
Handsacre. *Staf* 4E 73
Handsworth. *S Yor* 2B 86
Handsworth. *W Mid* 1E 61
Handy Cross. *Buck* 2G 37
Hanford. *Dors* 1D 14
Hanford. *Stoke* 1C 72
Hangersley. *Hants* 2G 15
Hanging Houghton. *Nptn* 3E 63
Hanging Langford. *Wilts* 3F 23
Hangleton. *Brig* 5D 26
Hangleton. *W Sus* 5B 26
Hanham. *S Glo* 4B 34
Hanham Green. *S Glo* 4B 34
Hankelow. *Ches E* 1A 72
Hankerton. *Wilts* 2E 35
Hankham. *E Sus* 5H 27
Hanley. *Stoke* 1C 72
Hanley Castle. *Worc* 1D 48
Hanley Childe. *Worc* 4A 60
Hanley Swan. *Worc* 1D 48
Hanley William. *Worc* 4A 60
Hanlith. *N Yor* 3B 98
Hanmer. *Wrex* 2G 71
Hannaborough. *Devn* 2F 11
Hannaford. *Devn* 4G 19
Hannah. *Linc* 3E 89
Hannington. *Hants* 1D 24
Hannington. *Nptn* 3F 63

Hayton—High Beech

Hayton. *Cumb* 5C 112 (nr. Aspatria)
Hayton. *Cumb* 4G 113 (nr. Brampton)
Hayton. *E Yor* 5C 100
Hayton. *Notts* 2E 87
Hayton's Bent. *Shrp* 2H 59
Haytor Vale. *Devn* 5A 12
Haytown. *Devn* 1D 11
Haywards Heath. *W Sus* 3E 27
Haywood. *S Lan* 4C 128
Hazelbank. *S Lan* 5B 128
Hazelbury Bryan. *Dors* 2C 14
Hazeleigh. *Essx* 5B 54
Hazeley. *Hants* 1F 25
Hazel Grove. *G Man* 2D 84
Hazelhead. *S Yor* 4B 92
Hazelslade. *Staf* 4E 73
Hazel Street. *Kent* 2A 28
Hazelton Walls. *Fife* 1F 137
Hazelwood. *Derbs* 1H 73
Hazlemere. *Buck* 2G 37
Hazler. *Shrp* 1G 59
Hazlerigg. *Tyne* 2F 115
Hazles. *Staf* 1E 73
Hazleton. *Glos* 4F 49
Hazon. *Nmbd* 4F 121
Heacham. *Norf* 2F 77
Headbourne Worthy. *Hants* 3C 24
Headcorn. *Kent* 1C 28
Headingley. *W Yor* 1C 92
Headington. *Oxon* 5D 50
Headlam. *Dur* 3E 105
Headless Cross. *Worc* 4E 61
Headley. *Hants* 3G 25 (nr. Haslemere)
Headley. *Hants* 5D 36 (nr. Kingsclere)
Headley. *Surr* 5D 38
Headley Down. *Hants* 3G 25
Headley Heath. *Worc* 3E 61
Headley Park. *Bris* 5A 34
Head of Muir. *Falk* 1B 128
Headon. *Notts* 3E 87
Heads Nook. *Cumb* 4F 113
Heage. *Derbs* 5A 86
Healaugh. *N Yor* 5D 104 (nr. Grinton)
Healaugh. *N Yor* 5H 99 (nr. York)
Heald Green. *G Man* 2C 84
Heale. *Devn* 2G 19
Healey. *G Man* 3G 91
Healey. *Nmbd* 4D 114
Healey. *N Yor* 1D 98
Healeyfield. *Dur* 5D 114
Healey Hall. *Nmbd* 4D 114
Healing. *NE Lin* 3F 95
Heamoor. *Corn* 3B 4
Heanish. *Arg* 4B 138
Heanor. *Derbs* 1B 74
Heanton Punchardon. *Devn* 3F 19
Heapham. *Linc* 2F 87
Heartsease. *Powy* 4D 58
Heasley Mill. *Devn* 3H 19
Heaste. *High* 2E 147
Heath. *Derbs* 4B 86
Heath and Reach. *C Beds* 3H 51
Heath Common. *W Sus* 4C 26
Heathcote. *Derbs* 4F 85
Heath Cross. *Devn* 3H 11
Heathencote. *Nptn* 1F 51
Heath End. *Derbs* 3A 74
Heath End. *Hants* 5D 36
Heath End. *W Mid* 5E 73
Heather. *Leics* 4A 74
Heatherfield. *High* 4D 155
Heatherton. *Derb* 2H 73
Heathfield. *Cambs* 1E 53
Heathfield. *Cumb* 5C 112
Heathfield. *Devn* 5B 12
Heathfield. *E Sus* 3G 27
Heathfield. *Ren* 3E 126
Heathfield. *Som* 3E 21 (nr. Lydeard St Lawrence)
Heathfield. *Som* 4E 21 (nr. Norton Fitzwarren)
Heath Green. *Worc* 3E 61
Heathhall. *Dum* 2A 112
Heath Hayes. *Staf* 4E 73
Heath Hill. *Shrp* 4B 72
Heath House. *Som* 2H 21
Heathrow (London) Airport. *G Lon* 3B 38
Heathstock. *Devn* 2F 13
Heath, The. *Norf* 3E 79 (nr. Buxton)
Heath, The. *Norf* 3B 78 (nr. Fakenham)
Heath, The. *Norf* 3D 78 (nr. Hevingham)
Heath, The. *Staf* 2E 73
Heath, The. *Suff* 2E 55
Heathton. *Shrp* 1C 60
Heathtop. *Derbs* 2F 73
Heath Town. *W Mid* 1D 60
Heatley. *G Man* 2B 84
Heatley. *Staf* 3E 73
Heaton. *Lanc* 3D 96
Heaton. *Staf* 4D 84
Heaton. *Tyne* 3F 115
Heaton. *W Yor* 1B 92
Heaton Moor. *G Man* 1C 84
Heaton's Bridge. *Lanc* 3C 90
Heaverham. *Kent* 5G 39
Heavitree. *Devn* 3C 12
Hebburn. *Tyne* 3G 115
Hebden. *N Yor* 3C 98
Hebden Bridge. *W Yor* 2H 91
Hebden Green. *Ches W* 4A 84
Hebing End. *Herts* 3D 52
Hebron. *Carm* 2F 43
Hebron. *Nmbd* 1E 115
Heck. *Dum* 1B 112
Heckdyke. *Notts* 1E 87
Heckfield. *Hants* 5F 37
Heckfield Green. *Suff* 3D 66
Heckfordbridge. *Essx* 3C 54
Heckington. *Linc* 1A 76
Heckmondwike. *W Yor* 2C 92
Heddington. *Wilts* 5E 35
Heddon. *Devn* 4G 19
Heddon-on-the-Wall. *Nmbd* 3E 115
Hedenham. *Norf* 1F 67
Hedge End. *Hants* 1C 16
Hedgerley. *Buck* 2A 38
Hedging. *Som* 4G 21
Hedley on the Hill. *Nmbd* 4D 115
Hednesford. *Staf* 4E 73
Hedon. *E Yor* 2E 95
Hegdon Hill. *Here* 5H 59
Heighington. *Darl* 2F 105
Heighington. *Linc* 4H 87
Heightington. *Worc* 3B 60
Heights of Brae. *High* 2H 157
Heights of Fodderty. *High* 2H 157
Heights of Kinlochewe. *High* 2C 156
Heiton. *Bord* 1B 120
Hele. *Devn* 2C 12 (nr. Exeter)
Hele. *Devn* 3D 10 (nr. Holsworthy)
Hele. *Devn* 2F 19 (nr. Ilfracombe)
Hele. *Torb* 2F 9
Helensburgh. *Arg* 1D 126
Helford. *Corn* 4E 5
Helhoughton. *Norf* 3A 78
Helions Bumpstead. *Essx* 1G 53
Helland. *Corn* 5A 10
Helland. *Som* 4G 21
Hellandbridge. *Corn* 5A 10
Hellesdon. *Norf* 4E 78
Hellesveor. *Corn* 2C 4
Hellidon. *Nptn* 5C 62
Hellifield. *N Yor* 4A 98
Hellingly. *E Sus* 4G 27
Hellington. *Norf* 5F 79
Helmdon. *Nptn* 1D 50
Helmingham. *Suff* 5D 66
Helmington Row. *Dur* 1E 105
Helmsdale. *High* 2H 165
Helmshore. *Lanc* 2F 91
Helmsley. *N Yor* 1A 100
Helperby. *N Yor* 3G 99
Helperthorpe. *N Yor* 2D 100
Helpringham. *Linc* 1A 76
Helpston. *Pet* 5A 76
Helsby. *Ches W* 3G 83
Helsey. *Linc* 3E 89
Helston. *Corn* 4D 4
Helstone. *Corn* 4A 10
Helton. *Cumb* 2G 103
Helwith. *N Yor* 4D 105
Helwith Bridge. *N Yor* 3H 97
Helygain. *Flin* 3E 82
Hemblington. *Norf* 4F 79
Hemel Hempstead. *Herts* 5A 52
Hemerdon. *Devn* 3B 8
Hemingbrough. *N Yor* 1G 93
Hemingby. *Linc* 3B 88
Hemingfield. *S Yor* 4D 93
Hemingford Abbots. *Cambs* 3B 64
Hemingford Grey. *Cambs* 3B 64
Hemingstone. *Suff* 5D 66
Hemington. *Leics* 3B 74
Hemington. *Nptn* 2H 63
Hemington. *Som* 1C 22
Hemley. *Suff* 1F 55
Hemlington. *Midd* 3B 106
Hempholme. *E Yor* 4E 101
Hempnall. *Norf* 1E 67
Hempnall Green. *Norf* 1E 67
Hempriggs. *High* 4F 169
Hemp's Green. *Essx* 3C 54
Hempstead. *Essx* 2G 53
Hempstead. *Medw* 4B 40
Hempstead. *Norf* 2D 78 (nr. Holt)
Hempstead. *Norf* 3G 79 (nr. Stalham)
Hempsted. *Glos* 4D 48
Hempton. *Norf* 3B 78
Hempton. *Oxon* 2C 50
Hemsby. *Norf* 4G 79
Hemswell. *Linc* 1G 87
Hemswell Cliff. *Linc* 2G 87
Hemsworth. *Dors* 2E 15
Hemsworth. *W Yor* 3E 93
Hem, The. *Shrp* 5B 72
Hemyock. *Devn* 1E 13
Henallt. *Carm* 3E 45
Henbury. *Bris* 4A 34
Henbury. *Ches E* 3C 84
Hendomen. *Powy* 1E 58
Hendon. *G Lon* 2D 38
Hendon. *Tyne* 4H 115
Hendra. *Corn* 3D 6
Hendre. *B'end* 3C 32
Hendreforgan. *Rhon* 3C 32
Hendy. *Carm* 5F 45
Heneglwys. *IOA* 3D 80
Henfeddau Fawr. *Pemb* 1G 43
Henfield. *S Glo* 4B 34
Henfield. *W Sus* 4D 26
Henford. *Devn* 3D 10
Hengoed. *Cphy* 2E 33
Hengoed. *Shrp* 2E 71
Hengrave. *Suff* 4H 65
Henham. *Essx* 3F 53
Heniarth. *Powy* 5D 70
Henlade. *Som* 4F 21
Henley. *Dors* 2B 14
Henley. *Shrp* 2G 59 (nr. Church Stretton)
Henley. *Shrp* 3H 59 (nr. Ludlow)
Henley. *Som* 3H 21
Henley. *Suff* 5D 66
Henley. *W Sus* 4G 25
Henley-in-Arden. *Warw* 4F 61
Henley-on-Thames. *Oxon* 3F 37
Henley's Down. *E Sus* 4B 28
Henley Street. *Kent* 4A 40
Henllan. *Cdgn* 1D 44
Henllan. *Den* 4C 82
Henllan. *Mon* 3F 47
Henllan Amgoed. *Carm* 3F 43
Henllys. *Torf* 2F 33
Henlow. *C Beds* 2B 52
Hennock. *Devn* 4B 12
Henny Street. *Essx* 2B 54
Henryd. *Cnwy* 3G 81
Henry's Moat. *Pemb* 2E 43
Hensall. *N Yor* 2F 93
Henshaw. *Nmbd* 3A 114
Hensingham. *Cumb* 3A 102
Henstead. *Suff* 2G 67
Hensting. *Hants* 4C 24
Henstridge. *Som* 1C 14
Henstridge Ash. *Som* 4C 22
Henstridge Bowden. *Som* 4B 22
Henstridge Marsh. *Som* 4C 22
Henton. *Oxon* 5F 51
Henton. *Som* 2H 21
Henwood. *Corn* 5C 10
Heogan. *Shet* 7F 173
Heol Senni. *Powy* 3C 46
Heol-y-Cyw. *B'end* 3C 32
Hepburn. *Nmbd* 2E 121
Hepple. *Nmbd* 4D 121
Hepscott. *Nmbd* 1F 115
Heptonstall. *W Yor* 2H 91
Hepworth. *Suff* 3B 66
Hepworth. *W Yor* 4B 92
Herbrandston. *Pemb* 4C 42
Hereford. *Here* 2A 48
Heribusta. *High* 1D 154
Heriot. *Bord* 4H 129
Hermiston. *Edin* 2E 129
Hermitage. *Dors* 2B 14
Hermitage. *Bord* 5H 119
Hermitage. *W Ber* 4D 36
Hermitage. *W Sus* 2F 17
Hermon. *Carm* 3G 45 (nr. Llandeilo)
Hermon. *Carm* 2D 44 (nr. Newcastle Emlyn)
Hermon. *IOA* 4C 80
Hermon. *Pemb* 1G 43
Herne. *Kent* 4F 41
Herne Bay. *Kent* 4F 41
Herne Common. *Kent* 4F 41
Herne Pound. *Kent* 5A 40
Herner. *Devn* 4F 19
Hernhill. *Kent* 4E 41
Herodsfoot. *Corn* 2G 7
Heronden. *Kent* 5G 41
Herongate. *Essx* 1H 39
Heronsford. *S Ayr* 1G 109
Heronsgate. *Herts* 1B 38
Heron's Ghyll. *E Sus* 3F 27
Herra. *Shet* 2H 173
Herriard. *Hants* 2E 25
Herringfleet. *Suff* 1G 67
Herringswell. *Suff* 4G 65
Herrington. *Tyne* 4G 115
Hersden. *Kent* 4G 41
Hersham. *Corn* 2C 10
Hersham. *Surr* 4C 38
Herstmonceux. *E Sus* 4H 27
Herston. *Dors* 5F 15
Herston. *Orkn* 8D 172
Hertford. *Herts* 4D 52
Hertford Heath. *Herts* 4D 52
Hertingfordbury. *Herts* 4D 52
Hesketh. *Lanc* 2C 90
Hesketh Bank. *Lanc* 2C 90
Hesketh Lane. *Lanc* 5F 97
Hesket Newmarket. *Cumb* 1E 103
Heskin Green. *Lanc* 3D 90
Hesleden. *Dur* 1B 106
Hesleyside. *Nmbd* 1B 114
Heslington. *York* 4A 100
Hessay. *York* 4H 99
Hessenford. *Corn* 3H 7
Hessett. *Suff* 4B 66
Hessilhead. *N Ayr* 4E 127
Hessle. *Hull* 2D 94
Hestaford. *Shet* 6D 173
Hest Bank. *Lanc* 3D 96
Hester's Way. *Glos* 3E 49
Heston. *G Lon* 3C 38
Hestwall. *Orkn* 6B 172
Heswall. *Mers* 2E 83
Hethe. *Oxon* 3D 50
Hethelpit Cross. *Glos* 3C 48
Hethersett. *Norf* 5D 78
Hethersgill. *Cumb* 3F 113
Hetherside. *Cumb* 3F 113
Hethpool. *Nmbd* 2C 120
Hett. *Dur* 1F 105
Hetton. *N Yor* 4B 98
Hetton-le-Hole. *Tyne* 5G 115
Hetton Steads. *Nmbd* 1E 121
Heugh. *Nmbd* 2D 115
Heugh-head. *Abers* 2A 152
Heveningham. *Suff* 3F 67
Hever. *Kent* 1F 27
Heversham. *Cumb* 1D 97
Hevingham. *Norf* 3D 78
Hewas Water. *Corn* 4D 6
Hewelsfield. *Glos* 5A 48
Hewish. *N Som* 5G 33
Hewish. *Som* 2H 13
Hewood. *Dors* 2G 13
Heworth. *York* 4A 100
Hexham. *Nmbd* 3C 114
Hextable. *Kent* 3G 39
Hexton. *Herts* 2B 52
Hexworthy. *Devn* 5G 11
Heybridge. *Essx* 1H 39 (nr. Brentwood)
Heybridge. *Essx* 5B 54 (nr. Maldon)
Heybridge Basin. *Essx* 5B 54
Heybrook Bay. *Devn* 4A 8
Heydon. *Cambs* 1E 53
Heydon. *Norf* 3D 78
Heydour. *Linc* 2H 75
Heylipol. *Arg* 4A 138
Heyop. *Powy* 3E 59
Heysham. *Lanc* 3D 96
Heyshott. *W Sus* 1G 17
Heytesbury. *Wilts* 2E 23
Heythrop. *Oxon* 3B 50
Heywood. *G Man* 3G 91
Heywood. *Wilts* 1D 22
Hibaldstow. *N Lin* 4C 94
Hickleton. *S Yor* 4E 93
Hickling. *Norf* 3G 79
Hickling. *Notts* 3D 74
Hickling Green. *Norf* 3G 79
Hickling Heath. *Norf* 3G 79
Hickstead. *W Sus* 3D 26
Hidcote Bartrim. *Glos* 1G 49
Hidcote Boyce. *Glos* 1G 49
Higford. *Shrp* 5B 72
High Ackworth. *W Yor* 3E 93
Higham. *Derbs* 5A 86
Higham. *Kent* 3B 40
Higham. *Lanc* 1G 91
Higham. *S Yor* 4D 92
Higham. *Suff* 2D 54 (nr. Ipswich)
Higham. *Suff* 4G 65 (nr. Newmarket)
Higham Dykes. *Nmbd* 2E 115
Higham Ferrers. *Nptn* 4G 63
Higham Gobion. *C Beds* 2B 52
Higham on the Hill. *Leics* 1A 62
Highampton. *Devn* 2E 11
Higham Wood. *Kent* 1G 27
High Angerton. *Nmbd* 1D 115
High Auldgirth. *Dum* 1G 111
High Bankhill. *Cumb* 5G 113
High Banton. *N Lan* 1A 128
High Barnet. *G Lon* 1D 38
High Beech. *Essx* 1F 39

High Bentham—Holbrook

High Bentham. *N Yor* 3F 97
High Bickington. *Devn* 4G 19
High Biggins. *Cumb* 2F 97
High Birkwith. *N Yor* 2H 97
High Blantyre. *S Lan* 4H 127
High Bonnybridge. *Falk* 2B 128
High Borrans. *Cumb* 4F 103
High Bradfield. *S Yor* 1G 85
High Bray. *Devn* 3G 19
Highbridge. *Cumb* 5E 113
Highbridge. *High* 5D 148
Highbridge. *Som* 2G 21
Highbrook. *W Sus* 2E 27
High Brooms. *Kent* 1G 27
High Bullen. *Devn* 4F 19
Highburton. *W Yor* 3B 92
Highbury. *Som* 2B 22
High Buston. *Nmbd* 4G 121
High Callerton. *Nmbd* 2E 115
High Carlingill. *Cumb* 4H 103
High Catton. *E Yor* 4B 100
High Church. *Nmbd* 1E 115
Highclere. *Hants* 5C 36
Highcliffe. *Dors* 3H 15
High Cogges. *Oxon* 5B 50
High Common. *Norf* 5B 78
High Coniscliffe. *Darl* 3F 105
High Crosby. *Cumb* 4F 113
High Cross. *Hants* 4F 25
High Cross. *Herts* 4D 52
High Dougarie. *N Ayr* 2C 122
High Easter. *Essx* 4G 53
High Eggborough. *N Yor* 2F 93
High Ellington. *N Yor* 1D 98
Higher Alham. *Som* 2B 22
Higher Ansty. *Dors* 2C 14
Higher Ashton. *Devn* 4B 12
Higher Ballam. *Lanc* 1B 90
Higher Bartle. *Lanc* 1D 90
Higher Bockhampton. *Dors* 3C 14
Higher Bojewyan. *Corn* 3A 4
High Ercall. *Telf* 4H 71
Higher Cheriton. *Devn* 2E 12
Higher Clovelly. *Devn* 4D 18
Higher Compton. *Plym* 3A 8
Higher Dean. *Devn* 2D 8
Higher Dinting. *Derbs* 1E 85
Higher Dunstone. *Devn* 5H 11
Higher End. *G Man* 4D 90
Higherford. *Lanc* 5A 98
Higher Gabwell. *Devn* 2F 9
Higher Halstock Leigh. *Dors* 2A 14
Higher Heysham. *Lanc* 3D 96
Higher Hurdsfield. *Ches E* 3D 84
Higher Kingcombe. *Dors* 3A 14
Higher Kinnerton. *Flin* 4F 83
Higher Melcombe. *Dors* 2C 14
Higher Penwortham. *Lanc* 2D 90
Higher Porthpean. *Corn* 3E 7
Higher Poynton. *Ches E* 2D 84
Higher Shotton. *Flin* 4F 83
Higher Shurlach. *Ches W* 3A 84
Higher Slade. *Devn* 2F 19
Higher Tale. *Devn* 2D 12
Highertown. *Corn* 4C 6
Higher Town. *IOS* 1B 4
Higher Town. *Som* 2C 20
Higher Vexford. *Som* 3E 20
Higher Walton. *Lanc* 2D 90
Higher Walton. *Warr* 2H 83
Higher Whatcombe. *Dors* 2D 14
Higher Wheelton. *Lanc* 2E 90
Higher Whiteleigh. *Corn* 3C 10
Higher Whitley. *Ches W* 3A 84
Higher Wincham. *Ches W* 3A 84
Higher Wraxall. *Dors* 2A 14
Higher Wych. *Wrex* 1G 71
Higher Yalberton. *Torb* 3E 9
High Etherley. *Dur* 2E 105
High Ferry. *Linc* 1C 76
Highfield. *E Yor* 1H 93
Highfield. *N Ayr* 4E 126
Highfield. *Tyne* 4E 115
Highfields Caldecote. *Cambs* 5C 64
High Garrett. *Essx* 3A 54
Highgate. *G Lon* 2D 39
Highgate. *N Ayr* 4E 127
Highgate. *Powy* 1D 58
High Grange. *Dur* 1E 105
High Green. *Cumb* 4F 103
High Green. *Norf* 5D 78
High Green. *Shrp* 2B 60
High Green. *S Yor* 1H 85
High Green. *W Yor* 3B 92
High Green. *Worc* 1D 49
Highgreen Manor. *Nmbd* 5C 120
High Halden. *Kent* 2C 28
High Halstow. *Medw* 3B 40
High Ham. *Som* 3H 21
High Harrington. *Cumb* 2B 102
High Haswell. *Dur* 5G 115
High Hatton. *Shrp* 3A 72
High Hawkser. *N Yor* 4G 107
High Hesket. *Cumb* 5F 113
High Hesleden. *Dur* 1B 106
High Hoyland. *S Yor* 3C 92
High Hunsley. *E Yor* 1C 94
High Hurstwood. *E Sus* 3F 27
High Hutton. *N Yor* 3B 100
High Ireby. *Cumb* 1D 102
High Keil. *Arg* 5A 122
High Kelling. *Norf* 1D 78
High Kilburn. *N Yor* 2H 99
High Knipe. *Cumb* 3G 103
High Lands. *Dur* 2E 105
Highlands, The. *Shrp* 2A 60
Highlane. *Ches E* 4C 84
Highlane. *Derbs* 2B 86
High Lane. *G Man* 2D 84
High Lane. *Here* 4A 60
High Laver. *Essx* 5F 53
Highlaws. *Cumb* 5C 112
Highleadon. *Glos* 3C 48
High Legh. *Ches E* 2A 84
Highleigh. *W Sus* 3G 17
High Leven. *Stoc T* 3B 106
Highley. *Shrp* 2B 60
High Littleton. *Bath* 1B 22
High Longthwaite. *Cumb* 5D 112
High Lorton. *Cumb* 2C 102
High Marishes. *N Yor* 2C 100
High Marnham. *Notts* 3F 87
High Melton. *S Yor* 4F 93
High Mickley. *Nmbd* 3D 115
Highmoor. *Cumb* 5D 112
High Moor. *Lanc* 3D 90
Highmoor. *Oxon* 3F 37
Highmoor Cross. *Oxon* 3F 37
Highmoor Hill. *Mon* 3H 33
High Mowthorpe. *N Yor* 3C 100
Highnam. *Glos* 4C 48
High Newport. *Tyne* 4G 115
High Newton. *Cumb* 1D 96
High Newton-by-the-Sea. *Nmbd* 2G 121
High Nibthwaite. *Cumb* 1B 96
High Offley. *Staf* 3B 72
High Ongar. *Essx* 5F 53
High Onn. *Staf* 4C 72
High Orchard. *Glos* 4D 48
High Park. *Mers* 3B 90
High Roding. *Essx* 4G 53
High Row. *Cumb* 1E 103
High Salvington. *W Sus* 5C 26
High Scales. *Cumb* 5C 112
High Shaw. *N Yor* 5B 104
High Shincliffe. *Dur* 5F 115
High Side. *Cumb* 1D 102
High Spen. *Tyne* 3E 115
Highsted. *Kent* 4D 40
High Stoop. *Dur* 5E 115
High Street. *Corn* 3D 6
High Street. *Suff* 5G 67
(nr. Aldeburgh)
High Street. *Suff* 2F 67
(nr. Bungay)
High Street. *Suff* 3G 67
(nr. Yoxford)
Highstreet Green. *Essx* 2A 54
High Street Green. *Suff* 5C 66
Highstreet Green. *Surr* 2A 26
Hightae. *Dum* 2B 112
High Throston. *Hart* 1B 106
Hightown. *Ches E* 4C 84
Hightown. *Mers* 4A 90
High Town. *Staf* 4D 73
Hightown Green. *Suff* 5B 66
High Toynton. *Linc* 4B 88
High Trewhitt. *Nmbd* 4E 121
High Valleyfield. *Fife* 1D 128
Highway. *Here* 1H 47
Highweek. *Devn* 5B 12
High Westwood. *Dur* 4E 115
Highwood. *Staf* 2E 73
Highwood. *Worc* 4A 60
High Worsall. *N Yor* 4A 106
Highworth. *Swin* 2H 35
High Wray. *Cumb* 5E 103
High Wych. *Herts* 4E 53
High Wycombe. *Buck* 2G 37
Hilborough. *Norf* 5H 77
Hilcott. *Wilts* 1G 23
Hildenborough. *Kent* 1G 27
Hildersham. *Cambs* 1F 53
Hilderstone. *Staf* 2D 72
Hilderthorpe. *E Yor* 3F 101
Hilfield. *Dors* 2B 14
Hilgay. *Norf* 1F 65
Hill. *S Glo* 2B 34
Hill. *Warw* 4B 62
Hill. *Worc* 1E 49
Hillam. *N Yor* 2F 93
Hillbeck. *Cumb* 3A 104
Hillberry. *IOM* 4C 108
Hillborough. *Kent* 4G 41
Hillbourne. *Pool* 3F 15
Hillbrae. *Abers* 4D 160
(nr. Aberchirder)
Hillbrae. *Abers* 1E 153
(nr. Inverurie)
Hillbrae. *Abers* 5F 161
(nr. Methlick)
Hill Brow. *Hants* 4F 25
Hillbutts. *Dors* 2E 15
Hillclifflane. *Derbs* 1G 73
Hillcommon. *Som* 4E 21
Hill Deverill. *Wilts* 2D 22
Hilldyke. *Linc* 1C 76
Hill End. *Dur* 1D 104
Hillend. *Fife* 1E 129
(nr. Inverkeithing)
Hill End. *Fife* 4C 136
(nr. Saline)
Hillend. *N Lan* 3B 128
Hill End. *N Yor* 4C 98
Hillend. *Shrp* 1C 60
Hillend. *Swan* 3D 30
Hillersland. *Glos* 4A 48
Hillerton. *Devn* 3H 11
Hillesden. *Buck* 3E 51
Hillesley. *Glos* 3C 34
Hillfarrance. *Som* 4E 21
Hill Furze. *Worc* 1E 49
Hill Gate. *Here* 3H 47
Hill Green. *Essx* 2E 53
Hillgreen. *W Ber* 4C 36
Hillhead. *Abers* 5C 160
Hill Head. *Hants* 2D 16
Hillhead. *S Ayr* 3D 116
Hillhead. *Torb* 3F 9
Hillhead of Auchentumb. *Abers* 3G 161
Hilliard's Cross. *Staf* 4F 73
Hilliclay. *High* 2D 168
Hillingdon. *G Lon* 2B 38
Hillington. *Norf* 3G 77
Hillington. *Ren* 3G 127
Hillmorton. *Warw* 3C 62
Hill of Beath. *Fife* 4D 136
Hill of Fearn. *High* 1C 158
Hill of Fiddes. *Abers* 1G 153
Hill of Keillor. *Ang* 4B 144
Hill of Overbrae. *Abers* 2F 161
Hill Ridware. *Staf* 4E 73
Hillsborough. *S Yor* 1H 85
Hillside. *Abers* 4G 153
Hillside. *Ang* 2G 145
Hillside. *Devn* 2D 8
Hillside. *Mers* 3B 90
Hillside. *Orkn* 5C 172
Hillside. *Shet* 5F 173
Hillside. *Shrp* 2A 60
Hill Side. *W Yor* 3B 92
Hillside. *Worc* 4B 60
Hillside of Prieston. *Ang* 5C 144
Hill Somersal. *Derbs* 2F 73
Hillstown. *Derbs* 4B 86
Hillstreet. *Hants* 1B 16
Hillswick. *Shet* 4D 173
Hill, The. *Cumb* 1A 96
Hill Top. *Dur* 2C 104
(nr. Barnard Castle)
Hill Top. *Dur* 5F 115
(nr. Durham)
Hill Top. *Dur* 4E 115
(nr. Stanley)
Hill Top. *Hants* 2C 16
Hill View. *Dors* 3E 15
Hill Wootton. *Warw* 4H 61
Hillyland. *Per* 1C 136
Hilmarton. *Wilts* 4F 35
Hilperton. *Wilts* 1D 22
Hilperton Marsh. *Wilts* 1D 22
Hilsea. *Port* 2E 17
Hilston. *E Yor* 1F 95
Hiltingbury. *Hants* 4C 24
Hilton. *Cambs* 4B 64
Hilton. *Cumb* 2A 104
Hilton. *Derbs* 2G 73
Hilton. *Dors* 2C 14
Hilton. *Dur* 2E 105
Hilton. *High* 5E 165
Hilton. *Shrp* 1B 60
Hilton. *Staf* 5E 73
Hilton. *Stoc T* 3B 106
Hilton of Cadboll. *High* 1C 158
Himbleton. *Worc* 5D 60
Himley. *Staf* 1C 60
Hincaster. *Cumb* 1E 97
Hinchcliffe Mill. *W Yor* 4B 92
Hinchwick. *Glos* 2G 49
Hinckley. *Leics* 1B 62
Hinderclay. *Suff* 3C 66
Hinderwell. *N Yor* 3E 107
Hindford. *Shrp* 2F 71
Hindhead. *Surr* 3G 25
Hindley. *G Man* 4E 90
Hindley. *Nmbd* 4D 114
Hindley Green. *G Man* 4E 91
Hindlip. *Worc* 5C 60
Hindolveston. *Norf* 3C 78
Hindon. *Wilts* 3E 23
Hindringham. *Norf* 2B 78
Hingham. *Norf* 5C 78
Hinksford. *Staf* 2C 60
Hinstock. *Shrp* 3A 72
Hintlesham. *Suff* 1D 54
Hinton. *Hants* 3H 15
Hinton. *Here* 2G 47
Hinton. *Nptn* 5C 62
Hinton. *Shrp* 5G 71
Hinton. *S Glo* 4C 34
Hinton Ampner. *Hants* 4D 24
Hinton Blewett. *Bath* 1A 22
Hinton Charterhouse. *Bath* 1C 22
Hinton-in-the-Hedges. *Nptn* 2D 50
Hinton Martell. *Dors* 2F 15
Hinton on the Green. *Worc* 1F 49
Hinton Parva. *Swin* 3H 35
Hinton St George. *Som* 1H 13
Hinton St Mary. *Dors* 1C 14
Hinton Waldrist. *Oxon* 2B 36
Hints. *Shrp* 3A 60
Hints. *Staf* 5F 73
Hinwick. *Bed* 4G 63
Hinxhill. *Kent* 1E 29
Hinxton. *Cambs* 1E 53
Hinxworth. *Herts* 1C 52
Hipley. *Hants* 1E 16
Hipperholme. *W Yor* 2B 92
Hipsburn. *Nmbd* 3G 121
Hipswell. *N Yor* 5E 105
Hiraeth. *Carm* 2F 43
Hirn. *Abers* 3E 153
Hirnant. *Powy* 3C 70
Hirst. *N Lan* 3B 128
Hirst. *Nmbd* 1F 115
Hirst Courtney. *N Yor* 2G 93
Hirwaen. *Den* 4D 82
Hirwaun. *Rhon* 5C 46
Hiscott. *Devn* 4F 19
Histon. *Cambs* 4D 64
Hitcham. *Suff* 5B 66
Hitchin. *Herts* 3B 52
Hittisleigh. *Devn* 3H 11
Hittisleigh Barton. *Devn* 3H 11
Hive. *E Yor* 1B 94
Hixon. *Staf* 3E 73
Hoaden. *Kent* 5G 41
Hoar Cross. *Staf* 3F 73
Hoarwithy. *Here* 3A 48
Hoath. *Kent* 4G 41
Hobarris. *Shrp* 3F 59
Hobbles Green. *Suff* 5G 65
Hobbs Cross. *Essx* 1F 39
Hobkirk. *Bord* 3H 119
Hobson. *Dur* 4E 115
Hoby. *Leics* 4D 74
Hockering. *Norf* 4C 78
Hockering Heath. *Norf* 4C 78
Hockerton. *Notts* 5E 86
Hockley. *Essx* 1C 40
Hockley. *Staf* 5G 73
Hockley. *W Mid* 3G 61
Hockley Heath. *W Mid* 3F 61
Hockliffe. *C Beds* 3H 51
Hockwold cum Wilton. *Norf* 2G 65
Hockworthy. *Devn* 1D 12
Hoddesdon. *Herts* 5D 52
Hoddlesden. *Bkbn* 2F 91
Hoddomcross. *Dum* 2C 112
Hodgeston. *Pemb* 5E 43
Hodley. *Powy* 1D 58
Hodnet. *Shrp* 3A 72
Hodsoll Street. *Kent* 4H 39
Hodson. *Swin* 3G 35
Hodthorpe. *Derbs* 3C 86
Hoe. *Norf* 4B 78
Hoe Gate. *Hants* 1E 17
Hoe, The. *Plym* 3A 8
Hoff. *Cumb* 3H 103
Hoffleet Stow. *Linc* 2B 76
Hogaland. *Shet* 4E 173
Hogben's Hill. *Kent* 5E 41
Hoggard's Green. *Suff* 5A 66
Hoggeston. *Buck* 3G 51
Hoggrill's End. *Warw* 1G 61
Hogha Gearraidh. *W Isl* 1C 170
Hoghton. *Lanc* 2E 90
Hoghton Bottoms. *Lanc* 2E 91
Hognaston. *Derbs* 5G 85
Hogsthorpe. *Linc* 3E 89
Hogstock. *Dors* 2E 15
Holbeach. *Linc* 3C 76
Holbeach Bank. *Linc* 3C 76
Holbeach Clough. *Linc* 3C 76
Holbeach Drove. *Linc* 4C 76
Holbeach Hurn. *Linc* 3C 76
Holbeach St Johns. *Linc* 4C 76
Holbeach St Marks. *Linc* 2C 76
Holbeach St Matthew. *Linc* 2D 76
Holbeck. *Notts* 3C 86
Holbeck. *W Yor* 1C 92
Holbeck Woodhouse. *Notts* 3C 86
Holberrow Green. *Worc* 5E 61
Holbeton. *Devn* 3C 8
Holborn. *G Lon* 2E 39
Holbrook. *Derbs* 1A 74
Holbrook. *S Yor* 2B 86
Holbrook. *Suff* 2E 55

Holburn—Hoveton

Holburn. *Nmbd* 1E **121**
Holbury. *Hants* 2C **16**
Holcombe. *Devn* 5C **12**
Holcombe. *G Man* 3F **91**
Holcombe. *Som* 2B **22**
Holcombe Brook. *G Man* 3F **91**
Holcombe Rogus. *Devn* 1D **12**
Holcot. *Nptn* 4E **63**
Holden. *Lanc* 5G **97**
Holdenby. *Nptn* 4D **62**
Holder's Green. *Essx* 3G **53**
Holdgate. *Shrp* 2H **59**
Holdingham. *Linc* 1H **75**
Holditch. *Dors* 2G **13**
Holemoor. *Devn* 2E **11**
Hole Street. *W Sus* 4C **26**
Holford. *Som* 2E **21**
Holker. *Cumb* 2C **96**
Holkham. *Norf* 1A **78**
Hollacombe. *Devn* 2D **11**
Holland. *Orkn* 2D **172**
Holland Fen. *Linc* 1B **76**
Holland Lees. *Lanc* 4D **90**
Holland-on-Sea. *Essx* 4F **55**
Holland Park. *W Mid* 5E **73**
Hollandstoun. *Orkn* 2G **172**
Hollesley. *Suff* 1G **55**
Hollinfare. *Warr* 1A **84**
Hollingbourne. *Kent* 5C **40**
Hollingbury. *Brig* 5E **27**
Hollingdon. *Buck* 3G **51**
Hollingrove. *E Sus* 3A **28**
Hollington. *Derbs* 1G **73**
Hollington. *E Sus* 4B **28**
Hollington. *Staf* 2E **73**
Hollington Grove. *Derbs* 2G **73**
Hollingworth. *G Man* 1E **85**
Hollins. *Derbs* 3H **85**
Hollins. *G Man* 4G **91** (nr. Bury)
Hollins. *G Man* 4G **91** (nr. Middleton)
Hollinsclough. *Staf* 4E **85**
Hollinswood. *Telf* 5A **72**
Hollinthorpe. *W Yor* 1D **93**
Hollinwood. *G Man* 4H **91**
Hollinwood. *Shrp* 2H **71**
Hollocombe. *Devn* 1G **11**
Holloway. *Derbs* 5H **85**
Hollow Court. *Worc* 5D **61**
Hollowell. *Nptn* 3D **62**
Hollow Meadows. *S Yor* 2G **85**
Hollows. *Dum* 2E **113**
Hollybush. *Cphy* 5E **47**
Hollybush. *E Ayr* 3C **116**
Hollybush. *Worc* 2C **48**
Holly End. *Norf* 5D **77**
Holly Hill. *N Yor* 4E **105**
Hollyhurst. *Ches E* 1H **71**
Hollym. *E Yor* 2G **95**
Hollywood. *Worc* 3E **61**
Holmacott. *Devn* 4F **19**
Holmbridge. *W Yor* 4B **92**
Holmbury St Mary. *Surr* 1C **26**
Holmbush. *Corn* 3E **7**
Holmcroft. *Staf* 3D **72**
Holme. *Cambs* 2A **64**
Holme. *Cumb* 2E **97**
Holme. *N Lin* 4C **94**
Holme. *N Yor* 1F **99**
Holme. *Notts* 5F **87**
Holme. *W Yor* 4B **92**
Holmebridge. *Dors* 4D **15**
Holme Chapel. *Lanc* 2G **91**
Holme Hale. *Norf* 5A **78**
Holme Lacy. *Here* 2A **48**
Holme Marsh. *Here* 5F **59**
Holmend. *Dum* 4C **118**
Holme next the Sea. *Norf* 1G **77**
Holme-on-Spalding-Moor. *E Yor* 1B **94**
Holme on the Wolds. *E Yor* 5D **100**
Holme Pierrepont. *Notts* 2D **74**
Holmer. *Here* 1A **48**
Holmer Green. *Buck* 1A **38**
Holmes. *Lanc* 3C **90**
Holme St Cuthbert. *Cumb* 5C **112**
Holmes Chapel. *Ches E* 4B **84**
Holmesfield. *Derbs* 3H **85**
Holmeswood. *Lanc* 3C **90**
Holmewood. *Derbs* 4B **86**
Holmfirth. *W Yor* 4B **92**
Holmhead. *E Ayr* 2E **117**
Holmisdale. *High* 4A **154**
Holm of Drumlanrig. *Dum* 5H **117**
Holmpton. *E Yor* 2G **95**
Holmrook. *Cumb* 5B **102**
Holmside. *Dur* 5F **115**
Holmwrangle. *Cumb* 5G **113**
Holne. *Devn* 2D **8**
Holsworthy. *Devn* 2D **10**
Holsworthy Beacon. *Devn* 2D **10**
Holt. *Dors* 2F **15**
Holt. *Norf* 2C **78**
Holt. *Wilts* 5D **34**
Holt. *Worc* 4C **60**
Holt. *Wrex* 5G **83**
Holtby. *York* 4A **100**
Holt End. *Hants* 3E **25**
Holt End. *Worc* 4E **61**
Holt Fleet. *Worc* 4C **60**
Holt Green. *Lanc* 4B **90**
Holt Heath. *Dors* 2F **15**
Holt Heath. *Worc* 4C **60**
Holton. *Oxon* 5E **50**
Holton. *Som* 4B **22**
Holton. *Suff* 3F **67**
Holton cum Beckering. *Linc* 2A **88**
Holton Heath. *Dors* 3E **15**
Holton le Clay. *Linc* 4F **95**
Holton le Moor. *Linc* 1H **87**
Holton St Mary. *Suff* 2D **54**
Holt Pound. *Hants* 2G **25**
Holtsmere End. *Herts* 4A **52**
Holtye. *E Sus* 2F **27**
Holwell. *Dors* 1C **14**
Holwell. *Herts* 2B **52**
Holwell. *Leics* 3E **75**
Holwell. *Oxon* 5H **49**
Holwell. *Som* 2C **22**
Holwick. *Dur* 2C **104**
Holworth. *Dors* 4C **14**
Holybourne. *Hants* 2F **25**
Holy City. *Devn* 2G **13**
Holy Cross. *Worc* 3D **60**
Holyfield. *Essx* 5D **53**
Holyhead. *IOA* 2B **80**
Holy Island. *Nmbd* 5H **131**
Holymoorside. *Derbs* 4H **85**
Holyport. *Wind* 4G **37**
Holystone. *Nmbd* 4D **120**
Holytown. *N Lan* 3A **128**
Holywell. *Cambs* 3C **64**
Holywell. *Dors* 2A **14**
Holywell. *Flin* 3D **82**
Holywell. *Glos* 2C **34**
Holywell. *Nmbd* 2G **115**
Holywell. *Warw* 4F **61**
Holywell Bay. *Corn* 3B **6**
Holywell Green. *W Yor* 3A **92**
Holywell Lake. *Som* 4E **20**
Holywell Row. *Suff* 3G **65**
Holywood. *Dum* 1G **111**
Homer. *Shrp* 5A **72**
Homer Green. *Mers* 4B **90**
Homersfield. *Suff* 2E **67**
Hom Green. *Here* 3A **48**
Homington. *Wilts* 4G **23**
Honeyborough. *Pemb* 4D **42**
Honeybourne. *Worc* 1G **49**
Honeychurch. *Devn* 2G **11**
Honeydon. *Bed* 5A **64**
Honey Hill. *Kent* 4F **41**
Honey Street. *Wilts* 5G **35**
Honey Tye. *Suff* 2C **54**
Honeywick. *C Beds* 3H **51**
Honiley. *Warw* 3G **61**
Honing. *Norf* 3F **79**
Honingham. *Norf* 4D **78**
Honington. *Linc* 1G **75**
Honington. *Suff* 3B **66**
Honington. *Warw* 1A **50**
Honiton. *Devn* 2E **13**
Honley. *W Yor* 3B **92**
Honnington. *Telf* 4B **72**
Hoo. *Suff* 5E **67**
Hoobrook. *Worc* 3C **60**
Hood Green. *S Yor* 4D **92**
Hooe. *E Sus* 5A **28**
Hooe. *Plym* 3B **8**
Hooe Common. *E Sus* 4A **28**
Hoo Green. *Ches E* 2B **84**
Hoohill. *Bkpl* 1B **90**
Hook. *Cambs* 1D **64**
Hook. *E Yor* 2A **94**
Hook. *G Lon* 4C **38**
Hook. *Hants* 1F **25** (nr. Basingstoke)
Hook. *Hants* 2D **16** (nr. Fareham)
Hook. *Pemb* 3D **43**
Hook. *Wilts* 3F **35**
Hook-a-Gate. *Shrp* 5G **71**
Hook Bank. *Worc* 1D **48**
Hooke. *Dors* 2A **14**
Hooker Gate. *Tyne* 4E **115**
Hookgate. *Staf* 2B **72**
Hook Green. *Kent* 2A **28** (nr. Lamberhurst)
Hook Green. *Kent* 3H **39** (nr. Longfield)
Hook Green. *Kent* 4H **39** (nr. Meopham)
Hook Norton. *Oxon* 2B **50**
Hook's Cross. *Herts* 3C **52**
Hook Street. *Glos* 2B **34**
Hookway. *Devn* 3B **12**
Hookwood. *Surr* 1D **26**
Hoole. *Ches W* 4G **83**
Hooley. *Surr* 5D **39**
Hooley Bridge. *G Man* 3G **91**
Hooley Brow. *G Man* 3G **91**
Hoo St Werburgh. *Medw* 3B **40**
Hooton. *Ches W* 3F **83**
Hooton Levitt. *S Yor* 1C **86**
Hooton Pagnell. *S Yor* 4E **93**
Hooton Roberts. *S Yor* 1B **86**
Hope. *Derbs* 2F **85**
Hope. *Flin* 5F **83**
Hope. *High* 2E **167**
Hope. *Powy* 5E **71**
Hope. *Shrp* 5F **71**
Hope. *Staf* 5F **85**
Hope Bagot. *Shrp* 3H **59**
Hope Bowdler. *Shrp* 1G **59**
Hopedale. *Staf* 5F **85**
Hope Green. *Ches E* 2D **84**
Hopeman. *Mor* 2F **159**
Hope Mansell. *Here* 4B **48**
Hopesay. *Shrp* 2F **59**
Hope's Green. *Essx* 2B **40**
Hopetown. *W Yor* 2D **93**
Hope under Dinmore. *Here* 5H **59**
Hopley's Green. *Here* 5F **59**
Hopperton. *N Yor* 4G **99**
Hop Pole. *Linc* 4A **76**
Hopstone. *Shrp* 1B **60**
Hopton. *Derbs* 5G **85**
Hopton. *Powy* 1E **59**
Hopton. *Shrp* 3F **71** (nr. Oswestry)
Hopton. *Shrp* 3H **71** (nr. Wem)
Hopton. *Staf* 3D **72**
Hopton. *Suff* 3B **66**
Hopton Cangeford. *Shrp* 2H **59**
Hopton Castle. *Shrp* 3F **59**
Hoptonheath. *Shrp* 3F **59**
Hopton Heath. *Staf* 3D **72**
Hopton on Sea. *Norf* 5H **79**
Hopton Wafers. *Shrp* 3A **60**
Hopwas. *Staf* 5F **73**
Hopwood. *Worc* 3E **61**
Horam. *E Sus* 4G **27**
Horbling. *Linc* 2A **76**
Horbury. *W Yor* 3C **92**
Horcott. *Glos* 5G **49**
Horden. *Dur* 5H **115**
Horderley. *Shrp* 2G **59**
Hordle. *Hants* 3A **16**
Hordley. *Shrp* 2F **71**
Horeb. *Carm* 3F **45** (nr. Brechfa)
Horeb. *Carm* 5E **45** (nr. Llanelli)
Horeb. *Cdgn* 1D **45**
Horfield. *Bris* 4B **34**
Horgabost. *W Isl* 8C **171**
Horham. *Suff* 3E **66**
Horkesley Heath. *Essx* 3C **54**
Horkstow. *N Lin* 3C **94**
Horley. *Oxon* 1C **50**
Horley. *Surr* 1D **27**
Horn Ash. *Dors* 2G **13**
Hornblotton Green. *Som* 3A **22**
Hornby. *Lanc* 3E **97**
Hornby. *N Yor* 4A **106** (nr. Appleton Wiske)
Hornby. *N Yor* 5F **105** (nr. Catterick Garrison)
Horncastle. *Linc* 4B **88**
Hornchurch. *G Lon* 2G **39**
Horncliffe. *Nmbd* 5F **131**
Horndean. *Hants* 1E **17**
Horndean. *Bord* 5E **131**
Horndon. *Devn* 4F **11**
Horndon on the Hill. *Thur* 2A **40**
Horne. *Surr* 1E **27**
Horner. *Som* 2C **20**
Horning. *Norf* 4F **79**
Horninghold. *Leics* 1F **63**
Horninglow. *Staf* 3G **73**
Horningsea. *Cambs* 4D **65**
Horningsham. *Wilts* 2D **22**
Horningtoft. *Norf* 3B **78**
Hornsbury. *Som* 1G **13**
Hornsby. *Cumb* 4G **113**
Hornsbygate. *Cumb* 4G **113**
Horns Corner. *Kent* 3B **28**
Horns Cross. *Devn* 4D **19**
Hornsea. *E Yor* 5G **101**
Hornsea Burton. *E Yor* 5G **101**
Hornsey. *G Lon* 2E **39**
Hornton. *Oxon* 1B **50**
Horpit. *Swin* 3H **35**
Horrabridge. *Devn* 2B **8**
Horringer. *Suff* 4H **65**
Horringford. *IOW* 4D **16**
Horrocks Fold. *G Man* 3F **91**
Horrocksford. *Lanc* 5G **97**
Horsbrugh Ford. *Bord* 1E **119**
Horsebridge. *Devn* 5E **11**
Horsebridge. *E Sus* 4G **27**
Horsebridge. *Hants* 3B **24**
Horse Bridge. *Staf* 5D **84**
Horsebrook. *Staf* 4C **72**
Horsecastle. *N Som* 5H **33**
Horsehay. *Telf* 5A **72**
Horseheath. *Cambs* 1G **53**
Horsehouse. *N Yor* 1C **98**
Horsell. *Surr* 5A **38**
Horseman's Green. *Wrex* 1G **71**
Horsenden. *Buck* 5F **51**
Horseway. *Cambs* 2D **64**
Horsey. *Norf* 3G **79**
Horsey. *Som* 3G **21**
Horsford. *Norf* 4D **78**
Horsforth. *W Yor* 1C **92**
Horsham. *W Sus* 2C **26**
Horsham. *Worc* 5B **60**
Horsham St Faith. *Norf* 4E **78**
Horsington. *Linc* 4A **88**
Horsington. *Som* 4C **22**
Horsley. *Derbs* 1A **74**
Horsley. *Glos* 2D **34**
Horsley. *Nmbd* 3D **11** (nr. Prudhoe)
Horsley. *Nmbd* 5C **120** (nr. Rochester)
Horsley Cross. *Essx* 3E **54**
Horsleycross Street. *Essx* 3E **54**
Horsleyhill. *Bord* 3H **119**
Horsleyhope. *Dur* 5D **114**
Horsley Woodhouse. *Derbs* 1A **74**
Horsmonden. *Kent* 1A **28**
Horspath. *Oxon* 5D **50**
Horstead. *Norf* 4E **79**
Horsted Keynes. *W Sus* 3E **27**
Horton. *Buck* 4H **51**
Horton. *Dors* 2F **15**
Horton. *Lanc* 4A **98**
Horton. *Nptn* 5F **63**
Horton. *Shrp* 2G **71**
Horton. *Som* 1G **13**
Horton. *S Glo* 3C **34**
Horton. *Staf* 5D **84**
Horton. *Swan* 4D **30**
Horton. *Wilts* 5F **35**
Horton. *Wind* 3B **38**
Horton Cross. *Som* 1G **13**
Horton-cum-Studley. *Oxon* 4D **50**
Horton Grange. *Nmbd* 2F **115**
Horton Green. *Ches W* 1G **71**
Horton Heath. *Hants* 1C **16**
Horton in Ribblesdale. *N Yor* 2H **97**
Horton Kirby. *Kent* 4G **39**
Hortonwood. *Telf* 4A **72**
Horwich. *G Man* 3E **91**
Horwich End. *Derbs* 2E **85**
Horwood. *Devn* 4F **19**
Hoscar. *Lanc* 3C **90**
Hose. *Leics* 3E **75**
Hosh. *Per* 1A **136**
Hosta. *W Isl* 1C **170**
Hoswick. *Shet* 9F **173**
Hotham. *E Yor* 1B **94**
Hothfield. *Kent* 1D **28**
Hoton. *Leics* 3C **74**
Houbie. *Shet* 2H **173**
Hough. *Arg* 4A **138**
Hough. *Ches E* 5B **84** (nr. Crewe)
Hough. *Ches E* 3C **84** (nr. Wilmslow)
Hougham. *Linc* 1F **75**
Hough Green. *Hal* 2G **83**
Hough-on-the-Hill. *Linc* 1G **75**
Houghton. *Cambs* 3B **64**
Houghton. *Cumb* 4F **113**
Houghton. *Hants* 3B **24**
Houghton. *Nmbd* 3E **115**
Houghton. *Pemb* 4D **43**
Houghton. *W Sus* 4B **26**
Houghton Bank. *Darl* 2F **105**
Houghton Conquest. *C Beds* 1A **52**
Houghton Green. *E Sus* 3D **28**
Houghton-le-Side. *Darl* 2F **105**
Houghton-le-Spring. *Tyne* 5G **115**
Houghton on the Hill. *Leics* 5D **74**
Houghton Regis. *C Beds* 3A **52**
Houghton St Giles. *Norf* 2B **78**
Houlsyke. *N Yor* 4E **107**
Hound. *Hants* 2C **16**
Hound Green. *Hants* 1F **25**
Houndslow. *Bord* 5C **130**
Houndsmoor. *Som* 4E **21**
Houndwood. *Bord* 3E **131**
Hounsdown. *Hants* 1B **16**
Hounslow. *G Lon* 3C **38**
Housay. *Shet* 4H **173**
Househill. *High* 3C **158**
Housetter. *Shet* 3E **173**
Houss. *Shet* 8E **173**
Houston. *Ren* 3F **127**
Housty. *High* 5D **168**
Houton. *Orkn* 7C **172**
Hove. *Brig* 5D **27**
Hoveringham. *Notts* 1E **74**
Hoveton. *Norf* 4F **79**

Hovingham—Inshegra

Hovingham. *N Yor* 2A **100**
How. *Cumb* 4G **113**
How Caple. *Here* 2B **48**
Howden. *E Yor* 2H **93**
Howden-le-Wear. *Dur* 1E **105**
Howe. *High* 2F **169**
Howe. *Norf* 5E **79**
Howe. *N Yor* 1F **99**
Howe Green. *Essx* 5H **53**
(nr. Chelmsford)
Howegreen. *Essx* 5B **54**
(nr. Maldon)
Howe Green. *Warw* 2H **61**
Howell. *Linc* 1A **76**
How End. *C Beds* 1A **52**
Howe of Teuchar. *Abers* 4E **161**
Howes. *Dum* 3C **112**
Howe Street. *Essx* 4G **53**
(nr. Chelmsford)
Howe Street. *Essx* 2G **53**
(nr. Finchingfield)
Howe, The. *Cumb* 1D **96**
Howe, The. *IOM* 5A **108**
Howey. *Powy* 5C **58**
Howgate. *Midl* 4F **129**
Howgill. *Lanc* 5H **97**
Howgill. *N Yor* 4C **98**
How Green. *Kent* 1F **27**
How Hill. *Norf* 4F **79**
Howick. *Nmbd* 3G **121**
Howle. *Telf* 3A **72**
Howle Hill. *Here* 3B **48**
Howleigh. *Som* 1F **13**
Howlett End. *Essx* 2F **53**
Howley. *Som* 2F **13**
Howley. *Warr* 2A **84**
Hownam. *Bord* 3B **120**
Howsham. *N Lin* 4D **94**
Howsham. *N Yor* 3B **100**
Howtel. *Nmbd* 1C **120**
Howt Green. *Kent* 4C **40**
Howton. *Here* 3H **47**
Howwood. *Ren* 3E **127**
Hoxne. *Suff* 3D **66**
Hoylake. *Mers* 2E **82**
Hoyland. *S Yor* 4D **92**
Hoylandswaine. *S Yor* 4C **92**
Hoyle. *W Sus* 4A **26**
Hubberholme. *N Yor* 2B **98**
Hubberston. *Pemb* 4C **42**
Hubbert's Bridge. *Linc* 1B **76**
Huby. *N Yor* 5E **99**
(nr. Harrogate)
Huby. *N Yor* 3H **99**
(nr. York)
Hucclecote. *Glos* 4D **48**
Hucking. *Kent* 5C **40**
Hucknall. *Notts* 1C **74**
Huddersfield. *W Yor* 3B **92**
Huddington. *Worc* 5D **60**
Huddlesford. *Staf* 5F **73**
Hudswell. *N Yor* 4E **105**
Huggate. *E Yor* 4C **100**
Hugglescote. *Leics* 4B **74**
Hughenden Valley. *Buck* 2G **37**
Hughley. *Shrp* 1H **59**
Hughton. *High* 4G **157**
Hugh Town. *IOS* 1B **4**
Hugus. *Corn* 4B **6**
Huish. *Devn* 1F **11**
Huish. *Wilts* 5G **35**
Huish Champflower. *Som* 4D **20**
Huish Episcopi. *Som* 4H **21**
Huisinis. *W Isl* 6B **171**
Hulcote. *Nptn* 5E **62**
Hulcott. *Buck* 4G **51**
Hulham. *Devn* 4D **12**
Hull. *Hull* 2D **94**
Hulland. *Derbs* 1G **73**
Hulland Moss. *Derbs* 1G **73**
Hulland Ward. *Derbs* 1G **73**
Hullavington. *Wilts* 3D **35**
Hullbridge. *Essx* 1C **40**
Hulme. *G Man* 1C **84**
Hulme. *Staf* 1D **72**
Hulme End. *Staf* 5F **85**
Hulme Walfield. *Ches E* 4C **84**
Hulverstone. *IOW* 4B **16**
Hulver Street. *Suff* 2G **67**
Humber. *Devn* 5C **12**
Humber. *Here* 5H **59**
Humber Bridge. *N Lin* 2D **94**
Humberside International Airport.
N Lin 3D **94**
Humberston. *NE Lin* 4G **95**
Humberstone. *Leic* 5D **74**
Humbie. *E Lot* 3A **130**
Humbleton. *E Yor* 1F **95**
Humbleton. *Nmbd* 2D **121**
Humby. *Linc* 2H **75**
Hume. *Bord* 5D **130**
Humshaugh. *Nmbd* 2C **114**
Huna. *High* 1F **169**
Huncoat. *Lanc* 1F **91**
Huncote. *Leics* 1C **62**
Hundall. *Derbs* 3A **86**
Hunderthwaite. *Dur* 2C **104**
Hundleby. *Linc* 4C **88**
Hundle Houses. *Linc* 5B **88**
Hundleton. *Pemb* 4D **42**
Hundon. *Suff* 1H **53**
Hundred Acres. *Hants* 1D **16**
Hundred House. *Powy* 5D **58**
Hundred, The. *Here* 4H **59**
Hungarton. *Leics* 5D **74**
Hungerford. *Hants* 1G **15**
Hungerford. *Shrp* 2H **59**
Hungerford. *Som* 2D **20**
Hungerford. *W Ber* 5B **36**
Hungerford Newtown. *W Ber* 4B **36**
Hunger Hill. *G Man* 4E **91**
Hungerton. *Linc* 2F **75**
Hungladder. *High* 1C **154**
Hungryhatton. *Shrp* 3A **72**
Hunmanby. *N Yor* 2E **101**
Hunmanby Sands. *N Yor* 2F **101**
Hunningham. *Warw* 4A **62**
Hunnington. *Worc* 2D **60**
Hunny Hill. *IOW* 4C **16**
Hunsdon. *Herts* 4E **53**
Hunsdonbury. *Herts* 4E **53**
Hunsingore. *N Yor* 4G **99**
Hunslet. *W Yor* 1D **92**
Hunslet Carr. *W Yor* 2D **92**
Hunsonby. *Cumb* 1G **103**
Hunspow. *High* 1E **169**
Hunstanton. *Norf* 1F **77**
Hunstanworth. *Dur* 5C **114**
Hunston. *Suff* 4B **66**
Hunston. *W Sus* 2G **17**
Hunstrete. *Bath* 5B **34**
Hunt End. *Worc* 4E **61**
Hunterfield. *Midl* 3G **129**
Hunters Forstal. *Kent* 4F **41**
Hunter's Quay. *Arg* 2C **126**
Huntham. *Som* 4G **21**
Hunthill Lodge. *Ang* 1D **144**
Huntingdon. *Cambs* 3B **64**
Huntingfield. *Suff* 3F **67**
Huntingford. *Wilts* 3D **22**
Huntington. *Ches W* 4G **83**
Huntington. *E Lot* 2A **130**
Huntington. *Here* 5E **59**
Huntington. *Staf* 4D **72**
Huntington. *Telf* 5A **72**
Huntington. *York* 4A **100**
Huntingtower. *Per* 1C **136**
Huntley. *Glos* 4C **48**
Huntley. *Staf* 1E **73**
Huntly. *Abers* 4C **160**
Huntlywood. *Bord* 5C **130**
Hunton. *Hants* 3C **24**
Hunton. *Kent* 1B **28**
Hunton. *N Yor* 5E **105**
Hunton Bridge. *Herts* 5A **52**
Hunt's Corner. *Norf* 2C **66**
Huntscott. *Som* 2C **20**
Hunt's Cross. *Mers* 2G **83**
Hunts Green. *Warw* 1F **61**
Huntsham. *Devn* 4D **20**
Huntshaw. *Devn* 4F **19**
Huntspill. *Som* 2G **21**
Huntstile. *Som* 3F **21**
Huntstrete. *Bath* 5B **34**
Huntworth. *Som* 3G **21**
Hunwick. *Dur* 1E **105**
Hunworth. *Norf* 2C **78**
Hurcott. *Som* 1G **13**
(nr. Ilminster)
Hurcott. *Som* 4A **22**
(nr. Somerton)
Hurdcott. *Wilts* 3G **23**
Hurdley. *Powy* 1E **59**
Hurdsfield. *Ches E* 3D **84**
Hurlet. *Glas* 3G **127**
Hurley. *Warw* 1G **61**
Hurley. *Wind* 3G **37**
Hurlford. *E Ayr* 1D **116**
Hurliston Green. *Lanc* 3B **90**
Hurn. *Dors* 3G **15**
Hursey. *Dors* 2H **13**
Hursley. *Hants* 4C **24**
Hurst. *G Man* 4H **91**
Hurst. *N Yor* 4D **104**
Hurst. *Som* 1H **13**
Hurst. *Wok* 4F **37**
Hurstbourne Priors. *Hants* 2C **24**
Hurstbourne Tarrant. *Hants* 1B **24**
Hurst Green. *Ches E* 1H **71**
Hurst Green. *E Sus* 3B **28**
Hurst Green. *Essx* 4D **54**
Hurst Green. *Lanc* 1E **91**
Hurst Green. *Surr* 5E **39**
Hurstley. *Here* 1G **47**
Hurstpierpoint. *W Sus* 4D **27**
Hurstway Common. *Here* 1F **47**
Hurst Wickham. *W Sus* 4D **27**
Hurstwood. *Lanc* 1G **91**
Hurtmore. *Surr* 1A **26**
Hurworth-on-Tees. *Darl* 3A **106**
Hurworth Place. *Darl* 3F **105**
Hury. *Dur* 3C **104**
Husbands Bosworth. *Leics* 2D **62**
Husborne Crawley. *C Beds* 2H **51**
Husthwaite. *N Yor* 2H **99**
Hutcherleigh. *Devn* 3D **9**
Hut Green. *N Yor* 2F **93**
Huthwaite. *Notts* 5B **86**
Huttoft. *Linc* 3E **89**
Hutton. *Cumb* 2F **103**
Hutton. *E Yor* 4E **101**
Hutton. *Essx* 1H **39**
Hutton. *Lanc* 2C **90**
Hutton. *N Som* 1G **21**
Hutton. *Bord* 4F **131**
Hutton Bonville. *N Yor* 4A **106**
Hutton Buscel. *N Yor* 1D **100**
Hutton Conyers. *N Yor* 2F **99**
Hutton Cranswick.
E Yor 4E **101**
Hutton End. *Cumb* 1F **103**
Hutton Gate. *Red C* 3C **106**
Hutton Henry. *Dur* 1B **106**
Hutton-le-Hole. *N Yor* 1B **100**
Hutton Magna. *Dur* 3E **105**
Hutton Mulgrave. *N Yor* 4F **107**
Hutton Roof. *Cumb* 2E **97**
(nr. Kirkby Lonsdale)
Hutton Roof. *Cumb* 1E **103**
(nr. Penrith)
Hutton Rudby. *N Yor* 4B **106**
Huttons Ambo. *N Yor* 3B **100**
Hutton Sessay. *N Yor* 2G **99**
Hutton Village. *Red C* 3D **106**
Hutton Wandesley.
N Yor 4H **99**
Huxham. *Devn* 3C **12**
Huxham Green. *Som* 3A **22**
Huxley. *Ches W* 4H **83**
Huyton. *Mers* 1G **83**
Hwlffordd. *Pemb* 3D **42**
Hycemoor. *Cumb* 1A **96**
Hyde. *Glos* 5D **49**
(nr. Stroud)
Hyde. *Glos* 3F **49**
(nr. Winchcombe)
Hyde. *G Man* 1D **84**
Hyde Heath. *Buck* 5H **51**
Hyde Lea. *Staf* 3D **72**
Hyde Park. *S Yor* 4F **93**
Hydestile. *Surr* 1A **26**
Hyndford Bridge. *S Lan* 5C **128**
Hynish. *Arg* 5A **138**
Hyssington. *Powy* 1F **59**
Hythe. *Hants* 2C **16**
Hythe. *Kent* 2F **29**
Hythe End. *Wind* 3B **38**
Hythie. *Abers* 3H **161**
Hyton. *Cumb* 1A **96**

I

Ianstown. *Mor* 2B **160**
Iarsiadar. *W Isl* 4D **171**
Ibberton. *Dors* 2C **14**
Ible. *Derbs* 5G **85**
Ibrox. *Glas* 3G **127**
Ibsley. *Hants* 2G **15**
Ibstock. *Leics* 4B **74**
Ibstone. *Buck* 2F **37**
Ibthorpe. *Hants* 1B **24**
Iburndale. *N Yor* 4F **107**
Ibworth. *Hants* 1D **24**
Icelton. *N Som* 5G **33**
Ichrachan. *Arg* 5E **141**
Ickburgh. *Norf* 1H **65**
Ickenham. *G Lon* 2B **38**
Ickenthwaite. *Cumb* 1C **96**
Ickford. *Buck* 5E **51**
Ickham. *Kent* 5G **41**
Ickleford. *Herts* 2B **52**
Icklesham. *E Sus* 4C **28**
Ickleton. *Cambs* 1E **53**
Icklingham. *Suff* 3G **65**
Ickwell. *C Beds* 1B **52**
Icomb. *Glos* 3H **49**
Idbury. *Oxon* 3H **49**
Iddesleigh. *Devn* 2F **11**
Ide. *Devn* 3B **12**
Ideford. *Devn* 5B **12**
Ide Hill. *Kent* 5F **39**
Iden. *E Sus* 3D **28**
Iden Green. *Kent* 2C **28**
(nr. Benenden)
Iden Green. *Kent* 2B **28**
(nr. Goudhurst)
Idle. *W Yor* 1B **92**
Idless. *Corn* 4C **6**
Idlicote. *Warw* 1A **50**
Idmiston. *Wilts* 3G **23**
Idole. *Carm* 4E **45**
Idridgehay. *Derbs* 1G **73**
Idrigill. *High* 2C **154**
Idstone. *Oxon* 3A **36**
Iffley. *Oxon* 5D **50**
Ifield. *W Sus* 2D **26**
Ifieldwood. *W Sus* 2D **26**
Ifold. *W Sus* 2B **26**
Iford. *E Sus* 5F **27**
Ifton Heath. *Shrp* 2F **71**
Ightfield. *Shrp* 2H **71**
Ightham. *Kent* 5G **39**
Iken. *Suff* 5G **67**
Ilam. *Staf* 5F **85**
Ilchester. *Som* 4A **22**
Ilderton. *Nmbd* 2E **121**
Ilford. *G Lon* 2F **39**
Ilford. *Som* 1G **13**
Ilfracombe. *Devn* 2F **19**
Ilkeston. *Derbs* 1B **74**
Ilketshall St Andrew. *Suff* 2F **67**
Ilketshall St Lawrence. *Suff* 2F **67**
Ilketshall St Margaret. *Suff* 2F **67**
Ilkley. *W Yor* 5D **98**
Illand. *Corn* 5C **10**
Illey. *W Mid* 2D **61**
Illidge Green. *Ches E* 4B **84**
Illington. *Norf* 2B **66**
Illingworth. *W Yor* 2A **92**
Illogan. *Corn* 4A **6**
Illogan Highway. *Corn* 4A **6**
Illston on the Hill. *Leics* 1E **62**
Ilmer. *Buck* 5F **51**
Ilmington. *Warw* 1H **49**
Ilminster. *Som* 1G **13**
Ilsington. *Devn* 5A **12**
Ilsington. *Dors* 3C **14**
Ilston. *Swan* 3E **31**
Ilton. *N Yor* 2D **98**
Ilton. *Som* 1G **13**
Imachar. *N Ayr* 5G **125**
Imber. *Wilts* 2E **23**
Immingham. *NE Lin* 3E **95**
Immingham Dock. *NE Lin* 3E **95**
Impington. *Cambs* 4D **64**
Ince. *Ches W* 3G **83**
Ince Blundell. *Mers* 4B **90**
Ince-in-Makerfield. *G Man* 4D **90**
Inchbae Lodge. *High* 2G **157**
Inchbare. *Ang* 2F **145**
Inchberry. *Mor* 3H **159**
Inchbraoch. *Ang* 3G **145**
Inchbrook. *Glos* 5D **48**
Incheril. *High* 2C **156**
Inchinnan. *Ren* 3F **127**
Inchlaggan. *High* 3D **148**
Inchmichael. *Per* 1E **137**
Inchnadamph. *High* 1G **163**
Inchree. *High* 2E **141**
Inchture. *Per* 1E **137**
Inchyra. *Per* 1D **136**
Indian Queens. *Corn* 3D **6**
Ingatestone. *Essx* 1H **39**
Ingbirchworth. *S Yor* 4C **92**
Ingestre. *Staf* 3D **73**
Ingham. *Linc* 2G **87**
Ingham. *Norf* 3F **79**
Ingham. *Suff* 3A **66**
Ingham Corner. *Norf* 3F **79**
Ingleborough. *Norf* 4D **76**
Ingleby. *Derbs* 3H **73**
Ingleby Arncliffe. *N Yor* 4B **106**
Ingleby Barwick. *Stoc T* 3B **106**
Ingleby Greenhow. *N Yor* 4C **106**
Ingleigh Green. *Devn* 2G **11**
Inglemire. *Hull* 1D **94**
Inglesbatch. *Bath* 5C **34**
Ingleton. *Dur* 2E **105**
Ingleton. *N Yor* 2F **97**
Inglewhite. *Lanc* 5E **97**
Ingoe. *Nmbd* 2D **114**
Ingol. *Lanc* 1D **90**
Ingoldisthorpe. *Norf* 2F **77**
Ingoldmells. *Linc* 4E **89**
Ingoldsby. *Linc* 2H **75**
Ingon. *Warw* 5G **61**
Ingram. *Nmbd* 3E **121**
Ingrave. *Essx* 1H **39**
Ingrow. *W Yor* 1A **92**
Ings. *Cumb* 5F **103**
Ingst. *S Glo* 3A **34**
Ingthorpe. *Rut* 5G **75**
Ingworth. *Norf* 3D **78**
Inkberrow. *Worc* 5E **61**
Inkford. *Worc* 3E **61**
Inkpen. *W Ber* 5B **36**
Inkstack. *High* 1E **169**
Innellan. *Arg* 3C **126**
Inner Hope. *Devn* 5C **8**
Innerleith. *Fife* 2E **137**
Innerleithen. *Bord* 1F **119**
Innerleven. *Fife* 3F **137**
Innermessan. *Dum* 3F **109**
Innerwick. *E Lot* 2D **130**
Innerwick. *Per* 4C **142**
Innsworth. *Glos* 3D **48**
Insch. *Abers* 1D **152**
Insh. *High* 3C **150**
Inshegra. *High* 3C **166**

Inshore—Ketsby

Inshore. *High* 1D **166**
Inskip. *Lanc* 1C **90**
Instow. *Devn* 3E **19**
Intwood. *Norf* 5D **78**
Inver. *Abers* 4G **151**
Inver. *High* 5F **165**
Inver. *Per* 4H **143**
Inverailort. *High* 5F **147**
Inveralligin. *High* 3H **155**
Inverallochy. *Abers* 2H **161**
Inveramsay. *Abers* 1E **153**
Inveran. *High* 4C **164**
Inveraray. *Arg* 3H **133**
Inverarish. *High* 5E **155**
Inverarity. *Ang* 4D **144**
Inverarnan. *Arg* 2C **134**
Inverarnie. *High* 5A **158**
Inverbeg. *Arg* 4C **134**
Inverbervie. *Abers* 1H **145**
Inverboyndie. *Abers* 2D **160**
Invercassley. *High* 3B **164**
Invercharnan. *High* 4F **141**
Inverchoran. *High* 3E **157**
Invercreran. *Arg* 4E **141**
Inverdruie. *High* 2D **150**
Inverebrie. *Abers* 5G **161**
Invereck. *Arg* 1C **126**
Inveresk. *E Lot* 2G **129**
Inveresragan. *Arg* 5D **141**
Inverey. *Abers* 5E **151**
Inverfarigaig. *High* 1H **149**
Invergarry. *High* 3F **149**
Invergeldie. *Per* 1G **135**
Invergordon. *High* 2B **158**
Invergowrie. *Per* 5C **144**
Inverguseran. *High* 3F **147**
Inverharroch. *Mor* 5A **160**
Inverie. *High* 3F **147**
Inverinan. *Arg* 2G **133**
Inverinate. *High* 1B **148**
Inverkeilor. *Ang* 4F **145**
Inverkeithing. *Fife* 1E **129**
Inverkeithny. *Abers* 4D **160**
Inverkip. *Inv* 2D **126**
Inverkirkaig. *High* 2E **163**
Inverlael. *High* 5F **163**
Inverliever Lodge. *Arg* 3F **133**
Inverliver. *Arg* 5E **141**
Inverloch. *High* 1F **141**
Inverlochlarig. *Stir* 2D **134**
Inverlussa. *Arg* 1E **125**
Inver Mallie. *High* 5D **148**
Invermarkie. *Abers* 5B **160**
Invermoriston. *High* 2G **149**
Invernaver. *High* 2H **167**
Inverneil House. *Arg* 1G **125**
Inverness. *High* 4A **158**
Inverness Airport. *High* 3B **158**
Invernettie. *Abers* 4H **161**
Inverpolly Lodge. *High* 2E **163**
Inverquhomery. *Abers* 4H **161**
Inverroy. *High* 5E **149**
Inversanda. *High* 3D **140**
Invershiel. *High* 2B **148**
Invershin. *High* 4C **164**
Invershore. *High* 5E **169**
Inversnaid. *Stir* 3C **134**
Inverugie. *Abers* 4H **161**
Inveruglas. *Arg* 3C **134**
Inverurie. *Abers* 1E **153**
Invervar. *Per* 4D **142**
Inverythan. *Abers* 4E **161**
Inwardleigh. *Devn* 3F **11**
Inworth. *Essx* 4B **54**
Iochdar. *W Isl* 4C **170**
Iping. *W Sus* 4G **25**
Ipplepen. *Devn* 2E **9**
Ipsden. *Oxon* 3E **37**
Ipstones. *Staf* 1E **73**
Ipswich. *Suff* 1E **55**
Irby. *Mers* 2E **83**
Irby in the Marsh. *Linc* 4D **88**
Irby upon Humber. *NE Lin* 4E **95**
Irchester. *Nptn* 4G **63**
Ireby. *Cumb* 1D **102**
Ireby. *Lanc* 2F **97**
Ireland. *Shet* 9E **173**
Ireleth. *Cumb* 2B **96**
Ireshopeburn. *Dur* 1B **104**
Ireton Wood. *Derbs* 1G **73**
Irlam. *G Man* 1B **84**
Irnham. *Linc* 3H **75**
Iron Acton. *S Glo* 3B **34**
Iron Bridge. *Cambs* 1D **65**
Ironbridge. *Telf* 5A **72**
Iron Cross. *Warw* 5E **61**
Ironville. *Derbs* 5B **86**
Irstead. *Norf* 3F **79**
Irthington. *Cumb* 3F **113**
Irthlingborough. *Nptn* 3G **63**
Irton. *N Yor* 1E **101**
Irvine. *N Ayr* 1C **116**
Irvine Mains. *N Ayr* 1C **116**
Isabella Pit. *Nmbd* 1G **115**
Isauld. *High* 2B **168**
Isbister. *Orkn* 6D **172**
Isbister. *Shet* 5G **173**
Isfield. *E Sus* 4F **27**
Isham. *Nptn* 3F **63**
Island Carr. *N Lin* 4C **94**
Islay Airport. *Arg* 4B **124**
Isle Abbotts. *Som* 4G **21**
Isle Brewers. *Som* 4G **21**
Isleham. *Cambs* 3F **65**
Isle of Man Airport. *IOM* 5B **108**
Isle of Thanet. *Kent* 4H **41**
Isle of Whithorn. *Dum* 5B **110**
Isleornsay. *High* 2F **147**
Isles of Scilly (St Mary's) Airport. *IOS* 1B **4**
Islesteps. *Dum* 2A **112**
Isleworth. *G Lon* 3C **38**
Isley Walton. *Leics* 3B **74**
Islibhig. *W Isl* 5B **171**
Islington. *G Lon* 2E **39**
Islington. *Telf* 3B **72**
Islip. *Nptn* 3G **63**
Islip. *Oxon* 4D **50**
Islwyn. *Cphy* 2F **33**
Isombridge. *Telf* 4A **72**
Istead Rise. *Kent* 4H **39**
Itchen. *Sotn* 1C **16**
Itchen Abbas. *Hants* 3D **24**
Itchen Stoke. *Hants* 3D **24**
Itchingfield. *W Sus* 3C **26**
Itchington. *S Glo* 3B **34**
Itlaw. *Abers* 3D **160**
Itteringham. *Norf* 2D **78**
Itteringham Common. *Norf* 3D **78**
Itton. *Devn* 3G **11**
Itton Common. *Mon* 2H **33**
Ivegill. *Cumb* 5F **113**
Ivelet. *N Yor* 5C **104**
Iverchaolain. *Arg* 2B **126**
Iver Heath. *Buck* 2B **38**
Iveston. *Dur* 4E **115**
Ivetsey Bank. *Staf* 4C **72**
Ivinghoe. *Buck* 4H **51**
Ivinghoe Aston. *Buck* 4H **51**
Ivington. *Here* 5G **59**
Ivington Green. *Here* 5G **59**
Ivybridge. *Devn* 3C **8**
Ivychurch. *Kent* 3E **29**
Ivy Hatch. *Kent* 5G **39**
Ivy Todd. *Norf* 5A **78**
Iwade. *Kent* 4D **40**
Iwerne Courtney. *Dors* 1D **14**
Iwerne Minster. *Dors* 1D **14**
Ixworth. *Suff* 3B **66**
Ixworth Thorpe. *Suff* 3B **66**

J

Jackfield. *Shrp* 5A **72**
Jack Hill. *N Yor* 4E **98**
Jacksdale. *Notts* 5B **86**
Jackton. *S Lan* 4G **127**
Jacobstow. *Corn* 3B **10**
Jacobstowe. *Devn* 2F **11**
Jacobswell. *Surr* 5A **38**
Jameston. *Pemb* 5E **43**
Jamestown. *Dum* 5F **119**
Jamestown. *Fife* 1E **129**
Jamestown. *High* 3G **157**
Jamestown. *W Dun* 1E **127**
Janetstown. *High* 2C **168**
(nr. Thurso)
Janetstown. *High* 3F **169**
(nr. Wick)
Jarrow. *Tyne* 3G **115**
Jarvis Brook. *E Sus* 3G **27**
Jasper's Green. *Essx* 3H **53**
Jaywick. *Essx* 4E **55**
Jedburgh. *Bord* 2A **120**
Jeffreyston. *Pemb* 4E **43**
Jemimaville. *High* 2B **158**
Jenkins Park. *High* 3F **149**
Jersey Marine. *Neat* 3G **31**
Jesmond. *Tyne* 3F **115**
Jevington. *E Sus* 5G **27**
Jingle Street. *Mon* 4H **47**
Jockey End. *Herts* 4A **52**
Jodrell Bank. *Ches E* 3B **84**
Johnby. *Cumb* 1F **103**
John o' Gaunts. *W Yor* 2D **92**
John o' Groats. *High* 1F **169**
John's Cross. *E Sus* 3B **28**
Johnshaven. *Abers* 2G **145**
Johnson Street. *Norf* 4F **79**
Johnston. *Pemb* 3D **42**
Johnstone. *Ren* 3F **127**
Johnstonebridge. *Dum* 5C **118**
Johnstown. *Carm* 4D **45**
Johnstown. *Wrex* 1F **71**
Joppa. *Edin* 2G **129**
Joppa. *S Ayr* 3D **116**
Jordan Green. *Norf* 3C **78**
Jordans. *Buck* 1A **38**
Jordanston. *Pemb* 1D **42**
Jump. *S Yor* 4D **93**
Jumpers Common. *Dors* 3G **15**
Juniper. *Nmbd* 4C **114**
Juniper Green. *Edin* 3E **129**
Jurby East. *IOM* 2C **108**
Jurby West. *IOM* 2C **108**
Jury's Gap. *E Sus* 4D **28**

K

Kaber. *Cumb* 3A **104**
Kaimend. *S Lan* 5C **128**
Kaimes. *Edin* 3F **129**
Kaimrig End. *Bord* 5D **129**
Kames. *Arg* 2A **126**
Kames. *E Ayr* 2F **117**
Kea. *Corn* 4C **6**
Keadby. *N Lin* 3B **94**
Keal Cotes. *Linc* 4C **88**
Kearsley. *G Man* 4F **91**
Kearsney. *Kent* 1G **29**
Kearstwick. *Cumb* 1F **97**
Kearton. *N Yor* 5C **104**
Kearvaig. *High* 1C **166**
Keasden. *N Yor* 3G **97**
Keason. *Corn* 2H **7**
Keckwick. *Hal* 2H **83**
Keddington. *Linc* 2C **88**
Keddington Corner. *Linc* 2C **88**
Kedington. *Suff* 1H **53**
Kedleston. *Derbs* 1H **73**
Kedlock Feus. *Fife* 2F **137**
Keekle. *Cumb* 3B **102**
Keelby. *Linc* 3E **95**
Keele. *Staf* 1C **72**
Keeley Green. *Bed* 1A **52**
Keeston. *Pemb* 3D **42**
Keevil. *Wilts* 1E **23**
Kegworth. *Leics* 3B **74**
Kehelland. *Corn* 2D **4**
Keig. *Abers* 2D **152**
Keighley. *W Yor* 5C **98**
Keilarsbrae. *Clac* 4A **136**
Keillmore. *Arg* 1E **125**
Keillor. *Per* 4B **144**
Keillour. *Per* 1B **136**
Keills. *Arg* 3C **124**
Keiloch. *Abers* 4F **151**
Keils. *Arg* 3D **124**
Keinton Mandeville. *Som* 3A **22**
Keir Mill. *Dum* 5A **118**
Keirsleywell Row. *Nmbd* 4A **114**
Keisby. *Linc* 3H **75**
Keisley. *Cumb* 2A **104**
Keiss. *High* 2F **169**
Keith. *Mor* 3B **160**
Keith Inch. *Abers* 4H **161**
Kelbrook. *Lanc* 5B **98**
Kelby. *Linc* 1H **75**
Keld. *Cumb* 3G **103**
Keld. *N Yor* 4B **104**
Keldholme. *N Yor* 1B **100**
Kelfield. *N Lin* 4B **94**
Kelfield. *N Yor* 1F **93**
Kelham. *Notts* 5E **87**
Kellacott. *Devn* 4E **11**
Kellan. *Arg* 4G **139**
Kellas. *Ang* 5D **144**
Kellas. *Mor* 3F **159**
Kellaton. *Devn* 5E **9**
Kelleth. *Cumb* 4H **103**
Kelling. *Norf* 1C **78**
Kellingley. *N Yor* 2F **93**
Kellington. *N Yor* 2F **93**
Kelloe. *Dur* 1A **106**
Kelloholm. *Dum* 3G **117**
Kells. *Cumb* 3A **102**
Kelly. *Devn* 4D **11**
Kelly Bray. *Corn* 5D **10**
Kelmarsh. *Nptn* 3E **63**
Kelmscott. *Oxon* 2A **36**
Kelsale. *Suff* 4F **67**
Kelsall. *Ches W* 4H **83**
Kelshall. *Herts* 2D **52**
Kelsick. *Cumb* 4C **112**
Kelso. *Bord* 1B **120**
Kelstedge. *Derbs* 4H **85**
Kelstern. *Linc* 1B **88**
Kelsterton. *Flin* 3E **83**
Kelston. *Bath* 5C **34**
Keltneyburn. *Per* 4E **143**
Kelton. *Dum* 2A **112**
Kelton Hill. *Dum* 4E **111**
Kelty. *Fife* 4D **136**
Kelvedon. *Essx* 4B **54**
Kelvedon Hatch. *Essx* 1G **39**
Kelvinside. *Glas* 3G **127**
Kelynack. *Corn* 3A **4**
Kemback. *Fife* 2G **137**
Kemberton. *Shrp* 5B **72**
Kemble. *Glos* 2E **35**
Kemerton. *Worc* 2E **49**
Kemeys Commander. *Mon* 5G **47**
Kemnay. *Abers* 2E **153**
Kempe's Corner. *Kent* 1E **29**
Kempley. *Glos* 3B **48**
Kempley Green. *Glos* 3B **48**
Kempsey. *Worc* 1D **48**
Kempsford. *Glos* 2G **35**
Kemps Green. *Warw* 3F **61**
Kempshott. *Hants* 1E **24**
Kempston. *Bed* 1A **52**
Kempston Hardwick. *Bed* 1A **52**
Kempton. *Shrp* 2F **59**
Kemp Town. *Brig* 5E **27**
Kemsing. *Kent* 5G **39**
Kemsley. *Kent* 4D **40**
Kenardington. *Kent* 2D **28**
Kenchester. *Here* 1H **47**
Kencot. *Oxon* 5A **50**
Kendal. *Cumb* 5G **103**
Kendleshire. *S Glo* 4B **34**
Kendray. *S Yor* 4D **92**
Kenfig. *B'end* 3B **32**
Kenfig Hill. *B'end* 3B **32**
Kengharair. *Arg* 4F **139**
Kenilworth. *Warw* 3G **61**
Kenknock. *Stir* 5B **142**
Kenley. *G Lon* 5E **39**
Kenley. *Shrp* 5H **71**
Kenmore. *High* 3G **155**
Kenmore. *Per* 4E **143**
Kenn. *Devn* 4C **12**
Kenn. *N Som* 5H **33**
Kennacraig. *Arg* 3G **125**
Kenneggy Downs. *Corn* 4C **4**
Kennerleigh. *Devn* 2B **12**
Kennet. *Clac* 4B **136**
Kennethmont. *Abers* 1C **152**
Kennett. *Cambs* 4G **65**
Kennford. *Devn* 4C **12**
Kenninghall. *Norf* 2C **66**
Kennington. *Kent* 1E **29**
Kennington. *Oxon* 5D **50**
Kennoway. *Fife* 3F **137**
Kennyhill. *Suff* 3F **65**
Kennythorpe. *N Yor* 3B **100**
Kenovay. *Arg* 4A **138**
Kensaleyre. *High* 3D **154**
Kensington. *G Lon* 3D **38**
Kenstone. *Shrp* 3H **71**
Kensworth. *C Beds* 4A **52**
Kensworth Common. *C Beds* 4A **52**
Kentallen. *High* 3E **141**
Kentchurch. *Here* 3H **47**
Kentford. *Suff* 4G **65**
Kent International Airport. *Kent* 4H **41**
Kentisbeare. *Devn* 2D **12**
Kentisbury. *Devn* 2G **19**
Kentisbury Ford. *Devn* 2G **19**
Kentmere. *Cumb* 4F **103**
Kenton. *Devn* 4C **12**
Kenton. *G Lon* 2C **38**
Kenton. *Suff* 4D **66**
Kenton Bankfoot. *Tyne* 3F **115**
Kentra. *High* 2A **140**
Kentrigg. *Cumb* 5G **103**
Kents Bank. *Cumb* 2C **96**
Kent's Green. *Glos* 3C **48**
Kent's Oak. *Hants* 4B **24**
Kent Street. *E Sus* 4B **28**
Kent Street. *Kent* 5A **40**
Kent Street. *W Sus* 3D **26**
Kenwick. *Shrp* 2G **71**
Kenwyn. *Corn* 4C **6**
Kenyon. *Warr* 1A **84**
Keoldale. *High* 2D **166**
Keppoch. *High* 1B **148**
Kepwick. *N Yor* 5B **106**
Keresley. *W Mid* 2H **61**
Keresley Newland. *Warw* 2H **61**
Keristal. *IOM* 4C **108**
Kerne Bridge. *Here* 4A **48**
Kerridge. *Ches E* 3D **84**
Kerris. *Corn* 4B **4**
Kerrow. *High* 5F **157**
Kerry. *Powy* 2D **58**
Kerrycroy. *Arg* 3C **126**
Kerry's Gate. *Here* 2G **47**
Kersall. *Notts* 4E **86**
Kersbrook. *Devn* 4D **12**
Kerse. *Ren* 4E **127**
Kersey. *Suff* 1D **54**
Kershopefoot. *Cumb* 1F **113**
Kersoe. *Worc* 2E **49**
Kerswell. *Devn* 2D **12**
Kerswell Green. *Worc* 1D **48**
Kesgrave. *Suff* 1F **55**
Kessingland. *Suff* 2H **67**
Kessingland Beach. *Suff* 2H **67**
Kestle. *Corn* 4D **6**
Kestle Mill. *Corn* 3C **6**
Keston. *G Lon* 4F **39**
Keswick. *Cumb* 2D **102**
Keswick. *Norf* 2F **79**
(nr. North Walsham)
Keswick. *Norf* 5E **78**
(nr. Norwich)
Ketsby. *Linc* 3C **88**

Kettering—Kintbury

Kettering. *Nptn* 3F 63
Ketteringham. *Norf* 5D 78
Kettins. *Per* 5B 144
Kettlebaston. *Suff* 5B 66
Kettlebridge. *Fife* 3F 137
Kettlebrook. *Staf* 5G 73
Kettleburgh. *Suff* 4E 67
Kettleholm. *Dum* 2C 112
Kettleness. *N Yor* 3F 107
Kettleshulme. *Ches E* 3D 85
Kettlesing. *N Yor* 4E 99
Kettlesing Bottom. *N Yor* 4E 99
Kettlestone. *Norf* 2B 78
Kettlethorpe. *Linc* 3F 87
Kettletoft. *Orkn* 4F 172
Kettlewell. *N Yor* 2B 98
Ketton. *Rut* 5G 75
Kew. *G Lon* 3C 38
Kewaigue. *IOM* 4C 108
Kewstoke. *N Som* 5G 33
Kexbrough. *S Yor* 4D 92
Kexby. *Linc* 2F 87
Kexby. *York* 4B 100
Keyford. *Som* 2C 22
Key Green. *Ches E* 4C 84
Key Green. *N Yor* 4F 107
Keyham. *Leics* 5D 74
Keyhaven. *Hants* 3B 16
Keyhead. *Abers* 3H 161
Keyingham. *E Yor* 2F 95
Keymer. *W Sus* 4E 27
Keynsham. *Bath* 5B 34
Keysoe. *Bed* 4H 63
Keysoe Row. *Bed* 4H 63
Key's Toft. *Linc* 5D 89
Keyston. *Cambs* 3H 63
Key Street. *Kent* 4C 40
Keyworth. *Notts* 2D 74
Kibblesworth. *Tyne* 4F 115
Kibworth Beauchamp. *Leics* 1D 62
Kibworth Harcourt. *Leics* 1D 62
Kidbrooke. *G Lon* 3F 39
Kidburngill. *Cumb* 2B 102
Kiddemore Green. *Staf* 5C 72
Kidderminster. *Worc* 3C 60
Kiddington. *Oxon* 3C 50
Kidd's Moor. *Norf* 5D 78
Kidlington. *Oxon* 4C 50
Kidmore End. *Oxon* 4E 37
Kidnal. *Ches W* 1G 71
Kidsgrove. *Staf* 5C 84
Kidstones. *N Yor* 1B 98
Kidwelly. *Carm* 5E 45
Kiel Crofts. *Arg* 5D 140
Kielder. *Nmbd* 5A 120
Kilbagie. *Fife* 4B 136
Kilbarchan. *Ren* 3F 127
Kilbeg. *High* 3E 147
Kilberry. *Arg* 3F 125
Kilbirnie. *N Ayr* 4E 126
Kilbride. *Arg* 1F 133
Kilbride. *High* 1D 147
Kilbucho Place. *Bord* 1C 118
Kilburn. *Derbs* 1A 74
Kilburn. *G Lon* 2D 38
Kilburn. *N Yor* 2H 99
Kilby. *Leics* 1D 62
Kilchattan. *Arg* 4A 132
(on Colonsay)
Kilchattan. *Arg* 4C 126
(on Isle of Bute)
Kilchattan Bay. *Arg* 4B 126
Kilchenzie. *Arg* 3A 122
Kilcheran. *Arg* 5C 140
Kilchiaran. *Arg* 3A 124
Kilchoan. *High* 4F 147
(nr. Inverie)
Kilchoan. *High* 2F 139
(nr. Tobermory)
Kilchoman. *Arg* 3A 124
Kilchrenan. *Arg* 1H 133
Kilconquhar. *Fife* 3G 137
Kilcot. *Glos* 3B 48
Kilcoy. *High* 3H 157
Kilcreggan. *Arg* 1D 126
Kildale. *N Yor* 4D 106
Kildary. *High* 1B 158
Kildermorie Lodge. *High* 1H 157
Kildonan. *Dum* 4F 109
Kildonan. *High* 1G 165
(nr. Helmsdale)
Kildonan. *High* 3C 154
(on Isle of Skye)
Kildonan. *N Ayr* 3E 123
Kildonnan. *High* 5C 146
Kildrummy. *Abers* 2B 152
Kildwick. *N Yor* 5C 98
Kilfillan. *Dum* 4H 109
Kilfinan. *Arg* 2H 125
Kilfinnan. *High* 4E 149
Kilgetty. *Pemb* 4F 43
Kilgour. *Fife* 3E 136
Kilgrammie. *S Ayr* 4B 116
Kilham. *E Yor* 3E 101
Kilham. *Nmbd* 1C 120
Kilkenneth. *Arg* 4A 138
Kilkhampton. *Corn* 1C 10
Killamarsh. *Derbs* 2B 86
Killandrist. *Arg* 4C 140
Killay. *Swan* 3F 31
Killean. *Arg* 5E 125
Killearn. *Stir* 1G 127
Killellan. *Arg* 4A 122
Killen. *High* 3A 158
Killerby. *Darl* 3E 105
Killichonan. *Per* 3C 142
Killiechronan. *Arg* 4G 139
Killiecrankie. *Per* 2G 143
Killilan. *High* 5B 156
Killimster. *High* 3F 169
Killin. *Stir* 5C 142
Killinghall. *N Yor* 4E 99
Killington. *Cumb* 1F 97
Killingworth. *Tyne* 2F 115
Killin Lodge. *High* 3H 149
Killinochonoch. *Arg* 4F 133
Killochyett. *Bord* 5A 130
Killundine. *High* 4G 139
Kilmacolm. *Inv* 3E 127
Kilmahog. *Stir* 3F 135
Kilmahumaig. *Arg* 4E 133
Kilmalieu. *High* 3C 140
Kilmaluag. *High* 1D 154
Kilmany. *Fife* 1F 137
Kilmarie. *High* 2D 146
Kilmarnock. *E Ayr* 1D 116
Kilmaron. *Fife* 2F 137
Kilmartin. *Arg* 4F 133
Kilmaurs. *E Ayr* 5F 127
Kilmelford. *Arg* 2F 133
Kilmeny. *Arg* 3B 124
Kilmersdon. *Som* 1B 22
Kilmeston. *Hants* 4D 24
Kilmichael Glassary. *Arg* 4F 133
Kilmichael of Inverlussa. *Arg* 1F 125
Kilmington. *Devn* 3F 13
Kilmington. *Wilts* 3C 22
Kilmoluag. *Arg* 4A 138
Kilmorack. *High* 4G 157
Kilmore. *Arg* 1F 133
Kilmore. *High* 3E 147
Kilmory. *Arg* 2F 125
Kilmory. *High* 1G 139
(nr. Kilchoan)
Kilmory. *High* 3B 146
(on Rùm)
Kilmory. *N Ayr* 3D 122
Kilmory Lodge. *Arg* 3E 132
Kilmote. *High* 2G 165
Kilmuir. *High* 4B 154
(nr. Dunvegan)
Kilmuir. *High* 1B 158
(nr. Invergordon)
Kilmuir. *High* 4A 158
(nr. Inverness)
Kilmuir. *High* 1C 154
(nr. Uig)
Kilmun. *Arg* 1C 126
Kilnave. *Arg* 2A 124
Kilncadzow. *S Lan* 5B 128
Kilndown. *Kent* 2B 28
Kiln Green. *Here* 4B 48
Kiln Green. *Wind* 4G 37
Kilnhill. *Cumb* 1D 102
Kilnhurst. *S Yor* 1B 86
Kilninian. *Arg* 4E 139
Kilninver. *Arg* 1F 133
Kiln Pit Hill. *Nmbd* 4D 114
Kilnsea. *E Yor* 3H 95
Kilnsey. *N Yor* 3B 98
Kilnwick. *E Yor* 5D 101
Kiloran. *Arg* 4A 132
Kilpatrick. *N Ayr* 3D 122
Kilpeck. *Here* 2H 47
Kilpin. *E Yor* 2A 94
Kilpin Pike. *E Yor* 2A 94
Kilrenny. *Fife* 3H 137
Kilsby. *Nptn* 3C 62
Kilspindie. *Per* 1E 136
Kilsyth. *N Lan* 2A 128
Kiltarlity. *High* 4H 157
Kilton. *Som* 2E 21
Kilton Thorpe. *Red C* 3D 107
Kilvaxter. *High* 2C 154
Kilve. *Som* 2E 21
Kilvington. *Notts* 1F 75
Kilwinning. *N Ayr* 5D 126
Kimberley. *Norf* 5C 78
Kimberley. *Notts* 1B 74
Kimblesworth. *Dur* 5F 115
Kimble Wick. *Buck* 5G 51
Kimbolton. *Cambs* 4H 63
Kimbolton. *Here* 4H 59
Kimcote. *Leics* 2C 62
Kimmeridge. *Dors* 5E 15
Kimmerston. *Nmbd* 1D 120
Kimpton. *Hants* 2A 24
Kimpton. *Herts* 4B 52
Kinbeachie. *High* 2A 158
Kinbrace. *High* 5A 168
Kinbuck. *Stir* 3G 135
Kincaple. *Fife* 2G 137
Kincardine. *Fife* 1C 128
Kincardine. *High* 5D 164
Kincardine Bridge. *Fife* 1C 128
Kincardine O'Neil. *Abers* 4C 152
Kinchrackine. *Arg* 1A 134
Kincorth. *Aber* 3G 153
Kincraig. *High* 3C 150
Kincraigie. *Per* 4G 143
Kindallachan. *Per* 3G 143
Kineton. *Glos* 3F 49
Kineton. *Warw* 5H 61
Kinfauns. *Per* 1D 136
Kingairloch. *High* 3C 140
Kingarth. *Arg* 4B 126
Kingcoed. *Mon* 5H 47
King Edward. *Abers* 3E 160
Kingerby. *Linc* 1H 87
Kingham. *Oxon* 3A 50
Kingholm Quay. *Dum* 2A 112
Kinghorn. *Fife* 1F 129
Kingie. *High* 3D 148
Kinglassie. *Fife* 4E 137
Kingledores. *Bord* 2D 118
Kingodie. *Per* 1F 137
King o' Muirs. *Clac* 4A 136
King's Acre. *Here* 1H 47
Kingsand. *Corn* 3A 8
Kingsash. *Buck* 5G 51
Kingsbarns. *Fife* 2H 137
Kingsbridge. *Devn* 4D 8
Kingsbridge. *Som* 3C 20
King's Bromley. *Staf* 4F 73
Kingsburgh. *High* 3C 154
Kingsbury. *G Lon* 2C 38
Kingsbury. *Warw* 1G 61
Kingsbury Episcopi. *Som* 4H 21
Kings Caple. *Here* 3A 48
Kingscavil. *W Lot* 2D 128
Kingsclere. *Hants* 1D 24
King's Cliffe. *Nptn* 1H 63
Kings Clipstone. *Notts* 4D 86
Kingscote. *Glos* 2D 34
Kingscott. *Devn* 1F 11
Kings Coughton. *Warw* 5E 61
Kingscross. *N Ayr* 3E 123
Kingsdon. *Som* 4A 22
Kingsdown. *Kent* 1H 29
Kingsdown. *Swin* 3G 35
Kingsdown. *Wilts* 5D 34
Kingseat. *Fife* 4D 136
Kingsey. *Buck* 5F 51
Kingsfold. *Lanc* 2D 90
Kingsfold. *W Sus* 2C 26
Kingsford. *E Ayr* 5F 127
Kingsford. *Worc* 2C 60
Kingsforth. *N Lin* 3D 94
Kingsgate. *Kent* 3H 41
King's Green. *Glos* 2C 48
Kingshall Street. *Suff* 4B 66
Kingsheanton. *Devn* 3F 19
King's Heath. *W Mid* 2E 61
Kings Hill. *Kent* 5A 40
Kingsholm. *Glos* 4D 48
Kingshouse. *High* 3G 141
Kingshouse. *Stir* 1E 135
Kingshurst. *W Mid* 2F 61
Kingskerswell. *Devn* 2E 9
Kingskettle. *Fife* 3F 137
Kingsland. *Here* 4G 59
Kingsland. *IOA* 2B 80
Kings Langley. *Herts* 5A 52
Kingsley. *Ches W* 3H 83
Kingsley. *Hants* 3F 25
Kingsley. *Staf* 1E 73
Kingsley Green. *W Sus* 3G 25
Kingsley Holt. *Staf* 1E 73
King's Lynn. *Norf* 3F 77
King's Meaburn. *Cumb* 2H 103
Kings Moss. *Mers* 4D 90
Kingsmuir. *Ang* 4D 145
Kingsmuir. *Fife* 3H 137
Kings Muir. *Bord* 1E 119
King's Newnham. *Warw* 3B 62
Kings Newton. *Derbs* 3A 74
Kingsnorth. *Kent* 2E 28
Kingsnorth. *Medw* 3C 40
King's Norton. *Leics* 5D 74
King's Norton. *W Mid* 3E 61
King's Nympton. *Devn* 1G 11
King's Pyon. *Here* 5G 59
Kings Ripton. *Cambs* 3B 64
King's Somborne. *Hants* 3B 24
King's Stag. *Dors* 1C 14
King's Stanley. *Glos* 5D 48
King's Sutton. *Nptn* 2C 50
Kingstanding. *W Mid* 1E 61
Kingsteignton. *Devn* 5B 12
Kingsteps. *High* 3D 158
King Sterndale. *Derbs* 3E 85
King's Thorn. *Here* 2A 48
Kingsthorpe. *Nptn* 4E 63
Kingston. *Cambs* 5C 64
Kingston. *Devn* 4C 8
Kingston. *Dors* 2C 14
(nr. Sturminster Newton)
Kingston. *Dors* 5E 15
(nr. Swanage)
Kingston. *E Lot* 1B 130
Kingston. *Hants* 2G 15
Kingston. *IOW* 4C 16
Kingston. *Kent* 5F 41
Kingston. *Mor* 2H 159
Kingston. *W Sus* 5B 26
Kingston Bagpuize. *Oxon* 2C 36
Kingston Blount. *Oxon* 2F 37
Kingston by Sea. *W Sus* 5D 26
Kingston Deverill. *Wilts* 3D 22
Kingstone. *Here* 2H 47
Kingstone. *Som* 1G 13
Kingstone. *Staf* 3E 73
Kingston Lisle. *Oxon* 3B 36
Kingston Maurward. *Dors* 3C 14
Kingston near Lewes. *E Sus* 5E 27
Kingston on Soar. *Notts* 3C 74
Kingston Russell. *Dors* 3A 14
Kingston St Mary. *Som* 4F 21
Kingston Seymour. *N Som* 5H 33
Kingston Stert. *Oxon* 5F 51
Kingston upon Hull. *Hull* 2D 94
Kingston upon Thames. *G Lon* 4C 38
King's Walden. *Herts* 3B 52
Kingswear. *Devn* 3E 9
Kingswells. *Aber* 3F 153
Kingswinford. *W Mid* 2C 60
Kingswood. *Buck* 4E 51
Kingswood. *Glos* 2C 34
Kingswood. *Here* 5E 59
Kingswood. *Kent* 5C 40
Kingswood. *Per* 5H 143
Kingswood. *Powy* 5E 71
Kingswood. *Som* 3E 20
Kingswood. *S Glo* 4B 34
Kingswood. *Surr* 5D 38
Kingswood. *Warw* 3F 61
Kingswood Common. *Staf* 5C 72
Kings Worthy. *Hants* 3C 24
Kingthorpe. *Linc* 3A 88
Kington. *Here* 5F 59
Kington. *S Glo* 2B 34
Kington. *Worc* 5D 61
Kington Langley. *Wilts* 4E 35
Kington Magna. *Dors* 4C 22
Kington St Michael. *Wilts* 4E 35
Kingussie. *High* 3B 150
Kingweston. *Som* 3A 22
Kinharrachie. *Abers* 5G 161
Kinhrive. *High* 1B 158
Kinkell Bridge. *Per* 2B 136
Kinknockie. *Abers* 4H 161
Kinkry Hill. *Cumb* 2G 113
Kinlet. *Shrp* 2B 60
Kinloch. *High* 5D 166
(nr. Loch More)
Kinloch. *High* 3A 140
(nr. Lochaline)
Kinloch. *High* 4C 146
(on Rùm)
Kinloch. *Per* 4A 144
Kinlochard. *Stir* 3D 134
Kinlochbervie. *High* 3C 166
Kinlocheil. *High* 1D 141
Kinlochewe. *High* 2C 156
Kinloch Hourn. *High* 3B 148
Kinloch Laggan. *High* 5H 149
Kinlochleven. *High* 2F 141
Kinloch Lodge. *High* 3F 167
Kinlochmoidart. *High* 1B 140
Kinlochmore. *High* 2F 141
Kinloch Rannoch. *Per* 3D 142
Kinlochspelve. *Arg* 1D 132
Kinloid. *High* 5E 147
Kinloss. *Mor* 2E 159
Kinmel Bay. *Cnwy* 2B 82
Kinmuck. *Abers* 2F 153
Kinnadie. *Abers* 4G 161
Kinnaird. *Per* 1E 137
Kinneff. *Abers* 1H 145
Kinnelhead. *Dum* 4C 118
Kinnell. *Ang* 3F 145
Kinnerley. *Shrp* 3F 71
Kinnernie. *Abers* 2E 152
Kinnersley. *Here* 1G 47
Kinnersley. *Worc* 1D 48
Kinnerton. *Powy* 4E 59
Kinnerton. *Shrp* 1F 59
Kinnesswood. *Per* 3D 136
Kinninvie. *Dur* 2D 104
Kinnordy. *Ang* 3C 144
Kinoulton. *Notts* 2D 74
Kinross. *Per* 3D 136
Kinrossie. *Per* 5A 144
Kinsbourne Green. *Herts* 4B 52
Kinsey Heath. *Ches E* 1A 72
Kinsham. *Here* 4F 59
Kinsham. *Worc* 2E 49
Kinsley. *W Yor* 3E 93
Kinson. *Bour* 3F 15
Kintbury. *W Ber* 5B 36

Laithkirk—Lees

Laithkirk. *Dur* 2C 104
Lake. *Devn* 3F 19
Lake. *IOW* 4D 16
Lake. *Wilts* 3G 23
Lake District. *Cumb* 3E 103
Lakenham. *Norf* 5E 79
Lakenheath. *Suff* 2G 65
Lakesend. *Norf* 1E 65
Lakeside. *Cumb* 1C 96
Laleham. *Surr* 4B 38
Laleston. *B'end* 3B 32
Lamancha. *Bord* 4F 129
Lamarsh. *Essx* 2B 54
Lamas. *Norf* 3E 79
Lamb Corner. *Essx* 2D 54
Lambden. *Bord* 5D 130
Lamberhead Green. *G Man* 4D 90
Lamberhurst. *Kent* 2A 28
Lamberhurst Quarter. *Kent* 2A 28
Lamberton. *Bord* 4F 131
Lambeth. *G Lon* 3E 39
Lambfell Moar. *IOM* 3B 108
Lambhill. *Glas* 3G 127
Lambley. *Nmbd* 4H 113
Lambley. *Notts* 1D 74
Lambourn. *W Ber* 4B 36
Lambourne End. *Essx* 1F 39
Lambourn Woodlands. *W Ber* 4B 36
Lambrook. *Som* 4F 21
Lambs Green. *Dors* 3E 15
Lambs Green. *W Sus* 2D 26
Lambston. *Pemb* 3D 42
Lamellion. *Corn* 2G 7
Lamerton. *Devn* 5E 11
Lamesley. *Tyne* 4F 115
Laminess. *Orkn* 4F 172
Lamington. *High* 1B 158
Lamington. *S Lan* 1B 118
Lamlash. *N Ayr* 2E 123
Lamonby. *Cumb* 1F 103
Lamorick. *Corn* 2E 7
Lamorna. *Corn* 4B 4
Lamorran. *Corn* 4C 6
Lampeter. *Cdgn* 1F 45
Lampeter Velfrey. *Pemb* 3F 43
Lamphey. *Pemb* 4E 43
Lamplugh. *Cumb* 2B 102
Lamport. *Nptn* 3E 63
Lamyatt. *Som* 3B 22
Lana. *Devn* 3D 10
(nr. Ashwater)
Lana. *Devn* 2D 10
(nr. Holsworthy)
Lanark. *S Lan* 5B 128
Lanarth. *Corn* 4E 5
Lancaster. *Lanc* 3D 97
Lanchester. *Dur* 5E 115
Lancing. *W Sus* 5C 26
Landbeach. *Cambs* 4D 64
Landcross. *Devn* 4E 19
Landerberry. *Abers* 3E 153
Landford. *Wilts* 1A 16
Land Gate. *G Man* 4D 90
Landhallow. *High* 5D 169
Landimore. *Swan* 3D 30
Landkey. *Devn* 3F 19
Landkey Newland. *Devn* 3F 19
Landore. *Swan* 3F 31
Landport. *Port* 2E 17
Landrake. *Corn* 2H 7
Landscove. *Devn* 2D 9
Land's End (St Just) Airport.
Corn 4A 4
Landshipping. *Pemb* 3E 43
Landulph. *Corn* 2A 8
Landywood. *Staf* 5D 73
Lane. *Corn* 2C 6
Laneast. *Corn* 4C 10
Lane Bottom. *Lanc* 1G 91
Lane End. *Buck* 2G 37
Lane End. *Hants* 4D 24
Lane End. *IOW* 4E 17
Lane End. *Wilts* 2D 22
Lane Ends. *Derbs* 2G 73
Lane Ends. *Dur* 1E 105
Lane Ends. *Lanc* 4G 97
Laneham. *Notts* 3F 87
Lanehead. *Dur* 5B 114
(nr. Cowshill)
Lane Head. *Dur* 3E 105
(nr. Hutton Magna)
Lane Head. *Dur* 2D 105
(nr. Woodland)
Lane Head. *G Man* 1A 84
Lanehead. *Nmbd* 1A 114
Lane Head. *W Yor* 4B 92
Lane Heads. *Lanc* 1C 90
Lanercost. *Cumb* 3G 113
Laneshaw Bridge. *Lanc* 5B 98
Laney Green. *Staf* 5D 72
Langais. *W Isl* 2D 170
Langal. *High* 2B 140
Langar. *Notts* 2E 74
Langbank. *Ren* 2E 127
Langbar. *N Yor* 4C 98
Langburnshiels. *Bord* 4H 119
Langcliffe. *N Yor* 3H 97
Langdale End. *N Yor* 5G 107
Langdon. *Corn* 3C 10
Langdon Beck. *Dur* 1B 104
Langdon Cross. *Corn* 4D 10
Langdon Hills. *Essx* 2A 40
Langdown. *Hants* 2C 16
Langdyke. *Fife* 3F 137
Langenhoe. *Essx* 4D 54
Langford. *C Beds* 1B 52
Langford. *Devn* 2D 12
Langford. *Essx* 5B 54
Langford. *Notts* 5F 87
Langford. *Oxon* 5H 49
Langford. *Som* 4F 21
Langford Budville. *Som* 4E 20
Langham. *Dors* 4C 22
Langham. *Essx* 2D 54
Langham. *Norf* 1C 78
Langham. *Rut* 4F 75
Langham. *Suff* 4B 66
Langho. *Lanc* 1F 91
Langholm. *Dum* 1E 113
Langland. *Swan* 4F 31
Langleeford. *Nmbd* 2D 120
Langley. *Ches E* 3D 84
Langley. *Derbs* 1B 74
Langley. *Essx* 2E 53
Langley. *Glos* 3F 49
Langley. *Hants* 2C 16
Langley. *Herts* 3C 52
Langley. *Kent* 5C 40
Langley. *Nmbd* 3B 114
Langley. *Slo* 3B 38
Langley. *Som* 4D 20
Langley. *Warw* 4F 61
Langley. *W Sus* 4G 25
Langley Burrell. *Wilts* 4E 35
Langleybury. *Herts* 5A 52
Langley Common. *Derbs* 2G 73
Langley Green. *Derbs* 2G 73
Langley Green. *Norf* 5F 79
Langley Green. *Warw* 4F 61
Langley Green. *W Sus* 2D 26
Langley Heath. *Kent* 5C 40
Langley Marsh. *Som* 4D 20
Langley Moor. *Dur* 5F 115
Langley Park. *Dur* 5F 115
Langley Street. *Norf* 5F 79
Langney. *E Sus* 5H 27
Langold. *Notts* 2C 86
Langore. *Corn* 4D 10
Langport. *Som* 4H 21
Langrick. *Linc* 1B 76
Langridge. *Bath* 5C 34
Langridgeford. *Devn* 4F 19
Langrigg. *Cumb* 5C 112
Langrish. *Hants* 4F 25
Langsett. *S Yor* 4C 92
Langshaw. *Bord* 1H 119
Langstone. *Hants* 2F 17
Langthorne. *N Yor* 5F 105
Langthorpe. *N Yor* 3F 99
Langthwaite. *N Yor* 4D 104
Langtoft. *E Yor* 3E 101
Langtoft. *Linc* 4A 76
Langton. *Dur* 3E 105
Langton. *Linc* 4B 88
(nr. Horncastle)
Langton. *Linc* 3C 88
(nr. Spilsby)
Langton. *N Yor* 3B 100
Langton by Wragby. *Linc* 3A 88
Langton Green. *Kent* 2G 27
Langton Herring. *Dors* 4B 14
Langton Long Blandford.
Dors 2E 15
Langton Matravers. *Dors* 5F 15
Langtree. *Devn* 1E 11
Langwathby. *Cumb* 1G 103
Langwith. *Derbs* 4C 86
Langworth. *Linc* 3H 87
Lanivet. *Corn* 2E 7
Lanjeth. *Corn* 3D 6
Lank. *Corn* 5A 10
Lanlivery. *Corn* 3E 7
Lanner. *Corn* 5B 6
Lanreath. *Corn* 3F 7
Lansallos. *Corn* 3F 7
Lansdown. *Bath* 5C 34
Lansdown. *Glos* 3E 49
Lanteglos Highway.
Corn 3F 7
Lanton. *Nmbd* 1D 120
Lanton. *Bord* 2A 120
Lapford. *Devn* 2H 11
Lapford Cross. *Devn* 2H 11
Laphroaig. *Arg* 5B 124
Lapley. *Staf* 4C 72
Lapworth. *Warw* 3F 61
Larachbeg. *High* 4A 140
Larbert. *Falk* 1B 128
Larden Green. *Ches E* 5H 83
Larel. *High* 3D 169
Largie. *Abers* 5D 160
Largiemore. *Arg* 1H 125
Largoward. *Fife* 3G 137
Largs. *N Ayr* 4D 126
Largue. *Abers* 4D 160
Largybeg. *N Ayr* 3E 123
Largymeanoch. *N Ayr* 3E 123
Largymore. *N Ayr* 3E 123
Larkfield. *Inv* 2D 126
Larkfield. *Kent* 5A 40
Larkhall. *Bath* 5C 34
Larkhall. *S Lan* 4A 128
Larkhill. *Wilts* 2G 23
Larling. *Norf* 2B 66
Larport. *Here* 2A 48
Lartington. *Dur* 3D 104
Lary. *Abers* 3H 151
Lasham. *Hants* 2E 25
Lashenden. *Kent* 1C 28
Lassodie. *Fife* 4D 136
Lasswade. *Midl* 3G 129
Lastingham. *N Yor* 5E 107
Latchford. *Herts* 3D 53
Latchford. *Oxon* 5E 51
Latchingdon. *Essx* 5B 54
Latchley. *Corn* 5E 11
Latchmere Green. *Hants* 5E 37
Lathbury. *Mil* 1G 51
Latheron. *High* 5D 169
Latheronwheel. *High* 5D 169
Lathom. *Lanc* 4C 90
Lathones. *Fife* 3G 137
Latimer. *Buck* 1B 38
Latteridge. *S Glo* 3B 34
Lattiford. *Som* 4B 22
Latton. *Wilts* 2F 35
Laudale House. *High* 3B 140
Lauder. *Bord* 5B 130
Laugharne. *Carm* 3H 43
Laughterton. *Linc* 3F 87
Laughton. *E Sus* 4G 27
Laughton. *Leics* 2D 62
Laughton. *Linc* 1F 87
(nr. Gainsborough)
Laughton. *Linc* 2H 75
(nr. Grantham)
Laughton Common. *S Yor* 2C 86
Laughton en le Morthen. *S Yor* 2C 86
Launcells. *Corn* 2C 10
Launceston. *Corn* 4D 10
Launcherley. *Som* 2A 22
Launton. *Oxon* 3E 50
Laurencekirk. *Abers* 1G 145
Laurieston. *Dum* 3D 111
Laurieston. *Falk* 2C 128
Lavendon. *Mil* 5G 63
Lavenham. *Suff* 1C 54
Laverhay. *Dum* 5D 118
Laversdale. *Cumb* 3F 113
Laverstock. *Wilts* 3G 23
Laverstoke. *Hants* 2C 24
Laverton. *Glos* 2F 49
Laverton. *N Yor* 2E 99
Laverton. *Som* 1C 22
Lavister. *Wrex* 5F 83
Law. *S Lan* 4B 128
Lawers. *Per* 5D 142
Lawford. *Essx* 2D 54
Lawhitton. *Corn* 4D 10
Lawkland. *N Yor* 3G 97
Lawley. *Shrp* 5A 72
Lawnhead. *Staf* 3C 72
Lawrenny. *Pemb* 4E 43
Lawshall. *Suff* 5A 66
Lawton. *Here* 5G 59
Laxey. *IOM* 3D 108
Laxfield. *Suff* 3E 67
Laxfirth. *Shet* 6F 173
Laxo. *Shet* 5F 173
Laxton. *E Yor* 2A 94
Laxton. *Nptn* 1G 63
Laxton. *Notts* 4E 86
Laycock. *W Yor* 5C 98
Layer Breton. *Essx* 4C 54
Layer-de-la-Haye. *Essx* 3C 54
Layer Marney. *Essx* 4C 54
Layland's Green. *W Ber* 5B 36
Laymore. *Dors* 2G 13
Laysters Pole. *Here* 4H 59
Layter's Green. *Buck* 1A 38
Laytham. *E Yor* 1H 93
Lazenby. *Red C* 3C 106
Lazonby. *Cumb* 1G 103
Lea. *Derbs* 5H 85
Lea. *Here* 3B 48
Lea. *Linc* 2F 87
Lea. *Shrp* 2F 59
(nr. Bishop's Castle)
Lea. *Shrp* 5G 71
(nr. Shrewsbury)
Lea. *Wilts* 3E 35
Leabrooks. *Derbs* 5B 86
Leachd. *Arg* 4H 133
Leachkin. *High* 4A 158
Leachpool. *Pemb* 3D 42
Leadburn. *Midl* 4F 129
Leadenham. *Linc* 5G 87
Leaden Roding. *Essx* 4F 53
Leaderfoot. *Bord* 1H 119
Leadgate. *Cumb* 5A 114
Leadgate. *Dur* 4E 115
Leadgate. *Nmbd* 4E 115
Leadhills. *S Lan* 3A 118
Leadingcross Green. *Kent* 5C 40
Lea End. *Worc* 3E 61
Leafield. *Oxon* 4B 50
Leagrave. *Lutn* 3A 52
Lea Hall. *W Mid* 2F 61
Lea Heath. *Staf* 3E 73
Leake. *N Yor* 5B 106
Leake Common Side. *Linc* 5C 88
Leake Fold Hill. *Linc* 5D 88
Leake Hurn's End. *Linc* 1D 76
Lealholm. *N Yor* 4E 107
Lealt. *Arg* 4D 132
Lealt. *High* 2E 155
Leam. *Derbs* 3G 85
Lea Marston. *Warw* 1G 61
Leamington Hastings. *Warw* 4B 62
Leamington Spa, Royal.
Warw 4H 61
Leamonsley. *Staf* 5F 73
Leamside. *Dur* 5G 115
Leargybreck. *Arg* 2D 124
Lease Rigg. *N Yor* 4F 107
Leasgill. *Cumb* 1D 97
Leasingham. *Linc* 1H 75
Leasingthorne. *Dur* 1F 105
Leasowe. *Mers* 1E 83
Leatherhead. *Surr* 5C 38
Leathley. *N Yor* 5E 99
Leaths. *Dum* 3E 111
Leaton. *Shrp* 4G 71
Leaton. *Telf* 4A 72
Lea Town. *Lanc* 1C 90
Leaveland. *Kent* 5E 40
Leavenheath. *Suff* 2C 54
Leavening. *N Yor* 3B 100
Leaves Green. *G Lon* 4F 39
Lea Yeat. *Cumb* 1G 97
Leazes. *Dur* 4E 115
Lebberston. *N Yor* 1E 101
Lechlade on Thames. *Glos* 2H 35
Leck. *Lanc* 2F 97
Leckford. *Hants* 3B 24
Leckfurin. *High* 3H 167
Leckgruinart. *Arg* 3A 124
Leckhampstead. *Buck* 2F 51
Leckhampstead. *W Ber* 4C 36
Leckhampstead Street. *W Ber* 4C 36
Leckhampton. *Glos* 4E 49
Leckmelm. *High* 4F 163
Leckwith. *V Glam* 4E 33
Leconfield. *E Yor* 5E 101
Ledaig. *Arg* 5D 140
Ledburn. *Buck* 3H 51
Ledbury. *Here* 2C 48
Ledgemoor. *Here* 5G 59
Ledgowan. *High* 3D 156
Ledicot. *Here* 4G 59
Ledmore. *High* 2G 163
Lednabirichen. *High* 4E 165
Lednagullin. *High* 2A 168
Ledsham. *Ches W* 3F 83
Ledsham. *W Yor* 2E 93
Ledston. *W Yor* 2E 93
Ledstone. *Devn* 4D 8
Ledwell. *Oxon* 3C 50
Lee. *Devn* 2E 19
(nr. Ilfracombe)
Lee. *Devn* 4B 20
(nr. South Molton)
Lee. *G Lon* 3F 39
Lee. *Hants* 1B 16
Lee. *Lanc* 4E 97
Lee. *Shrp* 2G 71
Leeans. *Shet* 7E 173
Leebotten. *Shet* 9F 173
Leebotwood. *Shrp* 1G 59
Lee Brockhurst. *Shrp* 3H 71
Leece. *Cumb* 3B 96
Leechpool. *Mon* 3A 34
Lee Clump. *Buck* 5H 51
Leeds. *Kent* 5C 40
Leeds. *W Yor* 1C 92
Leeds Bradford International Airport.
W Yor 5E 98
Leedstown. *Corn* 3D 4
Leegomery. *Telf* 4A 72
Lee Head. *Derbs* 1E 85
Leek. *Staf* 5D 85
Leekbrook. *Staf* 5D 85
Leek Wootton. *Warw* 4G 61
Lee Mill. *Devn* 3B 8
Leeming. *N Yor* 1E 99
Leeming Bar. *N Yor* 5F 105
Lee Moor. *Devn* 2B 8
Lee Moor. *W Yor* 2D 92
Lee-on-the-Solent. *Hants* 2D 16
Lees. *Derbs* 2G 73

Little Dunham—Llanfair

Little Dunham. *Norf* 4A 78
Little Dunkeld. *Per* 4H 143
Little Dunmow. *Essx* 3G 53
Little Easton. *Essx* 3G 53
Little Eaton. *Derbs* 1A 74
Little Eccleston. *Lanc* 5D 96
Little Ellingham. *Norf* 1C 66
Little Elm. *Som* 2C 22
Little End. *Essx* 5F 53
Little Everdon. *Nptn* 5C 62
Little Eversden. *Cambs* 5C 64
Little Faringdon. *Oxon* 5H 49
Little Fencote. *N Yor* 5F 105
Little Fenton. *N Yor* 1F 93
Littleferry. *High* 4F 165
Little Fransham. *Norf* 4B 78
Little Gaddesden. *Herts* 4H 51
Little Garway. *Here* 3H 47
Little Gidding. *Cambs* 2A 64
Little Glemham. *Suff* 5F 67
Little Glenshee. *Per* 5G 143
Little Gransden. *Cambs* 5B 64
Little Green. *Suff* 3C 66
Little Green. *Wrex* 1G 71
Little Grimsby. *Linc* 1C 88
Little Habton. *N Yor* 2B 100
Little Hadham. *Herts* 3E 53
Little Hale. *Linc* 1A 76
Little Hallingbury. *Essx* 4E 53
Littleham. *Devn* 4E 19 (nr. Bideford)
Littleham. *Devn* 4D 12 (nr. Exmouth)
Little Hampden. *Buck* 5G 51
Littlehampton. *W Sus* 5B 26
Little Haresfield. *Glos* 5D 48
Little Harrowden. *Nptn* 3F 63
Little Haseley. *Oxon* 5E 51
Little Hatfield. *E Yor* 5F 101
Little Hautbois. *Norf* 3E 79
Little Haven. *Pemb* 3C 42
Little Hay. *Staf* 5F 73
Little Hayfield. *Derbs* 2E 85
Little Haywood. *Staf* 3E 73
Little Heath. *W Mid* 2H 61
Little Heck. *N Yor* 2F 93
Littlehempston. *Devn* 2E 9
Little Herbert's. *Glos* 3E 49
Little Hereford. *Here* 4H 59
Little Horkesley. *Essx* 2C 54
Little Hormead. *Herts* 3E 53
Little Horsted. *E Sus* 4F 27
Little Horton. *W Yor* 1B 92
Little Horwood. *Buck* 2F 51
Little Houghton. *Nptn* 5F 63
Littlehoughton. *Nmbd* 3G 121
Little Houghton. *S Yor* 4E 93
Little Hucklow. *Derbs* 3F 85
Little Hulton. *G Man* 4F 91
Little Irchester. *Nptn* 4G 63
Little Kelk. *E Yor* 3E 101
Little Kimble. *Buck* 5G 51
Little Kineton. *Warw* 5H 61
Little Kingshill. *Buck* 2G 37
Little Langdale. *Cumb* 4E 102
Little Langford. *Wilts* 3F 23
Little Laver. *Essx* 5F 53
Little Lawford. *Warw* 3B 62
Little Leigh. *Ches W* 3A 84
Little Leighs. *Essx* 4H 53
Little Leven. *E Yor* 5E 101
Little Lever. *G Man* 4F 91
Little Linford. *Mil* 1G 51
Little London. *Buck* 4E 51
Little London. *E Sus* 4G 27
Little London. *Hants* 2B 24 (nr. Andover)
Little London. *Hants* 1E 24 (nr. Basingstoke)
Little London. *Linc* 3D 76 (nr. Long Sutton)
Little London. *Linc* 3B 76 (nr. Spalding)
Little London. *Norf* 2E 79 (nr. North Walsham)
Little London. *Norf* 1G 65 (nr. Northwold)
Little London. *Norf* 2D 78 (nr. Saxthorpe)
Little London. *Norf* 1F 65 (nr. Southery)
Little London. *Powy* 2C 58
Little Longstone. *Derbs* 3F 85
Little Malvern. *Worc* 1C 48
Little Maplestead. *Essx* 2B 54
Little Marcle. *Here* 2B 48
Little Marlow. *Buck* 3G 37
Little Massingham. *Norf* 3G 77
Little Melton. *Norf* 5D 78
Littlemill. *Abers* 4H 151
Littlemill. *E Ayr* 3D 116
Littlemill. *High* 4D 158
Little Mill. *Mon* 5G 47
Little Milton. *Oxon* 5E 50
Little Missenden. *Buck* 1A 38
Littlemoor. *Derbs* 4A 86
Littlemoor. *Dors* 4B 14
Littlemore. *Oxon* 5D 50
Little Mountain. *Flin* 4E 83
Little Musgrave. *Cumb* 3A 104
Little Ness. *Shrp* 4G 71
Little Neston. *Ches W* 3F 83
Little Newcastle. *Pemb* 2D 43
Little Newsham. *Dur* 3E 105
Little Oakley. *Essx* 3F 55
Little Oakley. *Nptn* 2F 63
Little Onn. *Staf* 4C 72
Little Ormside. *Cumb* 3A 104
Little Orton. *Cumb* 4E 113
Little Orton. *Leics* 5H 73
Little Ouse. *Norf* 2F 65
Little Ouseburn. *N Yor* 3G 99
Littleover. *Derb* 2H 73
Little Packington. *Warw* 2G 61
Little Paxton. *Cambs* 4A 64
Little Petherick. *Corn* 1D 6
Little Plumpton. *Lanc* 1B 90
Little Plumstead. *Norf* 4F 79
Little Ponton. *Linc* 2G 75
Littleport. *Cambs* 2E 65
Little Posbrook. *Hants* 2D 16
Little Potheridge. *Devn* 1F 11
Little Preston. *Nptn* 5C 62
Little Raveley. *Cambs* 3B 64
Little Reynoldston. *Swan* 4D 31
Little Ribston. *N Yor* 4F 99
Little Rissington. *Glos* 4G 49
Little Rogart. *High* 3E 165
Little Rollright. *Oxon* 2A 50
Little Ryburgh. *Norf* 3B 78
Little Ryle. *Nmbd* 3E 121
Little Ryton. *Shrp* 5G 71
Little Salkeld. *Cumb* 1G 103
Little Sampford. *Essx* 2G 53
Little Sandhurst. *Brac* 5G 37
Little Saredon. *Staf* 5D 72
Little Saxham. *Suff* 4G 65
Little Scatwell. *High* 3F 157
Little Shelford. *Cambs* 5D 64
Little Shoddesden. *Hants* 2A 24
Little Singleton. *Lanc* 1B 90
Little Smeaton. *N Yor* 3F 93
Little Snoring. *Norf* 2B 78
Little Sodbury. *S Glo* 3C 34
Little Somborne. *Hants* 3B 24
Little Somerford. *Wilts* 3E 35
Little Soudley. *Shrp* 3B 72
Little Stainforth. *N Yor* 3H 97
Little Stainton. *Darl* 2A 106
Little Stanney. *Ches W* 3G 83
Little Staughton. *Bed* 4A 64
Little Steeping. *Linc* 4D 88
Littlester. *Shet* 4G 173
Little Stoke. *Staf* 2D 72
Littlestone-on-Sea. *Kent* 3E 29
Little Stonham. *Suff* 4D 66
Little Stretton. *Leics* 5D 74
Little Stretton. *Shrp* 1G 59
Little Strickland. *Cumb* 3G 103
Little Stukeley. *Cambs* 3B 64
Little Sugnall. *Staf* 2C 72
Little Sutton. *Ches W* 3F 83
Little Sutton. *Linc* 3D 76
Little Swinburne. *Nmbd* 2C 114
Little Tew. *Oxon* 3B 50
Little Tey. *Essx* 3B 54
Little Thetford. *Cambs* 3E 65
Little Thirkleby. *N Yor* 2G 99
Little Thornage. *Norf* 2C 78
Little Thornton. *Lanc* 5C 96
Littlethorpe. *Leics* 1C 62
Littlethorpe. *N Yor* 3F 99
Little Thorpe. *W Yor* 2B 92
Little Thurlow. *Suff* 5F 65
Little Thurrock. *Thur* 3H 39
Littleton. *Ches W* 4G 83
Littleton. *Hants* 3C 24
Littleton. *Som* 3H 21
Littleton. *Surr* 1A 26 (nr. Guildford)
Littleton. *Surr* 4B 38 (nr. Staines)
Littleton Drew. *Wilts* 3D 34
Littleton Pannell. *Wilts* 1E 23
Littleton-upon-Severn. *S Glo* 3A 34
Little Torboll. *High* 4E 165
Little Torrington. *Devn* 1E 11
Little Totham. *Essx* 4B 54
Little Town. *Cumb* 3D 102
Littletown. *Dur* 5G 115
Littletown. *High* 5E 165
Little Town. *Lanc* 1E 91
Little Twycross. *Leics* 5H 73
Little Urswick. *Cumb* 2B 96
Little Wakering. *Essx* 2D 40
Little Walden. *Essx* 1F 53
Little Waldingfield. *Suff* 1C 54
Little Walsingham. *Norf* 2B 78
Little Waltham. *Essx* 4H 53
Little Warley. *Essx* 1H 39
Little Washbourne. *Glos* 2E 49
Little Weighton. *E Yor* 1C 94
Little Wenham. *Suff* 2D 54
Little Wenlock. *Telf* 5A 72
Little Whelnetham. *Suff* 5A 66
Little Whittingham Green. *Suff* 3E 67
Littlewick Green. *Wind* 4G 37
Little Wilbraham. *Cambs* 5E 65
Littlewindsor. *Dors* 2H 13
Little Wisbeach. *Linc* 2A 76
Little Witcombe. *Glos* 4E 49
Little Witley. *Worc* 4B 60
Little Wittenham. *Oxon* 2D 36
Little Wolford. *Warw* 2A 50
Littleworth. *Bed* 1A 52
Littleworth. *Glos* 2G 49
Littleworth. *Oxon* 2B 36
Littleworth. *Staf* 4E 73 (nr. Cannock)
Littleworth. *Staf* 3B 72 (nr. Eccleshall)
Littleworth. *Staf* 3D 72 (nr. Stafford)
Littleworth. *W Sus* 3C 26
Littleworth. *Worc* 4D 61 (nr. Redditch)
Littleworth. *Worc* 1D 49 (nr. Worcester)
Little Wratting. *Suff* 1G 53
Little Wymington. *Nptn* 4G 63
Little Wymondley. *Herts* 3C 52
Little Wyrley. *Staf* 5E 73
Little Yeldham. *Essx* 2A 54
Littley Green. *Essx* 4G 53
Litton. *Derbs* 3F 85
Litton. *N Yor* 2B 98
Litton. *Som* 1A 22
Litton Cheney. *Dors* 3A 14
Liurbost. *W Isl* 5F 171
Liverpool. *Mers* 1F 83
Liverpool John Lennon Airport. *Mers* 2G 83
Liversedge. *W Yor* 2B 92
Liverton. *Devn* 5B 12
Liverton. *Red C* 3E 107
Liverton Mines. *Red C* 3E 107
Livingston. *W Lot* 3D 128
Livingston Village. *W Lot* 3D 128
Lixwm. *Flin* 3D 82
Lizard. *Corn* 5E 5
Llaingoch. *IOA* 2B 80
Llaithddu. *Powy* 2C 58
Llampha. *V Glam* 4C 32
Llan. *Powy* 5A 70
Llanaber. *Gwyn* 4F 69
Llanaelhaearn. *Gwyn* 1C 68
Llanaeron. *Cdgn* 4D 57
Llanafan. *Cdgn* 3F 57
Llanafan-fawr. *Powy* 5B 58
Llanafan-fechan. *Powy* 5B 58
Llanallgo. *IOA* 2D 81
Llanandras. *Powy* 4F 59
Llananno. *Powy* 3C 58
Llanarmon. *Gwyn* 2D 68
Llanarmon Dyffryn Ceiriog. *Wrex* 2D 70
Llanarmon-yn-Ial. *Den* 5D 82
Llanarth. *Cdgn* 5D 56
Llanarth. *Mon* 4G 47
Llanarthne. *Carm* 3F 45
Llanasa. *Flin* 2D 82
Llanbabo. *IOA* 2C 80
Llanbadarn Fawr. *Cdgn* 2F 57
Llanbadarn Fynydd. *Powy* 3C 58
Llanbadarn-y-garreg. *Powy* 1E 46
Llanbadoc. *Mon* 5G 47
Llanbadrig. *IOA* 1C 80
Llanbeder. *Newp* 2G 33
Llanbedr. *Gwyn* 3E 69
Llanbedr. *Powy* 3F 47 (nr. Crickhowell)
Llanbedr. *Powy* 1E 47 (nr. Hay-on-Wye)
Llanbedr-Dyffryn-Clwyd. *Den* 5D 82
Llanbedrgoch. *IOA* 2E 81
Llanbedrog. *Gwyn* 2C 68
Llanbedr Pont Steffan. *Cdgn* 1F 45
Llanbedr-y-cennin. *Cnwy* 4G 81
Llanberis. *Gwyn* 4E 81
Llanbethery. *V Glam* 5D 32
Llanbister. *Powy* 3D 58
Llanblethian. *V Glam* 4C 32
Llanboidy. *Carm* 2G 43
Llanbradach. *Cphy* 2E 33
Llanbrynmair. *Powy* 5A 70
Llanbydderi. *V Glam* 5D 32
Llancadle. *V Glam* 5D 32
Llancarfan. *V Glam* 4D 32
Llancatal. *V Glam* 5D 32
Llancayo. *Mon* 5G 47
Llancloudy. *Here* 3H 47
Llancoch. *Powy* 3E 58
Llancynfelyn. *Cdgn* 1F 57
Llandaff. *Card* 4E 33
Llandanwg. *Gwyn* 3E 69
Llandarcy. *Neat* 3G 31
Llandawke. *Carm* 3G 43
Llanddaniel-Fab. *IOA* 3D 81
Llanddarog. *Carm* 4F 45
Llanddeiniol. *Cdgn* 3E 57
Llanddeiniolen. *Gwyn* 4E 81
Llandderfel. *Gwyn* 2B 70
Llanddeusant. *Carm* 3A 46
Llanddeusant. *IOA* 2C 80
Llanddew. *Powy* 2D 46
Llanddewi. *Swan* 4D 30
Llanddewi Brefi. *Cdgn* 5F 57
Llanddewi'r Cwm. *Powy* 1D 46
Llanddewi Rhydderch. *Mon* 4G 47
Llanddewi Velfrey. *Pemb* 3F 43
Llanddewi Ystradenni. *Powy* 4D 58
Llanddoged. *Cnwy* 4H 81
Llanddona. *IOA* 3E 81
Llanddowror. *Carm* 3G 43
Llanddulas. *Cnwy* 3B 82
Llanddwywe. *Gwyn* 3E 69
Llanddyfnan. *IOA* 3E 81
Llandecwyn. *Gwyn* 2F 69
Llandefaelog Fach. *Powy* 2D 46
Llandefaelog-tre'r-graig. *Powy* 2E 47
Llandefalle. *Powy* 2E 46
Llandegfan. *IOA* 3E 81
Llandegla. *Den* 5D 82
Llandegley. *Powy* 4D 58
Llandegveth. *Mon* 2G 33
Llandeilo. *Carm* 3G 45
Llandeilo Graban. *Powy* 1D 46
Llandeilo'r Fan. *Powy* 2B 46
Llandeloy. *Pemb* 2C 42
Llandenny. *Mon* 5H 47
Llandevaud. *Newp* 2H 33
Llandevenny. *Mon* 3G 33
Llandilo. *Pemb* 2F 43
Llandinabo. *Here* 3A 48
Llandinam. *Powy* 2C 58
Llandissilio. *Pemb* 2F 43
Llandogo. *Mon* 5A 48
Llandough. *V Glam* 4C 32 (nr. Cowbridge)
Llandough. *V Glam* 4E 33 (nr. Penarth)
Llandovery. *Carm* 2A 46
Llandow. *V Glam* 4C 32
Llandre. *Cdgn* 2F 57
Llandrillo. *Den* 2C 70
Llandrillo-yn-Rhos. *Cnwy* 2H 81
Llandrindod. *Powy* 4C 58
Llandrindod Wells. *Powy* 4C 58
Llandrinio. *Powy* 4E 71
Llandsadwrn. *Carm* 2G 45
Llandudno. *Cnwy* 2G 81
Llandudno Junction. *Cnwy* 3G 81
Llandudoch. *Pemb* 1B 44
Llandw. *V Glam* 4C 32
Llandwrog. *Gwyn* 5D 80
Llandybie. *Carm* 4G 45
Llandyfaelog. *Carm* 4E 45
Llandyfan. *Carm* 4G 45
Llandyfriog. *Cdgn* 1D 44
Llandyfrydog. *IOA* 2D 80
Llandygai. *Gwyn* 3E 81
Llandygwydd. *Cdgn* 1C 44
Llandynan. *Den* 1D 70
Llandyrnog. *Den* 4D 82
Llandysilio. *Powy* 4E 71
Llandyssil. *Powy* 1D 58
Llandysul. *Cdgn* 1E 45
Llanedeyrn. *Card* 3F 33
Llaneglwys. *Powy* 2D 46
Llanegryn. *Gwyn* 5F 69
Llanegwad. *Carm* 3F 45
Llaneilian. *IOA* 1D 80
Llanelian-yn-Rhos. *Cnwy* 3A 82
Llanelidan. *Den* 5D 82
Llanelieu. *Powy* 2E 47
Llanellen. *Mon* 4G 47
Llanelli. *Carm* 3E 31
Llanelltyd. *Gwyn* 4G 69
Llanelly. *Mon* 4F 47
Llanelly Hill. *Mon* 4F 47
Llanelwedd. *Powy* 5C 58
Llanelwy. *Den* 3C 82
Llanenddwyn. *Gwyn* 3E 69
Llanengan. *Gwyn* 3B 68
Llanerch. *Powy* 1F 59
Llanerchymedd. *IOA* 2D 80
Llanerfyl. *Powy* 5C 70
Llaneuddog. *IOA* 2D 80
Llanfachraeth. *IOA* 2C 80
Llanfaelog. *IOA* 3C 80
Llanfaelrhys. *Gwyn* 3B 68
Llanfaenor. *Mon* 4H 47
Llanfaes. *IOA* 3F 81
Llanfaes. *Powy* 3D 46
Llanfaethlu. *IOA* 2C 80
Llanfaglan. *Gwyn* 4D 80
Llanfair. *Gwyn* 3E 69
Llanfair. *Here* 1F 47

Longborough—Loxley Green

Longborough. Glos 3G 49
Long Bredy. Dors 3A 14
Longbridge. Warw 4G 61
Longbridge. W Mid 3E 61
Longbridge Deverill. Wilts 2D 22
Long Buckby. Nptn 4D 62
Long Buckby Wharf. Nptn 4D 62
Longburgh. Cumb 4E 112
Longburton. Dors 1B 14
Long Clawson. Leics 3E 74
Longcliffe. Derbs 5G 85
Long Common. Hants 1D 16
Long Compton. Staf 3C 72
Long Compton. Warw 2A 50
Longcot. Oxon 2A 36
Long Crendon. Buck 5E 51
Long Crichel. Dors 1E 15
Longcroft. Cumb 4D 112
Longcroft. Falk 2A 128
Longcross. Surr 4A 38
Longdale. Cumb 4H 103
Longdales. Cumb 5G 113
Longden. Shrp 5G 71
Longden Common. Shrp 5G 71
Long Ditton. Surr 4C 38
Longdon. Staf 4E 73
Longdon. Worc 2D 48
Longdon Green. Staf 4E 73
Longdon on Tern. Telf 4A 72
Longdown. Devn 3B 12
Longdowns. Corn 5B 6
Long Drax. N Yor 2G 93
Long Duckmanton. Derbs 3B 86
Long Eaton. Derbs 2B 74
Longfield. Kent 4H 39
Longfield Hill. Kent 4H 39
Longford. Derbs 2G 73
Longford. Glos 3D 48
Longford. G Lon 3B 38
Longford. Shrp 2A 72
Longford. Telf 4B 72
Longford. W Mid 2H 61
Longforgan. Per 1F 137
Longformacus. Bord 4C 130
Longframlington. Nmbd 4F 121
Long Gardens. Essx 2B 54
Long Green. Ches W 3G 83
Long Green. Worc 2D 48
Longham. Dors 3F 15
Longham. Norf 4B 78
Long Hanborough. Oxon 4C 50
Longhedge. Wilts 2D 22
Longhill. Abers 3H 161
Longhirst. Nmbd 1F 115
Longhope. Glos 4B 48
Longhope. Orkn 8C 172
Longhorsley. Nmbd 5F 121
Longhoughton. Nmbd 3G 121
Long Itchington. Warw 4B 62
Longlands. Cumb 1D 102
Longlane. Derbs 2G 73
Long Lane. Telf 4A 72
Longlane. W Ber 4C 36
Long Lawford. Warw 3B 62
Long Lease. N Yor 4G 107
Longley Green. Worc 5B 60
Long Load. Som 4H 21
Longmanhill. Abers 2E 161
Long Marston. Herts 4G 51
Long Marston. N Yor 4H 99
Long Marston. Warw 1G 49
Long Marton. Cumb 2H 103
Long Meadow. Cambs 4E 65
Long Meadowend. Shrp 2G 59
Long Melford. Suff 1B 54
Longmoor Camp. Hants 3F 25
Longmorn. Mor 3G 159
Longmoss. Ches E 3C 84
Long Newnton. Glos 2E 35
Longnewton. Bord 2H 119
Long Newton. Stoc T 3A 106
Longney. Glos 4C 48
Longniddry. E Lot 2H 129
Longnor. Shrp 5G 71
Longnor. Staf 4E 85
(nr. Leek)
Longnor. Staf 4C 72
(nr. Stafford)
Longparish. Hants 2C 24
Longpark. Cumb 3F 113
Long Preston. N Yor 4H 97
Longridge. Lanc 1E 90
Longridge. Staf 4D 72
Longridge. W Lot 3C 128
Longriggend. N Lan 2B 128
Long Riston. E Yor 5F 101
Longrock. Corn 3C 4
Longsdon. Staf 5D 84
Longshaw. G Man 4D 90
Longshaw. Staf 1E 73
Longside. Abers 4H 161
Longslow. Shrp 2A 72
Longstanton. Cambs 4C 64
Longstock. Hants 3B 24
Longstowe. Cambs 5C 64
Long Stratton. Norf 1D 66
Long Street. Mil 1F 51
Longstreet. Wilts 1G 23
Long Sutton. Hants 2F 25
Long Sutton. Linc 3D 76
Long Sutton. Som 4H 21
Longthorpe. Pet 1A 64
Long Thurlow. Suff 4C 66
Longthwaite. Cumb 2F 103
Longton. Lanc 2C 90
Longton. Stoke 1D 72
Longtown. Cumb 3E 113
Longtown. Here 3G 47
Longville in the Dale. Shrp 1H 59
Long Whatton. Leics 3B 74
Longwick. Buck 5F 51
Long Wittenham. Oxon 2D 36
Longwitton. Nmbd 1D 115
Longworth. Oxon 2B 36
Longyester. E Lot 3B 130
Lonmore. High 4B 154
Looe. Corn 3G 7
Loose. Kent 5B 40
Loosegate. Linc 3C 76
Loosley Row. Buck 5G 51
Lopcombe Corner. Wilts 3A 24
Lopen. Som 1H 13
Loppington. Shrp 3G 71
Lorbottle. Nmbd 4E 121
Lorbottle Hall. Nmbd 4E 121
Lordington. W Sus 2F 17
Loscoe. Derbs 1B 74
Loscombe. Dors 3A 14
Losgaintir. W Isl 8C 171
Lossiemouth. Mor 2G 159
Lossit. Arg 4A 124
Lostock Gralam. Ches W 3A 84
Lostock Green. Ches W 3A 84
Lostock Hall. Lanc 2D 90
Lostock Junction. G Man 4E 91
Lostwithiel. Corn 3F 7
Lothbeg. High 2G 165
Lothersdale. N Yor 5B 98
Lothianbridge. Midl 3G 129
Lothianburn. Edin 3F 129
Lothmore. High 2G 165
Lottisham. Som 3A 22
Loudwater. Buck 1A 38
Loughborough. Leics 4C 74
Loughor. Swan 3E 31
Loughton. Essx 1F 39
Loughton. Mil 2G 51
Loughton. Shrp 2A 60
Lound. Linc 4H 75
Lound. Notts 2D 86
Lound. Suff 1H 67
Lount. Leics 4A 74
Louth. Linc 2C 88
Love Clough. Lanc 2G 91
Lovedean. Hants 1E 17
Lover. Wilts 4H 23
Loversall. S Yor 1C 86
Loves Green. Essx 5G 53
Loveston. Pemb 4E 43
Lovington. Som 3A 22
Low Ackworth. W Yor 3E 93
Low Angerton. Nmbd 1D 115
Low Ardwell. Dum 5F 109
Low Ballochdoan. S Ayr 2F 109
Lowbands. Glos 2C 48
Low Barlings. Linc 3H 87
Low Bell End. N Yor 5E 107
Low Bentham. N Yor 3F 97
Low Borrowbridge. Cumb 4H 103
Low Bradfield. S Yor 1G 85
Low Bradley. N Yor 5C 98
Low Braithwaite. Cumb 5F 113
Low Brunton. Nmbd 2C 114
Low Burnham. N Lin 4A 94
Lowca. Cumb 2A 102
Low Catton. E Yor 4B 100
Low Coniscliffe. Darl 3F 105
Low Coylton. S Ayr 3D 116
Low Crosby. Cumb 4F 113
Low Dalby. N Yor 1C 100
Lowdham. Notts 1D 74
Low Dinsdale. Darl 3A 106
Lowe. Shrp 2G 71
Low Ellington. N Yor 1E 98
Lower Amble. Corn 1D 6
Lower Ansty. Dors 2C 14
Lower Arboll. High 5F 165
Lower Arncott. Oxon 4E 50
Lower Ashton. Devn 4B 12
Lower Assendon. Oxon 3F 37
Lower Auchenreath. Mor 2A 160
Lower Badcall. High 4B 166
Lower Ballam. Lanc 1B 90
Lower Basildon. W Ber 4E 36
Lower Beeding. W Sus 3D 26
Lower Benefield. Nptn 2G 63
Lower Bentley. Worc 4D 61
Lower Beobridge. Shrp 1B 60
Lower Bockhampton. Dors 3C 14
Lower Boddington. Nptn 5B 62
Lower Bordean. Hants 4E 25
Lower Brailes. Warw 2B 50
Lower Breakish. High 1E 147
Lower Broadheath. Worc 5C 60
Lower Brynamman. Neat 4H 45
Lower Bullingham. Here 2A 48
Lower Bullington. Hants 2C 24
Lower Burgate. Hants 1G 15
Lower Cam. Glos 5C 48
Lower Catesby. Nptn 5C 62
Lower Chapel. Powy 2D 46
Lower Cheriton. Devn 2E 12
Lower Chicksgrove. Wilts 3E 23
Lower Chute. Wilts 1B 24
Lower Clopton. Warw 5F 61
Lower Common. Hants 2E 25
Lower Cumberworth. W Yor 4C 92
Lower Darwen. Bkbn 2E 91
Lower Dean. Bed 4H 63
Lower Dean. Devn 2D 8
Lower Diabaig. High 2G 155
Lower Dicker. E Sus 4G 27
Lower Dounreay. High 2B 168
Lower Down. Shrp 2F 59
Lower Dunsforth. N Yor 3G 99
Lower East Carleton. Norf 5D 78
Lower Egleton. Here 1B 48
Lower Ellastone. Derbs 1F 73
Lower End. Nptn 4F 63
Lower Everleigh. Wilts 1G 23
Lower Eype. Dors 3H 13
Lower Failand. N Som 4A 34
Lower Faintree. Shrp 2A 60
Lower Farringdon. Hants 3F 25
Lower Foxdale. IOM 4B 108
Lower Frankton. Shrp 2F 71
Lower Froyle. Hants 2F 25
Lower Gabwell. Devn 2F 9
Lower Gledfield. High 4C 164
Lower Godney. Som 2H 21
Lower Gravenhurst. C Beds 2B 52
Lower Green. Essx 2E 53
Lower Green. Norf 2B 78
Lower Green. Staf 5D 72
Lower Green. W Ber 5B 36
Lower Halstow. Kent 4C 40
Lower Hardres. Kent 5F 41
Lower Hardwick. Here 5G 59
Lower Hartshay. Derbs 5A 86
Lower Hawthwaite. Cumb 1B 96
Lower Hayton. Shrp 2H 59
Lower Hergest. Here 5E 59
Lower Heyford. Oxon 3C 50
Lower Heysham. Lanc 3D 96
Lower Higham. Kent 3B 40
Lower Holbrook. Suff 2E 55
Lower Holditch. Dors 2G 13
Lower Hordley. Shrp 3F 71
Lower Horncroft. W Sus 4B 26
Lower Kilcott. Glos 3C 34
Lower Killeyan. Arg 5A 124
Lower Kingcombe. Dors 3A 14
Lower Kingswood. Surr 5D 38
Lower Kinnerton. Ches W 4F 83
Lower Langford. N Som 5H 33
Lower Largo. Fife 3G 137
Lower Layham. Suff 1D 54
Lower Ledwyche. Shrp 3H 59
Lower Leigh. Staf 2E 73
Lower Lemington. Glos 2H 49
Lower Lenie. High 1H 149
Lower Ley. Glos 4C 48
Lower Llanfadog. Powy 4B 58
Lower Lode. Glos 2D 49
Lower Lovacott. Devn 4F 19
Lower Loxhore. Devn 3G 19
Lower Loxley. Staf 2E 73
Lower Lydbrook. Glos 4A 48
Lower Lye. Here 4G 59
Lower Machen. Newp 3F 33
Lower Maes-coed. Here 2G 47
Lower Meend. Glos 5A 48
Lower Milovaig. High 3A 154
Lower Moor. Worc 1E 49
Lower Morton. S Glo 2B 34
Lower Mountain. Flin 5F 83
Lower Nazeing. Essx 5D 53
Lower Netchwood. Shrp 1A 60
Lower Nyland. Dors 4C 22
Lower Oakfield. Fife 4D 136
Lower Oddington. Glos 3H 49
Lower Ollach. High 5E 155
Lower Penarth. V Glam 5E 33
Lower Penn. Staf 1C 60
Lower Pennington. Hants 3B 16
Lower Peover. Ches W 3B 84
Lower Pilsley. Derbs 4B 86
Lower Pitkerrie. High 1C 158
Lower Place. G Man 3H 91
Lower Quinton. Warw 1G 49
Lower Rainham. Medw 4C 40
Lower Raydon. Suff 2D 54
Lower Seagry. Wilts 3E 35
Lower Shelton. C Beds 1H 51
Lower Shiplake. Oxon 4F 37
Lower Shuckburgh. Warw 4B 62
Lower Sketty. Swan 3F 31
Lower Slade. Devn 2F 19
Lower Slaughter. Glos 3G 49
Lower Soudley. Glos 4B 48
Lower Stanton St Quintin. Wilts 3E 35
Lower Stoke. Medw 3C 40
Lower Stondon. C Beds 2B 52
Lower Stonnall. Staf 5E 73
Lower Stow Bedon. Norf 1B 66
Lower Street. Norf 2E 79
Lower Strensham. Worc 1E 49
Lower Sundon. C Beds 3A 52
Lower Swanwick. Hants 2C 16
Lower Swell. Glos 3G 49
Lower Tale. Devn 2D 12
Lower Tean. Staf 2E 73
Lower Thurlton. Norf 1G 67
Lower Thurnham. Lanc 4D 96
Lower Thurvaston. Derbs 2G 73
Lowertown. Corn 4D 4
Lower Town. Here 1B 48
Lower Town. IOS 1B 4
Lower Town. Pemb 1D 42
Lower Tysoe. Warw 1B 50
Lower Upham. Hants 1D 16
Lower Upnor. Medw 3B 40
Lower Vexford. Som 3E 20
Lower Walton. Warr 2A 84
Lower Wear. Devn 4C 12
Lower Weare. Som 1H 21
Lower Welson. Here 5E 59
Lower Whatcombe. Dors 2D 14
Lower Whitley. Ches W 3A 84
Lower Wield. Hants 2E 25
Lower Withington. Ches E 4C 84
Lower Woodend. Buck 3G 37
Lower Woodford. Wilts 3G 23
Lower Wraxall. Dors 2A 14
Lower Wych. Ches W 1G 71
Lower Wyche. Worc 1C 48
Lowesby. Leics 5E 74
Lowestoft. Suff 1H 67
Loweswater. Cumb 2C 102
Low Etherley. Dur 2E 105
Lowfield Heath. W Sus 1D 26
Lowford. Hants 1C 16
Low Fulney. Linc 3B 76
Low Gate. Nmbd 3C 114
Lowgill. Cumb 5H 103
Lowgill. Lanc 3F 97
Low Grantley. N Yor 2E 99
Low Green. N Yor 4E 98
Low Habberley. Worc 3C 60
Low Ham. Som 4H 21
Low Hameringham. Linc 4C 88
Low Hawkser. N Yor 4G 107
Low Hesket. Cumb 5F 113
Low Hesleyhurst. Nmbd 5E 121
Lowick. Cumb 1B 96
Lowick. Nptn 2G 63
Lowick. Nmbd 1E 121
Lowick Bridge. Cumb 1B 96
Lowick Green. Cumb 1B 96
Low Knipe. Cumb 3G 103
Low Leighton. Derbs 2E 85
Low Lorton. Cumb 2C 102
Low Marishes. N Yor 2C 100
Low Marnham. Notts 4F 87
Low Mill. N Yor 5D 106
Low Moor. Lanc 5G 97
Low Moor. W Yor 2B 92
Low Moorsley. Tyne 5G 115
Low Newton-by-the-Sea. Nmbd 2G 121
Lownie Moor. Ang 4D 145
Lowood. Bord 1H 119
Low Row. Cumb 3G 113
(nr. Brampton)
Low Row. Cumb 5C 112
(nr. Wigton)
Low Row. N Yor 5C 104
Lowsonford. Warw 4F 61
Low Street. Norf 5C 78
Lowther. Cumb 2G 103
Lowthorpe. E Yor 3E 101
Lowton. Devn 2G 11
Lowton. G Man 1A 84
Lowton. Som 1E 13
Lowton Common. G Man 1A 84
Low Torry. Fife 1D 128
Low Toynton. Linc 3B 88
Low Valleyfield. Fife 1C 128
Low Westwood. Dur 4E 115
Low Whinnow. Cumb 4E 112
Low Wood. Cumb 1C 96
Low Worsall. N Yor 4A 106
Low Wray. Cumb 4E 103
Loxbeare. Devn 1C 12
Loxhill. Surr 2B 26
Loxhore. Devn 3G 19
Loxley. S Yor 2H 85
Loxley. Warw 5G 61
Loxley Green. Staf 2E 73

Loxton. N Som ...1G 21
Loxwood. W Sus ...2B 26
Lubcroy. High ...3A 164
Lubenham. Leics ...2E 62
Lubinvullin. High ...2F 167
Luccombe. Som ...2C 20
Luccombe Village. IOW ...4D 16
Lucker. Nmbd ...1F 121
Luckett. Corn ...5D 11
Luckington. Wilts ...3D 34
Lucklawhill. Fife ...1G 137
Luckwell Bridge. Som ...3C 20
Lucton. Here ...4G 59
Ludag. W Isl ...7C 170
Ludborough. Linc ...1B 88
Ludchurch. Pemb ...3F 43
Luddenden. W Yor ...2A 92
Luddenden Foot. W Yor ...2A 92
Luddenham. Kent ...4D 40
Ludderburn. Cumb ...5F 103
Luddesdown. Kent ...4A 40
Luddington. N Lin ...3B 94
Luddington. Warw ...5F 61
Luddington in the Brook. Nptn ...2A 64
Ludford. Linc ...2A 88
Ludford. Shrp ...3H 59
Ludgershall. Buck ...4E 51
Ludgershall. Wilts ...1A 24
Ludgvan. Corn ...3C 4
Ludham. Norf ...4F 79
Ludlow. Shrp ...3H 59
Ludstone. Shrp ...1C 60
Ludwell. Wilts ...4E 23
Ludworth. Dur ...5G 115
Luffenhall. Herts ...3C 52
Luffincott. Devn ...3D 10
Lugar. E Ayr ...2E 117
Luggate Burn. E Lot ...2C 130
Lugg Green. Here ...4G 59
Luggiebank. N Lan ...2A 128
Lugton. E Ayr ...4F 127
Lugwardine. Here ...1A 48
Luib. High ...1D 146
Luib. Stir ...1D 135
Lulham. Here ...1H 47
Lullington. Derbs ...4G 73
Lullington. E Sus ...5G 27
Lullington. Som ...1C 22
Lulsgate Bottom. N Som ...5A 34
Lulsley. Worc ...5B 60
Lulworth Camp. Dors ...4D 14
Lumb. Lanc ...2G 91
Lumb. W Yor ...2A 92
Lumby. N Yor ...1E 93
Lumphanan. Abers ...3C 152
Lumphinnans. Fife ...4D 136
Lumsdaine. Bord ...3E 131
Lumsden. Abers ...1B 152
Lunan. Ang ...3F 145
Lunanhead. Ang ...3D 145
Luncarty. Per ...1C 136
Lund. E Yor ...5D 100
Lund. N Yor ...1G 93
Lundie. Ang ...5B 144
Lundin Links. Fife ...3G 137
Lundy Green. Norf ...1E 67
Lunna. Shet ...5F 173
Lunning. Shet ...5G 173
Lunnon. Swan ...4E 31
Lunsford. Kent ...5B 40
Lunsford's Cross. E Sus ...4B 28
Lunt. Mers ...4B 90
Luppitt. Devn ...2E 13
Lupridge. Devn ...3D 8
Lupset. W Yor ...3D 92
Lupton. Cumb ...1E 97
Lurgashall. W Sus ...3A 26
Lurley. Devn ...1C 12
Lusby. Linc ...4C 88
Luscombe. Devn ...3D 9
Luson. Devn ...4C 8
Luss. Arg ...4C 134
Lussagiven. Arg ...1E 125
Lusta. High ...3B 154

Lustleigh. Devn ...4A 12
Luston. Here ...4G 59
Luthermuir. Abers ...2F 145
Luthrie. Fife ...2F 137
Lutley. Staf ...2C 60
Luton. Devn ...2D 12
(nr. Honiton)
Luton. Devn ...5C 12
(nr. Teignmouth)
Luton. Lutn ...3A 52
Luton (London) Airport. Lutn ...3B 52
Lutterworth. Leics ...2C 62
Lutton. Devn ...3B 8
(nr. Ivybridge)
Lutton. Devn ...2C 8
(nr. South Brent)
Lutton. Linc ...3D 76
Lutton. Nptn ...2A 64
Lutton Gowts. Linc ...3D 76
Lutworthy. Devn ...1A 12
Luxborough. Som ...3C 20
Luxley. Glos ...3B 48
Luxulyan. Corn ...3E 7
Lybster. High ...5E 169
Lydbury North. Shrp ...2F 59
Lydcott. Devn ...3G 19
Lydd. Kent ...3E 29
Lydden. Kent ...1G 29
(nr. Dover)
Lydden. Kent ...4H 41
(nr. Margate)
Lyddington. Rut ...1F 63
Lydd (London Ashford) Airport.
Kent ...3E 29
Lydd-on-Sea. Kent ...3E 29
Lydeard St Lawrence. Som ...3E 21
Lyde Green. Hants ...1F 25
Lydford. Devn ...4F 11
Lydford Fair Place. Som ...3A 22
Lydgate. G Man ...4H 91
Lydgate. W Yor ...2H 91
Lydham. Shrp ...1F 59
Lydiard Millicent. Wilts ...3F 35
Lydiate. Mers ...4B 90
Lydiate Ash. Worc ...3D 61
Lydlinch. Dors ...1C 14
Lydmarsh. Som ...2G 13
Lydney. Glos ...5B 48
Lydstep. Pemb ...5E 43
Lye. W Mid ...2D 60
Lye Green. Buck ...5H 51
Lye Green. E Sus ...2G 27
Lye Head. Worc ...3B 60
Lye, The. Shrp ...1A 60
Lyford. Oxon ...2B 36
Lyham. Nmbd ...1E 121
Lylestone. N Ayr ...5E 127
Lymbridge Green. Kent ...1F 29
Lyme Regis. Dors ...3G 13
Lyminge. Kent ...1F 29
Lymington. Hants ...3B 16
Lyminster. W Sus ...5B 26
Lymm. Warr ...2A 84
Lympne. Kent ...2F 29
Lympsham. Som ...1G 21
Lympstone. Devn ...4C 12
Lynaberack Lodge. High ...4B 150
Lynbridge. Devn ...2H 19
Lynch. Som ...2C 20
Lynchat. High ...3B 150
Lynch Green. Norf ...5D 78
Lyndhurst. Hants ...2B 16
Lyndon. Rut ...5G 75
Lyne. Bord ...5F 129
Lyne. Surr ...4B 38
Lyneal. Shrp ...2G 71
Lyne Down. Here ...2B 48
Lyneham. Oxon ...3A 50
Lyneham. Wilts ...4F 35
Lyneholmeford. Cumb ...2G 113
Lynemouth. Nmbd ...5G 121
Lyne of Gorthleck. High ...1H 149
Lyne of Skene. Abers ...2E 153

Lynesack. Dur ...2D 105
Lyness. Orkn ...8C 172
Lyng. Norf ...4C 78
Lyngate. Norf ...2E 79
(nr. North Walsham)
Lyngate. Norf ...3F 79
(nr. Worstead)
Lynmouth. Devn ...2H 19
Lynn. Staf ...5E 73
Lynn. Telf ...4B 72
Lynsted. Kent ...4D 40
Lynstone. Corn ...2C 10
Lynton. Devn ...2H 19
Lynwilg. High ...2C 150
Lyon's Gate. Dors ...2B 14
Lyonshall. Here ...5F 59
Lytchett Matravers. Dors ...3E 15
Lytchett Minster. Dors ...3E 15
Lyth. High ...2E 169
Lytham. Lanc ...2B 90
Lytham St Anne's. Lanc ...2B 90
Lythe. N Yor ...3F 107
Lythes. Orkn ...9D 172
Lythmore. High ...2C 168

M

Mabe Burnthouse. Corn ...5B 6
Mabie. Dum ...2A 112
Mablethorpe. Linc ...2E 89
Macbiehill. Bord ...4E 129
Macclesfield. Ches E ...3D 84
Macclesfield Forest. Ches E ...3D 85
Macduff. Abers ...2E 160
Machan. S Lan ...4A 128
Macharioch. Arg ...5B 122
Machen. Cphy ...3F 33
Machrie. N Ayr ...2C 122
Machrihanish. Arg ...3A 122
Machroes. Gwyn ...3C 68
Machynlleth. Powy ...5G 69
Mackerye End. Herts ...4B 52
Mackworth. Derb ...2H 73
Macmerry. E Lot ...2H 129
Madderty. Per ...1B 136
Maddington. Wilts ...2F 23
Maddiston. Falk ...2C 128
Madehurst. W Sus ...4A 26
Madeley. Staf ...1B 72
Madeley. Telf ...5A 72
Madeley Heath. Staf ...1B 72
Madeley Heath. Worc ...3D 60
Madford. Devn ...1E 13
Madingley. Cambs ...4C 64
Madley. Here ...2H 47
Madresfield. Worc ...1D 48
Madron. Corn ...3B 4
Maenaddwyn. IOA ...2D 80
Maenclochog. Pemb ...2E 43
Maendy. V Glam ...4D 32
Maenporth. Corn ...4E 5
Maentwrog. Gwyn ...1F 69
Maen-y-groes. Cdgn ...5C 56
Maer. Staf ...2B 72
Maerdy. Carm ...3G 45
Maerdy. Cnwy ...1C 70
Maerdy. Rhon ...2C 32
Maesbrook. Shrp ...3F 71
Maesbury. Shrp ...3F 71
Maesbury Marsh. Shrp ...3F 71
Maes-glas. Flin ...3D 82
Maesgwyn-Isaf. Powy ...4D 70
Maeshafn. Den ...4E 82
Maesllyn. Cdgn ...1D 44
Maesmynis. Powy ...1D 46
Maesteg. B'end ...2B 32
Maestir. Cdgn ...1F 45
Maesybont. Carm ...4F 45
Maesycrugiau. Carm ...1E 45
Maesycwmmer. Cphy ...2E 33
Maesyrhandir. Powy ...1C 58
Magdalen Laver. Essx ...5F 53
Maggieknockater. Mor ...4H 159

Magham Down. E Sus ...4H 27
Maghull. Mers ...4B 90
Magna Park. Leics ...2C 62
Magor. Mon ...3H 33
Magpie Green. Suff ...3C 66
Magwyr. Mon ...3H 33
Maidenbower. W Sus ...2D 27
Maiden Bradley. Wilts ...3D 22
Maidencombe. Torb ...2F 9
Maidenhayne. Devn ...3F 13
Maidenhead. Wind ...3G 37
Maiden Law. Dur ...5E 115
Maiden Newton. Dors ...3A 14
Maidens. S Ayr ...4B 116
Maiden's Green. Brac ...4G 37
Maidensgrove. Oxon ...3F 37
Maidenwell. Corn ...5B 10
Maidenwell. Linc ...3C 88
Maiden Wells. Pemb ...5D 42
Maidford. Nptn ...5D 62
Maids Moreton. Buck ...2F 51
Maidstone. Kent ...5B 40
Maidwell. Nptn ...3E 63
Mail. Shet ...9F 173
Maindee. Newp ...3G 33
Mainsforth. Dur ...1A 106
Mains of Auchindachy. Mor ...4B 160
Mains of Auchnagatt. Abers ...4G 161
Mains of Drum. Abers ...4F 153
Mains of Edingight. Mor ...3C 160
Mainsriddle. Dum ...4G 111
Mainstone. Shrp ...2E 59
Maisemore. Glos ...3D 48
Major's Green. Worc ...3F 61
Makeney. Derbs ...1A 74
Makerstoun. Bord ...1A 120
Malacleit. W Isl ...1C 170
Malaig. High ...4E 147
Malaig Bheag. High ...4E 147
Malborough. Devn ...5D 8
Malcoff. Derbs ...2E 85
Malcolmburn. Mor ...3A 160
Malden Rushett. G Lon ...4C 38
Maldon. Essx ...5B 54
Malham. N Yor ...3B 98
Maligar. High ...2D 155
Malinslee. Telf ...5A 72
Mallaig. High ...4E 147
Malleny Mills. Edin ...3E 129
Mallows Green. Essx ...3E 53
Malltraeth. IOA ...4D 80
Mallwyd. Gwyn ...4A 70
Malmesbury. Wilts ...3E 35
Malmsmead. Devn ...2A 20
Malpas. Ches W ...1G 71
Malpas. Corn ...4C 6
Malpas. Newp ...2F 33
Malswick. Glos ...3C 48
Maltby. S Yor ...1C 86
Maltby. Stoc T ...3B 106
Maltby le Marsh. Linc ...2D 88
Malt Lane. Arg ...3H 133
Malton. N Yor ...2B 100
Malvern Link. Worc ...1C 48
Malvern Wells. Worc ...1C 48
Mamble. Worc ...3A 60
Mamhilad. Mon ...5G 47
Manaccan. Corn ...4E 5
Manafon. Powy ...5D 70
Manaton. Devn ...4A 12
Manby. Linc ...2C 88
Mancetter. Warw ...1H 61
Manchester. G Man ...1C 84
Manchester International Airport.
G Man ...2C 84
Mancot. Flin ...4F 83
Manea. Cambs ...2D 65
Maney. W Mid ...1F 61
Manfield. N Yor ...3F 105
Mangotsfield. S Glo ...4B 34
Mangurstadh. W Isl ...4C 171
Mankinholes. W Yor ...2H 91
Manley. Ches W ...3H 83

Manmoel. Cphy ...5E 47
Mannal. Arg ...4A 138
Mannerston. Falk ...2D 128
Manningford Bohune. Wilts ...1G 23
Manningford Bruce. Wilts ...1G 23
Manningham. W Yor ...1B 92
Mannings Heath. W Sus ...3D 26
Mannington. Dors ...2F 15
Manningtree. Essx ...2E 54
Mannofield. Aber ...3G 153
Manorbier. Pemb ...5E 43
Manorbier Newton. Pemb ...5E 43
Manordeilo. Carm ...3G 45
Manor Park. G Lon ...2F 39
Manorowen. Pemb ...1D 42
Manselton. Swan ...3F 31
Mansell Gamage. Here ...1G 47
Mansell Lacy. Here ...1H 47
Mansergh. Cumb ...1F 97
Mansewood. Glas ...3G 127
Mansfield. E Ayr ...3F 117
Mansfield. Notts ...4C 86
Mansfield Woodhouse. Notts ...4C 86
Mansriggs. Cumb ...1B 96
Manston. Dors ...1D 14
Manston. Kent ...4H 41
Manston. W Yor ...1D 92
Manston Airport. Kent ...4H 41
Manswood. Dors ...2E 15
Manthorpe. Linc ...4H 75
(nr. Bourne)
Manthorpe. Linc ...2G 75
(nr. Grantham)
Manton. N Lin ...4C 94
Manton. Notts ...3C 86
Manton. Rut ...5F 75
Manton. Wilts ...5G 35
Manuden. Essx ...3E 53
Maperton. Som ...4B 22
Maplebeck. Notts ...4E 86
Maple Cross. Herts ...1B 38
Mapledurham. Oxon ...4E 37
Mapledurwell. Hants ...1E 25
Maplehurst. W Sus ...3C 26
Maplescombe. Kent ...4G 39
Mapperley. Derbs ...1B 74
Mapperley. Notts ...1C 74
Mapperley Park. Notts ...1C 74
Mapperton. Dors ...3A 14
(nr. Beaminster)
Mapperton. Dors ...3E 15
(nr. Poole)
Mappleborough Green. Warw ...4E 61
Mappleton. Derbs ...1F 73
Mappleton. E Yor ...5G 101
Mapplewell. S Yor ...4D 92
Mappowder. Dors ...2C 14
Maraig. W Isl ...7E 171
Marazion. Corn ...3C 4
Marbhig. W Isl ...6G 171
Marbury. Ches E ...1H 71
March. Cambs ...1D 64
Marcham. Oxon ...2C 36
Marchamley. Shrp ...3H 71
Marchington. Staf ...2F 73
Marchington Woodlands. Staf ...3F 73
Marchwiel. Wrex ...1F 71
Marchwood. Hants ...1B 16
Marcross. V Glam ...5C 32
Marden. Here ...1A 48
Marden. Kent ...1B 28
Marden. Wilts ...1F 23
Marden Beech. Kent ...1B 28
Marden Thorn. Kent ...1B 28
Mardu. Shrp ...2E 59
Mardy. Mon ...4G 47
Marefield. Leics ...5E 75
Mareham le Fen. Linc ...4B 88
Mareham on the Hill. Linc ...4B 88
Marehay. Derbs ...1A 74
Marehill. W Sus ...4B 26
Maresfield. E Sus ...3F 27
Marfleet. Hull ...2E 95
Marford. Wrex ...5F 83
Margam. Neat ...3A 32
Margaret Marsh. Dors ...1D 14

Margaret Roding. Essx 4F 53
Margaretting. Essx 5G 53
Margaretting Tye. Essx 5G 53
Margate. Kent 3H 41
Margery. Surr 5D 38
Margnaheglish. N Ayr 2E 123
Marham. Norf 5G 77
Marhamchurch. Corn 2C 10
Marholm. Pet 5A 76
Marian Cwm. Den 3C 82
Mariandyrys. IOA 2F 81
Marian-glas. IOA 2E 81
Mariansleigh. Devn 4H 19
Marian-y-de. Gwyn 2C 68
Marine Town. Kent 3D 40
Marion-y-mor. Gwyn 2C 68
Marishader. High 2D 155
Marjoriebanks. Dum 1B 112
Mark. Dum 4G 109
Mark. Som 2G 21
Markbeech. Kent 1F 27
Markby. Linc 3D 89
Mark Causeway. Som 2G 21
Mark Cross. E Sus 2G 27
Markeaton. Derb 2H 73
Market Bosworth. Leics 5B 74
Market Deeping. Linc 4A 76
Market Drayton. Shrp 2A 72
Market End. Warw 2H 61
Market Harborough. Leics 2E 63
Markethill. Per 5B 144
Market Lavington. Wilts 1F 23
Market Overton. Rut 4F 75
Market Rasen. Linc 2A 88
Market Stainton. Linc 2B 88
Market Weighton. E Yor 5C 100
Market Weston. Suff 3B 66
Markfield. Leics 4B 74
Markham. Cphy 5E 47
Markinch. Fife 3E 137
Markington. N Yor 3E 99
Marksbury. Bath 5B 34
Mark's Corner. IOW 3C 16
Marks Tey. Essx 3C 54
Markwell. Corn 3H 7
Markyate. Herts 4A 52
Marlborough. Wilts 5G 35
Marlcliff. Warw 5E 61
Marldon. Devn 2E 9
Marle Green. E Sus 4G 27
Marlesford. Suff 5F 67
Marley Green. Ches E 1H 71
Marley Hill. Tyne 4F 115
Marlingford. Norf 5D 78
Mar Lodge. Abers 5E 151
Marloes. Pemb 4B 42
Marlow. Buck 3G 37
Marlow. Here 3G 59
Marlow Bottom. Buck 3G 37
Marlow Common. Buck 3G 37
Marlpit Hill. Kent 1F 27
Marlpits. E Sus 3F 27
Marlpool. Derbs 1B 74
Marnhull. Dors 1C 14
Marnoch. Abers 3C 160
Marnock. N Lan 3A 128
Marple. G Man 2D 84
Marr. S Yor 4F 93
Marrel. High 2H 165
Marrick. N Yor 5D 105
Marros. Carm 4G 43
Marsden. Tyne 3G 115
Marsden. W Yor 3A 92
Marsett. N Yor 1B 98
Marsh. Buck 5G 51
Marsh. Devn 1F 13
Marshall Meadows. Nmbd 4F 131
Marshalsea. Dors 2G 13
Marshalswick. Herts 5B 52
Marsham. Norf 3D 78
Marshaw. Lanc 4E 97
Marsh Baldon. Oxon 2D 36
Marsh Benham. W Ber 5C 36
Marshborough. Kent 5H 41

Marshbrook. Shrp 2G 59
Marshbury. Essx 4G 53
Marshchapel. Linc 1C 88
Marshfield. Newp 3F 33
Marshfield. S Glo 4C 34
Marshgate. Corn 3B 10
Marsh Gibbon. Buck 3E 51
Marsh Green. Devn 3D 12
Marsh Green. Kent 1F 27
Marsh Green. Staf 5C 84
Marsh Green. Telf 4A 72
Marsh Lane. Derbs 3B 86
Marshside. Kent 4G 41
Marshside. Mers 3B 90
Marsh Side. Norf 1G 77
Marsh Street. Som 2C 20
Marsh, The. Powy 1F 59
Marsh, The. Shrp 3A 72
Marshwood. Dors 3G 13
Marske. N Yor 4E 105
Marske-by-the-Sea. Red C 2D 106
Marston. Ches W 3A 84
Marston. Here 5F 59
Marston. Linc 1F 75
Marston. Oxon 5D 50
Marston. Staf 3D 72
(nr. Stafford)
Marston. Staf 4C 72
(nr. Wheaton Aston)
Marston. Warw 1G 61
Marston. Wilts 1E 23
Marston Doles. Warw 5B 62
Marston Green. W Mid 2F 61
Marston Hill. Glos 2G 35
Marston Jabbett. Warw 2A 62
Marston Magna. Som 4A 22
Marston Meysey. Wilts 2G 35
Marston Montgomery. Derbs 2F 73
Marston Moretaine. C Beds 1H 51
Marston on Dove. Derbs 3G 73
Marston St Lawrence. Nptn 1D 50
Marston Stannett. Here 5H 59
Marston Trussell. Nptn 2D 62
Marstow. Here 4A 48
Marsworth. Buck 4H 51
Marten. Wilts 5A 36
Marthall. Ches E 3C 84
Martham. Norf 4G 79
Marthwaite. Cumb 5H 103
Martin. Hants 1F 15
Martin. Kent 1H 29
Martin. Linc 4B 88
(nr. Horncastle)
Martin. Linc 5A 88
(nr. Metheringham)
Martindale. Cumb 3F 103
Martin Dales. Linc 4A 88
Martin Drove End. Hants 4F 23
Martinhoe. Devn 2G 19
Martinhoe Cross. Devn 2G 19
Martin Hussingtree.
   Worc 4C 60
Martin Mill. Kent 1H 29
Martinscroft. Warr 2A 84
Martin's Moss. Ches E 4C 84
Martinstown. Dors 4B 14
Martlesham. Suff 1F 55
Martlesham Heath.
   Suff 1F 55
Martletwy. Pemb 3E 43
Martley. Worc 5B 60
Martock. Som 1H 13
Marton. Ches E 4C 84
Marton. Cumb 2B 96
Marton. E Yor 4G 101
(nr. Bridlington)
Marton. E Yor 1E 95
(nr. Hull)
Marton. Linc 2F 87
Marton. Midd 3C 106
Marton. N Yor 3G 99
(nr. Boroughbridge)
Marton. N Yor 1B 100
(nr. Pickering)

Marton. Shrp 3G 71
(nr. Myddle)
Marton. Shrp 5E 71
(nr. Worthen)
Marton. Warw 4B 62
Marton Abbey. N Yor 3H 99
Marton-le-Moor. N Yor 2F 99
Martyr's Green. Surr 5B 38
Martyr Worthy. Hants 3D 24
Marwood. Devn 3F 19
Marybank. High 3G 157
(nr. Dingwall)
Marybank. High 1B 158
(nr. Invergordon)
Maryburgh. High 3H 157
Maryfield. Corn 3A 8
Maryhill. Glas 3G 127
Marykirk. Abers 2F 145
Marylebone. G Lon 2D 39
Marylebone. G Man 4D 90
Marypark. Mor 5F 159
Maryport. Cumb 1B 102
Maryport. Dum 5E 109
Marystow. Devn 4E 11
Mary Tavy. Devn 5F 11
Maryton. Ang 3C 144
(nr. Kirriemuir)
Maryton. Ang 3F 145
(nr. Montrose)
Marywell. Abers 4C 152
Marywell. Ang 4F 145
Masham. N Yor 1E 98
Mashbury. Essx 4G 53
Masongill. N Yor 2F 97
Masons Lodge. Abers 3F 153
Mastin Moor. Derbs 3B 86
Mastrick. Aber 3G 153
Matching. Essx 4F 53
Matching Green. Essx 4F 53
Matching Tye. Essx 4F 53
Matfen. Nmbd 2D 114
Matfield. Kent 1A 28
Mathern. Mon 2A 34
Mathon. Here 1C 48
Mathry. Pemb 1C 42
Matlaske. Norf 2D 78
Matlock. Derbs 4G 85
Matlock Bath. Derbs 5G 85
Matterdale End. Cumb 2E 103
Mattersey. Notts 2D 86
Mattersey Thorpe. Notts 2D 86
Mattingley. Hants 1F 25
Mattishall. Norf 4C 78
Mattishall Burgh. Norf 4C 78
Mauchline. E Ayr 2D 117
Maud. Abers 4G 161
Maudlin. Corn 2E 7
Maugersbury. Glos 3G 49
Maughold. IOM 2D 108
Maulden. C Beds 2A 52
Maulds Meaburn. Cumb 3H 103
Maunby. N Yor 1F 99
Maund Bryan. Here 5H 59
Mautby. Norf 4G 79
Mavesyn Ridware. Staf 4E 73
Mavis Enderby. Linc 4C 88
Mawbray. Cumb 5B 112
Mawdesley. Lanc 3C 90
Mawdlam. B'end 3B 32
Mawgan. Corn 4E 5
Mawgan Porth. Corn 2C 6
Maw Green. Ches E 5B 84
Mawla. Corn 4B 6
Mawnan. Corn 4E 5
Mawnan Smith. Corn 4E 5
Mawsley Village. Nptn 3F 63
Mawthorpe. Linc 3D 88
Maxey. Pet 5A 76
Maxstoke. Warw 2G 61
Maxted Street. Kent 1F 29
Maxton. Kent 1G 29
Maxton. Bord 1A 120
Maxwellheugh. Bord 1B 120
Maxwelltown. Dum 2A 112

Maxworthy. Corn 3C 10
Mayals. Swan 4F 31
Maybole. S Ayr 4C 116
Maybush. Sotn 1B 16
Mayen. Mor 4C 160
Mayes Green. Surr 2C 26
Mayfield. E Sus 3G 27
Mayfield. Midl 3G 129
Mayfield. Per 1C 136
Mayfield. Staf 1F 73
Mayford. Surr 5A 38
Mayhill. Swan 3F 31
Mayland. Essx 5C 54
Maylandsea. Essx 5C 54
Maynard's Green. E Sus 4G 27
Maypole. IOS 1B 4
Maypole. Kent 4G 41
Maypole. Mon 4H 47
Maypole Green. Norf 1G 67
Maypole Green. Suff 5B 66
Maywick. Shet 9E 173
Mead. Devn 1C 10
Meadgate. Bath 1B 22
Meadle. Buck 5G 51
Meadowbank. Ches W 4A 84
Meadowfield. Dur 1F 105
Meadow Green. Here 5B 60
Meadowmill. E Lot 2H 129
Meadows. Nott 2C 74
Meadowtown. Shrp 5F 71
Meadwell. Devn 4E 11
Meaford. Staf 2C 72
Mealabost. W Isl 4G 171
(nr. Borgh)
Mealabost. W Isl 4G 171
(nr. Stornoway)
Meal Bank. Cumb 5G 103
Mealrig. Cumb 5C 112
Mealsgate. Cumb 5D 112
Meanwood. W Yor 1C 92
Mearbeck. N Yor 3H 97
Meare. Som 2H 21
Meare Green. Som 4F 21
(nr. Curry Mallet)
Meare Green. Som 4G 21
(nr. Stoke St Gregory)
Mears Ashby. Nptn 4F 63
Measham. Leics 4H 73
Meath Green. Surr 1D 27
Meathop. Cumb 1D 96
Meaux. E Yor 1D 94
Meavy. Devn 2B 8
Medbourne. Leics 1E 63
Medburn. Nmbd 2E 115
Meddon. Devn 1C 10
Meden Vale. Notts 4C 86
Medlam. Linc 5C 88
Medlicott. Shrp 1G 59
Medmenham. Buck 3G 37
Medomsley. Dur 4E 115
Medstead. Hants 3E 25
Medway Towns. Medw 4B 40
Meerbrook. Staf 4D 85
Meer End. W Mid 3G 61
Meers Bridge. Linc 2D 89
Meesden. Herts 2E 53
Meeson. Telf 3A 72
Meeth. Devn 2F 11
Meeting Green. Suff 5G 65
Meeting House Hill. Norf 3F 79
Meidrim. Carm 2G 43
Meifod. Powy 4D 70
Meigle. Per 4B 144
Meikle Earnock. S Lan 4A 128
Meikle Kilchattan Butts. Arg 4B 126
Meikleour. Per 5A 144
Meikle Tarty. Abers 1G 153
Meikle Wartle. Abers 5E 160
Meinciau. Carm 4E 45
Meir. Stoke 1D 72
Meir Heath. Staf 1D 72
Melbourn. Cambs 1D 53
Melbourne. Derbs 3A 74
Melbourne. E Yor 5B 100
Melbury Abbas. Dors 4D 23

Melbury Bubb. Dors 2A 14
Melbury Osmond. Dors 2A 14
Melbury Sampford. Dors 2A 14
Melby. Shet 6C 173
Melchbourne. Bed 4H 63
Melcombe Bingham. Dors 2C 14
Melcombe Regis. Dors 4B 14
Meldon. Devn 3F 11
Meldon. Nmbd 1E 115
Meldreth. Cambs 1D 53
Melfort. Arg 2F 133
Melgarve. High 4G 149
Meliden. Den 2C 82
Melinbyrhedyn. Powy 1H 57
Melincourt. Neat 5B 46
Melin-y-coed. Cnwy 4H 81
Melin-y-ddol. Powy 5C 70
Melin-y-wig. Den 1C 70
Melkington. Nmbd 5E 131
Melkinthorpe. Cumb 2G 103
Melkridge. Nmbd 3A 114
Melksham. Wilts 5E 35
Mellangaun. High 5C 162
Melldalloch. Arg 2H 125
Mellguards. Cumb 5F 113
Melling. Lanc 2E 97
Melling. Mers 4B 90
Melling Mount. Mers 4C 90
Mellis. Suff 3C 66
Mellon Charles. High 4C 162
Mellon Udrigle. High 4C 162
Mellor. G Man 2D 85
Mellor. Lanc 1E 91
Mellor Brook. Lanc 1E 91
Mells. Som 2C 22
Melmerby. Cumb 1H 103
Melmerby. N Yor 1C 98
(nr. Middleham)
Melmerby. N Yor 2F 99
(nr. Ripon)
Melplash. Dors 3H 13
Melrose. Bord 1H 119
Melsonby. N Yor 4E 105
Meltham. W Yor 3A 92
Meltham Mills. W Yor 3B 92
Melton. E Yor 2C 94
Melton. Suff 5E 67
Meltonby. E Yor 4B 100
Melton Constable. Norf 2C 78
Melton Mowbray. Leics 4E 75
Melton Ross. N Lin 3D 94
Melvaig. High 5B 162
Melverley. Shrp 4F 71
Melverley Green. Shrp 4F 71
Melvich. High 2A 168
Membury. Devn 2F 13
Memsie. Abers 2G 161
Memus. Ang 3D 144
Menabilly. Corn 3E 7
Menai Bridge. IOA 3E 81
Mendham. Suff 2E 67
Mendlesham. Suff 4D 66
Mendlesham Green. Suff 4C 66
Menethorpe. N Yor 3B 100
Menheniot. Corn 2G 7
Menithwood. Worc 4B 60
Menna. Corn 3D 6
Mennock. Dum 4H 117
Menston. W Yor 5D 98
Menstrie. Clac 4H 135
Menthorpe. N Yor 1H 93
Mentmore. Buck 4H 51
Meole Brace. Shrp 4G 71
Meols. Mers 2E 83
Meon. Hants 2D 16
Meonstoke. Hants 4E 24
Meopham. Kent 4H 39
Meopham Green. Kent 4H 39
Meopham Station. Kent 4H 39
Mepal. Cambs 2D 64
Meppershall. C Beds 2B 52
Merbach. Here 1G 47
Mercaston. Derbs 1G 73
Merchiston. Edin 2F 129

Mere—Milton Combe

Mere. *Ches E* 2B **84**
Mere. *Wilts* 3D **22**
Mere Brow. *Lanc* 3C **90**
Mereclough. *Lanc* 1G **91**
Mere Green. *W Mid* 1F **61**
Mere Green. *Worc* 4D **60**
Mere Heath. *Ches W* 3A **84**
Mereside. *Bkpl* 1B **90**
Meretown. *Staf* 3B **72**
Mereworth. *Kent* 5A **40**
Meriden. *W Mid* 2G **61**
Merkadale. *High* 5C **154**
Merkland. *S Ayr* 5B **116**
Merkland Lodge. *High* 1A **164**
Merley. *Pool* 3F **15**
Merlin's Bridge. *Pemb* 3D **42**
Merridge. *Som* 3F **21**
Merrington. *Shrp* 3G **71**
Merrion. *Pemb* 5D **42**
Merriott. *Som* 1H **13**
Merrivale. *Devn* 5F **11**
Merrow. *Surr* 5B **38**
Merrybent. *Darl* 3F **105**
Merry Lees. *Leics* 5B **74**
Merrymeet. *Corn* 2G **7**
Mersham. *Kent* 2E **29**
Merstham. *Surr* 5D **39**
Merston. *W Sus* 2G **17**
Merstone. *IOW* 4D **16**
Merther. *Corn* 4C **6**
Merthyr. *Carm* 3D **44**
Merthyr Cynog. *Powy* 2C **46**
Merthyr Dyfan. *V Glam* 4E **32**
Merthyr Mawr. *B'end* 4B **32**
Merthyr Tudful. *Mer T* 5D **46**
Merthyr Tydfil. *Mer T* 5D **46**
Merthyr Vale. *Mer T* 5D **46**
Merton. *Devn* 1F **11**
Merton. *G Lon* 4D **38**
Merton. *Norf* 1B **66**
Merton. *Oxon* 4D **50**
Meshaw. *Devn* 1A **12**
Messing. *Essx* 4B **54**
Messingham. *N Lin* 4B **94**
Metcombe. *Devn* 3D **12**
Metfield. *Suff* 2E **67**
Metherell. *Corn* 2A **8**
Metheringham. *Linc* 4H **87**
Methil. *Fife* 4F **137**
Methilhill. *Fife* 4F **137**
Methley. *W Yor* 2D **93**
Methley Junction. *W Yor* 2D **93**
Methlick. *Abers* 5F **161**
Methven. *Per* 1C **136**
Methwold. *Norf* 1G **65**
Methwold Hythe. *Norf* 1G **65**
Mettingham. *Suff* 1F **67**
Metton. *Norf* 2D **78**
Mevagissey. *Corn* 4E **6**
Mexborough. *S Yor* 4E **93**
Mey. *High* 1E **169**
Meysey Hampton. *Glos* 2G **35**
Miabhag. *W Isl* 8D **171**
Miabhaig. *W Isl* 7C **171**
(nr. Cliasmol)
Miabhaig. *W Isl* 4C **171**
(nr. Timsgearraidh)
Mial. *High* 1G **155**
Michaelchurch. *Here* 3A **48**
Michaelchurch Escley. *Here* 2G **47**
Michaelchurch-on-Arrow.
Powy 5E **59**
Michaelston-le-Pit. *V Glam* 4E **33**
Michaelston-y-Fedw.
Newp 3F **33**
Michaelstow. *Corn* 5A **10**
Michelcombe. *Devn* 2C **8**
Micheldever. *Hants* 3D **24**
Micheldever Station.
Hants 2D **24**
Michelmersh. *Hants* 4B **24**
Mickfield. *Suff* 4D **66**
Micklebring. *S Yor* 1C **86**
Mickleby. *N Yor* 3F **107**
Micklefield. *W Yor* 1E **93**
Micklefield Green. *Herts* 1B **38**
Mickleham. *Surr* 5C **38**
Mickleover. *Derb* 2H **73**
Micklethwaite. *Cumb* 4D **112**
Micklethwaite. *W Yor* 5D **98**
Mickleton. *Dur* 2C **104**
Mickleton. *Glos* 1G **49**
Mickletown. *W Yor* 2D **93**
Mickle Trafford.
Ches W 4G **83**
Mickley. *N Yor* 2E **99**
Mickley Green. *Suff* 5H **65**
Mickley Square. *Nmbd* 3D **115**
Mid Ardlaw. *Abers* 2G **161**
Midbea. *Orkn* 3D **172**
Mid Beltie. *Abers* 3D **152**
Mid Calder. *W Lot* 3D **129**
Mid Clyth. *High* 5E **169**
Middle Assendon. *Oxon* 3F **37**
Middle Aston. *Oxon* 3C **50**
Middle Barton. *Oxon* 3C **50**
Middlebie. *Dum* 2D **112**
Middle Chinnock. *Som* 1H **13**
Middle Claydon. *Buck* 3F **51**
Middlecliffe. *S Yor* 4E **93**
Middlecott. *Devn* 4H **11**
Middle Drums. *Ang* 3E **145**
Middle Duntisbourne. *Glos* 5E **49**
Middle Essie. *Abers* 3H **161**
Middleforth Green. *Lanc* 2D **90**
Middleham. *N Yor* 1D **98**
Middle Handley. *Derbs* 3B **86**
Middle Harling. *Norf* 2B **66**
Middlehope. *Shrp* 2G **59**
Middle Littleton. *Worc* 1F **49**
Middle Maes-coed. *Here* 2G **47**
Middlemarsh. *Dors* 2B **14**
Middle Marwood. *Devn* 3F **19**
Middle Mayfield. *Staf* 1F **73**
Middlemoor. *Devn* 5E **11**
Middlemuir. *Abers* 4F **161**
(nr. New Deer)
Middlemuir. *Abers* 3G **161**
(nr. Strichen)
Middle Rainton. *Tyne* 5G **115**
Middle Rasen. *Linc* 2H **87**
Middlesbrough. *Midd* 3B **106**
Middlesceugh. *Cumb* 5E **113**
Middleshaw. *Cumb* 1E **97**
Middlesmoor. *N Yor* 2C **98**
Middles, The. *Dur* 4F **115**
Middlestone. *Dur* 1F **105**
Middlestone Moor. *Dur* 1F **105**
Middle Stoughton. *Som* 2H **21**
Middlestown. *W Yor* 3C **92**
Middle Street. *Glos* 5C **48**
Middle Taphouse. *Corn* 2F **7**
Middleton. *Ang* 4E **145**
Middleton. *Arg* 4A **138**
Middleton. *Cumb* 1F **97**
Middleton. *Derbs* 4F **85**
(nr. Bakewell)
Middleton. *Derbs* 5G **85**
(nr. Wirksworth)
Middleton. *Essx* 2B **54**
Middleton. *G Man* 4G **91**
Middleton. *Hants* 2C **24**
Middleton. *Hart* 1C **106**
Middleton. *Here* 4H **59**
Middleton. *IOW* 4B **16**
Middleton. *Lanc* 4D **96**
Middleton. *Midl* 4G **129**
Middleton. *Norf* 4F **77**
Middleton. *Nptn* 1F **63**
Middleton. *Nmbd* 1F **121**
(nr. Belford)
Middleton. *Nmbd* 1D **114**
(nr. Morpeth)
Middleton. *N Yor* 5D **98**
(nr. Ilkley)
Middleton. *N Yor* 1B **100**
(nr. Pickering)
Middleton. *Per* 3D **136**
Middleton. *Shrp* 3H **59**
(nr. Ludlow)
Middleton. *Shrp* 3F **71**
(nr. Oswestry)
Middleton. *Suff* 4G **67**
Middleton. *Swan* 4D **30**
Middleton. *Warw* 1F **61**
Middleton. *W Yor* 2D **92**
Middleton Cheney. *Nptn* 1D **50**
Middleton Green. *Staf* 2D **73**
Middleton Hall. *Nmbd* 2D **121**
Middleton-in-Teesdale. *Dur* 2C **104**
Middleton One Row. *Darl* 3A **106**
Middleton-on-Leven. *N Yor* 4B **106**
Middleton-on-Sea. *W Sus* 5A **26**
Middleton on the Hill. *Here* 4H **59**
Middleton-on-the-Wolds.
E Yor 5D **100**
Middleton Priors. *Shrp* 1A **60**
Middleton Quernhow. *N Yor* 2F **99**
Middleton St George. *Darl* 3A **106**
Middleton Scriven. *Shrp* 2A **60**
Middleton Stoney. *Oxon* 3D **50**
Middleton Tyas. *N Yor* 4F **105**
Middletown. *Cumb* 4A **102**
Middle Town. *IOS* 1B **4**
Middletown. *Powy* 4F **71**
Middle Tysoe. *Warw* 1B **50**
Middle Wallop. *Hants* 3A **24**
Middlewich. *Ches E* 4B **84**
Middle Winterslow. *Wilts* 3H **23**
Middlewood. *Corn* 5C **10**
Middlewood. *S Yor* 1H **85**
Middle Woodford. *Wilts* 3G **23**
Middlewood Green. *Suff* 4C **66**
Middleyard. *Glos* 5D **48**
Middlezoy. *Som* 3G **21**
Middridge. *Dur* 2F **105**
Midelney. *Som* 4H **21**
Midfield. *High* 2F **167**
Midford. *Bath* 5C **34**
Mid Garrary. *Dum* 2C **110**
Midge Hall. *Lanc* 2D **90**
Midgeholme. *Cumb* 4H **113**
Midgham. *W Ber* 5D **36**
Midgley. *W Yor* 2A **92**
(nr. Halifax)
Midgley. *W Yor* 3C **92**
(nr. Horbury)
Midhopestones. *S Yor* 1G **85**
Midhurst. *W Sus* 4G **25**
Mid Kirkton. *N Ayr* 4C **126**
Mid Lambrook. *Som* 1H **13**
Midland. *Orkn* 7C **172**
Mid Lavant. *W Sus* 2G **17**
Midlem. *Bord* 2H **119**
Midney. *Som* 4A **22**
Midsomer Norton. *Bath* 1B **22**
Midton. *Inv* 2D **126**
Midtown. *High* 5C **162**
(nr. Poolewe)
Midtown. *High* 2F **167**
(nr. Tongue)
Midville. *Linc* 5C **88**
Midway. *Derbs* 3H **73**
Mid Yell. *Shet* 2G **173**
Migdale. *High* 4D **164**
Migvie. *Abers* 3B **152**
Milborne Port. *Som* 1B **14**
Milborne St Andrew.
Dors 3D **14**
Milborne Wick. *Som* 4B **22**
Milbourne. *Nmbd* 2E **115**
Milbourne. *Wilts* 3E **35**
Milburn. *Cumb* 2H **103**
Milbury Heath. *S Glo* 2B **34**
Milby. *N Yor* 3G **99**
Milcombe. *Oxon* 2C **50**
Milden. *Suff* 1C **54**
Mildenhall. *Suff* 3G **65**
Mildenhall. *Wilts* 5H **35**
Milebrook. *Powy* 3F **59**
Milebush. *Kent* 1B **28**
Mile End. *Cambs* 2F **65**
Mile End. *Essx* 3C **54**
Mileham. *Norf* 4B **78**
Mile Oak. *Brig* 5D **26**
Miles Green. *Staf* 5C **84**
Miles Hope. *Here* 4H **59**
Milesmark. *Fife* 1D **128**
Mile Town. *Kent* 3D **40**
Milfield. *Nmbd* 1D **120**
Milford. *Derbs* 1A **74**
Milford. *Devn* 4C **18**
Milford. *Powy* 1C **58**
Milford. *Staf* 3D **72**
Milford. *Surr* 1A **26**
Milford Haven.
Pemb 4D **42**
Milford on Sea. *Hants* 3A **16**
Milkwall. *Glos* 5A **48**
Milkwell. *Wilts* 4E **23**
Milland. *W Sus* 4G **25**
Millbank. *High* 2D **168**
Mill Bank. *W Yor* 2A **92**
Millbeck. *Cumb* 2D **102**
Millbounds. *Orkn* 4E **172**
Millbreck. *Abers* 4H **161**
Millbridge. *Surr* 2G **25**
Millbrook. *C Beds* 2A **52**
Millbrook. *Corn* 3A **8**
Millbrook. *G Man* 1D **85**
Millbrook. *Sotn* 1B **16**
Mill Common. *Suff* 2G **67**
Mill Corner. *E Sus* 3C **28**
Milldale. *Staf* 5F **85**
Millden Lodge. *Ang* 1E **145**
Milldens. *Ang* 3E **145**
Millearn. *Per* 2B **136**
Mill End. *Buck* 3F **37**
Mill End. *Cambs* 5F **65**
Millend. *Glos* 2C **34**
(nr. Dursley)
Mill End. *Glos* 4G **49**
(nr. Northleach)
Mill End. *Herts* 2D **52**
Millerhill. *Midl* 3G **129**
Miller's Dale. *Derbs* 3F **85**
Millers Green. *Derbs* 5G **85**
Millerston. *N Lan* 3H **127**
Millfield. *Abers* 4B **152**
Millfield. *Pet* 1A **64**
Millgate. *Lanc* 3G **91**
Mill Green. *Essx* 5G **53**
Mill Green. *Norf* 2D **66**
Mill Green. *Shrp* 3A **72**
Mill Green. *Staf* 3E **73**
Mill Green. *Suff* 1C **54**
Millhalf. *Here* 1F **47**
Millhall. *E Ren* 4G **127**
Millhayes. *Devn* 2F **13**
(nr. Honiton)
Millhayes. *Devn* 1E **13**
(nr. Wellington)
Millhead. *Lanc* 2D **97**
Millheugh. *S Lan* 4A **128**
Mill Hill. *Bkbn* 2E **91**
Mill Hill. *G Lon* 1D **38**
Millholme. *Cumb* 5G **103**
Millhouse. *Arg* 2A **126**
Millhouse. *Cumb* 1E **103**
Millhousebridge. *Dum* 1C **112**
Millhouses. *S Yor* 2H **85**
Millikenpark. *Ren* 3F **127**
Millington. *E Yor* 4C **100**
Millington Green. *Derbs* 1G **73**
Mill Knowe. *Arg* 3B **122**
Mill Lane. *Hants* 1F **25**
Millmeece. *Staf* 2C **72**
Mill of Craigievar.
Abers 2C **152**
Mill of Fintray. *Abers* 2F **153**
Mill of Haldane. *W Dun* 1F **127**
Millom. *Cumb* 1A **96**
Millow. *C Beds* 1C **52**
Millpool. *Corn* 5B **10**
Millport. *N Ayr* 4C **126**
Mill Side. *Cumb* 1D **96**
Mill Street. *Norf* 4C **78**
(nr. Lyn)
Mill Street. *Norf* 4C **78**
(nr. Swanton Morley)
Millthorpe. *Derbs* 3H **8**
Millthorpe. *Linc* 2A **7**
Millthrop. *Cumb* 5H **10**
Milltimber. *Aber* 3F **15**
Milltown. *Abers* 3G **15**
(nr. Corgarff)
Milltown. *Abers* 2B **152**
(nr. Lumsden)
Milltown. *Corn* 3F **7**
Milltown. *Derbs* 4A **86**
Milltown. *Devn* 3F **19**
Milltown. *Dum* 2E **113**
Milltown. *Mor* 4C **160**
Milltown of Aberdalgie. *Per* 1C **136**
Milltown of Auchindoun. *Mor* 4A **160**
Milltown of Campfield. *Abers* 3D **152**
Milltown of Edinville. *Mor* 4G **159**
Milltown of Towie. *Abers* 2B **152**
Milnacraig. *Ang* 3B **144**
Milnathort. *Per* 3D **136**
Milngavie. *E Dun* 2G **127**
Milnholm. *Stir* 1A **128**
Milnrow. *G Man* 3H **91**
Milnthorpe. *Cumb* 1D **97**
Milnthorpe. *W Yor* 3D **92**
Milson. *Shrp* 3A **60**
Milstead. *Kent* 5D **40**
Milston. *Wilts* 2G **23**
Milthorpe. *Nptn* 1D **50**
Milton. *Ang* 4C **144**
Milton. *Cambs* 4D **65**
Milton. *Cumb* 2C **50**
(nr. Banbury)
Milton. *Cumb* 3G **113**
(nr. Brampton)
Milton. *Cumb* 1E **97**
(nr. Crooklands)
Milton. *Derbs* 3H **73**
Milton. *Dum* 2F **111**
(nr. Crocketford)
Milton. *Dum* 4H **109**
(nr. Glenluce)
Milton. *E Ayr* 2D **116**
Milton. *Glas* 2G **127**
Milton. *High* 3F **157**
(nr. Achnasheen)
Milton. *High* 4G **155**
(nr. Applecross)
Milton. *High* 5G **157**
(nr. Drumnadrochit)
Milton. *High* 1B **158**
(nr. Invergordon)
Milton. *High* 4H **157**
(nr. Inverness)
Milton. *High* 3F **169**
(nr. Wick)
Milton. *Mor* 2C **160**
(nr. Cullen)
Milton. *Mor* 2F **151**
(nr. Tomintoul)
Milton. *N Som* 5G **33**
Milton. *Notts* 3E **86**
Milton. *Oxon* 2C **36**
Milton. *Pemb* 4E **43**
Milton. *Port* 3E **17**
Milton. *Som* 4H **21**
Milton. *Stir* 3E **135**
(nr. Aberfoyle)
Milton. *Stir* 4D **134**
(nr. Drymen)
Milton. *Stoke* 5D **84**
Milton. *W Dun* 2F **127**
Milton Abbas. *Dors* 2D **14**
Milton Abbot. *Devn* 5E **11**
Milton Auchlossan. *Abers* 3C **152**
Milton Bridge. *Midl* 3F **129**
Milton Bryan. *C Beds* 2H **51**
Milton Clevedon. *Som* 3B **22**
Milton Coldwells. *Abers* 5G **161**
Milton Combe. *Devn* 2A **8**

Milton Common—Mountain Street

Milton Common. *Oxon* 5E **51**
Milton Damerel. *Devn* 1D **11**
Miltonduff. *Mor* 2F **159**
Milton End. *Glos* 5G **49**
Milton Ernest. *Bed* 5H **63**
Milton Green. *Ches W* 5G **83**
Milton Hill. *Devn* 5C **12**
Milton Hill. *Oxon* 2C **36**
Milton Keynes. *Mil* 2G **51**
Milton Keynes Village. *Mil* 2G **51**
Milton Lilbourne. *Wilts* 5G **35**
Milton Malsor. *Nptn* 5E **63**
Milton Morenish. *Per* 5D **142**
Milton of Auchinhove. *Abers* 3C **152**
Milton of Balgonie. *Fife* 3F **137**
Milton of Barras. *Abers* 1H **145**
Milton of Campsie. *E Dun* 2H **127**
Milton of Cultoquhey. *Per* 1A **136**
Milton of Cushnie. *Abers* 2C **152**
Milton of Finavon. *Ang* 3D **145**
Milton of Gollanfield. *High* 3B **158**
Milton of Lesmore. *Abers* 1B **152**
Milton of Leys. *High* 4A **158**
Milton of Tullich. *Abers* 4A **152**
Milton on Stour. *Dors* 4C **22**
Milton Regis. *Kent* 4C **40**
Milton Street. *E Sus* 5G **27**
Milton-under-Wychwood. *Oxon* 4A **50**
Milverton. *Som* 4E **20**
Milverton. *Warw* 4H **61**
Milwich. *Staf* 2D **72**
Mimbridge. *Surr* 4A **38**
Minard. *Arg* 4G **133**
Minchington. *Dors* 1E **15**
Minchinhampton. *Glos* 5D **49**
Mindrum. *Nmbd* 1C **120**
Minehead. *Som* 2C **20**
Minera. *Wrex* 5E **83**
Minety. *Wilts* 2F **35**
Minffordd. *Gwyn* 2E **69**
Mingarrypark. *High* 2A **140**
Mingary. *High* 2G **139**
Mingearraidh. *W Isl* 6C **170**
Miningsby. *Linc* 4C **88**
Minions. *Corn* 5C **10**
Minishant. *S Ayr* 3C **116**
Minllyn. *Gwyn* 4A **70**
Minnigaff. *Dum* 3B **110**
Minorca. *IOM* 3D **108**
Minskip. *N Yor* 3F **99**
Minstead. *Hants* 1A **16**
Minsted. *W Sus* 4G **25**
Minster. *Kent* 4H **41** (nr. Ramsgate)
Minster. *Kent* 3D **40** (nr. Sheerness)
Minsteracres. *Nmbd* 4D **114**
Minsterley. *Shrp* 5F **71**
Minster Lovell. *Oxon* 4B **50**
Minsterworth. *Glos* 4C **48**
Minterne Magna. *Dors* 2B **14**
Minterne Parva. *Dors* 2B **14**
Minting. *Linc* 3A **88**
Mintlaw. *Abers* 4H **161**
Minto. *Bord* 2H **119**
Minton. *Shrp* 1G **59**
Minwear. *Pemb* 3E **43**
Minworth. *W Mid* 1F **61**
Miodar. *Arg* 4B **138**
Mirehouse. *Cumb* 3A **102**
Mireland. *High* 2F **169**
Mirfield. *W Yor* 3C **92**
Miserden. *Glos* 5E **49**
Miskin. *Rhon* 3D **32**
Misson. *Notts* 1D **86**
Misterton. *Leics* 2C **62**
Misterton. *Notts* 1E **87**
Misterton. *Som* 2H **13**
Mistley. *Essx* 2E **54**
Mistley Heath. *Essx* 2E **55**
Mitcham. *G Lon* 4D **39**
Mitcheldean. *Glos* 4B **48**
Mitchell. *Corn* 3C **6**
Mitchel Troy. *Mon* 4H **47**
Mitcheltroy Common. *Mon* 5H **47**
Mitford. *Nmbd* 1E **115**
Mithian. *Corn* 3B **6**
Mitton. *Staf* 4C **72**
Mixbury. *Oxon* 2E **50**
Mixenden. *W Yor* 2A **92**
Mixon. *Staf* 5E **85**
Moat. *Cumb* 2F **113**
Moats Tye. *Suff* 5C **66**
Mobberley. *Ches E* 3B **84**
Mobberley. *Staf* 1E **73**
Moccas. *Here* 1G **47**
Mochdre. *Cnwy* 3H **81**
Mochdre. *Powy* 2C **58**
Mochrum. *Dum* 5A **110**
Mockbeggar. *Hants* 2G **15**
Mockerkin. *Cumb* 2B **102**
Modbury. *Devn* 3C **8**
Moddershall. *Staf* 2D **72**
Modsarie. *High* 2G **167**
Moelfre. *Cnwy* 3B **82**
Moelfre. *IOA* 2E **81**
Moelfre. *Powy* 3D **70**
Moffat. *Dum* 4C **118**
Moggerhanger. *C Beds* 1B **52**
Mogworthy. *Devn* 1B **12**
Moira. *Leics* 4H **73**
Molash. *Kent* 5E **41**
Mol-chlach. *High* 2C **146**
Mold. *Flin* 4E **83**
Molehill Green. *Essx* 3F **53**
Molescroft. *E Yor* 5E **101**
Molesden. *Nmbd* 1E **115**
Molesworth. *Cambs* 3H **63**
Moll. *High* 5E **155**
Molland. *Devn* 4B **20**
Mollington. *Ches W* 3F **83**
Mollington. *Oxon* 1C **50**
Mollinsburn. *N Lan* 2A **128**
Monachty. *Cdgn* 4E **57**
Monachyle. *Stir* 2D **134**
Monar Lodge. *High* 4E **156**
Monaughty. *Powy* 4E **59**
Monewden. *Suff* 5E **67**
Moneydie. *Per* 1C **136**
Moneyrow Green. *Wind* 4G **37**
Moniaive. *Dum* 5G **117**
Monifieth. *Ang* 5E **145**
Monikie. *Ang* 5E **145**
Monimail. *Fife* 2E **137**
Monington. *Pemb* 1B **44**
Monk Bretton. *S Yor* 4D **92**
Monken Hadley. *G Lon* 1D **38**
Monk Fryston. *N Yor* 2F **93**
Monk Hesleden. *Dur* 1B **106**
Monkhide. *Here* 1B **48**
Monkhill. *Cumb* 4E **113**
Monkhopton. *Shrp* 1A **60**
Monkland. *Here* 5G **59**
Monkleigh. *Devn* 4E **19**
Monknash. *V Glam* 4C **32**
Monkokehampton. *Devn* 2F **11**
Monkseaton. *Tyne* 2G **115**
Monks Eleigh. *Suff* 1C **54**
Monk's Gate. *W Sus* 3D **26**
Monk's Heath. *Ches E* 3C **84**
Monk Sherborne. *Hants* 1E **24**
Monkshill. *Abers* 4E **161**
Monksilver. *Som* 3D **20**
Monks Kirby. *Warw* 2B **62**
Monk Soham. *Suff* 4E **66**
Monk Soham Green. *Suff* 4E **66**
Monkspath. *W Mid* 3F **61**
Monks Risborough. *Buck* 5G **51**
Monksthorpe. *Linc* 4D **88**
Monk Street. *Essx* 3G **53**
Monkswood. *Mon* 5G **47**
Monkton. *Devn* 2E **13**
Monkton. *Kent* 4G **41**
Monkton. *Pemb* 4D **42**
Monkton. *S Ayr* 2C **116**
Monkton Combe. *Bath* 5C **34**
Monkton Deverill. *Wilts* 3D **22**
Monkton Farleigh. *Wilts* 5D **34**
Monkton Heathfield. *Som* 4F **21**
Monktonhill. *S Ayr* 2C **116**
Monkton Up Wimborne. *Dors* 1F **15**
Monkton Wyld. *Dors* 3G **13**
Monkwearmouth. *Tyne* 4H **115**
Monkwood. *Dors* 3H **13**
Monkwood. *Hants* 3E **25**
Monmarsh. *Here* 1A **48**
Monmouth. *Mon* 4A **48**
Monnington on Wye. *Here* 1G **47**
Monreith. *Dum* 5A **110**
Montacute. *Som* 1H **13**
Montford. *Arg* 3C **126**
Montford. *Shrp* 4G **71**
Montford Bridge. *Shrp* 4G **71**
Montgarrie. *Abers* 2C **152**
Montgarswood. *E Ayr* 2E **117**
Montgomery. *Powy* 1E **58**
Montgreenan. *N Ayr* 5E **127**
Montrave. *Fife* 3F **137**
Montrose. *Ang* 3G **145**
Monxton. *Hants* 2B **24**
Monyash. *Derbs* 4F **85**
Monymusk. *Abers* 2D **152**
Monzie. *Per* 1A **136**
Moodiesburn. *N Lan* 2H **127**
Moon's Green. *Kent* 3C **28**
Moonzie. *Fife* 2F **137**
Moor. *Som* 1H **13**
Moor Allerton. *W Yor* 1C **92**
Moorbath. *Dors* 3H **13**
Moorby. *Linc* 4B **88**
Moorcot. *Here* 5F **59**
Moor Crichel. *Dors* 2E **15**
Moor Cross. *Devn* 3C **8**
Moordown. *Bour* 3F **15**
Moore. *Hal* 2H **83**
Moorend. *Dum* 2D **112**
Moor End. *E Yor* 1B **94**
Moorend. *Glos* 5C **48** (nr. Dursley)
Moorend. *Glos* 4D **48** (nr. Gloucester)
Moorends. *S Yor* 3G **93**
Moorgate. *S Yor* 1B **86**
Moorgreen. *Hants* 1C **16**
Moorgreen. *Notts* 1B **74**
Moor Green. *Wilts* 5D **34**
Moorhaigh. *Notts* 4C **86**
Moorhall. *Derbs* 3H **85**
Moorhampton. *Here* 1G **47**
Moorhouse. *Cumb* 4E **113** (nr. Carlisle)
Moorhouse. *Cumb* 4D **112** (nr. Wigton)
Moorhouse. *Notts* 4E **87**
Moorhouse. *Surr* 5F **39**
Moorhouses. *Linc* 5B **88**
Moorland. *Som* 3G **21**
Moorlinch. *Som* 3H **21**
Moor Monkton. *N Yor* 4H **99**
Moor of Granary. *Mor* 3E **159**
Moor Row. *Cumb* 3B **102** (nr. Whitehaven)
Moor Row. *Cumb* 5D **112** (nr. Wigton)
Moorsholm. *Red C* 3D **107**
Moorside. *Dors* 1C **14**
Moorside. *G Man* 4H **91**
Moor, The. *Kent* 3B **28**
Moortown. *Devn* 3D **10**
Moortown. *Hants* 2G **15**
Moortown. *IOW* 4C **16**
Moortown. *Linc* 1H **87**
Moortown. *Telf* 4A **72**
Moortown. *W Yor* 1D **92**
Morangie. *High* 5E **165**
Morar. *High* 4E **147**
Morborne. *Cambs* 1A **64**
Morchard Bishop. *Devn* 2A **12**
Morcombelake. *Dors* 3H **13**
Morcott. *Rut* 5G **75**
Morda. *Shrp* 3E **71**
Morden. *G Lon* 4D **38**
Mordiford. *Here* 2A **48**
Mordon. *Dur* 2A **106**
More. *Shrp* 1F **59**
Morebath. *Devn* 4C **20**
Morebattle. *Bord* 2B **120**
Morecambe. *Lanc* 3D **96**
Morefield. *High* 4F **163**
Moreleigh. *Devn* 3D **8**
Morenish. *Per* 5C **142**
Moresby Parks. *Cumb* 3A **102**
Morestead. *Hants* 4D **24**
Moreton. *Dors* 4D **14**
Moreton. *Essx* 5F **53**
Moreton. *Here* 4H **59**
Moreton. *Mers* 1E **83**
Moreton. *Oxon* 5E **51**
Moreton. *Staf* 4B **72**
Moreton Corbet. *Shrp* 3H **71**
Moretonhampstead. *Devn* 4A **12**
Moreton-in-Marsh. *Glos* 2H **49**
Moreton Jeffries. *Here* 1B **48**
Moreton Morrell. *Warw* 5H **61**
Moreton on Lugg. *Here* 1A **48**
Moreton Pinkney. *Nptn* 1D **50**
Moreton Say. *Shrp* 2A **72**
Moreton Valence. *Glos* 5C **48**
Morfa. *Cdgn* 5C **56**
Morfa Bach. *Carm* 4D **44**
Morfa Bychan. *Gwyn* 2E **69**
Morfa Glas. *Neat* 5B **46**
Morfa Nefyn. *Gwyn* 1B **68**
Morganstown. *Card* 3E **33**
Morgan's Vale. *Wilts* 4G **23**
Morham. *E Lot* 2B **130**
Moriah. *Cdgn* 3F **57**
Morland. *Cumb* 2G **103**
Morley. *Ches E* 2C **84**
Morley. *Derbs* 1A **74**
Morley. *Dur* 2E **105**
Morley. *W Yor* 2C **92**
Morley St Botolph. *Norf* 1C **66**
Morningside. *Edin* 2F **129**
Morningside. *N Lan* 4B **128**
Morningthorpe. *Norf* 1E **66**
Morpeth. *Nmbd* 1F **115**
Morrey. *Staf* 4F **73**
Morridge Side. *Staf* 5E **85**
Morridge Top. *Staf* 4E **85**
Morrington. *Dum* 1F **111**
Morris Green. *Essx* 2H **53**
Morriston. *Swan* 3F **31**
Morston. *Norf* 1C **78**
Mortehoe. *Devn* 2E **19**
Morthen. *S Yor* 2B **86**
Mortimer. *W Ber* 5E **37**
Mortimer's Cross. *Here* 4G **59**
Mortimer West End. *Hants* 5E **37**
Mortomley. *S Yor* 1H **85**
Morton. *Cumb* 1F **103** (nr. Calthwaite)
Morton. *Cumb* 4E **113** (nr. Carlisle)
Morton. *Derbs* 4B **86**
Morton. *Linc* 3H **75** (nr. Bourne)
Morton. *Linc* 1F **87** (nr. Gainsborough)
Morton. *Linc* 4F **87** (nr. Lincoln)
Morton. *Norf* 4D **78**
Morton. *Notts* 5E **87**
Morton. *Shrp* 3E **71**
Morton. *S Glo* 2B **34**
Morton Bagot. *Warw* 4F **61**
Morton Mill. *Shrp* 3H **71**
Morton-on-Swale. *N Yor* 5A **106**
Morton Tinmouth. *Dur* 2E **105**
Morvah. *Corn* 3B **4**
Morval. *Corn* 3G **7**
Morvich. *High* 3E **165** (nr. Golspie)
Morvich. *High* 1B **148** (nr. Shiel Bridge)
Morvil. *Pemb* 1E **43**
Morville. *Shrp* 1A **60**
Morwenstow. *Corn* 1C **10**
Morwick Hall. *Nmbd* 4G **121**
Mosborough. *S Yor* 2B **86**
Moscow. *E Ayr* 5F **127**
Mose. *Shrp* 1B **60**
Mosedale. *Cumb* 1E **103**
Moseley. *W Mid* 2E **61** (nr. Birmingham)
Moseley. *W Mid* 5D **72** (nr. Wolverhampton)
Moseley. *Worc* 5C **60**
Moss. *Arg* 4A **138**
Moss. *High* 2A **140**
Moss. *S Yor* 3F **93**
Moss. *Wrex* 5F **83**
Mossatt. *Abers* 2B **152**
Moss Bank. *Mers* 1H **83**
Mossbank. *Shet* 4F **173**
Mossblown. *S Ayr* 2D **116**
Mossbrow. *G Man* 2B **84**
Mossburnford. *Bord* 3A **120**
Mossdale. *Dum* 2D **110**
Mossedge. *Cumb* 3F **113**
Mossend. *N Lan* 3A **128**
Mossgate. *Staf* 2D **72**
Moss Lane. *Ches E* 3D **84**
Mossley. *Ches E* 4C **84**
Mossley. *G Man* 4H **91**
Mossley Hill. *Mers* 2F **83**
Moss of Barmuckity. *Mor* 2G **159**
Mosspark. *Glas* 3G **127**
Mosspaul. *Bord* 5G **119**
Moss Side. *Cumb* 4C **112**
Moss Side. *G Man* 1C **84**
Moss-side. *High* 3C **158**
Moss Side. *Lanc* 1B **90** (nr. Blackpool)
Moss Side. *Lanc* 2D **90** (nr. Preston)
Moss Side. *Mers* 4B **90**
Moss-side of Cairness. *Abers* 2H **161**
Mosstodloch. *Mor* 2H **159**
Mosswood. *Nmbd* 4D **114**
Mossy Lea. *Lanc* 3D **90**
Mosterton. *Dors* 2H **13**
Moston. *Shrp* 3H **71**
Moston Green. *Ches E* 4B **84**
Mostyn. *Flin* 2D **82**
Mostyn Quay. *Flin* 2D **82**
Motcombe. *Dors* 4D **22**
Mothecombe. *Devn* 4C **8**
Motherby. *Cumb* 2F **103**
Motherwell. *N Lan* 4A **128**
Mottingham. *G Lon* 3F **39**
Mottisfont. *Hants* 4B **24**
Mottistone. *IOW* 4C **16**
Mottram in Longdendale. *G Man* 1D **85**
Mottram St Andrew. *Ches E* 3C **84**
Mott's Mill. *E Sus* 2G **27**
Mouldsworth. *Ches W* 3H **83**
Moulin. *Per* 3G **143**
Moulsecoomb. *Brig* 5E **27**
Moulsford. *Oxon* 3D **36**
Moulsoe. *Mil* 1H **51**
Moulton. *Ches W* 4A **84**
Moulton. *Linc* 3C **76**
Moulton. *Nptn* 4E **63**
Moulton. *N Yor* 4F **105**
Moulton. *Suff* 4F **65**
Moulton. *V Glam* 4D **32**
Moulton Chapel. *Linc* 4B **76**
Moulton Eugate. *Linc* 4B **76**
Moulton St Mary. *Norf* 5F **79**
Moulton Seas End. *Linc* 3C **76**
Mount. *Corn* 2F **7** (nr. Bodmin)
Mount. *Corn* 3B **6** (nr. Newquay)
Mountain Ash. *Rhon* 2D **32**
Mountain Cross. *Bord* 5E **129**
Mountain Street. *Kent* 5E **41**

Mountain Water—Newark-on-Trent

Mountain Water. *Pemb* 2D 42
Mount Ambrose. *Corn* 4B 6
Mountbenger. *Bord* 2F 119
Mountblow. *W Dun* 2F 127
Mount Bures. *Essx* 2C 54
Mountfield. *E Sus* 3B 28
Mountgerald. *High* 2H 157
Mount Hawke. *Corn* 4B 6
Mount High. *High* 2A 158
Mountjoy. *Corn* 2C 6
Mount Lothian. *Midl* 4F 129
Mountnessing. *Essx* 1H 39
Mounton. *Mon* 2A 34
Mount Pleasant. *Buck* 2E 51
Mount Pleasant. *Ches E* 5C 84
Mount Pleasant. *Derbs* 1H 73
(nr. Derby)
Mount Pleasant. *Derbs* 4G 73
(nr. Swadlincote)
Mount Pleasant. *E Sus* 4F 27
Mount Pleasant. *Fife* 2E 137
Mount Pleasant. *Hants* 3A 16
Mount Pleasant. *Norf* 1B 66
Mount Skippett. *Oxon* 4B 50
Mountsorrel. *Leics* 4C 74
Mount Stuart. *Arg* 4C 126
Mousehole. *Corn* 4B 4
Mouswald. *Dum* 2B 112
Mow Cop. *Ches E* 5C 84
Mowden. *Darl* 3F 105
Mowhaugh. *Bord* 2C 120
Mowmacre Hill. *Leic* 5C 74
Mowsley. *Leics* 2D 62
Moy. *High* 5B 158
Moylgrove. *Pemb* 1B 44
Moy Lodge. *High* 5G 149
Muasdale. *Arg* 5E 125
Muchalls. *Abers* 4G 153
Much Birch. *Here* 2A 48
Much Cowarne. *Here* 1B 48
Much Dewchurch. *Here* 2H 47
Muchelney. *Som* 4H 21
Muchelney Ham. *Som* 4H 21
Much Hadham. *Herts* 4E 53
Much Hoole. *Lanc* 2C 90
Muchlarnick. *Corn* 3G 7
Much Marcle. *Here* 2B 48
Muchrachd. *High* 5E 157
Much Wenlock. *Shrp* 1A 60
Mucking. *Thur* 2A 40
Muckleford. *Dors* 3B 14
Mucklestone. *Staf* 2B 72
Muckleton. *Norf* 2H 77
Muckleton. *Shrp* 3H 71
Muckley. *Shrp* 1A 60
Muckley Corner. *Staf* 5E 73
Muckton. *Linc* 2C 88
Mudale. *High* 5F 167
Muddiford. *Devn* 3F 19
Mudeford. *Dors* 3G 15
Mudford. *Som* 1A 14
Mudgley. *Som* 2H 21
Mugdock. *Stir* 2G 127
Mugeary. *High* 5D 154
Mugginton. *Derbs* 1G 73
Muggintonlane End. *Derbs* 1G 73
Muggleswick. *Dur* 4D 114
Mugswell. *Surr* 5D 38
Muie. *High* 3D 164
Muirden. *Abers* 3E 160
Muirdrum. *Ang* 5E 145
Muiredge. *Per* 1E 137
Muirend. *Glas* 3G 127
Muirhead. *Ang* 5C 144
Muirhead. *Fife* 3E 137
Muirhead. *N Lan* 3H 127
Muirhouses. *Falk* 1D 128
Muirkirk. *E Ayr* 2F 117
Muir of Alford. *Abers* 2C 152
Muir of Fairburn. *High* 3G 157
Muir of Fowlis. *Abers* 2C 152
Muir of Miltonduff. *Mor* 3F 159
Muir of Ord. *High* 3H 157
Muir of Tarradale. *High* 3H 157
Muirshearlich. *High* 5D 148
Muirtack. *Abers* 5G 161
Muirton. *High* 2B 158
Muirton. *Per* 1D 136
Muirton of Ardblair. *Per* 4A 144
Muirtown. *Per* 2B 136
Muiryfold. *Abers* 3E 161
Muker. *N Yor* 5C 104
Mulbarton. *Norf* 5D 78
Mulben. *Mor* 3A 160
Mulindry. *Arg* 4B 124
Mullach Charlabhaigh. *W Isl* 3E 171
Mullacott. *Devn* 2F 19
Mullion. *Corn* 5D 5
Mullion Cove. *Corn* 5D 4
Mumbles. *Swan* 4F 31
Mumby. *Linc* 3E 89
Munderfield Row. *Here* 5A 60
Munderfield Stocks. *Here* 5A 60
Mundesley. *Norf* 2F 79
Mundford. *Norf* 1H 65
Mundham. *Norf* 1F 67
Mundon. *Essx* 5B 54
Munerigie. *High* 3E 149
Muness. *Shet* 1H 173
Mungasdale. *High* 4D 162
Mungrisdale. *Cumb* 1E 103
Munlochy. *High* 3A 158
Munsley. *Here* 1B 48
Munslow. *Shrp* 2H 59
Murchington. *Devn* 4G 11
Murcot. *Worc* 1F 49
Murcott. *Oxon* 4D 50
Murdishaw. *Hal* 2H 83
Murieston. *W Lot* 3D 128
Murkle. *High* 2D 168
Murlaggan. *High* 4C 148
Murra. *Orkn* 7B 172
Murrayfield. *Edin* 2F 129
Murray, The. *S Lan* 4H 127
Murrell Green. *Hants* 1F 25
Murroes. *Ang* 5D 144
Murrow. *Cambs* 5C 76
Mursley. *Buck* 3G 51
Murthly. *Per* 5H 143
Murton. *Cumb* 2A 104
Murton. *Dur* 5G 115
Murton. *Nmbd* 5F 131
Murton. *Swan* 4E 31
Murton. *York* 4A 100
Musbury. *Devn* 3F 13
Muscoates. *N Yor* 1A 100
Muscott. *Nptn* 4D 62
Musselburgh. *E Lot* 2G 129
Muston. *Leics* 2F 75
Muston. *N Yor* 2E 101
Mustow Green. *Worc* 3C 60
Muswell Hill. *G Lon* 2D 39
Mutehill. *Dum* 5D 111
Mutford. *Suff* 2G 67
Muthill. *Per* 2A 136
Mutterton. *Devn* 2D 12
Muxton. *Telf* 4B 72
Mwmbwls. *Swan* 4F 31
Mybster. *High* 3D 168
Myddfai. *Carm* 2A 46
Myddle. *Shrp* 3G 71
Mydroilyn. *Cdgn* 5D 56
Myerscough. *Lanc* 1C 90
Mylor Bridge. *Corn* 5C 6
Mylor Churchtown. *Corn* 5C 6
Mynachlog-ddu. *Pemb* 1F 43
Mynydd-bach. *Mon* 2H 33
Mynydd Isa. *Flin* 4E 83
Mynyddislwyn. *Cphy* 2E 33
Mynydd Llandegai. *Gwyn* 4F 81
Mynydd Mechell. *IOA* 1C 80
Mynydd-y-briw. *Powy* 3D 70
Mynyddygarreg. *Carm* 5E 45
Mynytho. *Gwyn* 2C 68
Myrebird. *Abers* 4E 153
Myrelandhorn. *High* 3E 169
Mytchett. *Surr* 1G 25
Mythe, The. *Glos* 2D 49
Mytholmroyd. *W Yor* 2A 92
Myton-on-Swale. *N Yor* 3G 99
Mytton. *Shrp* 4G 71

N

Naast. *High* 5C 162
Na Buirgh. *W Isl* 8C 171
Naburn. *York* 5H 99
Nab Wood. *W Yor* 1B 92
Nackington. *Kent* 5F 41
Nacton. *Suff* 1F 55
Nafferton. *E Yor* 4E 101
Na Gearrannan. *W Isl* 3D 171
Nailbridge. *Glos* 4B 48
Nailsbourne. *Som* 4F 21
Nailsea. *N Som* 4H 33
Nailstone. *Leics* 5B 74
Nailsworth. *Glos* 2D 34
Nairn. *High* 3C 158
Nalderswood. *Surr* 1D 26
Nancegollan. *Corn* 3D 4
Nancledra. *Corn* 3B 4
Nangreaves. *G Man* 3G 91
Nanhyfer. *Pemb* 1E 43
Nannerch. *Flin* 4D 82
Nanpantan. *Leics* 4C 74
Nanpean. *Corn* 3D 6
Nanstallon. *Corn* 2E 7
Nant-ddu. *Powy* 4D 46
Nanternis. *Cdgn* 5C 56
Nantgaredig. *Carm* 3E 45
Nantgarw. *Rhon* 3E 33
Nant Glas. *Powy* 4B 58
Nantglyn. *Den* 4C 82
Nantgwyn. *Powy* 3B 58
Nantlle. *Gwyn* 5E 81
Nantmawr. *Shrp* 3E 71
Nantmel. *Powy* 4C 58
Nantmor. *Gwyn* 1F 69
Nant Peris. *Gwyn* 5F 81
Nantwich. *Ches E* 5A 84
Nant-y-bai. *Carm* 1A 46
Nant-y-bwch. *Blae* 4E 47
Nant-y-Derry. *Mon* 5G 47
Nant-y-dugoed. *Powy* 4B 70
Nant-y-felin. *Cnwy* 3F 81
Nantyffyllon. *B'end* 2B 32
Nantyglo. *Blae* 4E 47
Nant-y-meichiaid. *Powy* 4D 70
Nant-y-moel. *B'end* 2C 32
Nant-y-Pandy. *Cnwy* 3F 81
Naphill. *Buck* 2G 37
Nappa. *Lanc* 4A 98
Napton on the Hill. *Warw* 4B 62
Narberth. *Pemb* 3F 43
Narberth Bridge. *Pemb* 3F 43
Narborough. *Leics* 1C 62
Narborough. *Norf* 4G 77
Narkurs. *Corn* 3H 7
Narth, The. *Mon* 5A 48
Narthwaite. *Cumb* 5A 104
Nasareth. *Gwyn* 1D 68
Naseby. *Nptn* 3D 62
Nash. *Buck* 2F 51
Nash. *Here* 4F 59
Nash. *Kent* 5G 41
Nash. *Newp* 3G 33
Nash. *Shrp* 3A 60
Nash Lee. *Buck* 5G 51
Nassington. *Nptn* 1H 63
Nasty. *Herts* 3D 52
Natcott. *Devn* 4C 18
Nateby. *Cumb* 4A 104
Nateby. *Lanc* 5D 96
Nately Scures. *Hants* 1F 25
Natland. *Cumb* 1E 97
Naughton. *Suff* 1D 54
Naunton. *Glos* 3G 49
Naunton. *Worc* 2D 49
Naunton Beauchamp. *Worc* 5D 60
Navenby. *Linc* 5G 87
Navestock Heath. *Essx* 1G 39
Navestock Side. *Essx* 1G 39
Navidale. *High* 2H 165
Nawton. *N Yor* 1A 100
Nayland. *Suff* 2C 54
Nazeing. *Essx* 5E 53
Neacroft. *Hants* 3G 15
Nealhouse. *Cumb* 4E 113
Neal's Green. *W Mid* 2H 61
Neap House. *N Lin* 3B 94
Near Sawrey. *Cumb* 5E 103
Neasden. *G Lon* 2D 38
Neasham. *Darl* 3A 106
Neath. *Neat* 2A 32
Neath Abbey. *Neat* 3G 31
Neatishead. *Norf* 3F 79
Neaton. *Norf* 5B 78
Nebo. *Cdgn* 4E 57
Nebo. *Cnwy* 5H 81
Nebo. *Gwyn* 5D 81
Nebo. *IOA* 1D 80
Necton. *Norf* 5A 78
Nedd. *High* 5B 166
Nedderton. *Nmbd* 1F 115
Nedging. *Suff* 1D 54
Nedging Tye. *Suff* 1D 54
Needham. *Norf* 2E 67
Needham Market. *Suff* 5C 66
Needham Street. *Suff* 4G 65
Needingworth. *Cambs* 3C 64
Needwood. *Staf* 3F 73
Neen Savage. *Shrp* 3A 60
Neen Sollars. *Shrp* 3A 60
Neenton. *Shrp* 2A 60
Nefyn. *Gwyn* 1C 68
Neilston. *E Ren* 4F 127
Neithrop. *Oxon* 1C 50
Nelly Andrews Green. *Powy* 5E 71
Nelson. *Cphy* 2E 32
Nelson. *Lanc* 1G 91
Nelson Village. *Nmbd* 2F 115
Nemphlar. *S Lan* 5B 128
Nempnett Thrubwell. *Bath* 5A 34
Nene Terrace. *Linc* 5B 76
Nenthall. *Cumb* 5A 114
Nenthead. *Cumb* 5A 114
Nenthorn. *Bord* 1A 120
Nercwys. *Flin* 4E 83
Neribus. *Arg* 4A 124
Nerston. *S Lan* 4H 127
Nesbit. *Nmbd* 1D 121
Nesfield. *N Yor* 5C 98
Ness. *Ches W* 3F 83
Nesscliffe. *Shrp* 4F 71
Neston. *Ches W* 3E 83
Neston. *Wilts* 5D 34
Nethanfoot. *S Lan* 5B 128
Nether Alderley. *Ches E* 3C 84
Netheravon. *Wilts* 2G 23
Nether Blainslie. *Bord* 5B 130
Netherbrae. *Abers* 3E 161
Netherbrough. *Orkn* 6C 172
Nether Broughton. *Leics* 3D 74
Netherburn. *S Lan* 5B 128
Nether Burrow. *Lanc* 2F 97
Netherbury. *Dors* 3H 13
Netherby. *Cumb* 2E 113
Nether Careston. *Ang* 3E 145
Nether Cerne. *Dors* 3B 14
Nether Compton. *Dors* 1A 14
Nethercote. *Glos* 3G 49
Nethercote. *Warw* 4C 62
Nethercott. *Devn* 3E 19
Nethercott. *Oxon* 3C 50
Nether Dallachy. *Mor* 2A 160
Nether Durdie. *Per* 1E 136
Nether End. *Derbs* 3G 85
Netherend. *Glos* 5A 48
Nether Exe. *Devn* 2C 12
Netherfield. *E Sus* 4B 28
Netherfield. *Notts* 1D 74
Nethergate. *Norf* 3C 78
Netherhampton. *Wilts* 4G 23
Nether Handley. *Derbs* 3B 86
Nether Haugh. *S Yor* 1B 86
Nether Heage. *Derbs* 5A 86
Nether Heyford. *Nptn* 5D 62
Netherhouses. *Cumb* 1B 96
Nether Howcleugh. *Dum* 3C 118
Nether Kellet. *Lanc* 3E 97
Nether Kinmundy. *Abers* 4H 161
Netherland Green. *Staf* 2F 73
Nether Langwith. *Notts* 3C 86
Netherlaw. *Dum* 5E 111
Netherley. *Abers* 4F 153
Nethermill. *Dum* 1B 112
Nethermills. *Mor* 3C 160
Nether Moor. *Derbs* 4A 86
Nether Padley. *Derbs* 3G 85
Netherplace. *E Ren* 4G 127
Nether Poppleton. *York* 4H 99
Netherseal. *Derbs* 4G 73
Nether Silton. *N Yor* 5B 106
Nether Stowey. *Som* 3E 21
Nether Street. *Essx* 4F 53
Netherstreet. *Wilts* 5E 35
Netherthird. *E Ayr* 3E 117
Netherthong. *W Yor* 4B 92
Netherton. *Ang* 3E 145
Netherton. *Cumb* 1B 102
Netherton. *Devn* 5B 12
Netherton. *Hants* 1B 24
Netherton. *Here* 3A 48
Netherton. *Mers* 1F 83
Netherton. *N Lan* 4A 128
Netherton. *Nmbd* 4D 121
Netherton. *Per* 3A 144
Netherton. *Shrp* 2B 60
Netherton. *Stir* 2G 127
Netherton. *W Mid* 2D 60
Netherton. *W Yor* 3C 92
(nr. Horbury)
Netherton. *W Yor* 3B 92
(nr. Huddersfield)
Netherton. *Worc* 1E 49
Nethertown. *Cumb* 4A 102
Nethertown. *High* 1F 169
Nethertown. *Staf* 4F 73
Nether Urquhart. *Fife* 3D 136
Nether Wallop. *Hants* 3B 24
Nether Wasdale. *Cumb* 4C 102
Nether Welton. *Cumb* 5E 113
Nether Westcote. *Glos* 3H 49
Nether Whitacre. *Warw* 1G 61
Netherwhitton. *Nmbd* 5F 121
Nether Winchendon. *Buck* 4F 51
Nether Worton. *Oxon* 2C 50
Nethy Bridge. *High* 1E 151
Netley. *Hants* 2C 16
Netley. *Shrp* 5G 71
Netley Marsh. *Hants* 1B 16
Nettlebed. *Oxon* 3F 37
Nettlebridge. *Som* 2B 22
Nettlecombe. *Dors* 3A 14
Nettlecombe. *IOW* 5D 16
Nettleden. *Herts* 4A 52
Nettleham. *Linc* 3H 87
Nettlestead. *Kent* 5A 40
Nettlestead Green. *Kent* 5A 40
Nettlestone. *IOW* 3E 16
Nettlesworth. *Dur* 5F 115
Nettleton. *Linc* 4E 94
Nettleton. *Wilts* 4D 34
Netton. *Devn* 4B 8
Netton. *Wilts* 3G 23
Neuadd. *Carm* 3H 45
Neuadd. *Powy* 5C 70
Neuk, The. *Abers* 4E 153
Nevendon. *Essx* 1B 40
Nevern. *Pemb* 1A 44
New Abbey. *Dum* 3A 112
New Aberdour. *Abers* 2F 161
New Addington. *G Lon* 4E 39
Newall. *W Yor* 5D 98
New Alresford. *Hants* 3D 24
New Alyth. *Per* 4B 144
Newark. *Orkn* 3G 172
Newark. *Pet* 5B 76
Newark-on-Trent. *Notts* 5E 87

New Arley. Warw 2G 61
Newarthill. N Lan 4A 128
New Ash Green. Kent 4H 39
New Balderton. Notts 5F 87
New Barn. Kent 4H 39
New Barnetby. N Lin 3D 94
Newbattle. Midl 3G 129
New Bewick. Nmbd 2E 121
Newbie. Dum 3C 112
Newbiggin. Cumb 2H 103
  (nr. Appleby)
Newbiggin. Cumb 3B 96
  (nr. Barrow-in-Furness)
Newbiggin. Cumb 5G 113
  (nr. Cumrew)
Newbiggin. Cumb 2F 103
  (nr. Penrith)
Newbiggin. Cumb 5B 102
  (nr. Seascale)
Newbiggin. Dur 5E 115
  (nr. Consett)
Newbiggin. Dur 2C 104
  (nr. Holwick)
Newbiggin. Nmbd 5C 114
Newbiggin. N Yor 5C 104
  (nr. Askrigg)
Newbiggin. N Yor 1F 101
  (nr. Filey)
Newbiggin. N Yor 1B 98
  (nr. Thoralby)
Newbiggin-by-the-Sea. Nmbd . . .1G 115
Newbigging. Ang 5D 145
  (nr. Monikie)
Newbigging. Ang 4B 144
  (nr. Newtyle)
Newbigging. Ang 5D 144
  (nr. Tealing)
Newbigging. Edin 2E 129
Newbigging. S Lan 5D 128
Newbigging-on-Lune.
  Cumb 4A 104
Newbold. Derbs 3A 86
Newbold. Leics 4B 74
Newbold on Avon. Warw 3B 62
Newbold on Stour. Warw 1H 49
Newbold Pacey. Warw 5G 61
New Bolingbroke. Linc 5C 88
Newborough. IOA 4D 80
Newborough. Pet 5B 76
Newborough. Staf 3F 73
Newbottle. Nptn 2D 50
Newbottle. Tyne 4G 115
New Boultham. Linc 3G 87
Newbourne. Suff 1F 55
New Brancepeth. Dur 5F 115
Newbridge. Cphy 2F 33
Newbridge. Cdgn 5E 57
Newbridge. Corn 3B 4
New Bridge. Dum 2G 111
Newbridge. Edin 2E 129
Newbridge. Hants 1A 16
Newbridge. IOW 4C 16
Newbridge. N Yor 1C 100
Newbridge. Pemb 1D 42
Newbridge. Wrex 1E 71
Newbridge Green. Worc 2D 48
Newbridge-on-Usk. Mon 2G 33
Newbridge-on-Wye. Powy 5C 58
New Brighton. Flin 4E 83
New Brighton. Hants 2F 17
New Brighton. Mers 1F 83
New Brinsley. Notts 5B 86
Newbrough. Nmbd 3B 114
New Broughton. Wrex 5F 83
New Buckenham. Norf 1C 66
Newbuildings. Devn 2A 12
Newburgh. Abers 1G 153
Newburgh. Fife 2E 137
Newburgh. Lanc 3C 90
Newburn. Tyne 3E 115
Newbury. W Ber 5C 36
Newbury. Wilts 2D 22
Newby. Cumb 2G 103

Newby. N Yor 2G 97
  (nr. Ingleton)
Newby. N Yor 1E 101
  (nr. Scarborough)
Newby. N Yor 3C 106
  (nr. Stokesley)
Newby Bridge. Cumb 1C 96
Newby Cote. N Yor 2G 97
Newby East. Cumb 4F 113
Newby Head. Cumb 2G 103
New Byth. Abers 3F 161
Newby West. Cumb 4E 113
Newby Wiske. N Yor 1F 99
Newcastle. B'end 3B 32
Newcastle. Mon 4H 47
Newcastle. Shrp 2E 59
Newcastle Emlyn. Carm 1D 44
Newcastle International Airport.
  Tyne 2E 115
Newcastleton. Bord 1F 113
Newcastle-under-Lyme.
  Staf 1C 72
Newcastle Upon Tyne.
  Tyne 3F 115
Newchapel. Pemb 1G 43
Newchapel. Powy 2B 58
Newchapel. Staf 5C 84
Newchapel. Surr 1E 27
New Cheriton. Hants 4D 24
Newchurch. Carm 3D 45
Newchurch. Here 5F 59
Newchurch. IOW 4D 16
Newchurch. Kent 2E 29
Newchurch. Lanc 1G 91
  (nr. Nelson)
Newchurch. Lanc 2G 91
  (nr. Rawtenstall)
Newchurch. Mon 2H 33
Newchurch. Powy 5E 58
Newchurch. Staf 3F 73
New Costessey. Norf 4D 78
Newcott. Devn 2F 13
New Cowper. Cumb 5C 112
Newcraighall. Edin 2G 129
New Crofton. W Yor 3D 93
New Cross. Cdgn 3F 57
New Cross. Som 1H 13
New Cumnock. E Ayr 3F 117
New Deer. Abers 4F 161
New Denham. Buck 2B 38
Newdigate. Surr 1C 26
New Duston. Nptn 4E 62
New Earswick. York 4A 100
New Edlington. S Yor 1C 86
New Elgin. Mor 2G 159
New Ellerby. E Yor 1E 95
Newell Green. Brac 4G 37
New Eltham. G Lon 3F 39
New End. Warw 4F 61
New End. Worc 5E 61
Newenden. Kent 3C 28
New England. Essx 1H 53
New England. Pet 5A 76
Newent. Glos 3C 48
New Ferry. Mers 2F 83
Newfield. Dur 4F 115
  (nr. Chester-le-Street)
Newfield. Dur 1F 105
  (nr. Willington)
New Forest. Hants 1H 15
Newfound. Hants 1D 24
New Fryston. W Yor 2E 93
New Galloway. Dum 2D 110
Newgate. Norf 1C 78
Newgate Street. Herts 5D 52
New Greens. Herts 5B 52
New Grimsby. IOS 1A 4
New Hainford. Norf 4E 78
Newhall. Ches E 1A 72
Newhall. Staf 3G 73
Newham. Nmbd 2F 121
New Hartley. Nmbd 2G 115
Newhaven. Derbs 4F 85

Newhaven. E Sus 5F 27
Newhaven. Edin 2F 129
New Haw. Surr 4B 38
New Hedges. Pemb 4F 43
New Herrington. Tyne 4G 115
Newhey. G Man 3H 91
New Holkham. Norf 2A 78
New Holland. N Lin 2D 94
Newholm. N Yor 3F 107
New Houghton. Derbs 4C 86
New Houghton. Norf 3G 77
Newhouse. N Lan 3A 128
New Houses. N Yor 2H 97
New Hutton. Cumb 5G 103
New Hythe. Kent 5B 40
Newick. E Sus 3F 27
Newingreen. Kent 2F 29
Newington. Edin 2F 129
Newington. Kent 2F 29
  (nr. Folkestone)
Newington. Kent 4C 40
  (nr. Sittingbourne)
Newington. Notts 1D 86
Newington. Oxon 2E 36
Newington Bagpath. Glos 2D 34
New Inn. Carm 2E 45
New Inn. Mon 5H 47
New Inn. N Yor 2H 97
New Inn. Torf 5G 47
New Invention. Shrp 3E 59
New Kelso. High 4B 156
New Lanark. S Lan 5B 128
Newland. Glos 5A 48
Newland. Hull 1D 94
Newland. N Yor 2G 93
Newland. Som 3B 20
Newland. Worc 1C 48
Newlandrig. Midl 3G 129
Newlands. Cumb 1E 103
Newlands. Essx 2C 40
Newlands. High 4B 158
Newlands. Nmbd 4D 115
Newlands. Staf 3E 73
Newlands of Geise. High 2C 168
Newlands of Tynet. Mor 2A 160
Newlands Park. IOA 2B 80
New Lane. Lanc 3C 90
New Lane End. Warr 1A 84
New Langholm. Dum 1E 113
New Leake. Linc 5D 88
New Leeds. Abers 3G 161
New Lenton. Nott 2C 74
New Longton. Lanc 2D 90
Newlot. Orkn 6E 172
New Luce. Dum 3G 109
Newlyn. Corn 4B 4
Newmachar. Abers 2F 153
Newmains. N Lan 4B 128
New Mains of Ury. Abers 5F 153
New Malden. G Lon 4D 38
Newman's Green. Suff 1B 54
Newmarket. Suff 4F 65
Newmarket. W Isl 4G 171
New Marske. Red C 2D 106
New Marton. Shrp 2F 71
New Micklefield. W Yor 1E 93
New Mill. Abers 4E 160
New Mill. Corn 3B 4
New Mill. Herts 4H 51
Newmill. Mor 3B 160
Newmill. Bord 3G 119
New Mill. W Yor 4B 92
New Mills. Corn 3C 6
New Mills. Derbs 2E 85
New Mills. Mon 5A 48
New Mills. Powy 5C 70
Newmills. E Ayr 1E 117
New Milton. Hants 3H 15
New Mistley. Essx 2E 54

New Moat. Pemb 2E 43
Newmore. High 3H 157
  (nr. Dingwall)
Newmore. High 1A 158
  (nr. Invergordon)
Newnham. Cambs 5D 64
Newnham. Glos 4B 48
Newnham. Hants 1F 25
Newnham. Herts 2C 52
Newnham. Kent 5D 40
Newnham. Nptn 5C 62
Newnham. Warw 4F 61
Newnham Bridge. Worc 4A 60
New Ollerton. Notts 4D 86
New Oscott. W Mid 1F 61
Newpark. Fife 2G 137
New Park. N Yor 4E 99
New Pitsligo. Abers 3F 161
New Polzeath. Corn 1D 6
Newport. Corn 4D 10
Newport. Devn 3F 19
Newport. E Yor 1B 94
Newport. Essx 2F 53
Newport. Glos 2B 34
Newport. High 1H 165
Newport. IOW 4D 16
Newport. Newp 3G 33
Newport. Norf 4H 79
Newport. Pemb 1E 43
Newport. Som 4G 21
Newport. Telf 4B 72
Newport-on-Tay. Fife 1G 137
Newport Pagnell. Mil 1G 51
Newpound Common.
  W Sus 3B 26
New Prestwick. S Ayr 2C 116
New Quay. Cdgn 5C 56
Newquay. Corn 2C 6
Newquay Cornwall Airport. Corn . . .2C 6
New Rackheath. Norf 4E 79
New Radnor. Powy 4E 58
New Rent. Cumb 1F 103
New Ridley. Nmbd 4D 114
New Romney. Kent 3E 29
New Rossington. S Yor 1D 86
New Row. Cdgn 3G 57
New Row. Lanc 1E 91
New Row. N Yor 3D 106
New Sauchie. Clac 4A 136
Newsbank. Ches E 4C 84
Newseat. Abers 5E 160
Newsham. Lanc 1D 90
Newsham. Nmbd 2G 115
Newsham. N Yor 3E 105
  (nr. Richmond)
Newsham. N Yor 1F 99
  (nr. Thirsk)
New Sharlston. W Yor 3D 93
Newsholme. E Yor 2H 93
Newsholme. Lanc 4H 97
New Shoreston. Nmbd 1F 121
New Springs. G Man 4D 90
Newstead. Notts 5C 86
Newstead. Bord 1H 119
New Stevenston. N Lan 4A 128
New Street. Here 5F 59
Newstreet Lane. Shrp 2A 72
New Swanage. Dors 4F 15
New Swannington. Leics 4B 74
Newthorpe. N Yor 1E 93
Newthorpe. Notts 1B 74
Newton. Arg 4H 133
Newton. B'end 4B 32
Newton. Cambs 1E 53
  (nr. Cambridge)
Newton. Cambs 4D 76
  (nr. Wisbech)
Newton. Ches W 4G 83
  (nr. Chester)
Newton. Ches W 5H 83
  (nr. Tattenhall)
Newton. Cumb 2B 96
Newton. Derbs 5B 86
Newton. Dors 1C 14

Newton. Dum 2D 112
  (nr. Annan)
Newton. Dum 5D 118
  (nr. Moffat)
Newton. G Man 1D 84
Newton. Here 2G 47
  (nr. Ewyas Harold)
Newton. Here 5H 59
  (nr. Leominster)
Newton. High 2B 158
  (nr. Cromarty)
Newton. High 4B 158
  (nr. Inverness)
Newton. High 5C 166
  (nr. Kylestrome)
Newton. High 4F 169
  (nr. Wick)
Newton. Lanc 2E 97
  (nr. Carnforth)
Newton. Lanc 4F 97
  (nr. Clitheroe)
Newton. Lanc 1C 90
  (nr. Kirkham)
Newton. Linc 2H 75
Newton. Mers 2E 83
Newton. Mor 2F 159
Newton. Norf 4H 77
Newton. Nptn 2F 63
Newton. Nmbd 3D 114
Newton. Notts 1D 74
Newton. Bord 2A 120
Newton. Shrp 1B 60
  (nr. Bridgnorth)
Newton. Shrp 2G 71
  (nr. Wem)
Newton. S Lan 3E 20
Newton. S Lan 3H 127
  (nr. Glasgow)
Newton. S Lan 1B 118
  (nr. Lanark)
Newton. Staf 3E 73
Newton. Suff 1C 54
Newton. Swan 4F 31
Newton. Warw 3C 62
Newton. W Lot 2D 129
Newton. Wilts 4H 23
Newton Abbot. Devn 5B 12
Newtonairds. Dum 1F 111
Newton Arlosh. Cumb 4D 112
Newton Aycliffe. Dur 2F 105
Newton Bewley. Hart 2B 106
Newton Blossomville. Mil 5G 63
Newton Bromswold. Bed 4G 63
Newton Burgoland. Leics 5A 74
Newton by Toft. Linc 2H 87
Newton Ferrers. Devn 4B 8
Newton Flotman. Norf 1E 66
Newtongrange. Midl 3G 129
Newton Green. Mon 2A 34
Newton Hall. Dur 5F 115
Newton Hall. Nmbd 3D 114
Newton Harcourt. Leics 1D 62
Newton Heath. G Man 4G 91
Newtonhill. Abers 4G 153
Newtonhill. High 4H 157
Newton Hill. W Yor 2D 92
Newton Ketton. Darl 2A 106
Newton Kyme. N Yor 5G 99
Newton-le-Willows. Mers 1H 83
Newton-le-Willows. N Yor 1E 98
Newton Longville. Buck 2G 51
Newton Mearns. E Ren 4G 127
Newtonmore. High 4B 150
Newton Morrell. N Yor 4F 105
Newton Mulgrave. N Yor 3E 107
Newton of Ardtoe. High 1A 140
Newton of Balcanquhal. Per 2D 136
Newton of Beltrees. Ren 4E 127
Newton of Falkland. Fife 3E 137
Newton of Mountblairy. Abers . . .3E 160
Newton of Pitcairns. Per 2C 136
Newton-on-Ouse. N Yor 4H 99
Newton-on-Rawcliffe. N Yor . . .5F 107
Newton on the Hill. Shrp 3G 71

Newton-on-the-Moor—Northstowe

Newton-on-the-Moor. *Nmbd* 4F 121
Newton on Trent. *Linc* 3F 87
Newton Poppleford. *Devn* 4D 12
Newton Purcell. *Oxon* 2E 51
Newton Regis. *Warw* 5G 73
Newton Reigny. *Cumb* 1F 103
Newton Rigg. *Cumb* 1F 103
Newton St Cyres. *Devn* 3B 12
Newton St Faith. *Norf* 4E 78
Newton St Loe. *Bath* 5C 34
Newton St Petrock. *Devn* 1E 11
Newton Solney. *Derbs* 3G 73
Newton Stacey. *Hants* 2C 24
Newton Stewart. *Dum* 3B 110
Newton Toney. *Wilts* 2H 23
Newton Tony. *Wilts* 2H 23
Newton Tracey. *Devn* 4F 19
Newton under Roseberry. *Red C* 3C 106
Newton Unthank. *Leics* 5B 74
Newton upon Ayr. *S Ayr* 2C 116
Newton upon Derwent. *E Yor* 5B 100
Newton Valence. *Hants* 3F 25
Newton-with-Scales. *Lanc* 1B 90
Newtown. *Abers* 2E 160
Newtown. *Cambs* 4H 63
Newtown. *Corn* 5C 10
Newtown. *Cumb* 5B 112 (nr. Aspatria)
Newtown. *Cumb* 3G 113 (nr. Brampton)
Newtown. *Cumb* 2G 103 (nr. Penrith)
Newtown. *Derbs* 2D 85
Newtown. *Devn* 4A 20
Newtown. *Dors* 2H 13 (nr. Beaminster)
New Town. *Dors* 1E 15 (nr. Sixpenny Handley)
New Town. *E Lot* 2H 129
Newtown. *Falk* 1C 128
Newtown. *Glos* 5B 48 (nr. Lydney)
Newtown. *Glos* 2E 49 (nr. Tewkesbury)
Newtown. *Hants* 1D 16 (nr. Bishop's Waltham)
Newtown. *Hants* 3G 25 (nr. Liphook)
Newtown. *Hants* 1A 16 (nr. Lyndhurst)
Newtown. *Hants* 5C 36 (nr. Newbury)
Newtown. *Hants* 4B 24 (nr. Romsey)
Newtown. *Hants* 2C 16 (nr. Warsash)
Newtown. *Hants* 1E 16 (nr. Wickham)
Newtown. *Here* 2A 48 (nr. Little Dewchurch)
Newtown. *Here* 1B 48 (nr. Stretton Grandison)
Newtown. *High* 3F 149
Newtown. *IOM* 4C 108
Newtown. *IOW* 3C 16
Newtown. *Lanc* 3D 90
New Town. *Lutn* 3A 52
Newtown. *Nmbd* 4E 121 (nr. Rothbury)
Newtown. *Nmbd* 2E 121 (nr. Wooler)
Newtown. *Pool* 3F 15
Newtown. *Powy* 1D 58
Newtown. *Rhon* 2D 32
Newtown. *Shrp* 2G 71
Newtown. *Som* 1F 13
Newtown. *Staf* 4D 84 (nr. Biddulph)
Newtown. *Staf* 5D 73 (nr. Cannock)
Newtown. *Staf* 4E 85 (nr. Longnor)
New Town. *W Yor* 2E 93
Newtown. *Wilts* 4E 23
Newtown-in-St Martin. *Corn* 4E 5
Newtown Linford. *Leics* 4C 74
Newtown St Boswells. *Bord* 1H 119
New Tredegar. *Cphy* 5E 47
Newtyle. *Ang* 4B 144
New Village. *E Yor* 1D 94
New Village. *S Yor* 4F 93
New Walsoken. *Cambs* 5D 76
New Waltham. *NE Lin* 4F 95
New Winton. *E Lot* 2H 129
New World. *Cambs* 1C 64
New Yatt. *Oxon* 4B 50
Newyears Green. *G Lon* 2B 38
New York. *Linc* 5B 88
New York. *Tyne* 2G 115
Nextend. *Here* 5F 59
Neyland. *Pemb* 4D 42
Nib Heath. *Shrp* 4G 71
Nicholashayne. *Devn* 1E 12
Nicholaston. *Swan* 4E 31
Nidd. *N Yor* 3F 99
Niddrie. *Edin* 2F 129
Niddry. *Edin* 2D 129
Nigg. *Aber* 3G 153
Nigg. *High* 1C 158
Nigg Ferry. *High* 2B 158
Nightcott. *Som* 4B 20
Nimmer. *Som* 1G 13
Nine Ashes. *Essx* 5F 53
Ninebanks. *Nmbd* 4A 114
Nine Elms. *Swin* 3G 35
Ninemile Bar. *Dum* 2F 111
Nine Mile Burn. *Midl* 4E 129
Ninfield. *E Sus* 4B 28
Ningwood. *IOW* 4C 16
Nisbet. *Bord* 2A 120
Nisbet Hill. *Bord* 4D 130
Niton. *IOW* 5D 16
Nitshill. *E Ren* 4G 127
Niwbwrch. *IOA* 4D 80
Noak Hill. *G Lon* 1G 39
Nobold. *Shrp* 4G 71
Nobottle. *Nptn* 4D 62
Nocton. *Linc* 4H 87
Nogdam End. *Norf* 5F 79
Noke. *Oxon* 4D 50
Nolton. *Pemb* 3C 42
Nolton Haven. *Pemb* 3C 42
No Man's Heath. *Ches W* 1H 71
No Man's Heath. *Warw* 5G 73
Nomansland. *Devn* 1B 12
Nomansland. *Wilts* 1A 16
Noneley. *Shrp* 3G 71
Nonikiln. *High* 1A 158
Nonington. *Kent* 5G 41
Nook. *Cumb* 2F 113 (nr. Longtown)
Nook. *Cumb* 1E 97 (nr. Milnthorpe)
Noranside. *Ang* 2D 144
Norbreck. *Bkpl* 5C 96
Norbridge. *Here* 1C 48
Norbury. *Ches E* 1H 71
Norbury. *Derbs* 1F 73
Norbury. *Shrp* 1F 59
Norbury. *Staf* 3B 72
Norby. *N Yor* 1G 99
Norby. *Shet* 6D 173
Norcross. *Lanc* 5C 96
Nordelph. *Norf* 5E 77
Norden. *G Man* 3G 91
Nordley. *Shrp* 1A 60
Norfolk Broads. *Norf* 5G 79
Norham. *Nmbd* 5F 131
Norland Town. *W Yor* 2A 92
Norley. *Ches W* 3H 83
Norleywood. *Hants* 3B 16
Normanby. *N Lin* 3B 94
Normanby. *N Yor* 1B 100
Normanby. *Red C* 3C 106
Normanby-by-Spital. *Linc* 2H 87
Normanby le Wold. *Linc* 1A 88
Norman Cross. *Cambs* 1A 64
Normandy. *Surr* 5A 38
Norman's Bay. *E Sus* 5A 28
Norman's Green. *Devn* 2D 12
Normanton. *Derb* 2H 73
Normanton. *Leics* 1F 75
Normanton. *Linc* 1G 75
Normanton. *Notts* 5E 86
Normanton. *W Yor* 2D 93
Normanton le Heath. *Leics* 4A 74
Normanton on Soar. *Notts* 3C 74
Normanton-on-the-Wolds. *Notts* 2D 74
Normanton on Trent. *Notts* 4E 87
Normoss. *Lanc* 1B 90
Norrington Common. *Wilts* 5D 35
Norris Green. *Mers* 1F 83
Norris Hill. *Leics* 4H 73
Norristhorpe. *W Yor* 2C 92
Northacre. *Norf* 1B 66
Northall. *Buck* 3H 51
Northallerton. *N Yor* 5A 106
Northam. *Devn* 4E 19
Northam. *Sotn* 1C 16
Northampton. *Nptn* 4E 63
North Anston. *S Yor* 2C 86
North Ascot. *Brac* 4A 38
North Aston. *Oxon* 3C 50
Northaw. *Herts* 5C 52
Northay. *Som* 1F 13
North Baddesley. *Hants* 4B 24
North Balfern. *Dum* 4B 110
North Ballachulish. *High* 2E 141
North Barrow. *Som* 4B 22
North Barsham. *Norf* 2B 78
Northbeck. *Linc* 1H 75
North Benfleet. *Essx* 2B 40
North Bersted. *W Sus* 5A 26
North Berwick. *E Lot* 1B 130
North Bitchburn. *Dur* 1E 105
North Blyth. *Nmbd* 1G 115
North Boarhunt. *Hants* 1E 16
North Bockhampton. *Dors* 3G 15
Northborough. *Pet* 5A 76
Northbourne. *Kent* 5H 41
Northbourne. *Oxon* 3D 36
North Bovey. *Devn* 4H 11
North Bowood. *Dors* 3H 13
North Bradley. *Wilts* 1D 22
North Brentor. *Devn* 4E 11
North Brewham. *Som* 3C 22
Northbrook. *Oxon* 3C 50
North Brook End. *Cambs* 1C 52
North Broomhill. *Nmbd* 4G 121
North Buckland. *Devn* 2E 19
North Burlingham. *Norf* 4F 79
North Cadbury. *Som* 4B 22
North Carlton. *Linc* 3G 87
North Cave. *E Yor* 1B 94
North Cerney. *Glos* 5F 49
North Chailey. *E Sus* 3E 27
Northchapel. *W Sus* 3A 26
North Charford. *Hants* 1G 15
North Charlton. *Nmbd* 2F 121
North Cheriton. *Som* 4B 22
North Chideock. *Dors* 3H 13
Northchurch. *Herts* 5H 51
North Cliffe. *E Yor* 1B 94
North Clifton. *Notts* 3F 87
North Close. *Dur* 1F 105
North Cockerington. *Linc* 1C 88
North Coker. *Som* 1A 14
North Collafirth. *Shet* 3E 173
North Common. *E Sus* 3E 27
North Commonty. *Abers* 4F 161
North Coombe. *Devn* 1B 12
North Cornelly. *B'end* 3B 32
North Cotes. *Linc* 4G 95
Northcott. *Devn* 3D 10 (nr. Boyton)
Northcott. *Devn* 1D 12 (nr. Culmstock)
Northcourt. *Oxon* 2D 36
North Cove. *Suff* 2G 67
North Cowton. *N Yor* 4F 105
North Craigo. *Ang* 2F 145
North Crawley. *Mil* 1H 51
North Cray. *G Lon* 3F 39
North Creake. *Norf* 2A 78
North Curry. *Som* 4G 21
North Dalton. *E Yor* 4D 100
North Deighton. *N Yor* 4F 99
North Dronley. *Ang* 5C 144
North Duffield. *N Yor* 1G 93
Northedge. *Derbs* 4A 86
North Elkington. *Linc* 1B 88
North Elmham. *Norf* 3B 78
North Elmsall. *W Yor* 3E 93
Northend. *Buck* 2F 37
North End. *E Yor* 1F 95
North End. *Essx* 4G 53 (nr. Great Dunmow)
North End. *Essx* 2A 54 (nr. Great Yeldham)
North End. *Hants* 5C 36
North End. *Leics* 4C 74
North End. *Linc* 1B 76
North End. *Norf* 1B 66
North End. *N Som* 5H 33
North End. *Port* 2E 17
Northend. *Warw* 5A 62
North End. *W Sus* 5C 26
North End. *Wilts* 2F 35
North Erradale. *High* 5B 162
North Evington. *Leic* 5D 74
North Fambridge. *Essx* 1C 40
North Fearns. *High* 5E 155
North Featherstone. *W Yor* 2E 93
North Feorline. *N Ayr* 3D 122
North Ferriby. *E Yor* 2C 94
Northfield. *Aber* 3F 153
Northfield. *Hull* 2D 94
Northfield. *Som* 3F 21
Northfield. *W Mid* 3E 61
Northfleet. *Kent* 3H 39
North Frodingham. *E Yor* 4F 101
Northgate. *Linc* 3A 76
North Gluss. *Shet* 4E 173
North Gorley. *Hants* 1G 15
North Green. *Norf* 2E 66
North Green. *Suff* 4F 67 (nr. Framlingham)
North Green. *Suff* 3F 67 (nr. Halesworth)
North Green. *Suff* 4F 67 (nr. Saxmundham)
North Greetwell. *Linc* 3H 87
North Grimston. *N Yor* 3C 100
North Halling. *Medw* 4B 40
North Hayling. *Hants* 2F 17
North Hazelrigg. *Nmbd* 1E 121
North Heasley. *Devn* 3H 19
North Heath. *W Sus* 3B 26
North Hill. *Corn* 5C 10
North Hinksey Village. *Oxon* 5C 50
North Holmwood. *Surr* 1C 26
North Huish. *Devn* 3D 8
North Hykeham. *Linc* 4G 87
Northiam. *E Sus* 3C 28
Northill. *C Beds* 1B 52
Northington. *Hants* 3D 24
North Kelsey. *Linc* 4D 94
North Kelsey Moor. *Linc* 4D 94
North Kessock. *High* 4A 158
North Killingholme. *N Lin* 3E 95
North Kilvington. *N Yor* 1G 99
North Kilworth. *Leics* 2D 62
North Kyme. *Linc* 5A 88
North Lancing. *W Sus* 5C 26
Northlands. *Linc* 5C 88
Northleach. *Glos* 4G 49
North Lee. *Buck* 5G 51
North Lees. *N Yor* 2E 99
Northleigh. *Devn* 3G 19 (nr. Barnstaple)
Northleigh. *Devn* 3E 13 (nr. Honiton)
North Leigh. *Kent* 1F 29
North Leigh. *Oxon* 4B 50
North Leverton. *Notts* 2E 87
Northlew. *Devn* 3F 11
North Littleton. *Worc* 1F 49
North Lopham. *Norf* 2C 66
North Luffenham. *Rut* 5G 75
North Marden. *W Sus* 1G 17
North Marston. *Buck* 3F 51
North Middleton. *Midl* 4G 129
North Middleton. *Nmbd* 2E 121
North Molton. *Devn* 4H 19
North Moor. *N Yor* 1D 100
Northmoor. *Oxon* 5C 50
Northmoor Green. *Som* 3G 21
North Moreton. *Oxon* 3D 36
Northmuir. *Ang* 3C 144
North Mundham. *W Sus* 2G 17
North Murie. *Per* 1E 137
North Muskham. *Notts* 5E 87
North Ness. *Orkn* 8C 172
North Newbald. *E Yor* 1C 94
North Newington. *Oxon* 2C 50
North Newnton. *Wilts* 1G 23
North Newton. *Som* 3F 21
Northney. *Hants* 2F 17
North Nibley. *Glos* 2C 34
North Oakley. *Hants* 1D 24
North Ockendon. *G Lon* 2G 39
Northolt. *G Lon* 2C 38
Northop. *Flin* 4E 83
Northop Hall. *Flin* 4E 83
North Ormesby. *Midd* 3C 106
North Ormsby. *Linc* 1B 88
Northorpe. *Linc* 4H 75 (nr. Bourne)
Northorpe. *Linc* 2B 76 (nr. Donington)
Northorpe. *Linc* 1F 87 (nr. Gainsborough)
North Otterington. *N Yor* 1F 99
Northover. *Som* 3H 21 (nr. Glastonbury)
Northover. *Som* 4A 22 (nr. Yeovil)
North Owersby. *Linc* 1H 87
Northowram. *W Yor* 2B 92
North Perrott. *Som* 2H 13
North Petherton. *Som* 3F 21
North Petherwin. *Corn* 4C 10
North Pickenham. *Norf* 5A 78
North Piddle. *Worc* 5D 60
North Poorton. *Dors* 3A 14
North Port. *Arg* 1H 133
Northport. *Dors* 4E 15
North Queensferry. *Fife* 1E 129
North Radworthy. *Devn* 3A 20
North Rauceby. *Linc* 1H 75
Northrepps. *Norf* 2E 79
North Rigton. *N Yor* 5E 99
North Rode. *Ches E* 4C 84
North Roe. *Shet* 3E 173
North Ronaldsay Airport. *Orkn* 2G 172
North Row. *Cumb* 1D 102
North Runcton. *Norf* 4F 77
North Sannox. *N Ayr* 5B 126
North Scale. *Cumb* 2A 96
North Scarle. *Linc* 4F 87
North Seaton. *Nmbd* 1F 115
North Seaton Colliery. *Nmbd* 1F 115
North Sheen. *G Lon* 3C 38
North Shian. *Arg* 4D 140
North Shields. *Tyne* 3G 115
North Shoebury. *S'end* 2D 40
North Shore. *Bkpl* 1B 90
North Side. *Cumb* 2B 102
North Skelton. *Red C* 3D 106
North Somercotes. *Linc* 1D 88
North Stainley. *N Yor* 2E 99
North Stainmore. *Cumb* 3B 104
North Stifford. *Thur* 2H 39
North Stoke. *Bath* 5C 34
North Stoke. *Oxon* 3E 36
North Stoke. *W Sus* 4B 26
Northstowe. *Cambs* 4D 64

Olveston—Parbrook

Olveston. *S Glo* 3B 34
Ombersley. *Worc* 4C 60
Ompton. *Notts* 4D 86
Omunsgarth. *Shet* 7E 173
Onchan. *IOM* 4D 108
Onecote. *Staf* 5E 85
Onehouse. *Suff* 5C 66
Onen. *Mon* 4H 47
Ongar Hill. *Norf* 3E 77
Ongar Street. *Here* 4F 59
Onibury. *Shrp* 3G 59
Onich. *High* 2E 141
Onllwyn. *Neat* 4B 46
Onneley. *Shrp* 1B 72
Onslow Green. *Essx* 4G 53
Onslow Village. *Surr* 1A 26
Onthank. *E Ayr* 1D 116
Openwoodgate. *Derbs* 1A 74
Opinan. *High* 1G 155
(nr. Gairloch)
Opinan. *High* 4C 162
(nr. Laide)
Orasaigh. *W Isl* 6F 171
Orbost. *High* 4B 154
Orby. *Linc* 4D 89
Orchard Hill. *Devn* 4E 19
Orchard Portman. *Som* 4F 21
Orcheston. *Wilts* 2F 23
Orcop. *Here* 3H 47
Orcop Hill. *Here* 3H 47
Ord. *High* 2E 147
Ordhead. *Abers* 2D 152
Ordie. *Abers* 3B 152
Ordiquish. *Mor* 3H 159
Ordley. *Nmbd* 4C 114
Ordsall. *Notts* 3E 86
Ore. *E Sus* 4C 28
Oreham Common. *W Sus* 4D 26
Oreton. *Shrp* 2A 60
Orford. *Suff* 1H 55
Orford. *Warr* 1A 84
Organford. *Dors* 3E 15
Orgil. *Orkn* 7B 172
Orgreave. *Staf* 4F 73
Oridge Street. *Glos* 3C 48
Orlestone. *Kent* 2D 28
Orleton. *Here* 4G 59
Orleton. *Worc* 4A 60
Orleton Common. *Here* 4G 59
Orlingbury. *Nptn* 3F 63
Ormacleit. *W Isl* 5C 170
Ormathwaite. *Cumb* 2D 102
Ormesby. *Midd* 3C 106
Ormesby St Margaret. *Norf* 4G 79
Ormesby St Michael. *Norf* 4G 79
Ormiscaig. *High* 4C 162
Ormiston. *E Lot* 3H 129
Ormsaigbeg. *High* 2F 139
Ormsaigmore. *High* 2F 139
Ormsary. *Arg* 2F 125
Ormsgill. *Cumb* 2A 96
Ormskirk. *Lanc* 4C 90
Orphir. *Orkn* 7C 172
Orpington. *G Lon* 4F 39
Orrell. *Lanc* 4D 90
Orrell. *Mers* 1F 83
Orrisdale. *IOM* 2C 108
Orsett. *Thur* 2H 39
Orslow. *Staf* 4C 72
Orston. *Notts* 1E 75
Orthwaite. *Cumb* 1D 102
Orton. *Cumb* 4H 103
Orton. *Mor* 3H 159
Orton. *Nptn* 3F 63
Orton. *Staf* 1C 60
Orton Longueville. *Pet* 1A 64
Orton-on-the-Hill. *Leics* 5H 73
Orton Waterville. *Pet* 1A 64
Orton Wistow. *Pet* 1A 64
Orwell. *Cambs* 5C 64
Osbaldeston. *Lanc* 1E 91
Osbaldwick. *York* 4A 100
Osbaston. *Leics* 5B 74
Osbaston. *Shrp* 3F 71
Osbournby. *Linc* 2H 75
Osclay. *High* 5E 169
Oscroft. *Ches W* 4H 83
Ose. *High* 4C 154
Osgathorpe. *Leics* 4B 74
Osgodby. *Linc* 1H 87
Osgodby. *N Yor* 1E 101
(nr. Scarborough)
Osgodby. *N Yor* 1G 93
(nr. Selby)
Oskaig. *High* 5E 155
Oskamull. *Arg* 4F 139
Osleston. *Derbs* 2G 73
Osmaston. *Derb* 2A 74
Osmaston. *Derbs* 1G 73
Osmington. *Dors* 4C 14
Osmington Mills. *Dors* 4C 14
Osmondthorpe. *W Yor* 1D 92
Osmotherley. *N Yor* 5B 106
Osnaburgh. *Fife* 2G 137
Ospisdale. *High* 5E 164
Ospringe. *Kent* 4E 40
Ossett. *W Yor* 2C 92
Ossington. *Notts* 4E 87
Ostend. *Essx* 1D 40
Ostend. *Norf* 2F 79
Osterley. *G Lon* 3C 38
Oswaldkirk. *N Yor* 2A 100
Oswaldtwistle. *Lanc* 2F 91
Oswestry. *Shrp* 3E 71
Otby. *Linc* 1A 88
Otford. *Kent* 5G 39
Otham. *Kent* 5B 40
Otherton. *Staf* 4D 72
Othery. *Som* 3G 21
Otley. *Suff* 5E 66
Otley. *W Yor* 5E 98
Otterbourne. *Hants* 4C 24
Otterburn. *Nmbd* 5C 120
Otterburn. *N Yor* 4A 98
Otterburn Camp. *Nmbd* 5C 120
Otterburn Hall. *Nmbd* 5C 120
Otter Ferry. *Arg* 1H 125
Otterford. *Som* 1F 13
Otterham. *Corn* 3B 10
Otterhampton. *Som* 2F 21
Otterham Quay. *Kent* 4C 40
Ottershaw. *Surr* 4B 38
Otterspool. *Mers* 2F 83
Otterswick. *Shet* 3G 173
Otterton. *Devn* 4D 12
Otterwood. *Hants* 2C 16
Ottery St Mary. *Devn* 3E 12
Ottinge. *Kent* 1F 29
Ottringham. *E Yor* 2F 95
Oughterby. *Cumb* 4D 112
Oughtershaw. *N Yor* 1A 98
Oughterside. *Cumb* 5C 112
Oughtibridge. *S Yor* 1H 85
Oughtrington. *Warr* 2A 84
Oulston. *N Yor* 2H 99
Oulton. *Cumb* 4D 112
Oulton. *Norf* 3D 78
Oulton. *Staf* 3B 72
(nr. Gnosall Heath)
Oulton. *Staf* 2D 72
(nr. Stone)
Oulton. *Suff* 1H 67
Oulton. *W Yor* 2D 92
Oulton Broad. *Suff* 1H 67
Oulton Street. *Norf* 3D 78
Oundle. *Nptn* 2H 63
Ousby. *Cumb* 1H 103
Ousdale. *High* 1H 165
Ousden. *Suff* 5G 65
Ousefleet. *E Yor* 2B 94
Ouston. *Dur* 4F 115
Ouston. *Nmbd* 4A 114
(nr. Bearsbridge)
Ouston. *Nmbd* 2D 114
(nr. Stamfordham)
Outer Hope. *Devn* 4C 8
Outertown. *Orkn* 7B 172
Outgate. *Cumb* 5E 103
Outhgill. *Cumb* 4A 104
Outlands. *Staf* 2B 72
Outlane. *W Yor* 3A 92
Out Newton. *E Yor* 2G 95
Out Rawcliffe. *Lanc* 5D 96
Outwell. *Norf* 5E 77
Outwick. *Hants* 1G 15
Outwood. *Surr* 1E 27
Outwood. *W Yor* 2D 92
Outwood. *Worc* 3D 60
Outwoods. *Leics* 4B 74
Outwoods. *Staf* 4B 72
Ouzlewell Green. *W Yor* 2D 92
Ovenden. *W Yor* 2A 92
Over. *Cambs* 3C 64
Over. *Ches W* 4A 84
Over. *Glos* 4D 48
Over. *S Glo* 3A 34
Over Burrows. *Derbs* 2G 73
Overbury. *Worc* 2E 49
Overcombe. *Dors* 4B 14
Over Compton. *Dors* 1A 14
Over End. *Cambs* 1H 63
Over Finlarg. *Ang* 4D 144
Overgreen. *Derbs* 3H 85
Over Green. *W Mid* 1F 61
Over Haddon. *Derbs* 4G 85
Over Hulton. *G Man* 4E 91
Over Kellet. *Lanc* 2E 97
Over Kiddington. *Oxon* 3C 50
Overleigh. *Som* 3H 21
Overley. *Staf* 4F 73
Over Monnow. *Mon* 4A 48
Over Norton. *Oxon* 3B 50
Over Peover. *Ches E* 3B 84
Overpool. *Ches W* 3F 83
Overscaig. *High* 1B 164
Overseal. *Derbs* 4G 73
Over Silton. *N Yor* 5B 106
Oversland. *Kent* 5E 41
Overstone. *Nptn* 4F 63
Over Stowey. *Som* 3E 21
Overstrand. *Norf* 1E 79
Over Stratton. *Som* 1H 13
Over Street. *Wilts* 3F 23
Overthorpe. *Nptn* 1C 50
Overton. *Aber* 2F 153
Overton. *Ches W* 3H 83
Overton. *Hants* 2D 24
Overton. *High* 5E 169
Overton. *Lanc* 4D 96
Overton. *N Yor* 4H 99
Overton. *Shrp* 2A 60
(nr. Bridgnorth)
Overton. *Shrp* 3H 59
(nr. Ludlow)
Overton. *Swan* 4D 30
Overton. *W Yor* 3C 92
Overton. *Wrex* 1F 71
Overtown. *Lanc* 2F 97
Overtown. *N Lan* 4B 128
Overtown. *Swin* 4G 35
Over Wallop. *Hants* 3A 24
Over Whitacre. *Warw* 1G 61
Over Worton. *Oxon* 3C 50
Oving. *Buck* 3F 51
Oving. *W Sus* 5A 26
Ovingdean. *Brig* 5E 27
Ovingham. *Nmbd* 3D 115
Ovington. *Dur* 3E 105
Ovington. *Essx* 1A 54
Ovington. *Hants* 3D 24
Ovington. *Norf* 5B 78
Ovington. *Nmbd* 3D 114
Owen's Bank. *Staf* 3G 73
Ower. *Hants* 2C 16
(nr. Holbury)
Ower. *Hants* 1B 16
(nr. Totton)
Owermoigne. *Dors* 4C 14
Owlbury. *Shrp* 1F 59
Owler Bar. *Derbs* 3G 85
Owlerton. *S Yor* 2H 85
Owlsmoor. *Brac* 5G 37
Owlswick. *Buck* 5F 51
Owmby. *Linc* 4D 94
Owmby-by-Spital. *Linc* 2H 87
Ownham. *W Ber* 4C 36
Owrytn. *Wrex* 1F 71
Owslebury. *Hants* 4D 24
Owston. *Leics* 5E 75
Owston. *S Yor* 3F 93
Owston Ferry. *N Lin* 4B 94
Owstwick. *E Yor* 1F 95
Owthorne. *E Yor* 2G 95
Owthorpe. *Notts* 2D 74
Owton Manor. *Hart* 2B 106
Oxborough. *Norf* 5G 77
Oxbridge. *Dors* 3H 13
Oxcombe. *Linc* 3C 88
Oxen End. *Essx* 3G 53
Oxenhall. *Glos* 3C 48
Oxenholme. *Cumb* 5G 103
Oxenhope. *W Yor* 1A 92
Oxen Park. *Cumb* 1C 96
Oxenpill. *Som* 2H 21
Oxenton. *Glos* 2E 49
Oxenwood. *Wilts* 1B 24
Oxford. *Oxon* 5D 50
Oxgangs. *Edin* 3F 129
Oxhey. *Herts* 1C 38
Oxhill. *Warw* 1B 50
Oxley. *W Mid* 5C 72
Oxley Green. *Essx* 4C 54
Oxley's Green. *E Sus* 3A 28
Oxlode. *Cambs* 2D 65
Oxnam. *Bord* 3B 120
Oxshott. *Surr* 4C 38
Oxspring. *S Yor* 4C 92
Oxted. *Surr* 5E 39
Oxton. *Mers* 2E 83
Oxton. *N Yor* 5H 99
Oxton. *Notts* 5D 86
Oxton. *Bord* 4A 130
Oxwich. *Swan* 4D 31
Oxwich Green. *Swan* 4D 31
Oxwick. *Norf* 3B 78
Oykel Bridge. *High* 3A 164
Oyne. *Abers* 1D 152
Oystermouth. *Swan* 4F 31
Ozleworth. *Glos* 2C 34

P

Pabail Iarach. *W Isl* 4H 171
Pabail Uarach. *W Isl* 4H 171
Pachesham. *Surr* 5C 38
Packers Hill. *Dors* 1C 14
Packington. *Leics* 4A 74
Packmoor. *Stoke* 5C 84
Packmores. *Warw* 4G 61
Packwood. *W Mid* 3F 61
Packwood Gullett. *W Mid* 3F 61
Padanaram. *Ang* 3D 144
Padbury. *Buck* 2F 51
Paddington. *G Lon* 2D 38
Paddington. *Warr* 2A 84
Paddlesworth. *Kent* 2F 29
Paddock. *Kent* 5D 40
Paddockhole. *Dum* 1D 112
Paddock Wood. *Kent* 1A 28
Paddolgreen. *Shrp* 2H 71
Padeswood. *Flin* 4E 83
Padiham. *Lanc* 1F 91
Padside. *N Yor* 4D 98
Padson. *Devn* 3F 11
Padstow. *Corn* 1D 6
Padworth. *W Ber* 5E 36
Page Bank. *Dur* 1F 105
Pagham. *W Sus* 3G 17
Paglesham Churchend. *Essx* 1D 40
Paglesham Eastend. *Essx* 1D 40
Paibeil. *W Isl* 2C 170
(on North Uist)
Paibeil. *W Isl* 8C 171
(on Taransay)
Paignton. *Torb* 2E 9
Pailton. *Warw* 2B 62
Paine's Corner. *E Sus* 3H 27
Painleyhill. *Staf* 2E 73
Painscastle. *Powy* 1E 47
Painshawfield. *Nmbd* 3D 114
Painsthorpe. *E Yor* 4C 100
Painswick. *Glos* 5D 48
Painter's Forstal. *Kent* 5D 40
Painthorpe. *W Yor* 3D 92
Pairc Shiaboist. *W Isl* 3E 171
Paisley. *Ren* 3F 127
Pakefield. *Suff* 1H 67
Pakenham. *Suff* 4B 66
Pale. *Gwyn* 2B 70
Palehouse Common. *E Sus* 4F 27
Palestine. *Hants* 2A 24
Paley Street. *Wind* 4G 37
Palgowan. *Dum* 1A 110
Palgrave. *Suff* 3D 66
Pallington. *Dors* 3C 14
Palmarsh. *Kent* 2F 29
Palmer Moor. *Derbs* 2F 73
Palmers Cross. *W Mid* 5C 72
Palmerstown. *V Glam* 5E 33
Palnackie. *Dum* 4F 111
Palnure. *Dum* 3B 110
Palterton. *Derbs* 4B 86
Pamber End. *Hants* 1E 24
Pamber Green. *Hants* 1E 24
Pamber Heath. *Hants* 5E 36
Pamington. *Glos* 2E 49
Pamphill. *Dors* 2E 15
Pampisford. *Cambs* 1E 53
Panborough. *Som* 2H 21
Panbride. *Ang* 5E 145
Pancakehill. *Glos* 4F 49
Pancrasweek. *Devn* 2C 10
Pandy. *Gwyn* 3A 70
(nr. Bala)
Pandy. *Gwyn* 5F 69
(nr. Tywyn)
Pandy. *Mon* 3G 47
Pandy. *Powy* 5B 70
Pandy. *Wrex* 2D 70
Pandy Tudur. *Cnwy* 4A 82
Panfield. *Essx* 3H 53
Pangbourne. *W Ber* 4E 37
Pannal. *N Yor* 4F 99
Pannal Ash. *N Yor* 4E 99
Pannanich. *Abers* 4A 152
Pant. *Shrp* 3E 71
Pant. *Wrex* 1F 71
Pantasaph. *Flin* 3D 82
Pant Glas. *Gwyn* 1D 68
Pant-glas. *Shrp* 2E 71
Pantgwyn. *Carm* 3F 45
Pantgwyn. *Cdgn* 1C 44
Pant-lasau. *Swan* 3F 31
Panton. *Linc* 3A 88
Pant-pastynog. *Den* 4C 82
Pantperthog. *Gwyn* 5G 69
Pant-teg. *Carm* 3E 45
Pant-y-Caws. *Carm* 2F 43
Pant-y-dwr. *Powy* 3B 58
Pant-y-ffridd. *Powy* 5D 70
Pantyffynnon. *Carm* 4G 45
Pantygasseg. *Torf* 5F 47
Pant-y-llyn. *Carm* 4G 45
Pant-yr-awel. *B'end* 3C 32
Pant y Wacco. *Flin* 3D 82
Panxworth. *Norf* 4F 79
Papa Stour Airport. *Shet* 6C 173
Papa Westray Airport. *Orkn* 2D 172
Papcastle. *Cumb* 1C 102
Papigoe. *High* 3F 169
Papil. *Shet* 8E 173
Papple. *E Lot* 2B 130
Papplewick. *Notts* 5C 86
Papworth Everard. *Cambs* 4B 64
Papworth St Agnes. *Cambs* 4B 64
Par. *Corn* 3E 7
Paramour Street. *Kent* 4G 41
Parbold. *Lanc* 3C 90
Parbrook. *Som* 3A 22

Parbrook—Pen-y-bryn

Parbrook. *W Sus* 3B 26
Parc. *Gwyn* 2A 70
Parcllyn. *Cdgn* 5B 56
Parc-Seymour. *Newp* 2H 33
Pardown. *Hants* 2D 24
Pardshaw. *Cumb* 2B 102
Parham. *Suff* 4F 67
Park. *Abers* 4E 153
Park. *Arg* 4D 140
Park. *Dum* 5B 118
Park Bottom. *Corn* 4A 6
Parkburn. *Abers* 5E 161
Park Corner. *E Sus* 2G 27
Park Corner. *Oxon* 3E 37
Parkend. *Glos* 5B 48
Park End. *Nmbd* 2B 114
Parkeston. *Essx* 2F 55
Parkfield. *Corn* 2H 7
Parkgate. *Ches W* 3E 83
Parkgate. *Cumb* 5D 112
Parkgate. *Dum* 1B 112
Park Gate. *Hants* 2D 16
Parkgate. *Surr* 1D 26
Park Gate. *Worc* 3D 60
Parkhall. *W Dun* 2F 127
Parkham. *Devn* 4D 19
Parkham Ash. *Devn* 4D 18
Parkhead. *Cumb* 5E 113
Parkhead. *Glas* 3H 127
Park Hill. *Mers* 4C 90
Parkhouse. *Mon* 5H 47
Parkhurst. *IOW* 3C 16
Park Lane. *G Man* 4F 91
Park Lane. *Staf* 5C 72
Parkmill. *Swan* 4E 31
Park Mill. *W Yor* 3C 92
Parkneuk. *Abers* 1G 145
Parkside. *N Lan* 4B 128
Parkstone. *Pool* 3F 15
Park Street. *Herts* 5B 52
Park Street. *W Sus* 2C 26
Park Town. *Oxon* 5D 50
Park Village. *Nmbd* 3H 113
Parkway. *Here* 2C 48
Parley Cross. *Dors* 3F 15
Parmoor. *Buck* 3F 37
Parr. *Mers* 1H 83
Parracombe. *Devn* 2G 19
Parrog. *Pemb* 1E 43
Parsonage Green. *Essx* 4H 53
Parsonby. *Cumb* 1C 102
Parson Cross. *S Yor* 1A 86
Parson Drove. *Cambs* 5C 76
Partick. *Glas* 3G 127
Partington. *G Man* 1B 84
Partney. *Linc* 4D 88
Parton. *Cumb* 2A 102
(nr. Whitehaven)
Parton. *Cumb* 4D 112
(nr. Wigton)
Parton. *Dum* 2D 111
Partridge Green. *W Sus* 4C 26
Parwich. *Derbs* 5F 85
Passenham. *Nptn* 2F 51
Passfield. *Hants* 3G 25
Passingford Bridge. *Essx* 1G 39
Paston. *Norf* 2F 79
Pasturefields. *Staf* 3D 73
Patchacott. *Devn* 3E 11
Patcham. *Brig* 5E 27
Patchetts Green. *Herts* 1C 38
Patching. *W Sus* 5B 26
Patchole. *Devn* 2G 19
Patchway. *S Glo* 3B 34
Pateley Bridge. *N Yor* 3D 98
Pathe. *Som* 3G 21
Pathfinder Village. *Devn* 3B 12
Pathhead. *Abers* 2G 145
Pathhead. *E Ayr* 3F 117
Pathhead. *Fife* 4E 137
Pathhead. *Midl* 3G 129
Pathlow. *Warw* 5F 61
Path of Condie. *Per* 2C 136
Pathstruie. *Per* 2C 136
Patmore Heath. *Herts* 3E 53
Patna. *E Ayr* 3D 116
Patney. *Wilts* 1F 23
Patrick. *IOM* 3B 108
Patrick Brompton. *N Yor* 5F 105
Patrington. *E Yor* 2G 95
Patrington Haven. *E Yor* 2G 95
Patrixbourne. *Kent* 5F 41
Patterdale. *Cumb* 3E 103
Pattiesmuir. *Fife* 1D 129
Pattingham. *Staf* 1C 60
Pattishall. *Nptn* 5D 62
Pattiswick. *Essx* 3B 54
Patton Bridge. *Cumb* 5G 103
Paul. *Corn* 4B 4
Paulerspury. *Nptn* 1F 51
Paull. *E Yor* 2E 95
Paulton. *Bath* 1B 22
Pauperhaugh. *Nmbd* 5F 121
Pave Lane. *Telf* 4B 72
Pavenham. *Bed* 5G 63
Pawlett. *Som* 2G 21
Pawston. *Nmbd* 1C 120
Paxford. *Glos* 2G 49
Paxton. *Bord* 4F 131
Payhembury. *Devn* 2D 12
Paythorne. *Lanc* 4H 97
Payton. *Som* 4E 20
Peacehaven. *E Sus* 5F 27
Peak Dale. *Derbs* 3E 85
Peak District. *Derbs* 2F 85
Peak Forest. *Derbs* 3F 85
Peak Hill. *Linc* 4B 76
Peakirk. *Pet* 5A 76
Pearsie. *Ang* 3C 144
Peasedown St John. *Bath* 1C 22
Peaseland Green. *Norf* 4C 78
Peasemore. *W Ber* 4C 36
Peasenhall. *Suff* 4F 67
Pease Pottage. *W Sus* 2D 26
Peaslake. *Surr* 1B 26
Peasley Cross. *Mers* 1H 83
Peasmarsh. *E Sus* 3C 28
Peasmarsh. *Som* 1G 13
Peasmarsh. *Surr* 1A 26
Peaston. *E Lot* 3H 129
Peastonbank. *E Lot* 3H 129
Peathill. *Abers* 2G 161
Peat Inn. *Fife* 3G 137
Peatling Magna. *Leics* 1C 62
Peatling Parva. *Leics* 2C 62
Peaton. *Arg* 1D 126
Peaton. *Shrp* 2H 59
Peats Corner. *Suff* 4D 66
Pebmarsh. *Essx* 2B 54
Pebworth. *Worc* 1G 49
Pecket Well. *W Yor* 2H 91
Peckforton. *Ches E* 5H 83
Peckham Bush. *Kent* 5A 40
Peckleton. *Leics* 5B 74
Pedair-ffordd. *Powy* 3D 70
Pedham. *Norf* 4F 79
Pedlinge. *Kent* 2F 29
Pedmore. *W Mid* 2D 60
Pedwell. *Som* 3H 21
Peebles. *Bord* 5F 129
Peel. *IOM* 3B 108
Peel. *Bord* 1G 119
Peel Common. *Hants* 2D 16
Peening Quarter. *Kent* 3C 28
Peggs Green. *Leics* 4B 74
Pegsdon. *C Beds* 2B 52
Pegswood. *Nmbd* 1F 115
Peinchorran. *High* 5E 155
Peinlich. *High* 3D 154
Pelaw. *Tyne* 3G 115
Pelcomb Bridge. *Pemb* 3D 42
Pelcomb Cross. *Pemb* 3D 42
Peldon. *Essx* 4C 54
Pelsall. *W Mid* 5E 73
Pelton. *Dur* 4F 115
Pelutho. *Cumb* 5C 112
Pelynt. *Corn* 3G 7
Pemberton. *Carm* 5F 45
Pembrey. *Carm* 5E 45
Pembridge. *Here* 5F 59
Pembroke. *Pemb* 4D 43
Pembroke Dock. *Pemb* 4D 42
Pembroke Ferry. *Pemb* 4D 43
Pembury. *Kent* 1H 27
Penallt. *Mon* 4A 48
Penally. *Pemb* 5F 43
Penalt. *Here* 3A 48
Penalum. *Pemb* 5F 43
Penare. *Corn* 4D 6
Penarth. *V Glam* 4E 33
Penbeagle. *Corn* 3C 4
Penberth. *Corn* 4B 4
Pen-bont Rhydybeddau. *Cdgn* 2F 57
Penbryn. *Cdgn* 5B 56
Pencader. *Carm* 2E 45
Pen-cae. *Cdgn* 5D 56
Pencaenewydd. *Gwyn* 1D 68
Pencaerau. *Neat* 3G 31
Pencaitland. *E Lot* 3H 129
Pencarnisiog. *IOA* 3C 80
Pencarreg. *Carm* 1F 45
Pencarrow. *Corn* 4B 10
Pencelli. *Powy* 3D 46
Pen-clawdd. *Swan* 3E 31
Pencoed. *B'end* 3C 32
Pencombe. *Here* 5H 59
Pencraig. *Here* 3A 48
Pencraig. *Powy* 3C 70
Pendeen. *Corn* 3A 4
Pendeford. *W Mid* 5D 72
Penderyn. *Rhon* 5C 46
Pendine. *Carm* 4G 43
Pendlebury. *G Man* 4F 91
Pendleton. *G Man* 1C 84
Pendleton. *Lanc* 1F 91
Pendock. *Worc* 2C 48
Pendoggett. *Corn* 5A 10
Pendomer. *Som* 1A 14
Pendoylan. *V Glam* 4D 32
Pendre. *B'end* 3C 32
Penegoes. *Powy* 5G 69
Penelewey. *Corn* 4C 6
Penffordd. *Pemb* 2E 43
Penffordd-Lâs. *Powy* 1A 58
Penfro. *Pemb* 4D 43
Pengam. *Cphy* 2E 33
Pengam. *Card* 4F 33
Penge. *G Lon* 3E 39
Pengelly. *Corn* 4A 10
Pengenffordd. *Powy* 2E 47
Pengorffwysfa. *IOA* 1D 80
Pengover Green. *Corn* 2G 7
Pengwern. *Den* 3C 82
Penhale. *Corn* 5D 5
(nr. Mullion)
Penhale. *Corn* 3D 6
(nr. St Austell)
Penhale Camp. *Corn* 3B 6
Penhallow. *Corn* 3B 6
Penhalvean. *Corn* 5B 6
Penhelig. *Gwyn* 1F 57
Penhill. *Swin* 3G 35
Penhow. *Newp* 2H 33
Penhurst. *E Sus* 4A 28
Peniarth. *Gwyn* 5F 69
Penicuik. *Midl* 3F 129
Peniel. *Carm* 3E 45
Penifiler. *High* 4D 155
Peninver. *Arg* 3B 122
Penisa'r Waun. *Gwyn* 4E 81
Penistone. *S Yor* 4C 92
Penketh. *Warr* 2H 83
Penkill. *S Ayr* 5B 116
Penkridge. *Staf* 4D 72
Penley. *Wrex* 2G 71
Penllech. *Gwyn* 2B 68
Penllergaer. *Swan* 3F 31
Pen-llyn. *IOA* 2C 80
Penmachno. *Cnwy* 5G 81
Penmaen. *Swan* 4E 31
Penmaenmawr. *Cnwy* 3G 81
Penmaenpool. *Gwyn* 4F 69
Penmaen Rhos. *Cnwy* 3A 82
Pen-marc. *V Glam* 5D 32
Penmark. *V Glam* 5D 32
Penmarth. *Corn* 5B 6
Penmon. *IOA* 2F 81
Penmorfa. *Gwyn* 1E 69
Penmynydd. *IOA* 3E 81
Penn. *Buck* 1A 38
Penn. *Dors* 3G 13
Penn. *W Mid* 1C 60
Pennal. *Gwyn* 5G 69
Pennan. *Abers* 2F 161
Pennant. *Cdgn* 4E 57
Pennant. *Den* 2C 70
Pennant. *Gwyn* 3B 70
Pennant. *Powy* 1A 58
Pennant Melangell. *Powy* 3C 70
Pennar. *Pemb* 4D 42
Pennard. *Swan* 4E 31
Pennerley. *Shrp* 1F 59
Pennington. *Cumb* 2B 96
Pennington. *G Man* 1A 84
Pennington. *Hants* 3B 16
Pennorth. *Powy* 3E 46
Penn Street. *Buck* 1A 38
Pennsylvania. *Devn* 3C 12
Pennsylvania. *S Glo* 4C 34
Penny Bridge. *Cumb* 1C 96
Pennycross. *Plym* 3A 8
Pennygate. *Norf* 3F 79
Pennyghael. *Arg* 1C 132
Penny Hill. *Linc* 3C 76
Pennylands. *Lanc* 4C 90
Pennymoor. *Devn* 1B 12
Pennyvenie. *E Ayr* 4D 117
Pennywell. *Tyne* 4G 115
Penparc. *Cdgn* 1C 44
Penparcau. *Cdgn* 2E 57
Penpedairheol. *Cphy* 2E 33
Penperlleni. *Mon* 5G 47
Penpillick. *Corn* 3E 7
Penpol. *Corn* 5C 6
Penpoll. *Corn* 3F 7
Penponds. *Corn* 3D 4
Penpont. *Corn* 5A 10
Penpont. *Dum* 5H 117
Penpont. *Powy* 3C 46
Penprysg. *B'end* 3C 32
Penquit. *Devn* 3C 8
Penrherber. *Carm* 1G 43
Penrhiw. *Pemb* 1C 44
Penrhiwceiber. *Rhon* 2D 32
Pen Rhiwfawr. *Neat* 4H 45
Penrhiw-llan. *Cdgn* 1D 44
Penrhiw-pal. *Cdgn* 1D 44
Penrhos. *Gwyn* 2C 68
Penrhos. *Here* 5F 59
Penrhos. *IOA* 2B 80
Penrhos. *Mon* 4H 47
Penrhos. *Powy* 4A 46
Penrhos Garnedd. *Gwyn* 3E 81
Penrhyn. *IOA* 1C 80
Penrhyn Bay. *Cnwy* 2H 81
Penrhyn-coch. *Cdgn* 2F 57
Penrhyndeudraeth. *Gwyn* 2F 69
Penrhyn Side. *Cnwy* 2H 81
Penrice. *Swan* 4D 31
Penrith. *Cumb* 2G 103
Penrose. *Corn* 1C 6
Penruddock. *Cumb* 2F 103
Penryn. *Corn* 5B 6
Pensarn. *Carm* 4E 45
Pen-sarn. *Gwyn* 3E 69
Pensax. *Worc* 4B 60
Pensby. *Mers* 2E 83
Penselwood. *Som* 3C 22
Pensford. *Bath* 5B 34
Pensham. *Worc* 1E 49
Penshaw. *Tyne* 4G 115
Penshurst. *Kent* 1G 27
Pensilva. *Corn* 2G 7
Pensnett. *W Mid* 2D 60
Penston. *E Lot* 2H 129
Penstone. *Devn* 2A 12
Pente-tafarn-y-fedw. *Cnwy* 4H 81
Pentewan. *Corn* 4E 6
Pentir. *Gwyn* 4E 81
Pentire. *Corn* 2B 6
Pentlepoir. *Pemb* 4F 43
Pentlow. *Essx* 1B 54
Pentney. *Norf* 4G 77
Penton Mewsey. *Hants* 2B 24
Pentraeth. *IOA* 3E 81
Pentre. *Powy* 1E 59
(nr. Church Stoke)
Pentre. *Powy* 2D 58
(nr. Kerry)
Pentre. *Powy* 2C 58
(nr. Mochdre)
Pentre. *Rhon* 2C 32
Pentre. *Shrp* 4F 71
Pentre. *Wrex* 2D 70
(nr. Llanfyllin)
Pentre. *Wrex* 1E 71
(nr. Rhosllanerchrugog)
Pentrebach. *Carm* 2B 46
Pentre-bach. *Cdgn* 1F 45
Pentrebach. *Mer T* 5D 46
Pentre-bach. *Powy* 2C 46
Pentrebach. *Swan* 5G 45
Pentre Berw. *IOA* 3D 80
Pentre-bont. *Cnwy* 5G 81
Pentrecagal. *Carm* 1D 44
Pentre-celyn. *Den* 5D 82
Pentre-clawdd. *Shrp* 2E 71
Pentreclwydau. *Neat* 5B 46
Pentre-cwrt. *Carm* 2D 45
Pentre Dolau Honddu. *Powy* 1C 46
Pentre-dwr. *Swan* 3F 31
Pentrefelin. *Carm* 3F 45
Pentrefelin. *Cdgn* 1G 45
Pentrefelin. *Cnwy* 3H 81
Pentrefelin. *Gwyn* 2E 69
Pentrefoelas. *Cnwy* 5A 82
Pentre Galar. *Pemb* 1F 43
Pentregat. *Cdgn* 5C 56
Pentre Gwenlais. *Carm* 4G 45
Pentre Gwynfryn. *Gwyn* 3E 69
Pentre Halkyn. *Flin* 3E 82
Pentre Hodre. *Shrp* 3F 59
Pentre-Llanrhaeadr. *Den* 4C 82
Pentre Llifior. *Powy* 1D 58
Pentrellwyn. *IOA* 2E 81
Pentre-llwyn-llwyd. *Powy* 5B 58
Pentre-llyn-cymmer. *Cnwy* 5B 82
Pentre Meyrick. *V Glam* 4C 32
Pentre-piod. *Gwyn* 2A 70
Pentre-poeth. *Newp* 3F 33
Pentre'r Beirdd. *Powy* 4D 70
Pentre'r-felin. *Powy* 2C 46
Pentre-ty-gwyn. *Carm* 2B 46
Pentre-uchaf. *Gwyn* 2C 68
Pentrich. *Derbs* 5A 86
Pentridge. *Dors* 1F 15
Pen-twyn. *Cphy* 5F 47
(nr. Oakdale)
Pentwyn. *Cphy* 5E 46
(nr. Rhymney)
Pentwyn. *Card* 3F 33
Pentyrch. *Card* 3E 32
Pentywyn. *Carm* 4G 43
Penuwch. *Cdgn* 4E 57
Penwithick. *Corn* 3E 7
Penwyllt. *Powy* 4B 46
Penybanc. *Carm* 4G 45
(nr. Ammanford)
Pen-y-banc. *Carm* 3G 45
(nr. Llandeilo)
Pen-y-bont. *Carm* 2H 43
Penybont. *Powy* 4D 58
(nr. Llandrindod Wells)
Pen-y-bont. *Powy* 3E 70
(nr. Llanfyllin)
Pen-y-Bont Ar Ogwr. *B'end* 3C 32
Penybontfawr. *Powy* 3C 70
Penybryn. *Cphy* 2E 33
Pen-y-bryn. *Pemb* 1B 44
Pen-y-bryn. *Wrex* 1E 71

Pen-y-cae. Powy	4B 46	Petsoe End. Mil	1G 51	Pilsgate. Pet	5H 75	Pittington. Dur	5G 115	Polbain. High	3E 1B
Penycae. Wrex	1E 71	Pett. E Sus	4C 28	Pilsley. Derbs	3G 85	Pitton. Swan	4D 30	Polbathic. Corn	3H 7
Pen-y-cae-mawr. Mon	2H 33	Pettaugh. Suff	5D 66	(nr. Bakewell)		Pitton. High	3H 23	Polbeth. W Lot	3D 12
Penycaerau. Gwyn	3A 68	Pett Bottom. Kent	5F 41	Pilsley. Derbs	4B 86	Pittswood. Kent	1H 27	Polbrock. Corn	2E
Pen-y-cefn. Flin	3D 82	Petteridge. Kent	1A 28	(nr. Clay Cross)		Pittulie. Abers	2G 161	Polchar. High	3C 15
Pen-y-clawdd. Mon	5H 47	Pettinain. S Lan	5C 128	Pilson Green. Norf	4F 79	Pittville. Glos	3E 49	Polebrook. Nptn	2H 63
Pen-y-coedcae. Rhon	3D 32	Pettistree. Suff	5E 67	Piltdown. E Sus	3F 27	Pitversie. Per	2D 136	Pole Elm. Worc	1D 48
Penycwm. Pemb	2C 42	Petton. Devn	4D 20	Pilton. Edin	2F 129	Pityme. Corn	1D 6	Polegate. E Sus	5G 27
Pen-y-Darren. Mer T	5D 46	Petton. Shrp	3G 71	Pilton. Nptn	2H 63	Pity Me. Dur	5F 115	Pole Moor. W Yor	3A 92
Pen-y-fai. B'end	3B 32	Petts Wood. G Lon	4F 39	Pilton. Rut	5G 75	Pixey Green. Suff	3E 67	Poles. High	4E 165
Penyffordd. Flin	4F 83	Pettycur. Fife	1F 129	Pilton. Som	2A 22	Pixley. Here	2B 48	Polesworth. Warw	5G 73
(nr. Mold)		Pettywell. Norf	3C 78	Pilton Green. Swan	4D 30	Place Newton. N Yor	2C 100	Polglass. High	3E 163
Pen-y-ffordd. Flin	2D 82	Petworth. W Sus	3A 26	Pimperne. Dors	2E 15	Plaidy. Abers	3E 161	Polgooth. Corn	3D 6
(nr. Prestatyn)		Pevensey. E Sus	5A 28	Pinchbeck. Linc	3B 76	Plaidy. Corn	3G 7	Poling. W Sus	5B 26
Penyffridd. Gwyn	5E 81	Pevensey Bay. E Sus	5A 28	Pinchbeck Bars. Linc	3A 76	Plain Dealings. Pemb	3E 43	Poling Corner. W Sus	5B 26
Pen-y-garn. Cdgn	2F 57	Pewsey. Wilts	5G 35	Pinchbeck West. Linc	3B 76	Plains. N Lan	3A 128	Polio. High	1B 158
Pen-y-garnedd. IOA	3E 81	Pheasants Hill. Buck	3F 37	Pinfold. Lanc	3B 90	Plainsfield. Som	3E 21	Polkerris. Corn	3E 7
Penygarnedd. Powy	3D 70	Philadelphia. Tyne	4G 115	Pinford End. Suff	5H 65	Plaish. Shrp	1H 59	Polla. High	3D 166
Pen-y-graig. Gwyn	2B 68	Philham. Devn	4C 18	Pinged. Carm	5E 45	Plaistow. Here	2B 48	Pollard Street. Norf	2F 79
Penygraig. Rhon	2C 32	Philiphaugh. Bord	2G 119	Pinhoe. Devn	3C 12	Plaistow. W Sus	2B 26	Pollicott. Buck	4F 51
Penygraigwen. IOA	2D 80	Phillack. Corn	3C 4	Pinkerton. E Lot	2D 130	Plaitford. Wilts	1A 16	Pollington. E Yor	3G 93
Pen-y-groes. Carm	4F 45	Philleigh. Corn	5C 6	Pinkneys Green. Wind	3G 37	Plas Llwyd. Cnwy	3B 82	Polloch. High	2B 140
Penygroes. Gwyn	5D 80	Philpstoun. W Lot	2D 128	Pinley. W Mid	3A 62	Plastow Green. Hants	5D 36	Pollok. Glas	3G 127
Penygroes. Pemb	1F 43	Phocle Green. Here	3B 48	Pinley Green. Warw	4G 61	Plas yn Cefn. Den	3C 82	Pollokshaws. Glas	3G 127
Pen-y-Mynydd. Carm	5E 45	Phoenix Green. Hants	1F 25	Pinmill. Suff	2F 55	Platt. Kent	5H 39	Pollokshields. Glas	3G 127
Penymynydd. Flin	4F 83	Pibsbury. Som	4H 21	Pinmore. S Ayr	5B 116	Platt Bridge. G Man	4E 90	Polmaily. High	5G 157
Penyrheol. Cphy	3E 33	Pibwrlwyd. Carm	4E 45	Pinner. G Lon	2C 38	Platt Lane. Shrp	2H 71	Polmassick. Corn	4D 6
Pen-yr-heol. Mon	4H 47	Pica. Cumb	2B 102	Pins Green. Worc	1C 48	Platts Common. S Yor	4D 92	Polmont. Falk	2C 128
Penyrheol. Swan	3E 31	Piccadilly. Warw	1G 61	Pinsley Green. Ches E	1H 71	Platt's Heath. Kent	5C 40	Polnessan. E Ayr	3D 116
Pen-y-Heolgerrig. Mer T	5D 46	Piccadilly Corner. Norf	2E 67	Pinvin. Worc	1E 49	Platt, The. E Sus	2G 27	Polnish. High	5F 147
Penysarn. IOA	1D 80	Piccotts End. Herts	5A 52	Pinwherry. S Ayr	1G 109	Plawsworth. Dur	5F 115	Polperro. Corn	3G 7
Pen-y-stryt. Den	5E 82	Pickering. N Yor	1B 100	Pinxton. Derbs	5B 86	Plaxtol. Kent	5H 39	Polruan. Corn	3F 7
Penywaun. Rhon	5C 46	Picket Piece. Hants	2B 24	Pipe and Lyde. Here	1A 48	Playden. E Sus	3D 28	Polscoe. Corn	2F 7
Penzance. Corn	3B 4	Picket Post. Hants	2G 15	Pipe Aston. Here	3G 59	Playford. Suff	1F 55	Polsham. Som	2A 22
Peopleton. Worc	5D 60	Pickford. W Mid	2G 61	Pipe Gate. Shrp	1B 72	Play Hatch. Oxon	4F 37	Polskeoch. Dum	4F 117
Peover Heath. Ches E	3B 84	Pickhill. N Yor	1F 99	Pipehill. Staf	5E 73	Playing Place. Corn	4C 6	Polstead. Suff	2C 54
Peper Harow. Surr	1A 26	Picklenash. Glos	3C 48	Piperhill. High	3C 158	Playley Green. Glos	2C 48	Polstead Heath. Suff	1C 54
Peplow. Shrp	3A 72	Picklescott. Shrp	1G 59	Pipe Ridware. Staf	4E 73	Plealey. Shrp	5G 71	Poltesco. Corn	5E 5
Pepper Arden. N Yor	4F 105	Pickletillem. Fife	1G 137	Pipers Pool. Corn	4C 10	Plean. Stir	1B 128	Poltimore. Devn	3C 12
Perceton. N Ayr	5E 127	Pickmere. Ches E	3A 84	Pipewell. Nptn	2F 63	Pleasington. Bkbn	2E 91	Polton. Midl	3G 129
Percyhorner. Abers	2G 161	Pickstock. Telf	3B 72	Pippacott. Devn	3F 19	Pleasley. Derbs	4C 86	Polwarth. Bord	4D 130
Perham Down. Wilts	2A 24	Pickwell. Devn	2E 19	Pipton. Powy	2E 47	Pledgdon Green. Essx	3F 53	Polyphant. Corn	4C 10
Periton. Som	2C 20	Pickwell. Leics	4E 75	Pirbright. Surr	5A 38	Plenmeller. Nmbd	3A 114	Polzeath. Corn	1D 6
Perkinsville. Dur	4F 115	Pickworth. Linc	2H 75	Pirnmill. N Ayr	5G 125	Pleshey. Essx	4G 53	Ponde. Powy	2E 46
Perlethorpe. Notts	3D 86	Pickworth. Rut	4G 75	Pirton. Herts	2B 52	Plockton. High	5H 155	Pondersbridge. Cambs	1B 64
Perranarworthal. Corn	5B 6	Picton. Ches W	3G 83	Pirton. Worc	1D 49	Plocrapol. W Isl	8D 171	Ponders End. G Lon	1E 39
Perranporth. Corn	3B 6	Picton. Flin	2D 82	Pisgah. Stir	3G 135	Ploughfield. Here	1G 47	Pond Street. Essx	2E 53
Perranuthnoe. Corn	4C 4	Picton. N Yor	4B 106	Pishill. Oxon	3F 37	Plowden. Shrp	2F 59	Pondtail. Hants	1G 25
Perranwell. Corn	5B 6	Pict's Hill. Som	4H 21	Pistyll. Gwyn	1C 68	Ploxgreen. Shrp	5F 71	Ponsanooth. Corn	5B 6
Perranzabuloe. Corn	3B 6	Piddington. Buck	5F 27	Pitagowan. Per	2F 143	Pluckley. Kent	1D 28	Ponsongath. Corn	5E 5
Perrott's Brook. Glos	5F 49	Piddington. Nptn	2G 37	Pitcairn. Per	3F 143	Plucks Gutter. Kent	4G 41	Ponsworthy. Devn	5H 11
Perry. W Mid	1E 61	Piddington. Oxon	4E 51	Pitcairngreen. Per	1C 136	Plumbland. Cumb	1C 102	Pontamman. Carm	4G 45
Perry Barr. W Mid	1E 61	Piddlehinton. Dors	3C 14	Pitcalnie. High	1C 158	Plumgarths. Cumb	5F 103	Pontantwn. Carm	4E 45
Perry Crofts. Staf	5G 73	Piddletrenthide. Dors	2C 14	Pitcaple. Abers	1E 152	Plumley. Ches E	3B 84	Pontardawe. Neat	5H 45
Perry Green. Essx	3B 54	Pidley. Cambs	3C 64	Pitchcombe. Glos	5D 48	Plummers Plain. W Sus	3D 26	Pontarddulais. Swan	5F 45
Perry Green. Herts	4E 53	Pidney. Dors	2C 14	Pitchcott. Buck	3F 51	Plumpton. Cumb	1F 103	Pontarfynach. Cdgn	3G 57
Perry Green. Wilts	3E 35	Pie Corner. Here	4A 60	Pitchford. Shrp	5H 71	Plumpton. E Sus	4E 27	Pont-ar-gothi. Carm	3F 45
Perry Street. Kent	3H 39	Piercebridge. Darl	3F 105	Pitch Green. Buck	5F 51	Plumpton. Nptn	1D 50	Pont ar Hydfer. Powy	3B 46
Perry Street. Som	2G 13	Pierowall. Orkn	3D 172	Pitch Place. Surr	5A 38	Plumpton Foot. Cumb	1F 103	Pontarllechau. Carm	3H 45
Perrywood. Kent	5E 41	Pigdon. Nmbd	1E 115	Pitcombe. Som	3B 22	Plumpton Green. E Sus	4E 27	Pontarsais. Carm	3E 45
Pershall. Staf	3C 72	Pightley. Som	3F 21	Pitcur. Per	5B 144	Plumpton Head. Cumb	1G 103	Pontblyddyn. Flin	4E 83
Pershore. Worc	1E 49	Pikehall. Derbs	5F 85	Pitfichie. Abers	2D 152	Plumstead. G Lon	3F 39	Pontbren Llwyd. Rhon	5C 46
Pertenhall. Bed	4H 63	Pikeshill. Hants	2A 16	Pitgrudy. High	4E 165	Plumstead. Norf	2D 78	Pont Cyfyng. Cnwy	5G 81
Perth. Per	1D 136	Pilford. Dors	2F 15	Pitkennedy. Ang	3E 145	Plumtree. Notts	2D 74	Pontdolgoch. Powy	1C 58
Perthy. Shrp	2F 71	Pilgrims Hatch. Essx	1G 39	Pitlessie. Fife	3F 137	Plumtree Park. Notts	2D 74	**Pontefract**. W Yor	2E 93
Perton. Staf	1C 60	Pilham. Linc	1F 87	Pitlochry. Per	3G 143	Plungar. Leics	2E 75	**Ponteland**. Nmbd	2E 115
Pertwood. Wilts	3D 23	Pill. N Som	4A 34	Pitmachie. Abers	1D 152	Plush. Dors	2C 14	Ponterwyd. Cdgn	2G 57
Peterborough. Pet	1A 64	Pillaton. Corn	2H 7	Pitmaduthy. High	1B 158	Plushabridge. Corn	5D 10	Pontesbury. Shrp	5G 71
Peterburn. High	5B 162	Pillaton. Staf	4D 72	Pitmedden. Abers	1F 153	Plwmp. Cdgn	5C 56	Pontesford. Shrp	5G 71
Peterchurch. Here	2G 47	Pillerton Hersey. Warw	1A 50	Pitminster. Som	1F 13	Plymouth. Plym	3A 8	Pontfadog. Wrex	2E 71
Petercultar. Aber	3F 153	Pillerton Priors. Warw	1A 50	Pitnacree. Per	3G 143	Plympton. Plym	3B 8	Pontfaen. Pemb	1E 43
Peterhead. Abers	4H 161	Pilleth. Powy	4E 59	Pitney. Som	4H 21	Plymstock. Plym	3B 8	Pont-faen. Powy	2C 46
Peterlee. Dur	5H 115	Pilley. Hants	3B 16	Pitroddie. Per	1E 136	Plymtree. Devn	2D 12	Pont-Faen. Shrp	2E 71
Petersfield. Hants	4F 25	Pilley. S Yor	4D 92	Pitscottie. Fife	2G 137	Pockley. N Yor	1A 100	Pontgarreg. Cdgn	5C 56
Petersfinger. Wilts	4G 23	Pillgwenlly. Newp	3G 33	Pitsea. Essx	2B 40	Pocklington. E Yor	5C 100	Pont-Henri. Carm	5E 45
Peter's Green. Herts	4B 52	Pilling. Lanc	5D 96	Pitsford. Nptn	4E 63	Pode Hole. Linc	3B 76	Ponthir. Torf	2G 33
Peters Marland. Devn	1E 11	Pilling Lane. Lanc	5C 96	Pitsford Hill. Som	3E 20	Podimore. Som	4A 22	Ponthirwaun. Cdgn	1C 44
Peterstone Wentlooge. Newp	3F 33	Pillowell. Glos	5B 48	Pitsmoor. S Yor	2A 86	Podington. Bed	4G 63	Pont-iets. Carm	5E 45
Peterston-super-Ely. V Glam	4D 32	Pill, The. Mon	3H 33	Pitstone. Buck	4H 51	Podmore. Staf	2B 72	Pontllanfraith. Cphy	2E 33
Peterstow. Here	3A 48	Pilning. S Glo	3A 34	Pitt. Hants	4C 24	Poffley End. Oxon	4B 50	Pontlliw. Swan	5G 45
Peter Tavy. Devn	5F 11	Pilsbury. Derbs	4F 85	Pitt Court. Glos	2C 34	Point Clear. Essx	4D 54	Pont Llogel. Powy	4C 70
Petham. Kent	5F 41	Pilsdon. Dors	3H 13	Pittentrail. High	3E 164	Pointon. Linc	2A 76	Pontlyfni. Gwyn	5D 80
Petherwin Gate. Corn	4C 10	Pilsgate. Pet		Pittenweem. Fife	3H 137	Pokesdown. Bour	3G 15	Pontlottyn. Cphy	5E 46
Petrockstowe. Devn	2F 11					Polbae. Dum	2H 109	Pontneddfechan. Neat	5C 46

Rescobie—Rook's Nest

Rescobie. *Ang* 3E 145
Rescorla. *Corn* 3E 7
(nr. Rosevean)
Rescorla. *Corn* 4D 6
(nr. St Ewe)
Resipole. *High* 2B 140
Resolfen. *Neat* 5B 46
Resolis. *High* 2A 158
Resolven. *Neat* 5B 46
Rest and be thankful. *Arg* 3B 134
Reston. *Bord* 3E 131
Restrop. *Wilts* 3F 35
Retford. *Notts* 2E 86
Retire. *Corn* 2E 6
Rettendon. *Essx* 1B 40
Revesby. *Linc* 4C 88
Rew. *Devn* 5D 8
Rewe. *Devn* 3C 12
Rew Street. *IOW* 3C 16
Rexon. *Devn* 4E 11
Reybridge. *Wilts* 5E 35
Reydon. *Suff* 3H 67
Reymerston. *Norf* 5C 78
Reynalton. *Pemb* 4E 43
Reynoldston. *Swan* 4D 31
Rezare. *Corn* 5D 10
Rhadyr. *Mon* 5G 47
Rhaeadr Gwy. *Powy* 4B 58
Rhandirmwyn. *Carm* 1A 46
Rhayader. *Powy* 4B 58
Rheindown. *High* 4H 157
Rhemore. *High* 3G 139
Rhenetra. *High* 3D 154
Rhewl. *Den* 1D 70
(nr. Llangollen)
Rhewl. *Den* 4D 82
(nr. Ruthin)
Rhewl. *Shrp* 2F 71
Rhewl-Mostyn. *Flin* 3D 82
Rhian. *High* 2C 164
Rhian Breck. *High* 3C 164
Rhicarn. *High* 1E 163
Rhiconich. *High* 3C 166
Rhicullen. *High* 1A 158
Rhidorroch. *High* 4F 163
Rhifail. *High* 4H 167
Rhigos. *Rhon* 5C 46
Rhilochan. *High* 3E 165
Rhiroy. *High* 5F 163
Rhitongue. *High* 3G 167
Rhiw. *Gwyn* 3B 68
Rhiwabon. *Wrex* 1F 71
Rhiwbina. *Card* 3E 33
Rhiwbryfdir. *Gwyn* 1F 69
Rhiwderin. *Newp* 3F 33
Rhiwlas. *Gwyn* 2B 70
(nr. Bala)
Rhiwlas. *Gwyn* 4E 81
(nr. Bangor)
Rhiwlas. *Powy* 2D 70
Rhodes. *G Man* 4G 91
Rhodesia. *Notts* 2C 86
Rhodes Minnis. *Kent* 1F 29
Rhodiad-y-Brenin. *Pemb* 2B 42
Rhondda. *Rhon* 2C 32
Rhonehouse. *Dum* 4E 111
Rhoose. *V Glam* 5D 32
Rhos. *Carm* 2D 45
Rhos. *Neat* 5H 45
Rhosaman. *Carm* 4H 45
Rhoscefnhir. *IOA* 3E 81
Rhoscolyn. *IOA* 3B 80
Rhos Common. *Powy* 4E 71
Rhoscrowther. *Pemb* 4D 42
Rhos-ddu. *Gwyn* 2B 68
Rhosdylluan. *Gwyn* 3A 70
Rhosesmor. *Flin* 4E 82
Rhos-fawr. *Gwyn* 2C 68
Rhosgadfan. *Gwyn* 5E 81
Rhosgoch. *IOA* 2D 80
Rhosgoch. *Powy* 1E 47
Rhos Haminiog. *Cdgn* 4E 57
Rhos-hill. *Pemb* 1B 44
Rhoshirwaun. *Gwyn* 3A 68
Rhoslan. *Gwyn* 1D 69
Rhoslefain. *Gwyn* 5E 69
Rhosllanerchrugog. *Wrex* 1E 71
Rhos Lligwy. *IOA* 2D 81
Rhosmaen. *Carm* 3G 45
Rhosmeirch. *IOA* 3D 80
Rhosneigr. *IOA* 3C 80
Rhos-on-Sea. *Cnwy* 2H 81
Rhossili. *Swan* 4D 30
Rhosson. *Pemb* 2B 42
Rhos, The. *Pemb* 3E 43
Rhostrenwfa. *IOA* 3D 80
Rhostryfan. *Gwyn* 5D 81
Rhostyllen. *Wrex* 1F 71
Rhoswiel. *Shrp* 2E 71
Rhosybol. *IOA* 2D 80
Rhos-y-brithdir. *Powy* 3D 70
Rhos-y-garth. *Cdgn* 3F 57
Rhos-y-gwaliau. *Gwyn* 2B 70
Rhos-y-llan. *Gwyn* 2B 68
Rhos-y-meirch. *Powy* 4E 59
Rhu. *Arg* 1D 126
Rhuallt. *Den* 3C 82
Rhubadach. *Arg* 2B 126
Rhubha Stoer. *High* 1E 163
Rhuddall Heath. *Ches W* 4H 83
Rhuddlan. *Cdgn* 1E 45
Rhuddlan. *Den* 3C 82
Rhue. *High* 4E 163
Rhulen. *Powy* 1E 47
Rhunahaorine. *Arg* 5F 125
Rhuthun. *Den* 5D 82
Rhuvoult. *High* 3C 166
Rhyd. *Gwyn* 1F 69
Rhydaman. *Carm* 4G 45
Rhydargaeau. *Carm* 3E 45
Rhydcymerau. *Carm* 2F 45
Rhydd. *Worc* 1D 48
Rhyd-Ddu. *Gwyn* 5E 81
Rhydding. *Neat* 3G 31
Rhydfudr. *Cdgn* 4E 57
Rhydlanfair. *Cnwy* 5H 81
Rhydlewis. *Cdgn* 1D 44
Rhydlios. *Gwyn* 2A 68
Rhydlydan. *Cnwy* 5A 82
Rhyd-meirionydd. *Cdgn* 2F 57
Rhydowen. *Cdgn* 1E 45
Rhyd-Rosser. *Cdgn* 4E 57
Rhydspence. *Powy* 1F 47
Rhydtalog. *Flin* 5E 83
Rhyd-uchaf. *Gwyn* 2B 70
Rhydwyn. *IOA* 2C 80
Rhyd-y-clafdy. *Gwyn* 2C 68
Rhydycroesau. *Shrp* 2E 71
Rhydyfelin. *Cdgn* 3E 57
Rhydyfelin. *Rhon* 3E 32
Rhyd-y-foel. *Cnwy* 3B 82
Rhyd-y-fro. *Neat* 5H 45
Rhydymain. *Gwyn* 3H 69
Rhyd-y-meirch. *Mon* 5G 47
Rhyd-y-meudwy. *Den* 5D 82
Rhydymwyn. *Flin* 4E 82
Rhyd-yr-onen. *Gwyn* 5F 69
Rhyd-y-sarn. *Gwyn* 1F 69
Rhyl. *Den* 2C 82
Rhymney. *Cphy* 5E 46
Rhymni. *Cphy* 5E 46
Rhynd. *Per* 1D 136
Rhynie. *Abers* 1B 152
Ribbesford. *Worc* 3B 60
Ribbleton. *Lanc* 1D 90
Ribby. *Lanc* 1C 90
Ribchester. *Lanc* 1E 91
Riber. *Derbs* 5H 85
Ribigill. *High* 3F 167
Riby. *Linc* 4E 95
Riccall. *N Yor* 1G 93
Riccarton. *E Ayr* 1D 116
Richards Castle. *Here* 4G 59
Richborough Port. *Kent* 4H 41
Richings Park. *Buck* 3B 38
Richmond. *G Lon* 3C 38
Richmond. *N Yor* 4E 105
Rickarton. *Abers* 5F 153
Rickerby. *Cumb* 4F 113
Rickerscote. *Staf* 3D 72
Rickford. *N Som* 1H 21
Rickham. *Devn* 5D 8
Rickinghall. *Suff* 3C 66
Rickleton. *Tyne* 4F 115
Rickling. *Essx* 2E 53
Rickling Green. *Essx* 3F 53
Rickmansworth. *Herts* 1B 38
Riddings. *Derbs* 5B 86
Riddlecombe. *Devn* 1G 11
Riddlesden. *W Yor* 5C 98
Ridge. *Dors* 4E 15
Ridge. *Herts* 5C 52
Ridge. *Wilts* 3E 23
Ridgebourne. *Powy* 4C 58
Ridge Lane. *Warw* 1G 61
Ridgeway. *Derbs* 5A 86
(nr. Alfreton)
Ridgeway. *Derbs* 2B 86
(nr. Sheffield)
Ridgeway. *Staf* 5C 84
Ridgeway Cross. *Here* 1C 48
Ridgeway Moor. *Derbs* 2B 86
Ridgewell. *Essx* 1H 53
Ridgewood. *E Sus* 3F 27
Ridgmont. *C Beds* 2H 51
Ridgwardine. *Shrp* 2A 72
Riding Mill. *Nmbd* 3D 114
Ridley. *Kent* 4H 39
Ridley. *Nmbd* 3A 114
Ridlington. *Norf* 2F 79
Ridlington. *Rut* 5F 75
Ridsdale. *Nmbd* 1C 114
Riemore Lodge. *Per* 4H 143
Rievaulx. *N Yor* 1H 99
Rift House. *Hart* 1B 106
Rigg. *Dum* 3D 112
Riggend. *N Lan* 2A 128
Rigsby. *Linc* 3D 88
Rigside. *S Lan* 1A 118
Riley Green. *Lanc* 2E 90
Rileyhill. *Staf* 4F 73
Rilla Mill. *Corn* 5C 10
Rillington. *N Yor* 2C 100
Rimington. *Lanc* 5H 97
Rimpton. *Som* 4B 22
Rimsdale. *High* 4H 167
Rimswell. *E Yor* 2G 95
Ringasta. *Shet* 10E 173
Ringford. *Dum* 4D 111
Ringing Hill. *Leics* 4B 74
Ringinglow. *S Yor* 2G 85
Ringland. *Norf* 4D 78
Ringlestone. *Kent* 5C 40
Ringmer. *E Sus* 4F 27
Ringmore. *Devn* 4C 8
(nr. Kingsbridge)
Ringmore. *Devn* 5C 12
(nr. Teignmouth)
Ring o' Bells. *Lanc* 3C 90
Ring's End. *Cambs* 5C 76
Ringsfield. *Suff* 2G 67
Ringsfield Corner. *Suff* 2G 67
Ringshall. *Buck* 4H 51
Ringshall. *Suff* 5C 66
Ringshall Stocks. *Suff* 5C 66
Ringstead. *Norf* 1G 77
Ringstead. *Nptn* 3G 63
Ringwood. *Hants* 2G 15
Ringwould. *Kent* 1H 29
Rinmore. *Abers* 2B 152
Rinnigill. *Orkn* 8C 172
Rinsey. *Corn* 4C 4
Riof. *W Isl* 4D 171
Ripe. *E Sus* 4G 27
Ripley. *Derbs* 1B 74
Ripley. *Hants* 3G 15
Ripley. *N Yor* 3E 99
Ripley. *Surr* 5B 38
Riplingham. *E Yor* 1C 94
Riplington. *Hants* 4E 25
Ripon. *N Yor* 2F 99
Rippingale. *Linc* 3H 75
Ripple. *Kent* 1H 29
Ripple. *Worc* 2D 48
Ripponden. *W Yor* 3A 92
Rireavach. *High* 4E 163
Risabus. *Arg* 5B 124
Risbury. *Here* 5H 59
Risby. *E Yor* 1D 94
Risby. *N Lin* 3C 94
Risby. *Suff* 4G 65
Risca. *Cphy* 2F 33
Rise. *E Yor* 5F 101
Riseden. *E Sus* 2H 27
Riseden. *Kent* 2B 28
Rise End. *Derbs* 5G 85
Risegate. *Linc* 2B 76
Riseholme. *Linc* 3G 87
Riseley. *Bed* 4H 63
Riseley. *Wok* 5F 37
Rishangles. *Suff* 4D 66
Rishton. *Lanc* 1F 91
Rishworth. *W Yor* 3A 92
Risley. *Derbs* 2B 74
Risley. *Warr* 1A 84
Risplith. *N Yor* 3E 99
Rispond. *High* 2E 167
Rivar. *Wilts* 5B 36
Rivenhall. *Essx* 4B 54
Rivenhall End. *Essx* 4B 54
River. *Kent* 1G 29
River. *W Sus* 3A 26
River Bank. *Cambs* 4E 65
Riverhead. *Kent* 5G 39
Rivington. *Lanc* 3E 91
Roach Bridge. *Lanc* 2D 90
Roachill. *Devn* 4B 20
Roade. *Nptn* 5E 63
Road Green. *Norf* 1E 67
Roadhead. *Cumb* 2G 113
Roadmeetings. *S Lan* 5B 128
Roadside. *High* 2D 168
Roadside of Catterline. *Abers* 1H 145
Roadside of Kinneff. *Abers* 1H 145
Roadwater. *Som* 3D 20
Road Weedon. *Nptn* 5D 62
Roag. *High* 4B 154
Roa Island. *Cumb* 3B 96
Roath. *Card* 4E 33
Roberton. *Bord* 3G 119
Roberton. *S Lan* 2B 118
Robertsbridge. *E Sus* 3B 28
Robertstown. *Mor* 4G 159
Robertstown. *Rhon* 5C 46
Roberttown. *W Yor* 2B 92
Robeston Back. *Pemb* 3E 43
Robeston Wathen. *Pemb* 3E 43
Robeston West. *Pemb* 4C 42
Robin Hood. *Lanc* 3D 90
Robin Hood. *W Yor* 2D 92
Robin Hood Airport Doncaster Sheffield.
S Yor 1D 86
Robinhood End. *Essx* 2H 53
Robin Hood's Bay. *N Yor* 4G 107
Roborough. *Devn* 1F 11
(nr. Great Torrington)
Roborough. *Devn* 2B 8
(nr. Plymouth)
Rob Roy's House. *Arg* 2A 134
Roby Mill. *Lanc* 4D 90
Rocester. *Staf* 2F 73
Roch. *Pemb* 2C 42
Rochdale. *G Man* 3G 91
Roche. *Corn* 2D 6
Rochester. *Medw* 4B 40
Rochester. *Nmbd* 5C 120
Rochford. *Essx* 1C 40
Rock. *Corn* 1D 6
Rock. *Nmbd* 2G 121
Rock. *W Sus* 4C 26
Rock. *Worc* 3B 60
Rockbeare. *Devn* 3D 12
Rockbourne. *Hants* 1G 15
Rockcliffe. *Cumb* 3E 113
Rockcliffe. *Dum* 4F 111
Rockcliffe Cross. *Cumb* 3E 113
Rock Ferry. *Mers* 2F 83
Rockfield. *High* 5G 165
Rockfield. *Mon* 4H 47
Rockford. *Hants* 2G 15
Rockgreen. *Shrp* 3H 59
Rockhampton. *S Glo* 2B 34
Rockhead. *Corn* 4A 10
Rockingham. *Nptn* 1F 63
Rockland All Saints. *Norf* 1B 66
Rockland St Mary. *Norf* 5F 79
Rockland St Peter. *Norf* 1B 66
Rockley. *Wilts* 4G 35
Rockwell End. *Buck* 3F 37
Rockwell Green. *Som* 1E 13
Rodborough. *Glos* 5D 48
Rodbourne. *Wilts* 3E 35
Rodd. *Here* 4F 59
Roddam. *Nmbd* 2E 121
Rodden. *Dors* 4B 14
Roddenloft. *E Ayr* 2D 117
Roddymoor. *Dur* 1E 105
Rode. *Som* 1D 22
Rodeheath. *Ches E* 4C 84
(nr. Congleton)
Rode Heath. *Ches E* 5C 84
(nr. Kidsgrove)
Rodel. *W Isl* 9C 171
Roden. *Telf* 4H 71
Rodhuish. *Som* 3D 20
Rodington. *Telf* 4H 71
Rodington Heath. *Telf* 4H 71
Rodley. *Glos* 4C 48
Rodmarton. *Glos* 2E 35
Rodmell. *E Sus* 5F 27
Rodmersham. *Kent* 4D 40
Rodmersham Green. *Kent* 4D 40
Rodney Stoke. *Som* 2H 21
Rodsley. *Derbs* 1G 73
Rodway. *Som* 2F 21
Rodway. *Telf* 4A 72
Rodwell. *Dors* 5B 14
Roecliffe. *N Yor* 3F 99
Roe Green. *Herts* 2D 52
Roehampton. *G Lon* 3D 38
Roffey. *W Sus* 2C 26
Rogart. *High* 3E 165
Rogate. *W Sus* 4G 25
Roger Ground. *Cumb* 5E 103
Rogerstone. *Newp* 3F 33
Roghadal. *W Isl* 9C 171
Rogiet. *Mon* 3H 33
Rogue's Alley. *Cambs* 5C 76
Roke. *Oxon* 2E 37
Rokemarsh. *Oxon* 2E 36
Roker. *Tyne* 4H 115
Rollesby. *Norf* 4G 79
Rolleston. *Leics* 5E 75
Rolleston. *Notts* 5E 87
Rolleston on Dove. *Staf* 3G 73
Rolston. *E Yor* 5G 101
Rolvenden. *Kent* 2C 28
Rolvenden Layne. *Kent* 2C 28
Romaldkirk. *Dur* 2C 104
Roman Bank. *Shrp* 1H 59
Romanby. *N Yor* 5A 106
Roman Camp. *W Lot* 2D 129
Romannobridge. *Bord* 5E 129
Romansleigh. *Devn* 4H 19
Romers Common. *Worc* 4H 59
Romesdal. *High* 3D 154
Romford. *Dors* 2F 15
Romford. *G Lon* 2G 39
Romiley. *G Man* 1D 84
Romsey. *Hants* 4B 24
Romsley. *Shrp* 2B 60
Romsley. *Worc* 3D 60
Ronague. *IOM* 4B 108
Rookby. *Cumb* 3B 104
Rookhope. *Dur* 5C 114
Rooking. *Cumb* 3F 103
Rookley. *IOW* 4D 16
Rooks Bridge. *Som* 1G 21
Rooksey Green. *Suff* 5B 66
Rook's Nest. *Som* 3D 20

Rookwood—St Erme

Rookwood. *W Sus* 3F **17**
Roos. *E Yor* 1F **95**
Roosebeck. *Cumb* 3B **96**
Roosecote. *Cumb* 3B **96**
Rootfield. *High* 3H **157**
Rootham's Green. *Bed* 5A **64**
Rootpark. *S Lan* 4C **128**
Ropley. *Hants* 3E **25**
Ropley Dean. *Hants* 3E **25**
Ropsley. *Linc* 2G **75**
Rora. *Abers* 3H **161**
Rorandle. *Abers* 2D **152**
Rorrington. *Shrp* 5F **71**
Rose. *Corn* 3B **6**
Roseacre. *Lanc* 1C **90**
Rose Ash. *Devn* 4A **20**
Rosebank. *S Lan* 5B **128**
Rosebush. *Pemb* 2E **43**
Rosedale Abbey. *N Yor* 5E **107**
Roseden. *Nmbd* 2E **121**
Rose Green. *Essx* 3C **54**
Rose Green. *Suff* 1C **54**
Rosehall. *High* 3B **164**
Rosehearty. *Abers* 2G **161**
Rose Hill. *E Sus* 4F **27**
Rose Hill. *Lanc* 1G **91**
Rosehill. *Shrp* 2A **72**
(nr. Market Drayton)
Rosehill. *Shrp* 4G **71**
(nr. Shrewsbury)
Roseisle. *Mor* 2F **159**
Rosemarket. *Pemb* 4D **42**
Rosemarkie. *High* 3B **158**
Rosemary Lane. *Devn* 1E **13**
Rosemount. *Per* 4A **144**
Rosenannon. *Corn* 2D **6**
Roser's Cross. *E Sus* 3G **27**
Rosevean. *Corn* 3E **6**
Rosewell. *Midl* 3F **129**
Roseworth. *Stoc T* 2B **106**
Roseworthy. *Corn* 3D **4**
Rosgill. *Cumb* 3G **103**
Roshven. *High* 1B **140**
Roskhill. *High* 4B **154**
Roskorwell. *Corn* 4E **5**
Rosley. *Cumb* 5E **112**
Roslin. *Midl* 3F **129**
Rosliston. *Derbs* 4G **73**
Rosneath. *Arg* 1D **126**
Ross. *Dum* 5D **110**
Ross. *Nmbd* 1F **121**
Ross. *Per* 1G **135**
Ross. *Bord* 3F **131**
Rossendale. *Lanc* 2F **91**
Rossett. *Wrex* 5F **83**
Rossington. *S Yor* 1D **86**
Rosskeen. *High* 2A **158**
Rossland. *Ren* 2F **127**
Ross-on-Wye. *Here* 3B **48**
Roster. *High* 4E **169**
Rostherne. *Ches E* 2B **84**
Rostholme. *S Yor* 4F **93**
Rosthwaite. *Cumb* 3D **102**
Roston. *Derbs* 1F **73**
Rosudgeon. *Corn* 4C **4**
Rosyth. *Fife* 1E **129**
Rothbury. *Nmbd* 4E **121**
Rotherby. *Leics* 4D **74**
Rotherfield. *E Sus* 3G **27**
Rotherfield Greys. *Oxon* 3F **37**
Rotherfield Peppard. *Oxon* 3F **37**
Rotherham. *S Yor* 1B **86**
Rothersthorpe. *Nptn* 5E **62**
Rotherwick. *Hants* 1F **25**
Rothes. *Mor* 4G **159**
Rothesay. *Arg* 3B **126**
Rothienorman. *Abers* 5E **160**
Rothiesholm. *Orkn* 5F **172**
Rothley. *Leics* 4C **74**
Rothley. *Nmbd* 1D **114**
Rothwell. *Linc* 1A **88**
Rothwell. *Nptn* 2F **63**
Rothwell. *W Yor* 2D **92**
Rothwell Haigh. *W Yor* 2D **92**
Rotsea. *E Yor* 4E **101**
Rottal. *Ang* 2C **144**
Rotten End. *Suff* 4F **67**
Rotten Row. *Norf* 4C **78**
Rotten Row. *W Ber* 4D **36**
Rotten Row. *W Mid* 3F **61**
Rottingdean. *Brig* 5E **27**
Rottington. *Cumb* 3A **102**
Roud. *IOW* 4D **16**
Rougham. *Norf* 3H **77**
Rougham. *Suff* 4B **66**
Rough Close. *Staf* 2D **72**
Rough Common. *Kent* 5F **41**
Roughcote. *Staf* 1D **72**
Rough Haugh. *High* 4H **167**
Rough Hay. *Staf* 3G **73**
Roughlee. *Lanc* 5H **97**
Roughley. *W Mid* 1F **61**
Roughsike. *Cumb* 2G **113**
Roughton. *Linc* 4B **88**
Roughton. *Norf* 2E **78**
Roughton. *Shrp* 1B **60**
Roundbush Green. *Essx* 4F **53**
Roundham. *Som* 2H **13**
Roundhay. *W Yor* 1D **92**
Round Hill. *Torb* 2F **9**
Roundhurst. *W Sus* 2A **26**
Round Maple. *Suff* 1C **54**
Round Oak. *Shrp* 2F **59**
Roundstreet Common. *W Sus* 3B **26**
Roundthwaite. *Cumb* 4H **103**
Roundway. *Wilts* 5F **35**
Roundyhill. *Ang* 3C **144**
Rousdon. *Devn* 3F **13**
Rousham. *Oxon* 3C **50**
Rous Lench. *Worc* 5E **61**
Routh. *E Yor* 5E **101**
Rout's Green. *Buck* 2F **37**
Row. *Corn* 5A **10**
Row. *Cumb* 1D **96**
(nr. Kendal)
Row. *Cumb* 1H **103**
(nr. Penrith)
Rowanburn. *Dum* 2F **113**
Rowanhill. *Abers* 3H **161**
Rowardennan. *Stir* 4C **134**
Rowarth. *Derbs* 2E **85**
Row Ash. *Hants* 1D **16**
Rowberrow. *Som* 1H **21**
Rowde. *Wilts* 5E **35**
Rowden. *Devn* 3G **11**
Rowen. *Cnwy* 3G **81**
Rowfoot. *Nmbd* 3H **113**
Row Green. *Essx* 3H **53**
Row Heath. *Essx* 4E **55**
Rowhedge. *Essx* 3D **54**
Rowhook. *W Sus* 2C **26**
Rowington. *Warw* 4G **61**
Rowland. *Derbs* 3G **85**
Rowland's Castle. *Hants* 1F **17**
Rowlands Gill. *Tyne* 4E **115**
Rowledge. *Surr* 2G **25**
Rowley. *Dur* 5D **115**
Rowley. *E Yor* 1C **94**
Rowley. *Shrp* 5F **71**
Rowley Hill. *W Yor* 3B **92**
Rowley Regis. *W Mid* 2D **60**
Rowlstone. *Here* 3G **47**
Rowly. *Surr* 1B **26**
Rowner. *Hants* 2D **16**
Rowney Green. *Worc* 3E **61**
Rownhams. *Hants* 1B **16**
Rowrah. *Cumb* 3B **102**
Rowsham. *Buck* 4G **51**
Rowsley. *Derbs* 4G **85**
Rowstock. *Oxon* 3C **36**
Rowston. *Linc* 5H **87**
Row, The. *Lanc* 2D **96**
Rowthorne. *Derbs* 4B **86**
Rowton. *Ches W* 4G **83**
Rowton. *Shrp* 2G **59**
(nr. Ludlow)
Rowton. *Shrp* 4F **71**
(nr. Shrewsbury)
Rowton. *Telf* 4A **72**
Row Town. *Surr* 4B **38**
Roxburgh. *Bord* 1B **120**
Roxby. *N Lin* 3C **94**
Roxby. *N Yor* 3E **107**
Roxton. *Bed* 5A **64**
Roxwell. *Essx* 5G **53**
Royal Leamington Spa. *Warw* 4H **61**
Royal Oak. *Darl* 2F **105**
Royal Oak. *Lanc* 4C **90**
Royal Oak. *N Yor* 2F **101**
Royal's Green. *Ches E* 1A **72**
Royal Tunbridge Wells. *Kent* 2G **27**
Royal Wootton Bassett. *Wilts* 3F **35**
Roybridge. *High* 5E **149**
Roydon. *Essx* 4E **53**
Roydon. *Norf* 2C **66**
(nr. Diss)
Roydon. *Norf* 3G **77**
(nr. King's Lynn)
Roydon Hamlet. *Essx* 5E **53**
Royston. *Herts* 1D **52**
Royston. *S Yor* 3D **92**
Royston Water. *Som* 1F **13**
Royton. *G Man* 4H **91**
Ruabon. *Wrex* 1F **71**
Ruaig. *Arg* 4B **138**
Ruan High Lanes. *Corn* 5D **6**
Ruan Lanihorne. *Corn* 4C **6**
Ruan Major. *Corn* 5E **5**
Ruan Minor. *Corn* 5E **5**
Ruarach. *High* 1B **148**
Ruardean. *Glos* 4B **48**
Ruardean Hill. *Glos* 4B **48**
Ruardean Woodside. *Glos* 4B **48**
Rubery. *W Mid* 3D **61**
Ruchazie. *Glas* 3H **127**
Ruckcroft. *Cumb* 5G **113**
Ruckinge. *Kent* 2E **29**
Ruckland. *Linc* 3C **88**
Rucklers Lane. *Herts* 5A **52**
Ruckley. *Shrp* 5H **71**
Rudbaxton. *Pemb* 2D **42**
Rudby. *N Yor* 4B **106**
Ruddington. *Notts* 2C **74**
Rudford. *Glos* 3C **48**
Rudge. *Shrp* 1C **60**
Rudge. *Wilts* 1D **22**
Rudge Heath. *Shrp* 1B **60**
Rudgeway. *S Glo* 3B **34**
Rudgwick. *W Sus* 2B **26**
Rudhall. *Here* 3B **48**
Rudheath. *Ches W* 3A **84**
Rudley Green. *Essx* 5B **54**
Rudloe. *Wilts* 4D **34**
Rudry. *Cphy* 3E **33**
Rudston. *E Yor* 3E **101**
Rudyard. *Staf* 5D **84**
Rufford. *Lanc* 3C **90**
Rufforth. *York* 4H **99**
Rugby. *Warw* 3C **62**
Rugeley. *Staf* 4E **73**
Ruglen. *S Ayr* 4B **116**
Ruilick. *High* 4H **157**
Ruisaurie. *High* 4G **157**
Ruishton. *Som* 4F **21**
Ruisigearraidh. *W Isl* 1E **170**
Ruislip. *G Lon* 2B **38**
Ruislip Common. *G Lon* 2B **38**
Rumbling Bridge. *Per* 4C **136**
Rumburgh. *Suff* 2F **67**
Rumford. *Corn* 1C **6**
Rumford. *Falk* 2C **128**
Rumney. *Card* 4F **33**
Rumwell. *Som* 4E **21**
Runcorn. *Hal* 2H **83**
Runcton. *W Sus* 2G **17**
Runcton Holme. *Norf* 5F **77**
Rundlestone. *Devn* 5F **11**
Runfold. *Surr* 2G **25**
Runhall. *Norf* 5C **78**
Runham. *Norf* 4G **79**
Runnington. *Som* 4E **20**
Runshaw Moor. *Lanc* 3D **90**
Runswick. *N Yor* 3F **107**
Runtaleave. *Ang* 2B **144**
Runwell. *Essx* 1B **40**
Ruscombe. *Wok* 4F **37**
Rushall. *Here* 2B **48**
Rushall. *Norf* 2D **66**
Rushall. *W Mid* 5E **73**
Rushall. *Wilts* 1G **23**
Rushbrooke. *Suff* 4A **66**
Rushbury. *Shrp* 1H **59**
Rushden. *Herts* 2D **52**
Rushden. *Nptn* 4G **63**
Rushenden. *Kent* 3D **40**
Rushford. *Devn* 5E **11**
Rushford. *Suff* 2B **66**
Rush Green. *Herts* 3C **52**
Rushlake Green. *E Sus* 4H **27**
Rushmere. *Suff* 2G **67**
Rushmere St Andrew. *Suff* 1E **55**
Rushmoor. *Surr* 2G **25**
Rushock. *Worc* 3C **60**
Rusholme. *G Man* 1C **84**
Rushton. *Ches W* 4H **83**
Rushton. *Nptn* 2F **63**
Rushton. *Shrp* 5A **72**
Rushton Spencer. *Staf* 4D **84**
Rushwick. *Worc* 5C **60**
Rushyford. *Dur* 2F **105**
Ruskie. *Stir* 3F **135**
Ruskington. *Linc* 5H **87**
Rusland. *Cumb* 1C **96**
Rusper. *W Sus* 2D **26**
Ruspidge. *Glos* 4B **48**
Russell's Water. *Oxon* 3F **37**
Russel's Green. *Suff* 3E **67**
Russ Hill. *Surr* 1D **26**
Russland. *Orkn* 6C **172**
Rusthall. *Kent* 2G **27**
Rustington. *W Sus* 5B **26**
Ruston. *N Yor* 1D **100**
Ruston Parva. *E Yor* 3E **101**
Ruswarp. *N Yor* 4F **107**
Rutherglen. *S Lan* 3H **127**
Ruthernbridge. *Corn* 2E **6**
Ruthin. *Den* 5D **82**
Ruthin. *V Glam* 4C **32**
Ruthrieston. *Aber* 3G **153**
Ruthven. *Abers* 4C **160**
Ruthven. *Ang* 4B **144**
Ruthven. *High* 5C **158**
(nr. Inverness)
Ruthven. *High* 4B **150**
(nr. Kingussie)
Ruthvoes. *Corn* 2D **6**
Ruthwaite. *Cumb* 1D **102**
Ruthwell. *Dum* 3C **112**
Ruxton Green. *Here* 4A **48**
Ruyton-XI-Towns. *Shrp* 3F **71**
Ryal. *Nmbd* 2D **114**
Ryall. *Dors* 3H **13**
Ryall. *Worc* 1D **48**
Ryarsh. *Kent* 5A **40**
Rychraggan. *High* 5G **157**
Rydal. *Cumb* 4E **103**
Ryde. *IOW* 3D **16**
Rye. *E Sus* 3D **28**
Ryecroft Gate. *Staf* 4D **84**
Ryeford. *Here* 3B **48**
Rye Foreign. *E Sus* 3D **28**
Rye Harbour. *E Sus* 4D **28**
Ryehill. *E Yor* 2F **95**
Rye Street. *Worc* 2C **48**
Ryhall. *Rut* 4H **75**
Ryhill. *W Yor* 3D **93**
Ryhope. *Tyne* 4H **115**
Ryhope Colliery. *Tyne* 4H **115**
Rylands. *Notts* 2C **74**
Rylstone. *N Yor* 4B **98**
Ryme Intrinseca. *Dors* 1A **14**
Ryther. *N Yor* 1F **93**
Ryton. *Glos* 2C **48**
Ryton. *N Yor* 2B **100**
Ryton. *Shrp* 5B **72**
Ryton. *Tyne* 3E **115**
Ryton. *Warw* 2A **62**
Ryton-on-Dunsmore. *Warw* 3A **62**
Ryton Woodside. *Tyne* 3E **115**

S

Saasaig. *High* 3E **147**
Sabden. *Lanc* 1F **91**
Sacombe. *Herts* 4D **52**
Sacriston. *Dur* 5F **115**
Sadberge. *Darl* 3A **106**
Saddell. *Arg* 2B **122**
Saddington. *Leics* 1D **62**
Saddle Bow. *Norf* 4F **77**
Saddlescombe. *W Sus* 4D **26**
Saddleworth. *G Man* 4H **91**
Sadgill. *Cumb* 4F **103**
Saffron Walden. *Essx* 2F **53**
Sageston. *Pemb* 4E **43**
Saham Hills. *Norf* 5B **78**
Saham Toney. *Norf* 5A **78**
Saighdinis. *W Isl* 2D **170**
Saighton. *Ches W* 4G **83**
Sain Dunwyd. *V Glam* 5C **32**
Sain Hilari. *V Glam* 4D **32**
St Abbs. *Bord* 3F **131**
St Agnes. *Corn* 3B **6**
St Albans. *Herts* 5B **52**
St Allen. *Corn* 3C **6**
St Andrews. *Fife* 2H **137**
St Andrews Major. *V Glam* 4E **33**
St Anne's. *Lanc* 2B **90**
St Ann's. *Dum* 5C **118**
St Ann's Chapel. *Corn* 5E **11**
St Ann's Chapel. *Devn* 4C **8**
St Anthony. *Corn* 5C **6**
St Anthony-in-Meneage. *Corn* 4E **5**
St Arvans. *Mon* 2A **34**
St Asaph. *Den* 3C **82**
Sain Tathan. *V Glam* 5D **32**
St Athan. *V Glam* 5D **32**
St Austell. *Corn* 3E **6**
St Bartholomew's Hill. *Wilts* 4E **23**
St Bees. *Cumb* 3A **102**
St Blazey. *Corn* 3E **7**
St Blazey Gate. *Corn* 3E **7**
St Boswells. *Bord* 1A **120**
St Breock. *Corn* 1D **6**
St Breward. *Corn* 5A **10**
St Briavels. *Glos* 5A **48**
St Brides. *Pemb* 3B **42**
St Bride's Major. *V Glam* 4B **32**
St Bride's Netherwent. *Mon* 3H **33**
St Bride's-super-Ely. *V Glam* 4D **32**
St Brides Wentlooge. *Newp* 3F **33**
St Budeaux. *Plym* 3A **8**
Saintbury. *Glos* 2G **49**
St Buryan. *Corn* 4B **4**
St Catherine. *Bath* 4C **34**
St Catherines. *Arg* 3A **134**
St Clears. *Carm* 3G **43**
St Cleer. *Corn* 2G **7**
St Clement. *Corn* 4C **6**
St Clether. *Corn* 4C **10**
St Colmac. *Arg* 3B **126**
St Columb Major. *Corn* 2D **6**
St Columb Minor. *Corn* 2C **6**
St Columb Road. *Corn* 3D **6**
St Combs. *Abers* 2H **161**
St Cross. *Hants* 4C **24**
St Cross South Elmham. *Suff* 2E **67**
St Cyrus. *Abers* 2G **145**
St David's. *Pemb* 2B **42**
St David's. *Per* 1B **136**
St Day. *Corn* 4B **6**
St Dennis. *Corn* 3D **6**
St Dogmaels. *Pemb* 1B **44**
St Dominick. *Corn* 2H **7**
St Donat's. *V Glam* 5C **32**
St Edith's Marsh. *Wilts* 5E **35**
St Endellion. *Corn* 1D **6**
St Enoder. *Corn* 3C **6**
St Erme. *Corn* 4C **6**

Sayers Common. *W Sus* 4D **26**
Scackleton. *N Yor* 2A **100**
Scadabhagh. *W Isl* 8D **171**
Scaftworth. *Notts* 1D **86**
Scagglethorpe. *N Yor* 2C **100**
Scaitcliffe. *Lanc* 2F **91**
Scaladal. *W Isl* 6D **171**
Scalasaig. *Arg* 4A **132**
Scalby. *E Yor* 2B **94**
Scalby. *N Yor* 5H **107**
Scalby Mills. *N Yor* 5H **107**
Scaldwell. *Nptn* 3E **63**
Scaleby. *Cumb* 3F **113**
Scaleby Hill. *Cumb* 3F **113**
Scale Houses. *Cumb* 5G **113**
Scales. *Cumb* 2B **96**
(nr. Barrow-in-Furness)
Scales. *Cumb* 2E **103**
(nr. Keswick)
Scalford. *Leics* 3E **75**
Scaling. *Red C* 3E **107**
Scaling Dam. *Red C* 3E **107**
Scalloway. *Shet* 8E **173**
Scalpaigh. *W Isl* 8E **171**
Scalpay House. *High* 1E **147**
Scamblesby. *Linc* 3B **88**
Scamodale. *High* 1C **140**
Scampston. *N Yor* 2C **100**
Scampton. *Linc* 3G **87**
Scaniport. *High* 5A **158**
Scapa. *Orkn* 7D **172**
Scapegoat Hill. *W Yor* 3A **92**
Scar. *Orkn* 3F **172**
Scarasta. *W Isl* 8C **171**
Scarborough. *N Yor* 1E **101**
Scarcliffe. *Derbs* 4B **86**
Scarcroft. *W Yor* 5F **99**
Scardroy. *High* 3E **156**
Scarfskerry. *High* 1E **169**
Scargill. *Dur* 3D **104**
Scarinish. *Arg* 4B **138**
Scarisbrick. *Lanc* 3B **90**
Scarning. *Norf* 4B **78**
Scarrington. *Notts* 1E **75**
Scarth Hill. *Lanc* 4C **90**
Scartho. *NE Lin* 4F **95**
Scarvister. *Shet* 7E **173**
Scatwell. *High* 3F **157**
Scaur. *Dum* 4F **111**
Scawby. *N Lin* 4C **94**
Scawby Brook. *N Lin* 4C **94**
Scawsby. *S Yor* 4F **93**
Scawton. *N Yor* 1H **99**
Scayne's Hill. *W Sus* 3E **27**
Scethrog. *Powy* 3E **46**
Scholar Green. *Ches E* 5C **84**
Scholes. *G Man* 4D **90**
Scholes. *W Yor* 2B **92**
(nr. Bradford)
Scholes. *W Yor* 4B **92**
(nr. Holmfirth)
Scholes. *W Yor* 1D **93**
(nr. Leeds)
Scholey Hill. *W Yor* 2D **93**
School Aycliffe. *Dur* 2F **105**
School Green. *Ches W* 4A **84**
School Green. *Essx* 2H **53**
Scissett. *W Yor* 3C **92**
Scleddau. *Pemb* 1D **42**
Scofton. *Notts* 2D **86**
Scole. *Norf* 3D **66**
Scolton. *Pemb* 2D **43**
Scone. *Per* 1D **136**
Sconser. *High* 5E **155**
Scoonie. *Fife* 3F **137**
Scopwick. *Linc* 5H **87**
Scoraig. *High* 4E **163**
Scorborough. *E Yor* 5E **101**
Scorrier. *Corn* 4B **6**
Scorriton. *Devn* 2D **8**
Scorton. *Lanc* 5E **97**
Scorton. *N Yor* 4F **105**
Sco Ruston. *Norf* 3E **79**
Scotbheinn. *W Isl* 3D **170**
Scotby. *Cumb* 4F **113**
Scotch Corner. *N Yor* 4F **105**
Scotforth. *Lanc* 3D **97**
Scot Hay. *Staf* 1C **72**
Scothern. *Linc* 3H **87**
Scotland End. *Oxon* 2B **50**
Scotlandwell. *Per* 3D **136**
Scot Lane End. *G Man* 4E **91**
Scotsburn. *High* 1B **158**
Scotsburn. *Mor* 2G **159**
Scotsdike. *Cumb* 2E **113**
Scots Gap. *Nmbd* 1D **114**
Scotstoun. *Glas* 3G **127**
Scotstown. *High* 2C **140**
Scotswood. *Tyne* 3F **115**
Scottas. *High* 3F **147**
Scotter. *Linc* 4B **94**
Scotterthorpe. *Linc* 4B **94**
Scottlethorpe. *Linc* 3H **75**
Scotton. *Linc* 1F **87**
Scotton. *N Yor* 5E **105**
(nr. Catterick Garrison)
Scotton. *N Yor* 4F **99**
(nr. Harrogate)
Scottow. *Norf* 3E **79**
Scoulton. *Norf* 5B **78**
Scounslow Green. *Staf* 3E **73**
Scourie. *High* 4B **166**
Scourie More. *High* 4B **166**
Scousburgh. *Shet* 10E **173**
Scout Green. *Cumb* 4G **103**
Scouthead. *G Man* 4H **91**
Scrabster. *High* 1C **168**
Scrafield. *Linc* 4C **88**
Scrainwood. *Nmbd* 4D **121**
Scrane End. *Linc* 1C **76**
Scraptoft. *Leic* 5D **74**
Scratby. *Norf* 4H **79**
Scrayingham. *N Yor* 3B **100**
Scredington. *Linc* 1H **75**
Scremby. *Linc* 4D **88**
Scremerston. *Nmbd* 5G **131**
Screveton. *Notts* 1E **75**
Scrivelsby. *Linc* 4B **88**
Scriven. *N Yor* 4F **99**
Scronkey. *Lanc* 5D **96**
Scrooby. *Notts* 1D **86**
Scropton. *Derbs* 2F **73**
Scrub Hill. *Linc* 5B **88**
Scruton. *N Yor* 5F **105**
Scuggate. *Cumb* 2F **113**
Sculamus. *High* 1E **147**
Sculcoates. *Hull* 1D **94**
Sculthorpe. *Norf* 2A **78**
Scunthorpe. *N Lin* 3B **94**
Scurlage. *Swan* 4D **30**
Sea. *Som* 1G **13**
Seaborough. *Dors* 2H **13**
Seabridge. *Staf* 1C **72**
Seabrook. *Kent* 2F **29**
Seaburn. *Tyne* 3H **115**
Seacombe. *Mers* 1F **83**
Seacroft. *Linc* 4E **89**
Seacroft. *W Yor* 1D **92**
Seadyke. *Linc* 2C **76**
Seafield. *High* 5G **165**
Seafield. *Midl* 3F **129**
Seafield. *S Ayr* 2C **116**
Seafield. *W Lot* 3D **128**
Seaford. *E Sus* 5F **27**
Seaforth. *Mers* 1F **83**
Seagrave. *Leics* 4D **74**
Seaham. *Dur* 5H **115**
Seahouses. *Nmbd* 1G **121**
Seal. *Kent* 5G **39**
Sealand. *Flin* 4F **83**
Seale. *Surr* 2G **25**
Seamer. *N Yor* 1E **101**
(nr. Scarborough)
Seamer. *N Yor* 3B **106**
(nr. Stokesley)
Seamill. *N Ayr* 5C **126**
Sea Mills. *Bris* 4A **34**
Sea Palling. *Norf* 3G **79**
Searby. *Linc* 4D **94**
Seasalter. *Kent* 4E **41**
Seascale. *Cumb* 4B **102**
Seaside. *Per* 1E **137**
Seater. *High* 1F **169**
Seathorne. *Linc* 4E **89**
Seathwaite. *Cumb* 3D **102**
(nr. Buttermere)
Seathwaite. *Cumb* 5D **102**
(nr. Ulpha)
Seatle. *Cumb* 1C **96**
Seatoller. *Cumb* 3D **102**
Seaton. *Corn* 3H **7**
Seaton. *Cumb* 1B **102**
Seaton. *Devn* 3F **13**
Seaton. *Dur* 4G **115**
Seaton. *E Yor* 5F **101**
Seaton. *Nmbd* 2G **115**
Seaton. *Rut* 1G **63**
Seaton Burn. *Tyne* 2F **115**
Seaton Carew. *Hart* 2C **106**
Seaton Delaval. *Nmbd* 2G **115**
Seaton Junction. *Devn* 3F **13**
Seaton Ross. *E Yor* 5B **100**
Seaton Sluice. *Nmbd* 2G **115**
Seatown. *Abers* 2C **160**
Seatown. *Dors* 3H **13**
Seatown. *Mor* 2C **160**
(nr. Cullen)
Seatown. *Mor* 1G **159**
(nr. Lossiemouth)
Seave Green. *N Yor* 4C **106**
Seaview. *IOW* 3E **17**
Seaville. *Cumb* 4C **112**
Seavington St Mary. *Som* 1H **13**
Seavington St Michael. *Som* 1H **13**
Seawick. *Essx* 4E **55**
Sebastopol. *Torf* 2F **33**
Sebergham. *Cumb* 5E **113**
Seckington. *Warw* 5G **73**
Second Coast. *High* 4D **162**
Sedbergh. *Cumb* 5H **103**
Sedbury. *Glos* 2A **34**
Sedbusk. *N Yor* 5B **104**
Sedgeberrow. *Worc* 2F **49**
Sedgebrook. *Linc* 2F **75**
Sedgefield. *Dur* 2A **106**
Sedgeford. *Norf* 2G **77**
Sedgehill. *Wilts* 4D **22**
Sedgley. *W Mid* 1D **60**
Sedgwick. *Cumb* 1E **97**
Sedlescombe. *E Sus* 4B **28**
Seend. *Wilts* 5E **35**
Seend Cleeve. *Wilts* 5E **35**
Seer Green. *Buck* 1A **38**
Seething. *Norf* 1F **67**
Sefton. *Mers* 4B **90**
Sefton Park. *Mers* 2F **83**
Segensworth. *Hants* 2D **16**
Seggat. *Abers* 4E **161**
Seghill. *Nmbd* 2F **115**
Seifton. *Shrp* 2G **59**
Seighford. *Staf* 3C **72**
Seilebost. *W Isl* 8C **171**
Seisdon. *Staf* 1C **60**
Seisiadar. *W Isl* 4H **171**
Selattyn. *Shrp* 2E **71**
Selborne. *Hants* 3F **25**
Selby. *N Yor* 1G **93**
Selham. *W Sus* 3A **26**
Selkirk. *Bord* 2G **119**
Sellack. *Here* 3A **48**
Sellafirth. *Shet* 2G **173**
Sellick's Green. *Som* 1F **13**
Sellindge. *Kent* 2F **29**
Selling. *Kent* 5E **41**
Sells Green. *Wilts* 5E **35**
Selly Oak. *W Mid* 2E **61**
Selmeston. *E Sus* 5G **27**
Selsdon. *G Lon* 4E **39**
Selsey. *W Sus* 3G **17**
Selsfield Common. *W Sus* 2E **27**
Selside. *Cumb* 5G **103**
Selside. *N Yor* 2G **97**
Selsley. *Glos* 5D **48**
Selsted. *Kent* 1G **29**
Selston. *Notts* 5B **86**
Selworthy. *Som* 2C **20**
Semer. *Suff* 1D **54**
Semington. *Wilts* 5D **35**
Semley. *Wilts* 4D **23**
Sempringham. *Linc* 2A **76**
Send. *Surr* 5B **38**
Send Marsh. *Surr* 5B **38**
Senghenydd. *Cphy* 2E **32**
Sennen. *Corn* 4A **4**
Sennen Cove. *Corn* 4A **4**
Sennicotts. *W Sus* 2G **17**
Sennybridge. *Powy* 3C **46**
Serlby. *Notts* 2D **86**
Sessay. *N Yor* 2G **99**
Setchey. *Norf* 4F **77**
Setley. *Hants* 2B **16**
Setter. *Shet* 3F **173**
Settiscarth. *Orkn* 6C **172**
Settle. *N Yor* 3H **97**
Settrington. *N Yor* 2C **100**
Seven Ash. *Som* 3E **21**
Sevenhampton. *Glos* 3F **49**
Sevenhampton. *Swin* 2H **35**
Sevenoaks. *Kent* 5G **39**
Sevenoaks Weald. *Kent* 5G **39**
Seven Sisters. *Neat* 5B **46**
Seven Springs. *Glos* 4E **49**
Severn Beach. *S Glo* 3A **34**
Severn Stoke. *Worc* 1D **48**
Sevington. *Kent* 1E **29**
Sewards End. *Essx* 2F **53**
Sewardstone. *Essx* 1E **39**
Sewell. *C Beds* 3H **51**
Sewerby. *E Yor* 3G **101**
Seworgan. *Corn* 5B **6**
Sewstern. *Leics* 3F **75**
Sgallairidh. *W Isl* 9B **170**
Sgarasta Mhor. *W Isl* 8C **171**
Sgiogarstaigh. *W Isl* 1H **171**
Sgreadan. *Arg* 4A **132**
Shabbington. *Buck* 5E **51**
Shackerley. *Shrp* 5C **72**
Shackerstone. *Leics* 5A **74**
Shackleford. *Surr* 1A **26**
Shadforth. *Dur* 5G **115**
Shadingfield. *Suff* 2G **67**
Shadoxhurst. *Kent* 2D **28**
Shadsworth. *Bkbn* 2E **91**
Shadwell. *Norf* 2B **66**
Shadwell. *W Yor* 1D **92**
Shaftesbury. *Dors* 4D **22**
Shafton. *S Yor* 3D **93**
Shafton Two Gates. *S Yor* 3D **93**
Shaggs. *Dors* 4D **14**
Shakesfield. *Glos* 2B **48**
Shalbourne. *Wilts* 5B **36**
Shalcombe. *IOW* 4B **16**
Shalden. *Hants* 2E **25**
Shaldon. *Devn* 5C **12**
Shalfleet. *IOW* 4C **16**
Shalford. *Essx* 3H **53**
Shalford. *Surr* 1B **26**
Shalford Green. *Essx* 3H **53**
Shallowford. *Devn* 2H **19**
Shallowford. *Staf* 3C **72**
Shalmsford Street. *Kent* 5E **41**
Shalstone. *Buck* 2E **51**
Shamley Green. *Surr* 1B **26**
Shandon. *Arg* 1D **126**
Shandwick. *High* 1C **158**
Shangton. *Leics* 1E **62**
Shankhouse. *Nmbd* 2F **115**
Shanklin. *IOW* 4D **16**
Shannochie. *N Ayr* 3D **122**
Shap. *Cumb* 3G **103**
Shapwick. *Dors* 2E **15**
Shapwick. *Som* 3H **21**
Sharcott. *Wilts* 1G **23**
Shardlow. *Derbs* 2B **74**
Shareshill. *Staf* 5D **72**
Sharlston. *W Yor* 3D **93**
Sharlston Common. *W Yor* 3D [illegible]3
Sharnal Street. *Medw* 3B [illegible]0
Sharnbrook. *Bed* 5G [illegible]
Sharneyford. *Lanc* 2G 9[illegible]
Sharnford. *Leics* 1B 6[illegible]
Sharnhill Green. *Dors* 2C 1[illegible]
Sharow. *N Yor* 2F **99**
Sharpe Green. *Lanc* 1D **90**
Sharpenhoe. *C Beds* 2A **52**
Sharperton. *Nmbd* 4D **120**
Sharpness. *Glos* 5B **48**
Sharp Street. *Norf* 3F **79**
Sharpthorne. *W Sus* 2E **27**
Sharrington. *Norf* 2C **78**
Shatterford. *Worc* 2B **60**
Shatton. *Derbs* 2G **85**
Shaugh Prior. *Devn* 2B **8**
Shavington. *Ches E* 5B **84**
Shaw. *G Man* 4H **91**
Shaw. *W Ber* 5C **36**
Shaw. *Wilts* 5D **35**
Shawbirch. *Telf* 4A **72**
Shawbury. *Shrp* 3H **71**
Shawdon Hall. *Nmbd* 3E **121**
Shawell. *Leics* 2C **62**
Shawford. *Hants* 4C **24**
Shawforth. *Lanc* 2G **91**
Shaw Green. *Lanc* 3D **90**
Shawhead. *Dum* 2F **111**
Shaw Mills. *N Yor* 3E **99**
Shawwood. *E Ayr* 2E **117**
Shearington. *Dum* 3B **112**
Shearsby. *Leics* 1D **62**
Shearston. *Som* 3F **21**
Shebbear. *Devn* 2E **11**
Shebdon. *Staf* 3B **72**
Shebster. *High* 2C **168**
Sheddocksley. *Aber* 3F **153**
Shedfield. *Hants* 1D **16**
Shedog. *N Ayr* 2D **122**
Sheen. *Staf* 4F **85**
Sheepbridge. *Derbs* 3A **86**
Sheep Hill. *Tyne* 4E **115**
Sheepscar. *W Yor* 1D **92**
Sheepscombe. *Glos* 4D **49**
Sheepstor. *Devn* 2B **8**
Sheepwash. *Devn* 2E **11**
Sheepwash. *Nmbd* 1F **115**
Sheepway. *N Som* 4H **33**
Sheepy Magna. *Leics* 5H **73**
Sheepy Parva. *Leics* 5H **73**
Sheering. *Essx* 4F **53**
Sheerness. *Kent* 3D **40**
Sheerwater. *Surr* 4B **38**
Sheet. *Hants* 4F **25**
Sheffield. *S Yor* 2H **85**
Sheffield Bottom. *W Ber* 5E **37**
Sheffield Green. *E Sus* 3F **27**
Shefford. *C Beds* 2B **52**
Shefford Woodlands. *W Ber* 4B **36**
Sheigra. *High* 2B **166**
Sheinton. *Shrp* 5A **72**
Shelderton. *Shrp* 3G **59**
Sheldon. *Derbs* 4F **85**
Sheldon. *Devn* 2E **12**
Sheldon. *W Mid* 2F **61**
Sheldwich. *Kent* 5E **40**
Sheldwich Lees. *Kent* 5E **40**
Shelf. *W Yor* 2B **92**
Shelfanger. *Norf* 2D **66**
Shelfield. *Warw* 4F **61**
Shelfield. *W Mid* 5E **73**
Shelford. *Notts* 1D **74**
Shelford. *Warw* 2B **62**
Shell. *Worc* 5D **60**
Shelley. *Suff* 2D **54**
Shelley. *W Yor* 3C **92**
Shell Green. *Hal* 2H **83**
Shellingford. *Oxon* 2B **36**
Shellow Bowells. *Essx* 5G **53**
Shelsley Beauchamp. *Worc* 4B **60**
Shelsley Walsh. *Worc* 4B **60**
Shelthorpe. *Leics* 4C **74**
Shelton. *Bed* 4H **63**

Starston. *Norf* 2E 67
Start. *Devn* 4E 9
Startforth. *Dur* 3D 104
Start Hill. *Essx* 3F 53
Startley. *Wilts* 3E 35
Stathe. *Som* 4G 21
Stathern. *Leics* 2E 75
Station Town. *Dur* 1B 106
Staughton Green. *Cambs* 4A 64
Staughton Highway. *Cambs* 4A 64
Staunton. *Glos* 3C 48
(nr. Cheltenham)
Staunton. *Glos* 4A 48
(nr. Monmouth)
Staunton in the Vale. *Notts* 1F 75
Staunton on Arrow. *Here* 4F 59
Staunton on Wye. *Here* 1G 47
Staveley. *Cumb* 5F 103
Staveley. *Derbs* 3B 86
Staveley. *N Yor* 3F 99
Staveley-in-Cartmel. *Cumb* 1C 96
Staverton. *Devn* 2D 9
Staverton. *Glos* 3D 49
Staverton. *Nptn* 4C 62
Staverton. *Wilts* 5D 34
Stawell. *Som* 3G 21
Stawley. *Som* 4D 20
Staxigoe. *High* 3F 169
Staxton. *N Yor* 2E 101
Staylittle. *Powy* 1A 58
Staynall. *Lanc* 5C 96
Staythorpe. *Notts* 5E 87
Stean. *N Yor* 2C 98
Stearsby. *N Yor* 2A 100
Steart. *Som* 2F 21
Stebbing. *Essx* 3G 53
Stebbing Green. *Essx* 3G 53
Stedham. *W Sus* 4G 25
Steel. *Nmbd* 4C 114
Steel Cross. *E Sus* 2G 27
Steelend. *Fife* 4C 136
Steele Road. *Bord* 5H 119
Steel Heath. *Shrp* 2H 71
Steen's Bridge. *Here* 5H 59
Steep. *Hants* 4F 25
Steep Lane. *W Yor* 2A 92
Steeple. *Dors* 4E 15
Steeple. *Essx* 5C 54
Steeple Ashton. *Wilts* 1E 23
Steeple Aston. *Oxon* 3C 50
Steeple Barton. *Oxon* 3C 50
Steeple Bumpstead. *Essx* 1G 53
Steeple Claydon. *Buck* 3E 51
Steeple Gidding. *Cambs* 2A 64
Steeple Langford. *Wilts* 3F 23
Steeple Morden. *Cambs* 1C 52
Steeton. *W Yor* 5C 98
Stein. *High* 3B 154
Steinmanhill. *Abers* 4E 161
Stelling Minnis. *Kent* 1F 29
Stembridge. *Som* 4H 21
Stemster. *High* 2D 169
(nr. Halkirk)
Stemster. *High* 2C 168
(nr. Westfield)
Stenalees. *Corn* 3E 6
Stenhill. *Devn* 1D 12
Stenhouse. *Edin* 2F 129
Stenhcusemuir. *Falk* 1B 128
Stenigot. *Linc* 2B 88
Stenscholl. *High* 2D 155
Stenso. *Orkn* 5C 172
Stenson. *Derbs* 3H 73
Stenson Fields. *Derbs* 2H 73
Stenton. *E Lot* 2C 130
Stenwith. *Linc* 2F 75
Steòrnabhagh. *W Isl* 4G 171
Stepaside. *Pemb* 4F 43
Stepford. *Dum* 1F 111
Stepney. *G Lon* 2E 39
Steppingley. *C Beds* 2A 52
Stepps. *N Lan* 3H 127
Sterndale Moor. *Derbs* 4F 85
Sternfield. *Suff* 4F 67

Stert. *Wilts* 1F 23
Stetchworth. *Cambs* 5F 65
Stevenage. *Herts* 3C 52
Stevenston. *N Ayr* 5D 126
Stevenstone. *Devn* 1F 11
Steventon. *Hants* 2D 24
Steventon. *Oxon* 2C 36
Steventon End. *Cambs* 1G 53
Stevington. *Bed* 5G 63
Stewartby. *Bed* 1A 52
Stewarton. *Arg* 4A 122
Stewarton. *E Ayr* 5F 127
Stewkley. *Buck* 3G 51
Stewkley Dean. *Buck* 3G 51
Stewley. *Som* 1G 13
Stewton. *Linc* 2C 88
Steynton. *Pemb* 4D 42
Stibb. *Corn* 1C 10
Stibbard. *Norf* 3B 78
Stibb Cross. *Devn* 1E 11
Stibb Green. *Wilts* 5H 35
Stibbington. *Cambs* 1H 63
Stichill. *Bord* 1B 120
Sticker. *Corn* 3D 6
Stickford. *Linc* 4C 88
Sticklepath. *Devn* 3G 11
Sticklinch. *Som* 3A 22
Stickling Green. *Essx* 2E 53
Stickney. *Linc* 5C 88
Stiffkey. *Norf* 1B 78
Stifford's Bridge. *Here* 1C 48
Stileway. *Som* 2H 21
Stillingfleet. *N Yor* 5H 99
Stillington. *N Yor* 3H 99
Stillington. *Stoc T* 2A 106
Stilton. *Cambs* 2A 64
Stinchcombe. *Glos* 2C 34
Stinsford. *Dors* 3C 14
Stiperstones. *Shrp* 5F 71
Stirchley. *Telf* 5B 72
Stirchley. *W Mid* 2E 61
Stirling. *Abers* 4H 161
Stirling. *Stir* 4G 135
Stirton. *N Yor* 4B 98
Stisted. *Essx* 3A 54
Stitchcombe. *Wilts* 5H 35
Stithians. *Corn* 5B 6
Stittenham. *High* 1A 158
Stivichall. *W Mid* 3H 61
Stixwould. *Linc* 4A 88
Stoak. *Ches W* 3G 83
Stobo. *Bord* 1D 118
Stobo Castle. *Bord* 1D 118
Stoborough. *Dors* 4E 15
Stoborough Green. *Dors* 4E 15
Stobs Castle. *Bord* 4H 119
Stobswood. *Nmbd* 5G 121
Stock. *Essx* 1A 40
Stockbridge. *Hants* 3B 24
Stockbridge. *W Yor* 5C 98
Stockbury. *Kent* 4C 40
Stockcross. *W Ber* 5C 36
Stockdalewath. *Cumb* 5E 113
Stocker's Head. *Kent* 5D 40
Stockerston. *Leics* 1F 63
Stock Green. *Worc* 5D 61
Stocking. *Here* 2B 48
Stockingford. *Warw* 1H 61
Stocking Green. *Essx* 2F 53
Stocking Pelham. *Herts* 3E 53
Stockland. *Devn* 2F 13
Stockland Bristol. *Som* 2F 21
Stockleigh English. *Devn* 2B 12
Stockleigh Pomeroy. *Devn* 2B 12
Stockley. *Wilts* 5F 35
Stocklinch. *Som* 1G 13
Stockport. *G Man* 2D 84
Stocksbridge. *S Yor* 1G 85
Stocksfield. *Nmbd* 3D 114
Stocks, The. *Kent* 3D 28
Stockstreet. *Essx* 3B 54
Stockton. *Here* 4H 59
Stockton. *Norf* 1F 67

Stockton. *Shrp* 1B 60
(nr. Bridgnorth)
Stockton. *Shrp* 5E 71
(nr. Chirbury)
Stockton. *Telf* 4B 72
Stockton. *Warw* 4B 62
Stockton. *Wilts* 3E 23
Stockton Brook. *Staf* 5D 84
Stockton Cross. *Here* 4H 59
Stockton Heath. *Warr* 2A 84
Stockton-on-Tees. *Stoc T* 3B 106
Stockton on Teme. *Worc* 4B 60
Stockton-on-the-Forest. *York* 4A 100
Stockwell Heath. *Staf* 3E 73
Stockwood. *Bris* 5B 34
Stock Wood. *Worc* 5E 61
Stodmarsh. *Kent* 4G 41
Stody. *Norf* 2C 78
Stoer. *High* 1E 163
Stoford. *Som* 1A 14
Stoford. *Wilts* 3F 23
Stogumber. *Som* 3D 20
Stogursey. *Som* 2F 21
Stoke. *Devn* 4C 18
Stoke. *Hants* 1C 24
(nr. Andover)
Stoke. *Hants* 2F 17
(nr. South Hayling)
Stoke. *Medw* 3C 40
Stoke. *W Mid* 3A 62
Stoke Abbott. *Dors* 2H 13
Stoke Albany. *Nptn* 2F 63
Stoke Ash. *Suff* 3D 66
Stoke Bardolph. *Notts* 1D 74
Stoke Bliss. *Worc* 4A 60
Stoke Bruerne. *Nptn* 1F 51
Stoke by Clare. *Suff* 1H 53
Stoke-by-Nayland. *Suff* 2C 54
Stoke Canon. *Devn* 3C 12
Stoke Charity. *Hants* 3C 24
Stoke Climsland. *Corn* 5D 10
Stoke Cross. *Here* 5A 60
Stoke D'Abernon. *Surr* 5C 38
Stoke Doyle. *Nptn* 2H 63
Stoke Dry. *Rut* 1F 63
Stoke Edith. *Here* 1B 48
Stoke Farthing. *Wilts* 4F 23
Stoke Ferry. *Norf* 1G 65
Stoke Fleming. *Devn* 4E 9
Stokeford. *Dors* 4D 14
Stoke Gabriel. *Devn* 3E 9
Stoke Gifford. *S Glo* 4B 34
Stoke Golding. *Leics* 1A 62
Stoke Goldington. *Mil* 1G 51
Stokeham. *Notts* 3E 87
Stoke Hammond. *Buck* 3G 51
Stoke Heath. *Shrp* 3A 72
Stoke Holy Cross. *Norf* 5E 79
Stokeinteignhead. *Devn* 5C 12
Stoke Lacy. *Here* 1B 48
Stoke Lyne. *Oxon* 3D 50
Stoke Mandeville. *Buck* 4G 51
Stokenchurch. *Buck* 2F 37
Stoke Newington. *G Lon* 2E 39
Stokenham. *Devn* 4E 9
Stoke on Tern. *Shrp* 3A 72
Stoke-on-Trent. *Stoke* 1C 72
Stoke Orchard. *Glos* 3E 49
Stoke Pero. *Som* 2B 20
Stoke Poges. *Buck* 2A 38
Stoke Prior. *Here* 5H 59
Stoke Prior. *Worc* 4D 60
Stoke Rivers. *Devn* 3G 19
Stoke Rochford. *Linc* 3G 75
Stoke Row. *Oxon* 3E 37
Stoke St Gregory. *Som* 4G 21
Stoke St Mary. *Som* 4F 21
Stoke St Michael. *Som* 2B 22
Stoke St Milborough. *Shrp* 2H 59
Stokesay. *Shrp* 2G 59
Stokesby. *Norf* 4G 79
Stokesley. *N Yor* 4C 106
Stoke sub Hamdon. *Som* 1H 13
Stoke Talmage. *Oxon* 2E 37

Stoke Town. *Stoke* 1C 72
Stoke Trister. *Som* 4C 22
Stoke Wake. *Dors* 2C 14
Stolford. *Som* 2F 21
Stondon Massey. *Essx* 5F 53
Stone. *Buck* 4F 51
Stone. *Glos* 2B 34
Stone. *Kent* 3G 39
Stone. *Som* 3A 22
Stone. *Staf* 2D 72
Stone. *Worc* 3C 60
Stonea. *Cambs* 1D 64
Stoneacton. *Shrp* 1H 59
Stone Allerton. *Som* 1H 21
Ston Easton. *Som* 1B 22
Stonebridge. *N Som* 1G 21
Stonebridge. *Surr* 2C 22
Stonebridge. *Surr* 1C 26
Stone Bridge Corner. *Pet* 5B 76
Stonebroom. *Derbs* 5B 86
Stonebyres. *S Lan* 5B 128
Stone Chair. *W Yor* 2B 92
Stone Cross. *E Sus* 5H 27
Stone Cross. *Kent* 2G 27
Stone-edge-Batch. *N Som* 4H 33
Stoneferry. *Hull* 1D 94
Stonefield. *Arg* 5D 140
Stonefield. *S Lan* 4H 127
Stonegate. *E Sus* 3A 28
Stonegate. *N Yor* 4E 107
Stonegrave. *N Yor* 2A 100
Stonehall. *Worc* 1D 49
Stonehaugh. *Nmbd* 2A 114
Stonehaven. *Abers* 5F 153
Stone Heath. *Staf* 2D 72
Stone Hill. *Kent* 2E 29
Stone House. *Cumb* 1G 97
Stonehouse. *Glos* 5D 48
Stonehouse. *Nmbd* 4H 113
Stonehouse. *S Lan* 5A 128
Stone in Oxney. *Kent* 3D 28
Stoneleigh. *Warw* 3H 61
Stoneley Green. *Ches E* 5A 84
Stonely. *Cambs* 4A 64
Stonepits. *Worc* 5E 61
Stoner Hill. *Hants* 4F 25
Stonesby. *Leics* 3F 75
Stonesfield. *Oxon* 4B 50
Stones Green. *Essx* 3E 55
Stone Street. *Kent* 5G 39
Stone Street. *Suff* 2C 54
(nr. Boxford)
Stone Street. *Suff* 2F 67
(nr. Halesworth)
Stonethwaite. *Cumb* 3D 102
Stoneyburn. *W Lot* 3C 128
Stoney Cross. *Hants* 1A 16
Stoneyford. *Devn* 2D 12
Stoneygate. *Leic* 5D 74
Stoneyhills. *Essx* 1D 40
Stoneykirk. *Dum* 4F 109
Stoney Middleton. *Derbs* 3G 85
Stoney Stanton. *Leics* 1B 62
Stoney Stoke. *Som* 3C 22
Stoney Stratton. *Som* 3B 22
Stoney Stretton. *Shrp* 5F 71
Stoneywood. *Aber* 2F 153
Stonham Aspal. *Suff* 5D 66
Stonnall. *Staf* 5E 73
Stonor. *Oxon* 3F 37
Stonton Wyville. *Leics* 1E 63
Stonybreck. *Shet* 1B 172
Stony Cross. *Devn* 4F 19
Stony Cross. *Here* 1C 48
(nr. Great Malvern)
Stony Cross. *Here* 4H 59
(nr. Leominster)
Stony Houghton. *Derbs* 4B 86
Stony Stratford. *Mil* 1F 51
Stoodleigh. *Devn* 4D 19
(nr. Barnstaple)
Stoodleigh. *Devn* 1C 12
(nr. Tiverton)
Stopham. *W Sus* 4B 26

Stopsley. *Lutn* 3B 52
Stoptide. *Corn* 1C 6
Storeton. *Mers* 2F 83
Stormontfield. *Per* 1D 136
Stornoway. *W Isl* 4G 171
Stornoway Airport. *W Isl* 4G 171
Storridge. *Here* 1C 48
Storrington. *W Sus* 4B 26
Storrs. *Cumb* 5E 103
Storth. *Cumb* 1D 97
Stotfield. *Mor* 1G 159
Stotfold. *C Beds* 2C 52
Stottesdon. *Shrp* 2A 60
Stoughton. *Leics* 5D 74
Stoughton. *Surr* 5A 38
Stoughton. *W Sus* 1G 17
Stoul. *High* 4F 147
Stoulton. *Worc* 1E 49
Stourbridge. *W Mid* 2C 60
Stourpaine. *Dors* 2D 14
Stourport-on-Severn.
    Worc 3C 60
Stour Provost. *Dors* 4C 22
Stour Row. *Dors* 4D 22
Stourton. *Staf* 2C 60
Stourton. *Warw* 2A 50
Stourton. *W Yor* 1D 92
Stourton. *Wilts* 3C 22
Stourton Caundle. *Dors* 1C 14
Stoven. *Suff* 2G 67
Stow. *Linc* 2H 75
(nr. Billingborough)
Stow. *Linc* 2F 87
(nr. Gainsborough)
Stow. *Bord* 5A 130
Stow Bardolph. *Norf* 5F 77
Stow Bedon. *Norf* 1B 66
Stowbridge. *Norf* 5F 77
Stow cum Quy. *Cambs* 4E 65
Stowe. *Glos* 5A 48
Stowe. *Shrp* 3F 59
Stowe. *Staf* 4F 73
Stowe-by-Chartley. *Staf* 3E 73
Stowell. *Som* 4B 22
Stowey. *Bath* 1A 22
Stowford. *Devn* 2G 19
(nr. Combe Martin)
Stowford. *Devn* 4D 12
(nr. Exmouth)
Stowford. *Devn* 4E 11
(nr. Tavistock)
Stowlangtoft. *Suff* 4B 66
Stow Longa. *Cambs* 3A 64
Stow Maries. *Essx* 1C 40
Stowmarket. *Suff* 5C 66
Stow-on-the-Wold. *Glos* 3G 49
Stowting. *Kent* 1F 29
Stowupland. *Suff* 5C 66
Straad. *Arg* 3B 126
Strachan. *Abers* 4D 152
Strangford. *Here* 3A 48
Stranraer. *Dum* 3F 109
Strata Florida. *Cdgn* 4G 57
Stratfield Mortimer. *W Ber* 5E 37
Stratfield Saye. *Hants* 5E 37
Stratfield Turgis. *Hants* 1E 25
Stratford. *Glos* 2D 49
Stratford. *G Lon* 2E 39
Stratford St Andrew. *Suff* 4F 67
Stratford St Mary. *Suff* 2D 54
Stratford sub Castle. *Wilts* 3G 23

Swinton—Thorncliffe

Swinton. *S Yor* 1B 86
Swithland. *Leics* 4C 74
Swordale. *High* 2H 157
Swordly. *High* 2H 167
Sworton Heath. *Ches E* 2A 84
Swyddffynnon. *Cdgn* 4F 57
Swyffrd. *Cphy* 2F 33
Swynnerton. *Staf* 2C 72
Swyre. *Dors* 4A 14
Sycharth. *Powy* 3E 70
Sychdyn. *Flin* 4E 83
Sychnant. *Powy* 3B 58
Sychtyn. *Powy* 5B 70
Syde. *Glos* 4E 49
Sydenham. *G Lon* 3E 39
Sydenham. *Oxon* 5F 51
Sydenham. *Som* 3G 21
Sydenham Damerel. *Devn* 5E 11
Syderstone. *Norf* 2H 77
Sydling St Nicholas. *Dors* 3B 14
Sydmonton. *Hants* 1C 24
Sydney. *Ches E* 5B 84
Syerston. *Notts* 1E 75
Syke. *G Man* 3G 91
Sykehouse. *S Yor* 3G 93
Sykes. *Lanc* 4F 97
Syleham. *Suff* 3E 66
Sylen. *Carm* 5F 45
Sylfaen. *Powy* 5D 70
Symbister. *Shet* 5G 173
Symington. *S Ayr* 1C 116
Symington. *S Lan* 1B 118
Symondsbury. *Dors* 3H 13
Symonds Yat. *Here* 4A 48
Synod Inn. *Cdgn* 5D 56
Syre. *High* 4G 167
Syreford. *Glos* 3F 49
Syresham. *Nptn* 1E 51
Syston. *Leics* 4D 74
Syston. *Linc* 1G 75
Sytchampton. *Worc* 4C 60
Sywell. *Nptn* 4F 63

T

Tabost. *W Isl* 6F 171 (nr. Cearsiadar)
Tabost. *W Isl* 1H 171 (nr. Suainebost)
Tachbrook Mallory. *Warw* 4H 61
Tackley. *Oxon* 3C 50
Tacleit. *W Isl* 4D 171
Tacolneston. *Norf* 1D 66
Tadcaster. *N Yor* 5G 99
Taddington. *Derbs* 3F 85
Taddington. *Glos* 2F 49
Taddiport. *Devn* 1E 11
Tadley. *Hants* 5E 36
Tadlow. *Cambs* 1C 52
Tadmarton. *Oxon* 2B 50
Tadwick. *Bath* 4C 34
Tadworth. *Surr* 5D 38
Tafarnaubach. *Blae* 4E 46
Tafarn-y-bwlch. *Pemb* 1E 43
Tafarn-y-Gelyn. *Den* 4D 82
Taff's Well. *Rhon* 3E 33
Tafolwern. *Powy* 5A 70
Taibach. *Neat* 3A 32
Tai-bach. *Powy* 3D 70
Taigh a Ghearraidh. *W Isl* 1C 170
Tain. *High* 5E 165 (nr. Invergordon)
Tain. *High* 2E 169 (nr. Thurso)
Tai-Nant. *Wrex* 1E 71
Tai'n Lon. *Gwyn* 5D 80
Tairbeart. *W Isl* 7D 171
Tairgwaith. *Neat* 4H 45
Takeley. *Essx* 3F 53
Takeley Street. *Essx* 3F 53
Talachddu. *Powy* 2D 46
Talacre. *Flin* 2D 82
Talardd. *Gwyn* 3A 70
Talaton. *Devn* 3D 12
Talbenny. *Pemb* 3C 42
Talbot Green. *Rhon* 3D 32
Taleford. *Devn* 3D 12
Talerddig. *Powy* 5B 70
Talgarreg. *Cdgn* 5D 56
Talgarth. *Powy* 2E 47
Talisker. *High* 5C 154
Talke. *Staf* 5C 84
Talkin. *Cumb* 4G 113
Talladale. *High* 1B 156
Talla Linnfoots. *Bord* 2D 118
Tallaminnock. *S Ayr* 5D 116
Tallarn Green. *Wrex* 1G 71
Tallentire. *Cumb* 1C 102
Talley. *Carm* 2G 45
Tallington. *Linc* 5H 75
Talmine. *High* 2F 167
Talog. *Carm* 2H 43
Talsarn. *Carm* 3A 46
Talsarn. *Cdgn* 5E 57
Talsarnau. *Gwyn* 2F 69
Talskiddy. *Corn* 2D 6
Talwrn. *IOA* 3D 81
Talwrn. *Wrex* 1E 71
Tal-y-bont. *Cdgn* 2F 57
Tal-y-Bont. *Cnwy* 4G 81
Tal-y-bont. *Gwyn* 3F 81 (nr. Bangor)
Tal-y-bont. *Gwyn* 3E 69 (nr. Barmouth)
Talybont-on-Usk. *Powy* 3E 46
Tal-y-cafn. *Cnwy* 3G 81
Tal-y-coed. *Mon* 4H 47
Tal-y-llyn. *Gwyn* 5G 69
Talyllyn. *Powy* 3E 46
Talysarn. *Gwyn* 5D 81
Tal-y-waenydd. *Gwyn* 1F 69
Talywain. *Torf* 5F 47
Talywern. *Powy* 5H 69
Tamerton Foliot. *Plym* 2A 8
Tamworth. *Staf* 5G 73
Tamworth Green. *Linc* 1C 76
Tandlehill. *Ren* 3F 127
Tandridge. *Surr* 5E 39
Tanerdy. *Carm* 3E 45
Tanfield. *Dur* 4E 115
Tanfield Lea. *Dur* 4E 115
Tangasdale. *W Isl* 8B 170
Tang Hall. *York* 4A 100
Tangiers. *Pemb* 3D 42
Tangley. *Hants* 1B 24
Tangmere. *W Sus* 5A 26
Tangwick. *Shet* 4D 173
Tankerness. *Orkn* 7E 172
Tankersley. *S Yor* 1H 85
Tankerton. *Kent* 4F 41
Tan-lan. *Cnwy* 4G 81
Tan-lan. *Gwyn* 1F 69
Tannach. *High* 4F 169
Tannadice. *Ang* 3D 145
Tanner's Green. *Worc* 3E 61
Tannington. *Suff* 4E 67
Tannochside. *N Lan* 3A 128
Tan Office Green. *Suff* 5G 65
Tansley. *Derbs* 5H 85
Tansley Knoll. *Derbs* 4H 85
Tansor. *Nptn* 1H 63
Tantobie. *Dur* 4E 115
Tanton. *N Yor* 3C 106
Tanvats. *Linc* 4A 88
Tanworth-in-Arden. *Warw* 3F 61
Tan-y-bwlch. *Gwyn* 1F 69
Tan-y-fron. *Cnwy* 4B 82
Tanyfron. *Wrex* 5E 83
Tan-y-goes. *Cdgn* 1C 44
Tanygrisiau. *Gwyn* 1F 69
Tan-y-pistyll. *Powy* 3C 70
Tan-yr-allt. *Den* 2C 82
Taobh a Chaolais. *W Isl* 7C 170
Taobh a Deas Loch Aineort. *W Isl* 6C 170
Taobh a Ghlinne. *W Isl* 6F 171
Taobh a Tuath Loch Aineort. *W Isl* 6C 170
Taplow. *Buck* 2A 38
Tapton. *Derbs* 3A 86
Tarbert. *Arg* 1E 125 (on Jura)
Tarbert. *Arg* 3G 125 (on Kintyre)
Tarbert. *W Isl* 7D 171
Tarbet. *Arg* 3C 134
Tarbet. *High* 4F 147 (nr. Mallaig)
Tarbet. *High* 4B 166 (nr. Scourie)
Tarbock Green. *Mers* 2G 83
Tarbolton. *S Ayr* 2D 116
Tarbrax. *S Lan* 4D 128
Tardebigge. *Worc* 4E 61
Tarfside. *Ang* 1D 145
Tarland. *Abers* 3B 152
Tarleton. *Lanc* 2C 90
Tarlogie. *High* 5E 165
Tarlscough. *Lanc* 3C 90
Tarlton. *Glos* 2E 35
Tarnbrook. *Lanc* 4E 97
Tarnock. *Som* 1G 21
Tarns. *Cumb* 5C 112
Tarporley. *Ches W* 4H 83
Tarpots. *Essx* 2B 40
Tarr. *Som* 3E 20
Tarrant Crawford. *Dors* 2E 15
Tarrant Gunville. *Dors* 1E 15
Tarrant Hinton. *Dors* 1E 15
Tarrant Keyneston. *Dors* 2E 15
Tarrant Launceston. *Dors* 2E 15
Tarrant Monkton. *Dors* 2E 15
Tarrant Rawston. *Dors* 2E 15
Tarrant Rushton. *Dors* 2E 15
Tarrel. *High* 5F 165
Tarring Neville. *E Sus* 5F 27
Tarrington. *Here* 1B 48
Tarsappie. *Per* 1D 136
Tarscabhaig. *High* 3D 147
Tarskavaig. *High* 3D 147
Tarves. *Abers* 5F 161
Tarvie. *High* 3G 157
Tarvin. *Ches W* 4G 83
Tasburgh. *Norf* 1E 66
Tasley. *Shrp* 1A 60
Taston. *Oxon* 3B 50
Tatenhill. *Staf* 3G 73
Tathall End. *Mil* 1G 51
Tatham. *Lanc* 3F 97
Tathwell. *Linc* 2C 88
Tatling End. *Buck* 2B 38
Tatsfield. *Surr* 5F 39
Tattenhall. *Ches W* 5G 83
Tatterford. *Norf* 3A 78
Tattersett. *Norf* 2H 77
Tattershall. *Linc* 5B 88
Tattershall Bridge. *Linc* 5A 88
Tattershall Thorpe. *Linc* 5B 88
Tattingstone. *Suff* 2E 55
Tattingstone White Horse. *Suff* 2E 55
Tattle Bank. *Warw* 4F 61
Tatworth. *Som* 2G 13
Taunton. *Som* 4F 21
Taverham. *Norf* 4D 78
Taverners Green. *Essx* 4F 53
Tavernspite. *Pemb* 3F 43
Tavistock. *Devn* 5E 11
Tavool House. *Arg* 1B 132
Taw Green. *Devn* 3G 11
Tawstock. *Devn* 4F 19
Taxal. *Derbs* 2E 85
Tayinloan. *Arg* 5E 125
Taynish. *Arg* 1F 125
Taynton. *Glos* 3C 48
Taynton. *Oxon* 4H 49
Taynuilt. *Arg* 5E 141
Tayport. *Fife* 1G 137
Tay Road Bridge. *Fife* 1G 137
Tayvallich. *Arg* 1F 125
Tealby. *Linc* 1A 88
Tealing. *Ang* 5D 144
Teams. *Tyne* 3F 115
Teangue. *High* 3E 147
Tebay. *Cumb* 4H 103
Tebworth. *C Beds* 3H 51
Tedburn St Mary. *Devn* 3B 12
Teddington. *Glos* 2E 49
Teddington. *G Lon* 3C 38
Tedsmore. *Shrp* 3F 71
Tedstone Delamere. *Here* 5A 60
Tedstone Wafer. *Here* 5A 60
Teesport. *Red C* 2C 106
Teesside. *Stoc T* 2C 106
Teeton. *Nptn* 3D 62
Teffont Evias. *Wilts* 3E 23
Teffont Magna. *Wilts* 3E 23
Tegryn. *Pemb* 1G 43
Teigh. *Rut* 4F 75
Teigncombe. *Devn* 4G 11
Teigngrace. *Devn* 5B 12
Teignmouth. *Devn* 5C 12
Telford. *Telf* 4A 72
Telham. *E Sus* 4B 28
Tellisford. *Som* 1D 22
Telscombe. *E Sus* 5F 27
Telscombe Cliffs. *E Sus* 5E 27
Tempar. *Per* 3D 142
Templand. *Dum* 1B 112
Temple. *Corn* 5B 10
Temple. *Glas* 3G 127
Temple. *Midl* 4G 129
Temple Balsall. *W Mid* 3G 61
Temple Bar. *Carm* 4F 45
Temple Bar. *Cdgn* 5E 57
Temple Cloud. *Bath* 1B 22
Templecombe. *Som* 4C 22
Temple Ewell. *Kent* 1G 29
Temple Grafton. *Warw* 5F 61
Temple Guiting. *Glos* 3F 49
Templehall. *Fife* 4E 137
Temple Hirst. *N Yor* 2G 93
Temple Normanton. *Derbs* 4B 86
Temple Sowerby. *Cumb* 2H 103
Templeton. *Devn* 1B 12
Templeton. *Pemb* 3F 43
Templeton. *W Ber* 5B 36
Templetown. *Dur* 5E 115
Tempsford. *C Beds* 5A 64
Tenandry. *Per* 2G 143
Tenbury Wells. *Worc* 4H 59
Tenby. *Pemb* 4F 43
Tendring. *Essx* 3E 55
Tendring Green. *Essx* 3E 55
Tenga. *Arg* 4G 139
Ten Mile Bank. *Norf* 1F 65
Tenterden. *Kent* 2C 28
Terfyn. *Cnwy* 3B 82
Terhill. *Som* 3E 21
Terling. *Essx* 4A 54
Ternhill. *Shrp* 2A 72
Terregles. *Dum* 2G 111
Terrick. *Buck* 5G 51
Terrington. *N Yor* 2A 100
Terrington St Clement. *Norf* 3E 77
Terrington St John. *Norf* 4E 77
Terry's Green. *Warw* 3F 61
Teston. *Kent* 5B 40
Testwood. *Hants* 1B 16
Tetbury. *Glos* 2D 35
Tetbury Upton. *Glos* 2D 35
Tetchill. *Shrp* 2F 71
Tetcott. *Devn* 3D 10
Tetford. *Linc* 3C 88
Tetney. *Linc* 4G 95
Tetney Lock. *Linc* 4G 95
Tetsworth. *Oxon* 5E 51
Tettenhall. *W Mid* 1C 60
Teversal. *Notts* 4B 86
Teversham. *Cambs* 5D 65
Teviothead. *Bord* 4G 119
Tewel. *Abers* 5F 153
Tewin. *Herts* 4C 52
Tewkesbury. *Glos* 2D 49
Teynham. *Kent* 4D 40
Teynham Street. *Kent* 4D 40
Thackthwaite. *Cumb* 2F 103
Thakeham. *W Sus* 4C 26
Thame. *Oxon* 5F 51
Thames Ditton. *Surr* 4C 38
Thames Haven. *Thur* 2B 41
Thamesmead. *G Lon* 2F 39
Thamesport. *Kent* 3C 40
Thamesport. *Medw* 3C 40
Thanington Without. *Kent* 5F 41
Thankerton. *S Lan* 1B 118
Tharston. *Norf* 1D 66
Thatcham. *W Ber* 5D 36
Thatto Heath. *Mers* 1H 83
Thaxted. *Essx* 2G 53
Theakston. *N Yor* 1F 99
Thealby. *N Lin* 3B 94
Theale. *Som* 2H 21
Theale. *W Ber* 4E 37
Thearne. *E Yor* 1D 94
Theberton. *Suff* 4G 67
Theddingworth. *Leics* 2D 62
Theddlethorpe All Saints. *Linc* 2D 88
Theddlethorpe St Helen. *Linc* 2D 89
Thelbridge Barton. *Devn* 1A 12
Thelnetham. *Suff* 3C 66
Thelveton. *Norf* 2D 66
Thelwall. *Warr* 2A 84
Themelthorpe. *Norf* 3C 78
Thenford. *Nptn* 1D 50
Therfield. *Herts* 2D 52
Thetford. *Linc* 4A 76
Thetford. *Norf* 2A 66
Thethwaite. *Cumb* 5E 113
Theydon Bois. *Essx* 1F 39
Thick Hollins. *W Yor* 3B 92
Thickwood. *Wilts* 4D 34
Thimbleby. *Linc* 3B 88
Thimbleby. *N Yor* 5B 106
Thingwall. *Mers* 2E 83
Thirlby. *N Yor* 1G 99
Thirlestane. *Bord* 5B 130
Thirn. *N Yor* 1E 98
Thirsk. *N Yor* 1G 99
Thirtleby. *E Yor* 1E 95
Thistleton. *Lanc* 1C 90
Thistleton. *Rut* 4G 75
Thistley Green. *Suff* 3F 65
Thixendale. *N Yor* 3C 100
Thockrington. *Nmbd* 2C 114
Tholomas Drove. *Cambs* 5D 76
Tholthorpe. *N Yor* 3G 99
Thomas Chapel. *Pemb* 4F 43
Thomas Close. *Cumb* 5F 113
Thomastown. *Abers* 4E 160
Thomastown. *Rhon* 3D 32
Thompson. *Norf* 1B 66
Thomshill. *Mor* 3G 159
Thong. *Kent* 3A 40
Thongsbridge. *W Yor* 4B 92
Thoralby. *N Yor* 1C 98
Thoresby. *Notts* 3D 86
Thoresway. *Linc* 1A 88
Thorganby. *Linc* 1B 88
Thorganby. *N Yor* 5A 100
Thorgill. *N Yor* 5E 107
Thorington. *Suff* 3G 67
Thorington Street. *Suff* 2D 54
Thorlby. *N Yor* 4B 98
Thorley. *Herts* 4E 53
Thorley Street. *Herts* 4E 53
Thorley Street. *IOW* 4B 16
Thormanby. *N Yor* 2G 99
Thorn. *Powy* 4E 59
Thornaby-on-Tees. *Stoc T* 3B 106
Thornage. *Norf* 2C 78
Thornborough. *Buck* 2F 51
Thornborough. *N Yor* 2E 99
Thornbury. *Devn* 2E 11
Thornbury. *Here* 5A 60
Thornbury. *S Glo* 3B 34
Thornby. *Cumb* 4D 112
Thornby. *Nptn* 3D 62
Thorncliffe. *Staf* 5E 85

Toller Whelme—Trewen

Toller Whelme. *Dors* 2A 14
Tollesbury. *Essx* 4C 54
Tolleshunt D'Arcy. *Essx* 4C 54
Tolleshunt Knights. *Essx* 4C 54
Tolleshunt Major. *Essx* 4C 54
Tollie. *High* 3H 157
Tollie Farm. *High* 1A 156
Tolm. *W Isl* 4G 171
Tolpuddle. *Dors* 3C 14
Tolstadh bho Thuath. *W Isl* 3H 171
Tolworth. *G Lon* 4C 38
Tomachlaggan. *Mor* 1F 151
Tomaknock. *Per* 1A 136
Tomatin. *High* 1C 150
Tombuidhe. *Arg* 3H 133
Tomdoun. *High* 3D 148
Tomich. *High* 1F 149
(nr. Cannich)
Tomich. *High* 1B 158
(nr. Invergordon)
Tomich. *High* 3D 164
(nr. Lairg)
Tomintoul. *Mor* 2F 151
Tomnavoulin. *Mor* 1G 151
Tomsleibhe. *Arg* 5A 140
Ton. *Mon* 2G 33
Tonbridge. *Kent* 1G 27
Tondu. *B'end* 3B 32
Tonedale. *Som* 4E 21
Tonfanau. *Gwyn* 5E 69
Tong. *Shrp* 5B 72
Tonge. *Leics* 3B 74
Tong Forge. *Shrp* 5B 72
Tongham. *Surr* 2G 25
Tongland. *Dum* 4D 111
Tong Norton. *Shrp* 5B 72
Tongue. *High* 3F 167
Tongue End. *Linc* 4A 76
Tongwynlais. *Card* 3E 33
Tonmawr. *Neat* 2B 32
Tonna. *Neat* 2A 32
Tonnau. *Neat* 2A 32
Ton-Pentre. *Rhon* 2C 32
Ton-Teg. *Rhon* 3D 32
Tonwell. *Herts* 4D 52
Tonypandy. *Rhon* 2C 32
Tonyrefail. *Rhon* 3D 32
Toot Baldon. *Oxon* 5D 50
Toot Hill. *Essx* 5F 53
Toot Hill. *Hants* 1B 16
Topcliffe. *N Yor* 2G 99
Topcliffe. *W Yor* 2C 92
Topcroft. *Norf* 1E 67
Topcroft Street. *Norf* 1E 67
Toppesfield. *Essx* 2H 53
Toppings. *G Man* 3F 91
Toprow. *Norf* 1D 66
Topsham. *Devn* 4C 12
Torbay. *Torb* 2F 9
Torbeg. *N Ayr* 3C 122
Torbothie. *N Lan* 3B 128
Torbryan. *Devn* 2E 9
Torcross. *Devn* 4E 9
Tore. *High* 3A 158
Torgyle. *High* 2F 149
Torinturk. *Arg* 3G 125
Torksey. *Linc* 3F 87
Torlum. *W Isl* 3C 170
Torlundy. *High* 1F 141
Tormarton. *S Glo* 4C 34
Tormitchell. *S Ayr* 5B 116
Tormore. *High* 3E 147
Tormore. *N Ayr* 2C 122
Tornagrain. *High* 4B 158
Tornaveen. *Abers* 3D 152
Torness. *High* 1H 149
Toronto. *Dur* 1E 105
Torpenhow. *Cumb* 1D 102
Torphichen. *W Lot* 2C 128
Torphins. *Abers* 3D 152
Torpoint. *Corn* 3A 8
Torquay. *Torb* 2F 9
Torr. *Devn* 3B 8
Torra. *Arg* 4B 124
Torran. *High* 4E 155
Torrance. *E Dun* 2H 127
Torrans. *Arg* 1B 132
Torranyard. *E Ayr* 5E 127
Torre. *Som* 3D 20
Torre. *Torb* 2E 9
Torridon. *High* 3B 156
Torrin. *High* 1D 147
Torrisdale. *Arg* 2B 122
Torrisdale. *High* 2G 167
Torrish. *High* 2G 165
Torrisholme. *Lanc* 3D 96
Torroble. *High* 3C 164
Torroy. *High* 4C 164
Torry. *Aber* 3G 153
Torryburn. *Fife* 1D 128
Torthorwald. *Dum* 2B 112
Tortington. *W Sus* 5B 26
Tortworth. *S Glo* 2C 34
Torvaig. *High* 4D 155
Torver. *Cumb* 5D 102
Torwood. *Falk* 1B 128
Torworth. *Notts* 2D 86
Toscaig. *High* 5G 155
Toseland. *Cambs* 4B 64
Tosside. *Lanc* 4G 97
Tostock. *Suff* 4B 66
Totaig. *High* 3B 154
Totardor. *High* 5C 154
Tote. *High* 4D 154
Totegan. *High* 2A 168
Tothill. *Linc* 2D 88
Totland. *IOW* 4B 16
Totley. *S Yor* 3H 85
Totnell. *Dors* 2B 14
Totnes. *Devn* 2E 9
Toton. *Derbs* 2B 74
Totronald. *Arg* 3C 138
Totscore. *High* 2C 154
Tottenham. *G Lon* 1E 39
Tottenhill. *Norf* 4F 77
Tottenhill Row. *Norf* 4F 77
Totteridge. *G Lon* 1D 38
Totternhoe. *C Beds* 3H 51
Tottington. *G Man* 3F 91
Totton. *Hants* 1B 16
Touchen-end. *Wind* 4G 37
Toulvaddie. *High* 5F 165
Towans, The. *Corn* 3C 4
Toward. *Arg* 3C 126
Towcester. *Nptn* 1E 51
Towednack. *Corn* 3B 4
Tower End. *Norf* 4F 77
Tower Hill. *Mers* 4C 90
Tower Hill. *W Sus* 3C 26
Towersey. *Oxon* 5F 51
Towie. *Abers* 2B 152
Towiemore. *Mor* 4A 160
Tow Law. *Dur* 1E 105
Town End. *Cambs* 1D 64
Town End. *Cumb* 4F 103
(nr. Ambleside)
Town End. *Cumb* 2H 103
(nr. Kirkby Thore)
Town End. *Cumb* 1D 96
(nr. Lindale)
Town End. *Cumb* 1C 96
(nr. Newby Bridge)
Town End. *Mers* 2G 83
Townend. *W Dun* 2F 127
Townfield. *Dur* 5C 114
Towngate. *Cumb* 5G 113
Towngate. *Linc* 4A 76
Town Green. *Lanc* 4B 90
Town Head. *Cumb* 4E 103
(nr. Grasmere)
Town Head. *Cumb* 3H 103
(nr. Great Asby)
Townhead. *Cumb* 1G 103
(nr. Lazonby)
Townhead. *Cumb* 1B 102
(nr. Maryport)
Townhead. *Cumb* 1H 103
(nr. Ousby)
Townhead. *Dum* 5D 111
Townhead of Greenlaw. *Dum* 3E 111
Townhill. *Fife* 1E 129
Townhill. *Swan* 3F 31
Town Kelloe. *Dur* 1A 106
Town Littleworth. *E Sus* 4F 27
Town Row. *E Sus* 2G 27
Towns End. *Hants* 1D 24
Townsend. *Herts* 5B 52
Townshend. *Corn* 3C 4
Town Street. *Suff* 2G 65
Town, The. *IOS* 1A 4
Town Yetholm. *Bord* 2C 120
Towthorpe. *E Yor* 3C 100
Towthorpe. *York* 4A 100
Towton. *N Yor* 1E 93
Towyn. *Cnwy* 3B 82
Toxteth. *Mers* 2F 83
Toynton All Saints. *Linc* 4C 88
Toynton Fen Side. *Linc* 4C 88
Toynton St Peter. *Linc* 4D 88
Toy's Hill. *Kent* 5F 39
Trabboch. *E Ayr* 2D 116
Traboe. *Corn* 4E 5
Tradespark. *High* 3C 158
Trafford Park. *G Man* 1B 84
Trallong. *Powy* 3C 46
Tranent. *E Lot* 2H 129
Tranmere. *Mers* 2F 83
Trantlebeg. *High* 3A 168
Trantlemore. *High* 3A 168
Tranwell. *Nmbd* 1E 115
Trapp. *Carm* 4G 45
Traquair. *Bord* 1F 119
Trash Green. *W Ber* 5E 37
Trawden. *Lanc* 1H 91
Trawscoed. *Powy* 2D 46
Trawsfynydd. *Gwyn* 2G 69
Trawsgoed. *Cdgn* 3F 57
Treaddow. *Here* 3A 48
Trealaw. *Rhon* 2D 32
Treales. *Lanc* 1C 90
Trearddur. *IOA* 3B 80
Treaslane. *High* 3C 154
Treator. *Corn* 1D 6
Trebanog. *Rhon* 2D 32
Trebanos. *Neat* 5H 45
Trebarber. *Corn* 2C 6
Trebartha. *Corn* 5C 10
Trebarwith. *Corn* 4A 10
Trebetherick. *Corn* 1D 6
Treborough. *Som* 3D 20
Trebudannon. *Corn* 2C 6
Trebullett. *Corn* 5D 10
Treburley. *Corn* 5D 10
Treburrick. *Corn* 1C 6
Trebyan. *Corn* 2E 7
Trecastle. *Powy* 3B 46
Trecenydd. *Cphy* 3E 33
Trecott. *Devn* 2G 11
Trecwn. *Pemb* 1D 42
Trecynon. *Rhon* 5C 46
Tredaule. *Corn* 4C 10
Tredavoe. *Corn* 4B 4
Tredegar. *Blae* 5E 47
Trederwen. *Powy* 4E 71
Tredington. *Glos* 3E 49
Tredington. *Warw* 1A 50
Tredinnick. *Corn* 2F 7
(nr. Bodmin)
Tredinnick. *Corn* 3G 7
(nr. Looe)
Tredinnick. *Corn* 1D 6
(nr. Padstow)
Tredogan. *V Glam* 5D 32
Tredomen. *Powy* 2E 46
Tredunnock. *Mon* 2G 33
Tredustan. *Powy* 2E 47
Treen. *Corn* 4A 4
(nr. Land's End)
Treen. *Corn* 3B 4
(nr. St Ives)
Treeton. *S Yor* 2B 86
Trefaldwyn. *Powy* 1E 58
Trefasser. *Pemb* 1C 42
Trefdraeth. *IOA* 3D 80
Trefdraeth. *Pemb* 1E 43
Trefecca. *Powy* 2E 47
Trefechan. *Mer T* 5D 46
Trefeglwys. *Powy* 1B 58
Trefeitha. *Powy* 2E 46
Trefenter. *Cdgn* 4F 57
Treffgarne. *Pemb* 2D 42
Treffynnon. *Flin* 3D 82
Treffynnon. *Pemb* 2C 42
Trefil. *Blae* 4E 46
Trefilan. *Cdgn* 5E 57
Trefin. *Pemb* 1C 42
Treflach. *Shrp* 3E 71
Trefnant. *Den* 3C 82
Trefonen. *Shrp* 3E 71
Trefor. *Gwyn* 1C 68
Trefor. *IOA* 2C 80
Treforest. *Rhon* 3D 32
Trefrew. *Corn* 4B 10
Trefriw. *Cnwy* 4G 81
Tref-y-Clawdd. *Powy* 3E 59
Trefynwy. *Mon* 4A 48
Tregada. *Corn* 4D 10
Tregadillett. *Corn* 4D 10
Tregare. *Mon* 4H 47
Tregarne. *Corn* 4E 5
Tregaron. *Cdgn* 5F 57
Tregarth. *Gwyn* 4F 81
Tregear. *Corn* 3C 6
Tregeare. *Corn* 4C 10
Tregeiriog. *Wrex* 2D 70
Tregele. *IOA* 1C 80
Tregeseal. *Corn* 3A 4
Tregiskey. *Corn* 4E 6
Tregole. *Corn* 3B 10
Tregolwyn. *V Glam* 4C 32
Tregonetha. *Corn* 2D 6
Tregonhawke. *Corn* 3A 8
Tregony. *Corn* 4D 6
Tregoodwell. *Corn* 4B 10
Tregorrick. *Corn* 3E 6
Tregoss. *Corn* 2D 6
Tregowris. *Corn* 4E 5
Tregoyd. *Powy* 2E 47
Tregrehan Mills. *Corn* 3E 7
Tre-groes. *Cdgn* 1E 45
Tregullon. *Corn* 2E 7
Tregurrian. *Corn* 2C 6
Tregynon. *Powy* 1C 58
Trehafod. *Rhon* 2D 32
Trehan. *Corn* 3A 8
Treharris. *Mer T* 2E 32
Treherbert. *Rhon* 2C 32
Trehunist. *Corn* 2H 7
Trekenner. *Corn* 5D 10
Trekenning. *Corn* 2D 6
Treknow. *Corn* 4A 10
Trelales. *B'end* 3B 32
Trelan. *Corn* 5E 5
Trelash. *Corn* 3B 10
Trelassick. *Corn* 3C 6
Trelawnyd. *Flin* 3C 82
Trelech. *Carm* 1G 43
Treleddyd-fawr. *Pemb* 2B 42
Trelewis. *Mer T* 2E 32
Treligga. *Corn* 4A 10
Trelights. *Corn* 1D 6
Trelill. *Corn* 5A 10
Trelissick. *Corn* 5C 6
Trellech. *Mon* 5A 48
Trelleck Grange. *Mon* 5H 47
Trelogan. *Flin* 2D 82
Trelystan. *Powy* 5E 71
Tremadog. *Gwyn* 1E 69
Tremail. *Corn* 4B 10
Tremain. *Cdgn* 1C 44
Tremaine. *Corn* 4C 10
Tremar. *Corn* 2G 7
Trematon. *Corn* 3H 7
Tremeirchion. *Den* 3C 82
Tremore. *Corn* 2E 6
Tremorfa. *Card* 4F 33
Trenance. *Corn* 2C 6
(nr. Newquay)
Trenance. *Corn* 1D 6
(nr. Padstow)
Trenarren. *Corn* 4E 7
Trench. *Telf* 4A 72
Trencreek. *Corn* 2C 6
Trendeal. *Corn* 3C 6
Trenear. *Corn* 5A 6
Treneglos. *Corn* 4C 10
Trenewan. *Corn* 3F 7
Trengune. *Corn* 3B 10
Trent. *Dors* 1A 14
Trentham. *Stoke* 1C 72
Trentishoe. *Devn* 2G 19
Trentlock. *Derbs* 2B 74
Treoes. *V Glam* 4C 32
Treorchy. *Rhon* 2C 32
Treorci. *Rhon* 2C 32
Tre'r-ddol. *Cdgn* 1F 57
Tre'r llai. *Powy* 5E 71
Trerulefoot. *Corn* 3H 7
Tresaith. *Cdgn* 5B 56
Trescott. *Staf* 1C 60
Trescowe. *Corn* 3C 4
Tresham. *Glos* 2C 34
Tresigin. *V Glam* 4C 32
Tresillian. *Corn* 4C 6
Tresimwn. *V Glam* 4D 32
Tresinney. *Corn* 4B 10
Treskillard. *Corn* 5A 6
Treskinnick Cross. *Corn* 3C 10
Tresmeer. *Corn* 4C 10
Tresparrett. *Corn* 3B 10
Tresparrett Posts. *Corn* 3B 10
Tressady. *High* 3D 164
Tressait. *Per* 2F 143
Tresta. *Shet* 6E 173
Treswell. *Notts* 3E 87
Treswithian. *Corn* 3D 4
Tre Taliesin. *Cdgn* 1F 57
Trethomas. *Cphy* 3E 33
Trethosa. *Corn* 3D 6
Trethurgy. *Corn* 3E 7
Tretio. *Pemb* 2B 42
Tretire. *Here* 3A 48
Tretower. *Powy* 3E 47
Treuddyn. *Flin* 5E 83
Trevadlock. *Corn* 5C 10
Trevalga. *Corn* 3A 10
Trevalyn. *Wrex* 5F 83
Trevance. *Corn* 1D 6
Trevanger. *Corn* 1D 6
Trevanson. *Corn* 1D 6
Trevarrack. *Corn* 3B 4
Trevarren. *Corn* 2D 6
Trevarrian. *Corn* 2C 6
Trevarrick. *Corn* 4D 6
Tre-vaughan. *Carm* 3E 45
(nr. Carmarthen)
Trevaughan. *Carm* 3F 43
(nr. Whitland)
Treveighan. *Corn* 5A 10
Trevellas. *Corn* 3B 6
Trevelmond. *Corn* 2G 7
Treverva. *Corn* 5B 6
Trevescan. *Corn* 4A 4
Trevethin. *Torf* 5F 47
Trevia. *Corn* 4A 10
Trevigro. *Corn* 2H 7
Trevilley. *Corn* 4A 4
Treviscoe. *Corn* 3D 6
Trevivian. *Corn* 4B 10
Trevone. *Corn* 1C 6
Trevor. *Wrex* 1E 71
Trevor Uchaf. *Den* 1E 71
Trew. *Corn* 4D 4
Trewalder. *Corn* 4A 10
Trewarlett. *Corn* 4D 10
Trewarmett. *Corn* 4A 10
Trewassa. *Corn* 4B 10
Treween. *Corn* 4C 10
Trewellard. *Corn* 3A 4
Trewen. *Corn* 4C 10

Trewennack. Corn 4D 5
Trewern. Powy 4E 71
Trewetha. Corn 5A 10
Trewidland. Corn 2G 7
Trewint. Corn 3B 10
Trewithian. Corn 5C 6
Trewoofe. Corn 4B 4
Trewoon. Corn 3D 6
Treworthal. Corn 5C 6
Trewyddel. Pemb 1B 44
Treyarnon. Corn 1C 6
Treyford. W Sus 1G 17
Triangle. Staf 5E 73
Triangle. W Yor 2A 92
Trickett's Cross. Dors 2F 15
Trimdon. Dur 1A 106
Trimdon Colliery. Dur 1A 106
Trimdon Grange. Dur 1A 106
Trimingham. Norf 2E 79
Trimley Lower Street. Suff 2F 55
Trimley St Martin. Suff 2F 55
Trimley St Mary. Suff 2F 55
Trimpley. Worc 3B 60
Trimsaran. Carm 5E 45
Trimstone. Devn 2F 19
Trinafour. Per 2E 142
Trinant. Cphy 2F 33
Tring. Herts 4H 51
Trinity. Ang 2F 145
Trinity. Edin 2F 129
Trisant. Cdgn 3G 57
Triscombe. Som 3E 21
Trislaig. High 1E 141
Trispen. Corn 3C 6
Tritlington. Nmbd 5G 121
Trochry. Per 4G 143
Troedrhiwdalar. Powy 5B 58
Troedrhiwfuwch. Cphy 5E 47
Troedrhiwgwair. Blae 5E 47
Troedyraur. Cdgn 1D 44
Troedyrhiw. Mer T 5D 46
Trondavoe. Shet 4E 173
Troon. Corn 5A 6
Troon. S Ayr 1C 116
Troqueer. Dum 2A 112
Troston. Suff 3A 66
Trottiscliffe. Kent 4H 39
Trotton. W Sus 4G 25
Troutbeck. Cumb 4F 103
(nr. Ambleside)
Troutbeck. Cumb 2E 103
(nr. Penrith)
Troutbeck Bridge. Cumb 4F 103
Troway. Derbs 3A 86
Trowbridge. Wilts 1D 22
Trowell. Notts 2B 74
Trowle Common. Wilts 1D 22
Trowley Bottom. Herts 4A 52
Trowse Newton. Norf 5E 79
Trudoxhill. Som 2C 22
Trull. Som 4F 21
Trumaisgearraidh. W Isl 1D 170
Trumpan. High 2B 154
Trumpet. Here 2B 48
Trumpington. Cambs 5D 64
Trumps Green. Surr 4A 38
Trunch. Norf 2E 79
Trunnah. Lanc 5C 96
Truro. Corn 4C 6
Trusham. Devn 4B 12
Trusley. Derbs 2G 73
Trusthorpe. Linc 2E 89
Tryfil. IOA 2D 80
Trysull. Staf 1C 60
Tubney. Oxon 2C 36
Tuckenhay. Devn 3E 9
Tuckhill. Shrp 2B 60
Tuckingmill. Corn 4A 6
Tuckton. Bour 3G 15
Tuddenham. Suff 3G 65
Tuddenham St Martin. Suff 1E 55
Tudeley. Kent 1H 27
Tudhoe. Dur 1F 105
Tudhoe Grange. Dur 1F 105

Tudorville. Here 3A 48
Tudweiliog. Gwyn 2B 68
Tuesley. Surr 1A 26
Tufton. Hants 2C 24
Tufton. Pemb 2E 43
Tugby. Leics 5E 75
Tugford. Shrp 2H 59
Tughall. Nmbd 2G 121
Tulchan. Per 1B 136
Tullibardine. Per 2B 136
Tullibody. Clac 4A 136
Tullich. Arg 2H 133
Tullich. High 4B 156
(nr. Lochcarron)
Tullich. High 1C 158
(nr. Tain)
Tullich. Mor 4H 159
Tullich Muir. High 1B 158
Tulliemet. Per 3G 143
Tulloch. Abers 5F 161
Tulloch. High 4D 164
(nr. Bonar Bridge)
Tulloch. High 5F 149
(nr. Fort William)
Tulloch. High 2D 151
(nr. Grantown-on-Spey)
Tulloch. Per 1C 136
Tullochgorm. Arg 4G 133
Tullybeagles Lodge. Per 5H 143
Tullymurdoch. Per 3A 144
Tullynessle. Abers 2C 152
Tumble. Carm 4F 45
Tumbler's Green. Essx 3B 54
Tumby. Linc 4B 88
Tumby Woodside. Linc 5B 88
Tummel Bridge. Per 3E 143
Tunbridge Wells, Royal. Kent 2G 27
Tunga. W Isl 4G 171
Tungate. Norf 3E 79
Tunley. Bath 1B 22
Tunstall. E Yor 1G 95
Tunstall. Kent 4C 40
Tunstall. Lanc 2E 97
Tunstall. Norf 5G 79
Tunstall. N Yor 5F 105
Tunstall. Staf 3B 72
Tunstall. Stoke 5C 84
Tunstall. Suff 5F 67
Tunstall. Tyne 4G 115
Tunstead. Derbs 3F 85
Tunstead. Norf 3E 79
Tunstead Milton. Derbs 2E 85
Tunworth. Hants 2E 25
Tupsley. Here 1A 48
Tupton. Derbs 4A 86
Turfholm. S Lan 1H 117
Turfmoor. Devn 2F 13
Turgis Green. Hants 1E 25
Turkdean. Glos 4G 49
Turkey Island. Hants 1D 16
Tur Langton. Leics 1E 62
Turleigh. Wilts 5D 34
Turin Moor. Pool 3E 15
Turnant. Here 3G 47
Turnastone. Here 2G 47
Turnberry. S Ayr 4B 116
Turnchapel. Plym 3A 8
Turnditch. Derbs 1G 73
Turners Hill. W Sus 2E 27
Turners Puddle. Dors 3D 14
Turnford. Herts 5D 52
Turnhouse. Edin 2E 129
Turnworth. Dors 2D 14
Turriff. Abers 4E 161
Tursdale. Dur 1A 106
Turton Bottoms. Bkbn 3F 91
Turtory. Mor 4C 160
Turves Green. W Mid 3E 61
Turvey. Bed 5G 63
Turville. Buck 2F 37
Turville Heath. Buck 2F 37
Turweston. Buck 2E 50
Tushielaw. Bord 3F 119
Tutbury. Staf 3G 73

Tutnall. Worc 3D 61
Tutshill. Glos 2A 34
Tuttington. Norf 3E 79
Tutts Clump. W Ber 4D 36
Tutwell. Corn 5D 11
Tuxford. Notts 3E 87
Twatt. Orkn 5B 172
Twatt. Shet 6E 173
Twechar. E Dun 2A 128
Tweedale. Telf 5B 72
Tweedmouth. Nmbd 4F 131
Tweedsmuir. Bord 2C 118
Twelveheads. Corn 4B 6
Twemlow Green. Ches E 4B 84
Twenty. Linc 3A 76
Twerton. Bath 5C 34
Twickenham. G Lon 3C 38
Twigworth. Glos 3D 48
Twineham. W Sus 3D 26
Twinhoe. Bath 1C 22
Twinstead. Essx 2B 54
Twinstead Green. Essx 2B 54
Twiss Green. Warr 1A 84
Twiston. Lanc 5H 97
Twitchen. Devn 3A 20
Twitchen. Shrp 3F 59
Two Bridges. Devn 5G 11
Two Bridges. Glos 5B 48
Two Dales. Derbs 4G 85
Two Gates. Staf 5G 73
Two Mile Oak. Devn 2E 9
Twycross. Leics 5H 73
Twyford. Buck 3E 51
Twyford. Derbs 3H 73
Twyford. Dors 1D 14
Twyford. Hants 4C 24
Twyford. Leics 4E 75
Twyford. Norf 3C 78
Twyford. Wok 4F 37
Twyford Common. Here 2A 48
Twynholm. Dum 4D 110
Twyning. Glos 2D 49
Twyning Green. Glos 2E 49
Twynllanan. Carm 3A 46
Twyn-y-Sheriff. Mon 5H 47
Twywell. Nptn 3G 63
Tyberton. Here 2G 47
Tyburn. W Mid 1F 61
Tyby. Norf 3C 78
Tycroes. Carm 4G 45
Tycrwyn. Powy 4D 70
Tydd Gote. Linc 4D 76
Tydd St Giles. Cambs 4D 76
Tydd St Mary. Linc 4D 76
Tye. Hants 2F 17
Tye Green. Essx 3F 53
(nr. Bishop's Stortford)
Tye Green. Essx 3A 54
(nr. Braintree)
Tye Green. Essx 2F 53
(nr. Saffron Walden)
Tyersal. W Yor 1B 92
Ty Issa. Powy 3D 70
Tyldesley. G Man 4E 91
Tyle. Carm 3G 45
Tyler Hill. Kent 4F 41
Tyler's Green. Buck 2G 37
Tyler's Green. Essx 5F 53
Tylorstown. Rhon 2D 32
Tylwch. Powy 2B 58
Ty-nant. Cnwy 1B 70
Tyndrum. Stir 5H 141
Tyneham. Dors 4D 15
Tynehead. Midl 4G 129
Tynemouth. Tyne 3G 115
Tyneside. Tyne 3F 115
Tyne Tunnel. Tyne 3G 115
Tyningham. E Lot 2C 130
Tynron. Dum 5H 117
Ty'n-y-bryn. Rhon 3D 32
Tyn-y-celyn. Wrex 2D 70

Tyn-y-cwm. Swan 5G 45
Tyn-y-ffridd. Powy 2D 70
Tynygongl. IOA 2E 81
Tynygraig. Cdgn 4F 57
Tyn-y-groes. Cnwy 3G 81
Ty'n-yr-eithin. Cdgn 4F 57
Tyn-y-rhyd. Powy 4C 70
Tyn-y-wern. Powy 3C 70
Tyrie. Abers 2G 161
Tyringham. Mil 1G 51
Tythecott. Devn 1E 11
Tythegston. B'end 4B 32
Tytherington. Ches E 3D 84
Tytherington. Som 2C 22
Tytherington. S Glo 3B 34
Tytherington. Wilts 2E 23
Tytherleigh. Devn 2G 13
Tywardreath. Corn 3E 7
Tywardreath Highway. Corn 3E 7
Tywyn. Cnwy 3G 81
Tywyn. Gwyn 5E 69

U

Uags. High 5G 155
Ubbeston Green. Suff 3F 67
Ubley. Bath 1A 22
Uckerby. N Yor 4F 105
Uckfield. E Sus 3F 27
Uckinghall. Worc 2D 48
Uckington. Glos 3E 49
Uckington. Shrp 5H 71
Uddingston. S Lan 3H 127
Uddington. S Lan 1A 118
Udimore. E Sus 4C 28
Udny Green. Abers 1F 153
Udny Station. Abers 1G 153
Udston. S Lan 4A 128
Udstonhead. S Lan 5A 128
Uffcott. Wilts 4G 35
Uffculme. Devn 1D 12
Uffington. Linc 5H 75
Uffington. Oxon 3B 36
Uffington. Shrp 4H 71
Ufford. Pet 5H 75
Ufford. Suff 5E 67
Ufton. Warw 4A 62
Ufton Nervet. W Ber 5E 37
Ugadale. Arg 3B 122
Ugborough. Devn 3C 8
Ugford. Wilts 3F 23
Uggeshall. Suff 2G 67
Ugglebarnby. N Yor 4F 107
Ugley. Essx 3F 53
Ugley Green. Essx 3F 53
Ugthorpe. N Yor 3E 107
Uidh. W Isl 9B 170
Uig. Arg 3C 138
Uig. High 2C 154
(nr. Balgown)
Uig. High 3B 154
(nr. Dunvegan)
Uigshader. High 4D 154
Uisken. Arg 2A 132
Ulbster. High 4F 169
Ulcat Row. Cumb 2F 103
Ulceby. Linc 3D 88
Ulceby. N Lin 3E 94
Ulceby Skitter. N Lin 3E 94
Ulcombe. Kent 1C 28
Uldale. Cumb 1D 102
Uley. Glos 2C 34
Ulgham. Nmbd 5G 121
Ullapool. High 4F 163
Ullenhall. Warw 4F 61
Ulleskelf. N Yor 1F 93
Ullesthorpe. Leics 2C 62
Ulley. S Yor 2B 86
Ullingswick. Here 1A 48
Ullinish. High 5C 154
Ullock. Cumb 2B 102
Ulpha. Cumb 5C 102
Ulrome. E Yor 4F 101

Ulsta. Shet 3F 173
Ulting. Essx 5B 54
Ulva House. Arg 5F 139
Ulverston. Cumb 2B 96
Ulwell. Dors 4F 15
Umberleigh. Devn 4G 19
Unapool. High 5C 166
Underbarrow. Cumb 5F 103
Undercliffe. W Yor 1B 92
Underdale. Shrp 4H 71
Underriver. Kent 5G 39
Under Tofts. S Yor 2H 85
Underton. Shrp 1A 60
Underwood. Newp 3G 33
Underwood. Notts 5B 86
Underwood. Plym 3B 8
Undley. Suff 2F 65
Undy. Mon 3H 33
Union Mills. IOM 4C 108
Union Street. E Sus 2B 28
Unstone. Derbs 3A 86
Unstone Green. Derbs 3A 86
Unthank. Cumb 5E 113
(nr. Carlisle)
Unthank. Cumb 5H 113
(nr. Gamblesby)
Unthank. Cumb 1F 103
(nr. Penrith)
Unthank End. Cumb 1F 103
Upavon. Wilts 1G 23
Up Cerne. Dors 2B 14
Upchurch. Kent 4C 40
Upcott. Devn 2F 11
Upcott. Here 5F 59
Upend. Cambs 5G 65
Up Exe. Devn 2C 12
Upgate. Norf 4D 78
Upgate Street. Norf 1C 66
Uphall. Dors 2A 14
Uphall. W Lot 2D 128
Uphall Station. W Lot 2D 128
Upham. Devn 2B 12
Upham. Hants 4D 24
Uphampton. Here 4F 59
Uphampton. Worc 4C 60
Up Hatherley. Glos 3E 49
Uphill. N Som 1G 21
Up Holland. Lanc 4D 90
Uplawmoor. E Ren 4F 127
Upleadon. Glos 3C 48
Upleatham. Red C 3D 106
Uplees. Kent 4D 40
Uploders. Dors 3A 14
Uplowman. Devn 1D 12
Uplyme. Devn 3G 13
Up Marden. W Sus 1F 17
Upminster. G Lon 2G 39
Up Nately. Hants 1E 25
Upottery. Devn 2F 13
Uppat. High 3F 165

Upper Affcot. Shrp 2G 59
Upper Arley. Worc 2B 60
Upper Armley. W Yor 1C 92
Upper Arncott. Oxon 4E 50
Upper Astrop. Nptn 2D 50
Upper Badcall. High 4B 166
Upper Bangor. Gwyn 3E 81
Upper Basildon. W Ber 4D 36
Upper Batley. W Yor 2C 92
Upper Beeding. W Sus 4C 26
Upper Benefield. Nptn 2G 63
Upper Bentley. Worc 4D 61
Upper Bighouse. High 3A 168
Upper Boddam. Abers 5D 160
Upper Boddington. Nptn 5B 62
Upper Bogside. Mor 3G 159
Upper Booth. Derbs 2F 85
Upper Borth. Cdgn 2F 57
Upper Boyndlie. Abers 2G 161
Upper Brailes. Warw 2B 50
Upper Breinton. Here 1H 47
Upper Broadheath. Worc 5C 60
Upper Broughton. Notts 3D 74
Upper Brynamman. Carm 4H 45

Upper Bucklebury—Walkerburn

Upper Bucklebury. *W Ber* 5D 36
Upper Bullington. *Hants* 2C 24
Upper Burgate. *Hants* 1G 15
Upper Caldecote. *C Beds* 1B 52
Upper Canterton. *Hants* 1A 16
Upper Catesby. *Nptn* 5C 62
Upper Chapel. *Powy* 1D 46
Upper Cheddon. *Som* 4F 21
Upper Chicksgrove. *Wilts* 4E 23
Upper Church Village. *Rhon* 3D 32
Upper Chute. *Wilts* 1A 24
Upper Clatford. *Hants* 2B 24
Upper Coberley. *Glos* 4E 49
Upper Coedcae. *Torf* 5F 47
Upper Cokeham. *W Sus* 5C 26
Upper Common. *Hants* 2E 25
Upper Cound. *Shrp* 5H 71
Upper Cudworth. *S Yor* 4D 93
Upper Cumberworth. *W Yor* 4C 92
Upper Cuttlehill. *Abers* 4B 160
Upper Cwmbran. *Torf* 2F 33
Upper Dallachy. *Mor* 2A 160
Upper Dean. *Bed* 4H 63
Upper Denby. *W Yor* 4C 92
Upper Derraid. *High* 5E 159
Upper Diabaig. *High* 2H 155
Upper Dicker. *E Sus* 5G 27
Upper Dinchope. *Shrp* 2G 59
Upper Dochcarty. *High* 2H 157
Upper Dounreay. *High* 2B 168
Upper Dovercourt. *Essx* 2F 55
Upper Dunsforth. *N Yor* 3G 99
Upper Dunsley. *Herts* 4H 51
Upper Eastern Green. *W Mid* 2G 61
Upper Elkstone. *Staf* 5E 85
Upper Ellastone. *Staf* 1F 73
Upper End. *Derbs* 3E 85
Upper Enham. *Hants* 2B 24
Upper Farmcote. *Shrp* 1B 60
Upper Farringdon. *Hants* 3F 25
Upper Framilode. *Glos* 4C 48
Upper Froyle. *Hants* 2F 25
Upper Gills. *High* 1F 169
Upper Glenfintaig. *High* 5E 149
Upper Godney. *Som* 2H 21
Upper Gravenhurst. *C Beds* 2B 52
Upper Green. *Essx* 2E 53
Upper Green. *W Ber* 5B 36
Upper Green. *W Yor* 2C 92
Upper Grove Common. *Here* 3A 48
Upper Hackney. *Derbs* 4G 85
Upper Hale. *Surr* 2G 25
Upper Halliford. *Surr* 4B 38
Upper Halling. *Medw* 4A 40
Upper Hambleton. *Rut* 5G 75
Upper Hardres Court. *Kent* 5F 41
Upper Hardwick. *Here* 5G 59
Upper Hartfield. *E Sus* 2F 27
Upper Haugh. *S Yor* 1B 86
Upper Hayton. *Shrp* 2H 59
Upper Heath. *Shrp* 2H 59
Upper Hellesdon. *Norf* 4E 79
Upper Helmsley. *N Yor* 4A 100
Upper Hengoed. *Shrp* 2E 71
Upper Hergest. *Here* 5E 59
Upper Heyford. *Nptn* 5D 62
Upper Heyford. *Oxon* 3C 50
Upper Hill. *Here* 5G 59
Upper Hindhope. *Bord* 4B 120
Upper Hopton. *W Yor* 3B 92
Upper Howsell. *Worc* 1C 48
Upper Hulme. *Staf* 4E 85
Upper Inglesham. *Swin* 2H 35
Upper Kilcott. *Glos* 3C 34
Upper Killay. *Swan* 3E 31
Upper Kirkton. *Abers* 5E 161
Upper Kirkton. *N Ayr* 4C 126
Upper Knockando. *Mor* 4F 159
Upper Knockchoilum. *High* 2G 149
Upper Lambourn. *W Ber* 3B 36
Upper Langford. *N Som* 1H 21
Upper Langwith. *Derbs* 4C 86
Upper Largo. *Fife* 3G 137
Upper Latheron. *High* 5D 169
Upper Layham. *Suff* 1D 54
Upper Leigh. *Staf* 2E 73
Upper Lenie. *High* 1H 149
Upper Lochton. *Abers* 4E 152
Upper Longdon. *Staf* 4E 73
Upper Longwood. *Shrp* 5A 72
Upper Lybster. *High* 5E 169
Upper Lydbrook. *Glos* 4B 48
Upper Lye. *Here* 4F 59
Upper Maes-coed. *Here* 2G 47
Upper Midway. *Derbs* 3G 73
Uppermill. *G Man* 4H 91
Upper Millichope. *Shrp* 2H 59
Upper Milovaig. *High* 4A 154
Upper Minety. *Wilts* 2F 35
Upper Mitton. *Worc* 3C 60
Upper Nash. *Pemb* 4E 43
Upper Netchwood. *Shrp* 1A 60
Upper Nobut. *Staf* 2E 73
Upper North Dean. *Buck* 2G 37
Upper Norwood. *W Sus* 4A 26
Upper Nyland. *Dors* 4C 22
Upper Oddington. *Glos* 3H 49
Upper Ollach. *High* 5E 155
Upper Outwoods. *Staf* 3G 73
Upper Padley. *Derbs* 3G 85
Upper Pennington. *Hants* 3B 16
Upper Poppleton. *York* 4H 99
Upper Quinton. *Warw* 1G 49
Upper Rissington. *Glos* 4H 49
Upper Rochford. *Worc* 4A 60
Upper Rusko. *Dum* 3C 110
Upper Sandaig. *High* 2F 147
Upper Sanday. *Orkn* 7E 172
Upper Sapey. *Here* 4A 60
Upper Seagry. *Wilts* 3E 35
Upper Shelton. *C Beds* 1H 51
Upper Sheringham. *Norf* 1D 78
Upper Skelmorlie. *N Ayr* 3C 126
Upper Slaughter. *Glos* 3G 49
Upper Sonachan. *Arg* 1H 133
Upper Soudley. *Glos* 4B 48
Upper Staploe. *Bed* 5A 64
Upper Stoke. *Norf* 5E 79
Upper Stondon. *C Beds* 2B 52
Upper Stowe. *Nptn* 5D 62
Upper Street. *Hants* 1G 15
Upper Street. *Norf* 4F 79
(nr. Horning)
Upper Street. *Norf* 4F 79
(nr. Hoveton)
Upper Street. *Suff* 2E 55
Upper Strensham. *Worc* 2E 49
Upper Studley. *Wilts* 1D 22
Upper Sundon. *C Beds* 3A 52
Upper Swell. *Glos* 3G 49
Upper Tankersley. *S Yor* 1H 85
Upper Tean. *Staf* 2E 73
Upperthong. *W Yor* 4B 92
Upperthorpe. *N Lin* 4A 94
Upper Thurnham. *Lanc* 4D 96
Upper Tillyrie. *Per* 3D 136
Upperton. *W Sus* 3A 26
Upper Tooting. *G Lon* 3D 38
Uppertown. *Derbs* 4H 85
(nr. Ashover)
Upper Town. *Derbs* 5G 85
(nr. Bonsall)
Upper Town. *Derbs* 5G 85
(nr. Hognaston)
Upper Town. *Here* 1A 48
Uppertown. *High* 1F 169
Upper Town. *N Som* 5A 34
Uppertown. *Nmbd* 2B 114
Uppertown. *Orkn* 8D 172
Upper Tysoe. *Warw* 1B 50
Upper Upham. *Wilts* 4H 35
Upper Upnor. *Medw* 3B 40
Upper Urquhart. *Fife* 3D 136
Upper Wardington. *Oxon* 1C 50
Upper Weald. *Mil* 2G 51
Upper Weedon. *Nptn* 5D 62
Upper Wellingham. *E Sus* 4F 27
Upper Whiston. *S Yor* 2B 86
Upper Wield. *Hants* 3E 25
Upper Winchendon. *Buck* 4F 51
Upperwood. *Derbs* 5G 85
Upper Woodford. *Wilts* 3G 23
Upper Wootton. *Hants* 1D 24
Upper Wraxall. *Wilts* 4D 34
Upper Wyche. *Here* 1C 48
Uppincott. *Devn* 2B 12
Uppingham. *Rut* 1F 63
Uppington. *Shrp* 5H 71
Upsall. *N Yor* 1G 99
Upsettlington. *Bord* 5E 131
Upshire. *Essx* 5E 53
Up Somborne. *Hants* 3B 24
Upstreet. *Kent* 4G 41
Up Sydling. *Dors* 2B 14
Upthorpe. *Suff* 3B 66
Upton. *Buck* 4F 51
Upton. *Cambs* 3A 64
Upton. *Ches W* 4G 83
Upton. *Corn* 2C 10
(nr. Bude)
Upton. *Corn* 5C 10
(nr. Liskeard)
Upton. *Cumb* 1E 102
Upton. *Devn* 2D 12
(nr. Honiton)
Upton. *Devn* 4D 8
(nr. Kingsbridge)
Upton. *Dors* 3E 15
(nr. Poole)
Upton. *Dors* 4C 14
(nr. Weymouth)
Upton. *E Yor* 4F 101
Upton. *Hants* 1B 24
(nr. Andover)
Upton. *Hants* 1B 16
(nr. Southampton)
Upton. *IOW* 3D 16
Upton. *Leics* 1A 62
Upton. *Linc* 2F 87
Upton. *Mers* 2E 83
Upton. *Norf* 4F 79
Upton. *Nptn* 4E 62
Upton. *Notts* 3E 87
(nr. Retford)
Upton. *Notts* 5E 87
(nr. Southwell)
Upton. *Oxon* 3D 36
Upton. *Pemb* 4E 43
Upton. *Pet* 5A 76
Upton. *Slo* 3A 38
Upton. *Som* 4H 21
(nr. Somerton)
Upton. *Som* 4C 20
(nr. Wiveliscombe)
Upton. *Warw* 5F 61
Upton. *W Yor* 3E 93
Upton. *Wilts* 3D 22
Upton Bishop. *Here* 3B 48
Upton Cheyney. *S Glo* 5B 34
Upton Cressett. *Shrp* 1A 60
Upton Crews. *Here* 3B 48
Upton Cross. *Corn* 5C 10
Upton End. *C Beds* 2B 52
Upton Grey. *Hants* 2E 25
Upton Heath. *Ches W* 4G 83
Upton Hellions. *Devn* 2B 12
Upton Lovell. *Wilts* 2E 23
Upton Magna. *Shrp* 4H 71
Upton Noble. *Som* 3C 22
Upton Pyne. *Devn* 3C 12
Upton St Leonards. *Glos* 4D 48
Upton Scudamore. *Wilts* 2D 22
Upton Snodsbury. *Worc* 5D 60
Upton upon Severn. *Worc* 1D 48
Upton Warren. *Worc* 4D 60
Upwaltham. *W Sus* 4A 26
Upware. *Cambs* 3E 65
Upwell. *Cambs* 5D 77
Upwey. *Dors* 4B 14
Upwick Green. *Herts* 3E 53
Upwood. *Cambs* 2B 64
Urafirth. *Shet* 4E 173
Uragaig. *Arg* 4A 132
Urchany. *High* 4C 158
Urchfont. *Wilts* 1F 23
Urdimarsh. *Here* 1A 48
Ure. *Shet* 4D 173
Ure Bank. *N Yor* 2F 99
Urgha. *W Isl* 8D 171
Urlay Nook. *Stoc T* 3B 106
Urmston. *G Man* 1B 84
Urquhart. *Mor* 2G 159
Urra. *N Yor* 4C 106
Urray. *High* 3H 157
Usan. *Ang* 3G 145
Ushaw Moor. *Dur* 5F 115
Usk. *Mon* 5G 47
Usselby. *Linc* 1H 87
Usworth. *Tyne* 4G 115
Utkinton. *Ches W* 4H 83
Uton. *Devn* 3B 12
Utterby. *Linc* 1C 88
Uttoxeter. *Staf* 2E 73
Uwchmynydd. *Gwyn* 3A 68
Uxbridge. *G Lon* 2B 38
Uyeasound. *Shet* 1G 173
Uzmaston. *Pemb* 3D 42

V

Valley. *IOA* 3B 80
Valley End. *Surr* 4A 38
Valley Truckle. *Corn* 4B 10
Valtos. *High* 2E 155
Van. *Powy* 2B 58
Vange. *Essx* 2B 40
Varteg. *Torf* 5F 47
Vatten. *High* 4B 154
Vaul. *Arg* 4B 138
Vauld,The. *Here* 1A 48
Vaynol. *Gwyn* 3E 81
Vaynor. *Mer T* 4D 46
Veensgarth. *Shet* 7F 173
Velindre. *Powy* 2E 47
Vellow. *Som* 3D 20
Velly. *Devn* 4C 18
Venhay. *Devn* 1A 12
Venn. *Devn* 4D 8
Venngreen. *Devn* 1D 11
Vennington. *Shrp* 5F 71
Venn Ottery. *Devn* 3D 12
Venn's Green. *Here* 1A 48
Venny Tedburn. *Devn* 3B 12
Venterdon. *Corn* 5D 10
Ventnor. *IOW* 5D 16
Vernham Dean. *Hants* 1B 24
Vernham Street. *Hants* 1B 24
Vernolds Common. *Shrp* 2G 59
Verwood. *Dors* 2F 15
Veryan. *Corn* 5D 6
Veryan Green. *Corn* 4D 6
Vicarage. *Devn* 4F 13
Vickerstown. *Cumb* 3A 96
Victoria. *Corn* 2D 6
Vidlin. *Shet* 5F 173
Viewpark. *N Lan* 3A 128
Vigo. *W Mid* 5E 73
Vigo Village. *Kent* 4H 39
Village Bay. *High* 3B 154
Vinehall Street. *E Sus* 3B 28
Vine's Cross. *E Sus* 4G 27
Viney Hill. *Glos* 5B 48
Virginia Water. *Surr* 4A 38
Virginstow. *Devn* 3D 11
Vobster. *Som* 2C 22
Voe. *Shet* 5E 173
Vole. *Som* 2G 21
Vowchurch. *Here* 2G 47
Vulcan Village. *Warr* 1H 83

W

Waberthwaite. *Cumb* 5C 102
Wackerfield. *Dur* 2E 105
Wacton. *Norf* 1D 66
Wadborough. *Worc* 1E 49
Wadbrook. *Devn* 2G 13
Waddesdon. *Buck* 4F 51
Waddeton. *Devn* 3E 9
Waddicar. *Mers* 1F 83
Waddingham. *Linc* 1G 87
Waddington. *Lanc* 5G 97
Waddington. *Linc* 4G 87
Waddon. *Devn* 5B 12
Wadebridge. *Corn* 1D 6
Wadeford. *Som* 1G 13
Wadenhoe. *Nptn* 2H 63
Wadesmill. *Herts* 4D 52
Wadhurst. *E Sus* 2H 27
Wadshelf. *Derbs* 3H 85
Wadsley. *S Yor* 1H 85
Wadsley Bridge. *S Yor* 1H 85
Wadswick. *Wilts* 5D 34
Wadwick. *Hants* 1C 24
Wadworth. *S Yor* 1C 86
Waen. *Den* 4C 82
(nr. Bodfari)
Waen. *Den* 4D 82
(nr. Llandyrnog)
Waen. *Den* 4B 82
(nr. Nantglyn)
Waen. *Powy* 1B 58
Waen Fach. *Powy* 4E 70
Waen Goleugoed. *Den* 3C 82
Wag. *High* 1H 165
Wainfleet All Saints. *Linc* 5D 89
Wainfleet Bank. *Linc* 5D 88
Wainfleet St Mary. *Linc* 5D 89
Wainhouse Corner. *Corn* 3B 10
Wainscott. *Medw* 3B 40
Wainstalls. *W Yor* 2A 92
Waitby. *Cumb* 4A 104
Waithe. *Linc* 4F 95
Wakefield. *W Yor* 2D 92
Wakerley. *Nptn* 1G 63
Wakes Colne. *Essx* 3B 54
Walberswick. *Suff* 3G 67
Walberton. *W Sus* 5A 26
Walbottle. *Tyne* 3E 115
Walby. *Cumb* 3F 113
Walcombe. *Som* 2A 22
Walcot. *Linc* 2H 75
Walcot. *N Lin* 2B 94
Walcot. *Swin* 3G 35
Walcot. *Telf* 4H 71
Walcot. *Warw* 5F 61
Walcote. *Leics* 2C 62
Walcot Green. *Norf* 2D 66
Walcott. *Linc* 5A 88
Walcott. *Norf* 2F 79
Walden. *N Yor* 1C 98
Walden Head. *N Yor* 1B 98
Walden Stubbs. *N Yor* 3F 93
Walderslade. *Medw* 4B 40
Walderton. *W Sus* 1F 17
Walditch. *Dors* 3H 13
Waldley. *Derbs* 2F 73
Waldridge. *Dur* 4F 115
Waldringfield. *Suff* 1F 55
Waldron. *E Sus* 4G 27
Wales. *S Yor* 2B 86
Walesby. *Linc* 1A 88
Walesby. *Notts* 3D 86
Walford. *Here* 3F 59
(nr. Leintwardine)
Walford. *Here* 3A 48
(nr. Ross-on-Wye)
Walford. *Shrp* 3G 71
Walford. *Staf* 2C 72
Walford Heath. *Shrp* 4G 71
Walgherton. *Ches E* 1A 72
Walgrave. *Nptn* 3F 63
Walhampton. *Hants* 3B 16
Walkden. *G Man* 4F 91
Walker. *Tyne* 3F 115
Walkerburn. *Bord* 1F 119

Welbury—Westmeston

Welbury. *N Yor* 4A **106**
Welby. *Linc* 2G **75**
Welches Dam. *Cambs* 2D **64**
Welcombe. *Devn* 1C **10**
Weld Bank. *Lanc* 3D **90**
Weldon. *Nptn* 2G **63**
Weldon. *Nmbd* 5F **121**
Welford. *Nptn* 2D **62**
Welford. *W Ber* 4C **36**
Welford-on-Avon. *Warw* 5F **61**
Welham. *Leics* 1E **63**
Welham. *Notts* 2E **87**
Welham Green. *Herts* 5C **52**
Well. *Hants* 2F **25**
Well. *Linc* 3D **88**
Well. *N Yor* 1E **99**
Welland. *Worc* 1C **48**
Wellbank. *Ang* 5D **144**
Well Bottom. *Dors* 1E **15**
Welldale. *Dum* 3C **112**
Wellesbourne. *Warw* 5G **61**
Well Hill. *Kent* 4F **39**
Wellhouse. *W Ber* 4D **36**
Welling. *G Lon* 3F **39**
Wellingborough. *Nptn* 4F **63**
Wellingham. *Norf* 3A **78**
Wellingore. *Linc* 5G **87**
Wellington. *Cumb* 4B **102**
Wellington. *Here* 1H **47**
Wellington. *Som* 4E **21**
Wellington. *Telf* 4A **72**
Wellington Heath. *Here* 1C **48**
Wellow. *Bath* 1C **22**
Wellow. *IOW* 4B **16**
Wellow. *Notts* 4D **86**
Wellpond Green. *Herts* 3E **53**
Wells. *Som* 2A **22**
Wellsborough. *Leics* 5A **74**
Wells Green. *Ches E* 5A **84**
Wells-next-the-Sea. *Norf* 1B **78**
Wells of Ythan. *Abers* 5D **160**
Wellswood. *Torb* 2F **9**
Wellwood. *Fife* 1D **129**
Welney. *Norf* 1E **65**
Welsford. *Devn* 4C **18**
Welshampton. *Shrp* 2G **71**
Welsh End. *Shrp* 2H **71**
Welsh Frankton. *Shrp* 2F **71**
Welsh Hook. *Pemb* 2D **42**
Welsh Newton. *Here* 4H **47**
Welsh Newton Common. *Here* 4A **48**
Welshpool. *Powy* 5E **70**
Welsh St Donats. *V Glam* 4D **32**
Welton. *Bath* 1B **22**
Welton. *Cumb* 5E **113**
Welton. *E Yor* 2C **94**
Welton. *Linc* 2H **87**
Welton. *Nptn* 4C **62**
Welton Hill. *Linc* 2H **87**
Welton le Marsh. *Linc* 4D **88**
Welton le Wold. *Linc* 2B **88**
Welwick. *E Yor* 2G **95**
Welwyn. *Herts* 4C **52**
Welwyn Garden City. *Herts* 4C **52**
Wem. *Shrp* 3H **71**
Wembdon. *Som* 3F **21**
Wembley. *G Lon* 2C **38**
Wembury. *Devn* 4B **8**
Wembworthy. *Devn* 2G **11**
Wemyss Bay. *Inv* 2C **126**
Wenallt. *Cdgn* 3F **57**
Wenallt. *Gwyn* 1B **70**
Wendens Ambo. *Essx* 2F **53**
Wendlebury. *Oxon* 4D **50**
Wendling. *Norf* 4B **78**
Wendover. *Buck* 5G **51**
Wendron. *Corn* 5A **6**
Wendy. *Cambs* 1D **52**
Wenfordbridge. *Corn* 5A **10**
Wenhaston. *Suff* 3G **67**
Wennington. *Cambs* 3B **64**
Wennington. *G Lon* 2G **39**
Wennington. *Lanc* 2F **97**
Wensley. *Derbs* 4G **85**
Wensley. *N Yor* 1C **98**
Wentbridge. *W Yor* 3E **93**
Wentnor. *Shrp* 1F **59**
Wentworth. *Cambs* 3D **65**
Wentworth. *S Yor* 1A **86**
Wenvoe. *V Glam* 4E **32**
Weobley. *Here* 5G **59**
Weobley Marsh. *Here* 5G **59**
Wepham. *W Sus* 5B **26**
Wereham. *Norf* 5F **77**
Wergs. *W Mid* 5C **72**
Wern. *Gwyn* 1E **69**
Wern. *Powy* 4E **46**
(nr. Brecon)
Wern. *Powy* 4E **71**
(nr. Guilsfield)
Wern. *Powy* 4B **70**
(nr. Llangadfan)
Wern. *Powy* 3E **71**
(nr. Llanymynech)
Wernffrwd. *Swan* 3E **31**
Wernyrheolydd. *Mon* 4G **47**
Werrington. *Corn* 4D **10**
Werrington. *Pet* 5A **76**
Werrington. *Staf* 1D **72**
Wervin. *Ches W* 3G **83**
Wesham. *Lanc* 1C **90**
Wessington. *Derbs* 5A **86**
West Aberthaw. *V Glam* 5D **32**
West Acre. *Norf* 4G **77**
West Allerdean. *Nmbd* 5F **131**
West Alvington. *Devn* 4D **8**
West Amesbury. *Wilts* 2G **23**
West Anstey. *Devn* 4B **20**
West Appleton. *N Yor* 5F **105**
West Ardsley. *W Yor* 2C **92**
West Arthurlie. *E Ren* 4F **127**
West Ashby. *Linc* 3B **88**
West Ashling. *W Sus* 2G **17**
West Ashton. *Wilts* 1D **23**
West Auckland. *Dur* 2E **105**
West Ayton. *N Yor* 1D **101**
West Bagborough. *Som* 3E **21**
West Bank. *Hal* 2H **83**
West Barkwith. *Linc* 2A **88**
West Barnby. *N Yor* 3F **107**
West Barns. *E Lot* 2C **130**
West Barsham. *Norf* 2B **78**
West Bay. *Dors* 3H **13**
West Beckham. *Norf* 2D **78**
West Bennan. *N Ayr* 3D **123**
Westbere. *Kent* 4F **41**
West Bergholt. *Essx* 3C **54**
West Bexington. *Dors* 4A **14**
West Bilney. *Norf* 4G **77**
West Blackdene. *Dur* 1B **104**
West Blatchington. *Brig* 5D **27**
Westborough. *Linc* 1F **75**
Westbourne. *Bour* 3F **15**
Westbourne. *W Sus* 2F **17**
West Bowling. *W Yor* 1B **92**
West Brabourne. *Kent* 1E **29**
West Bradford. *Lanc* 5G **97**
West Bradley. *Som* 3A **22**
West Bretton. *W Yor* 3C **92**
West Bridgford. *Notts* 2C **74**
West Briggs. *Norf* 4F **77**
West Bromwich. *W Mid* 1D **61**
Westbrook. *Here* 1F **47**
Westbrook. *Kent* 3H **41**
Westbrook. *Wilts* 5E **35**
West Buckland. *Devn* 3G **19**
(nr. Barnstaple)
West Buckland. *Devn* 4C **8**
(nr. Thurlestone)
West Buckland. *Som* 4E **21**
West Burnside. *Abers* 1G **145**
West Burrafirth. *Shet* 6D **173**
West Burton. *N Yor* 1C **98**
West Burton. *W Sus* 4B **26**
Westbury. *Buck* 2E **50**
Westbury. *Shrp* 5F **71**
Westbury. *Wilts* 1D **22**
Westbury Leigh. *Wilts* 2D **22**
Westbury-on-Severn. *Glos* 4C **48**
Westbury on Trym. *Bris* 4A **34**
Westbury-sub-Mendip. *Som* 2A **22**
West Butsfield. *Dur* 5E **115**
West Butterwick. *N Lin* 4B **94**
Westby. *Linc* 3G **75**
West Byfleet. *Surr* 4B **38**
West Caister. *Norf* 4H **79**
West Calder. *W Lot* 3D **128**
West Camel. *Som* 4A **22**
West Carr. *N Lin* 4H **93**
West Chaldon. *Dors* 4C **14**
West Challow. *Oxon* 3B **36**
West Charleton. *Devn* 4D **8**
West Chelborough. *Dors* 2A **14**
West Chevington. *Nmbd* 5G **121**
West Chiltington. *W Sus* 4B **26**
West Chiltington Common. *W Sus* 4B **26**
West Chinnock. *Som* 1H **13**
West Chisenbury. *Wilts* 1G **23**
West Clandon. *Surr* 5B **38**
West Cliffe. *Kent* 1H **29**
Westcliff-on-Sea. *S'end* 2C **40**
West Clyne. *High* 3F **165**
West Coker. *Som* 1A **14**
Westcombe. *Som* 3B **22**
(nr. Evercreech)
Westcombe. *Som* 4H **21**
(nr. Somerton)
West Compton. *Dors* 3A **14**
West Compton. *Som* 2A **22**
West Cornforth. *Dur* 1A **106**
Westcot. *Oxon* 3B **36**
Westcott. *Buck* 4F **51**
Westcott. *Devn* 2D **12**
Westcott. *Surr* 1C **26**
Westcott Barton. *Oxon* 3C **50**
West Cowick. *E Yor* 2G **93**
West Cranmore. *Som* 2B **22**
West Croftmore. *High* 2D **150**
West Cross. *Swan* 4F **31**
West Cullerlie. *Abers* 3E **153**
West Culvennan. *Dum* 3H **109**
West Curry. *Corn* 3C **10**
West Curthwaite. *Cumb* 5E **113**
Westdean. *E Sus* 5G **27**
West Dean. *W Sus* 1G **17**
West Dean. *Wilts* 4A **24**
West Deeping. *Linc* 5A **76**
West Derby. *Mers* 1F **83**
West Dereham. *Norf* 5F **77**
West Down. *Devn* 2F **19**
Westdowns. *Corn* 4A **10**
West Drayton. *G Lon* 3B **38**
West Drayton. *Notts* 3E **86**
West Dunnet. *High* 1E **169**
West Ella. *E Yor* 2D **94**
West End. *Bed* 5G **63**
West End. *Cambs* 1D **64**
West End. *Dors* 2E **15**
West End. *E Yor* 3E **101**
(nr. Kilham)
West End. *E Yor* 1E **95**
(nr. Preston)
West End. *E Yor* 1C **94**
(nr. South Cove)
West End. *E Yor* 4F **101**
(nr. Ulrome)
West End. *G Lon* 2D **39**
West End. *Hants* 1C **16**
West End. *Herts* 5C **52**
West End. *Kent* 4F **41**
West End. *Lanc* 3D **96**
West End. *Linc* 1C **76**
West End. *Norf* 4G **79**
West End. *N Som* 5H **33**
West End. *N Yor* 4D **98**
West End. *S Glo* 3C **34**
West End. *S Lan* 5C **128**
West End. *Surr* 4A **38**
West End. *Wilts* 4E **23**
West End. *Wind* 4G **37**
West End. *Worc* 2F **49**
West End Green. *Hants* 5E **37**
Westenhanger. *Kent* 2F **29**
Wester Aberchalder. *High* 2H **149**
Wester Balgedie. *Per* 3D **136**
Wester Brae. *High* 2A **158**
Wester Culbeuchly. *Abers* 2D **160**
Westerdale. *High* 3D **168**
Westerdale. *N Yor* 4D **106**
Wester Dechmont. *W Lot* 2D **128**
Wester Fearn. *High* 5D **164**
Westerfield. *Suff* 1E **55**
Wester Galcantray. *High* 4C **158**
Westergate. *W Sus* 5A **26**
Wester Gruinards. *High* 4C **164**
Westerham. *Kent* 5F **39**
Westerleigh. *S Glo* 4B **34**
Westerloch. *High* 3F **169**
Wester Mandally. *High* 3E **149**
Wester Rarichie. *High* 1C **158**
Wester Shian. *Per* 5F **143**
Westerton. *Ang* 3F **145**
Westerton. *Dur* 1F **105**
Westerton. *W Sus* 2G **17**
Westerwick. *Shet* 7D **173**
West Farleigh. *Kent* 5B **40**
West Farndon. *Nptn* 5C **62**
West Felton. *Shrp* 3F **71**
Westfield. *Cumb* 2A **102**
Westfield. *E Sus* 4C **28**
Westfield. *High* 2C **168**
Westfield. *Norf* 5B **78**
Westfield. *N Lan* 2A **128**
Westfield. *W Lot* 2C **128**
Westfields. *Dors* 2C **14**
Westfields of Rattray. *Per* 4A **144**
West Fleetham. *Nmbd* 2F **121**
Westford. *Som* 1E **13**
West Garforth. *W Yor* 1D **93**
Westgate. *Dur* 1C **104**
Westgate. *Norf* 1B **78**
Westgate. *N Lin* 4A **94**
Westgate on Sea. *Kent* 3H **41**
West Ginge. *Oxon* 3C **36**
West Grafton. *Wilts* 5H **35**
West Green. *Hants* 1F **25**
West Grimstead. *Wilts* 4H **23**
West Grinstead. *W Sus* 3C **26**
West Haddlesey. *N Yor* 2F **93**
West Haddon. *Nptn* 3D **62**
West Hagbourne. *Oxon* 3D **36**
West Hagley. *Worc* 2C **60**
West Hall. *Cumb* 3G **113**
Westhall. *Suff* 2G **67**
West Hallam. *Derbs* 1B **74**
Westhall Terrace. *Ang* 5D **144**
West Halton. *N Lin* 2C **94**
Westham. *Dors* 5B **14**
Westham. *E Sus* 5H **27**
West Ham. *G Lon* 2E **39**
Westham. *Som* 2H **21**
Westhampnett. *W Sus* 2G **17**
West Handley. *Derbs* 3A **86**
West Hanney. *Oxon* 2C **36**
West Hanningfield. *Essx* 1B **40**
West Hardwick. *W Yor* 3E **93**
West Harnham. *Wilts* 4G **23**
West Harptree. *Bath* 1A **22**
West Harting. *W Sus* 4F **25**
West Harton. *Tyne* 3G **115**
West Hatch. *Som* 4F **21**
Westhay. *Som* 2H **21**
Westhead. *Lanc* 4C **90**
West Head. *Norf* 5E **77**
West Heath. *Hants* 1D **24**
(nr. Basingstoke)
West Heath. *Hants* 1G **25**
(nr. Farnborough)
West Helmsdale. *High* 2H **165**
West Hendred. *Oxon* 3C **36**
West Heslerton. *N Yor* 2D **100**
West Hewish. *N Som* 5G **33**
Westhide. *Here* 1A **48**
Westhill. *Abers* 3F **153**
West Hill. *Devn* 3D **12**
West Hill. *E Yor* 3F **101**
Westhill. *High* 4B **58**
West Hill. *N Som* 4H **33**
West Hill. *W Sus* 2E **27**
West Hoathly. *W Sus* 2E **27**
West Holme. *Dors* 4D **15**
Westhope. *Here* 5G **59**
Westhope. *Shrp* 2G **59**
West Horndon. *Essx* 2H **39**
Westhorp. *Nptn* 5C **62**
Westhorpe. *Linc* 2B **75**
Westhorpe. *Suff* 4C **66**
West Horrington. *Som* 2A **22**
West Horsley. *Surr* 5B **38**
West Horton. *Nmbd* 1E **121**
West Hougham. *Kent* 1G **29**
Westhoughton. *G Man* 4E **91**
Westhouse. *N Yor* 2F **97**
Westhouses. *Derbs* 5B **86**
West Howe. *Bour* 3F **15**
Westhumble. *Surr* 5C **38**
West Huntspill. *Som* 2G **21**
West Hyde. *Herts* 1B **38**
West Hynish. *Arg* 5A **138**
West Hythe. *Kent* 2F **29**
West Ilsley. *W Ber* 3C **36**
West Itchenor. *W Sus* 2G **17**
West Keal. *Linc* 4C **88**
West Kennett. *Wilts* 5G **35**
West Kilbride. *N Ayr* 5D **126**
West Kingsdown. *Kent* 4G **39**
West Kington. *Wilts* 4D **34**
West Kirby. *Mers* 2E **82**
West Knapton. *N Yor* 2C **100**
West Knighton. *Dors* 4C **14**
West Knoyle. *Wilts* 3D **22**
West Kyloe. *Nmbd* 5G **131**
Westlake. *Devn* 3C **8**
West Lambrook. *Som* 1H **13**
West Langdon. *Kent* 1H **29**
West Langwell. *High* 3D **164**
West Lavington. *W Sus* 4G **25**
West Lavington. *Wilts* 1F **23**
West Layton. *N Yor* 4E **105**
West Leake. *Notts* 3C **74**
West Learmouth. *Nmbd* 1C **120**
Westleigh. *Devn* 4E **19**
(nr. Bideford)
Westleigh. *Devn* 1D **12**
(nr. Tiverton)
West Leigh. *Devn* 2G **11**
(nr. Winkleigh)
Westleigh. *G Man* 4E **91**
West Leith. *Buck* 4H **51**
Westleton. *Suff* 4G **67**
West Lexham. *Norf* 4H **77**
Westley. *Shrp* 5F **71**
Westley. *Suff* 4H **65**
Westley Waterless. *Cambs* 5F **65**
West Lilling. *N Yor* 3A **100**
West Lingo. *Fife* 3G **137**
Westlington. *Buck* 4F **51**
Westlinton. *Cumb* 3E **113**
West Linton. *Bord* 4E **129**
West Littleton. *S Glo* 4C **34**
West Looe. *Corn* 3G **7**
West Lulworth. *Dors* 4D **14**
West Lutton. *N Yor* 3D **100**
West Lydford. *Som* 3A **22**
West Lyng. *Som* 4G **21**
West Lynn. *Norf* 4F **77**
West Mains. *Per* 2B **136**
West Malling. *Kent* 5A **40**
West Malvern. *Worc* 1C **48**
Westmancote. *Worc* 2E **49**
West Marden. *W Sus* 1F **17**
West Markham. *Notts* 3E **86**
Westmarsh. *Kent* 4G **41**
West Marsh. *NE Lin* 4F **95**
West Marton. *N Yor* 4A **98**
West Meon. *Hants* 4E **25**
West Mersea. *Essx* 4D **54**
Westmeston. *E Sus* 4E **27**

Whitewall Corner. N Yor 2B 100
White Waltham. Wind 4G 37
Whiteway. Glos 4E 49
Whitewell. Lanc 5F 97
Whitewell Bottom. Lanc 2G 91
Whiteworks. Devn 5G 11
Whitewreath. Mor 3G 159
Whitfield. D'dee 5D 144
Whitfield. Kent 1H 29
Whitfield. Nptn 2E 50
Whitfield. Nmbd 4A 114
Whitfield. S Glo 2B 34
Whitford. Devn 3F 13
Whitford. Flin 3D 82
Whitgift. E Yor 2B 94
Whitgreave. Staf 3C 72
Whithorn. Dum 5B 110
Whiting Bay. N Ayr 3E 123
Whitington. Norf 1G 65
Whitkirk. W Yor 1D 92
Whitland. Carm 3G 43
Whitleigh. Plym 3A 8
Whitletts. S Ayr 2C 116
Whitley. N Yor 2F 93
Whitley. Wilts 5D 35
Whitley Bay. Tyne 2G 115
Whitley Chapel. Nmbd 4C 114
Whitley Heath. Staf 3C 72
Whitley Lower. W Yor 3C 92
Whitley Thorpe. N Yor 2F 93
Whitlock's End. W Mid 3F 61
Whitminster. Glos 5C 48
Whitmore. Dors 2F 15
Whitmore. Staf 1C 72
Whitnage. Devn 1D 12
Whitnash. Warw 4H 61
Whitney. Here 1F 47
Whitrigg. Cumb 4D 112
(nr. Kirkbride)
Whitrigg. Cumb 1D 102
(nr. Torpenhow)
Whitsbury. Hants 1G 15
Whitsome. Bord 4E 131
Whitson. Newp 3G 33
Whitstable. Kent 4F 41
Whitstone. Corn 3C 10
Whittingham. Nmbd 3E 121
Whittingslow. Shrp 2G 59
Whittington. Derbs 3B 86
Whittington. Glos 3F 49
Whittington. Lanc 2F 97
Whittington. Shrp 2F 71
Whittington. Staf 2C 60
(nr. Kinver)
Whittington. Staf 5F 73
(nr. Lichfield)
Whittington. Warw 1G 61
Whittington. Worc 5C 60
Whittington Barracks. Staf 5F 73
Whittlebury. Nptn 1E 51
Whittleford. Warw 1H 61
Whittle-le-Woods. Lanc 2D 90
Whittlesey. Cambs 1B 64
Whittlesford. Cambs 1E 53
Whittlestone Head. Bkbn 3F 91
Whitton. N Lin 2C 94
Whitton. Nmbd 4E 121
Whitton. Powy 4E 59
Whitton. Bord 2B 120
Whitton. Shrp 3H 59
Whitton. Stoc T 2A 106
Whittonditch. Wilts 4A 36
Whittonstall. Nmbd 4D 114
Whitway. Hants 1C 24
Whitwell. Derbs 3C 86
Whitwell. Herts 3B 52
Whitwell. IOW 5D 16
Whitwell. N Yor 5F 105
Whitwell. Rut 5G 75
Whitwell-on-the-Hill. N Yor 3B 100
Whitwick. Leics 4B 74
Whitwood. W Yor 2E 93
Whitworth. Lanc 3G 91
Whixall. Shrp 2H 71

Whixley. N Yor 4G 99
Whoberley. W Mid 3G 61
Whorlton. Dur 3E 105
Whorlton. N Yor 4B 106
Whygate. Nmbd 2A 114
Whyle. Here 4H 59
Whyteleafe. Surr 5E 39
Wibdon. Glos 2A 34
Wibtoft. Warw 2B 62
Wichenford. Worc 4B 60
Wichling. Kent 5D 40
Wick. Bour 3G 15
Wick. Devn 2E 13
Wick. High 3F 169
Wick. Som 2F 21
(nr. Bridgwater)
Wick. Som 1G 21
(nr. Burnham-on-Sea)
Wick. Som 4H 21
(nr. Somerton)
Wick. S Glo 4C 34
Wick. V Glam 4C 32
Wick. W Sus 5B 26
Wick. Wilts 4G 23
Wick. Worc 1E 49
Wick Airport. High 3F 169
Wicken. Cambs 3E 65
Wicken. Nptn 2F 51
Wicken Bonhunt. Essx 2E 53
Wickenby. Linc 2H 87
Wicken Green Village. Norf 2H 77
Wickersley. S Yor 1B 86
Wicker Street Green. Suff 1C 54
Wickford. Essx 1B 40
Wickham. Hants 1D 16
Wickham. W Ber 4B 36
Wickham Bishops. Essx 4B 54
Wickhambreaux. Kent 5G 41
Wickhambrook. Suff 5G 65
Wickhamford. Worc 1F 49
Wickham Green. Suff 4C 66
Wickham Heath. W Ber 5C 36
Wickham Market. Suff 5F 67
Wickhampton. Norf 5G 79
Wickham St Paul. Essx 2B 54
Wickham Skeith. Suff 4C 66
Wickham Street. Suff 4C 66
Wick Hill. Wok 5F 37
Wicklewood. Norf 5C 78
Wickmere. Norf 2D 78
Wick St Lawrence. N Som 5G 33
Wickwar. S Glo 3C 34
Widdington. Essx 2F 53
Widdrington. Nmbd 5G 121
Widdrington Station. Nmbd 5G 121
Widecombe in the Moor. Devn 5H 11
Widegates. Corn 3G 7
Widemouth Bay. Corn 2C 10
Wide Open. Tyne 2F 115
Widewall. Orkn 8D 172
Widford. Essx 5G 53
Widford. Herts 4E 53
Widham. Wilts 3F 35
Widmer End. Buck 2G 37
Widmerpool. Notts 3D 74
Widnes. Hal 2H 83
Widworthy. Devn 3F 13
Wigan. G Man 4D 90
Wigbeth. Dors 2F 15
Wigborough. Som 1H 13
Wiggaton. Devn 3E 12
Wiggenhall St Germans. Norf 4E 77
Wiggenhall St Mary Magdalen.
Norf 4E 77
Wiggenhall St Mary the Virgin.
Norf 4E 77
Wiggenhall St Peter. Norf 4F 77
Wiggens Green. Essx 1G 53
Wigginton. Herts 4H 51
Wigginton. Oxon 2B 50
Wigginton. Staf 5G 73
Wigglesworth. N Yor 4H 97
Wiggonby. Cumb 4D 112

Wiggonholt. W Sus 4B 26
Wighill. N Yor 5G 99
Wighton. Norf 1B 78
Wightwick. Staf 1C 60
Wigley. Hants 1B 16
Wigmore. Here 4G 59
Wigmore. Medw 4C 40
Wigsley. Notts 3F 87
Wigsthorpe. Nptn 2H 63
Wigston. Leics 1D 62
Wigtoft. Linc 2B 76
Wigton. Cumb 5D 112
Wigtown. Dum 4B 110
Wigtwizzle. S Yor 1G 85
Wike. W Yor 5F 99
Wilbarston. Nptn 2F 63
Wilberfoss. E Yor 4B 100
Wilburton. Cambs 3D 65
Wilby. Norf 2C 66
Wilby. Nptn 4F 63
Wilby. Suff 3E 67
Wilcot. Wilts 5G 35
Wilcott. Shrp 4F 71
Wilcove. Corn 3A 8
Wildboarclough. Ches E 4D 85
Wilden. Bed 5H 63
Wilden. Worc 3C 60
Wildern. Hants 1C 16
Wilderspool. Warr 2A 84
Wilde Street. Suff 3G 65
Wildhern. Hants 1B 24
Wildmanbridge. S Lan 4B 128
Wildmoor. Worc 3D 60
Wildsworth. Linc 1F 87
Wildwood. Staf 3D 72
Wilford. Nott 2C 74
Wilkesley. Ches E 1A 72
Wilkhaven. High 5G 165
Wilkieston. W Lot 3E 129
Wilksby. Linc 4B 88
Willand. Devn 1D 12
Willaston. Ches E 5A 84
Willaston. Ches W 3F 83
Willaston. IOM 4C 108
Willen. Mil 1G 51
Willenhall. W Mid 3A 62
(nr. Coventry)
Willenhall. W Mid 1D 60
(nr. Wolverhampton)
Willerby. E Yor 1D 94
Willerby. N Yor 2E 101
Willersey. Glos 2G 49
Willersley. Here 1G 47
Willesborough. Kent 1E 28
Willesborough Lees. Kent 1E 29
Willesden. G Lon 2D 38
Willesleigh. Devn 3F 19
Willesley. Wilts 3D 34
Willett. Som 3E 20
Willey. Shrp 1A 60
Willey. Warw 2B 62
Willey Green. Surr 5A 38
Williamscot. Oxon 1C 50
Willian. Herts 2C 52
Willingale. Essx 5F 53
Willingdon. E Sus 5G 27
Willingham. Cambs 3D 64
Willingham by Stow. Linc 2F 87
Willingham Green. Cambs 5F 65
Willington. Bed 1B 52
Willington. Derbs 3G 73
Willington. Dur 1E 105
Willington. Tyne 3G 115
Willington. Warw 2A 50
Willington Corner. Ches W 4H 83
Willisham Tye. Suff 5C 66
Willitoft. E Yor 1H 93
Williton. Som 2D 20
Willoughbridge. Staf 1B 72
Willoughby. Linc 3D 88
Willoughby. Warw 4C 62
Willoughby-on-the-Wolds.
Notts 3D 74
Willoughby Waterleys. Leics 1C 62
Willoughton. Linc 1G 87

Willow Green. Worc 5B 60
Willows Green. Essx 4H 53
Willsbridge. S Glo 4B 34
Willslock. Staf 2E 73
Wilmcote. Warw 5F 61
Wilmington. Bath 5B 34
Wilmington. Devn 3F 13
Wilmington. E Sus 5G 27
Wilmington. Kent 3G 39
Wilmslow. Ches E 2C 84
Wilnecote. Staf 5G 73
Wilney Green. Norf 2C 66
Wilpshire. Lanc 1E 91
Wilsden. W Yor 1A 92
Wilsford. Linc 1H 75
Wilsford. Wilts 3G 23
(nr. Amesbury)
Wilsford. Wilts 1G 23
(nr. Devizes)
Wilsill. N Yor 3D 98
Wilsley Green. Kent 2B 28
Wilson. Here 3A 48
Wilson. Leics 3B 74
Wilsontown. S Lan 4C 128
Wilstead. Bed 1A 52
Wilsthorpe. E Yor 3F 101
Wilsthorpe. Linc 4H 75
Wilstone. Herts 4H 51
Wilton. Cumb 3B 102
Wilton. N Yor 1C 100
Wilton. Red C 3C 106
Wilton. Bord 3H 119
Wilton. Wilts 5A 36
(nr. Marlborough)
Wilton. Wilts 3F 23
(nr. Salisbury)
Wimbish. Essx 2F 53
Wimbish Green. Essx 2G 53
Wimblebury. Staf 4E 73
Wimbledon. G Lon 3D 38
Wimblington. Cambs 1D 64
Wimboldsley. Ches W 4A 84
Wimborne Minster. Dors 2F 15
Wimborne St Giles. Dors 1F 15
Wimbotsham. Norf 5F 77
Wimpole. Cambs 1D 52
Wimpstone. Warw 1H 49
Wincanton. Som 4C 22
Winceby. Linc 4C 88
Wincham. Ches W 3A 84
Winchburgh. W Lot 2D 129
Winchcombe. Glos 3F 49
Winchelsea. E Sus 4D 28
Winchelsea Beach. E Sus 4D 28
Winchester. Hants 4C 24
Winchet Hill. Kent 1B 28
Winchfield. Hants 1F 25
Winchmore Hill. Buck 1A 38
Winchmore Hill. G Lon 1E 39
Wincle. Ches E 4D 84
Windermere. Cumb 5F 103
Winderton. Warw 1B 50
Windhill. High 4H 157
Windle Hill. Ches W 3F 83
Windlesham. Surr 4A 38
Windley. Derbs 1H 73
Windmill. Derbs 3F 85
Windmill Hill. E Sus 4H 27
Windmill Hill. Som 1G 13
Windrush. Glos 4G 49
Windsor. Wind 3A 38
Windsor Green. Suff 5A 66
Windyedge. Abers 4G 153
Windygates. Fife 3F 137
Windyharbour. Ches E 3C 84
Windyknowe. W Lot 3C 128
Wineham. W Sus 3D 26
Winestead. E Yor 2G 95
Winfarthing. Norf 2D 66
Winford. IOW 4D 16
Winford. N Som 5A 34
Winforton. Here 1F 47
Winfrith Newburgh. Dors 4D 14
Wing. Buck 3G 51

Wing. Rut 5F 75
Wingate. Dur 1A 106
Wingates. G Man 4E 91
Wingates. Nmbd 5F 121
Wingerworth. Derbs 4A 86
Wingfield. C Beds 3A 52
Wingfield. Suff 3E 67
Wingfield. Wilts 1D 22
Wingfield Park. Derbs 5A 86
Wingham. Kent 5G 41
Wingmore. Kent 1F 29
Wingrave. Buck 4G 51
Winkburn. Notts 5E 85
Winkfield. Brac 3A 38
Winkfield Row. Brac 4G 37
Winkhill. Staf 5E 85
Winklebury. Hants 1E 24
Winkleigh. Devn 2G 11
Winksley. N Yor 2E 99
Winkton. Dors 3G 15
Winlaton. Tyne 3E 115
Winlaton Mill. Tyne 3E 115
Winless. High 3F 169
Winmarleigh. Lanc 5D 96
Winnal Common. Here 2H 47
Winnard's Perch. Corn 2D 6
Winnersh. Wok 4F 37
Winnington. Ches W 3A 84
Winnington. Staf 2B 72
Winnothdale. Staf 1E 73
Winscales. Cumb 2B 102
Winscombe. N Som 1H 21
Winsford. Ches W 4A 84
Winsford. Som 3C 20
Winsham. Devn 3F 19
Winsham. Som 2G 13
Winshill. Staf 3G 73
Winsh-wen. Swan 3F 31
Winskill. Cumb 1G 103
Winslade. Hants 2E 25
Winsley. Wilts 5C 34
Winslow. Buck 3F 51
Winson. Glos 5F 49
Winson Green. W Mid 2E 61
Winsor. Hants 1B 16
Winster. Cumb 5F 103
Winster. Derbs 4G 85
Winston. Dur 3E 105
Winston. Suff 4D 66
Winstone. Glos 5E 49
Winswell. Devn 1E 11
Winterborne Clenston. Dors 2D 14
Winterborne Herringston. Dors 4B 14
Winterborne Houghton. Dors 2D 14
Winterborne Kingston. Dors 3D 14
Winterborne Monkton. Dors 4B 14
Winterborne St Martin. Dors 4B 14
Winterborne Stickland. Dors 2D 14
Winterborne Whitechurch.
Dors 2D 14
Winterborne Zelston. Dors 3E 15
Winterbourne. S Glo 3B 34
Winterbourne. W Ber 4C 36
Winterbourne Abbas. Dors 3B 14
Winterbourne Bassett. Wilts 4G 35
Winterbourne Dauntsey. Wilts 3G 23
Winterbourne Earls. Wilts 3G 23
Winterbourne Gunner. Wilts 3G 23
Winterbourne Monkton. Wilts 4F 35
Winterbourne Steepleton. Dors 4B 14
Winterbourne Stoke. Wilts 2F 23
Winterbrook. Oxon 3E 36
Winterburn. N Yor 4B 98
Winter Gardens. Essx 2B 40
Winterhay Green. Som 1G 13
Winteringham. N Lin 2C 94
Winterley. Ches E 5B 84
Wintersett. W Yor 3D 93
Winterton. N Lin 3C 94
Winterton-on-Sea. Norf 4G 79
Winthorpe. Linc 4E 89
Winthorpe. Notts 5E 87
Winton. Bour 3F 15
Winton. Cumb 3A 104